LEARNING TO TEACH
IN THE PRIMARY SCHOOL

How can you becom ? What do
you need to know?

Flexible, effective standing of
their pupils and how ironments
for learning, and the

This 2nd edition c tion of the
qualified teacher sta g both the
taught component a t provides
an accessible and e needs to
acquire in order to g

Written by experts essential
concepts and skills,

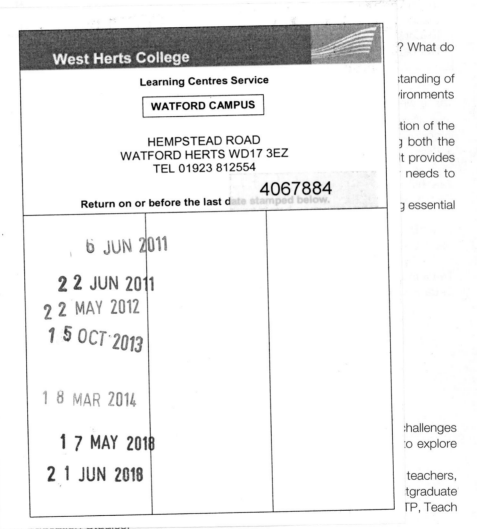

■ approaching planr
■ assessment for lea
■ e-learning NEW
■ inclusive approach
■ personalised learn
■ research and furth
■ responding to eth
■ teaching modern 1
■ the professional st
■ understanding ear
■ working with other

Each unit offers a rar challenges
– new to this edition to explore
topics in more detail.

This comprehensiv teachers,
including those on und tgraduate
teacher training course TP, Teach
First), plus those stud

James Arthur is Professor of Education and Civic Engagement at the University of Birmingham, UK.
Teresa Cremin (née Grainger) is Professor of Education at the Open University (Literacy), UK.

THE LEARNING TO TEACH IN THE PRIMARY SCHOOL SERIES

Series Editor: Teresa Cremin, the Open University

The *Learning to Teach in the Primary School Series* has been designed to accompany this core textbook.

Teaching is an art form. It demands not only knowledge and understanding of the core areas of learning, but also the ability to teach these creatively and effectively and foster learner creativity in the process. The series draws upon recent research, which indicates the rich potential of creative teaching and learning, and explores what it means to teach creatively in the primary phase. It also responds to the evolving nature of subject teaching in a wider, more imaginatively framed twenty-first-century primary curriculum.

These well-informed, lively texts offer support for students and practising teachers who want to develop more flexible, responsive and creative approaches to teaching and learning. The books highlight the importance of the research base underpinning teaching, and teachers' own creative engagement, sharing a wealth of innovative ideas to enrich pedagogy and practice.

Teaching English Creatively
Teresa Cremin

Teaching Science Creatively
Dan Davies and Ian Milne

Teaching Mathematics Creatively
Linda Pound and Trisha Lee

LEARNING TO TEACH IN THE PRIMARY SCHOOL

2nd Edition

Edited by
**James Arthur and
Teresa Cremin**

Routledge
Taylor & Francis Group

LONDON AND NEW YORK

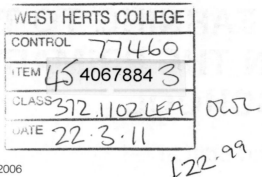
First edition published 2006
by Routledge

This edition published 2010
by Routledge
2 Park Square, Milton Park, Abingdon, Oxon OX14 4RN

Simultaneously published in the USA and Canada
by Routledge
270 Madison Ave, New York, NY 10016

Routledge is an imprint of the Taylor & Francis Group, an informa business

© 2010 selection and editorial material, James Arthur and Teresa Cremin;
individual chapters, the contributors

Typeset in Times New Roman by
Florence Production Ltd, Stoodleigh, Devon
Printed and bound in Great Britain by
The MPG Books Group

British Library Cataloguing in Publication Data
A catalogue record for this book is available from the British Library

Library of Congress Cataloging in Publication Data
Learning to teach in the primary school / edited by James Arthur and
Teresa Cremin. — 2nd ed.
        p. cm.
    Includes bibliographical references and index.
    1. Elementary school teaching – Great Britain.   2. Elementary teaching –
Great Britain.   3. Elementary school teachers – Training of – Great Britain.
I. Arthur, James, 1957   II. Cremin, Teresa.
LB1556.7.G7L43 2010
372.1102 – dc22   2009039574

ISBN10: 0–415–57492–7 (hbk)
ISBN10: 0–415–48790–0 (pbk)
ISBN10: 0–203–85462–4 (ebk)

ISBN13: 978–0–415–57492–1 (hbk)
ISBN13: 978–0–415–48790–0 (pbk)
ISBN13: 978–0–203–85462–4 (ebk)

CONTENTS

1 BECOMING A TEACHER   7

1.1 Primary teaching: a personal perspective   8
COLIN RICHARDS

■ 'acrostic' teaching ■ a sense of style ■ teaching: science, craft or art?
■ enactive, pre-active and post-active primary teaching ■ the personal qualities
and knowledge required of primary teachers ■ the purposes of primary
teaching ■ the importance of primary teaching

1.2 Professionalism and trainee teachers   18
DENIS HAYES

■ standards for trainee teachers ■ QTS standards for professional attributes:
relationships with children, frameworks, communicating and working with
others ■ evidence of success: checklist for professional attributes

2 EXPLORING THE NATURE OF LEARNING AND TEACHING   29

2.1 Child development   30
SANDRA SMIDT

■ child development: what is it and why does it matter? ■ some key figures
■ some current and recent research: neuroscience, the *Researching Effective Pedagogy
in the Early Years* (REPEY) project, the *Cambridge Primary Review*, the Early Years
Foundation Stage, the *Children's Plan* (2008) ■ the implications of all this

■ managing yourself ■ developing a CBP ■ making an early impact on your class ■ conveying your expectations: rules and routines ■ rewards and sanctions ■ using routines to maximise on-task activity ■ classroom layout ■ coping with challenging behaviour

deploy support most effectively? ■ developing a partnership approach:
communication, collaboration and co-construction ■ using teaching assistants
to support transition

ILLUSTRATIONS

FIGURES

TABLES

TASKS

TASKS ■ ■ ■ ■

CONTRIBUTORS

Carrie Ansell is Senior Lecturer in Primary and Early Years English at Bath Spa University, where she is presently course coordinator. She has worked in primary education for over 20 years, primarily in primary schools that had a multilingual and culturally diverse population. Her main research interests are in the field of linguistic diversity and bilingualism.

James Arthur is Professor of Education and Civic Engagement at the University of Birmingham. He has written on the relationship between theory and practice in education, particularly the links between communitarianism, social virtues, citizenship and education. His publications include *Education with Character: The Moral Economy of Schooling*, *Social Literacy, Citizenship, and the National Curriculum*, *Teaching Citizenship Education through History*, *Subject Mentoring in the Secondary School*, all published by Routledge, and *Schools and Community: The Communitarian Agenda in Education* (RoutledgeFalmer), *The Thomist Tradition in Education* and *The Ebbing Tide* (both Gracewing), *Teaching Citizenship in the Secondary School* (Routledge/David Fulton), and many articles and chapters in books.

Richard Bailey is an international acknowledged authority on education and sport. A former teacher in both primary and secondary schools and a teacher trainer, he has been a professor at Canterbury University, Roehampton University and most recently at Birmingham University. Richard has undertaken funded research in every continent of the world. He works with UNESCO as Expert Adviser for Physical Education, the World Health Organisation, the European Union and many similar agencies. He has carried out research on behalf of the English and Scottish governments, and numerous educational and sports agencies. In 2004 he was selected by delegates from more than 200 countries to act as Rapporteur for UNESCO's Athens Declaration. He is author of more than 100 publications, including books, academic and professional articles and monographs. Recent books include the *Routledge Physical Education Reader*, the *Sage Handbook of the Philosophy of Education*, *The Philosophy of Education: An Introduction* and *Physical Education for Learning* (both Continuum).

Jonathan Barnes is Senior Lecturer in Primary Education at Canterbury Christ Church University and teaches cross-curricular music and geography courses. He has wide experience in further, secondary and primary education both in England and in the developing world. His international work has resulted in a strong intercultural and global character to his teaching materials. He has written a wide range of books and articles for teachers on music, citizenship, Kenya, castles, technology, history, geography, cultural connections and creativity. He is particularly interested in promoting experience-led, cross-curricular and creative thinking in the primary school.

Eve Bearne's research interests while at the University of Cambridge, Faculty of Education, have been concerned with diversity and inclusion, specifically gender, language and literacy. She edited *Differentiation and Diversity* (Routledge) and has written and edited a range of books about language, literacy and inclusion.

Des Bowden has worked at Newman University College for some 20 years and has worked in Sierra Leone, Namibia and Malawi. His current interests focus on primary education and primary teacher education through the development of international links with The Gambia.

Carrie Cable is Senior Lecturer in Education at the Open University and Director of a DCSF-funded longitudinal research project examining the learning and teaching of languages in primary schools. Carrie has been involved in course development and research relating to primary and early years practitioners for many years. Other research interests include the role of bilingual teaching assistants in mediating children's learning. Co-edited books include *Professionalism in the Early Years* with Linda Miller (Hodder Education) and, with Linda Miller and Gill Goodliff, *Working with Children in the Early Years* and *Supporting Children's Learning in the Early Years* (both Routledge).

Simon Catling is Professor of Education and the Research Leader for the Department of Early Childhood and Primary Education in the Westminster Institute of Education, Oxford Brookes University. After teaching in primary schools in inner London for 12 years, he has worked in initial and continuing Teacher Education programmes and in Educational Studies. A past President of the Geographical Association, his research and teaching interests are in curriculum, teaching and learning with a particular interest in children's geographies and geographical education in primary schooling. He has published widely in this area for children, teachers and teacher educators. His latest publications are *Teaching Primary Geography*, co-authored with Tessa Willy (Learning Matters) and a new edition of Collins' Mapstart series.

Roland Chaplain is a chartered psychologist, working as Senior Lecturer in Psychology and Education at the University of Cambridge and as a consultant on behaviour management to various schools and local authorities. He teaches courses in applied social psychology, motivation, behaviour management and behaviour difficulties. He has previous experience as a teacher, head teacher and head of psychological services. His books include *Teaching Without Disruption* (Routledge), *Challenging Behaviour* (Pearson) and *Researching Special Educational Needs* (Routledge/David Fulton). He is a specialist adviser on teacher stress and children's behaviour for the British Psychological Society.

Pam Copeland has worked at Newman University College for some 18 years, having been a successful primary teacher previously. She has an enthusiastic and committed interest in the development of primary school teachers and latterly secondary school citizenship teachers. She has visited Gambian schools and worked in The Gambia College.

Teresa Cremin (previously known professionally as Grainger) is Professor of Education at the Open University. Teresa, who is involved in research, teaching and consultancy, has published widely on various aspects of language and literacy. Her most recent text, *Teaching English Creatively* (Routledge), is the first in the series she is editing which accompanies this textbook. Teresa is currently co-editing an international handbook on literacy and learning for Wiley Blackwells and is working on a new book on Critical Perspectives on Teaching Writing with Routledge co-edited with Deborah Myhill. Teresa has served as President of the United Kingdom Literacy Association (2007–9), and of the United Kingdom Reading Association (2001–2) and as editor of the journal, *Reading Literacy and Language* (1998–2003). She is currently a Trustee of UKLA, Booktrust and the Poetry Archive. Her current research focuses upon teachers' literate

John Meadows has worked for over 25 years in primary education in schools, training centres and university initial teacher training. He is a course director for a flexible PGCE primary course and teaches and organises the science and ICT elements of that course. His research interests are currently focused on innovations in science teaching at a European and global level. His recent publications include *Science and ICT in the Primary School* (Routledge/David Fulton), two chapters in Inman and Rogers' *Building a Sustainable Future: Challenges for Initial Teacher Training* (CCCI/WWF-UK) and a chapter, with J. Mintz, in Inman and Rogers' *Teachers for a Better World* (CCCI/WWF/London South Bank University).

Jane Medwell is Director of Teacher Education at the Institute of Education, University of Warwick. She has been a lecturer in other universities and a teacher in primary schools. She has conducted research in the effective teaching of literacy, IT and literacy, writing and handwriting as well as teacher education.

Elaine Millard began her career as an English teacher working in a variety of 11–18 comprehensive schools in Sheffield and Nottingham. From 1988 to 1990 she worked as an advisory teacher for Nottingham LEA, preparing both primary and secondary schools for the introduction of National Curriculum English. In 1991 she joined Sheffield University's School of Education and was one of the main originators of its influential Master's Degree in Literacy. Elaine is Past Chair of the National Association for the Teaching of English and is currently Visiting Professor at BCU, Birmingham, where she is supporting research in the fields of gender, literacy and creativity.

Anny Northcote is Senior Lecturer in primary English and primary languages on PGCE courses at Bath Spa University. She previously spent many years working in London as a classroom teacher and as an adviser for supporting bilingual learners, before moving into higher education, teaching language and literacy on primary initial teacher education courses at London Metropolitan University. Her main interests are in the areas of linguistic diversity and children's literature, including research into bilingual children's reading.

Cathie Pearce is Research Fellow at the Institute of Education. Having been Senior Lecturer in Education for some years at Manchester Metropolitan University, she moved to a full-time research post. Her research interests include the relationship between theory and practice, inclusion, subjectivity, reflexivity and difference. She has had a broad range of teaching experiences in inner-city primary schools. Her doctoral thesis 'Experiencing and Experimenting with Pedagogies and Research' was completed in 2007. She is an active member of CARN (Collaborative Action Research Network).

Alison Pickering taught in primary schools in inner London and Sydney, Australia, prior to her appointment as deputy head teacher of a primary school in Richmond-upon-Thames. She is currently Course Director for undergraduate routes into teaching at the School of Education, Kingston University. Her main areas of interest are primary science, cross-curricular approaches to learning and creative approaches to assessment.

Colin Richards is Emeritus Professor, University of Cumbria, and Visiting Professor at the Universities of Leicester, Warwick and Newcastle and at the National Institute of Education in Singapore. He was a primary class teacher, deputy head teacher and lecturer in education before becoming an HMI in 1983. After inspecting schools in the North East of England, he became Staff Inspector (Curriculum) in 1987. From 1994 to 1996 he was Ofsted's Specialist Adviser in Primary Education. Since leaving the Inspectorate he has maintained a keen interest in the issues of standards, the primary curriculum and school inspection. He has published widely and is a frequent contributor to the national press, particularly the *Times Educational Supplement* and *Education*

Journal. As well as being a small-school enthusiast, he is Chair of governors of a Cumbrian secondary school and a fervent lover of the Lake District in which he lives. He greatly treasures the epithet 'an old-fashioned HMI', bestowed on him by a former chief inspector of schools.

Carol Robinson is Senior Research Fellow at the University of Brighton. She is a qualified teacher and has previously taught in a number of schools and pupil referral units. Carol is an experienced research fellow, having been involved in a number of research projects since completing her PhD in 1996. Her current research interests focus around learner voice and the personalisation of learning and she has written widely in this area. One of her recent publications includes a research report, *Children and their Primary Schools: Pupils' Voices*, which formed part of the *Cambridge Primary Review* of education in England.

Sue Rogers is currently Head of Department of Learning Curriculum and Communication at the Institute of Education, London. Her research interests include early childhood pedagogy, play as an aesthetic and affective experience in the early childhood curriculum, post-structuralist approaches to analysing classroom processes and academic identity. She has published widely in the field of early childhood, including *Inside Role-play in Early Childhood Education*, with Julie Evans, and *Rethinking Play and Pedagogy in Early Childhood Education* (both Routledge).

Janet Rose is Senior Lecturer in Early Childhood Studies at the University of Gloucestershire and an early years specialist in child development. She also runs the MEd degree in Early Years and is currently researching student experiences of active learning in early years contexts. Other research interests include action research and the adult role.

John Ryan is Senior Lecturer in the Department of Education and Professional Studies at Newman University College. John has been an assistant head teacher in a primary school and has completed the NPQH. He is in the process of completing his doctorate. His research interests include the identity of primary practitioners, pupil voice and citizenship.

Kieron Sheehy is Senior Lecturer in the Centre for Childhood, Development and Learning at the Open University. He researches and publishes in the areas of inclusive education and technology, and child development.

Sandra Smidt has been involved in education for many years, as a primary teacher, head teacher of an inner-city London infants' school, local authority and Ofsted inspector and adult educator in several universities. From 1996 to 1999 she was in South Africa, where she led a national pilot project working with a team of young people, determining what the minimal standards should be for those working with children under the statutory school age. This was a life-changing experience, making her aware of just how western in attitude and ethos most of the published research and writing on early childhood education has been. Since her retirement she has been involved primarily in writing.

Janet Tod is Emeritus Professor of Education at Canterbury Christ Church University. She is a chartered educational and clinical psychologist and qualified speech therapist. Following her recent retirement as Head of Department for Educational Research, she has continued to be actively involved in research and publication in the area of special educational needs and inclusion. She is best known for work in the area of IEPs (individual education plans) and dyslexia. She has recently co-authored, with Simon Ellis, *Behaviour for Learning* (Routledge), which seeks to support teachers in developing proactive approaches to behaviour management.

Samantha Twiselton is Head of Early Years and Primary Initial Professional Studies at the University of Cumbria and is a member of the British Educational Research Association Council. She was recently involved in facilitating the advisory group for the *Independent Review of the*

Primary Curriculum (Rose Review). She was a primary classroom teacher for a number of years. Her PhD was in the development of teacher knowledge and expertise in initial teacher education. She lives in the Lake District with her husband and two children and will one day find enough time to actually get out there and walk in it.

Ben Whitney is Professional Leader/Adviser (Attendance and Child Welfare) at Wolverhampton City Council. He supervises the team of Education Welfare Officers and Parenting Workers and is involved in EWO training across the West Midlands. He previously worked in similar roles for Staffordshire LA and has written widely on education welfare issues, including *Protecting Children* (RoutledgeFalmer) and *A Guide to School Attendance* (Routledge/David Fulton). He was a member of the group responsible for producing *Learning to Protect*, a resource pack published by the NSPCC for use in initial teacher training.

Elizabeth Wood is Professor of Education at the University of Exeter. Her research interests include the role of play in early learning, progression and continuity in play, teachers' professional knowledge and practice, and curriculum, pedagogy and assessment in early childhood. She was consultant to the National Union of Teachers on developing their play policy in 2007, and has worked with DCSF on play, learning and pedagogy. She has an international reputation for her research on play. Her publications include *Play and Learning in Early Childhood Settings*, with P. Broadhead and J. Howard (Sage), *The Routledge Reader in Early Childhood* and *Play, Learning and the Early Childhood Curriculum*, with J. Attfield (Paul Chapman).

David Wray taught in primary schools for ten years and is currently Professor of Literacy Education at the University of Warwick. He has published over 30 books on aspects of literacy teaching and is best known for his work on developing teaching strategies to help pupils access the curriculum through literacy. This has resulted in such innovations as the Extending Interactions with Texts (EXIT) model to guide the teaching of reading to learn, and writing frames to help with the writing of factual text types. His work has been made an integral part of the National Literacy Strategy at both primary and secondary levels. His major publications include *Extending Literacy*, and *English 7–11* (both Routledge), *Developing Children's Non-Fiction Writing* (Scholastic), *Writing Frames and Writing across the Curriculum* (University of Reading/ Language Information Centre), *Literacy in the Secondary School* (Routledge/David Fulton) and *Teaching Literacy Effectively* (RoutledgeFalmer).

Dominic Wyse is Senior Lecturer in Primary and Early Years Education at the University of Cambridge and Fellow of Churchill College, Cambridge. He is a member of the Centre for Commonwealth Education at the University of Cambridge. Dominic's research focuses on primary and early years education, particularly in relation to curriculum policy and pedagogy for the teaching of English, language and literacy. His current research includes the wREPLACE project (place-based identity in reading and writing) and a project on pedagogy and leadership in Tanzania. His interest in educational innovation has led to research on creativity and curriculum innovation, including in secondary schools. He gave evidence in relation to the National Curriculum to the House of Commons Committee for Children, Schools and Families, and has appeared on BBC *Newsnight* and BBC Radio 4 *Today* to discuss reading pedagogy. Dominic is co-editor, with Richard Andrews and Jim Hoffman, of *The International Handbook of English, Language, and Literacy Teaching* (Routledge) and is a Deputy Executive Editor of the *Cambridge Journal of Education*. He is also editor of the forthcoming series of books about Primary Education to be published by Routledge. He is a member of the editorial boards of *Teaching and Teacher Education: An International Journal of Research and Studies* and *Writing and Literacy*, and The Editorial Commissioning and Advisory Board of the Teacher Training Resource Bank.

ACKNOWLEDGEMENTS

The editors would like to thank Helen Pritt and Emma Joyes from Routledge, who have been an invaluable support in undertaking this substantial second edition. In addition, they would like to acknowledge David Wray's contribution to the introduction and to the construction of the first edition of this book. Furthermore, the editors are indebted to Elizabeth Melville for her unstinting support and attention to detail. Each of the original and new authors involved in writing units for this book is also gratefully thanked for their time and talent.

INTRODUCTION

James Arthur and Teresa Cremin

WHAT IS PRIMARY TEACHING?

Teaching in primary schools has sometimes been thought of as having a somewhat lower status than 'real' teaching – that is, teaching a proper subject in a proper school, which means a secondary school. Primary teaching, so the folklore tells us, is just looking after young children until they get to the 'proper' school – showing them how to hold a pencil, wiping their noses, telling them a story or two, but not actually teaching them too much of real importance. Those (fairly rare) teachers who have made the change from teaching in secondary schools to primary schools often find that parents, even pupils, ask them why they have 'come down here', the idea that someone might voluntarily choose primary teaching over secondary being a hard one to grasp.

Thankfully, at least in official quarters, the image of primary teaching has changed and we now recognise that primary school is a crucial period, perhaps the most crucial, in children's learning. During this time children have to be taught those complex skills that are the foundation of all the learning they will do in the rest of their lives. It is primary teachers who teach children to read, to write, to manipulate numbers and to observe, record and question their experiences of the world, and who provide them with opportunities that stimulate their imaginations and expand their worlds. It is also primary teachers who help to foster positive attitudes and creative learning dispositions, as well as develop children's interpersonal skills and collaborative capacities. Far from being seen as childminders with little expertise, primary teachers are now viewed as professional learning enablers, possessing a wide subject knowledge base and a rich understanding of child development and teaching and learning, both within and beyond the classroom.

Even when the complexity of the job is recognised, there are still a number of different ways of conceptualising what makes a good primary teacher. A description that is often used is that primary teaching is a vocation – rather like the priesthood, you have to have a calling in order to be a good primary teacher. This view produces such ideas as the belief that good teachers are born, not made, and that to become a teacher all you really need to do is to work for a while alongside another experienced teacher and copy what he or she does. This used to be referred to as a 'sitting with Nellie' approach to becoming a teacher. It does have the merit that, if Nellie *is* a good teacher, watching and copying what she does will almost certainly pass on some pretty good habits of classroom practice.

But what if Nellie's classroom changes, as classrooms have changed, radically, over the past 20 years? If Nellie is to remain effective as a teacher and make learning meaningful, relevant and engaging to the young, those good habits will need to change as well. And the trouble with habits, as all those nail-biters and chocoholics among you will know, is that they can be extraordinarily resistant to change. Nellie will need to have an understanding about why she does what she does, why it works now but might not work in the future, and how she will go about changing and developing her practice. Having a sense of vocation will only get her so far. Successful teaching needs more than a feeling of being 'born to teach' and it is also true that many teachers develop into highly effective practitioners without ever feeling such an inner calling.

Another popular way of conceptualising teaching is to describe it as a craft, with the implication that it consists of an integrated collection of skilful activities. Other crafts include such activities as plumbing and wood-turning, both very skilful in their own right (and in some cases more lucrative as careers than primary teaching!). A craft view of teaching does allow for changes in practice to a much greater extent than might a vocation view. In the same way that plumbers have to change their practices to accommodate innovations (such as plastic rather than copper piping), so teachers have to adapt their skills to cope with the changing nature of literacy, for example in our new media age. Naturally, there is a large element of craft involved in the role of the primary teacher. For most beginning teachers, learning these craft elements looms pretty large in their early experiences of teaching. Learning to talk to large groups of pupils in an authoritative yet approachable way, learning to ask questions, learning to model curiosity and artistry, learning to plan appropriate activities for all the children in a class, learning how to write informative reports to parents about the progress of their offspring – all these have a significant craft element to them, and many beginning teachers see their principal aim in their first few years of teaching as mastering these and other skills and becoming craftsmen/women of the classroom. Yet this is not all there is to successful primary teaching, nor to the process of becoming a successful teacher. The two simple facts that set teaching apart from other crafts are the two Cs – consequence and complexity.

Let us take consequence first. What is the consequence of a plumber failing to do a job properly? Well, the worst-case scenario is a flooded house, which may be costly to put right but, in the end, is usually repairable. But the consequence of a teacher failing a pupil or group of pupils can be much, much more serious. Failing children can easily develop a self-image that incorporates failure – a view of themselves that can persist throughout their lives and radically limit the development of their potential. Teachers who fail to teach their pupils to read or write, or who fail to foster their positive attitudes to learning, do far more damage than any plumber who fails to connect two pipes together properly. The consequences of teaching are greater and longer lasting than those of most other crafts.

In terms of complexity, the craft of teaching also outdoes most others. Indeed, teaching is so complex an activity that it is sometimes almost impossible to predict what will happen as you engage in it. A plumber might weld together two pipes and, 99 times out of 100, if the job is done carefully, the result will be the same. A teacher, on the other hand, can teach the same lesson twice to different groups of pupils, and with one achieve success but with the other have a disaster. Why? Well it might be because the groups were different, with different personalities, abilities, interests, aptitudes and moods. The performance of the teacher may also have been subtly different, depending on their mood and/or their capacity to respond flexibly. In addition, other variables such as the physical environment, the time of day and the previous knowledge of the children may alter the curriculum experience. The point here is that any act of teaching is an incredibly complicated affair – there are so many things that can influence it. One of the key characteristics of really effective teachers is the ability to hold a lot of this complexity in their minds as they plan, develop and evaluate their teaching. Another significant difference between the craft of teaching and craft activities such as pottery or plumbing is that, while pipes are inert, children have personalities of their own. They are unique young thinkers, with their own thoughts, interests and needs.

By concentrating on practical teaching skills and methods – the mechanics of teaching – it is possible to produce a mechanistic 'teacher' who is able to manage a class and instruct pupils with a fair show of competence. The emphasis here is on what the teacher can do (a trade), rather than what the teacher is and can become (an educator). You need to be aware of the wider social setting, to have the flexibility to anticipate change, and to adapt your teaching methods to new demands and different learners.

Teaching in a primary school is, above all, a professional and artistic enterprise. Pupils spend a large part of the day with their teachers, and so you will have significant opportunities to influence them. The time spent by pupils in the company of teachers is inevitably personal and formative. Good teachers are connected to their pupils, for at the heart of the practice of education is the relationship between teacher and pupil. It is this relationship that sets the tone for everything that happens in the classroom and it is this relationship that influences the development of positive attitudes and dispositions as well as knowledge, skills and understanding.

For all these reasons, when we talk about teaching, we use the notion of professional decision making to represent it.

So our third way of conceptualising primary teaching, and the approach we use in this book, is teaching as a professional activity. This term implies a number of attributes within the teacher, including:

■ high levels of relevant knowledge about what is being taught and the children to whom it is being taught;
■ knowledge of, and skill in using, a range of strategies to enable learning;
■ the capacity to engage flexibly and thoughtfully in the classroom, taking into account the needs and responses of the learners as they develop and manifest themselves;
■ an understanding of the importance of learners' attitudes towards what they are learning and an ability to influence and develop these attitudes;
■ the ability and willingness to learn from a variety of sources about effective teaching and to adapt practices to fit this ongoing learning.

It is one of the aims of this book to help you begin to develop such professional attributes, dispositions and competences.

HOW CAN THIS BOOK HELP ME?

From what we have just said, you may already have realised that the book you are holding is not a collection of 'tips for the beginning teacher'. You will find within its pages a great deal of very practical advice about primary teaching, but the book goes far beyond this. In compiling it, we aimed to give you practical advice, but also a rationale for why such advice might be useful, where it comes from, on what basis it has been formulated and how you might evaluate its usefulness. In short, this book is intended to be both practical and theoretical, an intention that reflects a view of teaching as a highly skilled and knowledgeable professional activity.

The book, therefore, will help move you on in your development as a professional by providing you with background insights into a range of issues that affect the decisions you make in the classroom, and illustrating how such insights affect your classroom practice. Our intention is that this book will work alongside the other experiences within your initial teacher training/education course, both in university- or college-based sessions and in the classroom.

WHAT'S IN THE BOOK?

The aim of this book is to provide vital support to student teachers and their tutors, particularly with reference to the professional studies part of the course and during the school placement element of their initial teacher education. It provides a practical introduction to the necessary knowledge, skills, understanding and attitudes that a student teacher will need to acquire and to the theories underpinning them.

The book is divided into key sections, each explaining critical issues, such as teaching and learning, curriculum and assessment. Each unit within these sections contains an introduction to the key concepts and several learning activities for student teachers presented in the form of tasks. Tasks that are appropriate for Master's level (M level) study are referred to as M level challenges and are signposted with the following icon:

There are also annotated lists of suggested reading for students and tutors who want to explore topics in more detail.

In addition, there is a companion website at www.routledge.com/textbooks/ltps2e, where you will find more activities, units from the first edition, weblinks for recommended websites, and editable versions of illustrations that are template lesson plans, forms and templates.

Section 1: Becoming a teacher

This section includes units:

■ examining the nature of teaching, both formal and informal;
■ exploring the standards required for QTS with particular emphasis on professional values.

Section 2: Exploring the nature of learning and teaching

This section includes units:

■ outlining theories of child development that you need to understand in order to provide appropriate learning opportunities for children;
■ examining conceptualisations of learning, and the implications of these for teaching;
■ discussing a range of insights into learning and appropriate teaching strategies that respond to these;
■ examining effective early years practice and the principles and theories underpinning this.

Section 3: Planning and managing learning

This section includes units focusing on:

■ planning classroom work, for medium and long-term periods;
■ planning for the short term, including lesson planning and evaluation;
■ managing and organising the classroom for learning;
■ managing children's behaviour;
■ organising effective classroom talk;
■ organising and managing learning outside the classroom.

Section 4: Approaches to the curriculum

This section includes units focusing on:

■ the aims of primary education;
■ conceptions of the school curriculum and its formal, informal and hidden aims;
■ the rationale for and framing of the National Curriculum in England;
■ the current Scottish Curriculum at the primary phase.

Section 5: Assessment

This section includes units examining:

■ the nature of ongoing, formative assessment of pupils' progress – assessment for learning;
■ approaches to summative assessment – assessment of learning.

Section 6: Diversity and inclusion

This section includes units on:

■ provision for inclusion and barriers to learning and participation;
■ responding to difference, diversity and differentiation;
■ responding to cultural diversity;
■ exploring gender differences and their impact upon school experience and achievement;
■ recognising and building upon children's linguistic diversity.

Section 7: Recent developments

This section includes units exploring:

■ learners' voices and the personalisation of learning;
■ languages learning and teaching;
■ creative teaching and teaching for creativity;
■ thinking skills and the concept of multiple intelligences;
■ provision for children who are gifted and talented;
■ e-learning within and beyond the classroom.

Section 8: Partnership in practice

This section includes units on:

■ the changing role of the primary teacher;
■ working in partnership with a range of adults in the classroom;
■ partnerships with parents to support learning and others;
■ the teachers' pastoral role and child protection issues.

Section 9: Your professional development

The final section of the book includes units on:

- applying for a job and what to expect in induction;
- professional development, career opportunities and further qualifications;
- connecting teaching and research, and considering further qualifications.

HOW CAN I USE THE BOOK?

There are a number of ways in which you might use this book. You might, of course, want to sit yourself comfortably and just read it from cover to cover. We anticipate, however, that, as gripping a read as this book is, you will probably not want to approach it in quite that way!

It is more likely that you will want to read units from the book separately. The book has been designed so that each unit, while written to be part of a coherent whole, is also free-standing. The book can, therefore, be used in a very flexible way. You might use a number of approaches.

- You might read a particular unit after you have touched upon similar material in a college or university session. The unit will then serve as a revision of material you may have covered in the session, and/or extend your understanding of this material.
- You might prepare for a particular college or university session by reading the relevant unit in advance. You are likely to find the session much more rewarding and useful if you have prepared in this way by developing your background knowledge of the area to be covered.
- You might find that, because of the pressure of time on a course of teacher training (as in the case of most PGCE courses, for example), there simply is not enough college or university time available to cover some issues in any more than an introductory manner. In this case, this book will help you ensure that you do not miss anything really important and you can read units to widen your understanding and expertise.

However you use this book, we hope it will help inspire in you the same passionate interest in education, and primary education in particular, that is felt by every one of the contributors. Education is an endlessly fascinating subject and, of course, teaching children is a highly challenging activity. Enjoy the experience – we hope it will be engaging and satisfying for all involved. We hope, too, that you will find this book supports you on your professional learning journey.

1

BECOMING A TEACHER

UNIT 1.1

PRIMARY TEACHING
A personal perspective

Colin Richards

INTRODUCTION

Primary teaching is an immensely complicated business. It involves the interplay of so many elements, including interpersonal, intellectual, physical, spiritual, even aesthetic dimensions. Neither is it one thing, but it changes in form and substance from hour to hour, lesson to lesson, class to class and year to year. Some people see it as scientific in orientation, involving the selection of the best ways to 'deliver' material to young minds; others stress its artistic side and place emphasis on the 'feel' or style of teaching. So what is this thing called primary teaching? It is the purpose of this introductory chapter to open this up for discussion.

OBJECTIVES

By the end of this unit you should be beginning to:

■ form a view of the nature of primary teaching;
■ develop an awareness of the personal qualities and skills you require as a primary teacher;
■ form views as to the purposes of primary teaching;
■ be overawed at the responsibility of being a primary school teacher.

'ACROSTIC' TEACHING

When you begin teaching you will be surprised at the range of different types of writing that the children are expected to engage in. Children have to learn to write narrative accounts, imaginative stories, descriptions of their 'experiments', diaries, letters, poems, etc. Many are introduced to acrostics and enjoy the challenge these present. What are acrostics? . . . They are poems or other compositions in which certain letters in each line form a word or words.

    I use an acrostic when giving an introductory talk to students at the beginning of their course of teacher education. You will notice that I don't call them 'trainees' and I don't talk of 'teacher training'. Like you, they are not being introduced to a simple straightforward activity in which they can be trained to perform like machine operators on a production line or like circus animals.

They are being inducted into a very complex professional activity – illustrated, for example, by the fact that this introductory text you are reading contains over 30 units and is just an introduction!

I present the following:

T . . . .
E . . . .
A . . . .
C . . . .
H . . . .
I . . . .
N . . . .
G . . . .

and ask the students to characterise primary teaching using eight adjectives corresponding to the eight letters.

Task 1.1.1 **THE NATURE OF PRIMARY TEACHING**

Try the task for yourself. What do you think primary teaching is like? What does it feel like? What kind of activity is it? Make your list and share it with fellow students.

Of course there are no right or wrong answers and an activity as complex as primary teaching cannot be captured in eight words.

As 'a starter for eight' I offer you (as I do my students) the following.

T iring: Primary teaching is very demanding work – demanding physically as you have to cope with a class of very active, growing human beings; demanding interpersonally as you have to deal with the myriad social interactions occurring in a crowded classroom; demanding intellectually as you have to translate complex ideas in your head into terms that children of a particular age can understand.

E xhilarating: Primary teaching is equally (but paradoxically) invigorating work – when both you and the children get 'fired' up with enthusiasm for a particular activity, project or piece of work.

A musing: Primary teaching is enlivened by countless amusing incidents during the course of a day. Some children are natural and conscious comedians; others are unintentionally so; primary classrooms provide endless scope for amusement. 'Never a dull moment' captures this characteristic.

C haotic: Primary teaching can appear (and sometimes is) chaotic as unforeseen circumstances arise and have to be coped with, as parents, the head teacher and children make conflicting demands that have somehow to be met, and as the daily business of managing the learning of 20 or 30 lively youngsters has to be conducted.

H ectic: Primary teaching occurs in an extremely busy place called a classroom, where a multitude of activities (some intended by the teachers, others unintended!) take place and where nothing or nobody stands still for long. Stamina, patience and ability to cope with the unexpected are at a premium.

I nspiring: Primary teaching can be inspiring. You can be inspired by the amazing abilities children can reveal, for example in the creative arts; you can be inspired by the personal qualities of kindness and consideration children can show one another; you can be inspired by the fact that children with unbelievably difficult home circumstances come to school and manage to learn at all; you can be inspired by the work of your colleagues in school from whom you can learn so much.

N ever-ending: Primary teaching is not a 'nine till three-thirty' occupation. In fact it's not so much an occupation as a way of life. It is never complete, never mastered, never perfected. There is always more to learn and more to do for the children in your class. Teaching can take over your whole life with its never-ending demands. but you have to learn to temper these demands with your own personal needs. Doing this can be conscience-wracking but is absolutely essential – to your own and, indirectly, your children's well-being.

G ratifying: Primary teaching can be intensely gratifying (despite some inevitable frustrations!). Teaching a child to read, seeing another child's delight on mastering a skill, telling a story that captivates the whole class, having a lesson that goes really well – such activities can and will give you tremendous satisfaction.

A SENSE OF STYLE

You can see from my acrostic that I believe that primary teaching is an extremely complex activity, whether considered in theoretical or practical terms. It's an amalgam of so many elements – interpersonal, intellectual, physical, spiritual, even aesthetic. It changes subtly in form, substance and 'feel' hour to hour, lesson to lesson, class to class, year to year. It involves notions such as 'respect', 'concern', 'care' and 'intellectual integrity', which are impossible to define but which are deeply influential in determining the nature of life in classrooms. The ends and means, aims and methods of teaching are inextricably interwoven. It is a moral enterprise as well as a practical activity. The word 'style' captures something of what I am trying to convey – a sense of considered professional judgement, of personal response, of quality, of distinctive style – which each practitioner, including you (!) needs to foster. Primary teaching involves far more than the routine reproduction of established procedures; it goes well beyond establishing and maintaining patterns of classroom organisation. It cannot be pinned down in a few straightforward sentences (or in a simple acrostic!).

TEACHING: SCIENCE, CRAFT OR ART?

Some educational researchers, such as Muijs and Reynolds (2001), argue that it is possible to create a science of teaching. They believe that it is possible to study teaching by comparing the results of different methods in terms of the outcomes they produce in children and thereby arrive at objective findings as to which teaching methods are effective in which contexts. You will come across books with titles like *Effective Teaching*, which claim to provide scientifically defensible evidence on which to base decisions about how to teach.

Some educationists, such as Marland (1975), regard teaching as essentially a craft – a set of difficult and complex techniques that can be picked up from, or taught by, skilled practitioners and that can be honed and perfected over the years. You will come across books with titles like *The Craft of the Classroom* that embody this approach.

Still others, such as Eisner (1979), regard teaching as essentially an art – a complex creative activity concerned with the promotion of human learning and involving imagination, sensitivity and personal response and an indefinable element of professional judgement, none of which can be taught directly by another person (though they can be learned indirectly). He talks of the need to 'recognise the contingent nature of educational practice, to savour its complexity, and to be not afraid to use whatever artistry we can master to deal with its problems' and he warns against 'pseudo-science' (p. 33).

Task 1.1.2 **TEACHING: SCIENCE, CRAFT OR ART?**

Based on your experience of teaching at school, at university or on this course, how would you characterise teaching – as science, art or craft? Try to justify your answer to fellow students.

Again, as in the response to Task 1.1.1, there are no absolutely right or wrong answers.

From what I have written already you will see that I characterise teaching as an art, although an art also involving some craft skills that can be taught and even trained for. I do not see that there can ever be an objective science of teaching involving the rigorous definition of methods and the clear measurement of outcomes. I believe that such a science is logically impossible since 'the power to teach' is a highly complex amalgam of judgement, technique and personal qualities whose assessment is inevitably subjective and can never be susceptible to quantification or measurement. But that perspective is my own personal one. Other educationists have different ideas of the nature of teaching, including some who subscribe to the notion of 'the science of the art of teaching'!

ENACTIVE, PRE-ACTIVE AND POST-ACTIVE PRIMARY TEACHING

What activities are involved in being a primary teacher? What should the balance be between the different kinds of activity?

To outsiders and perhaps to most primary age children (though we don't know because we haven't asked them!) 'teaching' conjures up an image of a teacher in front of class describing, explaining, instructing or demonstrating something to his or her pupils. This is enactive teaching – teaching in action, the full frontal interaction of teacher and children. Of course, enactive teaching doesn't only take place in classrooms – it occurs in the hall, in the school grounds and on school trips. Nor does it always involve direct interaction with a class of children – the teacher may be teaching individuals or groups or may be setting up activities where children learn for themselves, for example. There has been a considerable amount of research into enactive teaching in English primary schools – referred to in other parts of this book. However, there is far more to teaching than enactive teaching, even though this is the core activity.

There is pre-active teaching involving the preparation and planning for children's learning, the organisation of the classroom, the collection and organisation of teaching resources, the management of visits or activities outside the classroom and the briefing of other adults who work with children. Interestingly, there has been little research into how primary teachers actually plan, prepare and organise their work. Pre-active teaching is essential to the success of enactive teaching – hence the emphasis on planning and managing learning in the third section of this book.

There is also post-active teaching, which involves considered reflection on practice, writing up evaluations, marking children's work, making assessments of children's progress and keeping records. At its best this feeds into pre-active teaching as reflection and assessment inform planning and preparation. There is plenty of advice available on assessment and record-keeping (see section

5) but again a dearth of research into how teachers actually engage in post-active teaching – you might consider undertaking some research of your own later in your career!

But there is still more to primary teaching as a professional activity. Teachers have to engage in a variety of extra-class activities – administrative tasks, staff meetings, clubs, consultations with parents and attendance at professional development courses, which relate indirectly to teaching but can't be fitted into my neat (too neat?) three-fold classification.

There was some interesting work carried out a decade or more ago by Campbell and Neill (1994) into the nature of primary teachers' work, especially the amount of time devoted to a variety of activities. The research makes interesting reading, although the categories the researchers used are rather different from my classification and the findings are dated. Campbell and Neill found that, on average, the 374 infant and junior teachers in their study spent 52.6 hours a week on professional activity – subdivided into 18.3 hours for teaching (i.e. enactive teaching), 15.7 hours for preparation/marking (i.e. an amalgam of pre-active and post-active teaching), 14.1 hours on administration, 7.2 hours on professional development (including staff meetings and reading) and 4.5 hours on a rag-bag of other activities that didn't fit into any of their other categories. Clearly this research gave the lie to the idea of primary teaching as a 'nine to three-thirty occupation'!

To many, including the researchers, one of the most surprising findings was the relatively small proportion of the teachers' total work time devoted to what I have called enactive teaching, that is, about a third. It is interesting to speculate whether the figures would be any different were the research to be conducted today. I doubt if there would be any substantial changes, despite recent government initiatives in reforming the school workforce. I believe that this is how it should be. Enactive teaching requires a large input of pre-active teaching if it is to be successful and it needs to be followed up by considerable, though somewhat less, post-active activity to ensure a professional cycle of planning – teaching – assessment – reflection – planning – teaching – assessment . . . ad infinitum. Remember, primary teaching is 'never-ending'!

THE PERSONAL QUALITIES AND KNOWLEDGE REQUIRED OF PRIMARY TEACHERS

> ## Task 1.1.3 **THE CHARACTERISTICS OF A GOOD TEACHER**
>
> In a small group consider what makes a good teacher and what knowledge and personal qualities are needed?
>
> Would children come up with same answers? Discuss the issue with a small group of primary-aged children.

There has been very little research into how children view good teachers. Over 40 years ago, Philip Taylor asked both primary- and secondary-aged children and received very similar answers from both. In his words:

> Pupils expect teachers to teach. They value lucid exposition, the clear statement of problems and guidance in their solution. Personal qualities of kindness, sympathy and patience are secondary, appreciated by pupils if they make the teacher more effective in carrying out his primary, intellectual task . . . there appears to be little demand by pupils that teachers shall be friends or temporary mothers and fathers.
>
> (Musgrove and Taylor, 1969: 17)

How do these findings compare with the results of your small group discussions?

The knowledge required to be a primary teacher has changed since the introduction of what was then teacher training in the nineteenth century, but the personal qualities needed have remained the same. The following paragraph in the introduction to the *Professional Standards* you are required to meet by the government (DfES/TTA, 2002) captures something of this demanding professional amalgam:

> teaching involves a lot more than care, mutual respect and well-placed optimism. It demands knowledge and practical skills; the ability to make informed judgements, and to balance pressures and challenges; practice and creativity; interest and effort; as well as an understanding of how children learn and develop.

> (p. 4)

In a letter published a few years ago in the *Times Educational Supplement*, I characterised the expectations of teachers held by the government and the wider society as representing:

> a set of demands which properly exemplified would need the omni-competence of Leonardo da Vinci, the diplomatic expertise of Kofi Annan, the histrionic skills of Julie Walters, the grim determination of Alex Ferguson and the saintliness of Mother Teresa, coupled with the omniscience of God.

Admittedly over the top (and with a very large tongue in cheek!), this does represent the inflated expectations of us as teachers. None of us is a perfect human being (nor for that matter are the children in our classes, their parents or our politicians), but those expectations are a powerful influence on how many teachers view themselves and on causing so many to feel guilty about falling short. We can aspire to educational sainthood but hardly hope to achieve it. However, in its pursuit we can at least aspire to show such qualities as 'care', 'respect', 'optimism', 'interest' and 'effort' – required of us, quite properly in my view, by officialdom.

The knowledge required of you as primary teachers is of seven kinds – each important though one (the second) is in my view more important than the others. You certainly need subject content knowledge – an understanding of the main concepts, principles, skills and content of the areas that you will have to teach. That's a tall order given that the curriculum you are required to teach in Key Stages 1 and 2 comprises 11 subjects as well as cross-curricular areas such as personal and social education and citizenship, and given that the curriculum required in the Foundation Stage comprises six broad areas of learning. You can't assume that you have the required subject knowledge as a result of your own education, whether at college and university. You will need to audit, and where necessary, top up your subject knowledge by reading or attending courses. Begin now if you haven't done this already.

The second kind of knowledge involves the application of subject knowledge in teaching your children – sometimes termed, rather grandly, 'pedagogical subject knowledge'. This crucially important area involves knowing how to make the knowledge, skills and understandings of subjects accessible and meaningful to children – how best to represent particular ideas; what illustrations to use; what demonstrations or experiments to employ; what stories to tell; what examples to draw on; what kind of explanations to offer; how to relate what needs to be taught to children's experiences or interests, and so on. You will begin to develop this applied expertise in your course of initial teacher education, you will need to add to it through continuing professional development and over time you will add to it from 'the wisdom of practice' – your colleagues' and hopefully your own. Application of subject knowledge also draws on knowledge of children's development, including aspects of how children learn and what motivates them; of developmental sequences (in as far as we can identify them); and of learning difficulties and other special needs (see sections 2 and 6 of this book).

You also need to develop curriculum knowledge, that is, knowledge of National Curriculum requirements; of national strategies and project materials; of policies, guidelines and schemes of work; and of the range of published materials and sources available as 'tools of the trade' to help you teach your class. You cannot be expected to keep abreast of developments in every area, but you can be expected to know to whom to turn for advice and to give advice in turn in any area of the curriculum where you act as a coordinator.

There are still other areas of professional knowledge you need to acquire. According to Shulman (1987), these include general pedagogical knowledge (including teaching strategies, techniques, classroom management and organisation), knowledge of educational contexts (ranging from the workings of small groups and the ways in which schools are organised, run, financed and governed, to the characteristics of communities and cultures) and knowledge of educational ends, purposes and values.

You can see that primary teaching involves much more than a knowledge of how to teach 'reading, writing and number'– a view too many politicians, local and national, seem to hold!

THE PURPOSES OF PRIMARY TEACHING

The state first provided elementary education for children of primary-school age in the latter half of the nineteenth century. The state system complemented a rather chaotic and ad hoc collection of schools established earlier by the churches. Now over 95 per cent of children aged four to eleven attend state primary schools and are taught by teachers employed by local education authorities but working to national requirements and guidelines, such as the National Curriculum and the Code of Practice for Children with Special Educational Needs.

Over that period of time, primary teaching has served a variety of purposes, although the relative importance of these has changed from time to time. As a primary teacher you will play a part in fulfilling these purposes. You will need to form your own view of their relative importance and decide how best to fulfil them or possibly subvert aspects of them.

One major purpose of primary teaching has been, and is, *instruction* – here broadly conceived to include the fostering of:

- procedural knowledge:
    - helping children to acquire and use information, e.g. learning and applying the four rules of number, learning how to spell, learning facts in science or history;
- conceptual knowledge:
    - helping children to understand ideas;
    - helping children to understand principles, e.g. learning how to conduct fair tests in science, learning the importance of chronology in history;
- skills acquisition:
    - helping children to acquire manipulative and other physical skills, such as cutting, handwriting or gymnastics;
    - helping children to acquire complex skills such as reading;
- metacognitive knowledge:
    - helping children to be more knowledgeable about how they learn and how they can improve their learning.

Over time, the relative importance of these components has changed. In the nineteenth century most emphasis was placed on *procedural knowledge* and *skills acquisition*, often of an elementary kind. The latter half of the twentieth century saw an increasing emphasis on *conceptual knowledge* and more advanced *skills acquisition*. Currently, there is a growing interest in fostering *metacognitive knowledge* (see section 2). As a primary teacher in the early part of the twenty-first century you will need to foster all four components – not an easy task!

A second major purpose of primary teaching has been, and is, *socialisation*. Children need to be introduced into a wider society than the home; they need to be able to relate to their peers and to work with them. They need to be inducted into the norms and values of British society. They need to be socialised into the 'strange' world of school, which operates very differently from most homes and involves a great deal of fundamental but often unacknowledged learning – graphically captured (for all time?) in Philip Jackson's brilliant first chapter in his book, *Life in Classrooms* (1968). As a teacher, especially if you are an early years teacher, you will be a most significant agent in children's socialisation. This process has always been a major purpose of primary teaching, especially in the nineteenth century, when large numbers of children entered formal education for the first time and had to be compelled to 'accept their place in society', as the Victorians might have put it. But it is still very significant today – partly as a result of our increasingly complex, rich multicultural society, in which the values of tolerance and respect for others are so much needed and where they can be fostered and reinforced from the minute children enter school. Contemporary children need to find a place – a comfortable, affirming place – in our society. Primary teaching needs to help them find it and make it their own.

Linked to socialisation is another function of primary teaching. Teachers are concerned with children's *welfare* – physical, mental, emotional and social. Primary schools are the most accessible 'outposts' of the welfare state as far as most parents and children are concerned. They are crucially important points of contact, especially for economically disadvantaged families. In the late nineteenth and early twentieth centuries primary teachers were particularly concerned for children's physical welfare – as illustrated by the introduction of school meals and medical inspections and the emphasis placed on physical training. In very recent years there has been a resurgence of concern about children's welfare. Now, under the *Every Child Matters* legislation, every primary teacher, including you, will have to work with other agents and agencies to promote children's well-being (see section 8). Especially in the area of welfare, it is not easy to decide on the limits of a teacher's care for their children (Nias, 1997). This is yet another dimension to primary teaching – no wonder your course of teacher education is so crowded and this book so long!

There is a fourth function of primary teaching – and one with which you may feel uncomfortable. Traditionally, primary teaching has also involved the *classification* of children in order to 'sort' them out for their secondary education. Classification wasn't a major purpose in Victorian times – the working-class children who were taught in the state elementary schools were not expected to go on to any form of secondary education. However, in the first three-quarters of the twentieth century, primary teachers played a major part in identifying children of different abilities and preparing them for different forms of secondary education – grammar, secondary modern and, to a far lesser extent, technical education. That classification function still applies in those parts of the country that retain selective schools. However, I would argue that, currently, a more insidious form of classification influences the practice of many primary teachers as a result of the introduction of national testing and the sorting of children into levels. Too often, children are described as 'level twos', 'level fours', etc., are classified as such, and are given a subtly different curriculum so that these levels begin to define them in ways that narrow their views of themselves and their ability to learn. As a primary teacher you will need to work within the system as it is, but you also have a professional duty to work to change it if, like me, you feel it works against the interests of children in your care.

Task 1.1.4 **THE PURPOSES OF PRIMARY TEACHING**

In pairs, consider the relative importance of the four purposes of primary teaching. Make a list of the kinds of activities teachers engage in related to each of the four purposes. Primary teachers in other countries do not necessarily see their role in these terms (see Alexander, 2000). Should any of these purposes *not* apply to primary teaching in the United Kingdom? Why not?

SUMMARY

The importance of primary teaching

I hope that, by now, you have realised how demanding primary teaching is and how important it is, especially to the children themselves. Philip Jackson reminds us that children spend around 7,000 hours in primary school spread over six or seven years of their young lives. There is no other activity that occupies as much of the child's time as that involved in attending school.

> Apart from the bedroom there is no single enclosure in which he spends a longer time than he does in the classroom. During his primary school years he is a more familiar sight to his teacher than to his father, and possibly even his mother.
>
> (Jackson, 1968: 5)

As a child's teacher you are an incredibly (and frighteningly!) significant person; your teaching will help shape attitudes to learning at a most sensitive period in children's development. After all:

> These seven years are among the most vivid of our existence. Every day is full of new experiences; the relatively static seems permanent; time seems to last much longer; *events and individuals leave deeper impressions and more lasting memories than later in life*. Without discussing what are the happiest years, we may at least agree that every stage of life should be lived for its own sake as happily and fully as possible. *We must above all respect this right on behalf of children, whose happiness is a good deal at the mercy of circumstances and people beyond their control.*
>
> (Scottish Education Department, 1946: 5; my italics)

To return to my acrostic, becoming a primary school teacher is demanding, difficult and exhausting and at times can be a fazing experience. But it is also immensely rewarding, incredibly fascinating, never for a moment boring (unless you make it so!), often very humorous and, because never-ending, always unfini . . .

Hopefully you are up for it?

ANNOTATED FURTHER READING

Alexander, R. (2000) *Culture and Pedagogy: International Comparisons in Primary Education*, Oxford: Blackwell.

A fascinating analysis of primary teaching as practised in France, Russia, India, the United States and England.

Campbell, R. and Neill, S. (1995) *Primary Teachers at Work*, London: Routledge.
> Though over a decade old, its findings provide plenty of food for thought as to the nature of the demands, responsibilities and work of English infant and junior teachers.

Cremin, T. (2009) 'Creative teachers, creative teaching', in A. Wilson (ed.) *Creativity in Primary Education*, 2nd edn, Exeter: Learning Matters, pp. 36–46.
> This explores the characteristics and personal qualities of creative teachers and creative primary teaching.

Jackson, P. (1968) *Life in Classrooms*, New York: Holt, Rinehart and Winston.
> This offers a complementary but rather different characterisation of teaching primary-aged children from that offered in this unit. Forty years on it is still the most evocative description of life as lived in classrooms.

Nias, J. (1989) *Primary Teachers Talking: A Study of Teaching at Work*, London: Routledge.
> This gets 'under the skin' of being a primary teacher and is based on in-depth interviews carried out over a number of years.

RELEVANT WEBSITES

TeacherNet: www.teachernet.gov.uk
Teacher Training Resource Bank: www.ttrb.ac.uk

Visit the companion website www.routledge.com/textbooks/ltps2e for:

■ links to useful websites relevant to this unit.

REFERENCES

Alexander, R. (2000) *Culture and Pedagogy: International Comparisons in Primary Education*, Oxford: Blackwell.

Campbell, R.J. and Neill, S. (1994) *Primary Teachers at Work*, London: Routledge.

Department for Education and Skills (DfES) and Teacher Training Agency (TTA) (2002) *Qualifying to Teach: Professional Standards for Qualified Teacher Status and Requirements for Initial Teacher Training*, London: DfES/TTA.

Eisner, E. (1979) *The Educational Imagination*, New York: Collier-Macmillan.

Jackson, P. (1968) *Life in Classrooms*, New York: Holt, Rinehart and Winston.

Marland, M. (1975) *The Craft of the Classroom*, London: Heinemann Educational.

Muijs, D. and Reynolds, D. (2001) *Effective Teaching: Evidence and Practice*, London: Paul Chapman.

Musgrove, F. and Taylor, P. (1969) *Society and the Teacher's Role*, London: Routledge and Kegan Paul.

Nias, J. (1997) 'Would schools improve if teachers cared less?', *Education 3–13*, 25(3): 11–22.

Scottish Education Department (1946) *Primary Education*, Edinburgh: His Majesty's Stationery Office.

Shulman, L. (1987) 'Knowledge and teaching: foundations of the new reforms', *Harvard Educational Review*, 57: 1–22.

PROFESSIONALISM AND TRAINEE TEACHERS

Denis Hayes

INTRODUCTION

In recent years, the focus has shifted from a consideration of whether teaching fulfils the necessary criteria (properly qualified and remunerated, a defined career structure, etc.) to the application of the positive values deemed to characterise a professional person in a variety of contexts. There are a number of aspects of professionalism that you must come to terms with in addition to teaching, such as caring for children, working with colleagues, dealing with parents, liaising with outside agencies, evaluating your progress as a teacher and contributing your expertise and knowledge to the team effort.

To help ensure continued professional competence, national standards for qualified teacher status (QTS) were established in the UK through what amounts to a national curriculum for pre-service education and training. For you to gain QTS, training providers (e.g. faculties of education) have to confirm that you have met all the required standards. In addition, an *induction year* has been established to monitor your progress during the first year as a newly qualified teacher.

As a trainee teacher on school placement, there are numerous ways of contributing practically to school life; however, it is the quality of your relationships that lies at the heart of your professionalism.

OBJECTIVES

This unit will help you:

■ examine the content of the Training and Development Agency for Schools' *Standards* document regarding professional attributes (TDA, 2007);
■ explore the practical implementation of standards 1–5;
■ identify sources of evidence for meeting each standard;
■ offer case studies that illuminate key issues.

The information provided in the unit will refer specifically to the following aspects of teacher behaviour as expressed through QTS standards 1–5, in which the acronym QTS is simplified to 'Q' followed by the number:

■ relationships with children and young people (Q1);

- ■ demonstrating the positive values, attitudes and behaviour you expect from children (Q2);
- ■ awareness of the professional duties of teachers and the statutory framework within which you work (Q3a);
- ■ awareness of the policies and practices of the workplace and sharing in collective responsibility for their implementation (Q3b);
- ■ communicating effectively with children, colleagues, parents and carers (Q4);
- ■ recognising and respecting the contribution that colleagues, parents and carers can make to the development and well-being of children and to raising their levels of attainment (Q5).

STANDARDS FOR TRAINEE TEACHERS

Meeting a professional standard is not simply a case of 'doing it once' to prove that you possess the ability or skills, but acting in such a way that these qualities are a recognisable part of your regular behaviour as a teacher. Consistency is a particularly important quality to possess in maintaining professional values and practice because colleagues and pupils in school must be confident that you will respond predictably and reasonably, even when under duress. Professional behaviour is the cornerstone of your work as a teacher, so must assume a high priority.

Practical considerations include arriving well before school begins, using time productively and gaining a solid reputation as an effective practitioner or, at least, someone with the potential to become one. Professionalism entails that you are transparent with every member of staff and empathise with individual concerns and dilemmas. Trainees who make an effort to be pleasant, show an interest in the children and establish a harmonious relationship with parents and carers not only endear themselves to all concerned, but are also trusted with a great deal of valuable information about pupils' lives out of school.

To underline the importance of professional conduct in administering the curriculum, a three-year study known as the *Cambridge Primary Review* and entitled: 'The condition and future of primary education in England' was undertaken by a team led by Robin Alexander on behalf of Esmee Fairburn Trust/ University of Cambridge (Alexander, 2009). The *Cambridge Primary Review* identified the purposes that the primary phase of education should serve, notably the values it should espouse; the curriculum and learning environment it should provide; and the conditions necessary to ensure the highest quality and address the future needs of children and society. A second report in the same year was the *Independent Review of the Primary Curriculum* (Rose Review) (Rose, 2009), which recommended a primary curriculum that was not based on discrete subjects (maths, science, history, etc.), but built around half a dozen or so areas of learning.

QTS STANDARDS FOR PROFESSIONAL ATTRIBUTES

All trainee teachers have to comply with the professional attributes as described in the *Professional Standards for Teachers: Qualified Teacher Status* (TDA, 2007). The following summaries relate specifically to each of the first five QTS standards for professional attributes; however, this division is purely for organisational reasons, as many of the standards are interdependent. For students who aspire to M level, there are two questions and discussion points in Task 1.2.1.

Task 1.2.1 **EDUCATIONAL POTENTIAL**

■ What do you understand by the phrase 'full educational potential'?
■ Discuss the assumption in Q1 that it is possible for a teacher to 'ensure' that every child has achieved his or her full educational potential?

Relationships with children

This section consists of two QTS standards: Q1 and Q2.

Q1: Have high expectations of children, including a commitment to ensuring that they can achieve their full educational potential and to establishing fair, respectful, trusting, supportive and constructive relationships with them.

You will note that there are three aspects of this QTS standard: (a) having high expectations; (b) ensuring pupils reach their potential; and (c) establishing good relationships. A high expectation is achieved through being clear in your mind about what you expect children to learn and also making it clear to them. It involves setting targets for individual pupils' learning, insisting on serious application to the task and encouraging appropriate standards of presentation of completed work. However, you should not confuse high expectations with unreasonable ones. For instance, setting tasks that are too demanding can quickly lead to pupil demoralisation and a lowering of self-esteem. The success with which you establish and maintain expectations will depend to a considerable extent on your ability to assess each pupil's knowledge and grasp of concepts. The greater your skill in assessment, the more precise you can be in setting work that suits a child's capability.

Your expectations should not only relate to academic success, but also extend to standards of behaviour. A small number of children choose to misbehave rather than to apply themselves to their work. Others do not apply themselves because they are confused about where the boundaries lie. Yet others may come from a home background in which success in school is not regarded as a priority. As the teacher you have to establish and maintain high expectations while taking account of the different factors that impinge upon achievement; namely, pupil motivation, confidence, natural ability, willingness to persevere, personality and even state of health. Your decisions about what is and what is not acceptable from each child will depend in part on these factors, but also on your own skill in teaching, maintaining interest and managing learning.

Ensuring that children achieve their full potential is accomplished through offering them practical support and reassurance, encouraging them to persevere and eliminating a fear of failure. It is also important to make sure that pupils have adequate time and resources to achieve goals, bearing in mind that some children work slowly and others much faster. In all cases, it is essential that you treat children with courtesy and consideration and show concern for their development as learners, providing them with benchmarks for success.

Discrimination is not allowed in schools on any basis. Furthermore, all teachers must recognise and respond effectively to equal opportunities issues and challenge incidents of bullying and harassment. Showing deliberate or unintentional bias towards pupils that can be construed as discriminatory leaves you open to charges of unprofessional conduct, so it is important to be as impartial as possible at all times through offering all children a fair chance to take advantage of your expertise and the available activities and resources.

It is not appropriate to label children due to circumstances beyond their control, such as home background or physical appearance. A teasing pleasantry about a child's looks or domestic circumstances may be more hurtful and do greater damage than you imagine. A useful antidote to discriminatory attitudes is to develop a positive attitude towards achievement and to adopt an 'all things are possible' working atmosphere in which children are resolute in facing challenges without fear of recrimination.

Strategies with children who have English as an additional language (EAL) include the use of steady, well-articulated speech, the availability of visual learning aids and making a special effort to involve all the children in creative activities. As some children may become frustrated by their inability to conform and contribute to classroom discussion, enlisting the help of a sympathetic child (a 'buddy') to help them to adjust, and the close involvement of teaching assistants who possess appropriate language skills, are desirable. It is important for you to remember that EAL children may be bright and articulate in their first tongue, so they should not be given a surfeit of trivial or repetitive tasks to keep them occupied on the assumption they are unable to cope with the more demanding work.

Establishing fair, respectful, trusting, supportive and constructive relationships with children is facilitated by speaking courteously and directly to the children; taking account of their personalities and dispositions; explaining complications patiently; being fair-minded and reasonable in dealing with issues; insisting on mutual respect; demonstrating that you like the children by using good eye contact, smiling often and responding positively to their comments; and celebrating their achievements by use of praise and, where appropriate, a tangible reward.

Task 1.2.2 **RELATING TO PUPILS**

In your mind divide your class list into three groups: (1) children that I enjoy teaching; (2) children that I don't relate to particularly well; and (3) children that I wish were in someone else's class. Over the next few days make a determined effort to view all children as (1) and resist the temptation to blame children in groups (2) and (3) for problems that arise. Monitor how adopting such a positive attitude transforms the way that you approach your teaching and your feelings about individuals.

Q2: Demonstrate the positive values, attitudes and behaviour they expect from children.

Standard Q2 consists of three elements: (a) demonstrating positive values; (b) demonstrating positive attitudes; and (c) demonstrating positive behaviour. The key word is 'demonstrating'; that is, the adult modelling the values, attitudes and behaviour that will offer children secure principles and practices on which to base their own actions. It would, for instance, be hypocritical to criticise a child for being noisy and bossy if you regularly exhibit such traits. Awareness that pupils are influenced by your conduct does not, of course, require that you should suppress your personality and behave artificially, but that immature behaviour is strictly off-limits.

In practice, demonstrating positive *values* to children can be achieved through exercising patience; showing fairness and sympathetic treatment during disputes; being polite towards children, even when they are being churlish; and a willingness to see both sides of an argument and arbitrate calmly. Demonstrating positive *attitudes* to children can be promoted through responding helpfully when they request assistance; being tolerant of sincere mistakes; applauding effort and hard work; trusting children to carry out tasks without close supervision; and being prepared to offer a second chance to children when they disappoint you. Demonstrating positive *behaviour* to children is done, first and foremost, by speaking and responding naturally (rather than 'teacherly'); being willing to confront wrong rather than pretending you did not notice; addressing the heart of the issue rather than attacking the person; being decisive when the facts are clear; showing that you enjoy learning; and responding enthusiastically to children.

Frameworks

The 'Frameworks' section of the QTS standards consists of a single Q-standard, Q3, sub-divided into Q3a and Q3b, emphasising duties, policies and practices.

Q3:
(a)   *Be aware of the professional duties of teachers and the statutory framework within which you work.*
(b)   *Be aware of the policies and practices of the workplace and share in collective responsibility for their implementation.*

Standard Q3 contains four distinct elements: (a) professional duties; (b) statutory framework; (c) policies and practices; and (d) collective responsibility. You have to take responsibility for your own professional development by keeping up to date with research and theories in teaching and possessing an understanding of school policies and practices in pastoral areas, personal safety matters and bullying. Although this standard only asks you to 'be aware of' and not to have a detailed working knowledge of the duties and practices, you need to possess sufficient insights to ensure that your work and conduct are influenced and guided by the stated requirements.

Being aware of the professional duties of teachers involves gaining information from the General Teaching Council for England (GTCE) about expectations of teachers and familiarity with the *School Teachers' Pay & Conditions Document 2007* (sections 72.1–72.12) for qualified teachers. The expectations are summarised as:

■   active teaching;
■   assessment and reporting duties;
■   communicating and consulting with parents;
■   providing guidance to pupils on educational and social matters;
■   contributing to the preparation and development of teaching material and to pastoral arrangements;
■   participating in national appraisal arrangements and in training and professional development schemes;
■   helping to sustain the discipline and health and safety dimensions of school life;
■   engaging in staff meetings;
■   providing limited 'cover' for absent colleagues.

You won't get bored!

The statutory framework within which teachers work necessitates that you know about your own rights and responsibilities in areas of equality of opportunity, health and safety, special educational needs (SEN), child protection and teacher employment; that you are familiar with the five key outcomes for children identified in *Every Child Matters* (DfES, 2005) – be healthy; stay safe; enjoy and achieve through learning; make a positive contribution to society; achieve economic well-being – and their implications; and that you know about the six areas of the Common Core of skills and knowledge for the children's workforce:

1   Effective communication and engagement with children, young people and their families and carers.
2   Child and young person development.
3   Safeguarding and promoting the welfare of the child.
4   Supporting transitions (e.g. from primary to secondary school).
5   Multi-agency working (e.g. the involvement of social services).
6   Sharing information (noting confidentiality and sensitivities). See Cheminais (2008).

As you become familiar with school documentation and discuss issues with subject leaders, SEN coordinators and other significant staff, recognise that, although policies exist as guidelines, they are not blueprints and particular instances still demand professional judgement as to the most appropriate action. Policies and practices do not always align perfectly.

The transition from being an outsider to an accepted member of the teaching team (the 'rite of passage') is never smooth (Eisenhart *et al.*, 1991). Although you may be given advice about how to behave in appropriate ways in school (enthusiastic, courteous and dependable) and general teaching skills (planning, motivating pupils, managing the class, assessing progress), the process of enculturation into the new school setting relies heavily on advice from the host teachers. The reality is that you may fit into one school placement setting with ease and yet struggle in the next, depending on your skill in accommodating the way things are done there and responding appropriately (Nias, 1989).

Task 1.2.3 **THE IMPACT ON THE SCHOOL OF YOUR PRESENCE**

Consider how your colleagues in school would respond if asked the following questions about you:

■ What is your prevailing countenance: gloomy, cheerful, unpredictable?
■ Do you seem pleased to be in the school?
■ Do you like the children?
■ What attempt do you make to be friendly to ancillary staff?

On the basis of these predicted responses make a conscious effort to improve in all four areas by:

■ sounding upbeat about life in general;
■ making positive comments about the work situation;
■ speaking warmly about the children and *to* the children;
■ determining to treat everyone in a friendly, non-patronising way.

Case study 1

Trudy, a mature trainee, determined that she was going to throw herself wholeheartedly into school life. She was highly conscientious and worked late every evening. Her file was immaculate and the tutor commended the quality of her teaching. In addition, Trudy volunteered to help with a lunchtime club and an after-school homework club. She was a bright presence around the school and interacted breezily with staff and parents. Initially, the class teacher was delighted to have such an exceptional student, but after a few weeks Trudy began to find difficulty with her teaching, became quite reclusive and looked permanently tired. The second half of the placement was much less successful than the first half and Trudy only just struggled through to the end. Instead of pacing herself, she had expended too much effort early on and simply ran out of steam.

Communicating and working with others

This section of the QTS standards consists of three Q-standards, Q4, Q5 and Q6, each of which emphasises the importance of teamwork and mutual support. The days of teachers working in isolation behind closed doors have long passed.

Q4: Communicate effectively with children, colleagues, parents and carers.

QTS standard Q4 invokes the need to communicate with four sets of people; three of the sets are considered separately (parents and carers are considered together), but it is worth remembering that there is also communication passing between them, so what is said to one person may have implications for another. For instance, what you say to a child in school will probably be repeated at home – not necessarily using the precise words or intonation that *you* used! There are numerous instances where custody of the child is shared between the two parents, which occasionally creates conflict about which parent is entitled to information about the child (e.g. who receives the child's end of year report).

Communicating effectively with *children* is achieved through speaking clearly; using appropriate vocabulary; providing necessary information and guidance; repeating key messages for the purpose of clarification; and using a variety of spoken, visual and kinaesthetic (hands-on) methods. Communicating effectively with *colleagues* is brought about by being adequately informed about the topic of conversation; asking appropriate questions at the right time; finding out from them things that cannot be discovered by other means; and offering your own perspectives on issues. Communicating effectively with *parents and carers* has become increasingly important in recent years. Legislation has established the rights of parents to be well informed about the curriculum offered by each school and to know about their children's progress through reports and informal access to teachers (see, for example, Beveridge, 2004). Parents are also supposed to be involved in formulating school policy and consulted about decisions that impact upon their children's learning. Part of school inspections involves inviting parents to comment on their satisfaction level with the school and their children's progress. As a trainee teacher, you can enhance communication by being available for consultation; well informed about children's progress; responding helpfully to parental questions while maintaining confidentiality; noting parent's concerns and passing them on to the host teacher; offering reassurance when concerns are raised; and being the sort of friendly, bright person that gives parents and carers (as well as colleagues) confidence in you.

It is worth viewing contact with parents as a wonderful opportunity to share information and celebrate achievement, ideas and concerns, in addition to giving them facts and figures about their children's academic attainment.

Q5: Recognise and respect the contribution that colleagues, parents and carers can make to the development and well-being of children, and to raising their levels of attainment.

Education is a joint effort between parents and teachers to ensure that children learn well, enjoy school and make the best possible progress, both academically and socially. Over time, schools have been expected to handle an increasing volume of curriculum change and deal with issues such

Task 1.2.4 **EXTERNAL FACTORS IN CHILDREN'S DEVELOPMENT**

■ What factors outside school influence children's development, well-being and attainment?
■ Discuss the proposition that pupil attainment is more greatly influenced by the quality of teaching than by innate ability.

as healthy eating, protecting the environment, emotional well-being, physical safety and (from 2009) sex education for pupils aged five years and over. It is therefore in teachers' own interests to involve parents, especially in key areas such as reading. The use of homework is another method by which links between home and school can become more secure, though it is worth noting that not all parents are willing or able to contribute a lot of time or effort in assisting their children, and excessive amounts of homework are burdensome.

A report for the DfES about the impact of parental involvement on pupils' education found that what parents do with their children at home is the single most significant factor in fostering academic success (Desforges and Abouchaar, 2003). Responsible parents teach their children particular sets of values, establish boundaries for their behaviour and show them the consequences of disobedience. They talk to their children and answer their questions. They show them books, introduce them to games and offer them opportunities to play alone and with friends. Once formal schooling begins, teachers assume some of the responsibility, but the closer your partnership with parents, the more likely that the children will benefit from the combined efforts of both parties.

Some schools provide training evenings for parents who are interested in knowing more about how they can help their children directly. The *Engaging Parents in Raising Achievement: Do Parents Know They Matter?* research project focused on the relationship between parental engagement and raising achievement (Specialist Schools and Academies Trust/Association of School and College Leaders, DCSF, 2007). The project set out to trial new ways of involving parents in schools – particularly those seen as hard to reach – and found that, where parents and teachers work together to improve learning, the gains in achievement are significant.

Recognising and respecting the contribution of *colleagues* to children's development, well-being and attainment can be greatly assisted through a close observation of experienced teachers and assistants at work; becoming knowledgeable about the contribution that other professionals can

Task 1.2.5 **RELATING TO ADULTS IN SCHOOL**

Keep a mental record of how many adults you communicate with in school in the following ways:

■ a nodding encounter;
■ exchanging a few words;
■ an extended conversation.

Over the following week, make an effort to improve the level of communication by moving more of (1) into (2) and (2) into (3). Monitor how participants' attitudes towards you alter and the impacts upon your confidence and sense of belonging.

make; liaising helpfully with teachers as they plan and evaluate programmes of work; and informing assistants of, and consulting with them about, their role in lessons, as well as regularly expressing your sincere – not patronising – thanks for their efforts.

EVIDENCE OF SUCCESS

Providing evidence that you have met the standards for professional attributes is not as straight-forward as with other areas of professional competence. For instance, whereas it is relatively simple to show that you have carried out an assessment of a child's work or differentiated activities in plans, it is far harder to demonstrate that you have treated pupils consistently or shown sensitivity towards parents and carers. Nevertheless, an ethic of care and concern for others and open, sincere relationships with adults and children should underpin all that you do and say as an emerging professional.

Evidence checklist for professional attributes

Give yourself a score out of ten for each of the following:

■ Your lesson plans, introductions, level of activities, encouragement to achieve and feedback to children clearly indicate your expectations of them.

■ You make every effort to ensure that each child has a fair share of your time and opportunity to access resources and ask questions.

■ You speak and react calmly to children, express an interest in them as significant individuals, show a healthy regard for their opinions and care for their needs.

■ You speak courteously to parents and show genuine interest in their opinions, offering helpful comment about their child's academic and social progress.

■ You are positive about school life by what you say and make an effort to contribute your expertise and practical support in extra-curricular activities.

■ You make every effort to work in harmony with support staff, involve them in your planning where appropriate and use their expertise to enhance pupil learning.

■ You are willing to listen to advice and act upon it, offer suggestions about improving your teaching and draw on the effective practice of others.

■ You are familiar with the legal requirements for teachers, the school policies for behaviour and health and safety, and exercise sensible judgement about their implementation.

Case study 2

Paul had been a successful manager before deciding to train as a teacher. He was used to being the person in charge and, despite his sparkling personality, found it hard to accept advice when he had relied on his own wits and instincts so much in the past. Paul had strong interpersonal skills and related well to other adults, especially parents and non-teaching staff, which occasionally distracted him from other classroom duties. The inexperienced class teacher in whose classroom Paul was placed was unsure about how to approach the situation, but the more experienced school mentor had no such qualms and spoke to Paul at length and unequivocally about the situation. Paul accepted the criticisms with grace and made a strenuous effort to sort out his priorities and time management. During his next and final school placement Paul was so well regarded that he was shortlisted for a vacancy and appointed at the school as a newly qualified teacher.

SUMMARY

Demonstrating professionalism as a trainee teacher encompasses far more than possessing the technical ability to teach. You need strong subject knowledge – but also the skills and strategies to engage children in learning, enthuse them about the work and give them opportunity for success. You need to teach consistently – but also to inject imagination and creativity into your lessons and empower children to do the same in their learning. You need to relate to colleagues – but also prove that you are reliable, flexible and willing to learn so that you can improve your practice. You need to relate to parents – but also demonstrate that you care about their children's success, motivation and personal well-being.

Professionalism as a trainee teacher is not conforming to a set of standards written by people who will never meet the pupils you teach. True professional behaviour is acting and responding in such a positive, responsible and determined way that, despite your inexperience, you are viewed and treated as an integral member of the staff team and have a beneficial impact on children's view of themselves that continues well after you have completed the placement. Now if that thought doesn't motivate you, it's hard to know what will!

ANNOTATED FURTHER READING

Arthur, J., Davison, J. and Lewis, M. (2005) *Professional Values and Practice: Achieving the Standards for QTS*, London: Routledge.
> A comprehensive description of what needs to be known, understood and demonstrated to achieve each standard.

Browne, A. and Haylock, D. (eds) (2004) *Professional Issues for Primary Teachers*, London: Paul Chapman.
> A text that deals thoroughly with the key professional issues faced by trainee teachers and practising teachers.

Day, C. (2004) *A Passion for Teaching*, London: Routledge.
> A powerful amalgam of ways in which teachers can bring commitment, enthusiasm, intellect and emotional energy into their teaching and relationships in school.

Hayes, D. (2008) *Primary Teaching Today: An Introduction*, London: Routledge.
> An honest and realistic exposure of the joys and demands of primary teaching.

Hayes, D. (2009) *Learning and Teaching in Primary Schools: Achieving QTS*, Exeter: Learning Matters.
> Offers a refreshingly different approach to the acquisition of QTS.

Nias, J. (1997) 'Would schools improve if teachers cared less?', *Education 3–13*, 25(3): 11–22.
> A thought-provoking article about the implications of caring for effective teaching.

RELEVANT WEBSITES

Cambridge Primary Review: www.primaryreview.org.uk
Every Child Matters: www.everychildmatters.gov.uk
Independent Review of the Primary Curriculum (Rose Review): www.dcsf.gov.uk/primarycurriculum review/

Visit the companion website www.routledge.com/textbooks/ltps2e for:

■ additional questions and task for this unit;
■ links to useful websites relevant to this unit.

REFERENCES

Alexander, R. (2009) *The Cambridge Primary Review*, 'The condition and future of primary education in England', Cambridge: University of Cambridge/Esmee Fairburn Trust.

Beveridge, S. (2004) *Children, Families and Schools: Developing Partnerships for Inclusive Education*, London: Routledge.

Cheminais, R. (2008) *Engaging Pupil Voice to Ensure that Every Child Matters*, London: Routledge.

Department for Children, Schools and Families (DCSF) (2007) *Engaging Parents in Raising Achievement: Do Parents Know They Matter?* London: Crown Copyright.

Department for Education and Skills (DfES) (2005) *Every Child Matters*, London: DfES Publications.

Desforges, C. and Abouchaar, A. (2003) *The Impact of Parental Involvement, Parental Support and Family Education on Pupil Achievement and Adjustment: A Literature Review*, Research Report 433 for the DfES, London: Queen's Printer Copyright.

Eisenhart, M., Behm, L. and Romagno, L. (1991) 'Learning to teach: developing expertise or rite of passage?', *Journal of Education for Teaching*, 17(1): 51–71.

Nias, D.J. (1989) *Primary Teachers Talking: A Study of Teaching as Work*, London: Routledge.

Rose, J. (2009) *Independent Review of the Primary Curriculum: Final Report*, London: DCSF. Available online at www.dcsf.gov.uk/primarycurriculumreview (accessed May 2009).

Training and Development Agency for Schools (TDA) (2007) *Professional Standards for Teachers: Qualified Teacher Status*, London: TDA.

2

EXPLORING THE NATURE OF LEARNING AND TEACHING

CHILD DEVELOPMENT

Sandra Smidt

INTRODUCTION

This is a unit about child development. It is designed to help you understand different theories about how children develop and learn, why they develop in different ways and what this means for you as a teacher.

As a teacher you will need to know as much as possible about each individual child you teach. Your knowledge of each child will come about through discovering as much as you can about each child's life history; through observing the children at work and at play; and through talking to them and the significant people in their lives. In addition, your knowledge will grow through knowing something about what is currently thought about how children in general develop and about why there are some patterns of development across culture and time, but why there are also enormous differences. Helen Penn (2005) tells us that where you live matters. We will return to this later.

In this unit we will examine some key themes:

■ the work of theorists who have had an influence on our education system and/or on our thinking;
■ the contributions of history, society and culture to development;
■ the significance of context to development;
■ recent and current research on aspects of child development and some subsequent legislation.

OBJECTIVES

By the end of this unit you should be able to:

■ explain why educators need to be knowledgeable about child development;
■ critique the work of some theorists in terms of respect for culture and context;
■ understand the concept of patterns of development and how and why these vary;
■ describe how context – in the sense of family, neighbourhood, culture and other factors – enables children to make sense of the world and of their place in it;
■ recognise each child as a competent and unique person, actively involved in making sense of all aspects of the physical, emotional and social worlds he or she inhabits;
■ refer to current and relevant legislation affecting children, their learning and their rights and assess the relevance of this to schools and teachers.

Task 2.1.1 **WHAT IS CHILD DEVELOPMENT?**

Take a moment to think about what you understand by the words 'child development' and then about why you think this is something that all educators need to be knowledgeable about. Did you come up with the names of any theorists, such as Piaget or Vygotsky, perhaps? Did you mention words like 'culture' or 'curiosity' or 'legislation'? Read on to find out more.

CHILD DEVELOPMENT: WHAT IS IT AND WHY DOES IT MATTER?

Here are two definitions of child development for you to think about. The first comes from Wikipedia and states that 'child development refers to the biological and psychological changes that occur in human beings between birth and the end of adolescence, as the individual progresses from dependency to increasing autonomy'. The second comes from the Inter-American Development Bank: Sustainable Development Department and states that 'child development is a multifaceted, integral, and continual process of change in which children become able to handle ever more complex levels of moving, thinking, feeling and relating to others'. Both definitions clearly imply some progression from dependency to independence; neither pays much attention to the effects of place, time, context, culture or society on development.

It is true that most texts on child development refer to children in the developed and prosperous world rather than to children in the developing world. In the first edition of this book, Tricia David (the respected previous author of this unit) (2006) drew attention to the work of William Kessen (written nearly 30 years ago), in which he talked of how each culture effectively 'invents' its children as each culture shapes both the childhoods and the futures of these children (Kessen, 1979). And since then writers like Bruner (2000) have continued to draw attention to the importance of context. He believed that the ways in which children are nurtured and reared within their own communities and homes, which reflect the values and beliefs and views of the world of those communities and homes, are important to the development of the children. The implication is that those working with children should be knowledgeable about, and respectful of, different values, beliefs, views of the world and styles of childrearing. Robert LeVine, writing of children in the advantaged North America describe such childhoods as being marked by the presence of

> numerous possessions earmarked as belonging to him (the child) alone; their number and variety increase as he gets older, permitting him to experience the boundaries of self represented in his physical environment . . . From infancy onwards the child is encouraged to characterize himself in terms of his favourite toys and foods and those he dislikes: his tastes, aversions and consumer preferences are viewed not only as legitimate but as essential aspects of his growing individuality – and a prized quality of an independent person.
>
> (LeVine, 2003: 95)

You might like to compare such a childhood with your own or with those of your own children or with that of one of the many African children orphaned through AIDS or affected by war.

In short, then, anyone who works with children needs to adopt a view of child development which might be described as sociocultural/historical, which means taking a view that examines the contexts of children and their development in terms of time, place and social grouping. This means reading the works of acknowledged child development theorists with a critical eye, paying attention to whether they focus on one kind of child from one kind of background, having experienced one style of child-rearing and one set of expectations. In the section that follows we will briefly examine the work of some of the best-known theorists and you will need to ask yourself whether their findings about how children develop and learn apply globally or not.

SOME KEY FIGURES

Task 2.1.2 **CHILD DEVELOPMENT THEORISTS**

Read through the list of names below and decide if you believe their approach to child development was largely individual or concerned more with the influences of society, history, culture and context. Make your own table of those you believe do take account of the importance of these factors and justify you choice. Your table should have two columns: (1) Theorist (2) Evidence that approach takes account of society, history, culture and context.

Theorist	Main focus of attention: select one of more of the following
Jean Piaget	A Swiss biologist who studied his own children individually and local children in groups. He was interested in cognitive development. He saw children as actively constructing meaning, or being able to make sense of the world, initially through their senses and movement and then through age-related stages of development. This stage model of development focused largely on the concept of 'readiness' for learning and on what children could not yet do. He was interested in both play and language development, but believed that *the role of the educator was to set up a learning environment in which there were challenging activities for the learners.* His stage model influenced the structure of our school system.
Lev Vygotsky	A Russian psychologist who was interested in how knowledge was passed on from generation to generation, which meant he was deeply concerned with culture. He shared with Piaget a belief in children as active learners, but believed that learning took place through the interactions learners had with more experienced others. He also shared with Piaget an interest in play as a mode of learning and placed tremendous emphasis on language. He said that children came to understand their world through their interactions with more experienced others and through the use of cultural tools – things such as language, art, music, symbols and signs, which had all been developed by groups in society. *For him the role of the educator was to know when and how to intervene in order to move the child on from what the child could do with help to what the child could do alone.* To explain this he developed the 'zone of proximal development' – the 'gap' between performance and potential.
Jerome Bruner	He was initially concerned with why so many young children failed in formal education in the UK. He was interested, too, in the interactions infants had with their primary caregivers (usually mothers) and in the rituals of early childhood – in the West, games like 'peekaboo'. He was

concerned to ensure that account was taken of context (as you will have seen from the earlier quotation). For him *the role of the educator was to establish what it was the learner was paying attention to and then to intervene, focused on this, to take learning forward.* This sharing of attention is crucial and leads the learner to be able to get deeply involved in whatever it is he or she is doing. In current parlance, it is referred to as 'sustained shared thinking'. Bruner developed the concept of 'scaffolding learning', in which the educator supports the child in taking small, measured steps to achieve a higher level of performance or learning.

Barbara Rogoff	An American researcher, deeply interested in the importance of groups and of culture, who looked at children in the developing world and saw how they learned through being active participants in the real-life events of their communities. She talked of these learners as 'apprentices' and of the learning happening through what she called 'guided participation'. Within the classroom setting this may lead to building a class culture of shared values, shared cultural tools and shared expectations. For her, *the role of the educator was to provide children in formal settings with life-like opportunities to gain first-hand experience.* Here, she was influenced by Vygotsky, who believed that children only achieved the ability to think abstractly after having considerable first-hand or everyday experience.
Urie Bronfennbrenner	He was an ecologist, concerned with describing the network of contexts available to all children. In his model, the child is at the centre and around the child is a *microsystem* made up of the home in which are the child, parents and, possibly, siblings; the religious setting in which are the child, peers and adults; the school or setting, in which are the child, educators and peers and the neighbourhood, in which are the child, adults and peers. The first concentric circle describes the *mesosystem*, which defines the interactions between home, school, neighbourhood and religious settings. Next is the *exosystem*, describing the impact (real or potential) of local industry, parents' workplaces, local government, mass media and school or setting management committee. Finally, and most remote from the child, are the *macrosystems*, which define the dominant beliefs and ideologies operating for that child and his or her family. Into this come things such as laws. Bronfennbrenner was not writing about education per se, but one might infer that *the role of the teacher here includes being aware of the complex developmental niches every child experiences and respecting each child's culture and language.*
Judy Dunn	Judy Dunn's research focused on developing understanding of very young children about the rules and laws relating to social interaction. Her study related to examining how children came to understand the rules and conventions governing interactions in families and, although it was situated within one smallish community or context, it has relevance more widely. Most interestingly, she showed how early in life children develop an understanding that others have feelings and needs. Dunn was not writing about schools, but her findings are relevant and the *implications for the role of the teacher are that all learning includes learning about the roles and the rules and the rituals of small and bigger groups.*

Sigmund Freud	Possibly the best-known name on this list and known for his work on trying to understand and describe emotional development. Through his work with adults he came to a stage model of emotional development that was (and still is) contentious and not universally accepted. Nonetheless, he was a key figure and exerted an enormous influence over those who followed. *For teachers there is the reminder that emotional development is as important as cognitive or other development and needs to be considered.*
Loris Malaguzzi	Based at Bologna University after the war, he helped peasant women in the Reggio Emilia region of Italy to set up a series of settings to provide educational opportunities for very young children. Underpinning his work was an ideology based on the notion of each child being both unique and competent and of every child having access to what he called 'a hundred languages' – by which he meant the resources (or cultural tools) to allow them to express their thoughts and feelings and theories in as many different ways as possible. *For him the role of the educator was to listen to children rather than to question or test them; to take their efforts seriously; and to give them access to as many of these languages as possible* – namely music, drawing, painting, dance, language, and so on.
Cummins, Baker and others	Many of you will have children in your class who have English as an additional language. There are many cognitive advantages to being bilingual and these include a greater awareness of how language itself operates, which can help with the development of literacy, enhance problem-solving skills and build recognition of the importance of both context and audience. Bilingual learners need access to their first language in the early years of acquiring English, because their developing English may not enable them to grasp more complex concepts as they do not yet have the English language as an efficient cultural tool. As a teacher you will want to encourage the use of a first language and show respect for it, while offering many opportunities for the children to learn English through meaningful and collaborative activities.

SOME CURRENT AND RECENT RESEARCH

Neuroscience

Many of you will know something about relatively recent research by neuroscientists into what happens in the human brain when learning takes place. Sophisticated imaging devices have made it possible for these researchers to track the tangle of neurons in the brain of the human infant and observe how connections between neurons are established whenever the child is exposed to some sensory output. Learning, it appears, is directly related to experience. But did we need the neuroscientists to tell us that? Alison Gopnik and her colleagues (1999) tell us that, as the human infant becomes able to utilise the new connections being built up through the use of physical movement and all their senses, they begin to take control of the movements of their eyes, of their hands and of their limbs. Since they live in a world peopled by others and interact with others whenever possible we might suggest that they are pre-programmed to be social. The neuroscientists give us food for thought, but some of their findings have been misinterpreted by the media and others, giving rise to some dubious practices, such as 'brain gym' (which is based on no real scientific findings), or to some serious misconceptions, trying to persuade us that 'enriched environments' provide ideal learning opportunities. In essence all children, growing up in all environments, learn from all their experiences. The provision of expensive toys and equipment is not a requirement for learning.

The *Researching Effective Pedagogy in the Early Years* (REPEY) project

The earlier research project, *Effective Provision of Pre-school Education* (EPPE) (1997–2003), examined a large number of early childhood settings and identified a number of factors that were significant in contributing to the quality of provision. The subsequent *Researching Effective Pedagogy in the Early Years* (REPEY) project focused more clearly on teaching or pedagogy and arrived at the conclusion that the most important factor in determining quality was the nature of adult–child interactions (Siraj-Blatchford *et al.*, 2002). Quality of provision was deemed high where children made the most progress and the activities were founded on solid principles of direct and first-hand experience. Here, children were able and helped to construct new understandings. In the views of the researchers, what characterised the quality they identified was the evidence of opportunities for children to become deeply involved in meaningful activities together with adults, both sharing meaning and engaged with understanding one another. They noted that the learning that took place through these interventions was particular in what they called *sustained shared thinking* between a pair (or a *dyad*) of learner and adult. This meant that, where an adult was able to focus on the child's interests and exploration rather than on a pre-set goal, the adult was able to intervene appropriately and sensitively and in this way help the child take the next step in learning.

Task 2.1.3 **SHARED THINKING**

Read the case study below and analyse it in terms of whether or not it seems to you to be an example of sustained shared thinking. To be an example of this it must show that the adult is not just questioning the child but is tuned in very carefully to what it is the child is paying attention to or interested in. Then think carefully about the effect of this on the child's learning and development.

Case study

Benedict, aged four, is sitting and looking out of the window of his classroom. There are various birds in the playground and he watches them intently. Rashida, the teaching assistant, has been working with Benedict over the past week because the class teacher feels he might be withdrawn from the other children, since she rarely sees him interact or hears him speak. Benedict gets up and goes across the room to fetch a pencil and a piece of paper. He takes them back to where he was sitting and very intently begins to draw and make marks on the piece of paper. Rashida continues to watch him. He keeps looking up at the birds and down at his piece of paper. After a while, Rashida goes over and says to him 'I love the birds. I love watching them.' And Ben answers her without hesitation. 'I think they are bored. They haven't got anything to play with.' Surprised, Rashida carries on the exchange. 'That's true. I never thought of that.' There is silence for a while and then Ben volunteers, 'I think they might like some toys. You know – a roundabout or a see-saw. I am trying to design one for them.' Rashida looks down at the paper and there, indeed, is an outline of what might become a see-saw for the bird. 'What a wonderful idea,' she responds. 'Perhaps you could get someone to help you make it because it would be a lot of work to do on your own.' Ben nods and then says, 'I would like to make it out of wood and Adebayo is really good at woodwork so I might ask him.' Later that day, the teacher notices that Ben and Adebayo are working together at the woodwork bench, communicating as they create both a roundabout and a see-saw for the birds.

The *Cambridge Primary Review*

The *Cambridge Primary Review* is an ongoing and wide-ranging enquiry into primary education in England. The work started in October 2006 and will publish its final report in 2010. Some of the interim findings are both interesting and significant and draw on four research reports. Two of these reports examine aspects of child development and they are the ones we will focus on. The report 2/1(a) *Children's Cognitive Development and Learning* (Goswami and Bryant, 2007) tells us that young children's learning is socially mediated and that families, carers, peers and educators all play significant roles in determining the effectiveness of learning. So the ways in which educators talk to children can influence memory, understanding and the motivation to learn. This report also tells us that, for children to be effective learners, they need to have had sound experiences in terms of language, perception and spatial development. The second report 2/1(b) was on social development and the roles of pupil–pupil interaction and collaboration in classroom learning and was carried out by Christine Howe and Neil Mercer (2007). You will not be surprised to learn that they found that talk and social interaction are key factors in social development and learning and that, in schools in England, there are few activities inviting collaboration, peer teaching or the development of negotiation and the sharing of ideas.

The Early Years Foundation Stage

The Early Years Foundation Stage (EYFS) framework became mandatory from September 2008 for all those in schools and other early years, Ofsted-registered settings attended by children from birth to the end of the academic year in which they turn five. The EYFS looks at the development of children from birth to the age of five and refers, of course, to the work and the findings of some of the people we have already referred to. It emphasises the fact that play is a very important mode of learning and that children should be learning primarily through play throughout this stage. Their definition of play may not coincide with mine, since they talk of adult-initiated play, whereas for me play is only play if it is self-chosen and self-directed. Adults can, of course, join in play or seek to interact with a child engaged in play. It is really important for you, as a teacher, to not only understand why play is so important as a way of learning, but also to be able to explain it to your colleagues and to parents. Play is not something trivial, nor is it always fun. People in traumatised and devastated communities have reported on the play that children there engage in and that is far from fun. Rather, play – which seems to be universal – is what children do when they find something that interests or excites or concerns or challenges them. When they want to find out about something, what they do is explore it using whatever means available to them. This activity, investigation, exploration or expression is play and because they have chosen to do it they will be very interested in it, spend a long time doing it and cannot fail. So play is only play when it is self-chosen. What is important to remember is that, in play, children do several cognitively significant things:

■ They almost always invent or make up rules and this is important because many of our abstract systems (written language, mathematics, physics, music and others) are rule bound. In language, for example, the rules are the grammar of the language.

■ They very often use one thing to stand for or represent another. This also relates to many of the abstract systems used in schooling that are symbolic (language uses sounds and letters to represents words, letters, ideas, concepts, and so on).

■ They often try out things in play – behaving 'as if . . .' or trying out 'what if . . .', and so on.

The *Children's Plan*

The *Children's Plan* (2008) is a government initiative that arose out of evidence published in 2007 showing that children in the UK fared worse than their counterparts in much of the developed world. The report seeks to improve 'childhood' per se through a series of goals and objectives. It states that it 'aims to make England the best place in the world for children and young people to grow up'. We cannot go into this plan in detail, but in terms of child development it does highlight some issues as follows:

■ The importance of parents and families in the development of children. We can extrapolate from this the importance of respecting the diversity of experiences children from different families have and that takes us back to Bruner's quotation earlier in this unit.

■ The importance of health and well-being in the development of children. Poverty continues to have a devastating effect on development and is something educators need to be aware of.

■ The effects, negative and positive, on development of things such as the internet, video games, excessive commercialism, risk taking, bullying, and so on. Children in England are thought to spend an inordinate amount of time watching screens of one sort or another, and of being restricted because of fears for their safety.

THE IMPLICATIONS OF ALL THIS

By now, you should have started to be able to think about what you can learn about how to teach children from knowing something about child development. What follows should help you consolidate this. We can say that:

■ *All learning is social: the roles of others in learning cannot be ignored.*
Social, in this sense, refers to more than the presence of others. It refers to the previous experiences of the learner and the use of socially and culturally constructed tools. So you as teacher will want to know as much as possible about the life and experiences of each learner before coming to your class. The 'others' who play a role in learning may be teachers, other adults and/or more experienced others, who may be peers or older children. For the educator the importance of this is to ensure that opportunities for interaction between children, and between children and adults, are planned for and exploited. For you this means thinking about where you and the other adults in your room will be and about how you will encourage learners to share, talk, negotiate and collaborate.

■ *Knowledge of and respect for cultural values and cultural tools is vital to successful learning.*
This implies that all involved in learning/teaching enterprises have to take time and effort to know what experiences and cultural tools their learners have had and ensure that, wherever possible, they have access to using these. You will need to know what languages the children in your class recognise, speak, read and/or write. You need to make as many cultural tools as possible available to the learners.

■   *Building a culture within the class or setting is important in developing the principles you bring to your teaching.*

This will allow you, with your learners, to develop an ethos of sustained shared attention, respect for one another, the use of shared cultural tools, and an environment where questioning, seeking for answers, making things and having a go are embedded. You are trying to create a culture of learners and learning.

■   *Language is the supreme but not the only cultural tool essential in planning and organising learning environments.*

Educators must plan for the use of spoken and written language and other symbolic systems or languages. The impact of this is to allow children to use their first language where this is the language in which they hold some concepts (both everyday and in some cases scientific or abstract) and to offer opportunities for all children to explore and represent things in ways other than in words. This brings us back to the 'hundred languages' of Malaguzzi. It also reminds us that a classroom should be a place buzzing with talk and not a silent place.

■   *Learning takes place through experience.*

The educator must plan and resource activities that are accessible and meaningful to the children. For the younger children, activities should offer first-hand and direct experience to allow for the development of everyday concepts, and for all children they should offer opportunities to create and use symbols, which should enable or enhance the ability to think abstractly.

■   *There are many ways or modes of learning and all need to be considered.*

Play (which we will come to next and which can be defined as where they are able to follow their own interests and create their own rules) may well be a dominant mode of learning for the younger children but not, sadly, for those in KS2. This is despite much work illustrating how much children learn through being in charge of following up their own interests. There are other important ways of learning. The search is always to find something that will motivate children, offer them a cognitive challenge, allow them to get deeply involved in what they are doing, and build on what they already know. Listening to stories, making music or expressing ideas through art or drama are all powerful ways of learning, as are climbing, sharing, negotiating and, vitally, questioning.

Task 2.1.4 **THEORY IN PRACTICE**

Organise a visit to spend time in one class in a school in which you are doing a placement or practice. Take a notebook with you and see if you can find examples of any of the important issues we have been able to highlight after our whistle-stop tour of some of the ideas of significant researchers and theorists.

Look for examples of any or all of the following:

■ learning through interaction;
■ adults listening to children;
■ adults scaffolding children's learning;
■ children having direct or first-hand experiences;
■ languages being explicitly recognised and respected;
■ adults giving helpful feedback;
■ adults and children sharing the focus of attention;
■ anything else you find positive.

■   *There are many ways or models of pedagogy or teaching.*

Those who adopt a sociocultural view of development and learning will be interested in developing a style of teaching that is interactive, uses cultural tools, focuses on the learner as a competent and curious individual, listens to the learner and thinks carefully about how to take learning forward through scaffolding, where there is sustained shared thinking. There are many modes of teaching, which include listening, making and sharing meaning, observing, giving feedback, modelling, answering, offering resources, and so on.

SUMMARY

In this very brief introduction to an extremely complex and fascinating area, we have only looked at the views of some people who have had an enormous influence on thinking about children, learning, development and childhoods. Running through this outline has been the concern to answer the question, 'Why do we, as educators, need to know anything at all about child development?' After an outline of the most important aspects of the work of writers and theorists, we have looked at some recent and relevant research and the implications of this for teachers. The unit ends with a summary of the contribution this all makes to educators. There are many books you can read on child development. Three are described briefly below.

ANNOTATED FURTHER READING

Donaldson, M. (1978) *Children's Minds*, London, Fontana.

> This is an accessible and important book that has not dated despite being written 30 years ago.

Gravelle, M. (ed.) (2000) *Planning for Bilingual Learners*, Stoke on Trent. Trentham Books.

> This is a book made up of many voices and offers a framework for those working with children who come with languages other than English. It is relevant because it refers back to recent research, including research into child development.

Smidt, S. (2009) *Introducing Vygotsky: A Guide for Practitioners and Students*, London and New York: Routledge.

> This is a book due to be published soon and has been written particularly for those working with or training to work with children in schools and other settings. It attempts to make some of the complex but fascinating ideas of Vygotsky and his followers accessible.

RELEVANT WEBSITES

Cambridge Primary Review: www.primaryreview.org.uk
Children's Plan: www.dcsf.gov.uk/childrensplan/
Early Years Foundation Stage framework: http://nationalstrategies.standards.dcsf.gov.uk/earlyyears
Effective Provision of Pre-school Education (EPPE): www.kl.ioe.ac.uk/schools/ecpe/eppe/
Every Child Matters: http://everychildmatters.gov.uk/
Wikipedia on child development: http://en..wikipedia.og/wiki/Child_development

Visit the companion website www.routledge.com/textbooks/ltps2e for:

■ additional questions and task for this unit;
■ links to useful websites relevant to this unit.

REFERENCES

Baker, C. (2000) *A Parents' and Teachers' Guide to Bilingualism*, 2nd edn, Clevedon: Multilingual Matters.

Bronfennbrenner, Urie (1979) *The Ecology of Human Development*, Cambridge, MA: Harvard University Press.

Bruner, Jerome (2000) 'Foreword', in J. DeLoache and A. Gottleib (eds) *A World of Babies: Imagined Childcare Guides for Seven Societies*, Cambridge: Cambridge University Press.

Cummins, Jim (2000) *Language, Power and Pedagogy. Bilingual Children in the Crossfire*, Clevedon: Multilingual Matters.

David, Tricia (2006) 'Looking at children', in J. Arthur, T. Grainger and D. Wray (eds) *Learning to Teach in the Primary School*, London and New York: Routledge.

Dunn, Judy (1993) *Young Children's Close Relationships: Beyond Attachment*, Newbury Park, CA: Sage.

Freud, Sigmund (1991) *Introductory Lectures on Psychoanalysis*, London: Penguin.

Gopnik, A., Melzoff, A. and Kuhl, P. (1999) *How Babies Think*, London: Weiden and Nicolson.

Goswani, U. and Bryant, P. (2007) *Children's Cognitive Development and Learning, Cambridge Primary Review: Research Survey 2/1(a)*, Cambridge: Cambridge University Press.

Howe, C. and Mercer, N. (2007) *Children's Social Development, Peer Interaction and Classroom Learning, Cambridge Primary Review: Survey 2/1(b)*, Cambridge: Cambridge University Press.

Kessen, W. (1979) 'The American child and other cultural inventions', *American Psychologist*, 34(10): 815–20.

LeVine, R. (2003) *Childhood Socialization: Comparative Studies of Parenting, Learning and Educational Change*, Hong Kong: Comparative Education Research Centre.

Malaguzzi, Loris (1984) *L'Occhio Se Salta Il Muro*, Giglio: Comune di Reggio Emilia.

Penn, Helen (2005) *Understanding Early Childhood*, Maidenhead: Open University Press/McGraw Hill.

Piaget, J. (1955) *Language and Thought of the Child*, London: Routledge and Kegan Paul.

Rogoff, Barbara (1990) *Apprenticeship in Thinking: Cognitive Development in Social Context*, Oxford: Oxford University Press.

Siraj-Blatchford, I., Sylva, K., Muttock, S., Gilden, R. and Bell, D. (2002) *Researching Effective Pedagogy in the Early Years* (REPEY), DfES Research Brief 356, London: DfES.

Vygotsky, Lev (1978) *Mind in Society: The Development of Higher Psychological Processes*, Cambridge, MA: Harvard University Press.

LOOKING AT LEARNING

David Wray

INTRODUCTION

Learning is paradoxical in nature. It can sometimes appear to be a very simple thing. All of us are learning all the time, after all, from the myriad experiences we encounter in our daily lives. I go to a new restaurant and I learn that even smoked salmon can be spoilt if you serve it with too much dill sauce; I read the newspaper and learn a little more about how Chelsea are threatening to take over the English footballing world; I play on my son's X-box and finally learn how to outwit that alien that's been shooting me in every one of my previous tries. Learning is so simple that we do not question its presence in how we go about our daily activities, for it is as natural to our existence as eating and drinking. Yet, when we encounter difficulties in learning something, we no longer take the learning process for granted. It is only then that our awareness of how we learn is heightened. Learning can suddenly seem very difficult indeed. I remember trying numerous ways of learning Latin declensions at school until it suddenly struck me I could make a nursery rhyme of them: Lupus, lupe, lupum, lupi, lupi, lupo. This revelation worked so well, I still have this (useless) knowledge down pat even now.

Learning is taken for granted as a natural process. Yet, as simple a process as it seems, understanding how we learn is not as straightforward. The existence of numerous definitions and theories of learning and the significant and, at times, vitriolic debates between adherents of particular theories vouch for the complexity of the process. A look, more or less randomly, at educational psychology textbooks will illustrate the differences between the views of the 'experts' about what exactly learning is and how we learn. In David Fontana's *Psychology for Teachers* (1985), for example, the author writes, 'Most psychologists would agree that learning is a relatively persistent change in an individual's possible behaviour due to experience' (p. 211). This definition reflects a behaviourist view of learning, for it equates learning with an outcome defined as behaviour. Contrast it with the remarks of Norah Morgan and Juliana Saxton in their *Teaching, Questioning and Learning* (1991), as they argue that:

> effective teaching depends upon recognizing that effective *learning* takes place when the students are active participants in 'what's going on'. And for effective teaching and learning to occur, teachers must structure their teaching to invite and sustain that active participation by providing experiences which 'get them thinking and feeling', 'get the adrenalin flowing' and which generate in students a need for expression.
>
> (p. 7)

and to reinforce those responses through an effective reinforcement schedule (Skinner, 1976: 161). An effective reinforcement schedule requires consistent repetition of the material. The material to be learned should be broken down into small, progressive sequences of tasks, and continuous positive reinforcement should be given. Without positive reinforcement, learned responses will quickly become extinct. This is because learners will continue to modify their behaviour until they do receive some positive reinforcement.

WHAT DOES MOTIVATION INVOLVE?

Behaviourists explain motivation in terms of schedules of positive and negative reinforcement. Just as receiving food pellets each time it pecks at a button teaches a pigeon to peck the button, pleasant experiences cause human learners to make the desired connections between specific stimuli and the appropriate responses. For example, a learner who receives verbal praise and good marks for correct answers is more likely to learn those answers effectively than one who receives little or no positive feedback for the same answers. Likewise, human learners tend to avoid responses that are associated with negative reinforcements, such as poor marks or negative feedback.

HOW SHOULD YOU TEACH?

Behaviourist teaching methods tend to rely on so-called 'skill and drill' exercises to provide the consistent repetition necessary for the effective reinforcement of response patterns. Other methods include question (stimulus) and answer (response) sequences in which questions are of gradually increasing difficulty, guided practice and regular reviews of material. Behaviourist methods also typically rely heavily on the use of positive reinforcements, such as verbal praise, good marks and prizes. Behaviourists test the degree of learning using methods that measure observable behaviour, such as tests and examinations.

Behaviourist teaching methods have proved most successful in areas where there is a 'correct' response or easily memorised material. For example, while behaviourist methods have proved to be successful in teaching structured material, such as facts and formulae, scientific concepts and foreign language vocabulary, their usefulness in teaching comprehension and composition, to name but two abilities demanded by current National Curricula, is questionable.

As an example of this kind of teaching, some of you will have experienced the use of 'language laboratories' when you were learning a foreign language. In the language lab, you were often presented with stretches of discourse in the target language, which you were required to repeat, and then you were given feedback on the accuracy of this repetition. This experience has been demonstrated to improve learners' knowledge of the particular discourse form, but not of how this should be adapted to other, real-life, situations. While I was in the sixth form at school, for instance, I worked with an enthusiastic language teacher who decided we should be introduced to Russian. Through extensive experience of language lab drills I learned (by rote) how to greet someone in Russian (Zdrastvwe Olga, kak tee posavaesh?), how to acknowledge such a greeting (Spasiba, kharasho, a ti?) and how to respond (Spasiba, kharasho) – these were spoken drills, so I never did know how this was written down! Unfortunately, the first and only time I tried this out on a Russian speaker, he was not called Olga, and did not acknowledge my greeting in the 'right' way, and thus left me floundering! My language behaviour was not sufficiently adaptable to cope with the real-life situation.

Behaviourist theories of learning have had a recent renaissance in the field of behaviour management, rather than in content and concept learning. Positive behaviour management is usually taken to involve rewarding acceptable behaviour in pupils (CBG – Catch them Being Good) and ignoring unacceptable. Thus, so the theory goes, pupils will be encouraged to repeat the acceptable behaviour and the unacceptable will gradually die away. Note that it has usually been argued that, theoretically, unacceptable behaviour, if met with a negative response by the teacher, may in fact be perceived by the pupil as having been rewarded (any attention being better than none for some pupils) and thus will not fade away but be continued. Ignoring it is better. This argument makes good sense theoretically, but you might find it difficult to implement practically!

It is also true, of course, that the reward (positive feedback) that a pupil gains following unacceptable behaviour may come not from the teacher but from others in the class. The class clown tends to get his or her rewards from peers rather than from teachers.

Task 2.2.1 **A BEHAVIOURIST APPROACH TO TEACHING**

Behaviourist approaches to teaching tend to rely on three basic principles:

1 Break down the desirable end behaviour into small steps.
2 Teach – that is, stimulate and reinforce – each of these steps in the learner.
3 Reinforce increasingly long chains of behaviour until the full end behaviour is finally achieved.

■ Think of a teaching event in which you might employ such a set of principles for your teaching. Share your suggestions with colleagues and discuss how applicable this approach might be to teaching.
■ Before reading the following section of this unit, discuss with your colleagues what you consider to be the main limitations of behaviourism as a theory of learning.

Task 2.2.2 **SKINNER VS. CHOMSKY**

One of the most significant challenges to behaviourist views of learning came in the field of language acquisition. Skinner's attempt to explain this from a behaviourist perspective came in 1957 in his book, *Verbal Behavior*. This produced a devastating review from noted linguist, Noam Chomsky. This review can be read at www.chomsky.info/articles/1967----.htm and a wider attack on behaviourism can be found at www.chomsky.info/articles/19711230.htm.

When you have read either, or both, of these articles, try to produce a bullet point summary of the differences between Skinner and Chomsky in terms of their views about learning.

Constructivism

BRIEF HISTORY

A dissatisfaction with behaviourism's strict focus on observable behaviour led educational psychologists such as Jean Piaget to demand an approach to learning theory that paid more attention to what went on 'inside the learner's head'. An approach developed that focused on mental processes rather than observable behaviour – cognition rather than action. Common to most constructivist approaches is the idea that knowledge comprises symbolic mental representations, such as propositions and images, together with a mechanism that operates on those representations. Knowledge is seen as something that is actively constructed by learners based on their existing cognitive structures.

Therefore, it relates strongly to their stage of cognitive development. Understanding the learner's existing intellectual framework is central to understanding the learning process.

The most influential exponent of constructivism was the Swiss child psychologist, Jean Piaget. Piaget rejected the idea that learning was the passive assimilation of given knowledge. Instead, he proposed that learning is a dynamic process comprising successive stages of adaptation to reality, during which learners actively construct knowledge by creating and testing their own theories of the world. Piaget's theory has two main strands: first, an account of the mechanisms by which cognitive development takes place; and, second, an account of the four main stages of cognitive development through which, he claimed, all children pass.

The basic principle underlying Piaget's theory is the principle of equilibration (balancing): all cognitive development progresses towards increasingly complex but *stable* mental representations of the world. Such stability is threatened by the input of new ideas and so equilibration takes place through a process of adaptation. One of the reasons why humans have often been quite resistant to new ideas is this inbuilt need for stability in their concepts of the world. Think about the centuries during which people were convinced that the sun orbited the earth, rather than vice versa. It was not until evidence of the falsity of such a belief was overwhelming that most people made the destabilising mental shift to a new set of ideas about the world.

Such adaptation might involve the assimilation of new information into existing cognitive structures or the accommodation of that information through the formation of new cognitive structures. As an example of this, consider what happens when you enter a novel situation – say, going into a new restaurant. Normally, although you have never been in this particular restaurant before, you will have experience of many similar environments, and thus know what to expect. You know the sequence of events (waiter brings menu; leaves you for a while; returns to ask for your order; if it's a posh restaurant a different waiter asks you what wine you would like to drink with the meal; etc., etc.) – you know what is expected of you. The 'new' aspects of this restaurant (location, orientation of the room, design of the menus, particular specialist dishes, where the loos are, etc.) are simply new elements of information that you need to assimilate into your mental maps of the world (Piaget used the term 'schema' to refer to one of these mental maps – the plural is variously written as 'schemata' or 'schemas', depending on how classical your education was). If, less usually, this restaurant is way outside your previous experience (suppose it's your first visit to a Japanese restaurant), the process of learning might be more radical. There may be details about the cutlery, plates, order of the courses, appropriate drinks, etc. to come to terms with, and these new features need to be accommodated into an expanded schema of 'restaurant'. Thus, learners adapt and develop by assimilating and accommodating new information into existing cognitive structures.

Piaget also suggested that there are four main stages in the cognitive development of children. In their first two years, children pass through a sensori-motor stage, during which they progress from cognitive structures dominated by instinctive drives and undifferentiated emotions (they do not care who picks them up as long as they satisfy the basic physical drives of hunger, comfort, etc.) to more organised systems of concrete concepts and differentiated emotions (not anyone will do as a food provider – it has to be Mum or Dad). At this stage, children's outlook is essentially egocentric in the sense that they are unable to take into account others' points of view. The second stage of development lasts until around seven years of age. Children begin to use language to make sense of reality. They learn to classify objects using different criteria and to manipulate numbers. Children's increasing linguistic skills open the way for greater levels of social action and communication with others. From the ages of seven to twelve years, children begin to develop logic, although they can only perform logical operations on concrete objects and events. In adolescence, children enter the formal operational stage, which continues throughout the rest of their lives. Children develop the ability to perform abstract intellectual operations, and reach emotional and intellectual maturity. They learn how to formulate and test abstract hypotheses without referring to concrete objects. Most importantly, children develop the capacity to appreciate others' points of view as well as their own.

Piaget's theory was widely accepted from the 1950s until the 1970s. Then researchers such as Margaret Donaldson began to find evidence that young children were not as limited in their thinking as Piaget had suggested. Researchers found that, when situations made 'human sense' (Donaldson's term) to children, they could engage in mental operations at a much higher level than Piaget had predicted. His theory, particularly that aspect related to the above stages of development, is not now as widely accepted, although it has had a significant influence on later theories of cognitive development. For instance, the idea of adaptation through assimilation and accommodation is still widely accepted, and incorporated into what is now known as 'schema theory', which we will revisit in the next unit of this book.

WHAT IS KNOWLEDGE?

Behaviourists maintain that knowledge is a passively absorbed repertoire of behaviours. Constructivists reject that claim, arguing instead that knowledge is actively constructed by learners and that any account of knowledge makes essential references to the cognitive structures within the learner's mind. Knowledge comprises a complex set of mental representations derived from past learning experiences. Each learner interprets experiences and information in the light of their existing knowledge, their stage of cognitive development, their cultural background, their personal history, and so on. Learners use these factors to organise their experience and to select and transform new information. Knowledge is therefore actively constructed by the learner rather than passively absorbed; it is essentially dependent on the standpoint from which the learner approaches it.

WHAT IS LEARNING?

Because knowledge is actively constructed, learning is defined as a process of active discovery. The role of the instructor is not to drill knowledge into learners through consistent repetition, or to goad them into learning through carefully employed rewards and punishments. Rather, the role of the teacher is to facilitate discovery by providing the necessary resources and by guiding learners as they attempt to assimilate new knowledge to old and to modify the old to accommodate the new. Teachers must thus take into account the knowledge that the learner currently possesses when deciding how to construct the curriculum and how to present, sequence and structure new material.

WHAT DOES MOTIVATION INVOLVE?

Unlike behaviourist learning theory, where learners are thought to be motivated by extrinsic factors such as rewards and punishment, constructivist learning theory sees motivation as largely intrinsic. Because it involves significant restructuring of existing cognitive structures, successful learning requires a major personal investment on the part of the learner. Learners must face up to the limitations of their existing knowledge and accept the need to modify or abandon existing beliefs. Without some kind of internal drive on the part of the learner to make these modifications, external rewards and punishments such as marks are unlikely to be sufficient.

HOW SHOULD YOU TEACH?

Constructivist teaching methods aim to assist learners in assimilating new information into existing knowledge, and to enable them to make the appropriate modifications to their existing intellectual

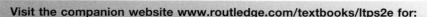
> **Visit the companion website www.routledge.com/textbooks/ltps2e for:**
>
> ■ additional questions and tasks for this unit;
> ■ links to useful websites relevant to this unit.

REFERENCES

Donaldson, M. (1978) *Children's Minds*, London: Fontana.

Fontana, D. (1985) *Psychology for Teachers*, London: Macmillan.

Joyce, B., Calhoun, E. and Hopkins, D. (1997) *Models of Learning: Tools for Teaching*, Buckingham: Open University Press.

Morgan, N. and Saxton, J. (1991) *Teaching Questioning and Learning*, London: Routledge.

Pritchard, A. (2008) *Ways of Learning*, London: David Fulton.

Skinner, B.F. (1976) *About Behaviourism*, New York: Vintage Books.

Vygotsky, L. (1978) *Mind in Society*, London: Harvard University Press.

Wood, D. (1988) *How Children Think and Learn*, Oxford: Blackwell.

FROM LEARNING TO TEACHING

David Wray

INTRODUCTION

In the previous unit we examined several important theories of learning, from behaviourism to social constructivism. It will probably have occurred to you that, in planning for the learning you hope and intend will take place in your classroom, you are guided not by a single theory of learning but in fact by elements of all these theories. There are useful elements within each of the theories reviewed in the previous unit, and indeed in other theoretical explorations of learning. Planning for teaching is not as simple as just deciding on the particular learning theory you wish to subscribe to. There are, however, a number of important insights into learning that can be used to underpin approaches to teaching and it is the purpose of this unit to outline these insights and then to develop some principles for teaching that can be derived from them.

OBJECTIVES

After reading this unit you should be able to:

■ discuss some important insights into the nature of learning and recognise the implications of these for teaching;
■ describe the basic elements of an apprenticeship approach to teaching, justify such an approach in terms of its foundation in research and theory, and suggest practical examples of the implementation of such an approach.

INSIGHTS INTO LEARNING

Four basic insights into the nature of the learning process have come from research over the past 20 years or so. Each of these has important implications for approaches to teaching.

Learning is a process of interaction between what is known and what is to be learned

It has become quite clear that, in order to do any real learning, we have to draw upon knowledge we already have about a subject. The more we know about the subject, the more likely it is that we shall learn any given piece of knowledge. Learning that does not make connections with our prior knowledge is learning at the level of rote only, and is soon forgotten once deliberate attempts to remember it have stopped.

Learning has been defined as 'the expansion and modification of existing ways of conceiving the world in the light of alternative ways (Wray and Medwell, 1991: 9). Such a constructivist approach to learning places great emphasis upon the ways in which prior knowledge is structured in the learner's mind and in which it is activated during learning. Theories about this, generally known as schema theories as they hypothesise that knowledge is stored in our minds in patterned ways (schema), suggest that learning depends, first, upon the requisite prior knowledge being in the mind of the learner and, second, upon it being brought to the forefront of the learner's mind.

As an example of this, in the field of learning through reading, try the following task.

Task 2.3.1 SCHEMAS AND READING

Look at the following story beginning:

The man was brought into the large white room. His eyes blinked in the bright light.

Try to picture in your mind the scene so far. Is the man sitting, lying or standing? Is he alone in the room? What sort of room is it? What might this story be going to be about?
Now read the next extract:

'Now, sit there', said the nurse. 'And try to relax.'

Has this altered your picture of the man or of the room? What is this story going to be about?

After the first extract you may have thought the story would be set in a hospital, or perhaps concern an interrogation. There are key words in the brief beginning that trigger off these expectations. After the second extract the possibility of a dentist's surgery may enter your mind, and the interrogation scenario fades.

Each item you read sparks off an idea in your mind, each one of which has its own associated schema, or structure of underlying ideas. It is unlikely, for example, that your picture of the room after the first extract had a plush white carpet on the floor. You construct a great deal from very little information.

Learning from the material you read is exactly like this. It is not simply a question of getting a meaning from what is on the page. When you read, you supply a good deal of the meaning to the page. The process is an interactive one, with the resultant learning being a combination of your previous ideas with new ones encountered in this text.

As another example of this, consider the following sentence:

Mary remembered her birthday money when she heard the ice-cream van coming.

Without trying too hard you can supply a great deal of information to the meaning of this, chiefly to do with Mary's intentions and feelings, but also to do with the appearance of the van and its driver's intentions. You probably do not immediately suspect him as a potential child molester! Notice that most of this seems so obvious that we barely give it much conscious thought. Our schemas for everyday events are so familiar that we do not notice when they are activated.

Now compare the picture you get from the following sentence:

Mary remembered her birthday money when she heard the bus coming.

What difference does this make to your picture of Mary, beyond the difference in her probable intentions? Most people say that she now seems rather older. Notice that this difference in understanding comes not so much from the words on the page as from the complex network of ideas that these words make reference to. These networks have been referred to as schemas and developments in our understanding of how they operate have had a great impact upon our ideas about the nature and teaching of reading comprehension.

Task 2.3.2 **THE IMPACT OF VARYING THE SCHEMA**

Try out the 'Mary' sentences above on some pupils you have access to (say between the ages of 6 and 11). Do they have the same responses to the sentences as you do? If not, this probably suggests that they have not yet developed the background schemas that you use in reading the sentences.

If they do make similar responses to you, you can extend the activity by using further variations on the original sentence. What schemas does the following activate, for example?

Mary remembered her gun when she heard the ice-cream van coming.

Or the following?

Mary remembered her stomach when she heard the ice-cream van coming.

Ask the pupils to think of their own variations and to explain the different impressions each leaves on the reader.

We have explored this issue through the example of reading, but the same interaction between the known and the new happens in any kind of learning. Many teachers have had the experience of asking a young child the apparently simple, mathematical question:

What is the difference between 6 and 9?

The answer they receive might be 3, or 'one number is upside down', or 'my brother is 9 and he's older than me 'cos I'm 6', depending upon the schema that is activated by the word 'difference'.

You may also have heard the story of the newly qualified teacher who began work with a class of 5–6 year olds in a rural school. She decided to begin her work with the class by using a topic she was reasonably confident they would be familiar with, so she showed them a picture of a cow. She asked the class, 'Now, who can tell me what this is?', but, to her consternation, not one of them could give her an answer, all of them looking faintly puzzled by the picture. After several equally fruitless attempts to get an answer to this simple question, she eventually became somewhat exasperated. 'Surely *somebody* can tell me what this is? You see them every day.' Eventually, one little boy raised his hand, not to give her an answer but to ask if he could look more closely at the picture. Baffled by now, she allowed him to come closer. He studied the picture for several moments before announcing in a tentative voice, 'I *think* it's an Aberdeen Angus cross heifer'.

In this case, the children actually possessed much more background knowledge – a richer schema – than the teacher. Their subsequent learning around this topic would be considerably different from that the teacher had planned.

Task 2.3.3 **CONFLICTING SCHEMAS**

It would be very useful to work with your colleagues to collect some more examples like this – where the schema being used by the teacher did not coincide with that being employed by the learners. Here are some examples from my own experience:

■ One 7-year-old boy once asked me 'How do you spell "friper"?' After some thought I had to admit this defeated me and I didn't know how to spell it. I asked him if he could tell me the sentence in which he wished to use this word. 'I like friper taters', came the reply!
■ One of my students was teaching in a South Wales school and had in his class a boy who was absent from school for a day. On his return, the student asked the boy what had been the problem. He replied, 'Badgers'. The student thought for a while and then took the boy to the class library and began to look for books about badgers, with the idea that they might possibly do a useful piece of project work on the subject. The boy looked increasingly puzzled and eventually stepped back and pointed to his ears, saying, 'Bad yers, sir.'

These are small examples, but if you can pool your experiences with other colleagues, you might collect a much wider range of activities. The challenge is to think of ways in which these misunderstandings (or 'misaligned schemas') might have been avoided by the teachers.

Learning is a social process

Ideas about learning have progressed significantly away from Piaget's purely 'lone scientist' view of learners as acting upon their environments, observing the results and then, through reflection, modifying or fine-tuning their schemas concerning these environments. Modern learning theory gives much greater recognition to the importance of social interaction and support and has a view of the learner as a social constructor of knowledge. In collaboration with others, learners establish:

■ *Shared consciousness*: a group working together can construct knowledge to a higher level than can the individuals in that group each working separately. The knowledge rests upon the group interaction.
■ *Borrowed consciousness*: individuals working alongside more knowledgeable others can 'borrow' their understanding of tasks and ideas to enable them to work successfully.

From a social constructivist perspective, the most important tool for learning is discussion, or discourse. A lot of research has been carried out to try to understand the qualities of discourse that enhance its effectiveness. Raphael and her colleagues, for example (Raphael *et al.*, 1992), have studied the discourse used by primary-aged pupils as they engaged in discussions about the books they had read. The question leading this research was: How do discussions about books influence 10–11-year-old pupils' ability to talk about literature? A great deal was revealed in the research about the role-played by the constitution of the groups, the books they discussed and the writing activities they were asked to complete as a follow-up. For example, it was found that the books chosen needed to have the potential for controversy and the power to elicit emotional responses. Furthermore, writing activities that allowed pupils more flexibility in their responses were more beneficial and led to more interesting discussions than those that demanded more structured responses. Finally, Raphael's research identified some of the more useful roles the teacher could play in such book discussions, such as modelling ways in which they could articulate their personal responses to literature.

The crucial role that the teacher plays in promoting the co-construction of knowledge in classrooms was also shown in the research of Forman *et al.* (1995), who studied the discourse of 11–12-year-old pupils and their teacher as they discussed mathematical problems. The classic pattern of classroom discussion has been found to consist largely of teachers initiating an exchange (usually by asking a question), a pupil responding (answering the question) and a teacher giving feedback on that response. This pattern is known as the Initiation – Response – Feedback (IRF) exchange and has been shown to account for up to 75 per cent of normal classroom discussion. In the Forman study, however, it was found that the pupils, rather than the teacher, were often engaged in evaluating each others' contributions, while the contributions of the teacher were often for the purpose of expanding upon pupils' contributions to the discussion. Similar patterns of discourse have been found in the sequence of research projects reported in Kumpulainen and Wray (2002) and suggest that group discussion, in changing the traditional patterns of classroom discourse, allows and encourages much greater involvement of pupils in learning.

Learning is a situated process

We learn everything in a context. That is not controversial. But modern learning theorists also suggest that what we learn is the context as much as any skills and processes that we use within that context (Lave and Wenger, 1991). Psychologists have sought in vain for 'generalisable skills' and all teachers are familiar with the problem of the transfer of learning. Why is it that a child who spells ten words correctly in a spelling test is likely to spell several of these wrongly when writing a story a short while afterwards? And why, to give an example from my own teaching experience, can a 10-year-old boy, who in class is absolutely hopeless with number work, maintain an extended, sensible discussion about horse-racing odds with peers in the playground. 'It's 9 to 4 on but it's going to soften.' Do *you* understand that statement? What will the odds move to if they 'soften'? 9 to 5 on, or 10 to 4 on? This mathematically challenged pupil had no problem with numbers of this kind. The answer to these conundrums is simply that the learning of skills such as spelling and number knowledge is so inextricably bound up with the context of learning that it cannot easily be applied outside this context.

Traditionally, education has often assumed a separation between learning and the use of learning, treating knowledge as a self-sufficient substance, theoretically independent of the situations in which it is learned and used. The primary concern of schools has often seemed to be the teaching of this substance, which comprised abstract, decontextualised, formal concepts. The activity and context in which learning took place were thus regarded as ancillary to learning – they were useful in terms of motivating the learners but not fundamental to the nature of the learning.

Recent investigations of learning, however, challenge this separation of what is learned from how it is learned and used. The activity in which knowledge is developed and deployed is now seen as an integral part of what is learned. Learning and cognition, it is now possible to argue, are fundamentally situated.

As an example of this, consider the work of Miller and Gildea (1987) on vocabulary teaching, in which they describe how children are taught words from dictionary definitions and a few exemplary sentences, and compare this method to the way vocabulary is normally learned outside school.

People generally learn words in the context of ordinary communication. This process is startlingly fast and successful. Miller and Gildea note that, by listening, talking and reading, the average 18 year old has learned vocabulary at a rate of about 5,000 words per year (13 per day) for over 16 years. By contrast, learning words from abstract definitions and sentences taken out of the context of normal use, the way vocabulary has often been taught, is slow and generally unsuccessful. There is barely enough classroom time to teach more than 100 to 200 words per year. Moreover, much of what is taught turns out to be almost useless in practice. Miller and Gildea give the following examples of pupils' uses of vocabulary acquired in this way:

■　Me and my parents correlate, because without them I wouldn't be here.
■　I was meticulous about falling off the cliff.
■　Mrs Morrow stimulated the soup.

Given the method, such mistakes seem unavoidable. Teaching from dictionaries assumes that definitions and example sentences are self-contained 'pieces' of knowledge. But words and sentences are not self-contained in this way. Using language would be almost impossible without the extra help that the context of an utterance provides. Take all the words in English that directly refer to other words or elements of context – termed by linguists 'indexical' words. Words such as here, now, next, tomorrow, afterwards and all pronouns are not just context-sensitive; they are completely context-dependent. Even words that seem to carry content rather than point to other words – words such as 'word' – are situated. I give you my word that a word, unless it is the Word of God, means what I choose it to mean – is, in a word, context-dependent, each of these 'words' meaning something quite different.

Experienced readers implicitly understand that words are situated. They, therefore, ask for the rest of the sentence or the context before committing themselves to an interpretation of a word. And then they go to dictionaries with situated examples of the usage in mind. The situation as well as the dictionary supports their interpretation. But the pupils who produced the sentences listed had no support from a normal communicative situation. In tasks such as theirs, dictionary definitions were assumed to be self-sufficient. The extra linguistic props that would structure, constrain and ultimately allow interpretation in normal communication were ignored.

All knowledge is like language. Its constituent parts refer to parts of the world and so are inextricably a product of the activity and situations in which they are produced. A concept, for example, will continually evolve every time it is used, because new situations, negotiations and activities inevitably recast it in a slightly different form. So a concept, like the meaning of a word, is always under construction. All learning is temporary and contextually situated. I remember being very puzzled in one of my early secondary school science lessons to be informed we were going to make a 'solution'. This sounded interesting: I had envisaged science as being exactly that – finding solutions to the problems of the natural world. When making the solution turned out to be simply a matter of mixing some blue crystals with water and watching them disappear, I could not help asking the teacher what that was the solution to!

Task 2.3.4 USING WORDS WITH VARIOUS MEANINGS

Think of some further examples of words and/or concepts that have a multiplicity of meanings depending on the contexts in which they occur. How might you go about teaching some of this diversity of meaning to your pupils?

Learning is a metacognitive process

While reading some particularly densely written background material before writing this unit, I noticed that it was becoming increasingly difficult for me to concentrate on what I was reading. My mind kept drifting to other, lighter, topics and several times I came to with a jerk to realise that I had understood nothing of the several paragraphs I thought I had 'read'. This was a metacognitive experience, and my comprehension monitoring had alternately lapsed and kicked into action. These terms are probably unfamiliar to many people, yet the processes to which they refer have been increasingly demonstrated to be of special importance in learning and in the operation of many intellectual activities. What do these terms mean?

There are two stages in the development of knowledge: first, its automatic unconscious acquisition (we learn things or how to do things, but do not know that we know these things) and, second, a gradual increase in active conscious control over that knowledge (we begin to know what we know and that there is more that we do not know). This distinction is essentially the difference between the cognitive and metacognitive aspects of knowledge and thought. The term *metacognition* is used to refer to cognition about cognition: thinking about your own thinking.

Metacognition can be differentiated into *metacognitive knowledge* and *metacognitive experience*. Metacognitive knowledge is the relatively stable information that we have about our own thinking processes. This knowledge may be about ourselves, about the tasks we are faced with and about possible strategies for tackling them. I may know, for example, that I have to read things at least twice before I will understand them, that it is much easier to understand texts if they are about a topic about which I already know something, or that it will help me remember information if I jot down key points as I read it.

Metacognitive experience refers to the mechanisms used by active learners as they regulate their own attempts to solve problems. These might include:

■ checking the outcome of what has already been attempted;
■ planning the next moves in response to a problem;
■ monitoring the effectiveness of these attempted actions;
■ testing, revising and evaluating strategies for learning.

Although it has been demonstrated that even quite young children can monitor their own activities when working on a simple problem, learners of any age are more likely to take active control of their own cognitive activities when they are faced with tasks of medium difficulty. This is not surprising, since it seems logical that with an easy task there is no need to devote too much attention to it, and with a task that is too hard there is a tendency to give up.

As an example of metacognition in action, we can consider the activity of reading. Good reading has been described as follows:

A good reader proceeds smoothly and quickly as long as his understanding of the material is complete. But as soon as he senses that he has missed an idea, that the track has been lost, he brings smooth progress to a blinding halt. Advancing more slowly, he seeks clarification in the subsequent material, examining it for the light it can throw on the earlier trouble spot. If still dissatisfied with his grasp, he returns to the point where the difficulty began and rereads the section more carefully. He probes and analyses phrases and sentences for their exact meaning; he tries to visualise abstruse descriptions; and through a series of approximations, deductions, and corrections he translates scientific and technical terms into concrete examples.

(Whimbey, 1975: 91)

While it is, of course, true that all readers do not follow precisely this sequence of actions, recent theories of reading have suggested similarly strategic models for the process. Most characterisations of the reading process include skills and activities that involve what is now termed metacognition. Some of the metacognitive activities involved in reading are:

■ clarifying your purposes for reading, that is, understanding the aim of a particular reading task;
■ identifying the important aspects of a text;
■ focusing attention on these aspects rather than on relatively trivial aspects;
■ monitoring ongoing activities to determine whether comprehension is taking place;
■ engaging in self-questioning to check whether your aims are being achieved;
■ taking corrective action if and when failures in comprehension are detected.

Reading for meaning, therefore, inevitably involves the metacognitive activity of comprehension monitoring, which entails keeping track of the success with which your comprehension is proceeding, ensuring that the process continues smoothly and taking remedial action if necessary.

Although mature readers typically engage in these processes as they read for meaning, it is usually not a conscious experience. Skilled readers tend to proceed on automatic pilot until a triggering event alerts them to a failure or problem in their comprehension. When alerted in this way, they must slow down and devote extra effort in mental processing to the area that is causing the problem. The events that trigger such action may vary widely. One common triggering event is the realisation that an expectation held about a text has not been confirmed by actual experience of the text. For example, in reading a sentence such as 'The old man the boats', the fourth and fifth words will probably cause a revision of your sense of understanding and therefore take longer to process.

Realising that you have failed to understand is only part of comprehension monitoring; you also have to know what to do when such failures occur. This involves making a number of strategic decisions such as:

■ reading on: reading more of the text to see if more information can be gained;
■ sounding out: examining letters and sounds carefully (this strategy is used most often by younger readers);
■ making an inference: guessing a meaning on the basis of textual clues and previous knowledge;
■ re-reading: reading the difficult section again;
■ suspending judgement: waiting to see if the text provides more clues.

Numerous research studies have examined the operation of metacognition in children's reading, that is, their monitoring of their own comprehension. Overall, there has been a remarkable consistency in the findings of these studies and it seems that:

Young children and poor readers are not nearly as adept as older children/adults and good readers, respectively, in engaging in planful activities either to make cognitive progress or to monitor it. Younger, less proficient learners are not nearly as 'resourceful' in completing a variety of reading and studying tasks important in academic settings.

(Garner, 1987: 59)

The above description has focused on reading, but this only parallels what we know about the importance of metacognition in all areas of learning. Self-awareness appears to be an essential ingredient in success in school. As John Holt put it:

Part of being a good student is learning to be aware of the state of one's mind and the degree of one's understanding. The good student may be one who often says that he does not understand, simply because he keeps a constant check on his understanding. The poor student, who does not, so to speak, watch himself trying to understand, does not know most of the time whether he understands or not.

(1969: 23)

This is a fundamental problem for young children: being much less aware of the operations of their own minds, and much less able to introspect to find out how their minds are working, they are thus less able to exert any conscious control over their own cognition. There is a strong implication that learning can be improved by increasing learners' awareness of their own mental processes.

PRINCIPLES FOR TEACHING

Arising from these insights we can derive some clear principles for teaching:

■ We need to ensure that learners have sufficient previous knowledge/understanding to enable them to learn new things, and to help them make explicit these links between what they already know and what they are learning.
■ We need to make provision for group interaction and discussion as teaching strategies, both in small, teacher-less groups and in groups working alongside experts.
■ We need to ensure meaningful contexts for learning, particularly in what are often called basic skills. This implies some kind of negotiation of the curriculum for learning. What is a meaningful context for teachers cannot be assumed automatically to be a meaningful context for learners.
■ We need to promote learners' knowledge and awareness of their own thinking and learning. This might be done by, for example, encouraging them to think aloud as they perform particular cognitive tasks.

TOWARDS A MODEL FOR TEACHING

Palincsar and Brown (1984) described a teaching procedure that began from the principles just outlined and that was based upon the twin ideas of 'expert scaffolding' and what they referred to as 'proleptic teaching': that is, teaching in anticipation of competence. This model arose from the Vygotskyan idea that children first experience a particular cognitive activity in collaboration with expert practitioners. The child is first a spectator as the majority of the cognitive work is done by the expert (parent or teacher), then a novice as he or she starts to take over some of the work under the close supervision of the expert. As the child grows in experience and capability of performing the task, the expert passes over greater and greater responsibility but still acts as a guide, assisting the child at problematic points. Eventually, the child assumes full responsibility for the task with the expert still present in the role of a supportive audience. Using this approach to teaching, children learn about the task at their own pace, joining in only at a level at which they are capable – or perhaps a little beyond this level so that the task continually provides sufficient challenge to be interesting. The approach is often referred to as an 'apprenticeship approach'. In the apprenticeship approach to reading, for example, the teacher and child begin by sharing a book together with, at first, most of the actual reading being done by the teacher. As the child develops confidence through repeated sharings of the book, he or she gradually takes over the reading until the teacher can withdraw entirely.

In mathematics learning Taylor and Cox (1997) have researched the effects of such apprenticeship approaches. They developed what they termed a 'socially assisted learning approach', which involved teachers modelling the ways they solved mathematical word problems, then encouraging learners to engage in such problem solving using several devices, such as the use of a reflection board in which teachers and pupils could share publicly their representation of a problem, peer collaboration, reflective questioning, scaffolding and quizzes. The pupils experiencing this approach did significantly better on word-problem tests than a control group who just received their normal mathematics teaching. When they analysed in a more detailed way the interactions of the teachers and the pupils, the researchers found that the support offered by the teacher was not a function of the number of questions or statements the teacher made, but rather that these questions/ statements came at the right time, when they served to scaffold understanding.

In explaining their results, Taylor and Cox (1997) speculated that success with this type of learning was a result of shared ownership of the learning, in which were expectations that:

■ all members of the group worked on the same aspect of the problem at the same time;
■ members externalised their thoughts, including possible wrong approaches and answers;
■ members came to agreement among themselves before proceeding;
■ as the teaching proceeded, more of the control of the activity was transferred from the adult to the children.

There appear to be four stages to the teaching process implied by these models.

Demonstration

During this stage, the expert models the skilful behaviour being taught. There is some evidence that learning can be assisted if this modelling is accompanied by a commentary by the expert, thinking aloud about the activities being undertaken. One relatively simple procedure is that of the teacher modelling how he or she tackles the skills being taught, for example, reading or writing in such a way that the learners have access to the thought processes that accompany these activities.

Joint activity

The expert and the learner share the activity. This may begin by the expert retaining responsibility for the difficult parts while the learner takes on the easy parts, while in some teaching strategies prior agreement is reached that participants will take turns at carrying out sections of the activity. The expert is always on hand to take full control if necessary. One of the best examples of this joint activity is that known as 'paired reading' (Morgan, 1986), in which the teacher (or parent) and the learner read aloud in unison until the learner signals that he or she is ready to go it alone. The teacher withdraws from the reading but is ready to rejoin if the learner shows signs of difficulty, such as prolonged pausing or reading errors.

Supported activity

The learner undertakes the activity alone, but under the watchful eye of the expert who is always ready to step in if necessary. In our work on the reading and writing of non-fiction (Wray and Lewis, 1997), we have found that this is the stage in the process that is most often neglected and teachers tend to move too rapidly from heavily supporting the children's work to asking them to work without support. Consequently, this is the stage at which most of our practical teaching strategies, such as writing frames, were aimed. Such scaffolding strategies play a key role in teaching approaches such as shared and guided reading.

Individual activity

The learner assumes sole responsibility for the activity. Some learners will, of course, move much more rapidly to this stage than others and the teacher needs to be sensitive to this. It is, arguably, equally as damaging to hold back learners by insisting they go through the same programme of support and practice as everyone else, as it is to rush learners through such a programme when they need a more extensive programme of support.

Task 2.3.5 **USING STAGED INTERACTIVE TEACHING**

Think of a skill you have taught in a primary school (or are planning to teach). Can you focus your teaching of this skill around the four steps of demonstration, joint activity, supported activity, individual activity? Jot down some notes on how you might use each of these stages in your teaching of this skill.

When you have done this activity, compare your approach to some of the examples given in Wray and Lewis (1997).

SUMMARY

In this unit, I have outlined four major insights that can be derived from a study of learning:

1 Learning is a process of interaction between what is known and what is to be learned.
2 Learning is a social process.
3 Learning is a situated process.
4 Learning is a metacognitive process.

Using these insights I have suggested four key principles for teaching:

1 We need to ensure that learners have sufficient previous knowledge/understanding to enable them to learn new things, and to help them make explicit these links between what they already know and what they are learning.
2 We need to make provision for group interaction and discussion as teaching strategies, both in small, teacher-less groups and in groups working alongside experts.
3 We need to ensure meaningful contexts for learning, particularly in what are often called basic skills.
4 We need to promote learners' knowledge and awareness of their own thinking and learning.

These principles are, I have argued, best exemplified by what can be termed an 'apprenticeship approach' to teaching. I hope you will be able to see applications for these principles in all your teaching. The apprenticeship approach has, after all, been used for years to teach all sorts of material to all sorts of people in the world outside school – 'just plain folks', in the terms used by some researchers. Its rediscovery by school teachers was long overdue.

ANNOTATED FURTHER READING

Lave, J. and Wenger, E. (1991) *Situated Learning: Legitimate Peripheral Participation*, Cambridge: University of Cambridge Press.

> This book contains an exploration of learning as participation in communities of practice. According to the authors, participation moves from the periphery to the 'centre'. Learning is, thus, not seen as the acquisition of knowledge by individuals so much as a process of *social* participation. This is a seminal text and opened up the concept of situated learning.

Mercer, N. and Hodgkinson, S. (eds) (2008) *Exploring Talk in School*, London: Sage.

> This book consists of a number of papers by leading international researchers who, drawing on the pioneering work of Douglas Barnes, consider ways of improving classroom talk. Chapters cover issues such as classroom communication and managing social relations; talk in science classrooms; using critical conversations in studying literature; exploratory talk and thinking skills; talking to learn and learning to talk in the mathematics classroom; and the 'emerging pedagogy' of the spoken word.

Mercer, N. and Littleton, K. (2007) *Dialogue and the Development of Children's Thinking*, London: Routledge.

> This book draws on extensive research to provide a fascinating account of the relationship between dialogue and children's learning development. It closely relates research findings to real-life classrooms, so that it is of practical value to teachers concerned that their children are offered the best possible learning opportunities. It provides a clear, accessible and well-illustrated case for the importance of dialogue in children's intellectual development.

Wray, D. (1994) *Literacy and Awareness*, Sevenoaks: Hodder & Stoughton.

> If you would like to know more about the concept of metacognition and, in particular, its relation to the teaching of literacy, this book represents a very good start. It includes chapters on metacognition and understanding in reading, awareness and writing, and language awareness.

RELEVANT WEBSITES

www.education.qld.gov.au/curriculum/learning/teaching/technology/pedagogy/index.html

> This site, maintained by the government of Queensland in Australia, is most useful because it gives access to the thinking underpinning the influential Productive Pedagogies project, which has defined and mapped all the characteristics of effective teaching in schools. Look at the Productive Pedagogies framework first of all, then chase down the research papers underpinning this if you are interested.

www.infed.org/

> The encyclopaedia of informal education contains a veritable cornucopia of material related to teaching and learning. As well as article length pieces on a variety of topics, it also has a comprehensive collection of links to take you further into the subject. If you consult no other information from the web about teaching and learning, do look at this site.

Visit the companion website www.routledge.com/textbooks/ltps2e for:

▪ additional questions and tasks for this unit;
▪ links to useful websites relevant to this unit.

REFERENCES

Forman, E.A., Stein, M.K., Brown, C. and Larreamendy-Joerns, J. (1995) 'The socialization of mathematical thinking: the role of institutional, interpersonal, and discursive contexts', Paper presented at the 77th annual conference of the American Educational Research Association, San Francisco.

Garner, R. (1987) *Metacognition and Reading Comprehension*, Norwood, NJ: Ablex.

Holt, J. (1969) *How Children Fail*, Harmondsworth: Penguin.

Kumpulainen, K. and Wray, D. (2002) *Classroom Interaction and Social Learning*, London: Routledge Falmer.

Lave, J. and Wenger, E. (1991) *Situated Learning*, Cambridge: Cambridge University Press.

Miller, G.A. and Gildea, P.M. (1987) 'How children learn words', *Scientific American*, 257(3): 94–9.

Morgan, R. (1986) *Helping Children Read*, London: Methuen.

Palincsar, A. and Brown, A. (1984) 'Reciprocal teaching of comprehension-fostering and comprehension-monitoring activities', *Cognition and Instruction*, 1(2): 117–75.

Raphael, T., McMahon, S.I., Goatley, V.J., Bentley, J.L. and Boyd, F.B. (1992) 'Research directions: literature and discussion in the reading program', *Language Arts*, 69: 55–61.

Taylor, J. and Cox, B.D. (1997) 'Microgenetic analysis of group-based solution of complex two-step mathematical word problems by fourth graders', *Journal of Learning Science*, 6: 183–226.

Whimbey, A. (1975) *Intelligence Can be Taught*, New York: Dutton.

Wray, D. and Lewis, M. (1997) *Extending Literacy*, London: Routledge.

Wray, D. and Medwell, J. (1991) *Literacy and Language in the Primary Years*, London: Routledge.

DEVELOPING YOUR TEACHING SKILLS

Samantha Twiselton

INTRODUCTION

> Any subject can be taught to any child at any age in some form that is honest.
>
> (Bruner, 1996)

This is a bold claim and quite daunting to anyone contemplating the skills that might be needed for effective primary teaching. Yet it is actually quite useful in helping us to understand what should be involved. This unit will look at the skills and knowledge required for you to be able to create and support successful learning experiences. It will focus in particular on the range of different factors that effective teachers need to consider when they decide what to do in the classroom.

OBJECTIVES

By the end of this unit you should be beginning to:

■ understand the importance of being aware of the underlying structures that underpin learning objectives;
■ understand some of the different types of knowledge involved in effective teaching;
■ be able to relate these to the decisions informing teachers' actions in the classroom;
■ develop strategies to help your own decision making in the classroom.

KNOWLEDGE AND LEARNING – FOR THE PUPIL AND THE TEACHER

According to Bruner and many others, learning involves the search for pattern, regularity and predictability. We can only make sense out of the confusion of information continuously bombarding our senses if we can *relate* the pieces of information to each other in some way. If a young child is presented with some bricks and the task of building a tower, this is only likely to be possible if he or she has had some other similar experiences to draw on (e.g. experimenting with bricks and learning something about how they balance, building other simple structures, etc.).

Input from a teacher should help children in the formation and discovery of the patterns and rules that are most likely to help them (1) make sense of the experience and (2) generalise it to other experiences. Complex tasks can be broken down into manageable smaller problems so that the learner can detect patterns and regularities that could not be discovered alone. So a task like building a tower with bricks can be made possible by the presence of a teacher who helps the pupil through decisions and actions in small steps, while still holding 'the bigger picture' of the ultimate goal of the tower in mind.

Bruner's claim in the opening quotation is linked to the idea that the ultimate aim of teaching a subject is to help children understand the basic principles that help define it, give it identity and allow other things to be related to it meaningfully. The 'fundamental ideas' of a subject are defined as those ideas that have the greatest breadth of applicability to new problems. This has a strong resonance with the notion of 'importance statements' as outlined in the recent *Independent Review of the Primary Curriculum* undertaken by Sir Jim Rose (Rose, 2009).

This approach to subject knowledge, focusing on the conceptual underpinning, rather than the content, is also a major aspect of the Rose Review, which promises to decongest and refine it so that the concepts and skills are not obscured by too much content. The international report, *Primary Curriculum Change: Directions of Travel in 10 Countries since 2005* (QCA, 2008), which is a major influence on this review, claims 'Across the 10 countries, there is a trend towards the application of knowledge through the use of concepts of "competences" or "skills" in the curriculum' and from this draws the following implication for the review: 'The primary review should note that several countries have recently made significant changes to their curriculum and associated policies in the light of new evidence and thinking about how children learn best'. The 2007 revision to the standards for classroom teachers, required for qualifying to teach in England (www.tda.gov.uk/partners/ittstandards.aspx) similarly reflects a renewed focus on a model of teacher knowledge that is broad and makes explicit connections between the subject, the learning environment and the learner.

Task 2.4.1 **AN EVIDENCE-BASED PROFESSION?**

Access the *Independent Review of the Primary Curriculum* website and look at the 'Thinking Primary' and 'Evidence Reports' web pages (www.qcda.gov.uk/15561.aspx and /17492.aspx respectively). Consider the extent to which the thinking reflected in these is supported by your experience of the curriculum in school. It is also useful to reflect on the notion of teaching as an 'evidence-based profession'. To what extent has this been your experience to date? Does M level study as part of a PGCE have a role to play in this?

An effective teacher will have an excellent grasp of these fundamental concepts and will be able to break down tasks in ways that will make them achievable, while still remaining consistent with the core ideas that underpin them. This means that core ideas are developed in nucleus as early as possible and are returned to with ever increasing complexity and sophistication in a 'spiral curriculum' as children's experience and understanding makes them ready for it.

The importance of underlying structures and the role of teachers in helping pupils to make connections is supported by the work of Medwell *et al.* (1998), in which they examined the work of teachers whose pupils made effective learning gains in literacy. In this they claim that effective teachers are much more likely to embed their teaching in a wider context and to show how specific aspects of literacy relate to each other. They assert that such teachers tend to make connections, both explicitly and implicitly, and to put features of language use into the broader context of texts. Medwell *et al.* found that the effective teachers tended to have more coherent belief systems that led them to pursue an embedded approach, where the more technical aspects of literacy were taught within a broader framework of meaningful contexts. This theme is echoed by the parallel study into effective teachers of numeracy undertaken by Askew *et al.* (1997), who characterise effective numeracy teachers as being 'connectionist-oriented', which involves a conscious awareness of connections and relationships.

So what does this mean in terms of the knowledge base required by you as a teacher and how this should be applied in the classroom? This can be a very alarming question for someone learning to be a primary school teacher, as there are so many different subjects in the primary curriculum, each having its own detailed requirements.

QUALITY VERSUS QUANTITY

The answer to this problem may be helped by Sternberg and Horvath's (1995) attempt to define what is involved in teacher expertise. They comment that there are a number of studies (e.g. Chi *et al.*, 1981; Larkin *et al.*, 1980) that show that it is not so much the *amount* of knowledge that the expert possesses but *how it is organised* in the memory. In general, experts are sensitive to the deep structures of the problems they solve – they are able to group problems together according to underlying principles. This supports Bruner's model. It seems that the key to being able to teach, for example, history or mathematics is not so much your knowing endless information about the subject as your understanding some of the key underlying principles and concepts that underpin it.

This is very much supported by my own study (Twiselton, 2000, 2003, 2004, 2006, 2007; Twiselton and Webb, 1998) of the types of knowledge and understanding that primary student teachers develop as they go through their initial teacher education (ITE) programme. I found that (partly dependent on how far through the programme they were) these students could be placed into one of three main categories (or points on a continuum) – Task Manager, Curriculum Deliverer or Concept/Skill Builder. The Task Managers (who were likely to be near the beginning of ITE) viewed their role in the classroom in terms of task completion, order and business – without any explicit reference to children's learning. The Curriculum Deliverers did see themselves as there to support learning, but only as dictated by an external source – a scheme, curriculum or lesson plan – and they struggled to give a rationale for *why what was being taught mattered* in any other terms. In contrast, the Concept/Skill Builders (likely to be at or near the end of ITE) were aware of the wider and deeper areas of understanding and skill needed by pupils that underpinned their learning objectives. Of the three types, the Concept/Skill Builders were much more likely to be able effectively, consistently and responsively to support learning at every stage of the learning experience. The most outstanding quality that separated the Concept/Skill Builders from the other two categories was their ability to see the 'bigger picture' and give a rationale for what they were attempting to do in terms of key principles and concepts. This would appear to be particularly important at a time when policy makers in England (e.g. *Every Child Matters* (2004), *Children's Plan* (2007), *Being the Best for Our Children* (2008)) are encouraging all who work with children to view their role within a broad, child-centred context that emphasises high levels of teacher knowledge and professionalism and aspires ultimately to make teaching an M level profession.

There are many indications that current policy is seeking to broaden the teacher role in a range of ways:

A combination of high expectations, innovative thinking and *a broad view of supporting children and young people* . . . personalisation – so that the *system fits to the individual rather than the individual having to fit to the system* . . . It is about having a system which will genuinely give high standards for all – the most effective teaching at school, which builds a detailed picture of what each *child already knows, and how they learn, to help them go further* . . . opportunities are built in for staff from different backgrounds to get to know each other, *cooperate, discuss and make joint decisions.*

(DfES, 2004; my italics)

The need for teachers to develop a broad and rich curriculum is strongly promoted. This is set alongside a notion of a very individualised, highly child-centred approach to supporting learning and a strong emphasis on multi-agency working and the sharing of expertise and information. All of this implies a notion of the teacher that goes well beyond the technician who delivers a prescribed curriculum – a model, it could be argued, that has dominated in the recent past.

This broad, more flexible and child-centred view of the teacher is welcome but is not without its challenges, particularly for those who are learning to teach. As a student teacher it is very easy to become so enmeshed in the practicalities of simply 'surviving' in the classroom that it is difficult to focus on underpinning concepts or how to connect these meaningfully to the needs of individual learners. The task below is designed to lead you through a process that will help you to begin to do this in stages, away from the hurly burly of the classroom, and the lesson plans (Figures 2.4.1 and 2.4.2) with commentary should help you to make the link back to the classroom and your planning.

Task 2.4.2 **LESSON PLANS 1**

■ Choose the subject you feel most confident in – e.g. 1: English; 2: science.
■ Choose a key area within it. – e.g. 1: poetry reading and writing; 2: solids, liquids and gases.
■ Write the key area in the middle of a piece of paper and write words and phrases you associate with it around the edge – e.g. 1: rhyme, rhythm, verses, language play, imagery; 2: evaporation and condensation, state, materials, properties.
■ In a different colour, write key words and phrases for all the ways in which this area is important – e.g. 1: it gives a pattern and meaning to chaotic experiences, it expresses emotion, it entertains, it conveys images, it communicates powerful ideas; 2: the changing properties of materials allow us to manipulate our environment, we can manufacture things using these changes, life on land requires the fresh water produced by evaporation and condensation.
■ Look at the words and phrases in the two different colours you have used. Is it possible to connect them? e.g. 1: rhyme and rhythm help to entertain and impose pattern and meaning, imagery is an effective way of communicating powerful ideas; 2: evaporation and condensation are important examples of key processes we use to manipulate the environment. If so, you are connecting the 'what' with the 'why' in the way the Concept/Skill Builders were doing.
■ Consider the implications for how these aspects of the subject should be taught to pupils. How can you ensure that they are presented with the 'why' sufficiently?

The next stage is to identify what other factors will be involved and how this translates into classroom practice. Figures 2.4.1 and 2.4.2 provide some examples of how a similar approach can

LESSON PLAN – YEAR 1/2 – MONDAY

DESIRED LEARNING OUTCOMES

T5/6	Recite stories with predictable and repeating patterns and describe story settings and incidents.
S2	Use awareness of grammar to decipher new words.
W3	Hear initial and final phonemes.

KEY LANGUAGE	USE OF ICT
Setting, character, phoneme, alliteration.	Clicker

ASSESSMENT [make reference to each section of the lesson]

Shared – yellow group – word choices.
Guided – red group – ability to make sentence orally and in writing.
Plenary – green group – explanation of choices.

USE OF OTHER ADULTS: **Mrs X to support green group in use of clicker.**

ANTICIPATED MISCONCEPTIONS/DIFFICULTIES: **Support with spelling strategies – reluctance to attempt unknown words – encourage to 'have a go' – use 'magic line'.**

	ACTIVITIES	COMMENTARY
Introduction Approx. timing – 10 minutes	**Introduce text.** **Look at cover – predict** what the characters are thinking (whiteboards). **Discuss title** – explain that we are going to be spending the week thinking about stories with a repeating pattern. Discuss why people like repeating patterns and why such stories are enjoyable. Explain that we are going to be looking at repeating texts so that we can have a go at writing our own later in the week.	*It is important that pupils are helped to understand the purposes of the texts they look at.* *It is also helpful if there is a concrete goal (e.g. writing their own story based on this one) that is introduced at the beginning and can give meaning and purpose to the week's activities.*

Whole-class work Use of additional support Approx. timing – 20 minutes	Read 'Bear Hunt' – encourage joining in. Cover up words with post-its – time out for words it could be. Show me – ideas. Look at sound effects – time out for more words beginning with 'sw' etc. *Additional support – Mrs X focused observation of yellow group word choices on feedback sheet.*	*It is important to emphasise those aspects of the text that define it and make it enjoyable – joining in with repetition is a good way to do this.* *Explain that sound effects might be used in the story the children write – it will be useful to have a bank of words and ideas they can use later.*
Guided group Red group Approx. timing – 20 minutes	1 Introduce 'Rosie's Walk' – explain similar to 'Bear Hunt' in some ways. 2 Strategy check – matching phonemes. 3 Look through text – tell a partner how is same? 4 Review/discuss. 5 Look at text – compare with 'Bear Hunt' – how different? What do we like about each one? 6 Review.	*Frame the whole discussion within the idea of eventually being able to take the best ideas from each book and use them in their own story.* *Remember to keep emphasising the features that make the text enjoyable.*
Independent work Approx timing – 20 minutes	Introduce independent work with whole class. Draw pictures for each stage of story. In pairs: blue group, green group – add simple captions underneath. Yellow group – clicker – put pictures in right order – find captions and paste.	*Explain that the independent work will help with planning their own stories later in the week.*
Plenary	Focus – green group. Blutack sentences on black board — green group read aloud.	*Explain that the captions will help when thinking of sentences for own stories later in the week.*

■ **Figure 2.4.1** Lesson plan – Year 1/2 – Monday

An editable version of Figure 2.4.1 is available on the companion website: www.routledge.com/textbooks/ltps2e

LESSON PLAN – YEAR 5 – TUESDAY

DESIRED LEARNING OUTCOMES

T3	Investigate how characters are presented through dialogue, action and description and through examining their relationship with other characters.
S4	Adapt writing for different audiences.

KEY LANGUAGE	USE OF ICT

Characterisation, empathy, perspective, imagery

ASSESSMENT [make reference to each section of the lesson]

Shared – yellow group – word choices.
Guided – red group – ability to make sentence orally and in writing.
Plenary – green group – explanation of choices.

USE OF OTHER ADULTS: Mrs X to support green group.

ANTICIPATED MISCONCEPTIONS/DIFFICULTIES: **Support with spelling strategies – reluctance to attempt unknown words.**

	ACTIVITIES	COMMENTARY
Introduction Approx. timing – 15 minutes	**Look at cover – predict what the characters are thinking (whiteboards). Use freeze frame and thought tracking to follow this up. Could include a hot seat activity.** **Map out 'Bear Hunt' – focus on one character – list words for each section to show how he is feeling.**	*In introducing the text yesterday it will have been important to explain it is going to be used to help consider how characters' perspectives change through the story so that they can write own story showing this.*

Whole-class work Approx. timing – 20 minutes	Read opening passages from 'The Shrieking Face' – look at how author builds up images of how Angus is feeling – time out – show me – write up key words, phrases, sentences. Ask for ideas for similar language for 'Bear Hunt' character. Teacher demo – 'He was feeling brave and adventurous – like a warrior going into battle.' Time out – paired ideas – supported composition. *Use of additional support –Mrs X focused observation of yellow group word choices on feedback sheet.*	*It is important that the discussion focuses on the effective use of language for conveying characters' perspectives. Pupils need to keep alive that the purpose is to help them use language effectively in their own stories.*
Guided group Approx. timing – 15 minutes	Red group – write opening sequence to new version – emphasise figurative language – use examples from shared work as starting point.	*Keep the reader's needs in mind at all times – read aloud and check for effectiveness.*
Independent work Approx timing – 15 minutes	Write key words on a story plan for each stage of the story. Write opening sequence.	*It is important that the pupils understand that this is going to be continued later in the week.*
Plenary – 10 minutes	Focus – green group. Blutack sentences on black board – green group read aloud – consider effectiveness.	*The focus should be on effectiveness and audience.*

Figure 2.4.2 Lesson plan – Year 5 – Tuesday

An editable version of Figure 2.4.2 is available on the companion website: www.routledge.com/textbooks/ltps2e

be taken through planning in Key Stage 1 and Key Stage 2. The commentary shows how the teaching can be directed by the underpinning rationale for the learning objectives.

The lesson plan in Figure 2.4.1 shows how a Key Stage 1 lesson can be explicitly and systematically underpinned by key concepts relating to meaning making, purpose and audience. The lesson plan in Figure 2.4.2 shows a very similar approach planned with Year 5.

Task 2.4.3 **LESSON PLANS 2**

Take a recent lesson plan – ideally one that is your own and that you have already taught. Focus on the learning outcomes that you planned for this lesson. Attempt to answer the following questions:

■ Why were these learning outcomes important for these children?
■ What importance/usefulness would this learning have beyond this lesson?
■ How was the above communicated to the children? Were they aware of why what they were learning mattered?

If you feel able to answer these questions with some confidence, the next step is to analyse the lesson chronologically to work out how well this was communicated at each stage. If possible, identify places where this could have been improved and how.

If you don't feel able to answer the above questions with confidence, the next step is to re-plan the lesson, starting with the learning outcomes and rewriting them in a way that you feel can be justified in terms of their importance. You then need to go through the rest of the plan to amend it to ensure this is clearly and meaningfully communicated to the children throughout the lesson.

OTHER TYPES OF TEACHER KNOWLEDGE

Any attempt to define all the different kinds of teacher knowledge required in effective practice is bound to hit the problem that the list can be infinitely extended. However, it is worth noting that most people agree that, however you describe it, the knowledge base is wide-ranging and varied and that different kinds of knowledge are required at different times. Tochon and Munby (1993) studied expert and novice teachers and found that a key characteristic that distinguished the experts was their ability to draw on a wide range of different kinds of knowledge (e.g. the subject, the plan, the individual pupil, the context, etc.) in making one teaching decision. The novices tended to think about one thing at a time and to stick quite rigidly to their plan, regardless of whether the pupil responses, the context, etc. supported this.

Lee Shulman (1987) has classified the knowledge base of teaching into seven categories: content knowledge (better known to us as subject knowledge), general pedagogical knowledge, curriculum knowledge, pedagogical content knowledge, knowledge of learners and their characteristics, knowledge of educational contexts and knowledge of educational ends. Others (e.g. Turner-Bisset, 1999) have expanded this list. The important thing for student teachers to note is not so much the items on the list (though these are useful) but the fact that they are so varied. It is the *drawing together and combining* of these varied factors that is important.

This is supported by both the above-mentioned Teacher Training Agency (TTA) studies in effective numeracy teachers (1997) and literacy teachers (1998). The Medwell *et al.* (1998) study found that the subject knowledge of the effective literacy teachers was only fully identifiable when it was embedded within a teaching context:

Our interpretation of what we have observed is that the effective teachers only knew their material by how they represented it to children . . . through experience of teaching it, their knowledge seemed to have been totally embedded in pedagogic practices.

(p. 24)

They also found that the effective teachers tended to have more coherent belief systems linked to the importance of communication, composition and understanding. This links with Bruner's views about the key components that are the fundamentals of the subject.

In the parallel effective numeracy teachers study (1997), Askew *et al.* characterised effective numeracy teachers as being 'connectionist-oriented'. They claimed that the highly effective teachers believed that being numerate required having a rich network of connections between different mathematical ideas.

COMBINING KNOWLEDGE

In Sternberg and Horvath's (1995) study of teaching expertise, three key features are identified. The first is *knowledge* and we have already considered their claim that the organisation of the knowledge around principles is the central factor. The second and third features are *efficiency* and *insight*. Efficiency is closely linked to experience in that the claim is that experts are much faster at processing information and making well-informed decisions, partly because what is initially effort-full and time consuming becomes effortless and automatic with practice. This is obvious and one of the most comforting pieces of advice that can be given to student teachers is that, as time goes on, many things that are difficult now become much easier. However, it is worth noting that Sternberg and Horvath also claim that experts typically spend a greater proportion of time trying to understand the problem, whereas novices spend more in actually trying out different solutions. Sometimes deciding the best response through more detailed analysis is a much more efficient way of dealing with problems than rushing in without clear judgement.

It can be argued that *insight*, Sternberg and Horvath's third feature of teacher expertise, involves a combination of the first two (knowledge and efficiency). Insight involves distinguishing information that is relevant to the problem solution from that which is irrelevant. This obviously provides the expert teacher with an insight into the situation, which will enable him or her to (1) make the most efficient use of the time available and (2) draw on the most useful areas of knowledge.

My study of student teachers (mentioned above) also involved examining how expert teachers operate. I did this through watching them teach, making detailed notes of their actions and words and interviewing them closely afterwards about how they decided what to do. The following extract is an example of the notes taken and Task 2.4.4 helps with understanding how this can be analysed to show how effective teachers constantly assess the situation in order to make the most effective response.

Task 2.4.4 **OBSERVING OTHER TEACHERS**

■ Read through observation notes 1 on page 76 and use the 'Assessment/response' column to make a note of any points at which the teacher (X) appears to be making an assessment or acting on the basis of an assessment made.

■ Repeat this with observation notes 2 on page 77 (from a different teacher).

■ What are the differences you notice between the two teachers?

Observation notes 1	Assessment/response
9.23 X is talking to child (C1) about her picture of a ladybird: 'Do you want to do some writing to tell everyone about this?' (C1 nods) 'What shall we write?' C1: The ladybird is sitting on a leaf. X: Excellent. Which side shall we start? C1: Over here. **9.25** X: You go ahead and write it and show me in a minute. X is explaining the spider's web pattern to a child (C2). **9.27** X: Can you make the lines go all along the web? It's very important you start at the left and finish on the right because we are practising for writing. Where's the left? Where will you start? (C2 shows her; she observes closely as C2 starts the web) X: Lovely, don't forget to keep your pencil on the line. Nice and slow. **9.30** X: What a lot of lovely writing. I can see some of the letters of your name. Where's the 'm'? C1: Here and here. X: You've done those beautifully. Can you read me your writing now? C1: The ladybird is sitting on the leaf. She has lots of children and they like flying. **9.32** X: Wow! You've added more to it! You told me earlier on that there was a 'l' at the beginning of ladybird. Where might the 'l' have gone here? (C1 points randomly and vaguely) X: Can you read it again and point to the words at the same time? (C1 moves her finger along the line from left to right, but there is no attempt to match up the writing with what she is saying) **9.34** X: Now I'll write my writing. Where shall I start? (C1 shows her; X writes the words and reads them as she does so) X: Let's read it again together. (They read it, X gently holds C1's finger and helps her to point to the words as they read)	

Observation notes 2	Assessment/response
10.10 TT to C1: What does that say? (Points from left to right over the label) (No answer from C1) TT: What does it start with? C1: It's a drink. TT: Yes, but what does it start with? C1: Don't know. TT: It's milk! 10.12 TT to the whole group: Take it in turns to choose a card – see if you can match it. (C2 takes a card) TT: What does that say? (C2 is looking at the picture) C2: Chocolate. TT: Good girl! Put it in the right place. 10.14 (C3 takes a card with a sandwich label) TT: What does that say? Have you got that? C3: It says pizza. TT: It's not pizza. What does it say? It says sandwich! 10.17 (C1 takes a card) TT: What does that card say? (No answer) TT: W . . . C1: Watermelon. TT: Brilliant! 10.19 (C2 takes a card) TT: What does it say? C2: Ice-cream. TT: Have you got ice-cream? (TT points to game card) C2: No. 10.20 TT: Well done!	

The second set of observation notes were taken from a student teacher (TT) during her first placement. The differences are notable. The student teacher assesses in a limited way and only uses a narrow range of strategies. The expert teacher is constantly assessing and responding and she uses a range of strategies in doing this. This supports Sternberg and Horvath's (1995) claims that effective teachers demonstrate knowledge, efficiency and insight through their ability to quickly process and analyse a learning experience and draw on a range of conceptual principles to make the best decisions for action.

SUMMARY

It does not require a chapter in a book to tell you that teaching is a very complicated business and that effective teaching requires a wide range of types of knowledge and a large number of skills. In this unit I have tried to elaborate on some of the more important components of teaching skills and to explore the implications of these for your teaching. It is important to close this unit with a reminder of the importance of quality over quantity. It is not the amount you know, or the number of teaching skills in which you have some competence, that are crucial. Your depth of knowledge and level of confidence in your skills is of much more importance. As you experience teaching, keep asking yourself the 'why' question and keep your eyes and ears open to children's responses. Deeper knowledge and surer confidence in your actions will follow if this becomes your natural mind-set.

ANNOTATED FURTHER READING

Askew, M., Brown, M., Rhodes, V., William, D. and Johnson, D. (1997) *Effective Teachers of Numeracy*, London: Teacher Training Agency.

This study was commissioned by the TTA as an enquiry into the characteristics (skills, knowledge and beliefs) of teachers identified as effective in teaching numeracy, and, indirectly, as an evidence base for the establishment of the standards for the award of qualified teacher status in the area of numeracy teaching. Its most significant finding was that the effective teachers of numeracy were those able to see and explain to pupils the rich connections between areas of numerical knowledge.

Elton-Chalcraft, S., Hansen, A. and Twiselton, S. (2008) *Doing Classroom Research*, Milton Keynes: Open University Press.

This book has been recently published partly to support those studying at M level as part of their initial teacher education programme. However, it has relevance for all who are undertaking school-based research and are interested in the development of teaching as an evidence-based profession.

Medwell, J., Wray, D., Poulson, L. and Fox, R. (1998) *Effective Teachers of Literacy*, London: Teacher Training Agency.

This was the parallel TTA study exploring the characteristics of effective teachers of literacy. One of its most important findings was that teacher subject knowledge in literacy was not a simple matter of what teachers knew about language. How they knew it, and the contexts in which they could apply it, were of much more significance.

Qualifications and Curriculum Authority (QCA) (2008) *Primary Curriculum Change: Directions of Travel in 10 Countries since 2005*, London: QCA.

This is a report of an international research project undertaken between January and March 2008 through the QCA's International Review of Curriculum and Assessment Frameworks Internet Archive (INCA) and the Eurydice network on education in Europe. The research was designed to provide a snapshot of changes to the curriculum since 2005 in a selection of countries. The research is intended to inform the *Independent Review of the Primary Curriculum* (Rose Review) in England.

Shulman, L.S. (1987) 'Knowledge and teaching: foundations of the new reform', *Harvard Educational Review*, 57(1): 1–22.
Lee Shulman might fairly claim to have invented the field of teachers' subject knowledge and his work has been the inspiration for numerous studies in a range of subject areas.

RELEVANT WEBSITES

Independent Review of the Primary Curriculum (Rose Review): *Final Report*: www.dcsf.gov.uk/primarycurriculumreview
You can also find a review of this report at:

www.ttrb.ac.uk/ViewArticle2.aspx?anchorId=17756&selectedId=17758&menu=17834&expanded=False&ContentId=15411
Thinking Primary and *Evidence Reports* from the above *Independent Review*: www.qcda.gov.uk/15561.aspx and www.qcda.gov.uk/17492.aspx
QCDA's *Big Picture of the Curriculum*: www.qcda.gov.uk/5856.aspx

Visit the companion website www.routledge.com/textbooks/ltps2e for:

■ additional questions and tasks for this unit;
■ editable figures from this unit;
■ links to useful websites relevant to this unit.

REFERENCES

Askew, M., Brown, M., Rhodes, V., William, D. and Johnson, D. (1997) *Effective Teachers of Numeracy*, London: Teacher Training Agency.
Bruner, J.S. (1996) *The Culture of Education*, Cambridge, MA: Harvard University Press.
Chi, M.T.H., Feltovich, J.P. and Glaser, R. (1981) 'Categorization and representation of physics problems by experts and novices', *Cognitive Science*, 5(2): 121–52.
Department for Education and Skills (DfES) (2004) *Five Year Strategy for Children and Learners*, London: DfES.
Larkin, J., McDermott, J., Simon, D. and Simon, A. (1980) 'Expert and novice performance in solving physics problems', *Science* 208: 1335–42.
Medwell, J., Wray, D., Poulson, L. and Fox, R. (1998) *Effective Teachers of Literacy*, London: Teacher Training Agency.
Qualifications and Curriculum Authority (QCA) (2008) *Primary Curriculum Change: Directions of Travel in 10 Countries since 2005*, London: QCA.
Rose, J. (2009) *Independent Review of the Primary Curriculum: Final Report*, London: DCSF. Available online at www.dcsf.gov.uk/primarycurriculumreview (accessed May 2009).
Shulman, L.S. (1987) 'Knowledge and teaching: foundations of the new reform', *Harvard Educational Review*, 57(1): 1–22.
Sternberg, R. and Horvath, J. (1995) 'A prototype view of expert learning', *Education Research*, 24(6): 9–17.
Tochon, F. and Munby. H. (1993) 'Novice and expert teachers' time epistemology: a wave function from didactics to pedagogy', *Teaching and Teacher Education*, 2: 205–18.
Turner-Bisset, R. (1999) 'Knowledge bases for teaching', *British Educational Research Journal*, 25(1): 39–55.
Twiselton, S. (2000) 'Seeing the wood for the trees: the National Literacy Strategy and initial teacher education; pedagogical content knowledge and the structure of subjects', *Cambridge Journal of Education*, 30(3): 391–403.

Twiselton, S. (2003) 'Beyond the curriculum: learning to teach primary literacy', in E. Bearne, H. Dombey and T. Grainger (eds) *Interactions in Language and Literacy in the Classroom*, Milton Keynes: Open University Press.

Twiselton, S. (2004) 'The role of teacher identities in learning to teach primary literacy', *Education Review: Special Edition: Activity Theory*, 56(2): 88–96.

Twiselton, S. (2006) 'The problem with English: the exploration and development of student teachers' English subject knowledge in primary classrooms', *Literacy*, 40(2): 88–96.

Twiselton, S. (2007) 'Seeing the wood for the trees: learning to teach beyond the curriculum. How can student teachers be helped to see beyond the National Literacy Strategy?' *Cambridge Journal of Education*, 37(4): 489–502.

Twiselton, S. and Webb. D (1998) 'The trouble with English: the challenge of developing subject knowledge in school', in C. Richards, N. Simco and S. Twiselton (eds) *Primary Teacher Education: High Standards? High Status?*, London: Falmer.

EARLY YEARS PRACTICE

Building on firm foundations

Sue Rogers and Janet Rose

INTRODUCTION

We have often heard student teachers say that 'all children do in the early years is play' and that 'early years teachers are just childminders'. Until relatively recently, early years education has suffered from low status, dogged by a wide range of misconceptions about how young children learn and the nature of work in early years settings.

However, the early years sector in the UK has seen an unprecedented period of development and change since the election of the New Labour government in 1997. The socio-political agenda to ameliorate the divisive and fragmented nature of early years provision in the UK is closely bound up with the desire to reduce child poverty and disadvantage and to encourage more lone parents (and in particular mothers) back to work. These aspirations have required a major 'root and branch' approach to services for young children and their families (Anning, 2006), and central to this has been the dual aim both to increase the quantity, and improve the quality, of early education and childcare provision.

Within this context our task in this unit is to challenge the popular conception that working with young children is easy and of less significance than formal schooling, and to convince you that, as primary school teachers, you need to understand how and in what ways children learn in the early years and the range of diverse experiences they are likely to have had on arrival in the primary school. We offer also a cautionary note: we acknowledge that a key aim of early years education is to build firm foundations for future learning in the primary school and beyond. However, the purpose of early years education is not simply a preparation for future life or for later schooling, but something that is important in its own right. Understanding this will enable you to build on the firm foundations established in the first five years and value the specific characteristics of young children as learners.

OBJECTIVES

This unit will help you to:

■ highlight key issues you ought to know about in relation to the early years;
■ eliminate any myths that may exist in your perspective of the early years;
■ emphasise the importance of the early years and outline key policy initiatives;
■ clarify the nature of early years practice.

EARLY YEARS POLICY

> Pre-school children have brains which are more active, more connected and more flexible than an adult's brain.
>
> (Riley, 2003: 3)

It is widely agreed that, from birth, children are powerful, creative and competent learners and that early years provision should capitalise on this at a time when they are particularly receptive, developmentally, to exploratory, imaginative and social activity. Key questions about what an appropriate curriculum and pedagogy for young children might look like and how, and in what ways adults can support the learning and development of children in the early years, have been the major preoccupations of policy makers and early years educators alike in recent years.

The considerable recognition now afforded to the early years of education by policy makers is indicative also of a wider appreciation of the fundamental significance of this phase of childhood in lifelong learning, a view underpinned by a large and robust research literature. For example, there is compelling recent evidence from the neurosciences that testifies to the profound way in which children's earliest experiences affect their developing potential with long-lasting implications (see, for example, Blakemore and Frith, 2006 and Gopnik *et al.*, 1999).

Increasingly, children under the age of five will have had experiences in one or more different early years contexts, whether they have been cared for by a nanny or childminder, or have experienced group settings such as day nurseries and/or pre-school nurseries or playgroups. Each of these settings will have provided a range of diverse experiences and in turn these will have affected the knowledge, skills and understanding that children bring with them to school. Plans to extend childcare funding to two year olds under the *Children's Plan*, coupled with the current economic climate and socio-political trends, are likely to increase further the likelihood of children spending time in settings other than the home. It is therefore imperative that teachers, particularly those working in Key Stage 1, are fully cognisant of the potential range of provision and that they understand the types of experiences these children will have had, in order to ease the transition process and be sensitive to the potential impact of these in helping young children to adapt and settle into the school environment. Indeed, the standards refer to the importance of teachers' understanding the impact of children's previous experiences.

THE EARLY YEARS FOUNDATION STAGE

Educational provision for children under five in the UK is offered within a wide range of diverse settings in both the maintained and private sectors. These settings include nursery classes, playgroups, childminders, children's centres and reception classes of primary schools. All of these settings now fall within the Foundation Stage, a distinctive phase for children from birth to statutory school age, currently described as 'the term after a child's fifth birthday'. Historically, the fragmented and patchy nature of educational provision has created difficulties and divisions for children, their families and practitioners alike.

In 2006, the Childcare Act provided the legal framework for the creation of the Early Years Foundation Stage (EYFS), implemented in 2008. The EYFS combines and replaces three earlier initiatives:

- *Birth to Three* framework (2002);
- *Curriculum Guidance for the Foundation Stage* (2003);
- *National Standards for Under Eights Day Care and Childminding* (2003).

The EYFS was developed in consultation with key stakeholders in the early years field, including practitioners, and is founded on evidence-based research on early years pedagogy, including international approaches. Two main principles are important here:

- The EYFS is intended to create a holistic and coherent approach to the care and education (sometimes referred to as 'educare') of young children – this represents a considerable and welcome development within the early years sector in recognition that the care and education of young children are inseparable and inextricably linked.
- The EYFS is a statutory framework, but it is not intended as a curriculum to be followed, as with the National Curriculum – rather, it is viewed as principles for practice across the early years sector.

Much of the EYFS is based on a commitment to 'developmentally appropriate practice', promoting activities that are in tune with the child's individual level of understanding and skills development. Though children are assessed individually, the sociocultural context of children's lives is also recognised, promoting contextually appropriate practice.

What is developmentally appropriate practice?

Developmentally appropriate practice requires both meeting children where they are – which means that teachers must get to know them well – and enabling them to reach goals that are both challenging and achievable. All teaching practices should be appropriate to children's age and developmental status, attuned to them as unique individuals, and responsive to the social and cultural contexts in which they live.

(Position Statement, NAEYC, 2009)

Early years practice is commonly associated with the term 'developmentally appropriate practice' (DAP), a term that has particular currency in the USA, but that has had a significant influence on early years education in the UK. Several authors endorse a developmental approach to the early years (Blenkin and Kelly, 1988), suggesting that education should primarily be concerned with 'human development' rather than knowledge acquisition. Elsewhere in this book, Bailey and Earl refer to the developmental tradition that 'emphasises the ways in which children develop physically, socially, emotionally and intellectually as a basis for planning and organising learning' (Unit 4.1). The *Cambridge Primary Review* in the UK has recently confirmed the importance of a developmentally appropriate curriculum for young learners, such as the need for active experience, multi-sensory approaches and pretend play to promote cognitive development (Goswami and Bryant, 2007). A longitudinal, cross-cultural study on pre-school experiences in ten different countries also shows that developmentally appropriate practice works best for younger children (Montie *et al.*, 2006). Clear links can also be found within the principles of EYFS and the principles behind DAP.

What is contextually appropriate practice?

> Practice grows out of political and economic conditions and traditions rather than from scientific research into child development.
>
> (Penn, 2008: 189)

Although DAP endorses a developmental perspective on children's education, we must be careful not to overemphasise the evidence from neuroscience and developmental psychology. Penn calls attention to the many assumptions there are in following a developmental approach, including the capacity to measure 'normality' and the 'compartmentalisation' of development into stages (2008: 14). Moreover, we need to consider not only developmental aspects but also the wider context and all the factors that may shape a child's learning and development. No framework or curriculum is 'value-free' or 'context-free' (Penn, 2008: 188). We therefore need to be conscious of the wide range of factors that may influence a child's experiences before entering Key Stage 1, not just their apparent developmental levels.

RHETORIC AND REALITY IN THE RECEPTION CLASS

The 'reception class' is the first class of primary school. It receives the new intake of children at age four or five. In England, Scotland and Wales, the statutory school starting age is the term after a child's fifth birthday. However, in practice, most children in England and Wales start school before the statutory age of five. Four distinct admission policies across the UK can be identified. These are: (1) at the statutory age (termly admission after the child's fifth birthday); (2) as 'rising fives' (termly admission in the term in which the child's fifth birthday occurs); (3) from roughly four and a half (two intakes per year); and (4) from four (one intake per year). Evidence suggests that, increasingly, schools favour one intake per year for its perceived benefits for summer-born children, although increases in the number of young four year olds entering school can be attributed to a range of factors, including falling rolls creating pressure for schools to fill places; pressure from parents for their children to start school earlier because of a lack of sufficient free, pre-school provision, but also for its perceived educational benefits; and the demands of the National Curriculum to ensure that children have sufficient time in school before formal assessment at seven.

Studies have highlighted the division between nursery and reception class practice, in spite of the fact that the Foundation Stage was designed precisely to overcome such divisions. A number of specific concerns have been identified and include diverse admission policies that may contribute to the uneven quality of provision for four year olds in reception classes; lower adult:child ratios in reception classes, which may reduce effective adult child interaction; a lack of appropriately trained staff in reception classes, which may lead to over-formal activities; and a reduction in the availability of choice of activity, outdoor access and time and space for active play (David, 1990; Adams *et al.*, 2004; Rogers and Evans, 2008). Others argue that the location of the reception class in school, unlike other separately managed pre-school settings, may result in features of a formal school curriculum percolating down to the teachers and children in the reception class. In turn, this can result in competing discourses of school improvement *versus* a distinctive pedagogy for early childhood (Aubrey, 2004).

Studies of reception class pedagogy explicitly endorse a nursery-style provision for four year olds and argue that there is no compelling evidence that starting school early has lasting educational benefits (Sharp, 2002; Adams *et al.*, 2004). Indeed, opponents of an early school starting age warn that over-formal education introduced too soon may be detrimental to children's social well-being and long-term attitude to learning. Yet it appears that children in reception classes may often experience a watered-down version of a Key Stage 1 class (Adams *et al.*, 2004). Indeed, tales have proliferated in the literature of children experiencing the literacy and numeracy hour earlier than they should in order to prepare them for Key Stage 1 (McInnes, 2002; Ofsted, 2003; Miller and Smith, 2004; Moyles, 2007; Whitebread and Coltman, 2008).

The emphasis on skill acquisition in reception classes can be to the detriment of children's motivation to learn, overemphasis on formal reading skills being a classic example of this trend. The *Cambridge Primary Review*, for example, has noted that any gains have been 'at the expense of [pupils'] enjoyment of reading' (Whetton *et al.*, 2007: 19). Young children's disposition to learning has been a critical factor identified in the literature for educational success (Katz, 1992), suggesting that the 'school-readiness' culture that permeates reception classes may be counter-effective. These issues are compounded by the increasing trend of four-year-old children entering reception classes who are encountering the effects of 'top down pressures' (Rogers and Rose, 2007). Such trends are unnecessary given the well-known evidence that children who start formal school at a later age eventually outstrip English children in academic achievement (Whetton *et al.*, 2007; Alexander, 2009).

As the *Cambridge Primary Review* has noted:

> the assumption that an early starting age is beneficial for children's later attainment is not well supported in the research and therefore remains open to question, whilst there are particular concerns about the appropriateness of provision for four year olds in school reception classes.
>
> (Riggall and Sharp, 2008)

Task 2.5.1 **SCHOOL STARTING AGE**

■ Read the article, Rogers, S. and Rose, J. (2007) 'Ready for reception? The advantages and disadvantages of single-point entry to school', *Early Years*, 27(1), March: 47–63.
■ Discuss the relative merits of an early school starting age in England.
■ Identify from your reading the advantages and disadvantages of a single-point entry and the practical implications of such a policy.

THE LEARNING ENVIRONMENT

A rich and varied environment supports children's learning and development. It gives them the confidence to explore and learn in secure and safe, yet challenging, indoor and outdoor spaces.

(EYFS, 2008, Commitment 3.3)

What is an appropriate learning environment for children in the early years? The debate about what constitutes an appropriate learning environment inevitably draws into its sphere the role of play.

The EYFS strongly endorses a play-based approach to learning in the early years. But, in practice, implementing a play-based approach can be problematic. First, teachers often feel under pressure to prepare children for formal learning and prioritise literacy and numeracy activities, as noted earlier, which may not be appropriate to developmentally appropriate practice. Second, it is not always clear how much structure to provide. Do children need manufactured and elaborate resources to play? Should play be tied to curriculum objectives or are the outcomes of play determined by the children? Third, what is the adult role in play? To what extent should adults intervene and when does intervention become interference?

Few would dispute the fact that one of the key ways in which children up to the age of five make human sense (Donaldson, 1978) of the world around them is through their play. We can see this in the earliest sensori-motor play observed in babies and toddlers, involving mainly exploratory activity through the senses and through action on objects. You might be familiar with the tendency of babies to put things in their mouths and throw things. At this stage, children are interested in the properties of things. Take, for example, Sam, who is ten months old. He is preoccupied with dropping objects from the top of the stairs repeatedly. Though this behaviour may be difficult for adults to tolerate, it is a vital part of Sam's development in his efforts to make sense of the world around him. He is learning about cause and effect, his impact on the world and trajectories (an early mathematical concept).

This exploratory play gradually changes as children approach their second birthdays, when a profound and uniquely human capacity comes to the fore of children's activity. This is the ability to pretend, seen first in the simple imitations of toddlers and later in the highly sophisticated social pretend play or role-play of four and five year olds. It is this social pretence that lays the foundations of many important life skills, such as problem solving, creative activity and interpersonal relations, as well as being enjoyable and life-enhancing to children as they play.

Of particular interest to those of you working in Key Stage 1 classes is research that demonstrates that children aged three to five engage in more pretend play than any other kind of play (see, for example, Corsaro, 2005). Not only is it more prevalent than other kinds of play, but it becomes highly complex, involving detailed planning and negotiation, and innovation. Developmentally speaking, there are good reasons for this. At around the age of four, we see children's imaginative play become more complex as they become more linguistically and socially expert. They have also discovered that other people have minds, and that what they think is not always what others think. This is the emergence of empathy growing out of a theory of mind acquired at around the age of three. All this is essential to successful pretend play and also developed within it.

The prevalence of this kind of play occurs precisely at the point at which children enter reception class settings in primary schools and continues to develop through to the role-play and other creative activities seen in primary school classrooms. In order to help children develop vivid imaginations, understand social relations and innovate (all transferable skills), it is essential that children are given ample opportunities to engage in social pretence with their peers at this age and, furthermore, that these experiences are built upon in Key Stage 1 and beyond.

In recognition of the importance of all types of play across the early years phase, early years settings are developed around the concept of 'free flow', continuous play provision both indoors and outdoors. Classrooms are organised into resource areas to which children have access throughout the day. This approach presupposes choice and autonomy on the part of children, who will have regular and sustained opportunities to access resources independently. Remember that Einstein believed that 'play is research.'

Task 2.5.2 **CHILD-INITIATED PLAY**

Read the following example of real-life practice and consider whether the teacher's aims fulfil her intention:

A teacher of six year olds is planning an art activity to develop their creative skills. She decides the children will make pine-cone turkeys and collects the range of materials they will use. She sits with a group and demonstrates how they will make them and explains exactly how the materials fit together in particular places to create the turkey. She then supports them in making them, allowing each child to choose five coloured feathers, which she encourages them to count. The children then make the turkeys, but need help with the glueing, sticking and making the pipe-cleaner feet. The children mostly watch the teacher during the whole activity.

(Woyke, 2001)

How you could turn this adult-led activity into one that is child-initiated and allows the child to be more active, creative and independent in the process?

The outdoor environment

Of particular importance since the introduction of the EYFS is the recognition that young children need regular access to outdoor play to enhance their well-being and development in all areas: physical, emotional, social, cognitive and creative. Research has shown that not only do young children prefer to play outside, but that they play in quite different ways in outdoor spaces. Rogers and Evans (2008) note that four and five year olds engaged in far more complex, sustained and socially developed role-play in outdoor spaces. Children displayed a wider range of social skills to establish and maintain social groups, stayed in character for longer periods, used open-ended props more creatively, and there were fewer conflicts between children and with adults. The incidence of mixed-gender play was also more frequently observed in the outdoor area.

THE ROLE OF THE ADULT IN PLAY

It is not simply the material resources that make for a stimulating and effective learning environment for young children. Knowledgeable, skilled and caring adults will create an environment that creates, nurtures and sustains a positive learning ethos that matches the dispositions and characteristics of young children and acknowledges and values cultural diversity and equity.

A recent research study by Rogers and Evans (2008) studied the role-play activity of four and five year olds in reception and Year 1 classes. They found that there was a mismatch between how children viewed their play and the way play was organised in the classroom. Typically, classrooms were set up with structured role-play areas around a particular theme or topic. For example, one classroom developed a shop, and another offered a café. Although these areas were resourced in elaborate and inviting ways, the children paid little attention to the theme, preferring instead to play games of their own choosing. In many instances, the play was difficult to contain and manage within the confines of the classroom. An alternative approach to role-play, well suited to children over the age of four and throughout the primary years, is open-ended play with suggestive rather than pre-specified props.

For example, Kelvin and his friends built a 'ship' from large bricks. They 'sailed' to a 'cave' made from a sheet draped over some chairs. In the 'cave' there were some keys, which they used to lock up the baddies. This example of sustained role-play involving five children lasted for at least 20 minutes. Kelvin, a child with identified special needs, emerged as a 'master player', leading the group and utilising language rarely heard in formal teaching activities. Social relationships were explored, formed and reformed in the course of the play as children negotiated roles and planned the course of the play.

In this simple example of role-play, we see a wide range of important learning and potential assessment opportunities for the observant adult. However, in order for this type of play to occur, the adult needs to take the following into consideration:

For young children, play is about:

■ exercising choice and control over what they do;
■ making and developing friendships;
■ pretending in a secure context;
■ experimenting with materials, ideas, time and place (here and now/fantasy and reality).

For adults, play may be a highly valued activity, but in practice it may be:

■ a holding task;
■ a reward for good work;
■ noisy and disruptive;
■ difficult to manage and irrational;
■ a low status activity.

Research shows that adults need to:

■ give children real choice about where, with whom, what and how they play;
■ give children space (indoors and outdoors) and uninterrupted time to play, revisit, rebuild and recreate ideas with adults and children;
■ show children we are interested in their play through co-construction, consultation and negotiation, observation and feedback;
■ be knowledgeable others and advocates for play;
■ develop outdoor spaces for playful learning where children can exercise greater choice over materials, location and play mates;
■ develop open-ended resources and spaces, enabling children to create play contexts and content;
■ provide time to play without unnecessary interruptions;
■ develop a learner-inclusive environment that encourages children's participation and decision making;
■ encourage *sustained shared thinking* between adults and children and between children.

(Adapted from Rogers and Evans, 2008)

Sustained shared thinking

Sustained shared thinking involves the adult being aware of the children's interests and understandings and the adult and children working together to develop an idea or skill. The adult shows genuine interest, offers encouragement, clarifies ideas and asks open questions. This supports and extends the children's thinking and helps children to make connections in learning.

(DfES, 2007)

Task 2.5.3 **SUSTAINED SHARED THINKING**

Read the following example of a real-life exchange between children and their teacher in a nursery. Evaluate the way in which the practitioner supported the children's thinking.

While playing outside, the children discovered a kitten (toy) stuck in the guttering of the barn area. The group was allowed time to discover the kitten and talk about how they thought it got there and how it could be rescued.

(P = practitioner)

Child B: Oh, poor kitty, I think she's stuck up there.

Child C: How did it get all the way up there?

P: Oh dear. How do you think the kitten got stuck up there in the first place?

Child A: He climbed up this pipe (pointing to the drainpipe), then went along here and got stuck in here.

Child C: He can't climb up there 'cos' he's not real! I think he must have been 'throwded' up there.

P: Who do you think might have done that?

Child C: I don't know but it's not very kind is it? They might have done it on accident.

Child A: Yeah, like this (he mimics throwing an imaginary object accidentally!)

Child E: My daddy 'throwed' the ball through the window by accident. Mummy was cross. He 'breaked' the window!

P: Yes, they might have done it by accident, I can't think that anyone would throw it up there on purpose. Well, I suppose we need to do some good thinking about what to do to help the kitten. How shall we do that do you think?

Child D: I know, I know! We can, we can ask Charlotte to climb up all the way.

Child A: Yeah, I seen Charlotte climb ladders to get that stuff off them tall shelves in the other room.

Child C: Or we can get Jill to do the ladder.

Child B: No, she 'don't really like 'um' (meaning ladders).

Child C: I know, we can find Graham, he's good with ladders and he fixes stuff.

Child E: Yeah, ask Graham to do it.

P: What do we need to ask Graham?

Child E: Ask him to get the ladders and climb up there.

P: Oh, I see.

Child D: He can climb all the way up to that pipe thing and put it (the kitten) in his pocket.

Child B: He 'don't' want to squash it though. That would hurt it, wouldn't it?

Child A: Poor kitty. I think he's very sad. I don't want him to be sad no more.

Child E: No.

P: Shall we decide what we think we should do then?

Group: Yeah!

P: Well, you had lots of thoughts and ideas; let's see if we can choose one idea to sort the problem out. You said we need to get a ladder, but who shall we ask to climb up it; you thought it could be Jill, Graham or Charlotte. Who do you think would be best to ask?

Child C: Graham.

Child A and E: Yeah, we can ask Graham.

P: What makes you think Graham will be best for the job of getting the kitten down?

Child E: He can climb ladders up really high.

Child D: Yeah, I 'seen' him before on ladders. He can put it (kitten) in his pocket gently, can't he?

Child B: He mustn't drop her or she'll have a headache and she might die!

P: I hope she doesn't do that! Okay, so you think Graham can climb the ladder and put the kitten in his pocket gently and bring it back down again?

Child A: Yeah, really gentle!

Child B: And then the kitten will live happily ever after!

(Bowery, 2008)

The *Effective Provision of Pre-school Education* (EPPE) project findings (Siraj-Blatchford, 2004; Sylva et al., 2004) suggested that the potential for learning through play can be extended by what the researchers have termed 'sustained shared thinking'. This process has officially been incorporated into the EYFS as noted in the quotation above. This essentially involves adults 'getting involved' in children's thinking, interacting in a shared (verbal or non-verbal) dialogue. In this way, as Siraj-Blatchford explains, adults can act as co-constructors to 'solve a problem, clarify a concept, evaluate activities or extend narratives' (2004: 147). Sustained shared thinking builds on other research that demonstrates the importance of meaningful, child-initiated and supportive interactions such as Bruner's (1986) work on scaffolding and learning as a communal activity inspired by Vygotsky, by Lave and Wenger's (1991) work on situated learning and by Schaffer's (1996) work on 'joint involvement episodes'. Apart from helping to develop children's learning, the adult needs to ensure that he or she is sensitive to the children's cues and levels of understanding, supporting them to make connections and transform their learning in a pleasurable and embedded way.

THE FOUNDATION STAGE PROFILE

The Foundation Stage Profile (FSP) is the precursor for the standard assessment tests (SATs) and is intended to provide a 'baseline assessment' of children starting school. Every government-funded setting, including schools, must complete an FSP for every child in their reception year or equivalent. Although each local authority has its own procedures for the collection of data from the FSP, in essence it requires reception class teachers to assess each child against the 13 assessment scales that are derived from the Early Learning Goals. It is intended that Year 1 teachers use the summary profiles to help inform them of individual children's learning and development. The results from these profiles are collected by local authorities and used to agree statutory targets. The Qualifications and Curriculum Authority (QCA) has stipulated that these summative assessments should be derived from the ongoing observations of consistent and independent behaviour undertaken largely in the context of children's self-initiated activities.

It should be noted that many have criticised these summative profiles and have questioned, among other things, their suitability, their effectiveness in feeding into teaching in Year 1, their oversimplification and the way in which they compartmentalise children's learning (BERA, 2003). The Assessment Reform Group (1999) has claimed that 'assessment which is specifically designed to promote learning is the single most powerful tool we have for both raising standards and empowering lifelong learners'. There is an increasing call for more formative styles of assessment to take priority. The *Researching Effective Pedagogy in the Early Years* (REPEY) project has also shown that effective formative assessment directly impacts upon the quality of learning (Siraj-Blatchford *et al.*, 2002).

An alternative form of assessment, namely 'Learning Journeys', is becoming increasingly common practice in early years settings. The EYFS makes reference to this style of assessment within the theme of the Enabling Environment. Such Learning Journeys are largely derived from 'learning stories' developed in New Zealand, whereby early years practitioners undergo regular assessment of children's natural activities, incorporating the observation, assessment and planning cycle within a framework of celebrating children's achievements. These are shared with both the children and parents, alongside discussion and decision making among the children and staff to plan, enrich and progress children's learning. This style of assessment follows a sociocultural model. It is collaboratively and community based and reflects the learner's personal development rather than performance indicators. It is undoubtedly assessment *for* learning rather than assessment *of* learning.

TRANSITION FROM THE FOUNDATION STAGE TO KEY STAGE 1

Transition from one key stage to another inevitably presents children and practitioners with both challenges and opportunities. It involves unlearning and relearning and the teacher's transition practice needs to take this into account. In conversation with reception class children, Rogers and Evans (2008) found that, for some, moving from the Foundation Stage to Key Stage 1 was an exciting prospect, signifying progress and achievement. For others, it was a source of anxiety, perceived as 'hard work', with fewer opportunities to play with friends.

Task 2.5.4 SUPPORTING TRANSITION

Undertake an audit of reception and Year 1 in a school from a child's perspective:

■ What do the children see in the Year 1 classroom that is the same as the reception classroom?
■ What is different?
■ What do the reception children experience that is the same as the Year 1 children?
■ What is different?

Now undertake an audit of transition procedures in the school:

■ What does the school do to reinforce the similarities?
■ What does the school do to accommodate the differences?

Evaluate your findings in terms of the suggestions made in this section about how teachers can support the transition process.

At any stage of education, transition is complex. It is not a straightforward linear process or for that matter a single event – it involves a complex web of shifting and diverse aspects that need to be taken into account by adults in the school. For example, a series of interactions takes place, invariably involving a change in status and culture and 'continued social activity in which the individual lives, and learns to cope, by adapting to the given social conditions' (Fabian, 2006: 13). Research shows that educational transitions are highly significant to pupils and can be a 'critical factor in determining children's future progress and development' (Fabian, 2006: 4).

With this in mind, it will be helpful to consider the following factors in order to ensure effective transition programmes:

■ Children need ample opportunity to become familiar with the new situation through visits to the setting and contact with the teacher.
■ 'Bridging' activities can form an important part of the process and 'create links between and actively involve children, parents, families, teachers, early childhood services, schools and the local community' (Fabian, 2006: 10).
■ Parents need to be properly informed and involved in the transition process.
■ Teachers have appropriate information about the children's prior development and experience (Margetts, 2002), as children may have experienced multiple transitions, e.g. childminder, day nursery, pre-school, home before starting school.
■ Children may also experience a variety of transitions across the school day, e.g. breakfast club, school, after-school club, childminder.

■   Transitions are bounded by a time period. However, the implications and repercussions of transition are not bound by time in the same way, i.e. children may move from reception to Year 1 within a few months, but the impact this has had on the child may last far longer than this.

■   Rules and rituals are significant issues in the transition process and assumptions are often made by adults that children will automatically understand these and their complexities.

■   The way in which individual children manage change from 'comfort zone' to new environment needs to be considered carefully by adults.

■   Research by Galton *et al.* (1999) recognised that some children may temporarily demonstrate a 'dip' in their learning during the transition period as they adjust to the new setting

SUMMARY

This unit has looked at, and should have helped you formulate a view on, the following key issues:

■ When should children start school?
■ In what ways do young children learn best?
■ Why is play important in early learning?
■ What is the nature of adult roles in early learning?

ANNOTATED FURTHER READING

Edgington, M. (2004) *The Foundation Stage Teacher*, **London: Sage.**
A useful practical text that will support students and newly qualified teachers to develop their understanding of the nature of teaching and learning in the Foundation Stage.

Moyles, J. (ed.) (2004) *The Excellence of Play*, **Buckingham: Open University Press.**
A collection of chapters on play in early years education. A good introduction to play theories and play in practice.

Rogers, S. and Evans, J. (2008) *Inside Role-play in Early Childhood Education: Researching Children's Perspectives*, **London: Routledge.**
An example of classroom research, this book investigates children's perspectives on play in reception classes. It includes introductory chapters on play theories and the nature of the reception class, methodology relating to researching with young children and many examples of children's perspectives of classroom experience.

Willan, J., Parker Rees, R. and Savage, J. (2007) *Early Childhood Studies*, **Exeter: Learning Matters.**
A highly accessible collection of chapters covering a wide range of topics in early childhood.

Wood, E. (ed.) (2008) *Routledge Reader of Early Childhood Education*, **London: Routledge.**
For those who would like more challenging reading, this book brings together a range of chapters and published articles on key issues and perspectives in early childhood education.

RELEVANT WEBSITES

Children's Workforce Development Council (CWDC): www.cwdcouncil.org.uk/eyfs
This contains information on the Early Years Foundation Stage.

National Strategies: http://nationalstrategies.standards.dcsf.gov.uk/earlyyears

Visit the companion website www.routledge.com/textbooks/ltps2e for:

■ links to useful websites relevant to this unit.

REFERENCES

Adams, S., Alexander, E., Drummond, M.J. and Moyles, J. (2004) *Inside the Foundation Stage: Recreating the Reception Year*, London: ATL.

Alexander, R.J. (2009) *Towards a New Primary Curriculum: A Report from the Cambridge Primary Review. Part 2. The Future*, Cambridge: University of Cambridge.

Anning, A. (2006) 'Early years education: mixed messages and conflicts', in D. Kassem, E. Mufti and J. Robinson (eds) *Education Studies: Issues and Critical Perspectives*, Maidenhead: Open University Press/McGraw-Hill, pp. 5–11.

Assessment Reform Group (1999) *Assessment for Learning: Beyond the Black Box*, Cambridge: Cambridge University Press.

Aubrey, C. (2004) 'Implementing the foundation stage in reception classes', *British Educational Research Journal*, 30(5): 633–56.

Blakemore, S. and Frith, U. (2005) *The Learning Brain: Lessons for Education*, Oxford: Blackwell.

Blenkin, G. and Kelly, A.V. (eds) (1988) *Early Childhood Education: A Developmental Curriculum*, London: Paul Chapman.

Bowery, E. (2008) 'Is there a place for the discrete teaching of thinking skills and dispositions in a pre-school curriculum?' Unpublished dissertation, University of Gloucestershire.

British Educational Research Association (BERA) (2003) *Early Years Research: Pedagogy, Curriculum and Adult Roles, Training and Professionalism*, Macclesfield: BERA.

Bruner, J. (1986) *Actual Minds, Possible Worlds*, Cambridge, MA: Harvard University Press.

Corsaro W.A. (2005) *The Sociology of Childhood*, 2nd edn, London: Pine Forge Press.

David, T. (1990) *Under Five – Under-educated?* Milton Keynes: Open University Press.

Department for Education and Skills (DfES) (2007) *Practice Guidance for the Early Years Foundation Stage*, Nottingham: DfES.

Donaldson, M. (1978) *Children's Minds*, Glasgow: Fontana.

Fabian, H. (2006) 'Informing transitions', in A.-W. Dunlop and H. Fabian, *Informing Transitions in the Early Years*, Milton Keynes: Open University Press.

Galton, M., Gray, J. and Ruddock, J. (1999) *The Impact of School Transitions and Transfers on Pupil Progress and Attainment*, Norwich: Crown Copyright.

Gopnik, A., Meltzoff, A. and Kuhl, P. (1999) *How Babies Think: The Science of Childhood*, London: Weidenfeld & Nicolson.

Goswami, U. and Bryant, P. (2007) *Children's Cognitive Development and Learning (Cambridge Primary Review: Research Survey 2/1(a))*, Cambridge: Cambridge University Press.

Katz, L.G. (1992) 'What should young children be learning?', in *ERIC Digest*, Urbana, IL: ERIC Clearinghouse on Elementary and Early Childhood Education. ED 290 554.

Lave, J. and Wenger, J. (1991) *Situated Learning: Legitimate Peripheral Participation*, Cambridge: Cambridge University Press.

Margetts, K. (2002) 'Planning transition programmes', in H. Fabian and A.W. Dunlop (eds) *Transition in the Early Years*, London: Routledge, pp. 111–22.

McInnes, K. (2002) 'What are the educational experiences of 4-year-olds? A comparative study of 4-year-olds in nursery and reception settings', *Early Years*, 22(2): 119–27.

Miller, L. and Smith, A.P. (2004) Practitioners' beliefs and children's experiences of literacy in four early years settings. *Early Years*, 24(2): 121–33.

Montie, J.E., Ziang, S. and Schqeinhart, L.J. (2006) 'Preschool experience in 10 countries: cognitive and language performance at age 7', *Early Childhood Research Quarterly*, 21: 313–31.

Moyles, J. (ed.) (2007) *Early Years Foundations: Meeting the Challenge*, Maidenhead: Open University Press/McGraw-Hill.

National Association for the Education of Young Children (NAEYC) (2009) *Developmentally Appropriate Practice in Early Childhood Programs Serving Children from Birth through Age 8*, Position Statement, Washington, DC: NAEYC.

Office for Standards in Education (Ofsted) (2003) *The Education of Six-year-olds in England, Denmark and Finland: An International Comparative Study*, HMI 1660, London: Ofsted.

Penn, H. (2008) *Understanding Early Childhood*, Maidenhead: Open University Press.

Riggall, A. and Sharp, C. (2008) *The Structure of Primary Education: England and Other Countries (Cambridge Primary Review: Research Survey 9/1)*, Cambridge: Cambridge University Press.

Riley, J.L. (ed.) (2003) *Learning in the Early Years: 3–7*, London: Paul Chapman/Sage.

Rogers, S. and Evans, J. (2008) *Inside Role-play in Early Education: Researching Children's Perspectives*, London: Routledge.

Rogers, S. and Rose, J. (2007) 'Ready for reception? The advantages and disadvantages of single-point entry to school', *Early Years*, 27(1), March: 47–63.

Schaffer, H.R. (1996) 'Joint involvement episodes as context for development', in H. Daniels (ed.) *An Introduction to Vygotsky*, London: Routledge.

Sharp, C. (2002) *School Starting Age: European Policy and Recent Research*, Conference paper, Slough: NFER.

Siraj-Blatchford, I. (2004) 'Educational disadvantage in the early years: how do we overcome it? Some lessons from research', *European Early Childhood Education Research Journal* 12(2): 5–20.

Siraj-Blatchford, I., Sylva, K., Muttock, S., Gilden, R. and Bell, D. (2002) *Researching Effective Pedagogy in the Early Years* (REPEY), DfES Research Brief 356, London: DfES.

Sylva, K., Melhuish, E.C., Sammons, P., Siraj-Blatchford, I. and Taggart, B. (2004) *The Effective Provision of Pre-school Education* (EPPE) *Project: Technical Paper 12 – The Final Report: Effective Pre-school Education*, London: DfES/Institute of Education, University of London.

Whetton, C., Ruddock, G. and Twist, L. (2007) *Standards in English Primary Education: The International Evidence (Cambridge Primary Review: Research Survey 4/2)*, Cambridge: Cambridge University Press.

Whitebread, D. and Coltman, P. (eds) (2008) *Teaching and Learning in the Early Years*, 3rd edn, London: Routledge.

Woyke, P.P. (2001) 'What does creativity look like in a developmentally appropriate preschool classroom?' *Earthworm*, 2(3): 15.

3

PLANNING AND MANAGING LEARNING

APPROACHING LONG- AND MEDIUM-TERM PLANNING

Jane Medwell

INTRODUCTION

The focus of this unit is longer-term planning: the termly and yearly plans you will use to prepare your teaching across the curriculum. This sort of planning includes long-term planning expressed as school policies and medium-term planning expressed as termly or half-termly planning sheets. Planning at this level is the basis of all your teaching but it is not something you will easily encounter during your initial training. You should take every opportunity to look at, discuss and question the medium- and long-term plans you encounter.

OBJECTIVES

By the end of this unit you should:

■ understand the difference between long-term and medium-term planning;
■ understand the purposes of long- and medium-term planning;
■ know the key features of long- and medium-term plans;
■ understand the range of issues considered when making long- and medium-term plans;
■ be confident in interpreting medium-term plans.

THE IMPORTANCE OF LONG-TERM PLANNING

Long-term planning can often seem like a 'given' in school. When you go to school placement, the planning is already there in the form of National Curriculum documents and school policies. This may even already have been translated into medium-term plans. However, it is important that you understand how long- and medium-term plans are developed and it is important that you can question the assumptions upon which such plans are based.

Long-term plans for a key stage are usually determined through whole-staff discussion, a process in which you may not be able to be involved. If you do not contribute to long-term planning, you will always teach what, and how, someone else has chosen, instead of participating in those decisions yourself. One of the most important parts of your newly qualified teacher (NQT) year will be the opportunity to participate in policy reviews.

What are you planning?

Long-term planning is the process whereby the school team decides how the curriculum is taught across the whole school or key stage. It shows:

■ exactly what the school curriculum is;
■ how the curriculum is covered in terms of breadth and depth;
■ how the curriculum is structured within year groups and across key stages;
■ how much time is allocated to each area of the curriculum in each year group.

The curriculum to be covered in state-maintained schools in England in the Early Years Foundation Stage (EYFS), Key Stage 1 or Key Stage 2 includes the statutory content of the National Curriculum for the relevant key stages. This includes the Early Learning Goals and, at Key Stages 1 and 2, the programmes of study and statements of attainment. The curriculum has been relatively stable for a number of years, but the current review means that there is likely to be change in the way that skills, knowledge and attitudes to be learned are set out. The curriculum must develop as the learning demands of society change.

The documents of the National Curriculum are available at http://curriculum.qcda.gov.uk/ and give a broad outline of the content of the curriculum, but not how it is to be taught. This is the role of long-term planning in school.

For each subject and for each key stage, programmes of study set out what pupils should be taught, and attainment targets set out the expected standards of pupils' performance. Schools choose how they organise their school curriculum to include the programmes of study. Teachers' planning for schemes of work usually starts with the programmes of study and the needs and abilities of their pupils. Level descriptions can help to determine the degree of challenge and progression for work across each year of a key stage.

Some key issues taken into consideration when planning long term are:

■ *breadth* – so that pupils experience the full range of curriculum areas and the key skills discussed above as well as any additional skills and learning identified as important in the school curriculum;
■ *depth* – so there are opportunities for in-depth learning and the chance for children to really develop their own understandings;
■ *coherence* – so that natural and meaningful links within and between some subjects are recognised and developed to help children learn as purposefully as possible;
■ *relevance* – so that pupils' activities relate to previous learning and so that they can understand how the learning is relevant to them;
■ *differentiation* – so the needs and progress of pupils are catered for;
■ *progression* – so learning develops through sequenced activities as children go through each term and school year, without undue repetition.

How will you plan to teach the content?

The content of the statutory curriculum and the needs of the children are two defining factors in what you teach. In long-term planning you also have to consider:

■ how much time is allocated to each area of the curriculum in each year group;
■ how the curriculum is structured within year groups and across key stages.

Task 3.1.1 **BEGINNING TO PLAN A TOPIC**

This task aims to get you to consider a popular topic, such as healthy living, where it appears in the National Curriculum and how this might be taught to children at Key Stage 2.

Go to the curriculum online at http://curriculum.qcda.gov.uk/key-stages-1-and-2/subjects/index.aspx and look at the Key Stage 2 personal, social and health education (PSHE) guidance. Identify the programme of study under 'Knowledge, skills and understanding':

Developing a healthy, safer lifestyle

3 Pupils should be taught:
   what makes a healthy lifestyle, including the benefits of exercise and healthy eating, what affects mental health, and how to make informed choices.

This is only a small part of the PSHE curriculum (which does not have statements of attainment).

Now identify what areas of the curriculum are related to this PSHE programme of study. Look at the programmes of study and attainment targets for science at Key Stage 2 and physical education (PE) at Key Stage 2.

How much time to allocate to learning in each subject, theme or key skill is an important area for negotiation. The working week in school includes activities such as collective worship and assemblies as well as lessons. It will not be possible to include every learning experience that teachers would like. For instance, a Key Stage 2 English coordinator might suggest the following allocation of time for English for all Key Stage 2 children:

■ 1 hour for literacy study every day (5 hours);
■ 10 minutes for daily handwriting practice (50 minutes);
■ 20 minutes for reading a story or poem to children (1 hour 40 minutes);
■ 20 minutes per week for speaking and listening planned into other curriculum areas;
■ time for setting and doing spelling tests (30 minutes);
■ a weekly drama session in the hall (40 minutes);
■ a daily 15-minute guided reading/reading activity rota time for all pupils (1 hour 15 minutes).

All these are worthy activities but, if all were to be timetabled, the English part of the curriculum could consume more than 10 hours a week in which there are only around 25 teaching hours! Each subject can always justify more time and school targets, such as a commitment to two hours' PE a week, must be taken into account. This is why long-term planning requires decisions about school priorities and about use of time for cross-curricular work.

Although the time available for teaching and learning is finite, there are a number of ways to plan this time so that it is used effectively and helps children to make links between their different areas of learning. Dividing school time rigidly into 'subjects', so that each subject has a weekly allocation, may not be the most effective way to use the time. For instance, rather than having a timed 'lesson' for developing the spiritual, moral, social and cultural (SMSC) lives of children, most schools plan to address this through a range of provision: school assemblies, collective worship, religious education and whole-school activities, as well as the rules and ethos of the school.

This does not mean that SMSC 'just happens' or that it is a less important aspect of school life than other subjects. The school has a clear policy and a detailed medium-term plan is derived from it. But it has decided that the best way to address SMSC is not through a weekly 'lesson'.

Some schools decide to 'block' subjects, so that children will have a meaningful block of time for a subject but may not have this subject every week of the year. Children may, for example, do art for one half term and design technology the next, or history one term and a geography topic the next. In this way, the material can be studied, explored and learned in depth, with an integrity and relevance that would not be possible in 15 minutes per week.

Some schools plan the whole curriculum in a cross-curricular way, so that the content of the National Curriculum is addressed, but it is done through learning themes or areas that are not designated subjects. Such schemes may be commercial programmes, such as the International Primary Curriculum or Mantle of the Expert Curriculum, where planning and support can be brought in by the school and adapted. Other schools do their cross-curricular planning in-house, planning content to make sure the coverage is complete, but arranging teaching for maximum creative opportunity. Two recent curriculum reviews have offered different suggestions, but both have identified the need to look across and beyond traditional subject boundaries. The *Independent Review of the Primary Curriculum* (Rose Review) can be found at www.dcsf.gov.uk/primarycurriculum review/. And the *Cambridge Primary Review*, an independent review conducted by the University of Cambridge, can be found at www.primaryreview.org.uk. Both these reviews will demand a total re-planning of the primary curriculum in schools, if the findings are adopted.

In Foundation Stage and Key Stage 1 it is very common to find that time is planned around the topic that is the focus of children's learning, with sessions not clearly 'labelled' as particular subjects. The curriculum planning is used to ensure a balanced curriculum, but the need for activities to make sense to the children is more important than the need for labels.

Another example of planning across the curriculum might be the introduction of the teaching of a primary language (teaching a foreign language) at Key Stages 1 or 2. This is an 'entitlement' for all children but is not yet a statutory part of the curriculum. Some schools address the allocation of time for primary languages (PL) by scheduling a regular PL slot for each class, or simply arranging a club out of school time. Other schools will 'block' PL teaching so that children do it more intensively in a particular term of the school year. In some schools the Year 6 children have a very intense PL programme in the last term of school, after standard assessment tests (SATs) and at the same time as transition to secondary school is considered. Other schools will look for opportunities for cross-curricular advantages. They might have a regular PL lesson for all children but also integrate PL into the school curriculum through assemblies about other cultures, writing to twin schools in English, answering the register in other languages and learning about the target country in geography. This does not actually eat up more curriculum time than the timetabled lesson but, through careful planning, gives the children a much broader experience. Decisions about how to allocate time to modern foreign languages (MFL) will depend not only on the learning goals and time available, but also on who will teach this aspect of the curriculum and what resources are needed. This is true across the curriculum.

In considering how to structure the curriculum within year groups and across key stages, you will have to consider the possibilities and resources available to you. The use of expensive resources that must be shared, such as information technology (IT) suites and halls, is an important considera-tion. Teacher time and expertise is also a valuable resource that needs to be planned effectively. A teacher who is particularly qualified, or expert in a subject such as music, a foreign language or sport, might well spend a good part of their time teaching a whole range of classes. This does not apply only to individual teachers who already have a particular skill or knowledge. Many schools ask teachers to develop particular specialisms, so that their teaching energy can be used effectively.

It may also be useful for teachers to concentrate on a smaller range of subjects, so that they can consolidate expertise and make planning and assessment manageable. Some schools will plan to make the teaching (including planning and assessment) manageable by using sets across classes or key stages, or by having teachers teach different parts of the curriculum to a range of classes. These sorts of decisions can help to make good use of expertise and to make the learning meaningful and relevant to children. When considering such arrangements, a school staff will weigh them against the lack of continuity caused by a change of teacher and the demands of moving children around between lessons.

The long-term planning undertaken by a school will be expressed through its policies, prospectus and development plan. You need to read these documents carefully. You will notice these documents will have review dates and will be regularly considered by staff so that changes to long-term planning can be made. There are some decisions that will be very clear to you as you work in school, but may not be written down – this can include the organisation of sets and groupings and the timing of the school day. If you choose your moment well, mentors and teachers will be happy to discuss these important, but often unwritten, parts of school policy.

Assessment and monitoring progress in long-term planning

One aspect of school planning that is relatively difficult to observe, but that has a real influence on long-term planning, is setting school targets. This happens at a number of levels. Schools, with the help of their local authority, set targets for the proportions of their pupils' targets expressed in National Curriculum levels and aim for children to make a planned rate of progress through the levels and sub-levels of the curriculum. Within school further targets are set for particular key stages and year groups. Each teacher is involved in the tracking of pupil progress against these expectations and will have a very clear understanding of the levels of progress made by their children.

School senior managers use the SAT results, optional tests in English and mathematics and a system of ongoing levelling, such as assessing of pupil progress (APP) to monitor pupils' progress towards these targets. SAT results are available to schools as summaries of data that can be used to monitor expectations and set targets for schools, key stages and individual year groups. These targets are negotiated with the head, subject coordinator and teachers, so that everyone is clear not only what is to be achieved, but what action can be taken to help children reach their targets. Such actions might include changes to staffing, such as changing the proportion of teaching assistance or special needs support, the provision of resources or the timing of booster classes, one-to-one tuition and other interventions. These decisions exemplify how national targets become school targets and influence long-term and medium-term planning. When you are in school, ask your mentor about the school's targets and your class teacher about pupil-tracking.

How the school assesses is also a matter for long-term planning. All schools required to follow the National Curriculum are also required to undertake statutory assessment and report to parents annually (although the arrangements are different in England, Wales and Scotland). However, schools also have to decide how they will conduct their assessment for learning, so that it is most useful and underpins teaching without generating unnecessary work or disrupting teaching. The school will have an assessment policy that is certainly worthy of your attention.

MEDIUM-TERM PLANNING

Medium-term plans will address the National Curriculum and the policies of the school, but will be much more specific than long-term planning. Medium-term planning might be half-termly or termly planning. Plans will be subject or theme specific, but also demonstrate links to other subjects. They will give you much more detail about:

■ the organisation and timetable of the particular class, and of any sets or other teaching arrangements;
■ learning objectives for the class and sets;
■ learning experiences and activities that will take place in the term or half term;
■ continuity and progression in learning – the way the learning is paced and broken up into manageable units.

Teachers have access to a good deal of support in their medium-term planning in the form of government schemes of work and frameworks of objectives, which are not statutory but are quite widely used. The Key Stage 1 and 2 Literacy and Mathematics Frameworks (see Primary National Strategies website below) usually form a part of the school's medium-term planning, although it is up to schools how closely they follow the suggestions. The units in these frameworks are useful for medium-term planning and can be grouped carefully so that some objectives are addressed repeatedly and some just once. These objectives are designed for medium-term planning and you would not expect to be able to address them in a single lesson. They are objectives for a sequence of lessons and more than one objective might be addressed in a single lesson.

The Primary National Strategies (http://nationalstrategies.standards.dcsf.gov.uk/primary) medium-term plans for maths and English for each year group incorporate a range of literacy and numeracy objectives. These units are very useful in grouping objectives in ways that make sense – for example, so that you plan to teach imperative sentences during a unit of work on instructions, rather than trying to teach a less appropriate sentence type. However, most teachers do not use these ready-made plans unadapted, as the plans cannot take account of the children in a particular class and their prior experience. Even so, the published plans are a very useful tool for shaping your own medium-term plans and the web-based format is helpful. As well as the frameworks, you would also need to consider other aspects of maths and English work and include planning for speaking and listening and cross-curricular links between English and maths and other subjects. It would be unfortunate to ignore the real opportunities for literacy and oracy offered by the study of geography, history or science, for instance.

Task 3.1.2 **USING SCHEMES OF WORK TO PLAN**

Look at the DCFS standards site, which contains the schemes of work available to schools: www.standards.dfes.gov.uk/schemes3/.

Follow up PSHE healthy living statement from the programmes of study for science and PE.

■ What units of work for science are relevant in each Key Stage 2 year (Years 3,4,5,6)?
■ What PE units are relevant?

Examine how the units are structured to ensure that the knowledge, skills and understanding are addressed as well as breadth of study.

■ What science and PE units of study would you specifically identify for a Year 4 class, if you were aiming to teach the PSHE programme of study about healthy living?

You can take this investigation further by looking at the literacy schemes of work and suggesting ways to link the science unit studied to the text types studied in each term, or look at the ICT scheme of work to find links between science and use of IT.

The schemes of work for foundation subjects and PL (www.standards.dfes.gov.uk/schemes3/) are also not statutory but are widely used. They demonstrate one way of organising medium-term plans for non-core subjects and are used flexibly in most schools. Schools often adapt these to meet their specific needs, local situation or available resources.

The medium-term plan will be written well before the start of the term or half term it applies to. In most cases it will be written by a group of teachers – either a key stage or year group team. The plan may well be based upon, or use elements from, a previous year's plan, but will never be simply copied again. The meetings where plans are written, or those where plans are reviewed, are some of the most useful meetings you can attend.

The role of the medium-term plan is:

■ to provide the detailed framework for classroom practice in a way that can be understood by everyone involved and can be scrutinised by coordinators, heads and inspectors (or taken up by a supply teacher, if necessary);

■ to identify the nature of work to be covered during the term or half term and ensure that it covers the requirements set out in the long-term plan;

■ to reflect the broad principles laid down in the school's policy for the subject and curriculum and ensure that agreed routines and teaching take place;

■ to detail the knowledge, skills and processes to be taught during the half term or term;

■ to involve all staff concerned with its teaching in both its writing and subsequent review;

■ to give clear guidance about the range of teaching styles and assessment techniques to be used.

For you, as a trainee, the medium-term plan has an additional role. It is there for you to discuss with your mentor, teacher, curriculum coordinators and teaching assistants. A detailed discussion of the medium-term plan is a very focused way of learning about how the class operates and is the first step in moving towards your responsibilities as a teacher. If you are able to discuss the medium-term plan for one subject with the teacher, you can then identify how you might be involved. Is there an activity you can plan, for instance?

The most important elements of a medium-term plan are:

■ title of the unit of work and identified curriculum areas;

■ objectives or learning outcomes: concepts, knowledge, skills and attitudes (related to the National Curriculum programme of study or EYFS curriculum);

■ key learning questions derived from objectives for pupils – these are not as simple as you might imagine; you must be well informed in the subject area and anticipate areas of uncertainty or confusion;

■ relevant attainment targets, level descriptions and a clear note of what you expect the majority of the class to achieve;

■ broad aspects of differentiation, such as how you differentiate for different sets or groups;

■ key vocabulary for pupils;

■ broad comments about activities: showing progression and organisation;

■ identified assessment tasks: summative and formative. These might include 'formal assessment tasks', such as a particular piece of writing, a quiz or a mind map at the end of a unit of work, but will also include the lesson outcomes as you go through the unit. These are important formative assessment opportunities.

In addition to these content-specific medium-term plans, most teachers have very carefully elaborated, but often unwritten, plans for the non-subject-based parts of the curriculum. You need to learn routines, resources, the rules of behaviour, standards and processes of marking and tokens of reward. You should know how your teacher works with the teaching assistants and how plans and assessments are shared among the teaching team. These aspects of class work may be enshrined in policies, but you may need to learn them through observation and discussion. These aspects of the curriculum – the unwritten curriculum – facilitate children's learning and knowing them marks you out as a teacher.

Task 3.1.3 **INFLUENCES ON PLANNING**

Think back to the last piece of medium-term planning in which you were involved. Try to isolate any aspects of the unwritten curriculum applying in your class that influenced your medium-term plans in any way. Examples of features you might suggest include:

■ availability of teaching assistants/other adults in the classroom;
■ physical aspects of the classroom, e.g. ready availability of a sink;
■ rewards systems operating in the class/school.

For each feature, describe how it influenced your planning, and what you might have done (or did do) to moderate the effects of this influence.

Task 3.1.4 **SHOULD THERE BE A CORE CURRICULUM?**

Read the government's *Independent Review of the Primary Curriculum* (Rose Review) (2009) and the report, *Towards a New Primary Curriculum*, which is part of the *Cambridge Primary Review* (2009) (see 'Annotated further reading' below for the web addresses). Decide on your view of the primary curriculum by considering the following issues:

■ Do you think there should be a core curriculum? What is the justification for a core curriculum (see *Independent Review*) or against a core curriculum (see *Cambridge Primary Review* report)?
■ What sort of core do you think could be justified, if any?
■ What is the difference between a 'domain' and an 'area of learning'?
■ Do you think the curriculum should be structured in the same way at Key Stages 1 and 2?
■ How should the structure of the curriculum differ at each key stage?

SUMMARY

Planning, teaching and assessment are often described as a cycle, because each process is dependent on the others. Teachers devote a considerable amount of their time and energy to planning effectively, something that has now been recognised in teachers' working conditions. There is no perfect teaching plan because there is no ideal class. Long-term plans are based on a National Curriculum that has caused widespread national discussion, but still needs to be made relevant and workable in the context of each school, through planning the curriculum, resources and teaching. Even when long-term plans are established, the medium-term plan has to take account of the particular class and situation. Having clear medium-term plans is a very good basis for writing the short-term plans you will be teaching from, but it does not mean that those medium-term plans are set in stone. You will find that sometimes teaching does not follow the expected plans, or some outcomes are not what you expect. All teachers make changes to their medium-term plans. They may change the rate at which they address issues, omit or add items or alter the manner or order in which topics are addressed. These changes do not indicate poor medium-term planning – they show that the teacher is making clear assessments of children's performance and evaluating the teaching techniques, pace and strategies necessary for the children to make progress.

ANNOTATED FURTHER READING

Alexander, R.J. (2009) *Towards a New Primary Curriculum: A Report from the Cambridge Primary Review*, Cambridge: University of Cambridge. Available online at www.primaryreview.org.uk/Publications/Publicationshome.html (accessed October 2009).

Rose, J. (2009) *Independent Review of the Primary Curriculum: Final Report*. Available online at www.dcsf.gov.uk/primarycurriculumreview (accessed October 2009).

This is usually known as the Rose Review, because of its coordinator, Sir Jim Rose. It has proposed a fairly radical overhaul of the primary national curriculum, yet its longer-term effects are not yet known and will depend, anyway, on political circumstances.

Both these reviews are important and invite the reader to ask fundamental questions about the nature of curriculum.

Medwell, J. (2008) *Successful Teaching Placement*, Exeter: Learning Matters.

This book covers in much greater detail issues of planning for work with pupils at various stages. It also discusses the implementation of these plans and strategies for successful teaching.

Qualifications and Curriculum Authority (QCA) *Customise Your Curriculum*. Available online at www.qcda.gov.uk/5198.aspx (accessed October 2009).

Customise your Curriculum is designed specifically to give examples of how teachers are taking ownership of the curriculum, shaping it and making it their own, by:

■ embedding aspects of English and mathematics in other subjects – giving pupils opportunities to use basic skills in rich, relevant and motivating contexts;

■ adapting units from the schemes of work – adjusting plans to better meet their children's needs;

■ combining units from different subjects – making learning more coherent, connecting essential skills, knowledge and understanding.

RELEVANT WEBSITES

Cambridge Primary Review: www.primaryreview.org.uk/

Department for Children, Schools and Families: www.dcsf.gov.uk/

> This has advice and links to aspects of policy, including the curriculum, assessing of pupil progress and curriculum consultation.

Early Years Foundation Stage: www.standards.dfes.gov.uk/eyfs/ or the Primary National Strategies website (see below).

Independent Review of the Primary Curriculum (Rose Review): www.dcsf.gov.uk/primarycurriculum review

International Primary Curriculum: www.internationalprimarycurriculum.com/

Mantle of the Expert: www.mantleoftheexpert.com/about-moe/faqs/what-about-the-international-primary-curriculum-and-mantle-of-the-expert/

> These two sites (above) have curriculum materials for commercial curricula.

National Curriculum (based on the 2000 version): http://curriculum.qcda.gov.uk

> As there have been small changes to the statements of attainment for English, this is now more up to date than the printed versions.

Primary National Strategies for Literacy and Mathematics: http://nationalstrategies.standards.dcsf. gov.uk/primary/

> There is also a great deal of planning advice on this site. The EYFS can also be found here at http://nationalstrategies.standards.dcsf.gov.uk/earlyyears.

Qualifications and Curriculum Authority/Department for Children, Schools and Family Schemes of Work: www.standards.dfes.gov.uk/schemes3/

> This site now hosts the QCA/DCSF schemes of work for the various subjects in the primary curriculum. The site states that:

> Many schools take the schemes of work as the starting point for their plans. They make their own decisions about how to make best use of this resource, remembering that the schemes are *not statutory*. Schools can use as much or as little as they wish and are free to devise their own ways of meeting the requirements of the national curriculum.

> There is also guidance here on how to plan with the schemes and adapt units of work.

Visit the companion website www.routledge.com/textbooks/ltps2e for:

■ additional questions and tasks for this unit;
■ links to useful websites relevant to this unit.

APPROACHING SHORT-TERM PLANNING

Jane Medwell

INTRODUCTION

The focus of this unit is short-term planning – the weekly and daily planning you will do to prepare your teaching across the curriculum. Planning at this level is one of your most onerous tasks during training, but it is one of your greatest learning experiences. As you build up your responsibility for planning, you will develop a real understanding of its central importance in teaching. This unit also refers to your use of information and communication technology (ICT) in teaching and underlines the importance of planning the use of ICT for both you and for the pupils.

OBJECTIVES

By the end of this unit you should:

■ understand the difference between medium-term and short-term planning;
■ understand the purposes of short-term planning;
■ know the key features of short-term plans;
■ be able to critically evaluate examples of short-term planning;
■ feel more confident to write your plans during school experiences.

THE IMPORTANCE OF SHORT-TERM PLANNING

All teachers undertake short-term planning and will do weekly and, sometimes, daily plans. As a trainee you will do both weekly and daily plans. You will base these on the medium- or long-term plans available to you in schools during your placement or, later in your training, on medium-term plans you may have made yourself. A short-term plan is your tool for adapting the broad objectives of the medium-term planning for the learning needs of your class. This means you may have to add or omit parts of the medium-term plan, rearrange the order in which work is done and plan the way you teach, in detail, so that all the children can learn.

The most obvious reason for planning your lessons carefully is to ensure that you offer children engaging and appropriate lessons. You have to ensure that your lessons address the teaching you have foreseen in medium-term plans in such a way that all the children in the class can understand

and explore the issues. As each child is different, you have to plan lessons that present information in ways suitable for all. This is the role of differentiation.

As a trainee, the creation of short-term plans also has a formative role for you and is a key training experience in itself. By writing a short-term plan, you are 'rehearsing' your lessons, anticipating challenges and working out exactly what you will do. By evaluating each short-term plan as the basis for the next, you are learning lessons from what you and the children have done. A cycle of planning, assessment, modification and more planning is the basis for children's learning. It is also the basis of yours!

Finally, short-term plans are also a way for you to be accountable, as a teacher and a trainee. Teachers write weekly plans so that they, or other teachers, can work from them and adapt them, but also so that head teachers, colleagues, inspectors and outside agencies can scrutinise and work with the plans. You will write plans so that your teacher and teaching assistants (TAs) can understand the plans and their roles in them. Teachers and mentors will be able to examine and advise you about these plans and those assessing your performance can gain insights into your professional thinking. If nothing else, this is good practice for an Ofsted-inspected future!

PLANNING FORMATS

The format of your plans will depend on a number of factors, including the age group you are teaching, your course requirements and school practices where you are teaching. You will probably find that completing some sort of grid on the word processor is easiest, but it is not essential – clarity is the main issue. There is no single, perfect planning format and you may find that you want to adapt your format to meet your training needs.

Teachers will usually have a weekly plan for each subject, domain or area of learning at Key Stages 1 and 2, although the strong links across the curriculum may dictate a topic or integrated plan. Some of these may be based on commercial schemes, such as the International Primary Curriculum, but will rarely be used unadapted to meet the needs of the children. In early Key Stage 1 and the Foundation Stage the weekly plan will usually be written by at least the teacher and TA. It may involve a larger team. It will address all the areas of development and will usually be planned around a theme. A good weekly planning format will include most or all of the following:

- weekly objectives related to daily tasks;
- references to the relevant curriculum documents;
- task objectives;
- texts, ICT and other resources to be used;
- a summary of each activity for each group, identifying differentiation;
- specific roles for TAs;
- key points for plenary sessions;
- assessment points, often linked to National Curriculum levels or sub-levels, assessment focuses or assessing pupil progress (APP) statements.

Weekly plans will break down learning and teaching in such a way that the children can achieve the learning objectives. This is a difficult skill because, as well as knowing everything necessary for medium-term planning, to do weekly plans you need to know what the children have already done, know and can do; the pace the children work at; their individual needs; and the likely response of the children to what you are planning. You will 'predict' these elements of the teaching for the week, but will find that you have to change or amend these weekly plans in response to the children's learning. This is good practice and shows you are using assessments to inform your plans.

It is a good idea to amend weekly plans by hand, so that observers can *see* that you are doing this.

Figure 3.2.1 shows an example of a format suitable for planning a sequence of lessons. Annotations under the figure give further details about the kinds of material you might include in each section of the plan.

An editable version of Figure 3.2.1 is available on the companion website: www.routledge.com/textbooks/ltps2e

Experienced teachers may teach from their weekly plans and as you gain experience you may too. When you start teaching you will plan your early lessons and parts of lessons on the basis of the teacher's weekly plans. As your placement progresses, you will be required to write weekly plans (or sequences of lesson plans) for core subjects. You may do this as part of a teaching team, but you will be expected to make a significant contribution and to lead the planning at this level before you can achieve the standards for the award of qualified teacher status (QTS).

One very important aspect of planning that is best addressed through weekly plans is the issue of routine activities such as guided group or individual reading and writing, storytelling, registration, distribution of maths games or books, story reading, book browsing, spelling tests, handwriting practice, tables practice, mark making, weather recording, show and tell and action rhyme times. These routines are easy to overlook but they are very important. Patterns of activity that are known to both child and adult are soothing, familiar and powerful learning activities. Your weekly plan needs to be checked to ensure these activities represent the balance you want and that they are planned.

Task 3.2.1 SCRUTINISING WEEKLY PLANNING

To do this task you will need a weekly plan and medium-term plan from your placement.

Ensure you know the answers to the following.

■ Which parts of the medium term plan does the weekly plan address?
■ Which parts of the relevant curriculum documents does this refer to?
■ How long will each lesson or session in the weekly plan be?

Focus on one part of the weekly plan, perhaps English, maths or science.

■ What resources are needed for the lessons in the weekly plan?
■ What is the balance of whole-class, group and individual work for this week?
■ What are the class management challenges for this week?

Discuss your chosen element of weekly planning with your teacher. Possible topics for discussion include the following.

■ How do you ensure that the learning is accessible to all the children in the class?
■ How do you differentiate for children who have SEN or are in the gifted and talented register?
■ What arrangements are made to include children with SEN?
■ What role will a TA or other adult play in these lessons and how will they know what to do?
■ What do you do if the children do not make the predicted learning gains in one week?
■ Will any of these sessions present particular management challenges?

What are the 'routine' activities in this week? Fill in the chart below and add other activities.

Activity	When	How long/ often	Resources	Content	Teacher action	Pupil response
Welcome/ weather, etc.						
Show and tell						
Action rhymes/ poems						
Story time						
Spelling test						
Tables practice						
Register						
Handwriting						

LESSON PLANNING

On the basis of weekly plans, you can construct detailed daily plans. The format depends on the age of the children and what you are planning for. The key elements that you should include are:

■ class/group taught;
■ time and duration of lesson;
■ objectives for the session or lesson;
■ reference to the relevant curriculum documents;
■ texts, ICT and other resources to be used;
■ structure and timings of the lesson;
■ summary of each activity for each group, identifying differentiation and what you expect teacher and children to do;
■ specific roles for teaching assistants and, usually, a plan for the TA;
■ details of teacher and child activity;
■ key vocabulary to be used;
■ key questions to be asked;

Term/Year:			Teaching group:		
Curriculum subject/Theme/Area(s) of learning:					
Broad learning objectives	Learning objectives	Key Activities	Resources	Cross-curricular opportunities	Planned method of assessment

Broad learning objectives:

Specific references to Early Learning Goals, National Curriculum, Primary National Strategies (PNS) (literacy or maths), Agreed Syllabus for Religious Education

Learning objectives: stating anticipated achievement in one or more of the following:

▨ attitudes (show . . .);
▨ skills (be able to . . .);
▨ knowledge (know that . . .);
▨ understanding (develop concept of . . .).

These form the basis of assessment and are judged through planned outcomes

Key activities should:

▨ enable learning objectives to be met;
▨ include a variety of experiences that progressively develop children's learning;
▨ recognise pupils' diverse needs (including pupils with special educational needs (SEN), more able and gifted pupils, and pupils with English as an additional language (EAL));
▨ take account of pupils' gender and ethnicity.

Resources should be:

▨ influenced by learning objectives;
▨ listed in detail;
▨ considered with health and safety in mind;
▨ related to displays where relevant.

Cross-curricular opportunities should develop significant and planned attitudes, skills, knowledge and understanding *across* the curriculum in, e.g.:

▨ English;
▨ ICT;
▨ PSHE/citizenship;
▨ other National Curriculum subjects/areas of learning where significant.

Planned method of assessment should include anticipated evidence:

▨ to demonstrate achievement of learning objectives, and to inform assessment and record keeping (may be observational, verbal, written or graphic evidence, depending on activity);
▨ to reflect a *range* of assessment methods.

▮ **Figure 3.2.1** An example format for planning a sequence of lessons

- key teaching points;
- identified outcomes (how will you assess whether the children have achieved their learning objectives?);
- notes of pupils' previous experience;
- cross-curricular links;
- identified health and safety issues (such as glue guns, the need to wear coats, etc.);
- an evaluation section;
- key points for plenary sessions;
- assessment points (who are you assessing and what do you want to know?);
- timings.

You may begin your training by doing lesson plans for every session you teach and, later, when you have more experience, move to teach from your weekly plans. However, always do individual lesson plans when your lesson is being observed, because it helps the observer to see your thinking (and helps you to do it!). You should also do lesson plans when you are teaching new ideas, when you are unsure of yourself or the children, or when you have a specific training target in mind. For instance, if you find it hard to manage time in your lessons with Key Stage 2, you will find that planning your lessons in detail, writing predicted times on the plans and reviewing them afterwards really helps you to manage time.

Planning an effective lesson

The research about planning is varied. Brophy and Good (1986) stressed that effective teachers demanded productive engagement with the task, prepared well and matched the tasks to the abilities of the children. Effective lessons tend to be those with a clear structure, with shared understandings about what is to be learned and why, where all children can do the activities and use the learning time effectively and where the teacher assesses progress and evaluates the lessons. All these elements of a successful lesson can be addressed through your planning by focusing on your lesson structure, management, lesson objectives, differentiation for learning and your use of evaluation of lesson plans. All these features will help you to make a lesson engaging and interesting.

Successful lessons have clear beginnings and strong conclusions with a certain amount of 'academic press' – that is, impetus to complete tasks within the given time. Learning time can be divided up so that it is used productively for learning and so that the parts of a lesson help children to progress through their tasks. However you structure your lesson, you should always make sure that lessons have a strong, clear structure and that the children know what this is. In this way the children can learn to use time effectively and experience 'academic press'.

Time spent learning, itself, is a significant factor in the effectiveness of lessons, with research suggesting that the most effective teachers are those who maximise learning time by reducing off-task chatter and managing the class effectively (Silcock, 1993). Transitions from whole class to group work, effective distribution of resources, and strategies for behaviour management are all parts of lessons where time can be saved through effective planning, thereby maximising learning time for pupils.

Learning to manage the pace of your lessons, so that the teaching and learning are lively and challenging but not rushed, takes time. It is fairly well established that the efficiency of experienced teachers allows them to perform complex procedures in a fraction of the time taken by novices – this is why you need to plan things experienced teachers do not even think about! If you find it difficult to maintain the pace of a lesson, you may want to plan in five-minute intervals and note down the times on your lesson plans.

Learning objectives are probably the most important points on a lesson plan. You should be absolutely clear about what you want the children to learn, understand or do as a result of your lesson. These lesson objectives must be reasonable and achievable. You may want to reference the PNS unit of work on your lesson plan, but phrase your lesson objective accurately so that the children can achieve it. A single lesson may address or contribute to a unit of work or to the achievement of an Early Learning Goal, but no lesson will completely cover one of these big objectives.

Most importantly, you must make sure your lesson objectives are meaningful. This means they must make sense in terms of the curriculum so that children are not simply learning a set of assorted skills and knowledge that may (or may not) make sense later. It also means that objectives must be clear to, and understood by, the children. A study of teachers of literacy (Wray *et al.*, 2001) found that effective teachers made sure that even young children understood the wider role of tasks in their learning. You will undoubtedly write up lesson objectives somewhere in the class, such as on the interactive whiteboard, a sheet of paper or a chart, but, unless you discuss these objectives with children and ensure the children know what they are learning and why, written objectives are just additional wallpaper.

Task 3.2.2 **SHARING LESSON OBJECTIVES?**

Sharing lesson objectives with the children has become one of the accepted markers of good teaching, and is certainly used by inspectors as a means of judging the effectiveness of a lesson. Yet its benefits are not universally accepted. Read the newspaper article on this topic by Philip Beadle (www.guardian.co.uk/education/2007/jan/16/schools.uk1). Beadle concludes his piece with the following:

> But why must children know what the objectives are at the beginning of the lesson? Why can't we ask them to guess what they are going to learn, or tell us what they learned at the end of the lesson? Why can't it be a surprise?

Try to compose *either* a reasoned rebuttal of Beadle's position, *or* a justification for his scepticism about the use of lesson objectives.

Your questioning is an important part of your teaching. The need to ask a range of open and closed questions has been well documented. Brophy and Good (1986) make recommendations from their review of research that include the need to ensure that questions are clear, that all children are asked questions, that the pace of questioning is adjusted to the task and that children are given sufficient wait time to answer. They also stress that it is important for questions to elicit correct answers, although, as new material is learned, the error rate will inevitably rise as a result of children being stretched. More recent characterisations of teaching have stressed the importance of teachers demonstrating, or modelling, the learner behaviour they wished to teach. This includes reading aloud to pupils, modelling comprehension strategies, modelling writing processes and thinking aloud as you solve mathematical problems. Plan the key points you want to make to the class, and the key questions and main skills you want to model. In this way you can make sure you teach what you intend to teach.

Questioning is only one approach to talk to classes and one that may place too much focus on the child. Alexander (2006) emphasises the importance of talk as a tool for learning. This involves the teacher having detailed knowledge of the lesson content and possibilities, but guiding discussion in ways that challenge and develop children's learning. However, there is no magic formula and different areas of learning may require different approaches to talk (Fisher, 2007).

Differentiation is the way you plan to meet the diverse learning needs of pupils. You will teach the knowledge, skills and understanding in ways that suit the pupils' abilities and previous experience. Differentiation is represented in different forms in your planning:

- *Presentation* – plan to use a variety of media to present ideas, and to offer vocabulary or extra diagrams to those who need more support. You will find ICT particularly helpful in preparing different types of presentation on paper, audio tape, screens or interactive whiteboards.
- *Content* – select appropriately so that there is content that suits most children with additional content available to some. For instance, some children may do six calculations where others complete ten. ICT, using the internet, can offer you a range of content.
- *Resources* – use resources that support pupils' needs, such as writing frames, language master-word banks or Spellmaster machines for poor spellers. For children with EAL, you might need to ensure that target vocabulary is available in a written form.
- *Grouping* – group pupils of similar ability for targeted support or pair children with a more able pupil, TA or language support teacher.
- *Task* – match tasks to pupils' abilities. This can mean different tasks for different pupils. It is sometimes a good idea to offer different tasks that address the same objectives to different pupils so that they can achieve success.
- *Support* – offer additional adult or peer assistance, from a TA, language support teacher or more experienced child.
- *Time* – giving more or less time to complete a given task can make the task more suitable to the particular pupils.

Differentiation sounds simple, but demands really good knowledge of the content, the children, resources and a range of teaching strategies. You will achieve appropriate differentiation by working closely with the teacher so that you find out what strategies are available and work for these children. Key resources to plan into your lessons will be TAs, language support staff and the individual education plans (IEPs) written for children with special needs.

Evaluation

Evaluation is a part of planning and also allows you to show you are able to improve your performance through self-evaluation. Evaluation means considering:

- how well the children achieved the learning objectives (assessment);
- how well you planned, taught and managed teaching in relation to your training targets.

Evaluations will usually be brief and will usually focus on two aspects: what you did and what the children learned. The most useful evaluations focus on particular aspects of your teaching and are the basis of your own training targets. You may be keen to record positive evaluations but less keen to focus on improvement. However, you should develop your ability to analyse your teaching, especially when you can see an area for improvement. When your evaluation comment identifies work to be done, always say what you propose to do in response. The very best planning is that which clearly uses evidence from children's previous attainment and leads on to influence the planning and teaching of the next session or lesson. This sort of evidence may be the annotations to a lesson plan you make in response to previous evaluations.

BUILDING PLANNING EXPERIENCE

Your early plans on a teaching experience may not be for whole lessons but for short parts of lessons or sessions, such as a whole-class phonics game, a guided reading session for a small group of children or a mental/oral starter in a maths lesson. Planning these parts of lessons gives you the chance to pay attention to detail and really concentrate on some important aspects of using plans such as:

■ ensuring you make your key points clearly;
■ maintaining a pace that is brisk and engaging but not so fast that the children are lost;
■ effective questioning and interactive teaching;
■ using resources such as the interactive whiteboard or phonics objects.

Planning parts of lessons and teaching them is a good start to building up responsibility for whole lessons.

Task 3.2.3 **PLANNING A MENTAL/ORAL STARTER**

Use the planner below to observe a mental/oral starter taught by your teacher. Then plan and evaluate a mental/oral starter or shared literacy session. This may be more detailed than you are used to but using such detail will help you to construct the mental 'scripts' you need to manage this complex task.

Planner for a mental oral starter, shared reading or shared writing session

Date		Group/ class	
Duration		NC/PNS reference	
Resources		Key vocabulary	
Activity			
Questions			
Less confident	Confident		More confident
Assessment			
Less confident	Confident		More confident
Evaluation			

PLANNING FOR OTHER ADULTS IN THE CLASS OR SETTING

To ensure you work well with TAs or other adults in class, you may use a set format to present clear expectations of what you would like the TA to do. This will usually include space for the TA to write assessment notes about how well the children achieved the objective. These notes may well affect your future planning.

Task 3.2.4 **INVOLVING A TEACHING ASSISTANT**

Arrange a specific time to talk to the TA in your placement class about a lesson in which he or she has assisted. Find out the following:

■ What does the TA think the objective of the session was?
■ What did the TA understand his or her role to be?
■ What key vocabulary did he or she use?
■ What resources did he or she prepare?
■ How did the TA know what to say and do?
■ What additional information would he or she like about class tasks?

When you have this information you will be able to use it to direct your communication with the TA in your lessons.

Figure 3.2.2 shows an example of a planning format suitable for use with a TA.

PLANNING AND ICT

ICT can assist you in your planning in two main ways. First, the computer is an invaluable tool for planning itself because it can help with the process and content of planning. Word processing allows you to produce and amend your plans swiftly and effectively. (Alternatively you can easily spend every evening colour coding, cross-referencing and wasting time.) The internet also offers you thousands of ready-made plans for almost any topic. These will not be instant solutions to the problems posed by your next lesson because they do not meet the needs of your particular class. However, they do present you with a spectacular range of ideas and formats. You need to use them, but not rely on them.

The second way in which ICT can be useful is in planning for pupil activity. If you are planning to use an interactive whiteboard (IWB) for your mental/oral starter in a maths lesson, you can make the lesson visually attractive (so that all eyes are attracted to it and are not distracted elsewhere). The content can be tailored to meet the whole range of abilities and the children can come out and be fully involved in the learning. You might use your computer to produce worksheets for some groups of children while others use calculators or roamers. To conclude the lesson, your plenary might include the IWB or a demonstration using a projected calculator. The ICT can make the lesson more effective, but only if you plan it carefully.

When you think of using ICT, do not concentrate only on the computer. Children can use audio or video recording to do speaking and listening, reading and writing activities. If children are presenting findings from group work, the visualiser might be the most accessible technology. Do not overlook the use of TV and radio materials. Like computer programmes, they are produced specifically for schools, have helpful teaching guidance and can be very useful if planned carefully.

Date .... Lesson focus ....
Activity (a brief account of the activity and the TA's role in any whole-class introduction, shared reading, mental/oral, etc.)
Resources needed
Key vocabulary to use • • • **Key questions to use** • • •
Objectives 1 2 3

For completion by the TA after group work:

Name		Can do	Needs help
	1		
	2		
	3		
	1		
	2		
	3		
	1		
	2		
	3		
	1		
	2		
	3		
	1		
	2		
	3		

■ **Figure 3.2.2** An example of a planning format for a teaching assistant (TA)

An editable version of Figure 3.2.2 is available on the companion website: www.routledge.com/textbooks/ltps2e

SUMMARY

Planning is one of the most time-consuming processes you will engage in, but planning well will help you to become a successful teacher. All successful teaching relies on teachers producing lessons that engage and motivate the children. This is partly down to selecting the right content and partly down to the way the content is dealt with. These issues are planning issues. Use your plans to rehearse and evaluate your lessons and you can appear confident, happy and interesting to your class of children.

ANNOTATED FURTHER READING

Gipps, C., Hargreaves, E. and McCallum, B. (2000) *What Makes a Good Primary School Teacher?*, London: RoutledgeFalmer

This accessible book offers an account of the range of teaching, assessing and feedback strategies used by individual 'expert' primary teachers and how they know or decide which strategy to bring into play, and when.

Wray, D., Medwell, J., Poulson, L. and Fox, R. (2001) *Teaching Literacy Effectively*, London: RoutledgeFalmer.

This book reports the findings of the *Effective Teachers of Literacy* project and includes several findings relating to the importance of good planning.

RELEVANT WEBSITES

Primary National Strategies: http://nationalstrategies.standards.dcsf.gov.uk/primary/

This site contains the frameworks for literacy and numeracy as well as plenty of 'exemplified units of work', that is, medium- and shorter-term plans for teaching.

TeacherNet: www.teachernet.gov.uk

This site offers access to over 2,000 lesson plans and has invaluable advice about many aspects of planning.

Visit the companion website www.routledge.com/textbooks/ltps2e for:

■ additional questions for this unit;
■ editable figures from this unit;
■ links to useful websites relevant to this unit.

REFERENCES

Alexander, R.J. (2006) *Towards Dialogic Teaching*, 3rd edn, Cambridge: Cambridge University Press/Dialogos.

Beadle, P. (2007) 'Shhh, let's not tell the kids what we're trying to do', *The Guardian*, 16 January. Available online at www.guardian.co.uk/education/2007/jan/16/schools.uk1 (accessed November 2009).

Brophy, J and Good, T. (1986) 'Teacher behaviour and student achievement', in M.C. Wittrock (ed.) *Handbook of Research In Teaching*, London: Collier Macmillan.

Fisher, R (2007) 'Dialogic teaching: developing thinking and metacognition through philosophical discussion', *Early Child Development and Care*, 177(6 and 7): 615–31.

Silcock, P. (1993) 'Can we teach effective teaching?', *Educational Review*, 45(1): 13–19.

Wray, D., Medwell, J., Poulson, L. and Fox, R. (2001) *Teaching Literacy Effectively*, London: RoutledgeFalmer.

ORGANISING YOUR CLASSROOM FOR LEARNING

Peter Kelly

INTRODUCTION

In this unit I link approaches to organising learning environments to views about how learning takes place, many of which have been discussed in earlier units. Learning is complex, and no one view can fully capture this complexity. However, each view of learning is helpful in understanding and planning for particular aspects of learning. I argue that a balanced approach to classroom organisation draws on each view of learning. Thus we should use different approaches to promote different types of learning.

OBJECTIVES

Having read this unit you will be able to:

- recognise the link between views about how learning takes place and approaches to organising your classroom;
- understand the key approaches to organising your classroom;
- recognise the scope and limitation of each of these approaches;
- identify appropriate approaches for a particular learning objectives.

ORGANISING LEARNING

How you organise your classroom says a great deal about how you view your children's learning. Colleagues, parents and, perhaps most importantly, children will read much about what you value from those features of classroom life for which you are responsible: the areas of the curriculum you choose to link and focus on, the lessons and activities you plan, the roles you ascribe to other adults in your classroom, how you group and seat the children, the decisions you allow children to take, the resources you provide and the ways in which you make them available, your use of display and of opportunities to learn outside the classroom and school, and so on.

Consider the range of options available to you in relation to just one of these: groupings. Children can be taught as a whole class, in groups or individually. In groups they might work collaboratively or be provided with differentiated individual tasks. Such tasks might be differentiated in terms of the level of challenge of the task or the level of support the group receives, and so on. Such features are not simple alternatives: those you choose to use and the circumstances in which you choose to use them will say something about your beliefs as a teacher, even if these are largely tacit and the decisions you make intuitive.

There is a lot of advice available on classroom organisation. This has not always been the case. It was not until the 1960s that the traditional model of teaching – that is, a teacher standing at the front of the classroom with the children sat facing, working on the same task at the same time – was challenged. Progressive approaches, developed largely from the ideas of Jean Piaget, suggested that children should be free to work at different speeds and in different ways, learning from first-hand experiences through active exploration and personal discovery. But traditionalists argued that such approaches were largely ineffective: there were things that children needed to be taught, such as spelling and grammar, which could not be discovered or left to chance. Thus began an enduring and polarised educational debate.

More recently, a loose consensus has prevailed, which recognises that certain approaches favour certain kinds of learning rather than one approach being best. Nevertheless, the range of approaches suggested can appear daunting. In fact it is relatively straightforward if you remain mindful of one thing: how you organise your classroom depends on how you believe children will learn in your classroom.

This unit considers classroom organisation in relation to four views of learning: basic skills acquisition; constructing understanding; learning together; and apprenticeship approaches.

Basic skills acquisition

Once a favourite of traditionalist knowledge transmission approaches, direct teaching dominates approaches to basic skills teaching in the Literacy and Mathematics Frameworks within the Primary National Strategies in England (DCSF, 2007). Originally conceived somewhat behaviouristically as teacher demonstration and pupil imitation, leading to a period of consolidation and practice, in these strategies direct teaching has been the recipient of a Vygotskyan make-over, becoming an interactive approach where the importance of high-quality dialogue and discussion between teachers and pupils is emphasised. However, this has been an issue with many teachers who have been less ready to move away from a teacher demonstration and pupil imitation model towards a more interactive one.

Learning as constructing understanding

Originating in the ideas of Jean Piaget, constructivism sees learners as theory builders, developing understandings to make sense of their observations and experiences, and modifying these understandings in the light of subsequent observations and experiences so that they become more generally useful and closer to accepted viewpoints. This perspective has had a huge impact on some curriculum areas, particularly science, in which a cottage industry grew in the 1980s researching the alternative understandings and misunderstandings, termed 'alternative frameworks', which children have of the phenomena they encounter. Phil Adey and Michael Shayer's Cognitive Acceleration through Science Education (CASE) has adapted and extended the constructivist approach (Adey et al., 1995). By challenging children's misunderstandings of phenomena, the CASE approach aims to develop the structure of their thinking.

Social learning

Social constructivists such as Jerome Bruner cite the ideas of the Russian theorist Lev Vygotsky in positing a central role for talking and listening in learning. Making sense and developing understanding, they assert, are essentially social processes that take place through talk. In the early 1990s, the National Oracy Project, which was unfortunately overshadowed by developments in literacy and numeracy, identified a whole range of ways in which participation with others in activities involving discussion can improve learning: it supports learners in constructing new meanings and understandings as they explore them in words; it allows learners to test out and criticise claims and different points of view as they speak and listen to others; and, importantly, talk provides raw material for learners' own thinking, because, for Vygotsky, thought is an internal, personal dialogue.

Learning as an apprenticeship

The work of social anthropologists such as Jean Lave and Etienne Wenger (Lave and Wenger, 1991; Wenger, 1998) has illuminated how people learn in everyday contexts. This has led them to reconsider school learning in sociocultural terms. Thus, there are many metaphors that we can adopt for our classrooms: the writer's workshop, the artist's studio, the scientist's laboratory, and so on. In each case, this view suggests, the children act as craft apprentices, engaging in the authentic activities of the community to which the metaphor pertains. So for children to think as, for example, historians, they have to be helped to act like historians by doing what historians do. The same is, of course, true for scientists or practitioners in any other area of enquiry.

Task 3.3.1 **LOOKING FOR LEARNING**

Think back to one particular day during a previous school placement. Write down briefly each of the learning activities the children engaged in during the day. Consider:

■ which areas of the curriculum were addressed and linked;
■ the planned lessons and activities;
■ the role adopted by the teacher and other adults in the classroom;
■ how the children were grouped and seated;
■ the decisions the children took;
■ the resources provided;
■ the use of display;
■ the opportunities for learning outside the classroom.

Now consider what these features suggest to you about the way in which the teacher (whether it was you or the class teacher) views learning.

Task 3.3.2 **CLASSROOM CULTURE**

Culture can be described most simply as 'the way we do things round here'. Critically reflect on your answers from Task 3.3.1. How does each of these things contribute to the classroom culture? To help, consider the following questions:

■ Is there a learning-centred culture or a working-centred one?
■ Is there a teacher-led culture that emphasises pupils acquiring new knowledge and skills, or a pupil-led culture that emphasises pupil participation in developing new knowledge and skills?
■ What metaphor best describes the classroom culture – a factory production line or perhaps a writer's study, an artist's studio or a scientist's laboratory?

You can explore these ideas further by reading Kelly (2005).

I will now turn to consider approaches relating to each of these views of learning.

CLASSROOM APPROACHES

Basic skills and direct interactive teaching

The Primary Frameworks in England promote direct interactive teaching. As a whole-class approach, this allows children to benefit from direct involvement with their teacher for sustained periods. But direct teaching and interaction are also important during individual, paired and group work.

The role of dialogue is emphasised: children are expected to play an active part in discussion by asking questions, contributing ideas and explaining and demonstrating their thinking to the class. However, many studies have found that teachers spend the majority of their time either explaining or using tightly structured questions. Such questions are mainly factual or closed in nature, and so fail to encourage and extend child contributions or to promote interaction and thinking.

New technologies have had, in recent years, a significant impact on direct interactive and whole-class teaching. These include interactive whiteboards, data projectors and remote devices such as infra-red keyboards and graphics tablets.

Good direct interactive teaching, as exemplified in some of the best examples of literacy and mathematics teaching using the Primary Frameworks, is achieved by balancing different approaches:

- *Directing and telling* – Sharing teaching objectives with the class, ensuring that children know what to do, and drawing attention to points over which they should take particular care.
- *Explaining and illustrating* – Giving accurate, well-paced explanations, and referring to previous work or methods.
- *Demonstrating* – Giving clear, well-structured demonstrations using appropriate resources and visual displays.
- *Questioning and discussing* – Ensuring all children take part; using open and closed questions; asking for explanations; giving time for children to think before answering; allowing children to talk about their answers in pairs before contributing them to the whole class; listening carefully to children's responses; responding constructively; and challenging children's assumptions to encourage thinking.
- *Exploring and investigating* – Asking children to pose problems or suggest a line of enquiry.
- *Consolidating and embedding* – Through a variety of activities in class and well-focused homework, opportunities are provided to practise and develop new learning; making use of this learning to tackle related problems and tasks.
- *Reflecting and evaluating* – Identifying children's errors, using them as positive teaching points by exploring them together; discussing children's reasons for choosing particular methods or resources; giving oral feedback on written work.
- *Summarising and reminding* – Reviewing during and towards the end of a lesson what has been taught and what children have learned; identifying and correcting misunderstandings; making links to other work; and giving children an insight into the next stage of their learning.

Direct interactive teaching approaches focus on knowledge and skills transmission and acquisition through active learning and interaction. In this they leave little room for learners to construct their own understandings of phenomena. This is where the following approach is useful.

Constructing understanding

Constructivists believe that learners build their understandings of the world from their experiences and observations. They suggest that children bring many misconceptions and misunderstandings to the classroom from their experiences of the world, and assert that the best way to change such misunderstandings is to challenge children to change them themselves through hands-on explorations. For example, in science children may, from their experiences at home, have formed the misconception that clothes make you warmer. An investigation in which chocolate is wrapped in fabric could be used to see if this causes the chocolate to melt. Such information might challenge the children's misconception, and the children would need to restructure their thinking to accommodate the new information that the chocolate is not warmed up; rather, it is prevented from cooling or warming as the outside temperature changes.

However, one of the problems here is that it is assumed that children will recognise the need to change their thinking or even that they will want to do it. An approach that takes the constructivist approach further is CASE (see page 119). This can be used to formalise the thinking and restructuring process as it contains certain key elements, which many teachers have adopted or adapted in their own classrooms:

- ▪ *Concrete preparation* – The problem is stated in terms that are understandable to the children; that is, so that they see it as a problem. For example, you might ask the children to talk to the person next to them and think about clothes they might choose to take on holiday to a very cold country with them and why.
- ▪ *Cognitive conflict* – Children are encouraged to consider a range of possible explanations for causes and effects that may interact in complex ways with each other. For example, children investigating the effects of clothing (identifying features such as fabric type, thickness and shape) on its suitability for a cold location could consider which feature or combination of features are central.
- ▪ *Social construction* – Now the children work together on the challenging activity to construct new joint understandings. In this, although the teacher asks probing questions to focus debate, the children do most of the thinking. So the children might share each others' discussions and try to come to a consensus.
- ▪ *Metacognition* – In this process the children are helped to become conscious of their own reasoning in order to understand it. In putting pupils in charge of their own learning it is important to enable them to articulate their own thinking and learning processes.
- ▪ *Bridging* – This is the conscious transfer of new ideas and understandings from the context in which they were generated to new but related contexts. So the children could apply their new shared understanding of clothing in cold countries to hot countries.

This approach focuses largely on the learning of the individual. Social learning approaches, which follow, focus more on what can be achieved by a group working together, with the view that what is done together the individual will eventually become able to do alone.

Social learning

ESTABLISHING GROUND RULES

Before engaging in social learning approaches, a number of ground rules need to be established with children. Rules to stop interruptions of all those involved in group work, adults or children, should be negotiated first. Thus children needing help might be encouraged to take greater responsibility for their learning by seeking support elsewhere, or by doing alternative work until support is available.

Such independent and self-directed learners can be referred to as *autonomous*. The American educationalist, Susan Bobbit Nolen (1995), considers three levels of autonomy. The first is when learners have autonomy or control over the strategies they use to carry out a task without the guidance of their teacher. Thus in mathematics a teacher might teach a variety of strategies for children to undertake three-digit multiplication. The children can then choose which one to use in tackling a problem. Similarly, children might choose the form of recording to use for a science exploration, and so on. At the second level, learners have control over the content of the curriculum, the things to be studied and learned, and the objectives of learning. Thus children might decide to explore something in its own right or set their own goals for their learning. They might choose an area or theme on history to research, an assignment to write, an experiment to do, or a book to read. This is learning for pleasure, following tangents and satisfying curiosities. At the third level, learners are able to judge things for themselves, after taking evidence and various views into account. Thus the children might make informed decisions about changes to school routines such as playtimes, spending money on new items for class or elections to the school council. They might tackle controversial issues in school and debate these, looking at the perspectives of different parties. This third level of autonomy goes beyond simple independence in accessing resources or completing the teachers' work, and has been called 'intellectual autonomy'. Learners who have intellectual autonomy think for themselves, link their thinking to their experiences and open their minds to new ideas.

Discussions during group work should be democratic: everyone has the right to a say, and for their contribution to be valued. This means that participants should:

■ listen attentively to the contributions of others without interrupting;
■ speak to each other, looking at the person to whom they are responding;
■ take turns and allow everyone an equal opportunity to speak;
■ be sensitive to each other's needs;
■ try to see things from other people's points of view, even if they disagree with their position;
■ give reasons for their views;
■ be prepared to change their viewpoint in the light of new information, and accept others doing the same.

Further, children should understand that it is disrespectful to others if they monopolise the talk or if they ridicule or are unkind about others or their views. Of course, it is often most effective when the children are allowed to come up with rules such as these themselves: with prompting they can be encouraged to address the key areas. A good place to develop these together with a regard for these democratic ways of working is the school council.

COLLABORATIVE GROUP WORK

Group tasks are most effective when children need to share their knowledge, skills and understandings to a common end through some form of problem-solving or open-ended task with one correct solution among many alternatives. In their activity, children's talk will centre initially on their actions, but should be moved towards their understandings.

Research (summarised in Bennett, 1995) suggests that the ideal size for groups engaging in collaborative work is four – pairs are too small for generating lots of ideas, threes tend to form a pair and exclude the third member, and groups bigger than four become harder for the children to manage, so it is less likely that everyone will be fully included. Similarly, mixed-gender and mixed-ability groups tend to be more inclusive, focused and generate the widest range of viewpoints and ideas.

There are two basic forms of task organisation for collaborative work: 'jigsaw' and 'group investigation'. The former requires each group member to complete a sub-task, which contributes to the whole group completing the assigned task. This might be the production of a picture, diagram or piece of writing about, say, Roman villas for a group display on that topic. In the second, all of the group work together on the same task, with each member of the group being assigned a different role. So the children might create a small dramatic episode portraying life in a Roman villa. Each child would play a different character and, in addition, one child might take on the role of director.

So, for example, a group might work together on a 'jigsaw' task to produce a leaflet welcoming newcomers and informing them about the school. Each child might survey a different group of children from across the school to find out what information newcomers would need and benefit from. Particular attention would be paid to the experiences of any newcomers to the school. Then the group would make decisions together about which areas to address, in what format, etc. Each child could then be allocated the task of developing an aspect of the leaflet, with these being finally brought together for the finished document.

DIALOGICAL ENQUIRY

Dialogical enquiries are discussions in which learners, through language and sometimes supported by written notes and prompts, jointly engage in:

- working towards a common understanding for all;
- asking questions and suggesting ideas relating to the evidence on which proposals are based;
- looking at issues and problems from as many different perspectives as possible;
- challenging ideas and perspectives in the light of contradictions and evidence so as to move the discussion forwards.

Examples include book clubs or reading circles, where children discuss their reading and produce new books together. Similarly, writing conferences are extremely valuable, in which writers discuss their writing with their peers. Of course, having such shared dialogues about texts will improve participants' ability to engage in such dialogues alone.

Other opportunities exist in developing home–school learning partnerships in children's work. Thus, in one example, parents of a particular group of young children read the same book with their children at home one evening. During the shared reading, parents wrote down the children's responses to the stories on post-it notes and fixed them to the relevant pages. Next day these notes became the starting points for discussion between the teacher and the group.

With older children, each child in a group reading the same book together might individually write a prediction of the next stage of the story. This writing might provide the starting point for a group discussion about the evidence for each prediction, likelihood and plausibility of each prediction and the group's preferred outcome. Such a discussion could equally be based on individual group members writing initially from the perspective of one of the characters of the story and providing that character's point of view. The discussion could then consider the story from this variety of perspectives.

In terms of interpretation of data, such discursive enquiries are important because they can link the process of enquiry to the big ideas of the subject. So, for example, in science, following an investigation of the conditions in which plants grow best, rather than children simply describing the conditions that are most favourable to healthy plant growth, the discussion can focus on ideas about why this might be the case. Perhaps the children's text of the data collected can be compared in their discussion to other writing they have done that has attempted to explain findings.

Learning through apprenticeship

Apprenticeship models of learning require groups of children to engage in the actual or authentic activities of particular groups. So, for science, children work as scientists, engaging in an enquiry for which the answer is not already known, using the key ideas and tools of science and sometimes working in partnership with others from the local community. For example, Year 5 and 6 children might set up a weather station or get involved in monitoring environmental changes in an environmental awareness campaign. In doing this they might involve members of the wider community, contact experts at the Met. Office for advice, and so on.

There are many other possibilities for authentic activities in schools. So, in mathematics Year 1 and 2 children might conduct a traffic survey in order to provide evidence for a letter to the council for some form of traffic control outside school, and Year 5 and 6 children might be helped to cost and plan a residential visit, while children in Years 3 and 4 could run a school stationery shop – ordering, pricing and selling goods in order to make a small profit. Similarly, in geography, children in Key Stage 2 might survey and research the school population growth using various indicators such as local birth rates, and could be encouraged to identify the implications of their findings. Finally, children from across the school could be involved in making a CD for sale following their composition of various items for a particular event, such as a school anniversary.

Sometimes it is important to look at particular areas of study in many different ways. For example, in an essentially historical study of the Battle of the Somme in 1916, older children could not only engage in an historical enquiry-based approach, be it text- or computer-based or involving the examination of original artefacts, but also look at events through the eyes of poets and novelists, or through the eyes of geographers or scientists. As such, the work of others might be explored, and the children might engage in original work themselves, not only in writing and poetry, but also through the media of music, dance, drama and painting. This would provide the children with a very full and rich learning experience.

Task 3.3.3 PLANNING FOR LEARNING 1

Consider how you might plan a series of lessons in one subject area so that a variety of the above approaches is used. For example, in looking at life processes in science in Years 1 and 2, you could consider the following:

■ *Constructing understanding*: growing sunflowers from seed in class, and exploring the conditions in which these grow best.
■ *Group work, discussion*: separate groups investigate the effects of one factor on plant growth, making hypotheses beforehand and discussing findings after.
■ *Authentic activity*: set up a garden centre in school, so that the children can grow a variety of plants to sell in time for the summer fair.
■ *Interactive direct teaching*: the children are taught how to write clear instructions so that they can provide buyers at the summer fair with instructions for caring for their plants.

Try doing this for another area of learning, for example data handling in mathematics at Year 4.

Task 3.3.4 **PLANNING FOR LEARNING 2**

Try out some of the activities you have planned for Task 3.3.3 with a group of children. Closely observe the children taking part in two different activities that you have planned, and try to answer the following:

■ How does their participation differ across the two activities?
■ Does one of the activities appear to engage them more than the other?

After the activities talk to the children involved and try to answer the following:

■ What did they think they had to do?
■ Why did they think they were doing these activities?
■ What did they think they learned?
■ How much did they enjoy them?
■ What did they remember most from the activities?

Now look at the work done by the children and critically reflect on this and the answers to the questions above: What does all this tell you about these children's learning?

SUMMARY

The approaches described in this unit are summarised in Figure 3.3.1.

Learning is complex, so much so that no one view of learning can fully express this complexity. It is only by considering learning in a variety of ways that we can begin to gain a fuller understanding of its nature, and it is only by planning for such a variety of approaches to address learning, as described in this unit, that we can provide rich and inclusive classroom experiences for our children.

ANNOTATED FURTHER READING

Hayes, D. (ed.) (2007) *Joyful Teaching and Learning in the Primary School*, Exeter: Learning Matters.
An interesting take on teaching creatively that looks at a range of approaches to teaching, learning and organisation in different subject areas of the primary curriculum. Chapters that focus particularly on literacy and mathematics teaching in this book include Arthur Shenton's 'The joyful teaching of reading' and Nick Pratt's 'The joy of mathematics'.

Kelly, P. (2005) *Using Thinking Skills in the Primary Classroom*, London: Sage.
A more detailed consideration of social learning and apprenticeship approaches, together with a wide range of examples and many suggestions for enhancing practice.

Osborn, M., Broadfoot, P., McNess, E., Planel, C., Ravn, B. and Triggs, P. (2003) *A World of Difference? Comparing Learners Across Europe*, Maidenhead, Open University Press.
International comparisons are always interesting in relation to classroom organisation. The ENCOMPASS project looked at primary teaching in Denmark, England and France and this book, which describes the project, has a chapter on classroom contexts as a reflection of national values.

Pratt, N. (2006) *Interactive Maths Teaching in the Primary School*, London: Paul Chapman.
A look at interactive mathematics teaching in detail.

Approaches to organising your classroom	Learning focus	Broad learning objectives	Strengths	Challenges
Primary Framework for literacy and mathematics in the Primary National Strategy (DCSF)	Basic skills acquisition	Primary Framework for literacy and mathematics objectives	An interactive approach where the importance of teacher modelling and high-quality dialogue between teachers and pupils is emphasised	Many teachers have had difficulty adopting fully interactive direct teaching; tendency to be used at whole class levels rather than with individuals or groups; little emphasis on learners own starting points
Many primary science schemes (including Nuffield Primary Science); Cognitive Acceleration in Science Education (Phil Adey and Michael Shayer)	Constructing understanding	To develop enquiry and investigative process skills; To develop children's own understandings of phenomena; To apply understandings to new contexts	Starts from children's ideas and perspectives, building on these using direct hands-on experience	Assumes children will notice experiences which don't fit their understandings, challenge their understandings and be able to restructure these to accommodate the new experiences
Group Work; Discussion; Dialogical Enquiry	Social learning	To develop collaborative and speaking and listening skills; To see things from different points of view; To develop critical and creative thinking; To develop children's own understandings of phenomena	Supports learners in constructing new meanings and understandings as they explore them together in words; allows learners to test out and criticize claims and different points of view as they speak and listen to others; and provides raw material for learners own thinking	Requires children to have certain basic skills and obey certain ground rules; sometimes difficult to organise; works best when children show areas of autonomous learning
Authentic Activity and Enquiry	Apprentice-ship	To encourage children to act and see the world as scientists, historians, archaeologists, poets, and so on	Outward looking, considering learning as something which takes you outside the classroom; inspiring and motivating	Requires significant time to allow it to happen; often needs access to good quality resources; teachers need to feel confident and have some expertise in the area of activity or enquiry or be able to get in someone who has

■ **Figure 3.3.1** Organising your classroom for learning

RELEVANT WEBSITES

Learning Outside the Classroom: www.lotc.org.uk/
    This DCSF site has a useful section on organising learning outside the classroom.

Reflective Teaching: www.rtweb.info/content/view/392/89/
    Andrew Pollard's website has a good section on classroom organisation.

Teachers Talking About Learning: www.unicef.org/teachers/build.htm
    This Unicef site provides an excellent archive of writings about child-friendly approaches to learning.

Visit the companion website www.routledge.com/textbooks/ltps2e for:

■ an additional task for this unit;
■ description of practice;
■ links to useful websites relevant to this unit.

REFERENCES

Adey, P., Shayer, M. and Yates, C. (1995) *Thinking Science*, London: Nelson.

Bennet, N. (1995) 'Managing learning through group work', in C. Desforges (ed.) *An Introduction to Teaching: Psychological Perspectives*, Oxford: Blackwell.

Bobbit Nolen, S. (1995) 'Teaching for autonomous learning', in C. Desforge (ed.) *An Introduction to Teaching: Psychological Perspectives*, Oxford: Blackwell.

Department for Children, Schools and Families (DCSF) (2007) *Primary Framework for Literacy and Mathematics*. Available online at www.standards.dfes.gov.uk/primaryframeworks/ (accessed October 2009).

Kelly, P. (2005) *Using Thinking Skills in the Primary Classroom*, London: Sage.

Lave, J. and Wenger, E. (1991) *Situated Learning: Legitimate Peripheral Participation*, Cambridge: Cambridge University Press.

Wenger, E. (1998) *Communities of Practice: Learning, Meaning and Identity*, Cambridge: Cambridge University Press.

MANAGING CLASSROOM BEHAVIOUR

Roland Chaplain

INTRODUCTION

This unit introduces you to a framework for developing behaviour management strategies. The effective management of pupil behaviour depends on a range of interrelated factors, including the organisational climate and aims of the school; your personality, socio-emotional competence and beliefs about the causes of behaviour; the academic and social development and dispositions of your pupils; and group dynamics.

OBJECTIVES

By the end of this unit you should understand:

- the multilevel nature of behaviour management in school;
- the value of a proactive classroom behaviour management plan (CBP);
- the importance of structural and organisational factors and interpersonal tactics in managing pupil behaviour;
- ways of responding to challenging behaviour.

FROM WHOLE-SCHOOL ISSUES TO CHALLENGING PUPILS

Managing classroom behaviour is not incidental to teaching and should be viewed in relation to wider aspects of behaviour management in school. All pupils should engage in positive behaviour in school to develop positive relationships, self-confidence and effective coping skills (DfES, 2003) and, furthermore, early intervention is recommended to prevent children from engaging in antisocial behaviour.

To facilitate this effectively requires attention to different levels of behaviour management, ranging from whole-school issues through classroom management to working with challenging individuals (Figure 3.4.1). Inconsistency between different levels offers pupils the opportunity to manipulate the system. Being an excellent class teacher means nothing if chaos reigns around you – the aftershock eventually gets through.

Schools are required to produce 'policies designed to promote good behaviour and discipline on the part of its pupils' (DfEE, 1998: 61.4) and should reflect the expectations of a school

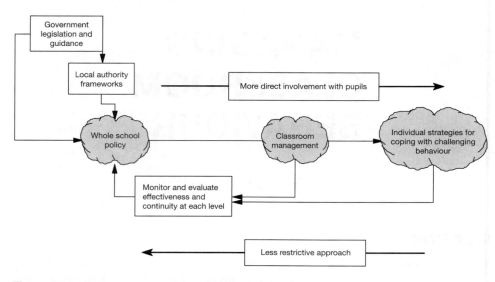

Figure 3.4.1 The multilevel model of behaviour management

Note: The whole school policy is the standard against which both classroom management and individual strategies are compared. As the management function moves from left to right, so does the level of intrusiveness or direct control over pupil behaviour.

community, inform practice, highlight valued behaviour and contribute to the school's organisational climate. The importance of behaviour policies in developing effective schools has been recognised for some time (c.f. Elton Report, 1989; DCSF, 2006). Chaplain (1995) suggested that behaviour policies should reflect the views and aspirations of *all* stakeholders in a school's community, including pupils, parents, staff and managers.

When the behaviour policy is well thought out, understood and applied consistently by all adults responsible for pupils, it can significantly reduce or eliminate many minor disruptive behaviours almost 'automatically'. There are a number of familiar school-wide routines (e.g. assemblies,

---

Task 3.4.1 **WHOLE-SCHOOL BEHAVIOUR POLICY**

Obtain a copy of the behaviour policy from your school and consider the following questions.

■ Are the core school rules explicit?
■ Do they encourage pupils to make a positive contribution to school?
■ Did pupils participate in developing the school's expectations?
■ To what extent do they match your own expectations for pupil behaviour?
■ What rewards exist for those pupils who behave as expected and what sanctions exist for those who do not?
■ Is there a clear hierarchy of rewards and sanctions?

Compare your school's policy with that of another trainee.

■ In what ways are they similar?
■ In what ways are they different?

Task 3.4.2 **ADHD?**

Attention deficit hyperactivity disorder (ADHD) is the most common childhood behavioural disorder (NHS, 2008) with 3–9 per cent of children suffering the condition. The causes of ADHD are not clear-cut and explanations include genetic, psychological and sociocultural factors. Examine the research evidence and decide to what extent it supports Barkley's (2005) view that the primary cause of ADHD results from difficulties in executive functioning of the brain (e.g. working memory, internal speech, emotion-regulation). What are the pedagogic implications of adopting such an explanation?

dress, timetable, movement, lining up, reporting, sanctions, rewards), which visibly reinforce what the school values. The behaviour policy should set the standard for all levels of behaviour management, providing uniformity, social identity and predictability for pupils and teachers alike. Nonetheless, teachers are individuals and each classroom has its own 'climate', which makes them distinctive – but preferably within an overall consistent framework.

TEACHER STRESS, PUPIL BEHAVIOUR AND CLASSROOM CONTROL

Research has consistently reported pupil misbehaviour as a significant stressor for both experienced and trainee teachers (Kyriacou and Sutcliffe, 1978; Borg, 1990; Chaplain, 1995, 2008; Dunham and Varma, 1998;). However, while teachers usually rate extreme behaviour (physical and verbal assault) as their biggest concern, such behaviour is not an everyday occurrence in the regular classroom. In contrast, low-level disruptive behaviours (e.g. talking out of turn, pupils getting out of their seats, not having equipment, fiddling with pens) are a familiar experience for many teachers (Elton Report, 1989; Ofsted, 2006), the cumulative effect of which can be very stressful. These 'daily hassles' (Kanner *et al.*, 1981) are usually offset by 'daily uplifts', most notably in the form of positive feedback from pupils – arguably the most rewarding aspect of teaching.

Task 3.4.3 **UNDERSTANDING DISRUPTIVE BEHAVIOUR**

■ What disruptive behaviours cause you most concern?
■ List them in order of priority, then write alongside how often you have observed or experienced them.
■ Consider the type of behaviour in relation to its frequency to understand its potential effect.
■ Now list the strategies you plan to use in order to cope with low-level disruptive behaviours?

Task 3.4.4 **EXPECTATIONS AND DISRUPTIVE BEHAVIOUR**

Qualified teachers are required to have high expectations for pupil behaviour (TDA, 2009), an observation reflecting a long history of research evidence that suggests teachers get what they expect from their pupils (Kuklinski and Weinstein, 2003). Critically evaluate the role of impression formation and non-verbal messages in the formation and mediation of teachers' expectations to children (Chaplain, 2003).

CAUSAL EXPLANATIONS OF MISBEHAVIOUR

What do you consider to be the main causes of disruptive behaviour?

▪ *Within pupil* – personality/temperament, part of growing up, children are: intrinsically naughty; out of control?

▪ *Within school* – irrelevant curriculum, teachers' incompetence, poorly managed schools, teachers' attitudes?

▪ *Within the community* – poor parenting, poverty, lack of discipline in the home/community/ society?

Consider the implications of your explanation. 'Within pupil' and 'within the community' factors are least under your control and hardest to change. In contrast, 'within school' factors are controllable by teachers and therefore easier to change. If you found yourself blaming factors outside your control, you are not alone – Lawrence *et al.* (1986) found that 78 per cent of teachers blamed misbehaviour on issues outside their control (see Miller *et al.*, 2000 for a pupil's perspectives on the causes of misbehaviour). The emphasis here will be on factors over which you have most control and how proactive planning can help you to become an effective classroom manager.

MANAGING YOURSELF

Verbal and non-verbal behaviours are the bread and butter of teaching; however, they are not always under your direct conscious control. You may plan to communicate something to someone but, when under pressure, fail because of emotional interference or lack of confidence (Chaplain, 2003). You have, no doubt, observed other people's habits when feeling under pressure – looking 'nervous', coughing, fidgeting or playing with their hair. I have observed teachers using the utterance 'ssh' or 'erm' when trying to gain the attention of the class – to no avail. They are busily 'ssh-ing' but the pupils carry on talking – something teachers often don't realise until I show them the video, which surprises them as they were not *aware* of their behaviour. They can remember pupils misbehaving, but nothing about their ineffective *habit*. We are all aware of being told to 'ssh' as a young child and it may indeed work effectively for some teachers – the problem arises when over-learned, 'automatic' responses are ineffective and we are unaware of using them. Other ineffective strategies retained from childhood that may emerge when we feel under pressure include shouting, screaming and losing our temper. Overcoming such behaviours requires first becoming aware of them (e.g. by videoing yourself), then identifying and practising alternative behaviours when not under pressure – taking an active role in self-regulation to enhance coping.

Believing you are able to influence important events in your life ('locus of control' – Rotter, 1966) is central to effective coping. People who believe they are able to influence important events (internal locus) tend to cope far better than those who believe other people make important decisions for them (external locus). I have met many trainee teachers reluctant to change classroom seating arrangements, despite being aware that existing arrangements are not working for them. Their reason for not asking to make changes is usually because they feel that, as it is someone else's classroom, it would be wrong to do so. However, their mentors are often as surprised as me that the trainees did not make such changes. This could be brought under the trainee's control simply by asking if it's OK to move things around to help them teach more effectively.

Belief in your capability to manage behaviour (teacher efficacy) affects how you cope with disruptive behaviour. A positive teacher efficacy means we think, feel and behave in a more confident manner (Woolfolk Hoy *et al.*, in press) making pupils feel secure and more likely to respond positively. Teachers are required to be *an authority* (knowledgeable) and *in authority* (able to manage pupils). The latter requires social competence (interpersonal skills and emotional control), which is something we can control and develop further with attention, effort and practice. We can also manipulate the classroom environment to reduce pressure on our personal resources.

I once observed a trainee teaching a maths lesson that involved the four rules of number. She admitted to being anxious (after the lesson) about teaching maths and had decided to write down all her workings on a card, which she held in her hand, checking everything before responding to children's answers or writing examples on the board. However, this behaviour prevented her from maximising interaction with the class (limited eye contact, staying near the whiteboard, talking with her back to the class) because she kept looking at the card. As the lesson progressed she began confirming pupils' answers to the most elementary calculations from her card (for fear of getting them wrong). Her anxiety arose from her (false) beliefs in her capability in maths (given the examples were all within her ability), undermining her ability to cope. To overcome this problem she was advised to write worked examples on a flip chart before the lesson (covering the answers with 'post-it' shapes). With the answers available but covered, she was able to scan the room, move to different parts of the classroom (getting pupils to remove the 'post-its') and so maintain the flow of the lesson and appear more confident.

Self-awareness and self-monitoring provide a useful starting point for considering how *all* your behaviours contribute to how you manage your class. Changing how you think, feel and behave is not always easy and may feel uncomfortable, but the potential benefits make it worthwhile.

Self-regulation in the classroom requires attention to what you say and how you say it; checking you are being understood; looking and feeling confident; self-belief; and communicating your authority and status as a teacher through verbal and non-verbal behaviour (Chaplain, 2003).

Task 3.4.5 IDENTIFYING YOUR POTENTIAL STRENGTHS AND WEAKNESSES

■ Make an audit of your resources (personal strengths) and concerns (potential stressors) about teaching.
■ Indicate ways in which you perceive them as a resource/concern.
■ Now identify which factors you believe you can change and those outside your control.
■ Consider what changes to make and how to deal with the unchangeable.

DEVELOPING A CBP

A CBP is not dissimilar to your lesson plan, but should focus on:

■ how you will organise your classroom for different lessons, including seating arrangements to *minimise off task* behaviour;
■ producing a classroom behaviour management profile – tactics to deter disruption (proactive); responses to pupils who occasionally slip off task (reorientation); and responses to more persistent off-task behaviour (reactive) (see Table 3.4.1);
■ rewards and sanctions you will use (check they are compatible with your school systems);
■ your verbal and non-verbal behaviour;
■ contextual priorities, e.g. challenging behaviour.

It should be informed by, and reflect the expectations of your school's behaviour policy.

How you structure your CBP is a matter of personal choice – you may have a separate plan or alternatively integrate with your general lesson plan. Do remember to keep a separate detailed record of different strategies you have tried and their success rate for future planning.

MAKING AN EARLY IMPACT ON YOUR CLASS

We form impressions of other people in a few seconds (Ambady and Rosenthal, 1993) and these impressions often remain unchanged for long periods of time. Hence the first part of your CBP should consider the type of impression you wish to make. In your early visits to the classroom you will be observing, which can feel uncomfortable as pupils are inquisitive and will want to know all about you, weighing you up. You will want to settle in and learn the ropes, but do not be too friendly with the pupils, as you will eventually have to establish your authority with the whole class. This is not to suggest you should be standoffish or hostile – just remember to convey your status and authority as a teacher. Your first lesson may be relaxed, with pupils being quite passive (Ball, 1980), but at some point they will test your ability to establish and maintain behavioural limits, so make sure you are clear about your expectations and convey them to your pupils.

It is essential to pay attention to detail, especially in your early lessons. Your CBP should detail how you will:

■ teach and reinforce your behavioural expectations (rules and routines);
■ use verbal and non-verbal behaviours to control the class – especially at critical points in the lesson (see Table 3.4.1);
■ reward required behaviour (see Table 3.4.2);
■ respond to disruptive behaviour (Table 3.4.2);
■ organise the physical layout of the classroom.

These procedures are not exclusive to early lessons since they represent good professional practice. Adjust your learning plans and CBP over time as your relationship with classes changes and you become more practised – experiment and rise to new challenges.

CONVEYING YOUR EXPECTATIONS: RULES AND ROUTINES

All lessons have similar patterns; for example, getting the attention of the class, conveying information, managing feedback, managing transitions, monitoring and responding to unwanted behaviour. Whether your teaching is enhanced or undermined by any or all of the above depends on devising and applying appropriate, enforceable and effective rules and routines. Rules set the limits to pupils' behaviour (Charles, 1999). While whole-school (core) rules are designed primarily to produce harmonious relationships among pupils, the main purpose of classroom rules is to maximise pupil engagement with learning (Savage, 1991). Effective rules provide pupils with a physically and psychologically safe, predictable environment (Chaplain, 2003) and work in a preventative way to establish and keep order and maintain momentum through the lesson. To gain maximum effect rules should be:

■ *Positively worded* – tell pupils what they *can do* rather than what they *cannot do*, e.g. 'be nice' as opposed to 'don't be nasty'. Negatively framed rules are not effective long term (Becker *et al.*, 1975).
■ *Few in number* – long lists of rules will not be remembered – focus on key concerns. Canter and Canter (2001) suggest four: follow directions; keep hands, feet and objects to yourself; no teasing or name-calling; no swearing. I would recommend no more than five.

■ **Table 3.4.1** Sample classroom behaviour management profile

Preventative tactics	Reorientation tactics	Reactive tactics
Make sure your lessons are interesting	Gaze – sustained eye contact to inform pupils you are aware of what they are doing	Caution – inform what will happen should the unwanted behaviour persist
Teach and reinforce rules and routines	Posture and gesture – use to complement gaze, e.g. raised eyebrow, raised first finger, hands on hips	Remove privileges, e.g. ban from use of the computer or miss a trip
Be clear about what behaviour you expect from your pupils – reinforce and check for understanding	Space invasion – the closer you are to pupils the more control you will have – do not hide behind your desk or 'glue' yourself to the whiteboard – the classroom is your domain to move around as you wish	Require pupil to complete extra work during break times
Be alert to changes based on perceptions of pupils' non-verbal and verbal behaviours (e.g. too quiet/too loud, eye movements, looking out of window)	Restate rules – remind pupils about what is expected	Time out as arranged with colleague or manager in advance – avoid having disruptive pupils wandering around the school – it is of no help to anybody
Scanning – think about positioning in respect of being able to see the whole class at all times to quickly respond to potential disruption	Use individual encouragement to get pupils back on task – 'You have been doing really well so far . . .'	Contract – agree with pupil specific expectations and record successes – review and adjust as necessary
Going up a gear in anticipation of a disruptive event, e.g. new pupils, time of year	Name-dropping – we are all sensitive to hearing our name even when there are several conversations going on – mentioning a non-attentive pupil's name while you are talking will usually get their attention – supplement this, if necessary, with gestures	Removal from class temporarily – working elsewhere in school or with another class
Being enthusiastic even when you're not!	Praising peers in the vicinity of someone off task can be effective, provided the pupil values being praised by you – usually most effective with younger pupils	Suspension from school
Manipulating classroom layout, e.g. planned seating arrangements	Humour – pupils like teachers with a sense of humour, so make use of yours – but not by ridiculing pupils – and ensure it is appropriate to pupils' levels of development	
Using appropriate reward systems for on-task behaviour	Maintain the flow of the lesson by carrying on teaching while moving round the room, using non-verbal gestures and removing anything being played with (e.g. pens) avoid being distracted from what you have to say	
Awareness of pupils' goals		
Getting lesson timings right		

Note: These are some examples of effective tactics, but you should experiment with new ideas and modify to suit your teaching styles and the expectations and agreed policies of the school.

■ *Realistic* – have rules that are age-appropriate, enforceable and achievable by your pupils.
■ *Focused on key issues* – personal safety, safety of others, cooperation and facilitating learning.
■ *Applied consistently* – intermittent or (unintended) selective reinforcement of rules will render them ineffective. For instance, if putting hands up to answer questions is a rule and you respond positively to those pupils who shout out a *very* competent answer, then reprimand someone else for shouting out an unsophisticated answer, you are sending out mixed and unhelpful messages to pupils about how much you value them.

When taking over a class from another teacher, it is important to consider his or her expectations in relation to your own and whether this will affect the way in which you establish your rules. If you adopt the rules of the existing teacher, do not assume the pupils will necessarily respond in the same way to you as they do to the existing teacher – they will not inevitably associate you with a particular rule, so make sure you teach explicitly the behaviour you expect, even if it means repeating what you believe they already know.

Make sure you display your rules prominently and keep reminding pupils about them until they are established. Be creative perhaps using cartoons or pictures to liven up your display.

Task 3.4.6 **RULES AND EXPECTATIONS**

■ Can you think of four or five rules that embody your behavioural expectations?
■ Look again at the school behaviour policy – are your expectations similar?
■ Discuss how your classroom teacher/mentor established his or her rules with your class.
■ Do you feel confident applying them?

REWARDS AND SANCTIONS

Rules alone do not guarantee good behaviour; they should be related to rewards and sanctions (Steer Report, 2005) and linked to consequences – this means *consistently* rewarding pupils who follow the rules and applying sanctions as a deterrent to those who do not. List your rewards and sanctions hierarchically (Table 3.4.2) and familiarise yourself with the sequence to avoid using higher-order sanctions prematurely, for example when you are under pressure. Furthermore, when threatening sanctions, always offer the opportunity to respond positively. For example, 'Joe, you have left your seat again despite knowing the rule. Now you can either sit down and stay there or stay in at break for five minutes.' Should Joe continue to ignore the rule say, 'Joe, you are already staying in for five minutes, now either sit down or you will be staying a further five minutes.' Whatever sanction you threaten, be sure to carry it through, otherwise you will be guaranteeing a future repetition of the unwanted behaviour. Share the rewards for positive behaviour with the whole class – with difficult pupils focus on catching them being good, however rare that might be in the early days. Encourage more withdrawn pupils to contribute by building waiting time into your questions: 'I am going to be asking about X in five minutes so start thinking about it now.' Teach more enthusiastic pupils to wait their turn without disengaging them from learning: 'Thanks for putting your hand up all the time, Henry, but I am going to ask someone else to answer this one.'

To be effective, rewards and sanctions need to be fit for purpose – the reward must be something the pupils like and the sanction(s) something they do not like. It is unwise to assume that *you* know what pupils like or do not like. You may have considered being sent to see the head as punishment, but some pupils enjoy the attention, or perceived status, or just missing a lesson.

■ **Table 3.4.2** Examples of hierarchical rewards and sanctions

Rewards	Example	Sanctions	Example
*Verbal praise private	Quiet word, 'John that's excellent work'	Gesture	Raised first finger, thumbs down
*Verbal praise public	Teacher and class applaud individual	Prolonged gaze	Hold eye contact (with frown)
Public display of positive behaviours	Star/points chart – cumulative points; gets postcard to parents	Rule reminder	'What do we do when we want to ask a question?'
Classroom awards	Certificates, badges or superstar of the day/week award	Physical proximity	Move closer to pupil – perhaps stand behind him/her – say nothing
Contact home (either for accumulated star/points or exceptional good behaviour)	Notes/cards/phone calls	Verbal reprimand	'I am very unhappy with your behaviour'
		Public display	Remove points from star chart
Special privileges	Helping around school, attending an event	Separate from group in class or keep back at playtime	Adjust length of time to suit needs/age of pupil
Tangible rewards	Book token, sweets, pens	Record name	Write name on board
School award	Certificates, tokens	Removal from classroom	Teach outside normal teaching area
		Refer to SMT	Send to deputy (as per school policy)
		Contact parents	Letter/phone home
		Invite parents to school	For informal/formal discussion
		Behavioural contract	Short, focused on specific expectations
		Separation from group	Individual teaching or special class
		Suspension	For an agreed period
		Review contract	As a basis for return
		Exclusion	

* Initially praise could be for every positive occurrence; over time change to intermittent praise to maintain effectiveness. Praise should be warm and natural, appropriate to pupil's level of development, varied and creative. However, at least until you have established a working relationship with the class you will usually operate a tangible reward scheme alongside praising the required behaviour – the reward being linked to either points, stars or raffle tickets. The raffle tickets are particularly effective since any pupil who earns at least one ticket has a chance of winning, unlike points systems where some individuals will conclude that they can never win a prize. Whenever you issue a point, star or ticket, praise the pupil's behaviour simultaneously. That way they will learn to associate praise from you with a rewarding experience. When issuing sanctions, do so in a way that suggests disappointment in having to do so rather than anger or contempt and refer to the behaviour not the pupil.

One way of discovering what pupils value is to ask them to complete an 'All about me' sheet in which they indicate their favourite subjects, hobbies, music, sports and learning styles. Plan to start each new day on a positive note, whatever happened the day before – feeling negative in advance will focus your attention on negative behaviour, which will produce a cyclical event – reflecting negativity in your behaviour, generating further negative pupil behaviour, and so on.

USING ROUTINES TO MAXIMISE ON-TASK ACTIVITY

Schools, like most organisations, operate through a series of established routines. While rules provide the framework for the conduct of lessons, they are few in number, so teachers therefore rely on many routines to provide the link between expectations and action. Routines are usually organised around times, places and contexts. Effective teachers spend considerable time in their early encounters with their classes teaching them routines (Emmer *et al.*, 1994), which, when practised, become automatic, leaving more time for teaching. Jones and Jones (1990) found that up to 50 per cent of some lessons was lost to non-teaching routines, such as getting out equipment and marking work, so efficient routines provide a real learning bonus. The following paragraphs consider key routines in more detail.

Entering the classroom

How pupils enter your classroom sets the scene for the lesson – charging noisily into a room is not the best way to start a lesson, so consider how you might control this initial movement. One way is to greet your pupils at the door, look pleased to see them and remind them what they are expected to do when they go into class. Have an engaging activity waiting for them that has a time limit, and is preferably linked to a reward. Physically standing by the door reduces the likelihood of pupils charging in but, if they do, call them back and make them repeat the procedure correctly.

Getting the attention of the class

This can be done by using verbal or other noises, silence or puppets.

■ *Using noises* – such as ringing bells, tapping the desk, clapping, asking pupils to show their hands or sit up straight. Which method you choose depends on your personal style and school policy. However, make sure that you explain beforehand what the signal is and what you want pupils to do when they hear it. I witnessed one teacher working with a 'lively' class use a tambourine to gain attention part way through the lesson, but the teacher had omitted to let pupils know beforehand. While it made everyone jump (including me), it was not associated with any required behaviour. A more effective method would have been to tell the class in advance, 'Whenever I bang the tambourine I want you all to stop what you are doing and look at me.'

■ *Using silence* – some teachers find they can gain attention using non-verbal signals, such as folding their arms, putting hands on hips, raising eyebrows or frowning. Using non-verbal signals can be very powerful – indeed the more you use non-verbal gestures and body language to manage behaviour the better, since it minimises disruption to the flow of your lesson. However, to be effective requires you to feel confident about your presence and to teach the pupils to associate a particular behaviour with a particular expectation.

■ *Using puppets* – a large figurative hand puppet can be very effective in behaviour management (see puppetsbypost.com). Introduce the puppet and say that it will only come out if everyone is quiet – because it suffers from headaches or is nervous. If the noise level gets too high put the puppet away. Hermit crab or snail puppets that only emerge if people are well behaved are also excellent! They can also be used as a reward, for example the best behaved group are allowed to have the puppet sitting at their table. Pupils are usually very attentive and empathetic towards puppets, so they can be used to aid the pupils' socio-emotional development. We have had excellent results when using them with pupils from Foundation Stage to Year 6.

Briefing

Take time to ensure that pupils understand exactly what is required from them at each stage of the lesson – unless you want those pupils who find it hard to pay attention wasting time asking other pupils what they should be doing. Taking time in your first lessons may be difficult if you are anxious about being in the spotlight – if this is so, use prompts to remind yourself to speak slowly and carefully (perhaps writing SLOW on your lesson notes). Write instructions, key words and questions on the board to support your verbal inputs – *do so before the lesson* so that you can maintain eye contact and scan the whole class while briefing them. You might also consider using consistent colour-coded writing to differentiate instructions, key words, questions, etc., so that pupils recognise more easily what is expected of them.

Distributing equipment

If done in advance, issuing equipment can cause a distraction, with pupils fiddling with it while you are talking, whereas issuing it after you have finished talking can disrupt a settled group. Choosing which one to use depends on how the class respond to you and each other. If you issue equipment in advance, make sure you tell pupils beforehand not to touch the equipment, rather than having to correct afterwards. Always check all your equipment before the lesson – do not assume that people will have returned the electrical experiment kit complete with full batteries and wires untangled, otherwise you may find yourself spending 20 minutes sorting it out, giving pupils the opportunity to misbehave.

Moving bodies

Often overlooked when planning lessons, keeping control of pupils on the move both in and out of the classroom requires careful planning if it is to be efficient and safe. Again make sure you specify in advance exactly what you require people to do (including supporting adults). If moving a class to a different location, think before the lesson about the group dynamics in the same way you would plan a learning activity. Plan where to position yourself in relation to the group to maintain your view of everyone you are responsible for. Reinforce those individuals who are behaving correctly to encourage the other pupils to copy them.

Checking for understanding

Throughout your lesson check that pupils are clear about what is expected. Where appropriate, support your verbal instructions with written ones – especially when working with pupils who have attention difficulties. Avoid repeatedly asking the same child or group and encourage all pupils to ask relevant questions if in doubt.

> ## Task 3.4.7 **CLASSROOM ROUTINES**
>
> ■ Think about the routines you consider important in your classroom and make a list.
> ■ How do you plan to teach them to your pupils?
> ■ Make a list of your key routines and rate them in terms of efficiency. Do they work? Could they be improved?

CLASSROOM LAYOUT

There is evidence to demonstrate a correlation between seating arrangements and pupil behaviour (Steer Report, 2005). For example, sitting boys with girls tends to reduce disruption (Merrett, 1993); children organised in rows tend to be less disruptive than when organised in groups (Wheldall and Lam, 1987). However, these findings need to be considered in relation to the nature of the learning task and the level of academic and social functioning of the children (see, for example, Finn and Pannozzo, 2004).

Movement around the classroom should be free-flowing. Where this is not the case there is a potential for disruption – some individuals will use every opportunity to push past, nudge or dislodge the chair or whiteboard of other pupils (Chaplain, 2003).

> ## Task 3.4.8 **CLASSROOM LAYOUT**
>
> ■ Consider the layout of your classroom. Is there sufficient room to move easily between the furniture?
> ■ Make a drawing of the classroom and cut out the various pieces of furniture. Try moving them around to see which arrangement gives the least disrupted flow around the room.
> ■ Where is the best place to stand to address the whole group? (Do not assume it is by the whiteboard.)
> ■ Monitor your movement during a lesson (video record or ask someone to record your movements) – do you spend equal amounts of time with each group?
> ■ How might you organise your tables so as to make the transition from group work to pairs most efficient?

COPING WITH CHALLENGING BEHAVIOUR

While having well-thought out rules, routines, rewards and sanctions will provide a secure structure for most pupils, some will persistently challenge your authority with behaviour ranging from physical and verbal aggression to defiance and refusal to work. The members of such groups are not homogeneous and range from pupils with temporary difficulties to those with persistent difficulties, such as ADHD or other behavioural emotional or social difficulty (BESD), who may require specialist interventions (see behaviour4learning.ac.uk).

There are a number of important general points to make in respect of coping with challenging behaviour. First, do not interpret such behaviour as a personal 'assault' – pupils seldom behave this way because they hate you and you will gain nothing from getting angry (however, this does not mean you should not reprimand pupils in an assertive way). Second, don't become obsessed with fitting pupils to descriptive categories (e.g. ADHD) – focus on understanding *the motive behind the behaviour* and record carefully what they do, when and where they do it – making sure you *include positive behaviour*, however infrequent. Keeping a record of positive behaviours not only provides an uplift when times are tense, but also gives useful insight into the pupil's currency – i.e. what motivates them to behave appropriately.

Keep things in perspective and do not lose your sense of humour. Managing challenging pupils can require considerable effort and inconsistent results can lead to frustration, which inhibits problem solving and creativity. It is not uncommon for teachers to question their own ability and lose confidence, which reflects in their behaviour – a change that pupils recognise and respond negatively to – making a difficult situation worse. Finding humour in the situation can be sufficient to influence events positively (Molnar and Lindquist, 1989). Focus on controlling your emotions and on believing that the situation can be coped with, if not completely controlled. Even situations that are so awful that you have to grin and bear it won't last forever. Do not be afraid to ask for help with extreme pupils. If you anticipate an aversive reaction (e.g. aggressive outburst) to a particular event, arrange for a supportive adult to be around in advance of that time. Fortunately, such occurrences are rare and most common behaviours can be dealt with through developing your knowledge of established interventions (see Harden *et al.*, 2003) for a recent overview), some of which are outlined below.

Dealing with challenging behaviour requires attention to several issues including:

■ *Being consistent* with whatever approach you adopt. Challenging pupils are looking for structure and security and will repeatedly challenge you until they realise you mean business. They act like people playing slot machines and will keep pressing your buttons until they hit the jackpot (make you angry). Do not let them – keep calm and focused. Remember, there are no quick fixes so prepare for the long haul!

■ *Classroom organisation* – seating arrangements. Position challenging pupils near the front so that there are no pupils between them and you to distract or provide an audience for a confrontation. This places you in close proximity while addressing the class, making monitoring and controlling their behaviour easier, for example through direct eye contact and using hand gestures. Putting aggressive pupils with groups for *all* activities is likely to create disruption, as they will cause arguments and fights, or make bullets for others to fire. This is not to suggest that they should live in isolation, but think about the nature of the learning task and (classroom permitting) try having them work on separate tables for individual tasks.

■ *Learning* – Carefully organise their time and the sequencing/size of their learning tasks. If concentration is an issue, break down their learning into smaller achievable progressive units, vary the tasks, emphasise visual learning, use colours and shapes to help them organise their work and change their tasks frequently. It is also helpful to have a clock visible and indicate how long they are required to stay on task; the clock provides a visual reference point and helps maintain focus. Specify exactly what you want them to do and provide visual reminders of important instructions.

■ *Support* – Where you have a teaching assistant, plan in advance who will deal with a disruptive pupil and who will take responsibility for the rest of the class – this eliminates ambiguity and inconsistency.

■ *Changing behaviour* – Focus on observable behaviour – avoid describing a pupil as 'always badly behaved'. List the behaviours causing concern then gather detailed observations of what occurs before the unwanted behaviour (antecedent), the behaviour itself and what happens afterwards (consequence), along with how frequently it occurs (see Figure 3.4.2).

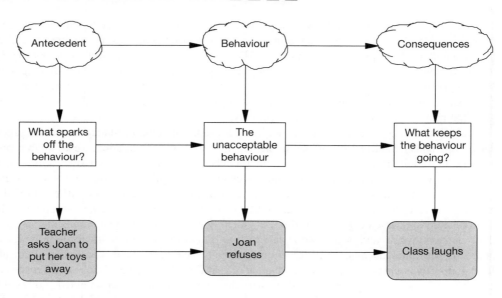

▪ **Figure 3.4.2** An A–B–C model of behaviour

Use your observations to hypothesise why the pupil is behaving in this way – in Figure 3.4.2 it could be the antecedent (asking Joan to put her toys away) or the consequences (other pupils laughing when she defies you). Next, decide what you want Joan to do instead of being defiant and what to reward her with for behaving appropriately. The process requires attention to detail and is outlined in Figure 3.4.3. (For detailed procedures of ways to develop pupils' self-regulation, see Chaplain and Freeman, 1998; Chaplain, 2003; Chaplain and Smith, 2006.)

SUMMARY

This unit has outlined some key factors to consider when developing your CBP. It is essential to keep in mind that effective classroom behaviour management is strongly influenced by whole-school attitudes and practices as well as your interpersonal skills and classroom organisation. Additional reading has been provided to assist you in extending your knowledge of the relevant areas, which you are strongly recommended to do in order to advance your behaviour management skills.

ANNOTATED FURTHER READING

Canter, L. and Canter, M. (2001) *Assertive Discipline: Positive Behavior Management for Today's Classroom)*, Los Angeles, CA: Canter & Associates.
A text offers helpful guidance on developing a discipline plan and managing difficult behaviour.

Chaplain, R. (2003) *Teaching Without Disruption in the Primary School: A Model for Managing Behaviour*, London: RoutledgeFalmer.
A comprehensive account of the theory and practice of behaviour management, including whole-school issues, classroom management and how to cope with difficult pupils.

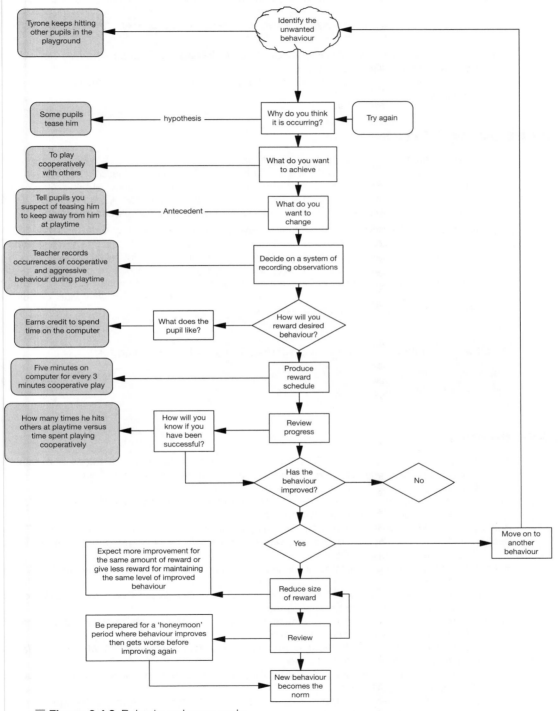

■ **Figure 3.4.3** Behaviour change cycle

Porter, L. (2000) *Behaviour in Schools: Theory and Practice for Teachers*, Buckingham: Open University Press.
A useful sourcebook reviewing some key theories on behaviour management, their underlying philosophy and recommended practices.

Robertson, J. (1996) *Effective Classroom Control: Understanding Teacher–Student Relationships*. London: Hodder and Stoughton.
Advice on establishing and maintaining authority in the classroom with an emphasis on non-verbal communication.

RELEVANT WEBSITES

Behaviour4Learning: www.behaviour4learning.ac.uk
Supported by the Training and Development Agency for Schools, this site contains up-to-date commentaries and reports on research and policy developments in respect of behaviour in schools. You will also find a link to the recent series of reports by the Practitioners' Group on school discipline and pupil behaviour announced in the *Children's Plan* (**www.dcsf.gov.uk/childrensplan/**).

Department for Children, Schools and Families: www.dcsf.gov.uk/behaviourandattendance/
This site contains advice and reference material for practitioners to reduce absenteeism and exclusions and improve behaviour. It includes information on the Behaviour and Education Support Teams, who are multi-agency teams that work closely with defined groups of schools to provide whole-school, group and individual support to address the needs of children and young people with emotional and behavioural problems. (For integrated, multi-agency working, see also **www.dcsf.gov.uk/every childmatters/strategy/deliveringservices1/iw/**.)

> **Visit the companion website www.routledge.com/textbooks/ltps2e for:**
>
> ■ additional questions and task for this unit;
> ■ links to useful websites relevant to this unit.

REFERENCES

Ambady, N. and Rosenthal, R. (1993) 'Half a minute: predicting teacher evaluations from thin slices of behaviour and physical attractiveness', *Journal of Personality and Social Psychology*, 64: 431–41.

Ball, S.J. (1980) 'Initial encounters in the classroom and the process of establishment', in P. Woods (ed.) *Pupil Strategies*, London: Croom Helm.

Barkley, R.A. (2005) *Attention Deficit Hyperactivity Disorder Handbook*, New York: Guilford Press.

Becker, W.C., Englemann, S. and Thomas, D.R. (1975) *Classroom Management*, Henley-on-Thames: Science Research Associates.

Borg, M.G. (1990) 'Occupational stress in British educational settings: a review', *Educational Research*, 10: 103–26.

Canter, L. and Canter, M. (2001) *Assertive Discipline: A Take Charge Approach for Today's Educator*, Los Angeles, CA: Lee Canter Associates.

Chaplain, R. (1995) 'Stress and job satisfaction: a study of English primary school teachers', *Educational Psychology*, 15(4): 473–91.

Chaplain, R. (2003) *Teaching Without Disruption in the Primary School: A Model for Managing Behaviour*, London: RoutledgeFalmer.

Chaplain, R. (2008) 'Stress and psychological distress among secondary trainee teachers', *Educational Psychology*, 28(2): 195–209.

Chaplain, R. and Freeman, A. (1998) *Coping with Difficult Children*, Cambridge: Pearson.

Chaplain, R. and Smith, S. (2006) *Challenging Behaviour*, Cambridge: Pearson.

Charles, C.M. (1999) *Building Classroom Discipline from Models to Practice*, 6th edn, New York: Longman.

Department for Children, Schools and Families (DCSF) (2006) *Educations and Inspections Act*, London: The Stationery Office.

Department for Education and Employment (DfEE) (1998) *School Standards and Framework Act*, London: DfEE.

Department for Education and Skills (DfES) (2003) *Every Child Matters*, London: DfES.

Dunham, J. and Varma, V. (1998) *Stress in Teachers: Past, Present and Future*, London: Whurr.

Elton Report (1989) *Discipline in Schools: Report of the Committee Chaired by Lord Elton*, London: HMSO.

Emmer, E.T., Evertson, C.M., Clements, B.S. and Worsham, M.E. (1994) *Classroom Management for Secondary Teachers*, 3rd edn, Upper Saddle River, NJ: Prentice Hall.

Finn, J. and Pannozzo, G. (2004) 'Classroom organization and student behavior in kindergarten, *Journal of Educational Research*, 98(2): 79–92.

Harden, A,. Thomas, J., Evans, J., Scanlon, M. and Sinclair, J. (2003) *Supporting Pupils with Emotional and Behavioural Difficulties (EBD) in Mainstream Primary Schools: A Systematic Review of Recent Research on Strategy Effectiveness (1999 to 2002)*, London: EPPI-Centre, Social Science Research Unit, Institute of Education, University of London.

Jones, V.F. and Jones, L.S. (1990) *Comprehensive Classroom Management*, 3rd edn, Needham: Allyn and Bacon.

Kanner, A.D., Coyne, J.C., Schaever, C. and Lazarus, R.S. (1981) 'Comparison of two modes of stress measurement: daily hassles and uplifts versus major life events', *Journal of Behavioural Medicine*, 4: 1–39.

Kuklinski, M. and Weinstein, R. (2003) 'Classroom and developmental differences in a path model of teacher expectancy effects', *Child Development*, 72(5): 1554–78.

Kyriacou, C. and Sutcliffe, J. (1978) 'Teacher stress: prevalence, sources and symptoms', *British Journal of Educational Psychology*, 48: 159–67.

Lawrence, J., Steed, D. and Young, P. (1986) *Disruptive Pupils – Disruptive Schools?*, London: Routledge.

Merrett, F. (1993) *Encouragement Works Best*, London: David Fulton.

Miller, A., Ferguson, E. and Byrne, I. (2000) 'Pupils' causal attributions for difficult classroom behaviour', *British Journal of Educational Psychology*, 70: 85–96.

Molnar, A. and Lindquist, B. (1989) *Changing Problem Behaviour*, San Francisco, CA: Jossey-Bass.

National Health Service (NHS) (2008) *Attention Deficit Hyperactivity Disorder* (Clinical guidelines CG72). Available online at www.nice.org.uk/CG072fullguideline (accessed October 2009).

Office for Standards in Education (Ofsted) (2006) *Improving Behaviour*, London: Ofsted.

Rotter, J.B. (1966) 'Generalised expectancies for internal versus external control of reinforcement', *Psychological Monographs*, 91: 482–97.

Savage, T. (1991) *Discipline for Self-control*, Upper Saddle River, NJ: Prentice Hall.

Steer, Sir Alan (2005) *Learning Behaviour: Lessons Learned* (Steer Report), London: DCSF/Institute of Education, University of London.

Training and Development Agency for Schools (TDA) (2009) *Professional Standards for Qualified Teacher Status and Requirements for Initial Teacher Training*, London: TDA. Available online at www.tda.gov.uk/teachers/professionalstandards/standards.aspx (accessed October 2009).

Wheldall, K. and Lam, Y.Y. (1987) 'Rows versus tables II: the effects of classroom seating arrangements on classroom disruption rate, *Educational Psychology*, 7(4): 303–12.

Woolfolk Hoy, A., Hoy, W.K., and Davis, H. (in press) 'Teachers' self-efficacy beliefs', in K. Wentzel and A. Wigfield (eds) Handbook *of Motivation in School*, Mahwah, NJ: Lawrence Erlbaum.

ORGANISING EFFECTIVE CLASSROOM TALK

Lyn Dawes

INTRODUCTION

> Discussion of reading, writing and numeracy in primary education sometimes fails to recognise the central importance of developing children's spoken communication. The primary skills of speaking and listening are essential in their own right and as a crucial platform for learning to read and write, to be numerate and, indeed, to be successful in virtually all of the learning children undertake at school and elsewhere.'
>
> (Sir Jim Rose, *Independent Review of the Primary Curriculum*, 2009)

In order to ensure effective classroom talk, we need to do two things. We need to make sure that we talk to children in ways that help them to learn. We also need to make sure that children are aware that their talk with teachers and with one another is extremely important if everyone is to benefit from classroom activities. Classroom organisation for talk involves creating a whole-class awareness of talk for learning, and generating everyday opportunities for children to talk about their learning to us, and to each other.

OBJECTIVES

This unit will help you to:

- consider the crucial importance of classroom talk for learning;
- identify ways that teachers use talk for learning;
- understand when and how to move between different sorts of talk;
- raise children's awareness of their classroom talk and its impact on others;
- integrate the Speaking and Listening objectives of the Primary Literacy Strategy throughout the curriculum.

THE CRUCIAL IMPORTANCE OF CLASSROOM TALK FOR LEARNING

Children learn not just through experience, but by talking about what they are doing. Talk precipitates thought as children share ideas and comment on what they observe. In this way, children help one another to generate new understanding and stimulate curiosity, imagination and interest. Children talking may articulate tentative or more firmly entrenched ideas, make suggestions or offer information. The chance to listen to children's talk allows us some useful insight into their thinking. In whole-class settings, talk with a teacher can provide children with new information. Even more importantly, children can hear and consider a range of alternative points of view. And classroom talk has the social function of helping the child to learn how effective communication goes on as ideas are raised and negotiated.

In primary classrooms even the most literate children are only just beginning to learn through reading and writing. Talk is the medium through which much learning goes on as children play, observe things and become involved in a range of activities. Teachers have the responsibility to make sure that every child has the opportunity to speak out in class as an everyday occurrence. This requires some organisation because, as educationalists, we cannot be satisfied with casual conversation; we need to organise the sort of educationally effective talk that we know will help everyone to develop, think and learn. So it is that we need to organise talk for learning. To do so we need to be able to say what *talk for learning* is, and to be able to describe what it sounds like and achieves.

WAYS THAT TEACHERS USE TALK FOR LEARNING: WHAT IS TALK FOR LEARNING?

We can start by saying what it is not. Every teacher is aware that classroom talk is not so easily focused on learning. Children are marvellous beings; imaginative, funny, charming and inconsequential, but also anarchic and self-centred. Classrooms put children in a social setting in which much is expected of them in terms of behaviour and concentration. They can, and do, use language in ways we find difficult. They contradict one another, are unkind, insensitive or rude; they come up with irrelevant or oblique comments; they shout, laugh or don't speak at all; they make jokes and distract others; they talk but do not listen; their concentration wavers and their thoughts drift off to their homes, games or friends. This is all fine – we want our children to be natural, chatty and confident. But we also want them to focus their minds on the educational task in hand. So we comment on talk in terms of behaviour: 'Everyone's being lovely and quiet' 'Stop talking now please' 'You need to listen, and you can't listen if you're talking.'

Classes do need to learn how to be quiet and attentive. They also need to learn how and why to talk to one another in ways that support learning.

Whole-class talk

Children's everyday experiences and their willingness to offer them for joint consideration by the class are invaluable resources. The class relies on the teacher to tap into the minds of others on their behalf. Ensuring access to this rich seam of imagination and information requires teachers to establish a positive relationship with children, based on an understanding that everyone's ideas will be valued. Developing an environment in which children feel that they can be open can be a slow process – but can be helped by direct teaching of the knowledge, skills and understanding needed to contribute to whole-class talk.

Group talk

Children's expectations of their contribution to group talk differ enormously from what we optimistically imagine. The moment adult attention is withdrawn, the group may find it very hard to focus on the artificial, complex and sometimes less than fascinating learning intentions that the curriculum demands. Again, direct tuition of talk skills and an understanding of why group talk is so important can help children to take part in effective discussions with one another, with no teacher present.

So what is talk for learning? Talk for learning is educationally effective talk; children learn from and through it. It is talk that is focused on the task in hand, is inclusive and equitable, and has the aim of helping everyone to gain new understanding. As teachers we cannot leave such talk to chance, because like everything else good that goes on in classrooms, it is unlikely to happen unless we organise it. We can consider ways of organising talk for learning in two common classroom contexts:

■ *dialogic teaching* – whole-class approach to talk between teacher and class;
■ *exploratory talk* – children working in groups with their classmates.

Much (though by no means all) talk for learning falls into these two contexts. A brief description of each follows, with references to further information and a summary of key points in Tables 3.5.1 and 3.5.2.

■ **Table 3.5.1** Dialogic teaching: talk between a teacher and a class of children

Purpose	Children summarise and share their thinking; express hypothetical ideas; admit to lack of understanding; listen to and reflect on other points of view; follow a line of reasoning. Exploring children's thoughts.
Organisation	Everyone can see and hear one another.
During dialogic teaching . . .	Children pay attention to each other's words; take extended turns; ask one another questions or challenge ideas; follow up on what they hear. The teacher chains responses into a coherent whole; orchestrates the talk; may speak very little themselves.
Talk tools	What is your opinion/idea . . .? Could you say more? Have you considered . . .? Choose someone who might contribute next . . . What if . . .? Remember what * said . . .? Who would like to challenge that . . .? What is your question/idea . . .? That's helpful because . . .
Ground rules	Children are prepared to explain their thinking; ask questions; admit lack of understanding; reason; listen attentively and follow the discussion. Teacher elicits contributions and maintains a focus on a line of thinking or reasoning.
Outcomes	Shared understanding and developing knowledge. Respect for ideas. Awareness of the limits of understanding, leading to productive questioning and learning.
Notes	Children may need input in active listening. Some may have an unwillingness to contribute or take an extended turn, and need positive support. There may be problems with admitting to lack of understanding. Children need to know that their contributions are of value to others.

Source: Mercer and Littleton (2007)

■ **Table 3.5.2** Exploratory talk: talk between groups of children with no adult support

Purpose	Inclusive talk to enable joint problem solving; sharing of ideas, opinions and reasons; negotiation.
Organisation	Three children seated near one another, around a table.
During exploratory talk . . .	All are invited to contribute; ideas and opinions are offered with reasons; information is shared; the group seeks to reach agreement; everyone listens; the group is on task.
Talk tools	What do you think? Why do you think that? I agree because . . . I disagree because . . . What do we know about . . .? I think . . . Shall we decide that . . . Wait a minute . . . But . . .
Ground rules	Everyone is invited to speak by others; contributions are treated with respect; reasons are asked for, and given; ideas are considered fully before agreement is reached.
Outcomes	Group agreement on a joint solution, idea or course of action. Group responsibility for decisions. Children support one another's thinking.
Notes	The task must necessitate discussion. Children need preparation; they must have an awareness of talk for learning, and have thought about and created a set of their own shared class ground rules for exploratory talk.

Source: Dawes (2008)

DIALOGIC TEACHING

Using dialogue as a way of thinking and learning has a long pedigree in education (Alexander, 2006; Scott and Asoko, 2006). Dialogic teaching can be described as teaching in which the teacher is aware of the power of dialogue and creates opportunities to engage every child in dialogue. For example, during whole-class work, children are expected to contribute not just brief answers but more lengthy explanations in which they go into detail about what they do, or do not, know or understand. Others listen attentively and are prepared to contribute themselves. In this way the class work together to discuss, reflect on and modify their ideas. The teacher orchestrates the discussion to lead children through a line of thinking. Crucially, there is time to deliberate and listen to tentative ideas. An effective lesson may contain dialogic episodes in addition to more authoritative episodes in which the teacher sums up or clarifies the discussion, and offers clear explanations.

What does dialogic teaching look and sound like?

During dialogic teaching, the class and teacher have the same aims for their learning, and are engaged in pursuit of knowledge and understanding through talk. Dialogic teaching is characterised by purposeful listening, a willingness to offer ideas or make problems with learning explicit, and teacher contributions that keep the children talking. This might mean that one child is encouraged to hold the floor, or another to talk about problems with their work in a way that helps their classmates to identify solutions or strategies. Contributions are linked to generate an overall 'bigger picture', through which children can make connections with previous learning. A feature of dialogue is that questions are raised, which, instead of leading to immediate and brief answers, lead to further questions, a discussion of detail or an admittance that more information is required. Such talk fosters children's natural curiosity.

EXPLORATORY TALK

Exploratory talk is talk in which children engage one another in a good discussion. They do this with no adult support. They are aware of the importance of their talk and take responsibility for their own learning and that of the others in their group. Each child is invited or encouraged to contribute. All information is shared. Opinions are backed up with reasons and discussed with respect. In addition, the talk may be hesitant as half-formed ideas are tentatively suggested, or particular points may be taken up and elaborated in some detail. Children may not be aware that this is what we require when we ask them to work in a group; direct teaching of the essential skills and understanding is necessary (Mercer and Littleton, 2007).

Exploratory talk requires shared motivation and purpose, which can be generated by direct teaching of the 'ground rules' that support discussion (Dawes *et al.*, 2003; Dawes and Sams, 2004). By creating and using their own class ground rules for talk, children are freed from having to negotiate social barriers and can really concentrate on engaging with the task in hand. Exploratory talk enables children in a group to achieve more than each child would alone, whatever their ability. Crucially, they simultaneously internalise the structures of reasoned, equitable discussion. By doing so, they learn a powerful and transferable way of thinking, which they can put to use when faced, alone, with a range of classroom and out-of-school problems.

What does exploratory talk look and sound like?

Children work closely in groups using questions as 'talk tools': 'What do you think?' 'Why do you think that?'; and as prompts: 'Can you say what you know about . . .' 'Tell us what happened . . .'; offering hypothetical ideas: 'What if . . .' 'But . . .'; elaborating on ideas: 'Yes, but remember when we did this before, we . . .'; and listening attentively to one another. The group of children is aware of the underlying rules that govern their discussion, and tries to adhere to them, in order to negotiate an agreement.

WHEN AND HOW TO MOVE BETWEEN TYPES OF TALK

We can plan talk for learning without being able to say how the talk will proceed in all classroom situations. We have to rely on our professional expertise to decide when and how to switch between types of talk. But we can generalise a little to say that:

■   *Whole-class introductory dialogue* requires authoritative input, such as clear instructions and information. Also we might use the sort of questions that simply check for items of knowledge: 'What did we do last week?' 'Remind us of the difference between an isosceles and equilateral triangle?' 'Where do herons lay their eggs?' Some of these questions might be targeted at individuals and often have a behavioural function; the question 'Jason, what is your answer to this?' is a way of ensuring Jason's involvement without actually saying 'Are you listening, Jason?!' After more than five minutes of such questions, children are not usually learning much. Some children always involve themselves with teacher's questions; some do just the opposite.

Introductions benefit from more complex dialogue in which we ask genuine questions: 'What do you already know about . . .' 'Has anyone heard of anything about this that might help us . . .?' 'What is your experience of this . . .?'

■ *Group work with no adult* requires children to engage one another in exploratory talk. The teacher's role is first to ensure that the children have been taught the structures of exploratory talk and, second, to listen in, support the children's work and move on. We can model exploratory talk as we move around the groups: 'Could you give a reason please?' 'Does anyone have any more information we can think about?'

A problem with exploratory talk is that a persuasive argument can sway a whole group into believing things that are not necessarily true. But since the talk is part of an ongoing classroom dialogue, the group is subsequently able to hear other ideas from their classmates, and can reconsider. Ideas established during discussion may not be firmly held until the child has had a chance to check them against practical experience and the ideas of others. Thinking about new ideas – 'weighing things up' and reflecting on how new ideas fit with one's own current thinking – is a learning process and an invaluable experience for a child. The chance to reject or accept an idea enables children to understand that they are responsible for their own learning and create their own ideas as they speak, listen and think with others.

■ *Whole-class closing plenary sessions* require dialogue that brings together the children's ideas from their group work linked into a coherent line of thinking. The teacher's role is to ensure that there is plenty time for talk, and to orchestrate the dialogue. In addition, there is often the necessity for some authoritative summary information. Dialogic teaching can be thought of as including episodes of talk and episodes of authoritative teacher input, which will later contribute to further dialogue. Plenary discussion should bring out children's thinking about new concepts, and also about the quality of the talk that took place in their group work. They can suggest who offered ideas, listened, asked an important question, and so on.

Task 3.5.1 **CHILDREN'S CLASSROOM TALK**

Listen carefully to children's classroom talk in two contexts – a whole class in discussion with the teacher; a small group discussion with no adult support. Ask yourself questions about the purpose, organisation and outcomes of the talk.

■ *Purpose*: What is the purpose of the talk? Is everyone aware of this purpose? Is the talk fulfilling its purpose?

■ *Organisation*: Who is organising the talk? How do people bid for turns? Who gets a turn and why? What happens to people who do not get a turn? Is any of the talk to do with behaviour management? Does the talk always stay on task?

■ *Outcomes*: What are the outcomes of the talk? What have different individuals learned about (1) the topic under discussion; (2) their position in the classroom; (3) how to communicate effectively with others?

RAISING CHILDREN'S AWARENESS OF TALK FOR LEARNING

Organising effective talk involves raising children's awareness of the power of spoken language. We must clarify the expectation that every child will contribute to the learning of others through sharing their thoughts. Some children may never have imagined that this is the case. Others may have a very good idea of why we ask them to contribute, but may find themselves unable to do so when faced with social pressures exerted on them – it is not easy to think aloud if you are at risk of being labelled 'teacher's pet'.

Episodes of dialogue contribute to awareness-raising, because we can model the sort of structures that make talk educationally effective. The phrases we use in whole-class talk, such as 'What do you think?' or 'Can you say a bit more about . . .?', are what we want children to say to each other. Encouraging someone to keep talking, making links between contributions, rephrasing and summing up are all skills children learn from experience, especially if they happen often and are explicitly discussed as talk strategies.

When children are in discussion in small groups, the teacher cannot know what every child is saying. It can be difficult for them – children in a group may bicker or simply ignore one another; they may feel that helping others is not helping their own learning, or that others are 'cheating' if they want to talk about their answers. It is instructive to ask children what they think of group work.

If we are honest, we know that group work can go wrong. The classroom becomes too noisy or little learning seems to be happening. But we know that talk is essential for learning. This is a real paradox and a problem for every teacher. We want to ensure effective group talk, because what is the alternative? We must insist on quiet. The command 'Stop talking!' immediately confines each child to their own thoughts . . . an uneasy silence reigns. Silence is a behaviour management strategy and not always conducive to developing minds. No doubt quiet has some value, but not if it is overused, and not when a child is trying to puzzle something out, explain something, use a recently heard word, ask a question or find out a missing piece of information. And silence cannot guarantee that children are thinking and learning about the topic in hand.

So, it is necessary to teach children 'talk lessons' – that is, children benefit from direct teaching about exploratory talk. We need to make explicit the usually hidden 'ground rules' that keep a discussion on track (Dawes, 2008).

What talk skills are needed? Simply put, children need to:

■ listen;
■ stay on task;
■ include everyone;
■ know how to challenge one another;
■ always respect contributions;
■ ask questions;
■ elaborate on what they hear;
■ offer their ideas with reasons.

This list of eight crucial skills can be used to devise lessons to focus on each skill in turn. There are plenty of contexts for talk in curriculum areas. Plenary discussions about the effectiveness of talk can help children to build up an awareness of their ability to contribute to one another's learning, and can help groups to establish an ethos of exploratory talk. Note that the child's own 'voice' (their accent, bilingualism, vocabulary and dialect) is valued, not diminished, by learning this further extension to their talk repertoire.

We can discuss and model relevant talk skills during introductory sessions, identify them as learning intentions, and review them during plenary sessions so that children can evaluate the difference good talk makes. Children need constant chances to reflect on what they have said and heard in order to examine what they have learned, and how, and who from. They need opportunities to identify particular talk episodes that helped them to understand, or caught their imagination, or made them feel puzzled. They need to acknowledge who it is that has contributed orally. It has to be made clear to children that knowledge and understanding are not simply contained in the teacher, computers or books, but in the class as a whole, and that, by talking and thinking together, such understandings can be profitably shared. They can usefully learn the term 'interthinking' – thinking aloud together – as a description of the spoken mechanism for creating joint understandings.

Task 3.5.2 **UNDERSTANDING INTERTHINKING**

Read 'Learning to think together and alone', in Mercer and Littleton (2007) *Dialogue and the Development of Children's Thinking*, pp. 55–82. Discuss with colleagues the value and purpose of interthinking and strategies for enabling children to talk about talk and their own thinking in school. How might you as the teacher model this?

Without shared ground rules, children in an unsupervised group will generally talk as they would in the playground or at home. Children unused to thinking that what they say is important are almost bound to misunderstand what we mean when we ask them to 'Talk about this with your group . . .' Indeed, they may believe that, if they talk about their work, they have somehow 'sold out'. For the child who wishes to talk about the task, the barriers may be insurmountable as more and more lures to join in with off-task conversation are thrown out. A group of children arguing about what happened at break time or discussing last night's television programmes instead of talking about the activity they are engaged in might not seem very unusual. After all, some talk has to be casual to act as a sort of social glue. But it is actually very worrying. If every chance to talk is a chance to forget about school work, children are unknowingly rejecting a major part of their learning throughout their primary years. This is unfair to them, especially since those most vulnerable to failure in the education system may well be those frittering away their time in class in superficial chatter.

Organising effective classroom talk requires planning – planning for the teaching of exploratory talk; planning for the creation of time to develop and consider ideas through dialogue;

Task 3.5.3 **CHILDREN'S RULES FOR CLASSROOM TALK**

Work with a group of three or four children. Ask them to discuss their ideas with you.

■ When they are working in a group with classmates, who do they like to work with and why? Who helps them to learn? Who stops them learning? What do they like or dislike about working in a group with other children? Why do they think that teachers ask them to work in groups?

■ Ask the children to suggest a list of five or six 'rules', which, if applied, would help a group to work well together. (Try to persuade them not to start these with the word 'Don't!) Compare their suggestions with the ground rules for exploratory talk in Table 3.5.2.

■ Have the same discussion with other groups, or with the whole class. Collate ideas to establish a class set of ground rules for exploratory talk. Check that everyone agrees with the rules and will try to follow them. Devise an activity that requires group discussion and ask the children to try to apply their rules. Evaluate the talk; did the rules help everyone to join in and share ideas? If not, can the class alter them?

and planning for group talk in which children can make the most of the opportunity to interthink. Of course, children do need to work individually sometimes. But sometimes the chance to discuss resources, ideas and problems can promote the sort of collaborative learning that is the advantage of being part of a class.

INTEGRATING SPEAKING AND LISTENING INTO THE PRIMARY CURRICULUM

The Speaking and Listening sections of the Literacy Strategy provide a structure for integrating effective talk into classroom activities.

Here, Year 4 is used as an example; objectives are available for Foundation Stage to Year 6 (www.standards.dfes.gov.uk/primaryframework/literacy, click 'Learning objectives' and you will be asked to specify a year group).

The following are some of the Year 4 learning objectives for Speaking, Listening and responding, and Group discussion and interaction:

- *Year 4 Speaking*
  Offer reasons and evidence for their views, considering alternative opinions.
  Respond appropriately to the contributions of others in the light of differing viewpoints.
  Use and reflect on some ground rules for sustaining talk and interactions.
- *Year 4 Listening and responding*
  Listen to a speaker, make notes on the talk and use notes to develop a role-play.
- *Year 4 Group discussion and interaction*
  Identify the main points of each speaker; compare their arguments and how they are presented.

We might assume that children will develop such talk skills and capacities as they work through curriculum activities. But direct tuition is essential. With the objectives as a structure, we can teach dedicated talk lessons that help children to develop the awareness of speaking and listening that might otherwise remain tacit. Having done this, we can then use the speaking and listening learning objectives during lessons in every other area of the curriculum, so that the talk skills are immediately put to use and their effectiveness made apparent.

Below is a brief example of this process. You will note that the objectives have been clustered and modified to suit this particular class, as you would do for your own class. In these examples, science is a context for the talk – talk has to have some context. Any curriculum area would do as well.

Example 1: Talk lesson, Year 4

(Context: Science 2: Different animals in different habitats)

LEARNING OBJECTIVES

To be able to:

- offer reasons and evidence for views, considering alternative opinions;
- listen to a speaker, making (mental) notes on the talk;
- identify the main points of each speaker; compare their arguments and how they are presented.

INTRODUCTION

Explain that the lesson is about speaking and listening as a good way of learning. Share learning objectives. Ask the children to use a dictionary and each other's ideas to find out and be able to explain what these words mean:

> reason   evidence   opinion   negotiate   articulate   discussion

Share what the children find out. Focus the class on using talk to discuss their ideas, respecting other points of view and negotiating agreement.

GROUP WORK

Spend a few minutes finding out everything the class already knows about hedgehogs. Provide and read these contradictory statements:

■   We need hedgehogs in our countryside.
■   It does not matter if hedgehogs become extinct.

Provide post-its. Ask children in their groups to think of three *reasons* to support each statement and to write each of their ideas on a separate post-it.

Once they have done this, decide on a group opinion with reasons for this decision.

WHOLE-CLASS DISCUSSION

Focus the children on active listening and ask them to try to remember something that they think particularly interesting as they listen to the class discussion.

Invite groups to provide their group opinion and reason. Once all opinions have been heard, ask children to comment on one another's ideas, using positive language and challenging others using the talk tool: 'I disagree because . . .'. Chain the discussion into coherent lines of thinking. Encourage children to nominate who they want to hear from next, and encourage children to take extended turns when talking. Sum up, or ask a child to sum up, the outcome of the discussion.

Collect up the post-its and display with the statements.

PLENARY

Ask children to reflect, recall and share examples of productive talk; who gave an *opinion* and what was their *reason*? How did your group *negotiate* ideas with another group? What were *key points* of the discussion? Can anyone offer to *compare* the ideas they heard? Who would you describe as *articulate*? Do you consider the class to have had a *productive discussion*? How do you know? What have we learned about *talk for learning*? What is important about talk for learning? How does it help us to *think*? In what ways is it difficult? How can we get round the problems to make sure that classroom talk helps us all to think and learn?

Provide resources and create hedgehog learning logs to continue the science learning.

Example 2: Science lesson, Year 4

LEARNING OBJECTIVES

To be able to:

- ■ offer reasons and evidence for views, considering alternative opinions;
- ■ listen to a speaker, making (mental) notes on the talk;
- ■ identify some starting ideas about the Science 4 topic of Friction.

INTRODUCTION

Share learning objectives, asking children to recall their ideas about the importance of talk for learning and how it might best proceed.

Ask the children to think about friction (give a brief example by rubbing hands); explain that we need to find out what everyone already knows so that it can be shared.

GROUP WORK

Ask groups to discuss the following *talking points* (Dawes, 2008) to decide whether their group thinks they are true or false; or are they unsure. Remind the groups of the importance of asking everyone for ideas, opinions and reasons. No writing should happen at this point.

TALKING POINTS: FRICTION

Are these statements true, false, or is your group unsure?

1   Grip is another word for friction.
2   Friction always happens when surfaces are moving against each other.
3   Friction is usually a nuisance.
4   Trainers have friction built into the soles.
5   You can't stop friction happening.
6   Bikes work because of friction.
7   Friction is a force.
8   Air resistance, which makes parachutes work, is a sort of friction.
9   There is no friction on the moon.
10 You can't slide on a carpet because of friction.

PLENARY

1   *Science*: Ask groups to contribute ideas about friction, especially if their group was unsure. Remind them that *uncertainty* is helpful because it is a way for everyone to learn. What were contradictory opinions? Ask groups to explain their ideas with reasons, noting who is providing the information.

2   *Speaking and listening*: Ask the class to suggest classmates who offered ideas, listened well, gave good reasons, summed up discussions and helped negotiation. Ask the same questions about talk as in the talk lesson. Help the children to understand that you have, as yet, done no teaching about friction; but that they have learned by sharing their understanding through speaking and listening.

Suggestions for further work using Speaking and Listening objectives

■ Identify and use specific speaking and listening objectives in curriculum lessons.

■ Choose one particular objective, teach it directly, then integrate it throughout a week.

■ Ask children to identify their particular problems with speaking and listening in class.

■ Make the link between speaking, listening, thinking and learning explicit at all times.

■ Encourage children to see that learning cannot happen unless certain sorts of speaking and listening go on – and unless voices are modulated, contributions thoughtful, and everyone in the class is included in discussions.

■ Create a 'speaking and listening for thinking and learning' display.

Task 3.5.4 **TALK FOR LEARNING**

■ Decide on a year group which interests you.

■ Look at the speaking, listening and group work learning objectives on the Standards website (www.standards.dfes.gov.uk/primaryframework/literacy). Choose one or two objectives and devise a talk lesson as in Example 1. You will need to think of a relevant context for talk, but keep the lesson focused on the talk, not the context!

■ Now choose a curriculum area, and devise a lesson that incorporates the skills and understanding from the talk lesson. Record your plenary questions, which will enable children to reflect on talk for learning, and to value one another's contribution to their learning.

■ Teach the lessons and evaluate them. Ask the children for their comments.

SUMMARY

We cannot just leave classroom talk to chance. Children arrive in our classrooms knowing how to talk, but may not have particularly considered the specialised sort of talk so important for classroom learning. Talk is such an everyday medium that children may take it for granted, not knowing that they can learn as much about talk as they do about reading and writing in classrooms. Talk can be so bound up with classroom behaviour that its crucial function of stimulating and developing thinking may be unclear to children.

Dialogic teaching is a means to move whole classes through steps of reasoning, hypothesis and deduction, by valuing contributions and encouraging reflection. And by teaching children how to engage one another in exploratory talk, we offer them a powerful means to work on their own thinking and that of others. Exploratory talk is educationally effective talk – talk for learning – and children need an awareness of that. The everyday occurrence of talk for learning can only happen if we organise classrooms by planning time for talk; ensuring that resources and activities merit discussion; and teaching the children how to talk to one another. The Speaking and Listening objectives of the Literacy Strategy provide a structure for integrating talk throughout curriculum learning. This can only happen once children are really aware of the importance of talk for learning. Effective teachers move between different types of talk as the lesson proceeds.

Engaging children in talk for learning helps teachers to develop effective classroom relationships. Talking about what they are doing with their group helps to motivate children and focus their interest. The busy hum of a classroom in which children are discussing their work – a sure sign of a well-organised teacher – is a happy feature of effective primary schools. Teachers want to hear children talking; it is an indication of learning, and a sign that children are practising the talk skills that will support their development throughout their education.

ANNOTATED FURTHER READING

Alexander, R. (2006) *Towards Dialogic Teaching*, York: Dialogos.
A short pamphlet-like text that offers practical support and sound advice about dialogic teaching.

Mercer, N. and Littleton, K. (2007) Dialogue and the Development of Children's Thinking: A Sociocultural Approach, London: Routledge.
An accessible and richly documented text that argues for the importance of spoken dialogue in children's intellectual development.

Rojas-Drummond, S. and Mercer, N. (2004) 'Scaffolding the development of effective collaboration and learning', *International Journal of Educational Research*, 39: 99–111.
A detailed research report that demonstrates the value of scaffolding learning through talk.

RELEVANT WEBSITES

The Speaking and Listening sections of the Literacy Strategy provide a structure for integrating effective talk into classroom activities. Objectives are available for Foundation Stage to Year 6:

www.standards.dfes.gov.uk/primaryframework/literacy
Click 'Learning objectives' and you will be asked to specify a year group.

Year 4 Science: Habitats: www.standards.dfes.gov.uk/schemes2/science/sci4b/sci4bq3?view=get

Year 4 Science: Friction: www.standards.dfes.gov.uk/schemes2/science/sci4e/sci4eq4?view=get

Visit the companion website www.routledge.com/textbooks/ltps2e for:

■ links to useful websites relevant to this unit.

REFERENCES

Alexander, R. (2006) *Towards Dialogic Teaching*, York: Dialogos.
Daniels, H. (2001) *Vygotsky and Pedagogy*, London: RoutledgeFalmer.
Dawes, L. (2008) 'Are these useful rules for discussion?'. Available online at http://thinkingtogether. educ.cam.ac.uk/resources/Are_these_useful_rules_for_discussion.pdf (accessed November 2009).
Dawes, L. and Sams, C. (2004) *Talk Box: Speaking and Listening Activities for Learning at Key Stage 1*, London: David Fulton.
Dawes, L., Mercer, N. and Wegerif, R. (2003) *Thinking Together: A Programme of Activities for Developing Speaking, Listening and Thinking Skills for Children aged 8–11*, Birmingham: Imaginative Minds.
Mercer, N. and Littleton, K. (2007) *Dialogue and the Development of Children's Thinking: A Sociocultural Approach*, London: Routledge.
Rose, J. (2009) *Independent Review of the Primary Curriculum: Final Report*, London: DCSF. Available online at www.dcsf.gov.uk/primarycurriculumreview (accessed May 2009).
Scott, P.H. and Asoko, H. (2006) 'Talk in science classrooms', in V. Wood-Robinson (ed.) *Association of Science Education Guide to Secondary Science Education*, Hatfield: Association for Science Education (ASE).

ORGANISING AND MANAGING LEARNING OUTSIDE THE CLASSROOM

Simon Catling

INTRODUCTION

Opportunities for learning outside the classroom are highly valued. Almost every primary school child studies in the school grounds on various occasions across different subjects during the year. Annually, several million off-site primary pupil visits take place. Providing experience for young children to learn through activities in the real world is important to primary teachers. The government's *Learning Outside the Classroom Manifesto* (DfES, 2006) has endorsed and emphasised the value and importance of extending children's learning into the school's grounds, the local environment and further afield. It supports a number of the aspects and expectations of the *Every Child Matters* strategy, including staying safe, enjoying and achieving, and economic well-being (Ofsted, 2008). Learning outside the classroom builds on the vital and engaging experiences initiated through work in the outdoor learning environment in the Foundation Stage (Parker, 2008; White, 2008).

OBJECTIVES

By the end of this unit you should be able to:

■ appreciate the value and benefits of out-of-classroom learning;
■ identify opportunities in your own planning and teaching where you can use out-of-classroom learning;
■ plan effectively for out-of-classroom learning.

These objectives reflect the requirements in the *Professional Standards* for trainee teachers, particularly in relation to planning for out-of-classroom work (standard Q24) and 'establishing a purposeful and safe learning environment conducive to learning' in such contexts (standard Q30) (TDA, 2007).

Case study 1

Jenni's Year 2 class are in the school grounds. As part of a springtime cross-subject project on growth and change in nature, she is using observational work in art. The children are using pencils, chalk or charcoal to make sketches of plants and buds. They are taking digital photographs, and will follow up this work by creating colour paintings from their sketches and photographs. Jenni argues that using such opportunities in their well-established school grounds enhances the children's learning through close observation, working *in situ* and showing care for the environment rather than bringing natural items into class, and challenging them to use good-quality resources from a young age. She says these challenges enable the children to concentrate and focus their interest.

Case study 2

Phil's class is in the local high street, doing fieldwork for their local geography study. Working with teaching assistants and parents, the Year 5 children are examining how well the local council, shops and other businesses have provided access for those with disabilities or infirmities. The children are mapping the accessibility of doorways, the help or hindrances of street furniture, and so forth, and using a rating scale to judge the quality of access. They work in groups, with a designated area to map. They are taking digital photographs of good and poor examples they see, to be used later in a display showing their findings and outlining their proposals for action. The children partly planned this fieldwork, which included developing awareness of the risks of undertaking studies along a street that many of them knew well. During his risk assessment Phil took photographs to show the children, so they could discuss potential hazards and how they would safely undertake their tasks. Phil uses sites outside school because he feels that, for geography, science and history, it is vital to go into the real world that these subjects are about. He argues that children can 'see further' by going outside because such fieldwork extends their observations in a disciplined and 'disciplinary' way.

Task 3.6.1 OUT-OF-CLASSROOM LEARNING

Consider your own experience of studying outside, whether with a class and teacher before or during your course, or as a primary or secondary school student.

■ Describe an activity you did, where you did it, and for how long.
■ List what you think you were intended to learn.
■ Reflect on what you feel you really learned from this out-of-class activity.

THE VALUE OF OUT-OF-CLASSROOM LEARNING

The essence of learning outside the classroom is the opportunity for 'first-hand experiences . . . to make subjects more vivid and interesting for pupils and enhance their understanding' (Ofsted, 2008: 7). Learning outside the classroom environment is a core dynamic in children's learning experience. There is strong support for the view that learning outside the classroom is vital for all children, adding value to their classroom experiences; that, well planned and taught, such learning enhances children's knowledge, understanding and skills across subjects; and that it fosters children's motivation, self-confidence and interpersonal learning (House of Commons Education and Skills Committee, 2005; DfES, 2006; O'Donnell *et al.*, 2006; Real World Learning Campaign, 2006; Council for Learning Outside the Classroom, 2008; Malone, 2008; Ofsted, 2008; Stagg *et al.*, 2009). While clear arguments have been made for the value of younger children's learning in the school grounds and off-site, there remains limited *research* into its benefits. Reviewing studies into the impact of fieldwork, visits off-site, working in the school grounds and outdoor adventure activities, Rickinson *et al.* (2004) drew several tentative conclusions (Figure 3.6.1), supported by Malone (2008).

Rickinson *et al.* (2004) examined the opportunities and gains that out-of-classroom learning offers, as have others (e.g. Braund and Reiss, 2004; Scoffham, 2004; Nundy, 2006; O'Donnell *et al.*, 2006; Council for Learning Outside the Classroom, 2008; Hoodless, 2008; Malone, 2008; Ofsted, 2008). Drawing on these studies we can identify various *foci* for learning outside alongside the *benefits* of such studies (Figure 3.6.2). You should note that the foci and benefits refer to cognitive outcomes, values and attitudes, *and* personal and interpersonal learning. We can also recognise the variety of *sites* that might be used (Figure 3.6.3).

The aims and value of out-of-classroom learning are:

- providing experiential and active learning in the environment;
- motivating children through novel, stimulating and enjoyable experiences;
- initiating or extending enquiry skills through 'real world' investigations;
- developing observational, recording and analytic skills *in situ*;
- developing knowledge and understanding in a 'real world' context;
- encouraging and enabling children to work cooperatively and develop relationships;
- fostering a 'feel' for the environment, through examining values and attitudes;
- building children's self-esteem and self-confidence through first-hand engagement and involvement in learning.

Inevitably, there are challenges in undertaking out-of-classroom activities. Figure 3.6.4 indicates some of these. Such challenges need to be resolved when organising working outside the

---

- Off-site fieldtrips are often memorable for children, even into adulthood.
- Younger children seem well motivated when working outside the classroom.
- For many children out-of-classroom activities enhance their knowledge and understanding of the topic(s) studied.
- Where children undertake environmental studies and/or become involved in school-based 'green initiatives' over time using the school grounds and/or off-site, their knowledge, understanding and valuing of the environment develops positively, enhancing their sense of environmental responsibility.
- Fieldtrips to particular sites may enhance children's positive attitudes to that site/area.
- Younger children's social and interpersonal skills can improve through ecological and field studies, particularly where they engage in collaborative tasks requiring cooperation, perseverance, initiative, reliability and leadership qualities; these tasks can also enhance children's self-esteem and self-confidence, supporting their emotional well-being.
- Children's involvement in school grounds 'greening' activities may have an overall positive impact on their general cognitive achievement.

■ **Figure 3.6.1** The impact of out-of-classroom learning on younger children

Examples of *foci* for out-of-classroom learning, about:

■ the natural environment, e.g. the school 'wild area';

■ human settlements, e.g. a local village or urban area study;

■ community activities, e.g. bulb planting in green spaces;

■ nature–society interactions, e.g. visits to nature reserves;

■ environmental issues, e.g. contentious planning proposals and developments;

■ oneself, e.g. in making a residential visit with peers for the first time;

■ others, e.g. through working together on small-group fieldwork tasks;

■ new skills, e.g. using quadrants, learned through activities led by field centre staff.

Examples of *benefits* resulting from out-of-classroom learning:

■ greater understanding of enquiry-based research, e.g. from investigating stream flow, erosion, transportation and deposition;

■ greater information about the local environment, e.g. through recognising historical features;

■ increased knowledge and understanding of geographical processes, e.g. people's use of shops;

■ recognition of personal values and feelings, e.g. in relation to your neighbourhood;

■ fostering attitudes to the future of an environment, e.g. a relic woodland, or to one's personal treatment of the environment;

■ developing new or improved skills, e.g. in orienteering and communication;

■ developing or reinforcing positive behaviours, e.g. in taking care not to leave litter or in working with others in community activities;

■ personal development, e.g. in building self-confidence through completing new challenges;

■ developing interpersonal skills and relationships, e.g. through team working on an outdoor project.

■ **Figure 3.6.2** Opportunities provided by learning outside the classroom

classroom. You need to remember that risk assessments and health and safety regulations are for your security as a teacher as well as for the children's safety. Planning out-of-classroom learning requires understanding the benefits such opportunities provide and finding ways to overcome the potential difficulties considerately and safely. Appreciating the value of out-of-classroom learning sets a positive basis for achieving this.

In a review of out-of-classroom learning across the primary and secondary sectors, Ofsted (2008) identified a number of elements enabling the achievement of good practice. These included:

■ An evident commitment to out-of-classroom learning in a school's leadership and policy, as a clear contribution to a broad, balanced and stimulating curriculum, and linked to a strong, even passionate, sense of common purpose among staff.

■ The use of learning outside the classroom as vital to motivating learners and to improving their progress and achievements, as well as raising their aspirations.

■ Use of the school's grounds and the local area, complemented by visits to other sites, as integral to all curriculum subjects and approaches.

■ Building on approaches within the Foundation Stage, developing a flexibility of movement between internal and external learning environments, such that children sense that these are natural and normal environments for learning.

The range of possible out-of-classroom *sites* that can be used to support, develop and motivate learning include:

- ■ the school grounds, play areas, habitats, equipment, gardens;
- ■ the built environment: suburban/urban areas around school, local streets, park, local shops, new developments;
- ■ the built environment: suburban/urban areas in contrasting localities;
- ■ the rural environment: landscapes, farmland, villages/hamlets;
- ■ wilderness areas;
- ■ rivers, streams, ponds, lakes, canals, waterfalls;
- ■ rural or city farms, botanic gardens;
- ■ parks, allotments, gardens;
- ■ industrial sites, waste disposal sites, reservoirs;
- ■ heritage sites, castles, historic houses and gardens;
- ■ museums, science centres, National Park centres, zoos;
- ■ field study centres, nature study centres, urban studies centres, science centres;
- ■ theatres, drama and dance workshops, art galleries;
- ■ planning offices, old people's homes, community centres;
- ■ shopping centres/malls, supermarkets;
- ■ libraries, local history and archive centres;
- ■ town halls, civic centres, tourist information centres;
- ■ sacred sites, places of worship.

■ **Figure 3.6.3** Possible sites for out-of-classroom activities

- ■ Working out of the classroom for differing periods of time, from a few minutes to half and whole days and on residential visits lasting overnight to a week or longer.
- ■ Making use of providers and sites for off-school learning, such as urban and field centres, museums, heritage sites, nature reserves, supermarkets and other businesses, the theatre and concert hall, rural and city farms, places of worship and places of cultural interest.
- ■ Clear organisation of the visit, with well-planned pre- and post-development in relation to the project or topic being studied, effectively resourced, such that all the children and adults are well acquainted with the purpose of the visit, preferably having been involved in aspects of its planning and organisation.
- ■ Approaches, organisation and activities that were inclusive of all children and planned appropriately to their needs.
- ■ An evaluation of the visit undertaken, considering benefits and limitations, what was learned that could be applied in future and what the learning gains were from the visit and activities for the children and the staff.

ORGANISING FOR LEARNING OUTSIDE THE CLASSROOM

This section discusses matters you need to consider, organise for and manage when working with children outside the classroom (DfES, 1998; Kimber and Smith, 1999; Braund and Reiss, 2004; Richardson, 2004; Council for Learning Outside the Classroom, 2008; Hoodless, 2008; McCreery *et al.*, 2008; Ofsted, 2008; Catling and Willy, 2009; Hoodless *et al.*, 2006; Stagg *et al.*, 2009).

Challenges	Possible concerns
Time	Organising out-of-classroom activities requires time and forethought, whether going into the school grounds, the neighbourhood or a distant locality. It may require rearranging the timetable.
Resources	Visits to museums and similar venues involve costs that may need to be obtained from parents. Taking children outside involves organising other adult support, and informing them about the activities they will supervise. Time is needed to walk to nearby sites, and public or private transport bookings must be made in advance. There is also overseeing the children on the bus/coach, having sick bags, etc. to consider.
Safety and health concerns	You must be fully acquainted with the school's and local authority's guidance on health and safety and follow procedures. Teachers and parents have heightened concerns about how safe children will be, whether from traffic, walking, farm visits, etc.
Personal confidence in taking children out	Taking children out requires confidence. Going into the school grounds, locally or further afield, means knowing what these places are like, what can be studied and how safely, and setting suitable challenges in the children's tasks.
Managing the children	A frequent concern is managing children's behaviour outside the classroom. It is vital that you are well prepared and that the children understand what is required of them. They need to understand the tasks they will do, perhaps because they have been involved in creating them. You need to be consistent with your classroom expectations, and the adults with you must know these and be consistent too. Ensure the children know how they must respond when you or their group adult wants their attention while out of the classroom.
Risk assessment	You must undertake a risk assessment of a potential, even familiar, site. Making judgements about risks involves taking responsibility for decisions about the possible hazards and ways to overcome them.
Regulations and requirements	The number of forms to complete and the regulations to check can be numerous when you take children off the school site. It involves obtaining permission from the head teacher/governors *and* possibly from someone in the local authority. Be organised well in advance.

■ **Figure 3.6.4** Possible challenges to out-of-classroom learning opportunities

Deciding why to go out of the classroom

First, you must consider *why* you might take the children out of the classroom for teaching and learning activities. As with all activities, this is about what you want the children to learn and why using the school grounds or going off-site will enhance and extend the children's learning. You need to consider the following questions:

■ How will working outside/off-site meet your *learning objectives/outcomes*?
■ Where does it fit into the *sequence* of activities planned for the study topic?

Task 3.6.2 **TAKING CHILDREN OUT OF THE CLASSROOM**

Using your own experience (see Task 3.6.1) and the information in Figures 3.6.1, 3.6.2, 3.6.3 and 3.6.4:

■ Give your reasons for including out-of-classroom activities in your teaching. What do you really want the children to learn from working outside the classroom, in the school grounds, locally and beyond? Consider how such benefits link across the curriculum.

■ Choose an out-of-classroom activity you might want to do and outline the benefits for the children for whom you would plan it. Note the challenges that you need to overcome and how you might achieve this.

Extending your analysis

■ Use the Ofsted (2008) evaluation of *Learning Outside the Classroom* to review the benefits and challenges you have noted. What further opportunities and barriers for schools and classes are noted? How is it suggested these can be overcome?

Task 3.6.3 **CRITIQUE THE VALUE OF OUT-OF-CLASSROOM LEARNING**

Malone's (2008) review of learning outside the classroom was structured around the 'domains' of children's cognitive learning, physical experiences, social interactions, emotional well-being and personal responses. She argued that it affects children's whole development. Knight (2009), focusing on the Forest Schools movement, implicitly notes the same domains but reflects also that outdoor learning benefits behaviour as well as relates to curiosity and creativity, and language and communication.

■ Explain how the points made in the section above illustrate these 'domains'.
■ What needs to be added, and why?
■ How might a critique be offered of the value of out-of-classroom learning?
■ What counter-balances are there to its benefits?

■ How does it contribute to the focus of study *at that time*?
■ What *relevant children's experience* does it draw on or develop? Or does it provide new experiences?

Deciding where to take the children

Having decided to provide learning out of the classroom, you must consider *where* you will take the children. You may look at a particular area or features in the school grounds for a science investigation; you might take the children into the local area as part of an enquiry they have planned; you could involve the children in an historical re-enactment at a country house, working with its education staff. In each case you need to have answered the following questions:

■ Where is the most appropriate *location/site/centre* to take the children for the learning you are planning?

■ Is it possible to take the children there *when* you want to (visits to centres, zoos, museums, etc. need booking *well* in advance)?

■ What *alternative sites* are there (if you cannot get your first choice)?

Meeting the school's policies for taking children outside

Before undertaking work outside, you must check who is responsible for giving permission (usually the head teacher) and what the school's policy is. Primary schools have policies for off-site visits and health and safety matters. Figure 3.6.5 indicates what you should find in a *School Visits* policy. This policy states how the school complies with government and local authority regulations for such visits (DfES, 1998), and gives the particular requirements the school has added that are relevant to its particular circumstances, for instance about what happens for a child unable to accompany a visit off-site. It will also cover safety matters if these are not cross-referenced to a separate policy.

Working in the school grounds means complying with good practice and common sense approaches to planning and organising your classroom teaching and to managing behaviour. The school will have a view on the support of other adults to work with you. You will need to check this if there is no statement in the School Visits policy.

When taking the children off-site for activities, for however long, there are organisational matters to check (Council for Learning Outside the Classroom, 2008; Stagg *et al.*, 2009). Use the *checklist* in Figure 3.6.6, particularly for when you are planning a visit to a site some distance away and need to travel by public transport or coach.

Checking the site

When you take the children into the school's grounds, you must check that the sites you use are appropriate and accessible. You should check if other staff intend to take children outside when you plan to. Do this properly in advance, not just in the playtime before you go out (when you might double-check).

If you plan to undertake fieldwork or a visit off-site, you must make a *reconnaissance* visit to the location first, whether it is a local site, a museum, a religious building, a field centre or

---

A School Visits policy should tell you about:

■ the value of working outside and off-site;

■ ways in which off-site studies support work across the curriculum;

■ possible sites and locations for working, e.g. in the grounds, off-site locally or at more distant locations, and about centres to visit;

■ local authority and school regulations and organisational requirements, such as permission forms, adult:pupil ratios, health and safety matters, letters to parents, etc.;

■ making site visits and undertaking risk assessment;

■ fieldwork resources;

■ countryside and urban codes for environmental care.

■ **Figure 3.6.5** Elements in a School Visits policy

An editable version of Figure 3.6.6 is available on the companion website: www.routledge.com/textbooks/ltps2e

Checklist items	Date started	Date completed
1 Check School Visits policy for off-site visits, including health and safety		
2 Identify reasons and objectives for working off-site		
3 Obtain permission from head teacher/governors/local authority		
4 Select location(s) for visit		
5 Check date(s)		
6 Undertake site visit and complete school risk assessment forms or obtain and review the site's own risk assessment for visiting parties		
7 Book visit with those who run the site/centre		
8 Book transport and check timings (as required)		
9 Collect contributions (if required) and keep accounts		
10 Write to parents about visit and request signed permission slips (unless already covered by school's approach)		
11 Introduce visit, purpose and activities to children; involve children in planning aspects of their work		
12 Ensure site staff know about any particular needs for your party, such as access for wheelchair users and children with particular educational needs		
13 Brief teachers, teaching assistants and other adults; allocate responsibilities for children and roles in case of emergency		
14 Know emergency procedures; access mobile phone; leave lists of participants, route and contact points in school		
15 Have plans in place for contingencies, such as where to eat lunch if it is wet, or what to do with the children if the coach breaks down		
16 Ensure awareness of key locations at the visit site, such as where the toilets, meeting places and kiosk or shop are, and which places are to be 'out-of-bounds' or time limited		
17 Organise resources/equipment and responsibility for return		
18 Make payments (as needed)		
19 Write letters of thanks (from children/yourself)		
20 Evaluate visit; note modifications for future site use; with the children, review what has been learned and gather their views about the site		

■ **Figure 3.6.6** A checklist for planning off-site work

anywhere else, and must have completed or seen and checked a *risk assessment form*, if necessary. If you are visiting a managed site, such as a country house or nature reserve, it is likely that the education staff will have undertaken their own risk assessment for school parties; it is vital that you see and review this to ensure that all the matters you have noted on your visit, and that you are aware of concerning your children, are accounted for properly and safely. This is essential because you must establish such matters as:

■ the suitability of the site (does the museum have what you want the children to study?);
■ its safety (are the pavements wide enough?);
■ booking the education staff (what will they do; how will they work with the children at the field centre?);
■ the suitability of the facilities (accessible toilets, somewhere to eat, a place to shelter in rain?).

Where necessary, you should complete the school's risk assessment form. Figure 3.6.7 shows an example. If you are uncertain about how to judge the probability and severity of the risks, ask more experienced staff for help. You may find that there is a completed risk assessment form in school for your proposed site and that you are not required to complete a new one. You must still make a site visit; it is useful practice to undertake your own risk assessment and compare it with the school's or centre's own.

Use these questions to find out the school's approach to taking children out of the classroom:

■ What is the school's policy on out-of-classroom activities and off-site visits?
■ Do you need agreement to take children out of the classroom to work in the school grounds? If so, from whom?
■ From whom do you need permission to take children off-site, locally or further afield?
■ Who can help you make bookings for visits and help you ensure that you have met all the needs and requirements for organising visits?
■ What do you do to visit the site, check its suitability and availability, and complete a risk assessment form?

You should also ensure in your organisation for an off-site visit that you have planned for emergencies. A contingency plan might cover such possible events as rain at an outdoor site (are you aware of nearby shelter?) or not having been informed of a change of plan at the site, and unforeseen occurrences, such as when the minibus or coach breaks down on the journey or a child becomes ill (who takes responsibility for the child and what do they do?). While you are not expected to plan for all eventualities, those that might occur (such as rain: check the weather forecast) ought to be planned for. You should always have one or more alternative activities for use at the site if tasks planned prove to be inappropriate or are completed more speedily than anticipated. You should know who to contact if you need to leave the site earlier than expected or if you are delayed.

MANAGING LEARNING OUT OF THE CLASSROOM

Planning teaching and learning outside the classroom

Planning a teaching session out of the classroom requires the same level and quality of planning as for any lesson. It is important to consider your teaching approach and the types of activities that the children will do. Figure 3.6.8 outlines five teaching approaches used in out-of-classroom studies (Kimber and Smith, 1999). When deciding your approach, be clear about your purpose and the level of children's active learning involvement that you want. Consider the merits of each approach.

RISK ASSESSMENT FORM				
Visit site:				
RA undertaken by:				
Date:		Season for proposed visit:		
No. of persons on visit: Adults:			Pupils:	
Location (mark on map)	Possible safety/ health hazards	Risk probability	Risk severity	Precautions/actions to reduce/remove risk
Overall risk: Decision whether to visit:				
Signed by assessor:		Signed by head teacher: Date:		

Risk assessment guidance

Level of risk	Probability of happening	Severity of outcome
Low (L)	Not likely or vary rare occurrence	None or very slight, perhaps involving minor First Aid
Medium (M)	Possible but might happen only occasionally	Chance of injury occurring
High (H)	Likely to happen, possibly often	Possible hospitalisation, or causes fatality/disability

■ **Figure 3.6.7** A risk assessment form

An editable version of Figure 3.6.7 is available on the companion website:
www.routledge.com/textbooks/ltps2e

Task 3.6.4 **EXAMINING A SCHOOL'S OUT-OF-CLASSROOM/VISITS POLICY**

Obtain or read through a school's School Visits policy (and its Health and Safety policy) to see what it states about working with children outside the classroom and off-site. Use the information in Figure 3.6.5 (see page 166) as a guide. Check the guidance on permission, ratios, organisation and risk assessment. Make your own list of points to check in other School Visits policies.

Extending your analysis

Use the guidance on *Health and Safety of Pupils on Educational Visits* (DfES, 1998) and the *Out and About Guidance* (Council for Learning Outside the Classroom, 2008) to review and extend your understanding of the school's policy. See the following websites to find these documents:

www.teachernet.gov.uk/learningoutsidetheclassroom
www.lotc.org.uk/Out-and-about-guidance

Possible teaching approaches

Site investigation: children undertake observations, measurements and recording to find out information, e.g. about particular artefacts in a museum, the use of shops in a local street, or river flow.

Enquiry-based research: children engage in planning the studies they undertake, the focus of and approaches to investigations, and the recording and follow-up, e.g. researching how a particular site is managed, or using interview questions they devise to investigate the roles of people in a religious centre.

Problem solving: children tackle a particular problem identified at a site, e.g. evidence in relation to a particular event in the past, mapping an area, or identifying ways to improve a site.

Re-enactment: children use role-play or dramatic recreations of people's lives, probably in costume, from a time in the past or from elsewhere in the world. This requires orientation to the context at the start and debriefing at the end about what has been learned.

Guided walk: children are guided around a site, e.g. a museum or historic building or on an urban or rural trail, where particular features, etc. are pointed out or they observe and record on a worksheet.

▨ **Figure 3.6.8** Five teaching approaches used in out-of-classroom studies

It is important to lead into the fieldwork or visit lesson/day, not least to ensure that the children come appropriately dressed for the activities they will do. In an *enquiry-based research* approach the children will have been involved in planning some or all of their tasks. For their study of a wasteland site, they might have identified, with their teacher, the specific questions and topics they will pursue at the site, have agreed the teams to undertake the tasks, and have organised the way they will measure, evaluate the quality and describe the potential of the site, so that they can bring back useful information for analysis and future planning. This may have taken several lessons prior to the fieldwork.

The fieldwork or visit itself needs to be carefully planned, whether it lasts half an hour or much of the day. Figure 3.6.9 provides an example of a lesson plan. There may be more detail in this plan than you usually provide, but it is important to be thorough, since planning for work outside the classroom and off-site is done less frequently. This example includes some key points that need to be planned into the lesson. Look particularly at the lesson sequence.

When planning to take children out of the classroom, consider these questions:

■ What do you want them to learn?
■ How can and will you organise the lesson?
■ Have you borne in mind safety aspects?
■ Have you the adult support you need and how are you using it?
■ Have you planned for the time available?

Vital to the effectiveness of your lesson will be your use of resources for activities and recording information, perceptions and what is seen. You may well have developed a survey sheet or questionnaire with the children, who will need clipboards and spare pens or have taken art materials. However, information and communication technology (ICT) offers a number of possibilities here. For instance, the use of digital still and video cameras enables records of views, activities (from pond-dipping to interviews) and items of particular interest to be brought back to the classroom for further analysis and evaluation. Tape recorders provide another alternative to writing answers. The use of a laptop computer to make notes or link to portable sampling technologies, such as stream-flow metres, can be used by some children and adults. Simpler technologies, such as compasses, should always be to hand, but they might be supported by GPS (global positioning system) technologies. These technological records enable evidence to be revisited in a variety of ways in the classroom following a visit. However, their use needs to be planned for in advance.

Managing the children

Among the challenges to making the most of out-of-classroom learning opportunities is managing the children in what is usually a less familiar situation (see Figure 3.6.4 on page 164). You should take account of the points made about managing children's classroom behaviour and group work in Units 3.4 and 3.5. Essential to managing children in out-of-classroom learning are the following five elements:

■ Ensure that you are well informed about the site and its opportunities and constraints and have planned well for the work the children will undertake (see above).

An editable version of Figure 3.6.9 is available on the companion website: www.routledge.com/textbooks/ltps2e

Subject: Geography – local area study	**Children**: 26 – Year 5
Context and focus: What does street furniture tell us about the place it is in?	**Time/duration**: 2 hours 15 minutes

Learning outcomes – children will be able to:
- ■ identify different categories of street furniture;
- ■ record the location of the street furniture accurately on a large-scale map;
- ■ give reasons for their judgements about the purpose and usefulness of street furniture.

Background to the current lesson:
- ■ Fifth lesson in local study unit, first off-site.
- ■ Children have fieldwork experience in school grounds and off-site.
- ■ Have recorded on maps but not used quality ratings.

Risk assessment outcome: Overall accident risk low.
- ■ Wide pavements to sites and along streets selected.
- ■ Traffic less heavy at time of day.
- ■ Large open space to meet at the centre of area, toilets nearby.

Lesson sequence (introduction, main activity, conclusion):

Introduction (20 mins)

1 Check children understand purpose of fieldwork: annotate a local map for types of street furniture, rating for usefulness, using key and rating scale agreed.

2 Review, through discussion, variety of street furniture they expect to see: signs (directions, information), posts (traffic lights, lighting), advertising notices (hoardings, A-stands), furniture (seats, benches) and safety fixtures (bollards, railings).

3 Check children have maps, keys, rating scales, clipboards. Ensure partners paired up, children know adult overseen by (five groups) and understand how to undertake tasks. Check they know their survey area. Toilet check.

Main activity (1 hour 30 mins)

4 Go out as a class, each group with adult, walk to open space by bank (15 mins). Check all present. Groups/adults move to areas.

5 On each street, group identifies street furniture, maps, rates. Pairs state rating judgements; group agrees fair-quality rating, record. In turn, pairs take photographs of selected street furniture. Repeat for two streets (45 mins).

6 At set time, regroup at open space. Count children. Children list three points on back of map about: level of usefulness of street furniture observed (15 mins).

7 Return (15 mins).

Conclusion (25 mins)

8 Pairs check maps/notes, ensure legible, symbols and rating judgements clear.

9 Plenary: pairs comment on variety/usefulness of street furniture. Discuss purpose, value and environmental impact of street furniture.

Next lesson: Same groups share information, prepare maps, ratings, comments on judgements about usefulness of street furniture in area surveyed; prepare report on role, quality, effectiveness of street furniture surveyed; make proposals for changes (if needed).

Support/differentiation:

Two TAs, two parent helpers responsible for groups of four children. Children in mixed pairs. Two children (slow at recording) with same TA. Two children (concentration and behaviour support) with me. Two children (ESL) with TA.

Assessment opportunities (observed by adults):
- ■ Do children identify a variety of street furniture types (using categories)?
- ■ Do children mark locations accurately on map (recording)?
- ■ Can children give reasons for some ratings (making judgements)?

Resources:	**Cross-curricular links**:
■ A4 map: survey streets; ■ street furniture key, rating key; ■ clipboards, digital cameras.	■ literacy – speaking and listening; ■ thinking skills – making judgements.

■ **Figure 3.6.9** An example of a fieldwork lesson plan

■ Use the expectations, standards and routines you have established with the class, so that the children know that there is consistency expected in the ways they work and behave in any learning and teaching environment with those in their classroom. If teaching staff and other adults at a centre will be working with the children, know about their ways of working and tell them about your expectations of the children.

■ Ensure that the children have been involved in the preparation for the work outside the classroom, whether it is only for a short while in the school's grounds or the local area or for a full day's visit to another location, such as a museum, field centre or nature reserve. This gives them much greater 'ownership' of the tasks and increases the likelihood that they will be focused and engaged.

■ Ensure that the other adults working with the children know and maintain the expectations and standards and are properly briefed on and understand the tasks and what is required of the children. If you have children with particular needs who may find working outside the classroom rather unfamiliar, challenging or even threatening, and whom you wish to monitor and support to keep on task, plan for the adults they will work with and vary the tasks to meet their needs.

■ Be clear to the children about the organisation of the work out of the classroom, so that they know when they are expected to listen and follow what they are asked to do, who to go to and what to do in an emergency (such as an urgent toilet need), and the timings of their activities, such as when they will have lunch (if part of the visit) and when they will change activities and gather to return to class or the school, including where to meet.

You may wish to organise the groups children are in, and the group work they will undertake, with them so that they work as effectively as they do in the classroom setting, or you might take the opportunity to provide fresh challenges, where you are confident that the children will respond positively to these. For such group work you will need to have briefed the adults working with them to ensure that they foster the interactive and dialogic nature of good group work to ensure mutually collaborative outcomes.

Following up work undertaken outside the classroom

The lesson plan in Figure 3.6.9 (see page 172) includes follow-up activities. These help to settle the children when they return to class and encourage them to think about key points from their research. You should do this, if only for a few minutes, when you arrive back before lunch or the end of the day, before the children disperse. As one in a series of lessons on the topic, you should plan to follow up out-of-classroom work over one or more lessons.

It is important for you to have considered the following questions:

■ How do I use the enthusiasm generated by the work outside the classroom?
■ How will the children work on the information they have gathered?
■ What types of outcome do I want to see?
■ What resources and support do they need to complete their work?

EVALUATING THE EXPERIENCE

You should always evaluate out-of-classroom studies. You may have collected new information from a museum, a field centre or a mosque to add to topic resources. You need to know what the children feel they gained from the experience. Such matters are important because you must appreciate how out-of-classroom learning has been beneficial for the children, how effectively it fitted into your planned learning sequence, whether the site is worth using again, and in what ways you might improve future out-of-classroom activities. You can evaluate the experience immediately, to record key points straight away, and at the end of the topic, when you judge how well such activities contributed overall to the children's learning. The questions to consider include:

- What was your own and the children's response to the out-of-classroom experience?
- What had the most or least impact, and what was learned from the tasks and site visited that was appropriate to the topic?
- What were the benefits and limitations of what you did?
- What would you change and why?
- Would you use this site again, and would you recommend a visit to the site to another teacher?

Learning outside the classroom is essential for every child (DfES, 2006). Using the school grounds and out-of-school sites, nearby and distant, enhances each primary curriculum subject. Some subjects, such as geography and science, require children to work outside to gather data for their studies at various times, but work in English, mathematics, history, religious education, art, design and technology, and ICT benefits from children using real-world experiences in their studies. In physical education, the outdoor environment, for sport and more adventurous activities, is an essential teaching and learning site.

Task 3.6.5 **PLANNING FOR OUT-OF-CLASSROOM LEARNING**

Either, for a unit you have taught *or* for one you might teach, *evaluate* or *plan* a sequence of three lessons:

- the lead-in lesson to the out-of-classroom studies;
- the lesson in the school grounds or off-site;
- the follow-up lesson after the out-of-classroom work.

Use the questions at the end of each sub-section above to help you in your evaluation or planning. Use Figure 3.6.8 (page 170) as a guide to selecting your approach to teaching and learning.

Extending the activity

Use one or more of the references for this unit to develop your understanding of planning and evaluation. Select one or more journals or magazines for one of the primary curriculum subjects and review an article that describes an out-of-classroom activity.

- How does it deepen your own understanding of effective lesson planning for learning outside the classroom?
- Which of the approaches given in Figure 3.6.8 does it reflect and why?

Task 3.6.6 **THE VALUE OF LEARNING OUTSIDE?**

Taking children out of the classroom to enhance their learning makes considerable demands on teachers. This unit has presented the benefits and value of such learning contexts. It has outlined the organisational and planning demands involved and noted some of the constraints on these. Ofsted (2008) notes that the out-of-classroom environment, whether on or off the school site, is much less well used than it could be.

■ What are the pragmatic and philosophical arguments that teachers and others might use to challenge the value of learning outside?
■ How would you critique and debate such arguments?
■ In which literature do you find the strongest arguments for learning outside the classroom made?

SUMMARY

Planning work outside the classroom must be based on a clear understanding and appreciation of its value. Teaching using the school grounds and off-site remains popular and is keenly valued by primary teachers, although there are safety concerns and organisational challenges. Teachers persist with out-of-classroom activities because they see the motivational and the cognitive and affective learning value for children.

■ Consider carefully why and when to take the children out of the classroom for learning and teaching.
■ Know the regulations and requirements that have to be met.
■ Visit every site you use before you take the children, however well you know it, and complete a risk assessment as necessary.
■ Know why and where out-of-classroom learning fits into the sequence of lessons and the children's learning, how you lead into the activities and how you follow up what has been done.
■ Thorough and careful planning and organisation enhance the experience for yourself and the children, and enable you to manage their behaviour in a motivating context.
■ Evaluate the children's experience and its place in a project's learning sequence.
■ Judge the benefits and limitations of your out-of-classroom teaching and apply your learning in future.

ANNOTATED FURTHER READING

Braund, M. and Reiss, M. (eds) (2004) *Learning Science Outside the Classroom*, London: Routledge Falmer.

This text provides a thorough outline of the ways in which science education can be enhanced through taking children into the school grounds and to water habitats, museums and field centres. It covers planning and safety matters.

Council for Learning Outside the Classroom (2008) *Out and About Guidance*. Available online at www.lotc.org.uk/Out-and-about-guidance (accessed November 2009).

The web-based guidance provided on this site covers the value and aims of out-of-classroom learning, organisational and planning aspects, site choices, practical matters and evaluation very thoroughly and there are invaluable links to many other resources and sites.

Department for Education and Skills (DfES) (1998) *Health and Safety of Pupils on Educational Visits*, London: DfES.

This handbook (updated periodically) provides guidance and information about organisation and safety planning for visits.

Department for Education and Skills (DfES) (2006) *Learning Outside the Classroom Manifesto*, Nottingham: DfES Publications. Available online at www.teachernet.gov.uk/learningoutsidethe classroom (accessed November 2009).

This document provides the rationale and encouragement to undertake learning outside the classroom.

Scoffham, S (ed.) (2004) *Primary Geography Handbook*, Sheffield: Geographical Association.

Chapter 10 outlines effective approaches to fieldwork teaching. The book includes many examples of ways to work with children in the school grounds and off-site, locally and further afield.

RELEVANT WEBSITES

Use these terms to search for websites providing information on learning outside the classroom, fieldwork organisation and places to visit: 'field study', 'field trips', 'field visits', 'fieldwork', 'site visits', 'outdoor learning', 'out-of-classroom learning' and 'learning outside the classroom'. They will lead you to websites providing a wide variety of out-of-classroom activities and locations.

Among those you should consult are:

Association for Science Education: www.ase.org.uk
Council for Learning Outside the Classroom: www.lotc.org.uk/Out-and-about-guidance
English Outdoor Council: www.englishoutdoorcouncil.org/
Geography Teaching Today: www.geographyteachingtoday.org.uk/fieldwork
Geographical Association: www.geography.org.uk
Growing Schools: www.teachernet.gov.uk/growingschools
Historical Association: www.history.org.uk
Learning Outside the Classroom: www.teachernet.gov.uk/learningoutsidetheclassroom
Learning Through Landscapes: www.ltl.org.uk
School Journeys Association: www.sja-online.org/
The Institute of Outdoor Education: www.outdoor-learning.org/

> **Visit the companion website www.routledge.com/textbooks/ltps2e for:**
>
> ■ additional questions and task for this unit;
> ■ editable figures from this unit;
> ■ links to useful websites relevant to this unit.

REFERENCES

Braund, M. and Reiss, M. (eds) (2004) *Learning Science Outside the Classroom*, London: RoutledgeFalmer.

Catling, S. and Willy, T. (2009) *Teaching Primary Geography*, Exeter: Learning Matters.

Council for Learning Outside the Classroom (2008) *Out and About Guidance*. Available online at www.lotc.org.uk/Out-and-about-guidance (accessed November 2009).

Department for Education and Skills (DfES) (1998) *Health and Safety of Pupils on Educational Visits*, London: DfES.

Department for Education and Skills (DfES) (2006) *Learning Outside the Classroom Manifesto*, Nottingham: DfES. Available online at www.lotc.org.uk (accessed November 2009).

Hoodless, P. (2008) *Teaching History in Primary Schools*, Exeter: Learning Matters.

Hoodless, P., Bermingham, S., McCreery, E. and Bowen, P. (2009) *Teaching Humanities in Primary Schools*, Exeter: Learning Matters.

House of Commons Education and Skills Committee (2005) *Education Outside the Classroom*, London: The Stationary Office.

Kimber, D. and Smith, M. (1999) 'Field work, visits and work outside the classroom', in M. Ashley (ed.) *Improving Teaching and Learning in the Humanities*, London: Falmer.

Knight, S. (2009) *Forest Schools and Outdoor Learning in the Early Years*, London: Sage.

Malone, K. (2008) *Every Experience Matters*, Report commissioned by Farming and Countryside Education for the UK Department for Children, Schools and Families, Woolagong, Australia. Available online at www.face-online.org.uk/index.php (accessed November 2009).

McCreery, E., Palmer, S. and Voiels, V. (2008) *Teaching Religious Education: Primary and Early Years*, Exeter: Learning Matters.

Nundy, S. (2006) 'Learning in the outdoors: geography or much more . . .?', *Primary Geographer*, 59: 4–6.

O'Donnell, L., Morris, M. and Wilson, R. (2006) *Education Outside the Classroom: An Assessment of Activity and Practice in Schools and Local Authorities*, Nottingham: DfES.

Office for Standards in Education (Ofsted) (2008) *Learning Outside the Classroom: How Far Should You Go?* Available online at www.ofsted.gov.uk (accessed November 2009).

Parker, C. (2008) '"This is the best day of my life! And I'm not leaving here until it's time to go home!" The outdoor learning environment', in D. Whitebread and P. Coltman (eds) *Teaching and Learning in the Early Years*, London: Routledge.

Real World Learning Campaign (2006) *Out-of-Classroom Learning: Practical Information and Guidance for Teachers*, Sandy: RSPB.

Richardson, P. (2004) 'Fieldwork', in S. Scoffham (ed.) *Primary Geography Handbook*, Sheffield: Geographical Association.

Rickinson, M., Dillon, J., Teamey, K., Morris, M., Young Choi, M., Sanders, D. and Benefield, P. (2004) *A Review of Research on Outdoor Learning*, Preston Montford: Field Studies Council.

Scoffham, S (ed.) (2004) *Primary Geography Handbook*, Sheffield: Geographical Association.

Stagg, C, Smith, P., Thomas, A. and Warn, C. (2009) *Off the Premises Handbook*, London: Optimus Education.

Training and Development Agency for Schools (TDA) (2007) *Professional Standards for Qualified Teacher Status and Requirements for Initial Teacher Training*, London: TDA. Available at www.tda.gov.uk/teachers/professionalstandards/standards.aspx (accessed November 2009).

White, J. (2008) *Playing and Learning Outdoors*, London: Routledge.

4 APPROACHES TO THE CURRICULUM

THE AIMS OF PRIMARY EDUCATION

Richard Bailey and Justine Earl

INTRODUCTION

This unit focuses on the aims of primary education. It encourages the reader to reflect upon aims that are inherent within different philosophies of education, as well as to consider his/her own views of the aims of primary education.

OBJECTIVES

By the end of this unit, you should:

- have a greater understanding of the aims of education and their relevance to practitioners;
- have reflected upon the relationship between educational aims and educational practice, and be familiar with some well-known historical examples;
- be able to consider the specific aims of primary education, as well as the values that underpin them;
- be able to form your own philosophy of primary education, and be aware of the practical implications of philosophical thinking in education.

WHAT ARE AIMS, AND WHY DO WE NEED THEM?

You might think that discussions of educational aims are not very practical or useful. You might also think that they are overly theoretical, when what you really need as a trainee teacher are workable strategies to help you survive in the classroom. We hope that it will become clear by the end of this unit that this is a mistaken view, as any sensible discussion about educational practice is always built on a foundation of aims. A teacher who is skilled in a technical sense, but who lacks a clear sense of their subject or lesson, will almost certainly offer the pupils an unsatisfactory experience. The same can be said for education as a whole.

Aims define the point of an activity: what it seeks to achieve; where it should go.

The difficulty is that there is no simple, overriding aim of education about which all of us – teachers, parents, academics, policy makers – can agree and to which we all aspire. There are numerous possible aims. Taken individually, these aims often seem legitimate and reasonable. Placed together, however, it often becomes apparent that some aims are incompatible with others. For example, in introducing its educational reforms in England and Wales in the 1980s, the government identified a number of principles, such as educational standards and excellence, parental choice and participation, professional accountability, market forces and consumer satisfaction, economy, efficiency and effectiveness (Le Métais, 1995). Some have suggested that there are real tensions between pairs of these principles. For example, the call for parental choice and the promotion of market forces may be incompatible with the demand for equality.

Skills and competencies are important if one wishes to become a good teacher. But they are really very little more than tools used to help realise some goal. Without this goal – this *aim* – the tools become rather pointless.

The solution to this apparent problem is not like the solution to a crossword puzzle, in which you simply need to find the correct answer. This is because educational aims are inseparable from educational *values* and *principles*. Values are concerns about what ought to be. A value can be understood as a belief that need not rely on facts or evidence. Values such as freedom, equality, the importance of the unique individual, the importance of community and of family, the defence of one's society, and social justice go beyond mere statements of fact towards more ambitious, yet more ill-defined aspirations. To make this point more clearly, look at Task 4.1.1.

Task 4.1.1 **WHICH AIMS?**

An international review of the stated aims of educational systems from around the world came up with the following composite list (Tabberer, 1997).

Excellence	Individual development
Social development	Personal qualities
Equal opportunity	National economy
Preparation for work	Basic skills
Foundation for further education	Knowledge/skills/understanding
Citizenship/community/democracy	Cultural heritage/literacy
Creativity	Environment
Health/physical/leisure	Lifelong education
Parental participation	

■ Give this list to friends and family and ask them to select what reflects most closely, for them, the main aims of education. Which aims are most frequently selected? Which are not selected at all?

■ If you are working in a school, ask to see a policy document that contains that school's aims. How do these aims reflect the list?

■ What is your view? Which aims do you think capture your personal philosophy?

Ultimately you, as a professional, will have to come to some judgement for yourself, as will every teacher. Clearly not all judgements are equally valid; we might well question the judgement of a teacher for whom the purpose of primary education is to bring about unconditional obedience to space aliens! However, at some stage, every teacher needs to ask him or herself, 'What am I trying to achieve?', 'What are my goals as a teacher?' and 'What are my aims of education?'

Values influence our aims, which, in turn, influence every aspect of the education we offer our pupils. Figure 4.1.1 illustrates one way of thinking about the relationship between values, aims and practice.

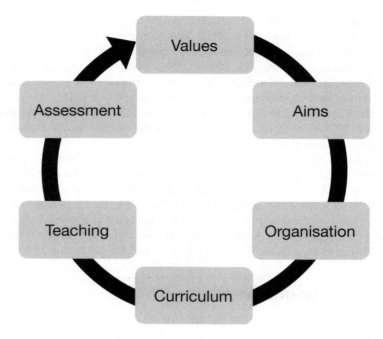

■ **Figure 4.1.1** The cycle of educational values
Source: Adapted from Le Métais (2004)

Values and aims direct decisions about school and class organisation (are pupils grouped according to age, ability or interest? How much say do parents and outside groups have? What is the nature of the authority of the teacher? Who is in charge?). Decisions of this sort will influence the type of curriculum offered (subject-based or theme-based? Broad and balanced or narrow and specialist? Which subjects receive most time, which receive least?), and these questions influence the selection of appropriate teaching styles and materials (teacher-centred or learner-centred? Memorising facts or problem solving? Teacher as authority, as friend, as resource?). Finally, the type of assessment strategies employed, if they are to have any purpose at all, need to reflect the aims of the education process.

In this era of national curricula and national strategies, it might seem surprising to be asked to reflect on the aims of education. Surely they are a given. And, of course, it would be a foolish trainee teacher who carried on oblivious to the policies and requirements of central government. But if we consider its stated aims, it is apparent why teachers' perspectives still have a role.

The National Curriculum for England (DfEE/QCA, 1999) does not commit itself to aims specifically for primary education. It does, however, give two broad aims for the curriculum, as a whole:

■ The school curriculum should aim to provide opportunities for all pupils to learn and to achieve.
■ The school curriculum should aim to promote pupils' spiritual, moral, social and cultural development and prepare pupils for the opportunities, responsibilities and experiences of adult life.

As they stand, these aims seem quite broad, and could reflect almost any educational system in the world. It is possible, however, to imagine some practices that would conflict with these aims, such as those that excluded sections of the pupil population, or those that offered only a narrow range of experiences. To some extent, then, you are working in a context in which aims are already in place, if only at a rather general level.

There are good reasons to suppose, however, that talk of aims will be relevant to you throughout your training. As a citizen, you have the same right as everyone else to hold and express your view on what education is for, and to contribute to the communal discussion about the aims and character of education. As a teacher, you have an even greater responsibility to be clear to yourself and others what your aims are, and be prepared to argue and defend them (Haydon, 1995). It is very difficult to identify universally shared values and aims. Committed professionals need to make decisions at each stage of the teaching process about how to interpret their values and aims in terms of practice. For this reason, we do not have one type of school, with one type of curriculum, teaching approach and assessment. And we do not yet have one narrow, prescriptive set of aims, to which all teachers must comply.

So, in response to the charge made at the beginning of this unit that talk of aims is not very practical, we are able to respond that we cannot even begin to decide what we should do in a particular situation without some idea of what it is we want to achieve.

AIMS AND PRACTICE: SOME HISTORICAL EXAMPLES

The point has already been made that educational practice cannot be separated from notions of aims. In order to exemplify this, we will consider the educational theories of three influential thinkers: Plato, Jean-Jacques Rousseau and John Dewey. These thinkers have been selected because each has had a significant influence on the way people think about the ways in which education should be conceived and carried out. Also, they have the virtue of coming from different places and times from our own. This distance should make it easier for us to talk about aims and practice, without being constrained by our assumptions of the way education *ought to be*.

Plato

The ancient Greek philosopher Plato (428–348 BCE) wrote about education in a number of his works, but his best-known treatment is in the book that has come to be known as *The Republic* (Bloom, 1991). Plato, a student of Socrates and the teacher of Aristotle, is said to have founded the first university – his Academy, near Athens.

Much of Plato's work is presented in the form of dialogues, or question and answer discussions, in which a student, or 'seeker', is led to uncover gaps in his or her reasoning by a teacher, or 'expert'. This method of teaching has come to be known as the 'Socratic Method' (after Plato's teacher), and characterises the presentation of educational ideas in *The Republic*, as well as Plato's view that such dialogues are a powerful method for developing a student's understanding as their subject knowledge comes through questioning, not teaching. Although this might at first appear a somewhat progressive teaching style, Plato makes it clear that the teacher–student relationship is not one of equals – the teacher is in control.

To understand Plato's educational theory, it is necessary to understand his views of politics. For him, the central issue is that of justice or right-living – the just person lives a life of harmony. This harmonious life expresses itself in two ways. First, as a member of a community, the just person lives a life that is appropriate to his or her social group. Soldiers, farmers, leaders and manufacturers all contribute to the just state, but each needs to stay in their place in the order: they need to know their place.

Second, just as the state needs order and harmony, so does the individual. We all have appetites and passions, as well as a capacity for reason and reflection. The different elements within us relate directly to the different roles within the state: our appetites (which equate to the producers) and our passions (the soldiers) must remain under the control of the higher, rational part (the leaders). When our appetites and passions overtake our reason, we become disturbed and disordered, just as a state becomes unstable if the lower orders take control from their leaders.

For Plato, then, the aim of education is to produce certain types of people, the just, and a certain type of state, the just society, in which each of the different elements keeps its proper place in the order. And how can we recognise where different people fit in this order? Plato's view is that humans are made up of a body, which is perishable, and a soul, which is immortal. Some souls are better than others. In Plato's terms, some of us have gold in our souls, while other progressively less worthy people have iron and bronze. The highest function of education, therefore, is to develop those with souls of gold (Moore, 1974) and lead them to see beyond superficial appearances towards an understanding of another level – the world of eternal, changeless reality.

So, how does this view of education translate into practice? First, if there really are different qualities of people, it follows that they will require different forms of schooling. Second, young children of quality who are not yet ready for the strains of philosophical training need to develop their senses and their love of beauty, order and harmony. Third, as children get older, they need to be inspired by tales of heroes and great leaders. Fourth, they need to ensure that their bodies are strong enough to house their souls, so the young need a period of rigorous physical training. Finally, only once the few have shown themselves to be fit will they be taught the secrets necessary for leadership. Only if these steps are followed will the state be kept safe, harmonious and just.

Rousseau

Jean-Jacques Rousseau (1712–78) was born in Switzerland and grew up in France. His book *Emile* (Bloom, 1979) is generally regarded as the most significant text on education since Plato's *Republic*. Rousseau lived shortly before the French Revolution, and his writing is often credited as being influential in setting the intellectual scene for that great political change. He worked variously as an engraver, a music teacher, a private tutor and a writer.

Rousseau's 'other' great book is *The Social Contract*, which begins with the famous and chilling lines: 'Man was born free, and he is everywhere in chains' (Cranston, 2004). This quotation captures his view that we are born good, but are corrupted by the evils of society. Rousseau called for an abandonment of the French society of his day, which he thought corrupt and unjust, and the emergence of a new kind of society, based on the real interests and engagement of its members (as opposed to just the aristocrats). The government, in this new system, would be based on what he called the 'General Will' – the rational, informed will of all members of society, guided by principles of 'liberty, equality and fraternity'. There is always a danger in such democratic structures that individuals and minority groups are exploited. So, Rousseau was forceful in advocating freedom of thought, independence and individualism of members and, of course, education.

Rousseau's *Emile* is a call for 'a return to nature', and his goal of education is the 'natural man' and an educational system 'according to nature'. Quite what he means by 'nature' is a matter of some interpretation. Certainly there is a strong 'green' element in Rousseau's writing. However, he means much more than modern environmentalism. In some parts of *Emile*, it seems that nature equates to the way things are in the natural world, within which children live as human animals. So, Rousseau stresses the importance of treating a child as a child, and not as a mini-adult (as was the fashion of his day). Children, he argued, do not share the faculties and needs of adults, so should not be treated as if they did. Ultimately, childhood should be characterised by a life of experience, rather than knowledge, of sensation rather than reason. In another part of *Emile*, it seems that Rousseau has a somewhat different understanding of the term 'nature'. Here, he places much greater emphasis on the natural person as one who has yet to be corrupted by society. A third view, offered by Rousseau's critics, is that his natural man is really the middle-class citizen of his new society, who is independent of thought, yet able to play a constructive part in society, without being overtaken by it (Moore, 1974).

The relationship between Rousseau's views of childhood and education, and modern, so-called 'child-centred' or progressive education, is clear. It is not surprising, then, that he has been blamed by some traditionalists for the anti-intellectual, anti-social forms of schooling that they claim have become endemic in recent decades. This is, perhaps, a little harsh, as Rousseau clearly recognised the need for both intellectual and social engagement – he stressed, however, that studying from books, initiation into academic disciplines and learning about the social world should occur when the individual is mature enough to benefit from them and not be corrupted by them. Before that time, during childhood, the child should be educated using personal experience.

Dewey

John Dewey (1859–1952) was born in an America that was evolving into a major industrial nation, yet was still influenced by the ethos of the frontier, with its emphasis on enterprise, independence and merit. He is acknowledged as one of the most influential educational philosophers of modern times, and, although he is sometimes portrayed as Rousseau's intellectual heir, and the father of modern child-centred education, he really marks a different tradition altogether.

Like both Plato and Rousseau before him, Dewey's views on education were greatly influenced by his views on children's nature. Born in the year in which Charles Darwin published *The Origin of Species*, Dewey saw humans as active, problem-solving creatures, who are continually seeking to overcome challenges from their environment. By the time they enter school, they have already experienced a great deal, and bring with them innate instincts to communicate, construct, inquire and express themselves. Children also bring their interests, and it is a basic task of the teacher to make use of these interests and instincts by guiding the child's activities at school. Dewey divides childhood into three developmental stages: the period of 'play', which is characterised by spontaneous child-led activity; the 'techniques' period, during which the child learns to follow simple procedures; and the period of 'reflective attention', when an overtly critical problem solving is developed. At each stage, the emphasis is on the child's activity, which gradually becomes more specific and outcome-orientated as the child grows older.

Underlying Dewey's philosophy is the aim of educating a certain type of person: an individual fit for a democracy. However, unlike the writers we met earlier, he is very suspicious of any theory of education that has an 'end' in mind, whether it be Plato's 'leader' or Rousseau's 'natural man'. For Dewey, education cannot really have an aim beyond itself: the end point of education is more education. This does not mean that Dewey thought of education as distinct from society; on the contrary, he was keen for schools to prepare for life in the 'real world'. Therefore, schools should present their pupils with real problems, which stem from their own interests. Many of these problems may originate in the social settings in which children work cooperatively and collaboratively. Education according to Dewey, therefore, is fundamentally concerned with developing children's innate interests and abilities by leading them to operate in the world of practical problems.

Task 4.1.2 **EDUCATIONAL AIMS AND PHILOSOPHIES 1**

Reflect upon the different visions of education offered by Plato, Rousseau and Dewey. Each has a distinctive view of education, and of its aims, as well as of childhood and children. Also, each, whether implicitly or explicitly, has a view of the role of *primary education* within their vision.

Outline the aims of primary education within each of these approaches. Can you recognise aspects of these aims in modern education and schooling? Consider, in particular, these contexts:

- the Foundation Stage;
- independent 'preparatory' schools;
- self-proclaimed 'child-centred' schools;
- the school with which you are most familiar.

Task 4.1.3 **EDUCATIONAL AIMS AND PHILOSOPHIES 2**

Reflect critically on the aspects you identified in Task 4.1.2. Consider how they impact on the learning experienced by the pupils in each context. Undertake further reading in order to make clearer connections between visions of education and actual practical examples.

WHAT ARE THE AIMS OF PRIMARY EDUCATION?

'Cheshire Puss,' she began, rather timidly . . . 'Would you tell me, please, which way I ought to go from here?' 'That depends a good deal on where you want to get to,' said the Cat. 'I don't much care where,' said Alice. 'Then it doesn't matter which way you go,' said the Cat. 'So long as I get somewhere,' Alice added as an explanation. 'Oh, you're sure to do that,' said the Cat, 'if you only walk long enough.'

(Lewis Carroll, *Alice's Adventures in Wonderland*)

Is there a quintessential character of 'primary' education? Are there aims that are special to the primary phase that set it apart from other aspects of pupils' learning and experience? One writer, reflecting on changing practices over the years and different approaches around the world, has been led to ponder: 'We encounter so little uniformity of practice that we might feel inclined to ask whether the word "primary" is anything more than a label denoting a stage of compulsory schooling' (Alexander, 1984: 11). Can that be all that is special about primary education: the age of the pupils? Or is there something else; is there something special and distinctive about the primary phase?

Historically, there have been some discrete traditions associated with primary education (see Alexander, 1984; Pollard and Tann, 1997):

- *The elementary tradition*: This is a form of educational practice and provision associated with a concentration on the so-called '3Rs' (reading, 'riting and 'rithmetic), and with a strict approach to discipline.

■ *The developmental tradition*: This approach emphasises the ways in which children develop physically, socially, emotionally and intellectually as a basis for planning and organising learning.

■ *The preparatory tradition*: This tradition sees primary education as a 'preparation' for later schooling, during which children learn the more traditional subject-based knowledge.

To some extent, these traditions need not be mutually exclusive. It is quite possible to envisage a school claiming to support all three approaches. For example, it might claim to be respectful of children's developmental needs, while still recognising their need to learn the basics of literacy and numeracy, as well as the foundations of good behaviour, so that they are prepared for the more traditional business of secondary schooling. But this would miss the purpose of the classification, which is to reflect upon the dominating aim – the driving purpose that defines and, to some extent, restricts what is offered in the name of primary education. Our imagined school might very well claim to represent all three traditions, but the true test comes when time and resources are limited, or when external inspectors demand evidence of its achievement. Does the school push forward its exemplary record in reading, writing and arithmetic, and flawless disciplinary record, or does it claim that it has devised a curriculum that is responsive to and respectful of each child's developmental needs, which means that not all children can read or add up because they are not all ready for these skills? Or does it boast of its outstanding SATs results or high success rate in winning places in selective secondary schools?

Task 4.1.4 SCHOOL AIMS AND EDUCATIONAL TRADITIONS

You have already been asked to read your school's policy documents.

■ To which tradition do you think they most closely belong?
■ What language in the policy document leads you to your conclusion?

Collaborate with colleagues on your course, and share your gathered policy documents.

■ Which themes are most evident, and which are least evident?

THE AIMS OF PRIMARY EDUCATION – RECENT DEVELOPMENTS

The English Qualifications and Curriculum Authority (QCA) has recently offered a statement of the aims of the curriculum, which are interesting to consider at this point. Three overall curriculum aims have been identified: that the curriculum will enable all young people to become:

■ *successful learners*, who enjoy learning, make progress and achieve;
■ *confident individuals*, who are able to live safe, healthy and fulfilling lives;
■ *responsible citizens*, who make a positive contribution to society.

These aims connect explicitly with the five *Every Child Matters* outcomes (2003) and the 2007 *Children's Plan*. The QCA has stated that clear aims are an essential component of a national curriculum. More importantly for you to consider here, it is also made clear that these aims should 'highlight the importance of the primary phase' (www.qca.org.uk). However, it is worth noting that these are the very same aims as offered for Key Stages 3 and 4. This raises some important questions for teachers, such as:

■   If the aims are fixed, can each school or teacher usefully reflect on the most appropriate aims in their local context?

■   To what extent are these aims especially relevant to the 'primary' stage?

The above aims are discussed in *A Big Picture of the Curriculum* (www.qcda.gov.uk/5856.aspx). This *Big Picture* emphasises the concept of the curriculum that goes beyond single-subject lessons. According to this approach, the curriculum becomes the 'entire planned learning experience' of the young person. This recognises the importance of events, the environment, routines, the extended school day and activities outside the classroom. Schools have been invited to join 'Curriculum Networks' in order to develop their own curriculum. Findings from these projects are then shared with other schools, via the web. There is an emphasis on schools shaping their work with their young learners to suit their own purposes, particular needs and context. The case studies offer a range of ideas and apparently flexible approaches. However, the *Big Picture* asks schools to answer the question, 'How well are we achieving our aims?' Yet, as we have seen, the aims are pre-set. It seems that a curriculum like this is not created, but rather adopted by schools.

Schools aiming to realise 'the big picture' are asked to answer the question of how well they are achieving their aims. The real starting point for curriculum revision in the school is 'How do we organise learning?' This organisation of learning, whether by subject (as is the case usually now), by areas of learning (as in the Foundation Stage curriculum), by skills, or by theme, must be evaluated in order to secure:

■   attainment and improved standards;

■   behaviour and attendance;

■   civic participation;

■   healthy lifestyle choices;

■   further involvement in education, employment or training.

This prescriptive approach to both the aims of the curriculum, and the means by which their success should be evaluated, apparently leaves little space for any other aims or values to play a part in curriculum design. It may have already occurred to you that, if the aims for the curriculum are to be statutory, teachers and schools need to know the values that underpin them. Only then will they be able to understand them sufficiently well to map out the curriculum content effectively.

So, a statement of curriculum aims such as that offered by QCA is in need of a clear rationale. The philosopher John White (2008) has suggested that, no matter how persuasive statements of aims may be, there is always a danger that they are simply an ordered list. It seems reasonable to claim that a school curriculum framework ought to relate to some vision of a worthwhile life, or at least of an idea of an educated person. An overall rationale, therefore, is needed, in order for the individual items to fit together within a larger framework. It is a matter of discussion whether or not the new reforms of the English curriculum are based on a set of aims that 'hang together' in a coherent and persuasive way. Certainly, the developers of the new English curriculum have not gone to the lengths of their colleagues in Northern Ireland in explaining the bigger picture, and the ways in which the stated aims, themes and activities contribute to it (see CCEA, 2007).

Task 4.1.5 **RELATING THE QCA AIMS TO YOUR OWN PHILOSOPHY**

In Task 4.1.1 you were asked to reflect on the aims of education in the broadest sense; on the stated aims of a particular school and on your own developing personal aims as a teacher. Revisit what you decided you want to achieve, and see how close your aims are to the three offered by QCA (see page 187).

■ How comfortable are you with the notion of statutory aims such as these?
■ What space is left for schools to allow their own aims and values to shape their choice of curriculum design?

Task 4.1.6 **STEPPING BEHIND THE 'VEIL OF IGNORANCE' 1**

For this task, you are going to be asked to carry out what philosophers call a 'thought experiment', which is an attempt to solve a problem using the power of your imagination and reasoning. This experiment comes from the philosopher John Rawls, whose book *A Theory of Justice* (1972) explored the fundamental principles of justice. Rawls was aware that we all have backgrounds, prejudices and vested interests that may distort our apprehension of these fundamental principles, so he proposed a way in which we could imagine how to choose these principles if we knew nothing about our present situation. This is what he calls the 'original position':

> I assume that the parties are situated behind a veil of ignorance. They do not know how the various alternatives will affect their own particular case and they're obliged to evaluate principles solely on the basis of general considerations. First of all, no one knows his place in society, his class position or social status; nor does he know his fortune in the distribution of natural assets or abilities, his intelligence and strength, and the like . . . It is taken for granted, however, that they know general facts about human society. They understand political affairs and the principles of economic theory; they know the basis of social organisation and the laws of human psychology. In fact, the parties are presumed to know whatever general facts affect the choice of the principles of justice.
>
> (Rawls, 1972: 136–7)

Now, step behind the 'veil of ignorance', and consider the aims of primary education. Imagining that you know nothing about your background, your place in society and your personal aspirations, outline a set of aims that reflect your interpretation of a reasonable and just primary education system.

Task 4.1.7 **STEPPING BEHIND THE 'VEIL OF IGNORANCE' 2**

Be prepared to justify your aims with your own clearly articulated rationale. You may be able to refer to your understandings gleaned from this unit as well as your own exploration of the national curricula on offer in the UK and in other countries.

THINKING ABOUT YOUR OWN PHILOSOPHY OF PRIMARY EDUCATION

> Education as such has no aims. Only persons, parents and teachers, etc. have aims, not an abstract idea like education.
>
> (Dewey, 1916: 107)

Studies suggest that most teachers enter the profession with a strong sense of values and aims (Thomas, 1995). You are probably the same. I hope that you have had the opportunity to reflect upon your own values and aims, and perhaps you have reconsidered them or modified them in some way. In reflecting on your own conceptions of the aims of primary education, two points need to be stressed. First, your aims come from somewhere; just as Plato, Rousseau and Dewey all reflect aspects of their culture and time in their philosophies of education, we cannot separate ourselves from our upbringing, schooling and cultural values. While we might like to think that we generate our views through raw intelligence and reason alone, the reality is that our individual beliefs often reflect our upbringing, previous experiences and social background. This is why we can find it difficult to change our aims, as their source can date back many years, and be closely associated with our conception of ourselves as people. Second, we need to remember that our aims will influence what we do, both inside and outside the classroom. Our aims are revealed in our behaviour and, thus, in our teaching (Pollard, 2002).

So aims are serious matters, and deserve critical examination. Tasks 4.1.6 and 4.1.7 encourage you do precisely this.

SUMMARY

To some extent, all teachers have to work within a framework of aims, prescribed by the National Curriculum, but there is plenty of room for the development and articulation of your personal views and philosophy. Aims help to give teachers a sense of direction and purpose in their professional work; different aims are associated with different teaching practices, curriculum organisation and assessment procedures. As such, they deserve serious consideration and examination.

ANNOTATED FURTHER READING

Pollard, A. and Tann, S. (1997) Reflective Teaching in the Primary School: A Handbook for the Classroom. London: Continuum.

This practical textbook has become something of a classic. Although it covers a great amount of material of relevance to primary practitioners, its implicit demand that we reflect upon our actions, and the thinking behind them, makes this a valuable resource for those wishing to consider aims in real-life contexts.

Pring, R. (2004) *Philosophy of Education: Aims, Theory, Common Sense and Research*, London: Continuum.

A challenging, thought-provoking series of chapters, examining different aspects of educational theory, and introducing the reader to a range of relevant authors and texts.

Walker, D.F. and Soltis, J.F. (2004) *Curriculum and its Aims*, New York: Teachers College Press.

This book from the US offers an accessible introduction to the issue of educational aims. It uses case studies to exemplify the practical implications of different theoretical positions, and offers a useful further reading section.

RELEVANT WEBSITES

A Big Picture of the Curriculum (QCA): www.qcda.gov.uk/5856.aspx
Cambridge Primary Review: www.primaryreview.org.uk
Children's Plan: www.dcsf.gov.uk/childrensplan/
Every Child Matters: www.dcsf.gov.uk/everychildmatters/
Philosophy of Education Society of Great Britain: www.philosophy-of-education.org/
Qualifications and Curriculum Development Agency (QCDA): www.qcda.gov.uk
The Encyclopaedia of Informal Education: www.infed.org/
Encyclopaedia of Philosophy of Education: http://web.archive.org/web/20010210002725/
      www.educacao.pro.br/entries.htm
The Ism Book: www.ismbook.com/
Philosophy of Education Societies:
United Kingdom – www.philosophy-of-education.org/
United States – http://philosophyofeducation.org/
Canada – www.philosophyofeducation.ca/
Australasia – www.pesa.org.au

Visit the companion website www.routledge.com/textbooks/ltps2e for:

■ additional questions and tasks for this unit;
■ links to useful websites relevant to this unit.

REFERENCES

Alexander, R. (1984) *Primary Teaching*, Eastbourne: Holt, Rinehart and Winston.
Bloom, A. (tr.) (1979) *Emile: or, On Education*, New York: Basic Books.
Bloom, A. (tr.) (1991) *The Republic of Plato*, New York: Basic Books.
Council for the Curriculum, Examinations and Assessment (CCEA) (2007) *The Statutory Curriculum at Key Stage 3: Rationale and Detail*, Belfast: CCEA.
Cranston, M. (tr.) (2004) *Jean-Jacques Rousseau: The Social Contract*, London: Penguin.
Department for Education and Employment/Qualifications and Curriculum Authority (DfEE/QCA) (1999) *English National Curriculum Handbook*, London: HMSO.
Dewey, J. (1916) *Democracy and Education*, New York: Free Press.
Haydon, G. (1995) 'Aims of education', in S. Capel, M. Leask and T. Turner (eds) *Learning to Teach in the Secondary School*, London: Routledge.
Le Métais, J. (1995) *Legislating for Change:School Reforms in England and Wales, 1979–1994*, Slough: NFER.
Le Métais, J. (2004) 'Values and aims in curriculum and assessment frameworks', in S. O'Donnell, C. Sargent, R. Brown, C. Andrews and J. Le Métais (eds) *INCA: The International Review of Curriculum and Assessment Frameworks Archive*, London: QCA.
Moore, T.W. (1974) *Educational Theory: An Introduction*, London: Routledge and Kegan Paul.
Pollard, A. (2002) *Reflective Teaching*, London: Continuum.
Pollard, A. and Tann, S. (1997) *Reflective Teaching in the Primary School: A Handbook for the Classroom*, London: Continuum.
Rawls, J. (1972) *A Theory of Justice*, Oxford: Clarendon Press.
Tabberer, R. (1997) 'Primary education: expectations and provision', in S. O'Donnell, C. Sargent, R. Brown, C. Andrews and J. Le Metais (eds) *INCA: The International Review of Curriculum and Assessment Frameworks Archive*, London: QCA.
Thomas, D. (1995) *Teachers' Stories*, Buckingham: Open University Press.
White, J. (2008) *Aims as Policy on English Primary Education (Cambridge Primary Review Research Survey 1/1)*, Cambridge: University of Cambridge Faculty of Education.

THE CURRICULUM

Dominic Wyse

INTRODUCTION

The nature of the primary curriculum has come under intense scrutiny over the last 15 years. In spite of all the controversy and change since 1988, you will see that the curriculum model remains largely the same as the first statutory curriculum from 1862. Once again, progressivism is on the march and there are some optimistic signs that things such as creativity will begin to play a much more important part in primary education. The unit concludes with a vision for the future primary curriculum.

OBJECTIVES

By the end of this unit you should:

- understand about the aims of the curricula at Foundation Stage and Key Stages 1 and 2;
- appreciate that the history of the curriculum is an important aspect of continuing debates;
- be starting to think about how teachers make professional decisions about the curriculum in the best interests of the children that they teach;
- have some ideas about how a future curriculum might look.

As part of your preparation for school experience, you will have become more familiar with national curricula. The Early Years Foundation Stage (EYFS) requirements (from birth to age five) are shown at the Department for Children, Families and Schools (DCFS) Primary National Strategies website (http://nationalstrategies.standards.dcsf.gov.uk/primary). For the later years, the requirements of the National Curriculum for Key Stages 1 and 2 (age 5–11: Year 1 to Year 6) are shown at the Qualifications and Curriculum Authority (QCA) website (http://curriculum.qcda.gov.uk/index.aspx), as are the requirements for secondary education. In spite of the importance of the National Curriculum in relation to what all primary teachers must teach, you may find that, once you start your school experience, the statutory requirements are rarely referred to. This is because schools' long-term and medium-term planning has often been discussed, agreed and written down over a considerable period of time. Once this thinking has been translated from the National Curriculum into teaching plans, the official documents are not really needed so much. This can make it difficult for student teachers to appreciate the links between the National Curriculum and school planning.

Another area in which it is sometimes difficult to see the links with the statutory documents is the extent to which some of the important opening statements of national curricula are genuinely reflected in classroom practice. These opening statements, such as principles and values, should be very important because, in theory, it is these that guide everything else in the documents, and in practice.

The aims for the EYFS are addressed in at least two sources (see Figure 4.2.1).

The 'overarching aim' of the EYFS isn't really a clear aim in its own right at all because it simply refers to the outcomes of *Every Child Matters* (ECM) (2003). *Every Child Matters* was a government initiative given legal force by the Children Act 2004. The lack of clarity of aims is added to by the additional *themes* and *principles* that are also meant to guide work in the early years. The lack of a succinct, clear, single set of aims for this stage of education is unfortunate. One significant feature of the EYFS is the Early Learning Goals that are assessed by the Foundation Stage Profile, which is a precursor to the statutory tests/exams at 7, 11 and 16. Many people remain unhappy that the children of England are tested more than those of any other country in the world.

The enactment of the Child Care Act 2006 meant that statutory control of the primary and secondary curriculum was augmented, for the first time in the history of education in England, by control of the early years curriculum. The curriculum for children in the early years is organised around six areas of learning and development.

4.4 Areas of learning and development

'Areas of learning and development' is one of the commitments to the EYFS principle of 'Learning and Development'. The commitment includes the practice guidance for all six areas of learning and development:

■ personal, social and emotional development;
■ communication, language and literacy;
■ mathematical development;
■ knowledge and understanding of the world;
■ physical development;
■ creative development.

The preamble, above, to the areas of learning and development is another example of the unnecessary complexity of the way that aims/principles/commitments/outcomes are stated. The conceptual organisation into broad areas of learning is helpful, but the traditional emphases are still obvious. Reading, writing, mathematics and science are priorities, and creativity appears at the bottom of the list. The order of a list may not seem to be particularly significant, but you will see that it reflects a common trend over more than 100 years.

Unlike the National Curriculum, which locates speaking and listening after reading and writing, in the Foundation Stage guidance communication and language come before literacy. It is certainly true that language development is an essential part of learning and, as such, should be an important feature of the curriculum. However, the special place of speaking and listening as something that is naturally acquired, and as the medium through which learning and teaching take place, makes it unique. Although this is quite controversial, in view of the fact that speaking and listening were neglected for many years, I think that it may be necessary to re-evaluate the balance between the modes. A more clearly specified language curriculum should differentiate with rigour between

THE PURPOSE AND AIMS OF THE EYFS

1.1 Every child deserves the best possible start in life and support to fulfil their potential. A child's experience in the early years has a major impact on their future life chances. A secure, safe and happy childhood is important in its own right, and it provides the foundation for children to make the most of their abilities and talents as they grow up. When parents choose to use early years services they want to know that provision will keep their children safe and help them to thrive. The Early Years Foundation Stage (EYFS) is the framework that provides that assurance.

1.2 The overarching aim of the EYFS is to help young children achieve the five *Every Child Matters* outcomes of staying safe, being healthy, enjoying and achieving, making a positive contribution, and achieving economic well-being by:

▪ setting the standards for the learning, development and care young children should experience when they are attending a setting outside their family home, ensuring that every child makes progress and that no child gets left behind;

▪ providing for equality of opportunity and anti-discriminatory practice and ensuring that every child is included and not disadvantaged because of ethnicity, culture or religion, home language, family background, learning difficulties or disabilities, gender or ability;

▪ creating the framework for partnership working between parents and professionals, and between all the settings that the child attends;

▪ improving quality and consistency in the early years sector through a universal set of standards that apply to all settings, ending the distinction between care and learning in the existing frameworks, and providing the basis for the inspection and regulation regime;

▪ laying a secure foundation for future learning through learning and development that is planned around the individual needs and interests of the child, and informed by the use of ongoing observational assessment.

(DCSF, 2008: 7)

The four themes of the EYFS
▪ A Unique Child
▪ Positive Relationships
▪ Enabling Environments
▪ Learning and Development

Each Theme is linked to an important Principle:

▪ A Unique Child

Every child is a competent learner from birth who can be resilient, capable, confident and self-assured.

▪ Positive Relationships

Children learn to be strong and independent from a base of loving and secure relationships with parents and/or a key person.

▪ Enabling Environments

The environment plays a key role in supporting and extending children's development and learning.

▪ Learning and Development

Children develop and learn in different ways and at different rates and all areas of Learning and Development are equally important and interconnected.
Each Principle is supported by four Commitments, which are shown on the poster that accompanies the materials. The Commitments describe how the Principles can be put into practice.
The Principles and their associated Commitments can also be found in the Principles into Practice cards in the resource section.

(DCSF 2009)

▪ **Figure 4.2.1** The aims of the Early Years Foundation Stage

language features that are likely to be naturally acquired, those that might benefit from more directed teaching as part of the English curriculum and those that should be covered as part of all curriculum subjects. If this were to be done, there would be a slight reduction in the curriculum content for the subject of English. This would be consistent with research evidence, which shows that reading and writing are not acquired as naturally as speaking and listening and benefit more from direct teaching.

The two aims and the subjects of the National Curriculum are stated in the Education Act 2002 (see Figures 4.2.2 and 4.2.3).

You can see from section 80(1)(a) that religious education and religious worship are singled out in the legal requirements for schools in England and Wales. We need to question whether the wording of the two aims is appropriate for twentieth-century England. For example, is pupils' 'spiritual' development correctly positioned as the first priority of the first of the two aims? White (2004) analyses the extent to which the National Curriculum actually does reflect its aims. I would emphasise the fact that it is not clear at all that the second aim, to prepare children for adult life, is being met.

Task 4.2.1 **RELIGIOUS EDUCATION, RELIGION AND THE CURRICULUM**

The Church of England and the Catholic Church have had a profound influence on the English education system, including involvement in the funding of schools; the legal necessity for a daily act of worship; and the place of religious education (RE) as a subject. Given that in most other countries this is not the case, and in some their national curricula are completely secular, to what extent do you think the influence of religion is a positive aspect of the curriculum in England?

When the National Curriculum was first proposed, there was overwhelming resistance to the fact that it should be introduced at all, as Haviland (1988) showed. However, one of the strong arguments mounted in favour of the National Curriculum was that pupils across England and Wales were receiving an uneven education, which could include considerable repetition of subject matter, a situation that could be exacerbated if children moved areas to different schools. There were also well-founded claims that some groups of children, particularly minority ethnic ones, were subject to low expectations reflected in the curricula that were delivered to them. A national curriculum was seen as a solution to these problems because it would ensure that all children had an *entitlement* to a continuous and coherent curriculum (one of four *purposes* of the National Curriculum). But exposing children to the *same* curriculum does not necessarily lead to the fulfilment of their entitlement. I would argue that a curriculum that is informed by pupils' interests, needs and rights is more likely to give them their entitlement than a uniform one that is legally imposed. Despite the resistance to the National Curriculum, it was introduced in 1988. Following many complaints that it was overburdening schools, it was revised in 1993, but the revisions did little to reduce the load. In spite of three significant reviews of the primary curriculum in 2009, the National Curriculum has remained very similar to the previous versions; to understand the reasons for this we need to look back in time.

HISTORY OF THE CURRICULUM

The idea of the curriculum being dominated by the 3Rs (Reading, wRiting and aRithmetic) is a very old one. In 1862, Parliament finally agreed a legal document called 'The Revised Code of

1862'. This introduced the idea that children over the age of seven would be examined in the 3Rs by an inspector. Children were grouped by age into different 'standards' that had certain requirements (see Table 4.2.1)

Teachers were paid eight shillings for each child who passed the examination of the 3Rs in their standard. A failure in any one of the 3Rs would mean that the grant was reduced by two

---

THE AIMS OF THE NATIONAL CURRICULUM

78 General requirements in relation to curriculum

(1) The curriculum for a maintained school or maintained nursery school satisfies the requirements of this section if it is a balanced and broadly based curriculum which –

    (a) promotes the spiritual, moral, cultural, mental and physical development of pupils at the school and of society, and

    (b) prepares pupils at the school for the opportunities, responsibilities and experiences of later life.

(2) The curriculum for any funded nursery education provided otherwise than at a maintained school or maintained nursery school satisfies the requirements of this section if it is a balanced and broadly based curriculum which –

    (a) promotes the spiritual, moral, cultural, mental and physical development of the pupils for whom the funded nursery education is provided and of society, and

    (b) prepares those pupils for the opportunities, responsibilities and experiences of later life.

80 Basic curriculum for every maintained school in England

(1) The curriculum for every maintained school in England shall comprise a basic curriculum which includes –

    (a) provision for religious education for all registered pupils at the school (in accordance with such of the provisions of Schedule 19 to the School Standards and Framework Act 1998 (c. 31) as apply in relation to the school),

    (b) a curriculum for all registered pupils at the school who have attained the age of three but are not over compulsory school age (known as 'the National Curriculum for England'),

    (c) in the case of a secondary school, provision for sex education for all registered pupils at the school, and

    (d) in the case of a special school, provision for sex education for all registered pupils at the school who are provided with secondary education.

(2) Subsection (1)(a) does not apply –

    (a) in relation to a nursery class in a primary school, or

    (b) in the case of a maintained special school (provision as to religious education in special schools being made by regulations under section 71(7) of the School Standards and Framework Act 1998).

(3) The Secretary of State may by order –

    (a) amend subsection (1) so as to add further requirements (otherwise than in relation to religious education or sex education),

    (b) amend subsection (1)(b) by substituting for the reference to compulsory school age (or to any age specified there by virtue of this paragraph) a reference to such other age as may be specified in the order, and

    (c) amend any provision included in subsection (1) by virtue of paragraph (a) of this subsection.

(Education Act 2002)

■ **Figure 4.2.2** The aims of the National Curriculum

THE SUBJECTS OF THE CURRENT NATIONAL CURRICULUM

83 Curriculum requirements for foundation stage

(1) For the foundation stage, the National Curriculum for England shall comprise the areas of learning and may specify in relation to them –

(a) the knowledge, skills and understanding which pupils of different abilities and maturities are expected to have by the end of the foundation stage (referred to in this Part as 'the early learning goals'),

(b) the matters, skills and processes which are required to be taught to pupils of different abilities and maturities during the foundation stage (referred to in this Part as 'educational programmes'), and

(c) assessment arrangements.

(2) The following are the areas of learning for the foundation stage –

(a) personal, social and emotional development,

(b) communication, language and literacy,

(c) mathematical development,

(d) knowledge and understanding of the world,

(e) physical development, and

(f) creative development.

(3) The Secretary of State may by order amend subsection (2).

84 Curriculum requirements for first, second and third key stages

(1) For the first, second and third key stages, the National Curriculum for England shall comprise the core and other foundation subjects specified in subsections (2) and (3), and shall specify attainment targets, programmes of study and assessment arrangements in relation to each of those subjects for each of those stages.

(2) The following are the core subjects for the first, second and third key stages –

(a) mathematics,

(b) English, and

(c) science.

(3) The following are the other foundation subjects for the first, second and third key stages –

(a) design and technology,

(b) information and communication technology,

(c) physical education,

(d) history,

(e) geography,

(f) art and design,

(g) music, and

(h) in relation to the third key stage –

(i) citizenship, and

(ii) a modern foreign language.

(4) In this section 'modern foreign language' means a modern foreign language specified in an order made by the Secretary of State or, if the order so provides, any modern foreign language.

(5) An order under subsection (4) may –

(a) specify circumstances in which a language is not to be treated as a foundation subject, and

(b) provide for the determination under the order of any question arising as to whether a particular language is a modern foreign language.

(6) The Secretary of State may by order amend subsections (2) to (5).

(Education Act 2002)

■ **Figure 4.2.3** The subjects of the current National Curriculum

■ **Table 4.2.1** The curriculum specified by the Revised Code of 1862

48.	Standard I	Standard II	Standard III	Standard IV	Standard V	Standard VI
Reading	Narrative in monosyllables.	One of the narratives next in order after monosyllables in an elementary reading book used in the school.	A short paragraph from an elementary reading book used in the school.	A short paragraph from a more advanced reading book used in the school.	A few lines of poetry from a reading book used in the first class of the school.	A short ordinary paragraph in a newspaper, or other modern narrative.
Writing	Form on blackboard or slate, from dictation, letters, capital and small, manuscript.	Copy in manuscript character a line of print.	A sentence from the same paragraph, slowly read once, and then dictated in single words.	A sentence slowly dictated once by a few words at a time, from the same book, but not from the paragraph read.	A sentence slowly dictated once, by a few words at a time, from a reading book used in the first class of the school.	Another short ordinary paragraph in a newspaper, or other modern narrative, slowly dictated once by a few words at a time.
Arithmetic	Form on blackboard or slate, from dictation, figures up to 20; name at sight figures up to 20; add and subtract figures up to 10; orally from examples on the blackboard.	A sum in simple addition or subtraction, and the multiplication table.	A sum in any simple rule as far as short division (inclusive).	A sum in compound rules (money).	A sum in compound rules (common weights and measures).	A sum in practice or bills of parcels.

shillings and eight pence. Four shillings was awarded for general merit and attendance. This system, known as 'payment by results', had two main problems: (1) the stress on the children due to the examination system; (2) the focus on the 3Rs resulting in a very narrow curriculum (Curtis and Boultwood, 1964). Payment by results was suspended from 1895, to be replaced by more freedom for primary teachers represented by the Education Act 1902 and the publication of the significant handbook *Suggestions for the Consideration of Teachers and Others Concerned in the Work of Public Elementary Schools*. Until 1926, the legal powers established in the Elementary Code meant that the Board of Education held the right to approve the school curriculum and timetable through the work of inspectors. In 1926, the regulations were revised and any reference to the subjects of the curriculum was removed (Cunningham, 2002).

It wasn't until much later, in the 1960s, that government began to take a strong interest in the curriculum once more. The idea of the primary curriculum as a 'secret garden' was coined by David Eccles (Minister of Education from 1954 to 1957 and again from 1959 to 1962) in a debate on the Crowther Report in the House of Commons in March 1960. It became a very powerful slogan, especially in the subsequent attempt by the government to set up a Curriculum Study Group in the Ministry of Education in the face of opposition from teacher unions. The result was the Schools Council for Curriculum Reform, which had more teacher representation and less dominance by civil servants than the Study Group. Shirley Williams, as Prime Minister James Callaghan's Secretary of State for Education and Science, initiated the Great Debate. She called local education authorities (LEAs) to account for the curriculum in a way that her broad powers under the 1944 Act entitled her to. These powers had not hitherto conventionally been exerted in respect of the curriculum, especially given post-war sensitivities about curriculum control in totalitarian states, and possibly some respect for the professional judgement of teachers (Cunningham, 2009, personal communication). Prime Minister James Callaghan's Ruskin College speech clearly signalled government's intention to take more control of the curriculum. As you saw at the beginning of the unit, this control was maximised in the Child Care Act 2006 and has steadily increased to the present day through the imposition of the national strategies. The 'secret garden' has become a national park.

Cunningham (2002) points out that LEA teachers' centres were an important catalyst for new ideas and practices and he claims that their influence has been unduly neglected by historians of the teaching profession. The year 1902 marked the beginning of progressivism, which through the first 70 years of the twentieth century was increasingly influenced by courses provided by LEAs. From my own point of view, I still remember the excitement of taking part in courses run by the Inner London Education Authority (ILEA) and later involvement in the Language in the National Curriculum (LINC) project while working in Bradford, and subsequent courses run by Kirklees LEA when I worked in Huddersfield. However, I'm not sure that the progressive ideas emerging from teachers' centres were as universally influential as had been suggested. Let me take an example from the teaching of English. 'The real book approach' is a progressive approach to the teaching of literacy that has frequently been blamed for alleged poor standards in reading, but the number of teachers who use such an approach is frequently exaggerated. Research (Wyse, 1998) has shown that, at various periods in time, only about 4 per cent of schools have confirmed that they use such progressive approaches to the teaching of literacy. Simpson (1996) confirms this figure in his comment that, in spite of the Plowden Report's (CACE, 1967) claim that many of the old beliefs about primary teaching had been 'blown away, only 4 per cent of schools had rejected streaming, which was in contradiction to the report's recommendations. This lack of change in teacher practice continued in spite of the fact that LEA teachers' centres and universities may have promoted progressive educational ideas. Alexander (1995) recognised this when he spoke about the change in the collective culture of schools contrasting with continuity in the privacy of classrooms'. And later his view that:

English primary education in 2000 is nineteenth-century elementary education modified – much modified, admittedly – rather than transformed. Elementary education is its centre of gravity. Elementary education provides its central point of reference. Elementary education is the form to which it most readily tends to regress.

(Alexander, 2000: 147)

One of the most damaging aspects of this is the separation of core and foundation subjects, which Alexander (2004) has called a crude '"basics" and the rest' curriculum, which you saw was first statutorily implemented in the revised code of 1862.

A NEW PROGRESSIVISM: CREATIVITY

The period since the Education Reform Act 1988, which first established the concept of a national curriculum, has been a bleak time. Heavy prescription through the National Curriculum, national strategies, testing, targets and league tables of test results have resulted in an impoverished curriculum (Wyse and Torrance, 2009). Amid this stormy landscape, a lifeline emerged in the unexpected form of another government report. The National Advisory Committee on Creative and Cultural Education (NACCCE) was established in February 1998 to make recommendations on the creative and cultural development of young people through formal and informal education. There were some powerful messages in the report:

> The real effect of the existing distinction between the core and foundation subjects now needs to be carefully assessed in the light of ten years' experience. It appears to have reduced the status of the arts and humanities and their effective impact in the school curriculum.
>
> (NACCCE, 1999: 75)

As a way of reducing the curriculum content and addressing the neglect of subjects such as music and art, the report recommended: 'In order to achieve parity, the existing distinction between core and foundation subjects should be removed' (p. 87). Unfortunately, this recommendation was not followed when the National Curriculum 2000 was put into place, nor has it been to date, as literacy, numeracy and information and communication technology (ICT) are the core curriculum. The NACCCE report seemed to strike a chord with many people in education who were deeply unhappy about the mechanistic and bloated curriculum that had been followed since 1988. In spite of overwhelming support for its message, politicians were not quick to act.

Excellence and Enjoyment: A Strategy for Primary Schools (DfES, 2003) subsumed the literacy and numeracy strategies and was the third major national strategy from the period between 1997 and 2003. It came on top of an unprecedented number of government interventions in primary education. In spite of teachers' feelings of 'intervention overload', it was anticipated keenly because of the growing consensus that educational policy in England was too prescriptive and that this was impacting negatively on creative teaching and creative learning. It was hoped that fundamental reforms might result in a more appropriate level of professional autonomy for teachers, including the opportunity to teach more creatively with fewer constraints.

The document did indeed include words like 'freedom' and 'empowerment' and on page 18, for the first time after the executive summary, the word 'creativity' appeared:

> 2.11 Some teachers question whether it is possible to exercise their curricular freedom, because of the priority the Government attaches to improving literacy and numeracy. But as Ofsted reports have shown, it is not a question of 'either', 'or'. Raising standards and making learning fun can and do go together. The best primary schools have developed timetables and teaching plans that combine creativity with strong teaching in the basics.
>
> (DfES, 2003: 18)

It is true that it is not impossible to teach creatively and to help children learn creatively in spite of government constraints, but there is a more important consideration: is the primary strategy the *best* way to achieve creativity? Is it reasonable that government should place more responsibility on primary schools and teachers without admitting their own failure to ensure an appropriate balance to the curriculum since 1997?

One of the most promising things to emerge following the NACCCE report was the Creative Partnerships initiative. The Department for Media, Culture and Sport (DCMS), Department for Education and Skills (DfES) and the Arts Council started funding Creative Partnerships in 2002. This released £110 million to support the development of 'creative learning' in approximately 900 primary and secondary schools in 36 areas of the country. The main aim has been to provide schoolchildren across England with the opportunity to develop creativity in learning and to take part in cultural activities of the highest quality.

To a certain extent, the success of Creative Partnerships represents progressivism beginning to take hold of the curriculum once more. The idea of putting creativity at the heart of the curriculum by teaching more holistically, thematically and by breaking down the barriers of the core subjects in particular, is in some ways reminiscent of early periods of progressivism. You may even hear some cynics suggesting that this is just another example of ideas coming in and out of fashion. While this is partially true, it fails to show understanding of the fact that this new creativity is built on a history of curriculum development and for that reason can never be identical to previous versions. Evidence of this is shown by Wyse and Spendlove (2007), whose research revealed teachers' complaints that, even with the extra funding from Creative Partnerships, the main barriers to creative teaching and learning were the statutory ones: the National Curriculum and the associated testing and inspection system.

Task 4.2.2 THINKING ABOUT NATIONAL CURRICULA

■ What changes would you like to see made to the curriculum?

■ What are your views about a subject-led curriculum?

■ Has the emphasis on English and maths since 1997 been a reasonable one?

■ In what ways are teachers developing a more creative curriculum?

■ Which aspects of the curriculum are you excited about teaching? Which ones are you less confident about? What will you do to improve your confidence?

THE FUTURE OF THE PRIMARY CURRICULUM

The year 2009 was historically another key moment for primary education. Sir Jim Rose published his final report on the curriculum that had been commissioned by government, the Select Committee for Children, Schools and Families completed its bi-partisan review of the primary curriculum, and the *Cambridge Primary Review* was published. Rose's interim report (2008) had some welcome features, the most important of which was the idea that 'an important aim of primary education is to instil a love of learning for its own sake' (Rose, 2008: 16). 'Love of learning' is an emotive phrase, but an appropriate one, which should be used as the basis for the systematic evaluation of the success or otherwise of changes to a curriculum. A rewarding curriculum that results in a love of learning depends on children being encouraged to make meaningful choices in their curriculum, which requires that teachers are empowered to enable such choices. The empowerment of teachers requires encouragement for each individual teacher in the primary school to develop interests and knowledge unique to them that may colour their teaching in ways that make the school experience for pupils more varied. This was recognised implicitly in the report: 'many believe that the Government, the QCA, Ofsted, and the National Strategies, or a combination of all four, effectively restrict their [teachers'] freedom' (p. 19). Steps need to be taken to mitigate this restriction on professional decision making.

There were other areas of the report that were less positive (an extended version of the following points, and the points made in the previous paragraph, can be found in Wyse *et al.*, 2009).

1   The idea of child-centred education was addressed somewhat sceptically in the report, yet such education has a sound cultural, philosophical and increasing empirical basis.

2   The voices of children themselves were absent from the report.

3   The suggestion to organise the curriculum into six areas of learning was promising, but the rationale for this and the specific wording and conception of these areas lacked rigour. The pragmatics of accepting that 'the aims and values for primary education must be seen in the light of the Children's Plan' (p. 15) were not a sufficient rationale for the development of an outstanding curriculum.

4   One could sympathise with Sir Jim Rose's comments on the review website (www.dcsf.gov.uk/primarycurriculumreview/), which suggested that the distinction between cross-curricular work and subject-based work had been polarised by some in the media. Yet the report also appeared to emphasise 'cross-curricular studies' merely as a vehicle for *applying* understanding learned in the context of subject teaching. Effective 'topic work' or theme-based work is in fact valuable in its own right as a coherent and intellectually defensible way to organise teaching in the primary classroom.

5   The idea that teaching pre-1988 was a 'do as you please' (p. 17) curriculum was an unfortunate caricature that cannot seriously be defended. It also neglects the fact that serious problems occurred post-1988 because of the introduction of the National Curriculum and the associated high-stakes testing system (Wyse *et al.*, 2008) (testing was something that the report would not address, claiming that the remit prevented this).

6   The review recognised that the curriculum is more than just subjects and linked areas of learning, for example it embraced links from schools to sites outside schools, and relationships with external partners to support learning. So it was unfortunate that matters of place, space, time and the design of schools, classrooms and other spaces for play, socialising and learning were given such minor consideration in the review. The first new schools built as a result of the Primary Capital Programme (a massive investment programme to renew at least half of all primary school buildings by 2022–23 in order to create twenty-first-century schools that are at the heart of their communities) will be opening at a time when the new primary curriculum is in effect. It is vital that these two policy initiatives be connected imaginatively and systematically if an education fit for the twenty-first century is to be achieved.

One of the most important things about the curriculum in future is that the model needs to be relevant from the early years up to the end of schooling and should genuinely prepare pupils for higher education and lifelong learning. As we have seen in this unit, the current model for early years differs from the model for primary years. I propose Figure 4.2.4 as a starting point for thinking about the curriculum.

A curriculum model that reflects learning and teaching throughout life needs to put the individual's 'self' at the centre. It is the individual person's motivation to learn and their interests that will sustain learning throughout life. A new curriculum will need to encourage teaching that explicitly encourages pupils to find areas of work that motivate them and to pursue these in depth, even at the very earliest stages of education. Children's rights to participate in all matters that affect

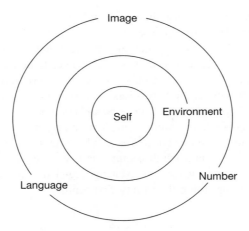

■ **Figure 4.2.4** Proposed curriculum model

them should not be an abstract item in the programmes of study for citizenship, but a daily reality in their lives (see Wyse (2003) for a discussion of the United Nations Convention on the Rights of the Child and the condemnation the UK's report received from the UN Committee on the Rights of the Child). Role-play and drama will be a recurrent medium for reflecting on the self and others. Physical development, including health, will be nurtured as part of this focus.

The environment in which learning takes place is vital to sustain the self. In spite of futuristic claims about learning electronically from home, a place called school will still be the main arena for learning, but it should be one that is not a grimy, damp, cold, boomy building: it should be architecturally inspiring. It should be a place where the crafts of life, such as the preparation and sharing of food and the performing of and listening to music are centre stage. The social interaction provided by the home and community will form an integrated link with the social interaction provided by the school's curriculum. Sights, sounds and exploration of the world, beginning with the immediate surroundings, will form part of the environmental curriculum. Investigations will take place, problems will be solved, and things will be made. All of this will be set in the context of active participation in working towards a sustainable environmental future for the world.

Learning centred on images – both still and moving, icons, logos, signs, symbols – will no longer be neglected in view of the dominant role these things have in our daily lives, and have done for many years. The counting and categorisation of entities ultimately leading to the beautiful abstraction of mathematical symbols will remain a powerful focus for learning about number. Language in all its linguistic contexts, including text and talk, will also remain a powerful focus and one that unites all other aspects of this curriculum.

Information technology (IT) will not be a subject. Do we have P and P, or paper and pencils, as a subject in the curriculum? No. IT will be central to the work of schools just as any other basic resource is. It will not be used as the latest solution to all our problems, but it will, whenever appropriate, enrich the possibilities for learning and teaching, and its natural influence will continue to grow.

Is my suggestion that we abandon the current subject-dominated core/foundation curriculum particularly radical? Not really. As one example of practice, the Royal Society for the encouragement of Arts, Manufactures and Commerce (RSA) has been working with schools developing their 'Opening Minds' curriculum for a number of years. Opening Minds is a curriculum that more than 500 schools have trialled. It is not based on subjects but a series of 'competences' that pupils are expected to acquire through curriculum content decided by schools. The RSA's conference in 2005 asked the question 'How special are subjects?' (RSA, 2005; Wyse, 2005). There was strong agreement from nearly all participants and speakers that not only were other models practically possible, but that there was an urgent need for changes to be made to the National Curriculum. As another example of alternative curricula, the primary curriculum developed by the International Baccalaureate Organisation (IBO) organises its curriculum around six themes. Consider, also, higher education, which offers hundreds of subjects, and continues to add new ones, that combine a range of understanding and skills that would benefit from preparation by a different curriculum model in schools. However, the reason that these changes have not been made before, and why the curriculum is still entrenched in the nineteenth century, is that it requires our political leaders to have the knowledge, understanding and courage to change legislation and revolutionise the primary education system in order to bring it into the twenty-first century.

Task 4.2.3 **OTHER NATIONAL CURRICULA**

Examine a national curriculum from another country. Discuss the similarities and differences between England's National Curriculum and that from the other country, then agree two or three changes that you think would be of benefit to the National Curriculum in England.

SUMMARY

In this unit we have discussed the aims of the curriculum at Foundation and Key Stages 1 and 2, and have explored how teachers make professional decisions about the curriculum for their pupils. It is recommended, therefore, that you build on these discussions by reading the recommendations below in order to widen your knowledge and understanding of the primary school curriculum.

ANNOTATED FURTHER READING

Bayliss, V., Bastiani, J., Cross, M., James, L. and Wyse, B. (2003) *Opening Minds: Taking Stock*, London: Royal Society for the encouragement of Arts, Manufacturers and Commerce.
An evaluation of a small sample of the schools that have used the RSA's Opening Minds curriculum. Shows how it can be done in practice and some of the potential pitfalls.

Kelly, A.V. (2009) *The Curriculum: Theory and Practice,* 6th edn, London: Sage.
An excellent overview of issues that combines comprehensive definitions with necessary political analysis. The comments about the increase in political interference with the curriculum, revealed through the author's reflections about the six editions of this book, are fascinating.

Rose, J. (2008) *The Independent Review of the Primary Curriculum: Interim Report*, London: DCSF. Available online at www.dcsf.gov.uk/primarycurriculumreview (accessed October 2009).
The interim report from the government-commissioned review of the primary curriculum by Sir Jim Rose.

RELEVANT WEBSITES

Cambridge Primary Review: www.primaryreview.org.uk/
This website contains links to the evidence for the large-scale, wide-ranging independent review of primary education headed by Robin Alexander and based at the University of Cambridge's Faculty of Education.

Children, Schools and Families Committee: www.publications.parliament.uk/pa/select.htm
This House of Commons Select Committee's report on the National Curriculum was one of the most important government education reports of the 2000s.

Every Child Matters: www.dcsf.gov.uk/everychildmatters/
This DCSF programme is aimed at improving outcomes for all children and young people.

International Review of Curriculum and Assessment Frameworks Internet Archive: www.inca.org.uk/
INCA's archive is a useful resource for comparing different countries.

National Curriculum: http://curriculum.qcda.gov.uk/index.aspx
This is the home of the National Curriculum for England.

National Strategies: http://nationalstrategies.standards.dcsf.gov.uk/
The Early Years Foundation Stage (EYFS) curriculum requirements are shown here.

Visit the companion website www.routledge.com/textbooks/ltps2e for:

■ additional questions and task for this unit;
■ links to useful websites relevant to this unit.

REFERENCES

Alexander, R.J. (ed.) (1995) *Versions of Primary Education*, London: Routledge and The Open University.

Alexander, R.J. (2000) *Culture and Pedagogy: International Comparisons in Primary Education*, Oxford: Blackwell.

Alexander, R.J. (2004) 'Still no pedagogy? Principle, pragmatism and compliance in primary education', *Cambridge Journal of Education*, 34(1): 7–33.

Central Advisory Council for Education (CACE) (1967) *Children and Their Primary Schools* (The Plowden Report), London: HMSO.

Cunningham, P. (2002) 'Progressivism, decentralisation and recentralisation: local education authorities and the primary curriculum, 1902–2002', *Oxford Review of Education*, 28(2–3), 217–33.

Curtis, S.J. and Boultwood, M.E.A. (1964) *An Introductory History of English Education since 1800*, 3rd edn, London: University Tutorial Press.

Department for Children, Schools and Families (DCSF) (2007) *Children's Plan*. Available online at www.dcsf.gov.uk/childrensplan/ (accessed November 2009).

Department for Children, Schools and Families (DCSF) (2008) *The Early Years Foundation Stage Statutory Framework*, Nottingham: DCFS.

Department for Children, Schools and Families (DCSF) (2009) *The National Strategies: Early Years: About the Themes and Principles*. Available online at http://nationalstrategies.standards.dcsf.gov.uk/eyfs/site/principles/index.htm (accessed November 2009).

Department for Education and Skills (DfEE) (2003) *Excellence and Enjoyment: A Strategy for Primary Schools*, Sudbury: DfEE.

Haviland, J. (1988) *Take Care, Mr Baker!* London: Fourth Estate.

National Advisory Committee on Creative and Cultural Education (NACCCE) (1999) *All Our Futures: Creativity, Culture and Education*, Sudbury: DfEE.

Office for Standards in Education (Ofsted) (2002) *The National Literacy Strategy: The First Four Years 1998–2002*, London: Ofsted.

Rose, J. (2008) *The Independent Review of the Primary Curriculum: Interim Report*, London: DCSF. Available online at www.dcsf.gov.uk/primarycurriculumreview (accessed October 2009).

Rose, J. (2009) *The Independent Review of the Primary Curriculum: Final Report*, London: DCSF. Available online at www.dcsf.gov.uk/primarycurriculumreview (accessed October 2009).

Royal Society for the encouragement of Arts, Manufactures and Commerce (RSA) (2005) *How Special Are Subjects? Are they the best way to structure a curriculum or can we do better?* London: Creative Partnerships/RSA.

Simpson, D. (1996) 'Progressivism and the development of primary education: an historical review', *History of Education Society Bulletin*, 58(Autumn): 55–63.

White, J. (ed.) (2004) *Rethinking the School Curriculum: Values, Aims and Purposes*, London: RoutledgeFalmer.

Wyse, D. (1998) *Primary Writing*, Buckingham: Open University Press.

Wyse, D. (ed.) (2003) *Introduction to Childhood Studies*, Oxford: Basil Blackwell.

Wyse, D. (2005) *Two Tears for the Primary Curriculum*, Paper presented at the How Special are Subjects? conference, Royal Society for the encouragement of Arts, Manufactures and Commerce (RSA), 6 April, London.

Wyse, D. and Spendlove, D. (2007) 'Partners in creativity: action research and creative partnerships', *Education 3–13*, 35(2): 181–91.

Wyse, D. and Torrance, H. (2009) 'The development and consequences of national curriculum assessment for primary education in England', *Educational Research*, 51(2): 213–28.

Wyse, D., McCreery, E. and Torrance, H. (2008) *The Trajectory and Impact of National Reform: Curriculum and Assessment in English Primary Schools (Cambridge Primary Review Research Survey 3/2)*, Cambridge: University of Cambridge Faculty of Education.

Wyse, D., Hilton, M., Burke, C. and Goswami, U. (eds) (2009) *A Response to the Independent Review of the Primary Curriculum: Interim Report (December 2008) by Sir Jim Rose*, Cambridge: PLACE Group.

THE NATIONAL CONTEXT FOR THE CURRICULUM

Maureen Lewis and Carrie Ansell

INTRODUCTION

Prior to the introduction of the National Curriculum in 1988, the school curriculum was largely determined at local level, but throughout the 1970s and 1980s public debate about education, schools and the curriculum grew. This debate culminated in the introduction of a statutory National Curriculum by the Department for Education and Science in 1988, which heralded an era of increasingly centralised control of education. During the last two decades, the National Curriculum and other non-statutory guidance (and the support structures and assessment associated with these) have become part of the mechanism by which government education policy becomes enacted within schools.

A school's curriculum involves a complex interplay of beliefs, attitudes, skills, knowledge and understanding. It is no surprise, therefore, that what is taught in our schools and how it is taught is a matter of debate between those who subscribe to different values, who have different aims for education, who have different views on the kind of knowledge that the curriculum should contain or who question whether a national curriculum is needed at all (see Kelly 2004, for detailed discussion of such issues).

The National Curriculum Handbook for Primary Teachers (DFEE/QCA, 2000) defines the curriculum as 'all the learning and other experiences that each school plans for its pupils' (p. 10). This definition, as with most issues connected to the curriculum, is disputed and alternative definitions exist, but for this unit we will use this official definition. Throughout this unit we will be discussing the National Curriculum and the *Statutory Framework for the Early Years Foundation Stage* and non-statutory guidance for England. For details of the curriculum in Wales and Northern Ireland, see www.accac.org.uk and www.ccea.org.uk. For details of the curriculum for Scotland see Unit 4.4 (Ellis).

OBJECTIVES

By the end of this unit you should:

■ understand the rationale and context for the emergence of a national curriculum;
■ be familiar with the current aims, structures and content of the National Curriculum/ Early Years Foundation Stage curriculum;

■ have examined the implementation of the non-statutory National Strategies for Literacy and Numeracy and the subsequent 'renewal' of their Frameworks of Teaching objectives, as a case study of moving from policy into curriculum practice;
■ have considered the advantages and disadvantages of a statutory national curriculum;
■ have reflected on possible future developments of the National Curriculum with reference to the QCA Futures agenda.

THE EMERGENCE OF A NATIONAL CURRICULUM

The Education Act 1944 did not lay down any requirements for the school curriculum (other than the inclusion of religious education). This gave schools and individual teachers great freedom to determine what was taught. There have been many significant educational and political changes during the last 60 years that have affected this position and some of the key events relating to the curriculum are outlined below.

The rise of progressive education

In the 1950s and 1960s, the 11+ examination was widely used to assess which type of school children would attend at the end of their primary years. In 1953, the first secondary comprehensive (non-selective) school opened and local education authorities (LEAs) began to abandon the 11+ examination. Changes aimed at modernising the primary and secondary curricula, such as the introduction of 'modern maths' and 'creative writing', began to be made. In 1967, the Plowden Report (CACE, 1967) argued for an active, experiential and child-centred curriculum for primary schools. This report both reflected and gave further impetus to changes that were already happening within some schools. Although the extent of progressive practice with primary schools in the 1960s and 1970s is difficult to quantify, this shift in thinking and practice brought to the fore the tensions between child-centred views of education and more traditional performance-based views.

The 'Great Debate'

The rise of progressive educational ideas and practices led to a public debate via parliamentary questions, newspaper articles and academic publications. New practices such as the introduction of mixed-ability classes, the use of competency-based assessment and the spread of informal and 'play'-based approaches in primary schools were attacked as leading to a decline in educational standards. In response, in 1974 the government set up the 'Assessment Performance Unit' to monitor standards in mathematics, English and science and to provide statistical evidence.

In 1976, the then Prime Minister, James Callaghan, opened what he called the 'Great Debate' on education in a speech, in which he discussed the need for changes in education. The major concerns at the time centred around beliefs that:

■ there was a general decline in educational standards;
■ the curriculum had become overcrowded;
■ there was an imbalance in the subjects being studied (too many students taking humanities and not enough studying science and technology);
■ there were variations in approaches to the curriculum between schools;
■ the curriculum did not meet the demands of a modern society.

Task 4.3.1 **CONCERNS ABOUT THE CURRICULUM**

Look at the list of concerns about the curriculum in 1976. Discuss the following questions:

■ Which of these concerns are under discussion in relation to today's schools?
■ What would you consider to be robust evidence to prove or disprove these concerns?
■ Do you consider that any of the concerns listed above have been 'solved' or have become less pressing since 1976?

The introduction of a core curriculum

Following the 'Great Debate', the government began to exercise some control over the curriculum. By 1980, LEAs had to produce detailed statements of their curricular policies and their schools had to make public their curricula.

Throughout the 1980s, the idea of a 'core curriculum', which gave greater attention to 'the basics', began to be promoted. Critics saw this as a narrowing of the curriculum, with the potential for a split between 'the basics' and the rest of the curriculum (which could be seen as less important). These decades of intense debate and increasing official control of the curriculum culminated in the Education Reform Act 1988, which introduced the National Curriculum for the first time. The curriculum contained the statutory statements and non-statutory guidance concerning the curriculum every child should study between the ages of 5 and 16. It set out the structural details of how the curriculum would operate:

■ core and foundation subjects to be studied by all pupils;
■ attainment targets defining progress through knowledge, skills and understanding in every subject;
■ programmes of study – the content, skills and processes that must be taught during each key stage;
■ assessment arrangements for assessing each pupil at or near the end of key stages.

The National Curriculum Council (NCC) and the Schools Examination and Curriculum Council (SEAC) were set up to oversee the new curriculum. These quangos later changed to the School Curriculum and Assessment Authority (SCAA) and latterly to the Qualifications and Curriculum Authority (QCA).

In 2000, the National Curriculum was revised. The subject content was slimmed down and citizenship was included for the first time; the aims, purposes and values were stated explicitly and further non-statutory guidance and learning across the curriculum guidelines were included. This revised document – *The National Curriculum Handbook for Primary Teachers in England* (DfES/QCA, 2000) – is currently in force. Figure 4.3.1 shows the content and assessment of the current National Curriculum and its division into key stages.

The early years curriculum

In 2000, the 'Foundation Stage' was introduced as a distinct phase for children aged three to five. The Education Act 2002 extended the National Curriculum to include the Foundation Stage, and

Key Stage	Age	Year	Statutory curriculum 2005	Other non-statutory areas and non-statutory guidelines	Statutory assessment
Foundation Stage	3–4		Statutory document – *The Early Years Foundation Stage* **6 areas of learning** • Personal, social and emotional development • Communication, language and literacy • Problem solving, reasoning and numeracy		The EYFS Profile (reception year)
	4–5	R	• Knowledge and understanding of the world • Physical development • Creative development Each area of learning has set of related **Early Learning Goals**		
Key Stage 1	5–6	1	Statutory document – *The National Curriculum Handbook for Primary Teachers in England*	• Personal social and health education (PSHE)	Teacher assessment and national tests in English and mathematics in Year 2
	6–7	2	**Core subjects** – English, mathematics, science **Foundation subjects** – design and technology, ICT, history,	• MFL – an entitlement from 2009 • Key skills –	
Key Stage 2	7–8	3	geography, art and design, music, physical education **Additional statutory areas** –	problem solving, communication, application of	National tests in core subjects (summer term, Year 6)
	8–9	4	Religious education. Content determined by LEA or faith foundation. QCA national	number, IT, working with others, improving	
	9–10	5	framework available, citizenship **General teaching requirements** – apply across all subjects and	own learning and performance • Thinking skills –	
	10–11	6	include inclusion, use of language, ICT and health and safety	enquiry, information processing, reasoning, creative thinking, evaluation	
Key Stage 3	11–12	7	As Key Stages 1 and 2 with addition of a modern foreign language (MFL)	As Key Stages 1 and 2 but MFL now statutory	National tests in core subjects (summer term, Year 9)

■ **Figure 4.3.1** Content and assessment of the current National Curriculum

the six areas of learning outlined in *Curriculum Guidance for the Foundation Stage* (QCA, 2000) became statutory for nursery and reception classes and early years settings receiving education grant funding. The new *Statutory Framework for the Early Years Foundation Stage* (DCSF, 2008) brings together and replaces the *Curriculum Guidance*, the *Birth to Three Matters* framework (2002) and the *National Standards for Under 8s Daycare and Childminding* (2003). The aim of this new framework, which early years providers began to use in September 2008, was to help children achieve the *Every Child Matters* (ECM) five outcomes – be healthy; stay safe; enjoy and achieve; make a positive contribution; and achieve economic well-being. It was developed alongside the renewed *Primary Framework for Literacy and Mathematics*. The Early Years Foundation Stage (EYFS) and the *Primary Framework* together enable nursery, reception and Key Stage 1 providers to see how the six areas of the EYFS link to literacy and mathematics in Key Stage 1.

A national assessment system for the Foundation Stage, replacing local baseline assessment schemes, was also introduced. Now called the Early Years Foundation Stage Profile, it requires all registered early years providers from September 2008 to assess each child in the academic year in which he or she reaches the age of five. Those criticising the EYFS have said that it is too prescriptive and that there are too many inappropriate Early Learning Goals on reading and writing. The argument is that these may encourage teachers to resort to using formal teaching methods with children who are far too young, in order to ensure goals are achieved. This, in turn, would cause increased stress for children. Comparisons have been made with the curriculum in Scandinavian countries, which wait until children are six or seven and where 'readiness' for school is assessed before introducing formal elements of reading and writing with little effect on standards.

THE AIMS AND STRUCTURES OF THE NATIONAL CURRICULUM

Values, aims, purposes and principles

Task 4.3.2 AIMS AND PURPOSES

When asked the purpose of education, young children often reply that its purpose is 'to help you get a job'. Do you think there are other purposes to education?

■ Reflect on what you think are the values, aims and purposes of education. Then read the section 'Values and purposes underpinning the school curriculum' in the *National Curriculum Handbook* (DfES/QCA, 2000).
■ Summarise the two aims and four purposes in the handbook. Compare your ideas with those.
■ Discuss why is it important to be explicit about the values and purposes underpinning any national curriculum.

The *Statutory Framework for the Early Years Foundation Stage* also sets out a list of purposes and aims along with a set of principles for early years education. These are grouped into four distinct themes: A Unique Child; Positive Relationships; Enabling Environments; Learning and Development. All practice is built around these guiding principles and they provide a context for teaching and learning in the EYFS.

Programmes of study, attainment targets and level descriptors

The *programmes of study* are legally binding statements that set out:

- the knowledge, skills and understanding that must be taught;
- the breadth of study – the contexts, activities, areas of study and range of experiences through which the knowledge, skills and understanding are taught.

In addition to the statutory National Curriculum programmes of study, further non-statutory National Strategies for English and mathematics, with frameworks giving detailed termly curriculum objectives and advice on how to deliver these objectives, were introduced in 1997 and 1998. The strategies merged to become the Primary National Strategy (PNS) in 2004 and the frameworks were revised in 2006. A case study on this is given later in this unit.

Attainment targets set out the criteria for the knowledge, skills and understanding that pupils are expected to have by the end of each key stage. Most attainment targets are divided into eight, progressively more challenging, level descriptors. These level descriptors provide the basis for making judgements about pupil performance and the expected attainment at each key stage is shown in Figure 4.3.2. There will always be some pupils who may move more slowly or more quickly through the levels because of their particular abilities and aptitudes.

National tests (see Section 5) at the end of each key stage (and teacher assessment at Key Stage 1) are used to assign levels. Schools inform parents of the individual results of these formal tests for their child and the overall school results are made public. Teachers also use the levels to assess children's work and moderate standards within the school.

Range of levels at which the great majority of pupils are expected to work		Expected attainment for the majority of the pupils at the end of the key stage	
Key Stage 1	1–3	At age 7	2
Key Stage 2	2–5	At age 11	4
Key Stage 3	3–7	At age 14	6

▪ **Figure 4.3.2** National Curriculum attainment target levels

---

Task 4.3.3 **ATTAINMENT TARGETS 1**

- Select one core subject and one foundation subject and examine the attainment target level descriptors for these. In each subject you have chosen, track one skill or one strand of knowledge through the level descriptors and note how it becomes more complex.
- If you have access to children's work, consider where you would place this in terms of the level descriptors.

Task 4.3.4 **ATTAINMENT TARGETS 2**

Discuss what you think are the advantages and disadvantages of assessing children's work as in Task 4.3.3, synthesising both theory and practice.

Schemes of work and other National Curriculum support materials

Schools are expected to show how they will deliver the National Curriculum through outlining their planning in *schemes of work*. There is no statutory way in which a school must set out its schemes of work and head teachers and teachers can plan their own schemes to take account of their own context and the choices available to them within the curriculum. For example, the breadth of study in history allows schools to select from seven possible ancient civilisations to study.

To support teachers in understanding how the programmes of study can be translated into practical schemes of work, the QCA provides exemplar schemes of work in all subject areas except for English and mathematics (where support with planning is provided via the PNS). Many schools have used these schemes of work to ease the planning burden and to familiarise themselves with the planning process. As they have become increasingly familiar with the programmes of study, schools have begun to develop and adapt the schemes of work.

The personalisation of centrally provided support materials is now officially encouraged. In *Excellence and Enjoyment* (2003) – the DfES statement of its vision for primary education – schools are encouraged to be more innovative and creative and use the freedom they have to plan a more flexible curriculum. On the QCA website and on the *National Curriculum in Action* website (see 'Relevant websites' at the end of this unit), there are examples of how to adapt and combine units along with case studies, showing the many different ways in which the programmes of study can be translated into practice. While many teachers find these resources helpful, critics see them as a way of controlling and strengthening the official approach to the curriculum. However, the encouragement for schools to be more flexible has been welcomed by most educationalists as evidence of a changing ethos after several years of increasingly centralised control.

THE NATIONAL STRATEGIES – A CASE STUDY OF POLICY INTO CURRICULUM PRACTICE

Comparing the initial implementation of the National Strategies for English and Mathematics (1997/1998), the revisions of the frameworks in 2006 and the related curriculum reviews is illustrative of the ways in which government policy becomes enacted within schools. It also indicates how the policy approaches to implementing new curriculum changes have begun to show some signs of change over the last few years.

As with the introduction of the National Curriculum, the National Strategies were conceived as a response to perceived low standards of attainment in reading and mathematics and concerns about how these were taught in school (see, for example, Ofsted, 1996). The strategies and their delivery structures were formed and written by a small group and briefly trialled before being launched nationally. To ensure the implementation of the strategies, the government put the following in place (adapted from Barber, 2000):

■ *A long term project plan* for both literacy and numeracy, setting out actions, responsibilities and deadlines.

■ *A substantial investment* sustained over the lifetime of the strategies and skewed towards those schools that need the most help.

■ *A project infrastructure* involving national direction from the government disseminated via regional directors, LEA strategy managers and LEA consultants who deliver training and offer targeted support. There are also school-based, expert teachers who model best practice for their peers.

■ *Public accountability* through challenging *targets* for SATs results and the publication of 'league tables'.

■ *A detailed teaching framework programme* and an expectation that every class would have a daily mathematics and literacy lesson.

■ *A professional-development programme* consisting of centrally provided courses and materials for school and LEA use.

■ *The provision of 'intensive support'* to schools where it was deemed the most progress was required and early intervention and catch-up programmes for children who had fallen behind.

■ *Regular monitoring* by Ofsted and LEAs and *external evaluation* by Ofsted and a team from the University of Toronto.

■ *A national curriculum and professional standards for initial teacher training*, requiring all providers to prepare trainee primary teachers to teach mathematics and literacy daily. Subsequently, in 2007, the Training and Development Agency for Schools announced that trainee teachers were required to meet 33 standards covering attributes, knowledge and understanding, and skills. The framework of the standards became progressive so that, at each career point, teachers would have to demonstrate increasing expertise and prove efficacy in relation to them.

Given this 'assertive, relatively controlling, and responsive set of strategies' (Barber, 2000) for implementation, it is no surprise that the majority of schools adopted the National Strategies into their curriculum in some form or other, even though they were not statutory. While some welcomed the strategies, there was also teacher resistance to the top-down implementation and increased government control of *how* teachers teach, the perceived loss of teacher professionalism and the negative impact an emphasis on literacy and numeracy had on the rest of the curriculum, as well as reservations about such some of the teaching methods advocated by the strategies.

The renewed *Primary Framework for Literacy and Mathematics* was introduced in both paper and electronic form in 2006 (DCSF, 2007). This policy change was accepted more readily than the original frameworks. This was because, by this time:

■ some of the pressure and support mechanisms had already begun to evolve;

■ the aims of the framework were wider, encouraging increased flexibility and creativity, and making them more acceptable to more teachers;

■ other developments, such as an emphasis on speaking and listening and assessment for learning, within longer units of work in literacy, came alongside the impetus for teachers to plan for personalised learning and address the ECM agenda, which conceived the vision of a 'rich, varied and exciting curriculum';

■ attempts towards consultations were undertaken in the writing of the new framework.

As part of the renewal process, a review of the teaching of reading took place to inform the new framework. Again, this process indicated some moves towards a more inclusive process, which offered extensive consultation opportunities, open to all. However, many felt only certain views were taken into account and outcomes proved controversial. The incorporation of the findings of the *Independent Review of the Teaching of Early Reading* (Rose, 2006) and the introduction of a new conceptual framework for reading known as the 'Simple View of Reading', provoked the strongest response. Many practitioners in schools, supported by researchers in this particular field of literacy, objected to being directed to teach reading to young children using a synthetic phonics approach.

In addition to this, controversies over standards and marking in 2008, along with findings from the report from the University of Cambridge team's *Primary Review* (2009) all seemed to signal that many educationalists had become disillusioned with the testing regime inherent in the English curriculum.

Changes made to the 2004 Key Stage 1 standard assessment tests (SATs) arrangements placed greater emphasis on 'building a picture' of the whole child through a range of assessment techniques.

Although league tables continued to be published based on the schools SATs results, these were beginning to be informed by a contextual value-added (CVA) score to show those schools that have added the most value, taking into account factors such as ethnicity and poverty. Since 2008, these scores now form part of the league tables.

This is by no means a perfect system, but shows something of a move forward from what was viewed as a purely top-down imposition.

This case study has shown how a perceived need for educational reform influences government policy – that standards will be raised by reforming how a curriculum subject is taught – and how this policy in turns leads to curriculum change through a detailed teaching programme, advice on how to deliver it and mechanisms to encourage participation. But even carefully constructed implementation plans have to change and evolve as later changes demonstrate. Processes have to be dynamic not static, inclusive not top down.

A CURRICULUM FOR THE TWENTY-FIRST CENTURY – THE DEBATE CONTINUES

Curriculum development never remains static for long and as society changes the kind of curriculum it wants and needs in its schools is likely to change also. In 2005, the QCA launched a debate about the future of the National Curriculum in *Futures: Meeting the Challenge*, which identified the following forces for curriculum change:

■ changes in society and the nature of work;
■ the impact of technology;
■ new understanding about learning;
■ the need for greater personalisation and innovation;
■ the increasing international dimension to life and work.

The report, and subsequent forum for discussion, stimulated debate about how best to prepare young people for a technologically advanced global world.

In December 2006, the Teaching and Learning in 2020 Review Group published their *2020 Vision* report of teaching and learning, with a focus on what personalised learning might look like in schools in 2020. The group described personalised learning as 'a highly structured and responsive approach to each child's and young person's learning, in order that all are able to progress, achieve and participate' (Teaching and Learning in 2020 Review Group, 2006). The recommendations included embedding assessment for learning, with pupils taking ownership of their learning, and engaging parents and carers in children's learning.

THE REVIEW OF THE CURRICULUM

After nearly two decades of the National Curriculum and governmental advice on *how* to teach as well as *what* to teach, the primary curriculum is under intense review and scrutiny again. The 'official' *Independent Review of the Primary Curriculum*, led by Sir Jim Rose, was set up in response to a request from the Secretary of State as part of the *Children's Plan* (December 2007). The aims of the review were:

■ to ensure that more time would be spent on the basics of reading and writing and mathematics;
■ to consider how well two of the milestones in the EYFS support a smooth transition into Key Stage 1;

■   to provide greater scope for flexibility and creativity in the curriculum;

■   to allow time for children to learn a modern foreign language (which will become statutory at Key Stage 2 by September 2010);

■   to address the disadvantages that summer-born children may experience during the transition between play-based early years learning and the primary phase.

The review, supported by the QCA, called for evidence nationally under five broad headings that reflected the remit given. Respondents to the review ranged from teachers, parents and governors to local authorities, universities and professional associations.

Criticism of the review focused on the narrow brief, lack of any real independence or intention to change the current testing regime inherent in the present curriculum and, in relation to literacy, the fundamental absence of speaking and listening, with the emphasis being on the 'basics' of reading and writing.

An independent review of the primary curriculum was also set up by Robin Alexander of Cambridge University in October 2006. The main purpose of the *Cambridge Primary Review* was:

> to begin to make a real difference to the character and quality of English primary education over the first decades of the 21st century, and to the contribution which that education makes to individual lives and the collective good, at a time of change, uncertainty and growing concern about the future.

The review commissioned research surveys around ten themes. Interim reports on this research have been published, several of which generated considerable debate, media interest and controversy (e.g. the three reports on Theme 3, on curriculum and assessment: Conroy *et al.*, 2008; Hall and Øzerk, 2008; Wyse *et al.*, 2008).

Task 4.3.5 **REFLECTING ON REVIEWS**

■ Despite purporting to be independent, it is hard to measure how truly consultative and independent both reviews (Rose/Cambridge) of the curriculum were. Reflect on your reading and discuss this with reference to scholarly argument.

■ Read and critically review some of the Theme 3 reports (see above) for the *Cambridge Primary Review*. What comparative beliefs and values underline the principles of each review?

WHERE NEXT? LEARNING TO LEARN

In the last few years there has already been growing interest in the aspects of learning currently to be found in the 'Learning across the National Curriculum' section of the current curriculum document. These aspects of learning include:

■   Key skills – problem solving, communication, application of number, information technology, working with others, improving own learning and performance.

■   Thinking skills – enquiry, information processing, reasoning, creative thinking, evaluation.

Campaigns to promote 'learning to learn' and research and development into this are under way by the DCSF (for example, *Excellence and Enjoyment: Learning and Teaching in the Primary Years* (2003) and a wide range of organisations and academics (for example, the Campaign for Learning; the Economic and Social Research Council's (ESRC) Learning How to Learn research project; and Claxton, 2002). Similarly, national organisations (such as the Royal Society for the encouragement of Arts, Manufactures and Commerce) and individuals are working with schools to develop more creative approaches to the curriculum (see Unit 7.3 (Cremin and Barnes) and Unit 4.2 (Wyse)).

More recently, the *Primary Curriculum Futures* report from the 2008 *Cambridge Primary Review* (Conroy et al., 2008) refers to the curriculum of the future having a focus on 'understanding for learning' and a shift away from traditional subjects towards integrated content. It identifies alternative curricula, such as the Somerset Critical Skills course, the Reggio Emilia approach and Philosophy for Children (see, for example, Haynes, 2002), which have as their underpinning beliefs creativity and children as self-determining agents of their learning.

This same report reviewed shared tendencies of schools that have established alternative curricula. It concluded that these schools spend less time using televisions and computers, and more time reading, with and to children, with greater emphasis on nurturing the imagination.

All these developments point to a new phase of curriculum development.

THE ADVANTAGES AND DISADVANTAGES OF A NATIONAL CURRICULUM

Now you have looked at why the National Curriculum was created and how it is structured and assessed, considered a case study of how government curriculum policy becomes practice and looked briefly at how the curriculum continues to change and evolve, you will probably have begun to form your own opinions on whether a national approach to the curriculum is a good idea. Those who support the introduction and continued development of a national curriculum and non-statutory guidance argue that it has a crucial role to play in addressing several educational issues. These include:

- *Providing an entitlement curriculum* for all pupils regardless of ability. The curriculum applies to all children and there is guidance on inclusion for children with special education needs, those for whom English is an additional language and pupils with disabilities.
- *Ensuring progress and continuity*, through subjects, between key stages and across schools.
- *Addressing inequality of provision* and educational opportunity between schools, by ensuring schools do not offer widely varying curricula.
- *Raising standards*. The curriculum levels provide a measure against which individual progress and attainment can be judged. They also provide national assessment data against which schools can be judged in comparison to schools with similar intakes.
- *Improving communication, transparency and accountability*. Parents and the wider public know what is taught in schools and the progress that can be expected. Schools must report on the progress of individuals to parents. Governments and local authorities can monitor the results of investments in professional development and curriculum innovations. Education is very costly and governments and the public have a right to know if their money is being spent effectively.

Those who have concerns about the role of a national curriculum point to:

■ *A lack of conceptual clarity* in the aims and purpose of the National Curriculum and a particular view of the nature of knowledge and how it is acquired and measured.

■ *The ideological dominance of the official views* and discourse. For example, at subject level an emphasis on Standard English and synthetic phonics, or at the conceptual level the implicit message that this is the only and correct approach to the curriculum.

■ *A diminution in teacher professionalism and autonomy* with teachers increasingly told what to teach and how to teach it, leaving no space for professional judgement.

■ *Restrictions on pupil choice and creativity*. The curriculum leaves little space for pupils to pursue areas of particular interest or go outside the proscribed curriculum. Critics argue whether this prepares children for the kind of flexible, self-motivating environments in which many will spend their adult working lives or whether it allows them to develop as fully rounded individuals.

■ *The crowded nature of the curriculum*, which can lead to superficial understanding in order to achieve coverage.

■ Concerns regarding *the reliability of national tests* and their impact on what is taught.

Task 4.3.6 **DO WE NEED A NATIONAL CURRICULUM?**

■ Consider the arguments for and against a national curriculum.
■ Which to you seem the most compelling? On balance do you consider we should retain or abandon or modify our National Curriculum?

Task 4.3.7 **ANALYSING YOUR VIEWS ON THE NATIONAL CURRICULUM**

Make use of argument from further reading and theory in order to analyse your views on the National Curriculum.

SUMMARY

This brief overview of the development of the National Curriculum shows the move from teacher and school autonomy to an increasingly centralised control of the curriculum and finally towards developing a new curriculum with an emphasis on creativity, innovation and personalisation. As society continues to evolve and technology to advance, new demands are made on the curriculum. Debates now focus on what is needed to be a creative and effective learner in the new 'knowledge society' (Hargreaves, 2003) and how digital and communication technologies can enable learners to collaborate and participate in this process. Qualities such as developing critical thinking skills, managing information and establishing relationships are being given high status.

After several years of a centrally controlled, content-driven curriculum, schools are now developing more autonomy within their curriculum. Keeping an entitlement curriculum for all that is relevant to young people's lives, ensuring personalisation, the emphasis on creativity and flexible learning skills and improving the five outcomes from *Every Child Matters* are now the challenges for all those engaged in curriculum development.

ANNOTATED FURTHER READING

Colwill, I. (2005) *What Has the National Curriculum Ever Done for Us?* Available online at www. qca.org.uk/futures/ (accessed October 2009).

In this article, the Director of the QCA curriculum division argues that the purposes of the National Curriculum are essentially democratic. He elaborates on the purposes of a national curriculum and discusses how future revision needs to take place. This article gives a useful insight into 'official' thinking about the curriculum.

Coulby, D. (2000) *Beyond the National Curriculum*, London: RoutledgeFalmer.

This gives an alternative view of the National Curriculum.

Johnson, M. (2007) *Subject to Change: New Thinking on the Curriculum*, London: ATL.

The foreword by Mick Waters from the QCA refers to a book that 'asks searching questions and provides serious argument. It is a positive book, looking for a better future for learning, and in so doing seeks out the treasure of the curriculum.'

Kelly, A.V. (2004) *The Curriculum: Theory and Practice*, 5th edn, London: Sage.

Kelly summarises the findings of curriculum research, and considers the nature and development of the curriculum and the importance of examining curriculum development. He takes a critical look at recent curriculum development and the introduction of the National Curriculum.

Pollard, A and Triggs, P. (2000) What Pupils Say: Changing Policy and Practice in Primary Education, London: Continuum.

A view of the curriculum from the pupils' perspective. This book looks at the impact of the introduction of the National Curriculum on pupils and their experiences in the classroom.

RELEVANT WEBSITES

Cambridge Primary Review: Final Report: www.primaryreview.org.uk

Campaign for Learning: www.campaign-for-learning.org.uk

Economic and Social Research Council's Learning How to Learn research project: www.tlrp.org/proj. phase11/phase2f.html

Independent Review of the Curriculum: Final Report (Rose Review): www.dcsf.gov.uk/primary curriculumreview

National Curriculum in Action: http://curriculum.qcda.gov.uk/key-stages-1-and-2/assessment/ nc-in-action

National Curriculum in Northern Ireland: www.ccea.org.uk

National Curriculum in Wales: www.accac.org.uk

National Strategies: http://nationalstrategies.standards.dcsf.gov.uk/

For reports and articles on the National Strategies, including a further summary of relevant research, see also: www.literacytrust.org.uk/database/primary/stratevaluation.html#Final

Primary Framework for Literacy and Mathematics: http://nationalstrategies.standards.dcsf.gov.uk/ primary/primaryframework

Qualifications and Curriculum Authority: www.qcda.gov.uk

Visit the companion website www.routledge.com/textbooks/ltps2e for:

■ links to useful websites relevant to this unit.

REFERENCES

Alexander, R.J. (2009) *Towards a New Primary Curriculum: A Report from the Cambridge Primary Review*, Cambridge: University of Cambridge. Available online at www.primaryreview.org.uk/ Publications/CambridgePrimaryReviewrep.html (accessed October 2009).

Barber, M. (2000) 'Large-scale reform is possible', *Education Week*, 25 November. Available online at www.edweek.org/ew/articles/2000/11/15/11barber.h20.html (accessed November 2009).

Central Advisory Council for Education (CACE) (1967) *Children and Their Primary Schools* (Plowden Report), London: HMSO.

Claxton, G. (2002) *Building Learning Power: Helping Young People Become Better Learners*, Bristol: TLO.

Conroy, J., Hulme, M. and Menter, I. (2008) *Primary Curriculum Futures (Cambridge Primary Review Research Survey 3/3)*, Cambridge: University of Cambridge Faculty of Education. Available online at www.primaryreview.org.uk/ (accessed October 2009).

Department for Children, Schools and Families (DCSF) (2003) *Excellence and Enjoyment: Learning and Teaching in the Primary Years*, London: DCSF.

Department for Children, Schools and Families (DCSF) (2007) *Primary Framework for Literacy and Mathematics*. Available online at www.standards.dfes.gov.uk/primaryframeworks/ (accessed October 2009).

Department for Education and Employment/Qualifications and Curriculum Authority (DEE/QCA) (2000) *The National Curriculum Handbook for Primary Teachers*, London: HMSO.

Department for Education and Skills (DfES) (2003) *Excellence and Enjoyment: A Strategy for Primary Schools*, London: DfES. Available online at http://nationalstrategies.standards.dcsf.gov.uk/ node/88755 (accessed November 2009).

Hall, K. and Øzerk, K. (2008) *Primary Curriculum and Assessment: England and Other Countries (Cambridge Primary Review Research Survey 3/1)*, Cambridge: University of Cambridge Faculty of Education. Available online at www.primaryreview.org.uk/ (accessed October 2009).

Hargreaves, A. (2003) *Teaching in the Knowledge Society*, Buckingham: Open University Press.

Haynes, J. (2002) *Children as Philosophers: Learning Through Enquiry and Dialogue in the Primary Classroom*, London: RoutledgeFalmer.

Kelly, A.V. (2004) *The Curriculum: Theory and Practice*, 5th edn, London: Sage.

Office for Standards in Education (Ofsted) (1996) *The Teaching of Reading in 45 Inner London Primary Schools: A Report by Her Majesty's Inspectors in Collaboration with the LEAs of Islington, Southwark and Tower Hamlets*, London: Ofsted.

Qualifications and Curriculum Authority (QCA) (2000) *Curriculum Guidance for the Foundation Stage*, London: QCA.

Qualifications and Curriculum Authority (QCA) (2005) *Futures: Meeting the Challenge*, London: QCA. Available online at www.qcda.org.uk/6073.aspx (accessed October 2009).

Rose, J. (2006) *Independent Review of the Teaching of Early Reading*, London: DfES. Available online at www.standards.dfes.gov.uk/phonics/report.pdf (accessed October 2009).

Teaching and Learning in 2020 Review Group (2006) *Statutory Framework for the Early Years Foundation Stage*, London: DCSF. Available online at http://nationalstrategies.standards. dcsf.gov.uk/node/151379 (accessed October 2009).

Wyse, D., McCreery, E. and Torrance, H. (2008) *The Trajectory and Impact of National Reform: Curriculum and Assessment in English Primary Schools (Cambridge Primary Review Research Survey 3/2)*, Cambridge: University of Cambridge Faculty of Education. Available online at www.primaryreview.org.uk/ (accessed October 2009).

THE SCOTTISH CONTEXT FOR THE CURRICULUM

Susan Ellis

INTRODUCTION

The curriculum in Scotland seeks to define and frame the core ideas and experiences that are most important for learning and teaching. The challenges involved in any such task are threefold: first, reaching a common agreement about what is important and fundamental can be problematic. Researchers, politicians, local authorities, teachers, head teachers, children, parents and employers may all have different views. The second challenge is to find a curriculum framework that provides support and direction but also allows flexibility. Allowing for flexibility is important so that the curriculum can respond to changes, both in the social context of education and to new research understandings of how children learn and how best to develop learning. The third challenge is to ensure that the curriculum intentions are not lost during implementation. This final challenge is perhaps the hardest to meet.

This unit describes how curriculum policy is made in Scotland and outlines some of the key implications and implementation issues of *Curriculum for Excellence*.

OBJECTIVES

By the end of this unit, you should be able to:

- explain the process of curriculum development in Scotland, who shapes the curriculum and how this is done;
- explain how this system came about and some of the advantages and disadvantages it offers;
- describe *Curriculum for Excellence*, why it was formed, how it is structured and how it is intended to shape practice and pedagogy in local authorities and primary schools;
- consider which aspects of the context of implementation may impede or facilitate change.

CURRICULUM POLICY IN SCOTLAND

Scotland has its own legislative framework for education. National policy is framed by the Scottish Government and education is the formal responsibility of the First Minister, who is answerable to the Scottish Parliament.

There is no legally enforceable 'national curriculum' in Scotland and any curriculum and assessment guidelines are non-statutory. This means that the curriculum is not a rigid, centrally determined programme of study. What *is* statutory is that the Minister for Education and Young People, local authorities and schools work together to improve the quality of school education, and that they report on their progress to the people of Scotland. The Education (National Priorities) (Scotland) Order 2000 places a duty on Scottish ministers to set, from time to time, national priorities in education. Local authorities must use these to frame their own objectives, which form the context for the schools' development plans, interpretations and delivery of the curriculum. The National Priorities give a general sense of direction for educational policy and curriculum development (see Figure 4.4.1). There are agreed quantitative measures and qualitative indicators to gauge how local authorities are progressing national priorities, and progress is reported to the Scottish Government by Her Majesty's Inspectorate for Education (HMIE).

There are other mechanisms for finding out whether the curriculum in Scotland is working effectively. The Scottish Survey of Achievement (SSA) provides sample-based information about overall levels of attainment, particularly in literacy and numeracy. This enables politicians to monitor the efficacy of their education policy and identify areas that need further investment or attention. Scotland also participates in several international studies of achievement, which allow education policies and practices to be examined against globally defined benchmarks. The Program for International Student Assessment (PISA) studies the attainment of 15-year-olds in maths, literacy and science in Organisation for Economic Cooperation and Development (OECD) countries, the Progress in International Reading Literacy Study (PIRLS) provides data on how nine and ten year olds perform in reading and the Trends in International Mathematics and Science Study (TIMSS) does this for

---

THE CURRENT NATIONAL PRIORITIES IN SCOTLAND

National Priority 1: Achievement and Attainment

To raise standards of educational attainment for all in schools, especially in the core skills of literacy and numeracy, and to achieve better levels in national measures of achievement, including examination results.

National Priority 2: Framework for Learning

To support and develop the skills of teachers [and] the self-discipline of pupils and enhance school environments so that they are conducive to teaching and learning.

National Priority 3: Inclusion and Equality

To promote equality and help every pupil benefit from education, with particular regard paid to pupils with disabilities and special educational needs, and to Gaelic and other lesser used languages.

National Priority 4: Values and Citizenship

To work with parents to teach pupils respect for self and one another and their interdependence with other members of their neighbourhood and society and to teach them the duties and responsibilities of citizenship in a democratic society.

National Priority 5: Learning for Life

To equip pupils with the foundation skills, attitudes and expectations necessary to prosper in a changing society and to encourage creativity and ambition.

■ **Figure 4.4.1** Scotland's National Priorities for Education

Source: www.ltscotland.org.uk/cpdscotland/fivenationalpriorities.asp

mathematics and science. Analyses of these, and of Scottish examination results, are published by the Scottish Qualifications Authority (SQA).

Curriculum policy and development is shaped by several bodies. HMIE publish school and local authority inspection reports, but also *Portrait of Current Practice* reports to promote improvements and stimulate reflection in Scottish education. Each report focuses on a specific curricular area and draws on the findings of inspections and examples of effective practice that have been showcased at HMIE conferences (HMIE, 2006a and b). They also publish an online digital resource for professional development, *Journey to Excellence* (www.hmie.gov.uk/documents/publication/hgiosjte.pdf), which exemplifies excellent practice and draws together professional knowledge and research. Schools and local authorities use these reports to help them identify and address emerging issues about curriculum organisation, teaching content and pedagogy.

Task 4.4.1 **IMPLICATIONS OF A NATIONAL CURRICULUM**

Find some recent HMIE *Portrait of Current Practice* reports on the Scottish Government website www.hmie.gov.uk/Publications.aspx. Choose a subject area in the primary curriculum that interests you. Read its *Portrait of Current Practice* report and consider:

■ how far the description of current practice matches your experience in schools;
■ how far the description matches the insights into the curriculum and pedagogy that you have gained from your reading about research and practice in this subject area.

Then, list three specific implications of the report for your own teaching in this area.

Learning and Teaching Scotland (LTS) provides national advice on curriculum policy and practice. It has responsibility for national research and development work and for delivering national initiatives, such as *Curriculum for Excellence*, and GLOW, the Scottish schools digital network.

The management of school education rests with the 32 local authorities in Scotland. Local authorities must interpret and deliver national priorities and curriculum guidelines to meet local needs, while taking account of advice from HMIE, SQA and LTS. Most local authorities offer support in the form of local development plans, courses for professional development, guidance on planning and assessment and, occasionally, coordinating working parties to create curriculum resources.

The curriculum in schools is the formal responsibility of the head teacher, who prepares development plans to show how the school will develop its curriculum to meet local and national priorities. The head teacher must ensure that teachers deliver a suitable curriculum and that appropriate frameworks for teaching, assessment, monitoring and reporting are in place.

POLICY ON TESTING AND ASSESSMENT

Recent experience in Scotland shows that an assessment policy can have unintended consequences. In 1991, the government introduced Scotland's first national assessment policy. It highlighted the importance of considering evidence from a variety of sources (including evidence from self- and peer assessments) to make informed decisions about a child's progress and 'next steps'. National tests in reading, writing and mathematics were to moderate teachers' professional judgements. They were to be sat only when the teacher judged a child to have attained a level and, if the national test result conflicted with the teacher's professional judgement, the latter took priority (SOEID, 1991).

Yet, this did not happen. Local authorities used test results to set targets for improving attainment in individual schools; there were numerous reports of children being rehearsed for tests and taking and retaking tests. In 2001, the Assessment is for Learning (AifL) programme was established to try to ensure that assessment improved the quality of teaching and learning in schools. Its first national initiative focused on embedding research findings about formative assessment into school practices (Black and Wiliam, 1998; Black *et al.*, 2002). It was based on the principles of large-scale organisational change (Ellis and Hayward, 2009) and had a noticeable impact on practice.

Local authorities generally have baseline assessments in place for literacy and numeracy, which help track pupil progress and inform personal learning plans. Schools and local authorities use internally and externally devised summative assessments for literacy and numeracy, attainment in which will continue to be a focus of all HMIE inspections.

Task 4.4.2 **THE SHAPE OF THE NATIONAL CURRICULUM IN SCOTLAND**

■ Using all the information given so far, draw a diagram to show how the curriculum is shaped and developed in Scotland.
■ Compare your diagram with that of a colleague on the course.

THE PRIMARY CURRICULUM

In Scotland, pupils enter school in the year of their fifth birthday. There is one intake per year, in August, and the ages of children at the start of Primary 1 range from four years six months to five years six months. Children leave primary school when they have completed Primary 7.

The past half-century has seen three distinct curriculum policy phases in Scotland. In the 1960s, curriculum advice was developed by COPE (the Committee on Primary Education) and its subcommittees, subject to final approval by the Consultative Council on the Curriculum. However, primary teachers had complete choice about what they taught and the mechanisms to ensure that curriculum recommendations were discussed and adopted by schools were weak. A report for the Scottish Education Department concluded that, six years after one key curriculum initiative, the *Primary Memorandum*, 'Few head teachers had done anything to formulate a policy for the planned implementation of the approaches suggested' (SED, 1971: 16).

There are many reasons why schools can be slow to adopt new initiatives. Eisner identifies a passive resistance, in which 'experienced teachers tend to . . . ride out the wave of enthusiasm, and then just float until the next wave comes' (1992: 616). There can also be a tendency for teachers to embrace aspects that concur with current practice, but overlook or dismiss ideas that require change, and for them to focus on activities, materials and classroom organisation rather than on the deeper pedagogical principles (Spillane, 2000). Certainly, when the next curriculum policy phase – the *5–14 Guidelines* – was launched in 1989, the emphasis on talking and listening in the *English Language Guidelines* was greeted with genuine surprise, despite several policy documents since 1965 advocating the importance of planned contexts for talk for both language development and for learning.

The *5–14 Guidelines* sought to ensure continuity, breadth and progression in the primary and early secondary curriculum by outlining key content that should be taught and that would be inspected by HMIE. Scotland had always had a history of consensual curriculum development and there was disquiet about this new concept of a centrally determined and imposed curriculum framework. It was described as 'a shift in policy-making style in Scotland, from debate followed by consensus to consultation followed by imposition' (Rodger, in Adams, 2003: 371). The model used for developing the *5–14 Guidelines* offered both advantages and disadvantages: They were based on a consensual understanding of 'existing good practice' rather than on more theoretical or research-based understandings. This ensured a reasonably good fit with many existing school practices, but did not challenge or ask fundamental questions of them. For example, changes in the teaching of reading came not from the *5–14 Guidelines*, but from the Early Intervention initiative sponsored by the Scottish Executive Education Department (Ellis and Friel, 2008). Another problem was that each curricular area was developed by a separate working party of specialist teachers who paid scant regard to cross-curricular themes or connections. This effectively promoted a compartmentalised curriculum at the expense of the previous, integrated, approaches epitomised by methodologies such as the *Scottish Storyline Method* (Bell, 2003; Bell and Harkness, 2006). Also, because nobody took an overview of the whole curriculum, there was serious curriculum overload.

The pressure for accountability created in the wake of the *5–14 Guidelines* meant that curriculum policy was taken seriously. Variability between schools decreased and there was a stronger emphasis on equity and attainment. Because schemes and worksheets provided easy evidence of coverage and progression, active learning and the *Scottish Storyline Method* (which migrated to Scandinavia, where it thrived) were abandoned at this time, although it is now being reintroduced to Scotland.

Dividing every subject area into discrete outcomes, each split into strands and then further into tiny slivers of attainment targets, fragmented the curriculum in a way that was never envisaged. Forward planning focused on mapping activities on to attainment targets and strands rather than on identifying the most appropriate learning priorities and contexts for the class. The framework discouraged integration and did not prompt teachers to contextualise work or help pupils to see connections and links. The sheer quantity of content created time pressures and stress, and squeezed out opportunities for play, self-directed learning, extended writing and problem-based learning. Teachers had little time to revisit, consolidate or explore ideas in depth.

In short, the *5–14 Guidelines* encouraged teachers to focus on curriculum content and on attainment. These are good things. However, they also created some learning environments that were dysfunctional; environments that de-skilled teachers and did not foster creativity or intellectual and emotional engagement. The National Debate on Education initiated in 2002 showed that the people of Scotland did not want a centralised, uniform curriculum. They wanted curriculum flexibility, breadth and depth, with quality teaching and quality materials to support teaching, but most of all they wanted a less crowded curriculum – one that would make learning more enjoyable and with better connections between the pre-five, primary, secondary and post-secondary stages.

THE CURRENT CURRICULUM: *CURRICULUM FOR EXCELLENCE*

In 2004, Peter Peacock, the Minister for Education and Young People, wrote:

> The curriculum in Scotland has many strengths . . . However, the various parts were developed separately and, taken together, they do not now provide the best basis for an excellent education for every child. The National Debate showed that people want a curriculum that will fully prepare today's children for adult life in the 21st century, be less crowded and better connected, and offer more choice and enjoyment.

(SEED, 2004)

This is an extraordinarily brave and frank statement for any government minister to make. It indicates a genuine desire to make the education system work for children and reflects confidence in the willingness and ability of the Scottish educational community to deliver effective change.

Curriculum For Excellence (SEED, 2004) represents the third curriculum policy phase in Scotland. It aims to provide a single curriculum for 3–18 year olds, supported by a simple and effective structure for assessment. It seeks to de-clutter the primary curriculum, to free up more time for young people to achieve and to allow teachers the freedom to exercise judgement on appropriate learning.

The starting point for *Curriculum for Excellence* is that the curriculum cannot focus solely on narrow definitions of attainment and progression or on detailed sets of teaching content and tasks. The four capacities that define the purposes of the curriculum (see Figure 4.4.2) focus attention on building social, emotional and intellectual capacity. *Curriculum for Excellence* extends the influence of curriculum policy beyond subject areas, giving explicit recognition to the importance

Successful learners

With
- enthusiasm and motivation for learning
- determination to reach high standards of achievement
- openness to new thinking and ideas

and able to
- use literacy, communication and numeracy skills
- use technology for learning
- think creatively and idependently
- learn independently and as part of a group
- make reasoned evaluations
- link and apply different kinds of learning in new situations

Confident individuals

With
- self respect
- a sense of physical, mental and emotional well-being
- secure values and beliefs
- ambition

and able to
- relate to others and manage themselves
- pursue a healthy and active lifestyle
- be self aware
- develop and communicate their own beliefs and view of the world
- live as independently as they can
- assess risk and take informed decisions
- achieve success in different areas of activity

To enable all young people to become

Responsible citizens

With
- respect for others
- commitment to participate responsibly in political, economic, social and cultural life

and able to
- develop knowledge and understanding of the world and Scotland's place in it
- understand different beliefs and cultures
- make informed choices and decisions
- evaluate environmental, scientific and technological issues
- develop informed, ethical views of complex issues

Effective contributors

With
- an enterprising attitude
- resilience
- self-reliance

and able to
- communicate in different ways and in different settings
- work in partnership and in teams
- take the initiative and lead
- apply critical thinking in new contexts
- create and develop
- solve problems

■ **Figure 4.4.2** The purposes of the curriculum from 3–18: the four capacities

Source: Learning and Teaching Scotland (2009)

Task 4.4.3 **THE PURPOSES OF THE CURRICULUM**

Look carefully at Figure 4.4.2 and think about one curricular area that you have seen taught in schools.

■ To what extent do you think the teaching delivered these purposes?
■ How would you change or adapt the teaching to enable it to better meet the purposes outlined in *Curriculum for Excellence*?

---

of interdisciplinary links, to the ethos and life of the school as a community within wider society and to the importance of providing opportunities for wider achievement.

In each subject area, *Curriculum for Excellence* details five levels of experiences and outcomes, covering the age range 3–18: Early (Pre-school and P1); First (by the end of P4 or earlier); Second (by the end of P7 or earlier); Third (S1–3) and Fourth (S4–6). The design, by defining the curriculum in terms of experiences as well as outcomes, seeks to promote smoother transitions between the nursery, primary and secondary sectors, focusing on coherent progression in both content *and* the types of learning experiences that children will meet.

The framework generally seeks to provide focus but not be so content-laden as to leave little space for innovative teaching or responding to children's interests and needs. The planning principles detailed by *Curriculum for Excellence* (challenge and enjoyment, breadth, progression, depth, personalisation and choice, coherence and relevance) emphasise the importance of analysing what is most appropriate for the pupils and the school context. This, it is hoped, will result in better progression, more purposeful learning activities, more choice and more enjoyment of learning, all of which are necessary to raise achievement. (Note the use of 'achievement', a wider term than the 'attainment' focus, which characterised discussion of the *5–14 Guidelines*.)

Curriculum for Excellence divides the curriculum into the following areas:

■ health and well-being;
■ mathematics and numeracy;
■ languages and literacy;
■ religious and moral education;
■ sciences;
■ social subjects;
■ technologies;
■ expressive arts.

Health and well-being, literacy and numeracy must be developed across learning, by every teacher, at every level, regardless of curriculum area or the formal exam focus of secondary school teachers.

Task 4.4.4 **CURRICULUM DEVELOPMENTS**

Find some reasonably experienced primary teachers to interview. Ask them about the curriculum developments they have experienced during their career.

■ How did the changes affect their work with the pupils, or their planning or thinking about teaching? What did they think of them at the time? How do they feel about them now?
■ What are the current curriculum issues? How do these teachers feel about them?

RESEARCH PERSPECTIVES

At its heart, *Curriculum for Excellence* recognises that learning is socially and culturally mediated. It has the potential to promote a school system and curriculum that draws explicitly on sociocultural and ethnographic research in addition to the cognitive research that has traditionally informed teaching content and pedagogy. This could create a new dialogue about education. For example, we know that literacy is not just cognitively but socially and culturally determined (Bearne and Marsh, 2007; Moss, 2007). Yet, despite clear evidence of this (gender and socio-economic status remain the strongest predictors of literacy attainment), the debates about the content of the literacy curriculum are almost exclusively focused on cognitive issues – the best way to teach phonics, comprehension or writing, for example. There are few arguments about the most effective specific curriculum adaptations that will address children's social and cultural needs as readers and writers.

By offering this broader base for the curriculum, *Curriculum for Excellence* also has the potential to deal more fluently with emerging policy concerns, which can rarely be framed solely in terms of cognition, pedagogy and teaching content. Certainly, *Curriculum for Excellence* accords with recent policy and research studies that highlight the impact of engagement on learning and attainment (Guthrie and Humenick, 2004).

Curriculum for Excellence demonstrates educational integrity by focusing on the issues that are central to the quality of children's lives. For example, research tells us that poor literacy skills are a major barrier to learning, contributing to increased absence from school, poor attitudes to learning, limited opportunities for employment and, for some, increased involvement with the criminal justice system. The loss to the economy from low literacy is estimated at over one and a

Task 4.4.5 *CURRICULUM FOR EXCELLENCE*

Curriculum for Excellence gives great scope for teachers, schools and local authorities to create a curriculum that works for them. It contrasts with the more centralised, top-down curriculum approaches in England or the USA. Top-down models can be seen negatively as ignoring the teaching capacity that exists in schools, positioning teachers as passive conduits for the curriculum and making curricular decisions highly vulnerable to single-issue pressure groups. They can also be seen positively as building capacity by compelling teachers to engage with new pedagogies, providing clear frameworks that focus decisions on evidence and mitigating the worst effects of a weak teacher.

Devolved curriculum models, such as *Curriculum for Excellence*, offer more potential to engage teachers and to capitalise on the good practice and emotional investment that already exists in schools. However, they may leave teachers unsupported in making evidence-based decisions or analysing curriculum changes, forcing them to rely on their own unexplored, and possibly limited, past experiences. Critics argue that the dream of teachers making clear judgements based on research and on robust analyses of evidence is simply that – a dream. Research studies on rolling out educational reforms, however, show that the contexts in which programmes are implemented are at least as important to their effectiveness as the design features of the programme (Datnow *et al.*, 2002); Eisner comments, 'Educators know experientially that context matters most in the "chemistry" that makes for educational effectiveness' (Eisner, 2004: 616).

■ What do you think are the important things to bear in mind when considering the pros and cons of each model for a specific context?

half billion pounds (KPMG Foundation, 2006). It is in direct response to such studies that *Curriculum for Excellence* makes literacy, along with health and well-being and numeracy, the responsibility of every teacher, in every sector, at every level.

ACHIEVING SUCCESS

In a rather depressing analysis, John MacBeath reminds us that the organisation and curriculum of schools has changed little since Victorian times (MacBeath, 2008: 940). Past predictions that schools and schooling would be revolutionised have all come to naught – 'The future never happened.' MacBeath holds little hope for radical, bottom-up curriculum change where learner experiences can forge new ways of seeing and learning in the curriculum. Policy change, he argues, always happens downwards: the design of buildings, school hierarchies, staffing structures, teaching arrangements, pedagogical conventions, planning and monitoring procedures and tests can only produce a certain type of curriculum and particular types of learning experiences.

Task 4.4.6 RADICAL CHANGE?

■ To what extent do you agree with MacBeath's analysis? How far does it concur with what you have read and experienced?

■ What four things would you change in the structure and organisation of primary schools that would revolutionise teaching and learning and ensure that *Curriculum for Excellence* succeeds? Justify your choices with reference to your own experience, research and theory.

■ Compare your ideas to those of a colleague.

Yet the existence of *Curriculum for Excellence* is clear evidence of the desire to create a curriculum that learners can influence, and there is plenty of research evidence of the need for such an approach to the curriculum. Brian Boyd has noted that 'Scotland has never been extreme with its educational innovations; [the Scottish approach] . . . has always been to integrate innovation firmly into traditional approaches (Humes and Bryce, 2003: 111). Past curriculum developments in Scotland have tended to be a process of evolution rather than revolution and the experience of implementing the *5–14 Guidelines* shows that we need to pay as much attention to the context of implementation as to the initial structures and frameworks. To be successful, *Curriculum for Excellence* has to challenge and change thinking at every level of the system so that the many different influences that determine how it is interpreted support rather than destroy its spirit.

Scotland has already begun to redefine the nature of accountability in national, local authority and school contexts: HMIE in Scotland has changed the inspection process to focus on the quality of self-evaluation. Scotland has learned, partly from the history of Ofsted inspections in England, that a perceived culture of criticism and blame encourages a defensive, mechanistic curriculum as teachers and head teachers seek protection by 'following guidelines to the letter'. It is hoped that the new inspection process will offer a more equal conversation and place real power in the hands of the head teacher.

Possibly the biggest change that *Curriculum for Excellence* requires is in the mindset and knowledge-base of teachers and head teachers. More freedom and flexibility needs teachers to have secure professional understandings and to take a constructivist, evidenced-based view of pupil learning, of their own pedagogy and of the school curriculum. The, albeit tacit, understanding in the *Curriculum for Excellence* architecture is that learning, pedagogy and curriculum design must be informed by research and developed through hard-nosed evaluation, each having a dynamic relationship to the others. To fully change the culture, we need a move towards research-orientated schools, in which significant curriculum innovation and evaluation is part of the job for teachers, head teachers and local authorities. Only this will provide the professional dialogue necessary for serious collaboration between the Scottish government, local authorities and teachers. For it to work, it is essential that everyone – educators, children, parents, the media, employers and politicians – sees and understands education as a complex process with many outcomes, rather than as a one-dimensional commodity.

If *Curriculum for Excellence* is successful, it may produce less uniform curricula and possibly a more diverse education system. Preventing the politicisation of the curriculum may be difficult. All public bodies now pay careful attention to how they are reported in the press and local authority councillors and schools must account for their actions. The temptation may be for them to promote their own initiatives as 'the best solution', reducing complex analyses to newspaper headlines. This will not help reflection and careful decision making. Calm analysis based on evaluations that acknowledge limitations and detail the complexity of the issues will be crucial.

The issue of evaluation raises many ethical questions. The best knowledge networks should analyse and share information about the innovations that don't work as well as those that do. When the Millennium Bridge across the River Thames in London was first built, it wobbled as pedestrians walked across it. After, we learned that 'wobbling bridges' are not uncommon, but the design error persists because comparatively little is known about them; no commercial company wishes to be associated with having built a wobbly bridge and they are not written up as case studies. The extent to which local authorities will be willing to openly discuss evaluations of unsuccessful or negative aspects of innovations will be determined by factors largely outside the control of educators, including the tone of the education discourse adopted by politicians, parents and the media.

Teachers will need to see their job differently in other ways, too. The image of the primary teacher as an isolated adult with a class of children has changed. The recommendations in the McCrone Report (2000) promoted a more social and research-based view of teaching. It recognised that teachers must discuss their practice with others and that time must be available for this. However, time is not enough. If primary teachers are to develop a strong and assertive professional voice, their discussions about learning need to be clearly evidence-based, and they need a sophisticated understanding of the different types of evidence and how it may be used. As curriculum designers, teachers need to focus on how their analyses of their class and school should interact with the timing, selection and balance of ideas in the curriculum, and accept that sometimes they may not get it right. As professionals they need to have open and honest dialogue with head teachers and local authority staff about the curriculum and how it is delivered, and identify local implementation policies that are enabling and those that are not.

We all need to recognise that teachers' learning is social and emotional as well as cognitive. Continuing professional development needs to enhance teachers' professional judgement and dialogue, alongside their knowledge, and ensure that head teachers actively support this process. Good leadership in schools needs to be seen in terms of building capacity at all levels, including the capacity of weak teachers. As one Scottish head teacher recently explained:

> Weak teachers are not made competent by being given work programmes or criticism; they just clam up and become passive. They need to talk, talk and talk some more about how they are teaching the children in their own class and get specific, tailored advice and help, including practical support and demonstrations, with explanations linked to that.

(Ellis and Hayward, 2009)

SUMMARY

The discussion of curriculum guidelines and how they are implemented can seem awfully dry and boring. There is a great temptation for student teachers to focus on the immediate job of teaching the children without thinking about 'the big picture'. It is part of every teacher's professional responsibility to think about what matters in education, and to ensure that the curriculum is working to deliver this. The key points from this unit are that curriculum guidelines are only one aspect of a complex, dynamic picture, and that the process of implementation is crucial.

ANNOTATED FURTHER READING

Bryce, T.G.K and Humes, W.M. (eds) (2008) *Scottish Education, Third Edition: Beyond Devolution*, Edinburgh: Edinburgh University Press.
   This is the most comprehensive text on Scottish education. Each chapter is designed to give an explanatory overview of policy and practice and identify key issues for the future.

Ellis, S. and Hayward, L. (2009) 'The answer's achievement, but what's the question?', in C. Mills, R. Cox and G. Moss (eds) *Language and Literacies in the Primary School*, London: Routledge.
   This chapter describes the policy context for the highly successful *Assessment is for Learning* intervention in Scotland and illustrates it with an example of how one school involved in the project raised writing achievement by focusing on teaching and learning.

Moss, G. (2007) *Literacy and Gender: Researching Texts, Contexts and Readers*, London: Routledge.
   This is an example of the sort of research that is challenging traditional, content-focused curriculum frameworks. Moss produces hard evidence of the need for teachers to pay attention to how children network around books and, in doing so, exemplifies just how complex the process of becoming literate actually is.

Scottish Executive Education Department (SEED) (2004): *A Curriculum for Excellence*, Edinburgh: HMSO.
   A highly readable document that sets out the framework for the new curriculum.

RELEVANT WEBSITES

Curriculum for Excellence: www.ltscotland.org.uk/curriculumforexcellence/index.asp
   For the *Curriculum for Excellence*, see also Scotland's Colleges website: www.sfeu.ac.uk/projects/curriculum_for_excellence and Learning Curve Education's website: www.curriculum-for-excellence.co.uk

GLOW: www.ltscotland.org.uk/glowscotland/index.asp
   GLOW is a core element of support for the *Curriculum for Excellence*.

Journey to Excellence: www.hmie.gov.uk/documents/publication/hgiosjte.pdf
   The online resource for professional development provided by HMIE.

Scottish Government: www.hmie.gov/Publications.aspx
   Contains links to *Portrait of Current Practice* reports.

Visit the companion website www.routledge.com/textbooks/ltps2e for:

■ additional questions and tasks for this unit;
■ links to useful websites relevant to this unit.

REFERENCES

Adams, F.R. (2003) '5–14: Origins, development and implementation', in T.G.K. Bryce and W.M. Humes (eds) *Scottish Education: Second Edition: Post-devolution*, Edinburgh: Edinburgh University Press, pp. 369–79.

Bell, S. (2003) *The Scottish Storyline Method*. Available online at www.storyline.org/ (accessed April 2009).

Bell, S. and Harkness, S. (2006) *Storyline: Promoting Language Across the Curriculum*, Royston: UKLA.

Bearne, E. and Marsh, J. (eds) (2007) *Literacy and Social Inclusion: Closing the Gap*, Stoke on Trent: Trentham Books.

Black, P. and Wiliam, D. (1998) *Inside the Black Box*, London: King's College.

Black, P., Harrison, C., Lee, G., Marshall, B. and Wiliam, D. (2002) *Working Inside the Black Box*, London: King's College.

Datnow, A., Hubbard, L. and Mehan, H. (2002) *Extending Educational Reform: From One School to Many*, New York: RoutledgeFalmer.

Eisner, E.W. (1992) 'Educational reform and the ecology of schooling', *Teachers College Record*, 93(4): 610–27.

Eisner, E.W. (2004) 'Artistry in teaching', *Cultural Commons*. Available online at www.culturalcommons.org/eisner.htm (accessed April 2009).

Ellis, S. and Friel, G. (2008) 'English language', in T.G.K. Bryce and W.M. Humes (eds) *Scottish Education: Third Edition: Beyond Devolution*, Edinburgh: Edinburgh University Press, pp. 344–9.

Ellis, S. and Hayward, L. (2009) 'The answer's achievement, but what's the question', in C. Mills, R. Cox and G. Moss (eds) *Language and Literacies in the Primary School*, London: Routledge.

Guthrie, J.T. and Humenick, N.M. (2004) 'Motivating students to read: evidence for classroom practices that increase reading motivation', in P. McCardle and V. Chhabra (eds) *The Voice of Evidence in Reading Research*, New York: Erlbaum, pp. 329–55.

Her Majesty's Inspectorate for Education (HMIE) (2006a) *Improving Scottish Education*, Edinburgh: SEED

Her Majesty's Inspectorate for Education (HMIE) (2006b) *HMIE Report to SEED on the Delivery of the National Priorities*, November, 2005. Available online at www.hmie.gov.uk/documents/publication/hmiednp.html (accessed April 2009).

Humes, W.M and Bryce, T.G.K (2003) 'The distinctiveness of Scottish education', in T.G.K. Bryce and W.M. Humes (eds) *Scottish Education: Second Edition: Post-Devolution*, Edinburgh: Edinburgh University Press, pp. 108–18.

KPMG Foundation (2006) *The Long Term Costs Of Literacy Difficulties*. Available online at www.kpmg.co.uk/about/foundation/index.cfm (accessed April 2009).

Learning and Teaching Scotland (2009) *Curriculum for Excellence: The Four Capacities.* Available online at www.ltscotland.org.uk/curriculumforexcellence/curriculumoverview/aims/fourcapacities.asp (accessed November 2009).

MacBeath, J. (2008) 'Do schools have a future?', in T.G.K. Bryce and W.M. Humes (eds) *Scottish Education: Third Edition: Beyond Devolution*, Edinburgh: Edinburgh University Press, pp. 939–48.

McCrone, G. (2000) *Report of the McCrone Inquiry into Professional Conditions of Service for Teachers*, Edinburgh: HMSO.

Moss, G. (2007) *Literacy and Gender: Researching Texts, Contexts and Readers*, London: Routledge.

Scottish Education Department (SED) (1971) *Primary Education: Organisation for Development*, Edinburgh: HMSO.

Scottish Executive Education Department (SEED) (2004) *A Curriculum for Excellence*, Edinburgh: HMSO.

Scottish Office Education and Industry Department (SOEID) (1991) *Curriculum and Assessment in Scotland: Assessment 5–14: Improving the Quality of Learning and Teaching*, Edinburgh: HMSO.

Spillane, J.P. (2000) 'Cognition and policy implementation: district policymakers and the reform of mathematics education', *Cognition and Instruction*, 18(2): 141–79.

5 ASSESSMENT

ASSESSMENT FOR LEARNING

Formative approaches

Caroline Gipps and Alison Pickering

INTRODUCTION

Assessment for learning (AFL) is a particular approach to assessment developed for teachers in classrooms. It is not the same as the standardised tests or SATs you may have to give, but rather is a way of using informal assessment during ordinary classroom activities to improve learning. Here, assessment is seen as an integral part of the learning and teaching process rather than being 'added on' for summative purposes. This approach brings with it a rather different relationship between teacher and learner than in traditional models of assessment, since the pupil needs to become involved in discussions about the tasks (learning objectives) the assessment criteria (success criteria), their performance and what they need to do to improve: the relationship is more of a partnership with both pupil and teacher playing a role. We know that with appropriate guidance children as young as six or seven can do this.

There are two key elements to AFL that this unit will go on to unpack: the nature of the feedback given to the learner to help him or her understand the quality of their work and next steps, and the active engagement of the learner.

The early work of the Assessment Reform Group (1999) and of Black and Wiliam (1998b) showed that improving learning through assessment depends on five, deceptively simple, key factors:

- the provision of effective feedback to pupils;
- the active involvement of pupils in their own learning;
- adjusting teaching to take account of the results of assessment;
- a recognition of the profound influence assessment has on the motivation and self-esteem of pupils, both of which are crucial influences on learning;
- the need for pupils to be able to assess themselves and understand how to improve.

Since the publication of the Assessment Reform Group's (ARG, 2002) summary of research-based principles of AFL, there has been a considerable impact on classroom practice. The ten principles of effective teaching and learning identified by the ARG are now posted on the QCA website (www.qcda.gov.uk/13440.aspx) and form the basis of current approaches to learning and teaching in many classrooms. The ARG identifies ten principles to guide teachers in implementing AFL in their classrooms. Some of these are addressed in this unit and suggestions are made for putting them into practice.

OBJECTIVES

By the end of the unit you should be able to:

■ understand the key factors that contribute to assessment for learning;
■ develop a range of strategies that will facilitate improved learning/teaching;
■ recognise that effective assessment is a powerful tool in raising achievement in the classroom.

ASSESSMENT FOR LEARNING: FROM THEORY TO PRACTICE

The ten principles of assessment for learning

ASSESSMENT FOR LEARNING SHOULD BE PART OF THE EFFECTIVE PLANNING OF TEACHING AND LEARNING

A teacher's planning should provide opportunities for both learner and teacher to obtain and use information about progress towards learning goals. It also has to be flexible to respond to initial and emerging ideas and skills. Planning should include strategies to ensure that learners understand the goals they are pursuing and the criteria that will be applied in assessing their work. How learners will receive feedback, how they will take part in assessing their learning and how they will be helped to make further progress should also be planned.

ASSESSMENT FOR LEARNING SHOULD FOCUS ON HOW PUPILS LEARN

The process of learning has to be in the minds of both learner and teacher when assessment is planned and when the evidence is interpreted. Learners should become as aware of the 'how' of their learning as they are of the 'what'.

ASSESSMENT FOR LEARNING SHOULD BE RECOGNISED AS CENTRAL TO CLASSROOM PRACTICE

Much of what teachers and learners do in classrooms can be described as assessment. That is, tasks and questions prompt learners to demonstrate their knowledge, understanding and skills. What learners say and do is then observed and interpreted, and judgements are made about how learning can be improved. These assessment processes are an essential part of everyday classroom practice and involve both teachers and learners in reflection, dialogue and decision making.

ASSESSMENT FOR LEARNING SHOULD BE REGARDED AS A KEY PROFESSIONAL SKILL FOR TEACHERS

Teachers require the professional knowledge and skills to: plan for assessment; observe learning; analyse and interpret evidence of learning; give feedback to learners; and support learners in self-assessment. Teachers should be supported in developing these skills through initial and continuing professional development.

ASSESSMENT FOR LEARNING SHOULD BE SENSITIVE AND CONSTRUCTIVE BECAUSE ANY ASSESSMENT HAS AN EMOTIONAL IMPACT

Teachers should be aware of the impact that comments, marks and grades can have on learners' confidence and enthusiasm and should be as constructive as possible in the feedback that they give. Comments that focus on the work rather than the person are more constructive for both learning and motivation.

ASSESSMENT FOR LEARNING SHOULD TAKE ACCOUNT OF THE IMPORTANCE OF LEARNER MOTIVATION

Assessment that encourages learning fosters motivation by emphasising progress and achievement rather than failure. Comparison with others who have been more successful is unlikely to motivate learners. It can also lead to their withdrawing from the learning process in areas where they have been made to feel they are 'no good'. Motivation can be preserved and enhanced by assessment methods that protect the learner's autonomy, provide some choice and constructive feedback, and create opportunity for self-direction.

ASSESSMENT FOR LEARNING SHOULD PROMOTE COMMITMENT TO LEARNING GOALS AND A SHARED UNDERSTANDING OF THE CRITERIA BY WHICH THEY ARE ASSESSED

For effective learning to take place, learners need to understand what it is they are trying to achieve – and want to achieve it. Understanding and commitment follows when learners have some part in deciding goals and identifying criteria for assessing progress. Communicating assessment criteria involves discussing them with learners, using terms that they can understand, providing examples of how the criteria can be met in practice and engaging learners in peer and self-assessment.

LEARNERS SHOULD RECEIVE CONSTRUCTIVE GUIDANCE ABOUT HOW TO IMPROVE

Learners need information and guidance in order to plan the next steps in their learning. Teachers should:

■ pinpoint the learner's strengths and advise on how to develop them;
■ be clear and constructive about any weaknesses and how they might be addressed;
■ provide opportunities for learners to improve upon their work.

ASSESSMENT FOR LEARNING DEVELOPS LEARNERS' CAPACITY FOR SELF-ASSESSMENT SO THAT THEY CAN BECOME REFLECTIVE AND SELF-MANAGING

Independent learners have the ability to seek out and gain new skills, new knowledge and new understandings. They are able to engage in self-reflection and to identify the next steps in their learning. Teachers should equip learners with the desire and the capacity to take charge of their learning through developing the skills of self-assessment.

ASSESSMENT FOR LEARNING SHOULD RECOGNISE THE FULL RANGE OF
ACHIEVEMENTS OF ALL LEARNERS

AFL should be used to enhance all learners' opportunities to learn in all areas of educational activity.
It should enable all learners to achieve their best and to have their efforts recognised.

(Adapted from ARG, 2002)

PLANNING FOR ASSESSMENT FOR LEARNING

Effective planning enables you to provide learning opportunities that match the needs of all the
children. It should include the following:

- Objectives that focus on learning. The task then becomes the vehicle for the learning.
- Strategies for finding out what the children already know so that you can pitch the learning/
  teaching at the appropriate level.
- An element of pupil choice.
- Ways in which you can share the 'bigger picture' with the children so that they know what
  they are aiming for.
- Mini-plenaries so that the children can regularly reflect back on the bigger picture.
- Opportunities for peer and self-assessment with and without teacher support.

Sharing the bigger picture

From the start, share the success criteria with your pupils. Articulate exactly what it is you will be
assessing. In writing, for example, a success criterion might be 'a descriptive piece of writing using
adjectives', but an assessment focus might include accurate presentation. This must be made clear
to the children.

Teachers and pupils can create the success criteria together. Figure 5.1.1 shows a pupil self-
assessment sheet for a history topic. You can display a large version on the wall and have an
individual copy for each child. There are three levels of attainment here, which can either be used
for pupil self-assessment or peer assessment.

What was it like to live here in the past?

Must

- understand that St Paul's School was different in the past;
- make comparisons between the school in the past and as it is today.

Should

- recognise features of the school building and know how it has changed over time;
- enquire about some of the people who have worked at the school (both pupils and staff) and
  understand differences in working conditions at different times;
- be able to use a range of historical sources in a variety of ways.

Could

- describe and compare features of the school and identify changes on a time line;
- select and combine information from different sources.

■ **Figure 5.1.1** Pupil self-assessment sheet

> ## Task 5.1.1 **PUPIL ASSESSMENT SHEET**
>
> Referring to Figure 5.1.1, choose another area of the curriculum and construct a similar sheet.

Discussion during the sessions and mini-plenaries

Discussions take place before, during and after each lesson so that the teacher can check the children's understanding and judge their progress. It also provides a vehicle for a continued sharing of the learning objectives. Here are some strategies for doing this:

■ Before the lesson have discussions with the children to ascertain what they already know about the subject in order that you can plan the work effectively to include different levels of understanding. Identify in your planning the children you wish to support in that lesson.

■ Once you have identified children's misconceptions or unexpected responses, you can follow up your individual discussion during the session to clarify these.

■ Monitor the children's progress throughout the lesson by asking them questions about the task and then sharing with them targets for the next steps in their learning.

■ At intervals during the session remind the children of the lesson objectives, then ask children to feed back to the class what they have found out so far and what they still have to do to complete the task.

■ Ask the children to evaluate their own progress against the success criteria given.

QUESTIONING

Effective questioning is the key to good teacher assessment; make sure you know which questions to use and when you will use them.

Teachers are always asking questions, but in order to develop higher-order thinking skills it is important to ask open-ended, child-centred questions (see Figure 5.1.2). The use of open questioning is critical in encouraging children to offer their own opinions. The teacher then acknowledges that these opinions are a valid response. This approach to questioning is much more productive than a closed questioning technique where only one response is deemed 'correct' by the teacher, leaving the children guessing what the teacher wants to hear rather than basing their response on their own ideas. Ask follow-up questions to make the children think more deeply. (For details of types of questioning in assessment observed in the classes of 'expert' primary teachers, see Gipps *et al.*, 2000.)

Thinking time

To encourage this process children must be given time to think more deeply before responding to questions.

Once you have asked a question, allow the children 'thinking time' before listening to their responses. This has a twofold effect. First, it encourages the more able to think more deeply and fosters higher-order thinking skills and, second, it builds the confidence of those pupils who take longer to respond. Teacher expectation is important here, expecting a response from every child. A useful technique for encouraging this is the use of 'discussion' or 'talk partners'. The child first shares their ideas with a partner before sharing their response with the teacher or the class. In this

Type of question	Responses
What do you notice about . . .?	Descriptive observations
What can you tell me about . . .?	Inviting recalled information but content chosen by the children
What does it remind you of?	Seeing patterns/analogies
Which things do you think belong together? Why do you think that?	Seeing patterns/classifying and creative explanations
What do you think will happen next?	Creative predictions
What happened after you did that?	Descriptive reasoning/cause and effect/conclusions
Why do you think that happened? I wonder why it did that?	Creative hypotheses/explanations
Do you think you could do it differently?	Evaluation/reflective analysis
I wonder what made you think that?	Reflective self-awareness/metacognition
Anything else? Or?	Neutral/inviting more of the responses listed above

■ **Figure 5.1.2** How open-ended questions encourage thinking skills
Source: de Bóo (1999)

way the children can test their ideas with their peers and perhaps adjust their thinking before offering a response, which in turn helps them feel more confident about voicing a response. During these peer discussions the teacher has an opportunity to find out any misconceptions that the children may hold or indeed areas of the topic that excite them. This information can then be fed into planning, making it more personalised.

Task 5.1.2 **QUESTIONING TO ENCOURAGE THINKING SKILLS 1**

■ Figure 5.1.2 shows a range of questions and the types of responses they are designed to promote. Apply this technique to a specific curriculum area.

■ Ask a colleague to observe your teaching session and comment on your inclusion of the following aspects of questioning. You could reciprocate by observing his or her teaching and then share your findings.

▪ Asking questions to assess the children's starting points in order to adapt learning and teaching.

▪ Asking a range of questions to develop understanding.

▪ Using thinking time and 'talk partners' to ensure all children are engaged in answering questions.

▪ Giving the children opportunities to ask questions before and after the session.

▪ Creating a question board related to a particular topic and encouraging children to 'post' on this.

▪ Having an agreed time to discuss the questions with the children.

> ### Task 5.1.3 QUESTIONING TO ENCOURAGE THINKING SKILLS 2
>
> Reflect on how the information you have obtained in Task 5.1.2 then impacted on your planning for this aspect of the curriculum.

PEER AND SELF-ASSESSMENT

An increased awareness of the role of the learner in the assessment process has led to changes in approaches to teaching involving more dialogue between pupils and teachers in the setting and adaptation of the assessment process. Learners are more aware not only of what they learn, but how they learn and what helps them learn. Pupils can assess themselves and can learn from their own and others' assessments. This in turn leads them to reflect on how they learn.

Children should be involved not only in their own, but also in peer assessment. This gives children a central role in learning and is a really important shift from the teacher having all the responsibility for assessment to a position of sharing goals, self-evaluation and setting their own targets (Black and Wiliam, 1998a).

This approach can be highly motivating but must be endorsed by a supportive classroom ethos, which should include clear guidelines for the children in terms of supporting and guiding each other's learning. First, there must be a clear focus and structure for the lesson. Children need a set of success and assessment criteria (see 'Planning for assessment for learning' above) by which to judge the success of their learning. These can be negotiated by yourself and the children. Try some of the following methods of engaging your children in their own assessment.

You can use 'Thumbs Up' to establish pupil understanding. A thumb up means that they have understood well, whereas a thumb down indicates no understanding, and a thumb sideways indicates a need for more help or time. This technique offers the teacher a quick indication of how the class has received the lesson.

'Traffic Lights' is another way for pupils to evaluate their learning against the learning objectives. They put a red, green or yellow dot against the learning objectives in a similar way to 'Thumbs Up', once again giving clear indications for target setting. After the children in the red, yellow, thumbs down or sideways categories have received additional adult input, they can reassess themselves against the objective and revise their response. These techniques also help you to decide when particular objectives need to be revisited.

'Pinks and Greens' again allows the pupils to assess themselves. In this example the child highlights two aspects of their work in green that they feel fulfil the success criteria and identify one target for improvement that they underline in pink. This approach can also be used by pupils to assess the work of their peers.

> ### Task 5.1.4 SELF-ASSESSMENT
>
> ■ Using the pupil self-assessment sheet created in Task 5.1.1, ask your pupils to reflect in their learning log on how well they are meeting the success criteria. Follow this up by asking them what they need to do to improve and if they have any further questions they wish to ask about the task.
> ■ Assess their peers using the 'Pinks and Greens' technique described above.

'The Learning Log' encourages children to reflect on the success criteria. The teacher allows time for the children to articulate to others how well they are meeting them. It also gives them the opportunity to ask questions of their own and even to extend the criteria for success.

FEEDBACK

As Black and Wiliam argue: 'Feedback to any pupil should be about the particular qualities of his or her work, with advice on what he or she can do to improve, and should avoid comparisons with other pupils' (1998b: 9).

Effective feedback to children provides information to support self-assessment and suggests steps that will lead to improvement. Feedback through written comments should refer back to the learning goals set at the beginning of the session and should be constructive. We know that many teachers focus on spelling, punctuation, grammar or the structure of the piece of work, often omitting or underplaying the objectives, so make sure that your comments relate directly to the learning and assessment objectives.

A useful way of thinking about/describing feedback is whether it is evaluative or descriptive (see Figure 5.1.3).

All too often, teachers provide evaluative feedback in the form of grades and short (usually non-specific) comments, praise or censure. This kind of feedback tells pupils whether they are doing okay or not, but it offers little direction for moving their learning forward. Regular critical evaluative feedback without guidance for how to improve can lower motivation and self-esteem. Descriptive feedback, on the other hand, relates to the task at hand, the learner's performance and what they might do to improve. (For details of feedback observed in the classrooms of 'expert' primary teachers, see Gipps *et al.*, 2000; for practical activities, see Clarke, 2003.)

The ideal situation is when the teacher can discuss and annotate work with the child present so that targets can be set together. However, this is not always possible so the teacher writes comments for the child to read. For these to be meaningful they must be linked clearly to the learning objectives and you must allow time on your plan for the child to read them. This can sometimes be forgotten and may therefore negate the value of the comments. Here is an example of written dialogue between teacher and pupil which leads to further reflection by the pupil:

Teacher comment: A really clear graph. I like the way it is set out. What do you think we should do with this information?

Evaluative feedback	<ul><li>Giving rewards and punishments</li><li>Expressing approval and disapproval.</li></ul>
Descriptive feedback	<ul><li>Telling children they are right or wrong</li><li>Describing why an answer is correct</li><li>Telling children what they have achieved and have not achieved</li><li>Specifying or implying a better way of doing something</li><li>Getting children to suggest ways they can improve.</li></ul>

■ **Figure 5.1.3** Evaluative and descriptive feedback strategies
Source: Gipps *et al.* (2000)

Pupil comment: See how much rubbish is in a bin, and see what thing is in there and how much of the things are in there. We should put up more recycle bins to keep the world safe. And we'll put them in the hall.

The teacher's comments have encouraged the child to interrogate the graph more fully.

RECOGNISING AND CELEBRATING CHILDREN'S WORK

You need to consider how a child's effort is recognised. Build in time for reflection at the end of the day or the week. In an early years setting, good work may be celebrated in a discussion at the end of the session, taking the opportunity to point out what makes it worthy of comment. Another method of highlighting good work is by taking photographs, providing a permanent reminder for both child and teacher. Teachers of younger children commonly write an accompanying explanation of the context of the piece and may include a record of any dialogue that has taken place. Some teachers simply display a chosen piece of work on the wall or on a bookstand so that everyone can share that pupil's success. The use of circle time is another opportunity to celebrate the products of sessions and is also an opportunity to assess pupil attitudes. These activities give the teacher an opportunity to focus on work that shows improvement and an understanding of subject progression. The activities are suitable for Key Stage 1 and 2 classrooms, but with the children becoming increasingly involved in the selection of good work. It is important that you consider how these activities will be tracked. Will they be tracked by the teacher or the pupil? Will you keep pupil profiles?

Task 5.1.5 QUESTIONS TO ASK YOURSELF IN RELATION TO YOUR PLANNING FOR AFL

■ Does the assessment allow children multiple ways to demonstrate their learning across the range of curriculum activities?

■ Does it assess the extent to which learning has taken place?

■ How do you ensure that feedback from assessments allows the children opportunities to develop and progress in their learning by linking your comments to agreed success criteria and indicating the next steps to encourage further learning?

■ How do assessment outcomes influence session planning and modifications to future curriculum planning?

■ How will you/should you keep track of this?

Task 5.1.6 PEER REFLECTION

You have had an opportunity to evaluate your practice in relation to pupil self-assessment and questioning. Now ask one of your peers to observe another lesson and comment on another two of the principles of AFL identified by the ARG. You can then observe your peer's class and share your comments to help each other learn.

SUMMARY

Assessment for learning as opposed to *assessment of learning* is part of ongoing learning and teaching and is not a 'bolt-on'. Its aim is to assess all areas of the curriculum as described in *Excellence and Enjoyment* (DfES, 2003). In order to achieve this it uses a wide range of strategies to secure a wider range of assessments. It is recognition of what a child can do and the identification of the next steps in their learning so that they can progress at a pace appropriate for them. This is done by a mixture of teacher-led assessment, negotiation and pupils sharing in the assessment process, so that they can eventually assess their own work and set appropriate targets. An exciting and controversial aspect of AFL is its use in summative assessment as outlined in the report of the Assessment Systems for the Future (ASF) project (2004), which highlights how the development of effective practice in formative assessment might impact on teacher's summative assessment.

The tasks in this unit address the following *Professional Standards* (TDA, 2008)

Teaching and learning

Q10 Have a knowledge and understanding of a range of teaching, learning and behaviour management strategies and know how to use and adapt them, including how to personalise learning and provide opportunities for all learners to achieve their potential.

Assessment and monitoring

Q12 Know a range of approaches to assessment, including the importance of formative assessment.

Planning

Q22 Plan for progression across the age and ability range for which they are trained, designing effective sequences within lessons and across series of lessons and demonstrating secure subject/curriculum knowledge.

Teaching

Q25 Teach lessons and sequences of lessons across the age and ability range for which they are trained in which they:
  (a) use a range of teaching strategies and resources . . . taking practical account of diversity and promoting equality and inclusion;
  (c) adapt their language to suit the learners they teach, introducing new ideas and concepts clearly, and using explanations, questions, discussions and plenaries effectively.

Assessing, monitoring and giving feedback

Q26 (a) Make effective use of a range of assessment, monitoring and recording strategies.
  (b) Assess the learning needs of those they teach in order to set challenging learning objectives.
Q27 Provide timely, accurate and constructive feedback on learners' attainment, progress and areas for development.
Q28 Support and guide learners to reflect on their learning, identify the progress they have made and identify their emerging learning needs.

Reviewing teaching and learning

Q29 Evaluate the impact of their teaching on the progress of all learners, and modify their planning and classroom practice where necessary.

ANNOTATED FURTHER READING

Briggs, M., Woodfield, A., Martin, C. and Swatton P. (2008) *Assessment for Learning and Teaching: Achieving QTS*, Exeter: Learning Matters.
Includes references to the Primary National Strategy and qualified teacher status standards for 2007.

Clarke, S. (2003) *Enriching Feedback in the Primary Classroom*, London: Hodder and Stoughton.
Written by an experienced practitioner, this book offers clear strategies for marking pupil work and giving effective feedback to the learner.

Gipps, C., McCallum, B. and Hargreaves, E. (2000) *What Makes a Good Primary School Teacher? Expert Classroom Strategies*, London: RoutledgeFalmer.
This book describes, in non-academic language, the teaching, assessment and feedback strategies used by experienced primary teachers.

RELEVANT WEBSITES

Assessment Reform Group's ten principles to guide classroom practice: www.qcda.gov.uk/13440.aspx
Also check the following links: assessment for learning guidance; overview documents; professional development; and case studies.

Qualifications and Curriculum Authority (QCA): www.qcda.gov.uk
The QCA is now the Qualifications and Curriculum Development Agency.

Visit the companion website www.routledge.com/textbooks/ltps2e for:

■ links to useful websites relevant to this unit.

REFERENCES

Assessment Reform Group (ARG) (1999) *Assessment for Learning, Beyond the Black Box*, London: ARG/Nuffield Foundation.

Assessment Reform Group (ARG) (2002) Assessment for Learning: 10 Research-based Principles to Guide Classroom Practice. Available online at www.qcda.gov.uk/13440.aspx (accessed November 2009).

Assessment Reform Group (ARG) (2004) *Report of the Assessment Systems for the Future Project*, London: ARG/Nuffield Foundation.

Black, P.J. and Wiliam, D. (1998a) 'Assessment and classroom learning', *Assessment in Education*, 5(1): 7–74.

Black, P.J. and Wiliam, D. (1998b) *Inside the Black Box: Raising Standards Through Classroom Assessment*, London: Kings College.

Clarke, S. (2003) *Enriching Feedback in the Primary Classroom*, London: Hodder and Stoughton.

Daugherty, R. (2008) 'Reviewing National Curriculum assessment in Wales: how can evidence inform the development of policy?', *Cambridge Journal of Education*, 38(1): 77–91.

Daugherty, R. (2009) 'National Curriculum assessment in Wales: adaptations and divergence', *Educational Research*, 51(2): 247–50.

de Bóo, M. (1999) *Using Science to Develop Thinking Skills at Key Stage 1*, London: National Association for Able Children in Education/David Fulton.

Department for Education and Skills (DfES) (2003) *Excellence and Enjoyment: A Strategy for Primary Schools*, London: DfES.

Gipps, C., McCallum, B. and Hargreaves, E. (2000) *What Makes a Good Primary School Teacher? Expert Classroom Strategies*, London: RoutledgeFalmer.

Training and Development Agency for Schools (TDA) (2008) *Professional Standards for Qualified Teacher Status and Requirements for Initial Teacher Training*, London: TDA.

ASSESSMENT AND LEARNING

Summative approaches

Kathy Hall and Kieron Sheehy

INTRODUCTION

In this unit you will have the chance to reflect on what summative assessment is, its uses and its potential impact on learners. You will also be able to consider some aspects of current policy on assessment. We start by considering some basic questions about summative assessment and by linking it with formative assessment. We will go on to identify purposes of summative assessment as well as sources of assessment evidence and we will explain what counts as good evidence of learning. We also consider standard assessment tests (SATs) in the context of summative assessment and we finish by inviting your views on current assessment policy.

OBJECTIVES

By the end of this unit you should be able to:

- define summative assessment and relate it to formative assessment;
- explain why it is important to assess learners in a variety of contexts and know the kinds of assessment tasks that are effective in generating good evidence of learning;
- identify ways in which schools might use summative assessment information to feed back into teaching and learning;
- describe some aspects of the national policy on assessment and offer an informed opinion about the current emphasis on different assessment purposes and approaches.

WHAT IS ASSESSMENT AND WHY DO IT?

Assessment means different things in different contexts and it is carried out for different purposes. There is no simple answer to what it is or why we do it. Indeed one of the most important messages that we would like you to take away from this unit is that assessment is not a simple or innocent term. Assessing learning is not a neutral or value-free activity – it is always bound up with attitudes, values, beliefs and sometimes prejudices on the part of those carrying out the assessment and on the part of those being assessed. When we make assessments of children's learning we are always influenced by what we bring with us in terms of our previous experiences, personal views and histories. Children's responses to assessment are influenced by what they bring with them – their previous experiences and their personal views.

Summative assessment sums up learning

Most recent sources on assessment refer to two important types. One is summative assessment, the other is formative assessment. Sometimes summative assessment is termed 'assessment of learning' (AOL) and in recent times formative assessment is associated with 'assessment for learning' (AFL). These newer terms are useful as they give an insight into the purpose of assessment that is involved in each case. In the previous unit (5.1) the area of formative assessment is addressed in more detail.

As the term implies, summative assessment tries to sum up a child's attainment in a given area of the curriculum. Summative assessment is retrospective: it looks back at what has been achieved, perhaps over a term, year or key stage. Formative assessment, on the other hand, is prospective: it looks forward to the next steps of learning. However, debate continues over whether and how summative and formative assessment should be distinguished (Threlfall, 2005; Black and Wiliam, 2007). As we explain in a moment, we consider that the use to which assessment information is put is also helpful in determining whether it is labelled summative or formative.

SOURCES OF ASSESSMENT EVIDENCE

Assessing learning is about collecting information or evidence about learners and making judgements about it. The evidence may be based on one or more of the following:

- what learners say;
- what learners do;
- what learners produce;
- what learners feel or think.

The information or evidence may come from learners' responses to a test, such as a spelling test; a classroom activity, such as a science investigation; a game or a puzzle; or a standard assessment task or test like the SATs. It may come from a task or activity that is collaborative, that is, one where several pupils work together on the same problem. It may come from a task that pupils do on their own without interacting with other children.

We suspect that you will have observed children and made judgements about them in many of those settings, and you may have noted down some of your observations and/or shared them with the class teacher or tutor when you were on teaching practice.

PURPOSES OF SUMMATIVE ASSESSMENT

As a new teacher you will be meeting children whom you have not taught, or may not have even met previously. In these situations you might wish to gain an overview of each pupil's progress. This is particularly so when children are transferring between different stages of schooling and the classwork is different. Summative assessment is used frequently in these contexts because obtaining a summary of what learners know or can do helps the teacher to decide what to teach next.

Summative assessment is carried out for several purposes. First, it provides you with a summary of learners' achievements that will inform your future teaching and of course your planning for future learning. (This is close to the notion of formative assessment described in Unit 5.1.) Second, it provides valid and accurate information that can be shared with parents about their children's progress. And, third, summatively assessing learning provides a numerical measurement that can be used in league tables – the purpose being to make schools accountable.

Before reading on, try to put these purposes in order of importance for yourself as a classroom teacher.

We suspect this exercise is not that simple to do. Assessing learners for the purpose of helping you to plan your teaching can't easily be accommodated alongside assessing learners for the purpose of rendering the school or class accountable through the publication of league tables. League tables call for assessment methods that are reliable, in that they are comparable across all schools and across the country as a whole, and valid, in that they offer an account of what is considered important to know at various stages of schooling. As Black *et al.* (2003: 2) note, these are 'exacting requirements'. Reliability and comparability are not major issues if, on the other hand, you are seeking evidence to help you decide what to teach next.

For the purpose of generating league tables, as Black *et al.* (2003) note, the main assessment methods are formal tests (not devised by teachers). These are usually isolated from day-to-day teaching and learning, and they are often carried out at special times of the year. In contrast, assessments designed to inform your teaching are usually more informal, they may be integrated into your ongoing teaching, and they are likely to be carried out in different ways by different teachers. In the light of the previous sentence, you may well wonder what the difference is between summative and formative assessment, and indeed some research challenges the distinction in the first place (Threlfall, 2005). However, in line with the work of Black and Wiliam (1998) we are reluctant to label the latter as formative assessment.

As we see it, the salient feature of formative assessment is that learners themselves use the information deriving from the assessment to bridge the gap between what they know and what they need to know (see Hall and Burke (2003) for a full discussion). Collecting information to inform your teaching is in itself no guarantee that learners will use this information to move forward in their learning.

PRODUCING GOOD EVIDENCE OF ACHIEVEMENT

It is important to appreciate that summative assessment can take a variety of forms – it need not, indeed should not, just be a written test. In addition, it is important for you as a teacher to try to anticipate how pupils might respond to the demands of an assessment task. In 1987, Desmond Nuttall wrote a paper describing the types of tasks or activities that are good for assessing learning. Such tasks, he says, should be concrete and within the experience of the individual; they should be presented clearly; and they should be perceived by the pupils as relevant to their current concerns.

Being able to respond to a task by using different methods, for example making, doing, talking and writing, allows learners to demonstrate their learning in a variety of ways. The value of varied approaches to assessing learning is that they help learners really show what they know or can do. For example, a learner who is not a very skilled writer may be better able to demonstrate their historical knowledge through talk or through a combination of written work and oral work. Think about your own history as a pupil – do you feel that a written test enabled you to demonstrate what you really knew? Would other ways have been more appropriate for assessing your competence in different curriculum areas?

The use of a variety of ways of assessing learning (often referred to as 'multiple response modes') allows adults to have evidence of learning from a variety of contexts, and to avoid making judgements about learning based on single sources of evidence, such as, say, a pencil and paper test. This results in information that is more accurate and trustworthy than results deriving from just one assessment in just one situation. You could say that it is more valid and dependable. By looking across several instances in which a child uses, say, reading, the teacher and teaching assistant gain valuable information about that child as a reader.

Judgements based on the use of a variety of sources of assessment information are of course more demanding on time and resources. This means teachers and policy makers have to consider the appropriate balance to obtain between validity and trustworthiness of assessment evidence on the one hand and manageability and cost on the other. Teachers' summative assessment appears to work well when they make decisions about the programme of work and what needs to be assessed within it, have helped develop the assessment criteria and can examine a range of pupil work (Harlen, 2005). Reviewing teachers' use of summative assessment, Harlen (2005) also highlighted a need for teachers to be aware of potential bias in their judgements – for example, a 'halo' effect, where one pupil characteristic (such as gender or an identification of special educational needs) may influence the teacher's judgement about their performance on academic tasks or activities.

Tick sheets and portfolios

Some teachers use 'tick sheets' to summarise a child's achievements at a point in schooling. This type of assessment is also summative. What is your view of this approach in the light of the previous section about good assessment evidence?

The tick sheet, yes/no approach might be manageable for very busy practitioners and could provide a useful overview of a child's learning. However, it is likely to be too crude to offer a really meaningful account of learning and usually it offers no source of evidence or little evidence regarding the context in which the assessment took place. Mary Jane Drummond, an expert on early years education, says that a tick sheet approach may hinder the production of a 'rich respectful account' (1999: 34) of a child's learning.

Portfolios offer a useful way of keeping evidence of learning. For example, your pupils might have an individual literacy portfolio into which they put lists of books read, written responses to stories, non-fiction writing, drawings or paintings in response to literature, and so on. They may include drafts of work as well as finished pieces of writing. You might then use this evidence to write short summary accounts of your pupils, which in turn could be used as a basis of discussion at a parents' evening.

As well as individual portfolios, some schools keep 'class' or 'school' portfolios where they put samples of pupil work. They may annotate the samples with reference to context and the standards met. So, for example, contextual annotations might include the date, whether the piece of work was the result of pupils collaborating or an individual working alone, whether the teacher helped or whether it was done independently. Annotations about the standard met might include a grade or a score and a comment indicating how closely the work met a National Curriculum standard or level description (see page 210). This kind of portfolio sometimes acts as a vehicle for teachers to share their interpretation of the standards, not just among themselves but also with parents and with pupils.

SUMMATIVE ASSESSMENT AND TEACHER ASSESSMENT

As well as the external testing regime of standard assessment tests (SATs), teachers assess and report on their pupils via teacher assessment – they are required to 'sum up' their pupils' attainments in relation to National Curriculum levels. As we noted earlier, in order to offer defensible and trustworthy accounts of their attainment, you need to assess pupils in a variety of contexts and in a variety of ways. But any assessment is only as good as the use to which it is put. Some writers refer to this concept as 'consequential validity', as what is considered important are the consequences of the assessment – what happens to the assessment information once it is collected. Is it used to inform teaching, to enable the production of league tables or to summarise achievement for parents, or for the next teacher?

Assessment information, including that obtained via SATs and, especially, teacher assessment, can be used in a way that supports teaching and learning. We will explain this with reference to the way some teachers use level descriptions.

Level descriptions are used in all four parts of the UK. They are summary statements that describe the types and range of performance that pupils are expected to demonstrate at various stages in their schooling. Teachers have to judge which level 'best fits' a child's performance for each area of the curriculum. This involves cross-checking against adjacent levels in a scale and considering the balance of strengths and weaknesses for each particular child.

What use is made of level descriptions? Does the process of allocating levels to pupils' achievements inform teaching and learning? A study conducted in six different schools in six different local education authorities (LEAs) in the north of England sought to understand how primary teachers were using level descriptions (Hall and Harding, 2002). On the basis of many interviews over two years with teachers and LEA assessment advisers and observations of assessment meetings, two contrasting approaches to the process of interpreting and using level descriptions in schools were identified. The approaches are described as *collaborative* and *individualistic.* To illustrate we will describe just two of the schools – East Street and West Street (not their real names), which show these contrasting tendencies.

A collaborative approach

East Street School is a large inner city primary school of 400+ pupils, all but 5 per cent of whom are from ethnic minority backgrounds. East Street has an assessment community that is highly collaborative, with teachers, parents and pupils having many opportunities to talk about assessment and how and why it is done. The staff frequently meet to discuss the purposes of assessment in general and of their ongoing teacher assessment in particular. They talk about what constitutes evidence of achievement in various areas of the curriculum and they compare their judgements of samples of pupil work. They use a range of tools, such as school portfolios and sample material from the Qualifications and Curriculum Authority (QCA), to help in their assessment tasks and to ensure that they are applying the level descriptions consistently. They strive to include pupils, parents and other teachers as part of that assessment community.

An individualistic approach

West Street School is a larger-than-average primary school serving a varied socio-economic area in a northern city. Pupils are drawn from a mixture of privately owned and council-maintained housing and the school has a sizeable number of pupils from educationally disadvantaged backgrounds. West Street reluctantly complies with the demands of national policy on assessment. Teachers here work largely in isolation from each other in interpreting and implementing assessment goals and, especially, in interpreting level descriptions and using portfolios and evidence. There is no real attempt to involve interested groups, such as parents and pupils, in assessment discussions. The staff tend to view national testing as an unhelpful, arduous intrusion.

What all of this tells us is that schools vary a great deal in how they implement national assessment policy. Some teachers reluctantly comply with the policy, while others make it work for the benefit of all interested parties in the school. To be more precise, some teachers use level descriptions in a way that supports assessment *for* learning and assessment *of* learning.

Task 5.2.1 ASSESSMENT – DIFFERENT APPROACHES

■ Study Table 5.2.1, which summarises the assessment approach in East Street and West Street schools.

■ Suggest some reasons for the difference in approach in the two schools.

■ Practice in most schools is probably somewhere in between these two. Make a note of which practices listed for East Street you are aware of from your experience in school recently.

■ **Table 5.2.1** Assessment communities and assessment individuals

	Collaborative (East Street School)	Individualistic (West Street School)
Goals	Compliant and accepting	Reluctant compliance and resistance
Processes	1 Level descriptions – interpretation is shared 2 Portfolio – in active use 3 Exemplification materials – owned by teachers; a mixture of school-devised and QCA materials 4 Evidence – planned collection; variety of modes; assessment embedded in teaching and learning; emphasis on the process 5 Common language of assessment 6 Commitment to moderation (cross-checking of interpretations of evidence)	1 Level descriptions – little or no sharing of interpretations 2 Portfolio – dormant 3 Exemplification materials – QCA not used; commercially produced materials used by some individuals 4 Evidence – not used much; assessment often bolted on to learning and teaching; emphasis on products 5 Uncertainty/confusion about terms 6 Weak or non-existent moderation
Personnel	Whole school; aspirations to enlarge the assessment community to include pupils, parents and other teachers	Year 2 teachers as individuals; no real grasp of the potential for enlarging the assessment community
Value system	Assessment seen as useful, necessary and integral to teaching and learning; made meaningful through collaboration	Assessment seen as 'imposed' and not meaningful at the level of the class teacher

To become a collaborative assessment community, staff need time to develop their expertise. They need time to talk about and share their practices in a culture that shares the expectation that adults too are valued learners.

SUMMATIVE ASSESSMENT AND SATS

Summative assessment does not just refer to the kinds of end of key stage assessment carried out in schools all over the country in Years 2 and 6. While those external tasks and tests, known as SATs, are indeed summative, they are not the only kind of summative assessment that goes on in schools. However, because of their 'high stakes' – that is, schools' ranking in league tables depends on them – they are accorded very high status in practice in schools and people sometimes make the mistake of assuming that summative assessments means SATs. Table 5.2.2 illustrates the range of SATs undertaken by pupils in English primary schools in 2004.

When presented in this way the amount of testing looks daunting. It has been pointed out that 'the total amount of compulsory testing is in fact only 17 hours spread over nine years – an average of not even 2 hours per year' (Whetton, 2004: 15). However, this statement does not reflect the impact that such assessments have on pupils or on practice within schools.

THE IMPACT OF 'HIGH STAKES' ASSESSMENT ON PUPILS

Many researchers on assessment, including ourselves, have written about the impact on pupils of different assessment purposes and practices (Harlen and Deakin Crick, 2002). The research shows that schools feel under pressure to get more of their pupils achieving at higher levels in national tests. This pushes some teachers, especially those who have classes about to take national tests, to spend more time and energy on helping pupils to get good at doing those tests. This is often referred to as 'teaching to the test' and it means there is less time to actually develop pupils' skills and understanding in the various areas of the curriculum.

This is exactly what we found in a recent study of Year 6 pupils in urban areas of disadvantage (Hall *et al.*, 2004). The external pencil and paper tests, which are designed to offer evidence to the

■ **Table 5.2.2** Primary SATs in England in 2004

■ Foundation Stage Profile (5 years old)	All pupils
■ Key Stage 1 tests (7 years old) English, maths	All pupils
■ Optional tests (8 years old) English, maths	Nearly all pupils
■ Optional tests (9 years old) English, maths	Nearly all pupils
■ Optional tests (10 years old) English, maths	Nearly all pupils
■ Key Stage 2 tests (11 years old) Results published English, maths	All pupils
■ Year 7 progress tests	Low attainers

Source: Adapted from Whetton (2004)

government about how schools are raising standards, received enormous attention in the daily life of pupils in the schools that were part of our study. Such is the perceived pressure in schools to do well in league tables that they sometimes feel unable to place sufficient emphasis on assessment designed to promote learning across the curriculum or on assessing learning through a variety of modes (see pages 248–50 of this unit). Summative assessment can even become seen as the goal of teaching. George W. Bush, a former President of the USA, visited an East London primary school. After listening to a story being read to the children, he commented on the importance of literacy to the teachers: 'You teach a child to read, and he or her (*sic*) will be able to pass a literacy test' (cited in Yandell, 2008).

In situations where passing a test is seen as the purpose of teaching, the children's learning experiences become focused towards this end. Yandell (2008) described how pupils, studying a play, were only given photocopies of the 'SATs' sections of the text and never read the play itself.

There are many other potential consequences for pupils. 'High stakes' tests can lead teachers to adopt transmission styles of teaching and thus disadvantage pupils who prefer other, more creative, ways of learning. Practice tests, when repeatedly undertaken, can have a negative impact on the self-esteem of lower-achieving pupils. Research from outside the UK suggests that pupils' expectations about the purpose of assessment reflects badly on summative approaches (Black, 2003), for example pupils believing that summative assessment was entirely for their school's and parents' benefit. Children who did less well in such assessments felt that their purpose was to make them work harder. It was a source of pressure that resulted in pupil anxiety and even fear.

Pupils used to a diet of summative assessments, based on written tests and on only a few curriculum areas (often numeracy and literacy) can take time in adapting to more formative approaches. The same can be true for teachers. For example, in response to calls for formative assessment, many teachers produce formal summative tests that mimic the statutory tests. This again reflects the perceived importance of SATs. Weeden *et al.* (2002) make the point that the more important a quantitative measure becomes, 'the more it is likely to distort the processes it is supposed to monitor' (p. 34).

'High stakes' testing might also influence the way you respond to and feel about the children in your class. 'How many teachers of young children are now able to listen attentively in a non-instrumental way without feeling guilty about the absence of criteria or the insistence of a target tugging at their sleeve' (Fielding, cited in Hill, 2007). There is clearly an emotional/affective factor that is often overlooked in seeking the objective viewpoint that summative assessments are seen as presenting. Robert Reinecke highlights this:

> Assessments, formal or informal, considered or casual, intentional or not, powerfully affect people, particularly students. The assessment climate that students experience is a crucial component of instruction and learning. Students' assessment experiences remain with them for a lifetime and substantially affect their capacity for future learning . . . emotional charge is part of the character of assessment information.
>
> (1998: 7)

For any assessment to have a positive impact on children's learning, the way in which performance results are used and communicated is vitally important.

DIFFERENCES IN TESTING ACROSS THE UK

Pupils in England and in Northern Ireland are subjected to more testing than their peers in other parts of the UK. However, after decades of external summative assessment there now appears to be a shift towards teacher assessment (Leung and Rea-Dickens, 2007). Teachers in Scotland, for instance, decide when their pupils are ready to take the external tests. Teachers at Key Stage 1 in Wales are no longer obliged to assess their pupils for the purpose of compiling league tables and teacher assessment is used for statutory reporting at ages 11 and 14 (Leung and Rea-Dickins, 2007). This followed a review of assessment practices, which questioned whether the hard data extracted by external assessments was worth the negative consequences (Daugherty, 2008, 2009). Teacher assessment is now used in Wales for statutory reporting at 11 and 14 years (Daugherty, 2008, 2009), with teachers working in 'cluster groups to maximise the consistency' of their assessments (Daugherty, 2008: 80). In England, external testing of children at 7 years is being replaced by teacher assessment and a pilot study is looking at a similar approach for 14 year olds (Black and Wiliam, 2007). Scotland has developed an overall approach that emphasises formative testing (for details of these approaches please see the 'Relevant websites' at the end of this unit).

The following is a short extract from an important policy document in England, *Excellence and Enjoyment: A Strategy for Primary Schools*. It tells you what head teachers think is the best way of summarising a learner's achievements:

> At our head teacher conferences, head teachers argued that a teacher's overall, rounded assessment of a child's progress through the year (taking into account the regular tests and tasks that children do) was a more accurate guide to a child's progress at this age [Key Stage 1] than their performance in one particular set of tasks and tests.
>
> (DfES, 2003: 2.29)

Because head teachers in England are so concerned about testing at Key Stage 1, the government decided to commission research to see whether an approach that focuses more on teachers' judgements about pupils' progress throughout the year could result in accurate and rigorous assessments. Currently, teacher assessment of progress across the key stage is the main focus, supported by tests in maths, reading and writing. A sample of schools is externally moderated each year, with the rest carrying out internal moderation exercises. Guidance recommends a standardisation to check consistency of judgements before assessments are made (DCSF, 2008). Once the teacher has concluded their assessments, internal moderation is carried out. Typically, this will be a sample or one or two pupils' work per teacher (DCSF, 2008). This practice is useful for formative aspects (see Unit 5.1) and also for teachers' in-school summative assessment. (See DCSF (2008) for details of standardisation and moderation processes.)

We are hopeful that England and Northern Ireland will continue to move away from their strong emphasis on external testing in favour of a greater focus on teachers' own judgements based on a range of modes of assessment.

Task 5.2.2 TESTING – WHAT DO YOU THINK?

■ Note down some advantages and disadvantages of testing all children at ages 7 and 11.
■ Why do you think England, in particular, places such a strong emphasis on external testing for accountability purposes?

We would suggest that external testing in primary schools is part of a wider social preoccupation with measuring, league tables and auditing. If you consider other social services, for example the health service and the police service, you find a similar push towards accountability in the form of league tables. England has experienced all of this to a greater degree than other parts of the UK. Education in England seems to be more politicised than in other parts of the UK and politicians in England are less inclined to be influenced by professional groups such as teachers and researchers. This means that, in turn, such groups have less power in educational decision making in England than their counterparts have in Scotland, Wales and Northern Ireland.

A CRITIQUE OF CURRENT ASSESSMENT APPROACHES

Dylan Wiliam, a researcher on assessment over many years, has expressed concern about the narrowing effect on the curriculum of teachers teaching to the test – a point we noted earlier in this unit. Here are some key questions he poses.

■ Why are pupils tested as individuals, when the world of work requires people who can work well in a team?
■ Why do we test memory, when in the real world engineers and scientists never rely on memory: if they're stuck, they look things up.
■ Why do we use timed tests when it is usually far more important to get things done right than to get things done quickly?

He favours an approach that would support teachers' own judgements of pupil achievement, and believes that this approach should replace all forms of testing, from the earliest stages through to GCSE and A-levels. He points out that this happens in Sweden. This is how he justifies his argument:

> In place of the current vicious spiral, in which only those aspects of learning that are easily measured are regarded as important, I propose developing a system of summative assessment based on moderated teacher assessment. A separate system, relying on 'light sampling' of the performance of schools, would provide stable and robust information for the purposes of accountability and policy-formation.
>
> (Wiliam, 2002: 61–2)

He goes on to say that his preferred approach 'would also be likely to tackle boys' underachievement, because the current "all or nothing" test at the end of a key stage encourages boys to believe that they can make up lost ground at the last minute' (pp. 61–2).

He envisages that there would be a large number of assessment tasks but not all pupils would undertake the same task. These good-quality assessment tasks would cover the entire curriculum and they would be allocated randomly. This would guard against teaching to the test or, as he puts it, 'the only way to teach to the test would be to teach the whole curriculum to every student' (p. 62).

He suggests that schools that taught only a limited curriculum, or concentrated on, say, the most able pupils, would be shown up as ineffective.

Task 5.2.3 A DIFFERENT APPROACH – WHAT DO YOU THINK?

■ What do you think of Wiliam's ideas?
■ Do you think his suggestions are more in line with what we know about learning and assessment, especially what we know about the impact of testing on pupils?
■ Do you think his suggestions are feasible?
■ How would these groups view his ideas: parents, pupils, teachers, politicians?

SUMMARY

In this unit we have sought to define and describe summative assessment and ways of using it. We have also highlighted the (mostly negative) impact on learners of testing, especially 'high stakes' testing. Whatever the national policy on external testing, as a class teacher you will have a powerful influence over how you assess your pupils. In turn, how you assess your pupils will have considerable influence on how they perform, on how motivated they become as learners and on how they feel about themselves as learners. You are likely to influence the kind of lifelong learners they become.

To recap the major points of the unit, we suggest that you revisit the learning objectives we noted on the first page. As you do this, you might consider the different ways in which you could demonstrate your understanding and knowledge of the topic.

ANNOTATED FURTHER READING

The following three articles provide evidence about the impact of 'high stakes' summative assessment on pupils and teachers, and on teaching and learning.

Hall, K., Collins, J., Benjamin, S., Sheehy, K. and Nind, M. (2004) 'SATurated models of pupildom: assessment and inclusion/exclusion', *British Educational Research Journal*, 30(6): 801–17.

Harlen, W. (2005) 'Teachers' summative practices and assessment for learning: tensions and synergies', *The Curriculum Journal*, 16(2): 207–24.

Reay, D. and Wiliam, D. (1999) '"I'll be a nothing": structure, agency and the construction of identity through assessment', *British Educational Research Journal*, 25(3): 343–54.

Although more than a decade old, the following article provides an excellent account of what makes a good test.

Gipps, C. (1994) Developments in educational assessment: what makes a good test? *Assessment in Education*, 1(3): 283–91.

RELEVANT WEBSITES

Assessment is for Learning (AifL): www.aifl-na.net

Information about National Assessments and examples of tasks, which are open to anyone to browse, can be found at this site.

Northern Ireland Curriculum: www.nicurriculum.org.uk/

Has information on Northern Ireland's curriculum and assessment arrangements.

Primary Assessment – Making Summative Assessment Work for You: www.teachers.tv/video/3360

Professor Wynne Harlen, whose work is referred to in this unit, takes part in a discussion of teacher's summative assessments.

Primary Assessment – The Welsh Experience: www.teachers.tv/video/3361

This looks at how teachers in Wales are assessing and moderating their work across phases, following the removal of statutory testing as Key Stages 2 and 3.

Qualification and Curriculum Authority (QCA): www.qcda.gov.uk/13581.aspx

The QCA's assessment web page.

Scottish Government site on Curriculum and Assessment: www.scotland.gov.uk/Topics/Education/Schools/curriculum

This is a useful source of further information regarding Assessment is for Learning (AifL).

Visit the companion website www.routledge.com/textbooks/ltps2e for:

■ additional questions and task for this unit;
■ links to useful websites relevant to this unit.

REFERENCES

Black, P. (2003) *Testing: Friend or Foe? Theory and Practice of Assessment and Testing*, London: RoutledgeFalmer.

Black, P. and Wiliam, D. (1998) *Inside the Black Box*, London: Kings College.

Black, P. and Wiliam, D. (2007) 'Large-scale assessment systems: design principles drawn from international comparisons', *Measurement: Interdisciplinary Research and Perspectives*, 5(1): 1–53.

Black, P., Harrison, C., Lee, C., Marshall, B. and Wiliam, D. (2003) *Assessment for Learning: Putting it into Practice*, Buckingham: Open University Press.

Department for Children, Schools and Families (DCSF) (2008) *Primary Framework for Literacy and Mathematics*. Available online at www.standards.dfes.gov.uk/primaryframeworks/ (accessed October 2009).

Department for Education and Skills (DfES) (2003) *Excellence and Enjoyment: A Strategy for Primary Schools*, London: DfES.

Drummond, M.J. (1999) 'Baseline assessment: a case for civil disobedience?', in C. Conner (ed.) *Assessment in Action in the Primary School*, London: Falmer, pp. 3–49.

Hall, K. and Burke, W. (2003) *Making Formative Assessment Work: Effective Practice in the Primary Classroom*, Buckingham: Open University Press.

Hall, K. and Harding, A. (2002) 'Level descriptions and teacher assessment: towards a community of assessment practice', *Educational Research*, 40(1): 1–16.

Hall, K., Collins, J., Benjamin, S., Sheehy, K. and Nind, M. (2004) 'SATurated models of pupildom: assessment and inclusion/exclusion', *British Educational Research Journal*, 30(6): 801–17.

Harlen, W. (2005) 'Trusting teachers' judgement: research evidence of the reliability and validity of teachers', *Research Papers in Education*, 20(3): 245–70.

Harlen, W. and Deakin-Crick, R. (2002) 'A systematic review of the impact of summative assessment and tests on students' motivation for learning' (EPPI-Centre Review, version 1.1), in *Research Evidence in Education Library*, London: EPPI-Centre, Social Science Research Unit, Institute of Education.

Hill, D. (2007) 'Critical teacher education, New Labour in Britain, and the global project of neoliberal capital', *Policy Futures in Education*, 5(2): 204–25.

Leung, C. and Rea-Dickins, P. (2007) 'Teacher assessment as policy instrument: contradictions and capacities', *Language Assessment Quarterly*, 4(1): 6–36.

Nuttall, D. (1987) 'The validity of assessments', *European Journal of the Psychology of Education*, 11(2): 109–18.

Reinecke, R.A. (1998) *Challenging the Mind, Touching the Heart: Best Assessment Practice*, Thousand Oaks, CA: Corwin Oaks.

Threlfall, J. (2005) 'The formative use of assessment information in planning: the notion of contingent planning', *British Journal of Educational Studies*, 53(1): 54–65.

Weedon, P., Winter, J. and Broadfoot, P. (2002) *Assessment: What's In It For Schools?*, London: RoutledgeFalmer.

Whetton, C. (2004) *Reflections on Fifteen Years of National Assessment: Lessons, Successes and Mistakes*, Paper presented at the 30th International Association for Educational Assessment Conference, Philadelphia, PA, 13–18 June.

Wiliam, D. (2002) 'What is wrong with our educational assessment and what can be done about it?', *Education Review*, 15(1): 57–62.

Yandell, J. (2008) 'Mind the gap: investigating test literacy and classroom literacy', *English in Education*, 42(1): 70–87.

6 DIVERSITY AND INCLUSION

PROVIDING FOR INCLUSION

Simon Ellis and Janet Tod

INTRODUCTION

This unit explores *inclusion* within the context of special educational needs (SEN) and disability. The authors accept that inclusion in its broadest sense is of relevance to *any* learners experiencing barriers to learning and participation (Booth and Ainscow, 2002). However, the term 'inclusion' continues to be most commonly used by policy makers, practitioners and parents to describe educational provision for children and young people with SEN in mainstream schools (Pirrie *et al.*, 2005).

In 1997, the newly elected Labour government expressed its commitment to inclusion via *Excellence for All Children* (DfEE, 1997a), effectively endorsing the internationally agreed principles of the Salamanca Statement (UNESCO, 1994). There followed a raft of new policy and guidance documents (e.g. DfES, 2001a), as well as revisions to existing documents to reflect this inclusive orientation (e.g. DfEE/QCA, 1999; DfES, 2001b). Although inclusion still remains firmly on the educational agenda for the twenty-first century, the 'tidal wave of inclusive intent' (O'Brien, 1998: 151) in policy and guidance that characterised the late 1990s has given way to concerns expressed (e.g. Warnock, 2005; MacBeath *et al.*, 2006) regarding the potential negative effects of a policy of inclusion on some individual pupils and the demands placed on schools.

OBJECTIVES

By the end of this unit you should have:

- an increased understanding of the rationale for inclusion in schools;
- a critical awareness of the policy initiatives that inform inclusive approaches for schools;
- reflected upon how to develop your own pedagogy with regard to inclusion;
- increased your range of strategies for achieving increased inclusion.

THE COMMITMENT TO INCLUSIVE EDUCATION

The Salamanca Statement (UNESCO, 1994) was a catalyst for much of the educational policy in the UK from the mid-1990s onwards. The Salamanca Statement was the outcome of a world conference on Special Needs Education, attended by representatives from 92 governments and 25 international organisations. It set out five proclaimed beliefs:

- every child has a fundamental right to education, and must be given the opportunity to achieve and maintain an acceptable level of learning;
- every child has unique characteristics, interests, abilities and learning needs;
- education systems should be designed and educational programmes implemented to take into account the wide diversity of these characteristics and needs;
- those with special educational needs must have access to regular schools, which should accommodate them within a child-centred pedagogy capable of meeting these needs;
- regular schools with this inclusive orientation are the most effective means of combating discriminatory attitudes, creating welcoming communities, building an inclusive society and achieving education for all; moreover, they provide an effective education to the majority of children and improve the efficiency and ultimately the cost-effectiveness of the entire education system.

(UNESCO, 1994: viii–ix)

The five beliefs contain principles alongside prescription as to how these principles might be realised. In many ways, some of the criticisms and tensions that have emerged in recent years regarding the implementation of a policy of inclusion are an inevitable result of this mixing of largely incontestable principles with prescription for methods of realisation that may be open to greater debate. The last two proclaimed beliefs are substantially rooted in prescription of method and are challenging in terms of the level of change demanded of existing education systems and structures.

Although the Salamanca Statement was a catalyst, the UK government's commitment to an inclusive approach was an evolution of an existing system. Since the Education Act 1981, which had implemented many of the recommendations of the Warnock Report (Warnock, 1978), the UK had followed a policy of integration. It is important to acknowledge that there are differences between inclusion and integration. Unlike integration, which implies a threshold to be crossed before the pupil is deemed suitable to be admitted, based on a concept of educational or social 'readiness' for placement in the mainstream school (Blamires, 1999), inclusion recognises the individual child's right to be included and carries the expectation that schools need to be prepared to change aspects of curriculum, assessment, pedagogy and groupings of pupils to facilitate this. Despite these important differences in the underlying principles, the policy of integration can be considered the forerunner of the policy of inclusion.

MEDICAL AND SOCIAL MODELS OF DISABILITY

The field of Special Education existed long before a policy of inclusion was adopted. It has its own traditions and heritage rooted in what is commonly known as the *medical model* of disability. Practice that developed early in the twentieth century placed the emphasis on diagnosis and labelling, originally carried out exclusively by doctors and psychologists, in order to determine provision. The medical model typically attributes difficulties in learning to deficiencies or impairments within the pupil. This model of disability, difficulty and difference has exerted a pervasive influence over many years within the education system and society in general.

Inclusive education is underpinned by a *social model* of disability, advocated initially by members of the Disability Rights movement. The social model of disability is concerned with the barriers that may exist in the nature of the setting or arise through the interaction between pupils and their contexts. This essential difference between social and medical models is captured in the Union of the Physically Impaired Against Segregation's (UPIAS) description of disability as:

The disadvantage or restriction of ability caused by a contemporary social organisation which takes little or no account of people who have physical impairments and thus excludes them from participation in the mainstream of social activities.

(UPIAS, 1976: 14)

In school contexts the influence of the medical model has led in the past to the 'over-individualising' of pupils' difficulties in learning. Embracing a social model represents a positive move, recognising that schools, through their culture, curriculum, pedagogy, policies, practices, organisation and structures, can either create or reduce barriers to learning and participation. At a practical level this has led schools and their teachers to refocus on classroom organisation, teaching materials, teaching style and differentiation as the means by which to include more children with learning difficulties and disabilities in mainstream settings.

The acceptance of a social model of disability poses a number of challenges. It is undoubtedly a necessary model, but Norwich (2002a) and others have argued that there is a risk that problems are 'over-socialised', with an emphasis placed on situational, generic barriers rather than recognising the reality of individual difficulties and disabilities. Norwich (2002a) has proposed a model based on bio-psycho-social perspectives that seeks to recognise the need to look at and address the barriers presented through contexts and conditions, but also accepts that, for some pupils, there are biological and psychological factors that need to be given due regard.

DEFINING EDUCATIONAL INCLUSION

Educational inclusion is a term that lacks adequate theorising or consensus about what it means in practice (Wearmouth *et al.,* 2005). However, for practitioners the definition of inclusion that is likely to be most pertinent is that used by the government. Within *Removing Barriers to Achievement*, the DfES stated:

Inclusion is about much more than the type of school that children attend: it is about the quality of their experience; how they are helped to learn, achieve and participate fully in the life of the school.

(DfES, 2004a: 25)

This gave a clear indication that, at policy level, placement in a mainstream school was not considered a defining feature of inclusion. This definition potentially allows for an experience of inclusion to be achieved in a mainstream primary school, a wide ability secondary school, a grammar school, a city academy, a special school or any other form of educational provision. Maintaining a consistent line from the earlier *Excellence for All Children* (DfEE, 1997a), *Removing Barriers to Achievement* stated: 'a small number of children have such severe and complex needs that they will continue to require special provision (DfES, 2004a: 37).

It is something of a staffroom and media myth that the government policy of inclusion called for the systematic closure of *all* special schools. However, national policy is interpreted at local level and there is considerable regional variation in the amount of specialist provision. For example, in a report for the Centre for Studies on Inclusive Education (CSIE), Norwich (2002b) identified that a disabled pupil in Manchester was more than seven times as likely to be placed in a segregated special school than a similar pupil in the London Borough of Newham.

The local authority in which you teach will have interpreted the national policy of inclusion and taken strategic decisions regarding the amount and role of any specialist provision.

A GOVERNMENT RATIONALE FOR INCLUSION

Within *Excellence for All Children* (DfEE, 1997a) the government set out its rationale for the adoption of an inclusive approach, stating:

> The ultimate purpose of SEN provision is to enable young people to flourish in adult life. There are therefore strong educational, as well as social and moral, grounds for educating children with SEN with their peers.
>
> (p. 43)

And

> The great majority of children with SEN will, as adults, contribute economically; all will contribute as members of society. Schools have to prepare all children for these roles. That is a strong reason for educating children with SEN, as far as possible with their peers.
>
> (p. 4)

You will notice that there are links with wider issues regarding the purpose of education; in particular its role in preparing pupils for adult life as members of society. The first quote reflects a concern for the individual; the second reflects the needs of society. Central to the ideology of inclusion is the belief that education makes a powerful contribution to the social construction of inclusive communities and an inclusive society. Inclusive education is concerned with human rights in that it promotes access to, and participation in, an appropriate mainstream community-based education. It offers the promise of increased opportunity to engage in lifelong learning and employment.

EVALUATING INCLUSION

When we think about inclusion and its efficacy as an educational approach it is necessary to consider how we are interpreting the term and the sorts of indicators that would demonstrate effective inclusive practice. Inclusion is a process that is influenced by a range of factors and has different meanings and outcomes for those involved. It might, for example, have a different meaning for a parent than a policy maker and be judged accordingly. The following task is designed to enable you to understand these different perspectives on inclusion within your school.

Task 6.1.1 **IS YOUR SCHOOL INCLUSIVE?**

Do you think your school is inclusive?

■ Think about the process by which you made that judgement.
■ If you were asked to gather evidence about the impact of inclusion in your school, what evidence would you look for and why?

In reflecting upon whether your school is inclusive you probably became aware that there are many different indicators to be considered, including indicators linked to policy development, changes in practice, and the experiences of the individual learner. In thinking about inclusion from your perspective it should now be clear that inclusion is a complex construct rather than a single indicator that you are required to achieve.

Ultimately, it is difficult and unhelpful to debate the effects of a policy of inclusion at the level of 'is inclusion working?' We could look at the number of pupils who are now in mainstream schools who were once previously in special schools. A larger number might be an indicator of a successful policy of inclusion, *if* we were to define inclusion solely in terms of placement in a mainstream school. Against this criterion, a local authority such as Newham, which reportedly (Norwich, 2002b) places few of its pupils in specialist provision, could be seen as doing better than one that continued to place a significant number in special schools. If, however, we were to define inclusion, as the government currently does, in terms of the pupil's experience, based on how they are helped to learn, achieve and participate fully in the life of the school, the evaluation criteria change. Such a definition recognises that there will be pupils with special educational needs who thrive, or fail to thrive, socially, emotionally and cognitively in mainstream schools, just as there will be in special schools. In this case, evaluation of the success of inclusion is based on the individual.

How to evaluate inclusion is an enduring issue. It is possible to evaluate at the level of:

■ *Principles*: Is inclusion generally felt to be the right and proper aspiration to pursue?
■ *Place*: Is there evidence of increased numbers of pupils placed in mainstream schools?
■ *Policy*: To what extent is national and local policy inclusive in its orientation?
■ *Practice*: To what extent are schools and their teachers becoming more inclusive in terms of curriculum and pedagogy?
■ *Person*: To what extent is the individual pupil's *experience* one of 'being included'?

It is, of course, possible for inclusion to be judged to be 'working' at the first four of these levels, but fail when judged against the fifth. It is significant, for example, that Ofsted (2004) noted that, although more mainstream schools saw themselves as inclusive, only a minority actually met special educational needs well (Wedell, 2008).

Despite ongoing practical concerns regarding the implementation of a policy of inclusion, there are clearly many pupils in mainstream schools who would once have unnecessarily been placed in specialist provision. Whether *all* pupils who are categorised as having SEN could be placed in mainstream schools is a difficult question to answer. It could be argued that aspiring to anything less than full mainstream inclusion effectively lets the education system 'off the hook' in terms of needing to change. Current government policy (e.g. DfES, 2004a) has been criticised for: 'expressing strong support for the principle of inclusion while, at the same time, qualifying this support to the point where it is hard to see any particular policy direction being indicated' (Croll and Moses, 2000: 2).

Equally, to pursue a policy of full mainstream inclusion as a way of driving change risks failing to deliver an appropriate education to some pupils who pass through the educational system before sufficient change has occurred.

Task 6.1.2 CRITICAL EVALUATIONS

The government interpretation of inclusion has been criticised for 'expressing strong support for the principle of inclusion while, at the same time, qualifying this support to the point where it is hard to see any particular policy direction being indicated' (Croll and Moses, 2000: 2).

■ Critically evaluate the descriptions of inclusive education used within a range of national guidance and policy documents. To what extent do you think Croll and Moses' criticism is valid?

CRITICISM OF INCLUSION

Educational inclusion has been developed more in response to a global moral imperative based on human rights than as an evidence-based rationale for an enhanced educational experience for all. The adoption and implementation of a policy of inclusion has brought with it a number of practical challenges and dilemmas.

It was Baroness Warnock's (2005) criticism of the policy of inclusion that perhaps grabbed the greatest attention, due to her earlier role in the development of practice in the field of SEN through the Warnock Report (Warnock, 1978). In her 2005 paper, *Special Educational Needs: A New Look*, Baroness Warnock (2005) argued that 'the idea of transforming talk of disability into talk of what children need in order to make progress has turned out to be a baneful one' (2005: 19) and 'the failure to distinguish various kinds of needs has been disastrous for many children' (2005: 20). She also made clear her view that inclusion in mainstream school could be detrimental for some pupils.

Prior to Baroness Warnock's comments on the subject, Ofsted (2004) had reported on special educational needs and inclusion. The report presented a varied picture of practice and voiced a number of concerns, including:

■ A minority of mainstream schools meet special needs very well, and others are becoming better at doing so.

■ Taking all the steps needed to enable pupils with SEN to participate fully in the life of the school and achieve their potential remains a significant challenge for many schools. Expectations of achievement are often neither well enough defined nor pitched high enough. Progress in learning remains slower than it should be for a significant number of pupils.

■ Few schools evaluate their provision for pupils with SEN systematically so that they can establish how effective the provision is and whether it represents value for money. The availability and use of data on outcomes for pupils with SEN continue to be limited.

■ Not enough use is made by mainstream schools of the potential for adapting the curriculum and teaching methods so that pupils have suitable opportunities to improve key skills.

■ The teaching seen of pupils with SEN was of varying quality, with a high proportion of lessons having shortcomings. Support by teaching assistants can be vital, but the organisation of it can mean that pupils have insufficient opportunity to develop their skills, understanding and independence.

■ Despite the helpful contributions by the national strategies, the quality of work to improve the literacy of pupils with SEN remains inconsistent.

(Ofsted, 2004: 5)

MacBeath *et al.* (2006) produced a detailed report entitled *The Costs of Inclusion* on behalf of the National Union of Teachers. Numerous concerns were raised about the effects of government policy on schools, teachers and pupils. The conclusion was that the current education system itself made it difficult to implement inclusion (Wedell, 2008). Perhaps more notable in terms of grabbing public interest was MacBeath's comment about inclusion to journalists: 'You might call it a form of abuse, in a sense, that those children are in a situation that's totally inappropriate for them' (BBC, 2006).

The growing and publicly aired concern regarding inclusion was enough to trigger a Select Committee review (House of Commons Education and Skills Committee, 2006). The subsequent report was critical of the lack of progress with regard to the proposal for training in relation to SEN set out in *Removing Barriers to Achievement* (DfES, 2004a). The government was also criticised for causing confusion through a changing definition of inclusion. The report urged the government, if it intended to continue to use the term in key policy documents, to work harder to define exactly what it means by inclusion. The Select Committee report also raised concern at the variations nationally in provision and attributed this to confusing messages within policy regarding the future and role of special schools.

Significantly the Select Committee also pointed to the potential tension experienced by schools between different strands of government educational policy, stating:

> SEN policy needs to be more explicitly considered in a broader education context and in light of existing education policies – not just those it sits comfortably with like *Every Child Matters*, personalisation, reading strategies, behaviour strategies, but also those it sits less comfortably with – specifically the continuing priority of raising standards for the majority with its emphasis on league tables and attainment targets and a system of increased choice and diversity for parents.
>
> (House of Commons Education and Skills Committee, 2006:18)

Though the Select Committee report has been viewed as critical of inclusion, it was a review of SEN provision. By implication, because the policy context for SEN provision is one of inclusion, it is inevitable that inclusion is criticised. In reality, a number of the structures and processes that are criticised have origins that pre-date the policy of inclusion and would probably have existed in similar form even if the government had continued with the policy of integration that existed prior to the adoption of a policy of inclusion.

Despite the concerns regarding how the government's policy of inclusion was operating for some pupils with SEN, the Select Committee report was clear:

> This Committee supports the principle of educators pursuing an ethos that fully includes all children – including those with SEN and disabilities – in the setting or settings that best meets their needs and helps them achieve their potential, preferably a good school within their local community.
>
> (p. 23)

THE DEVELOPMENT OF INCLUSIVE CLASSROOM PRACTICE

In thinking about your own practice it is necessary to be aware of the changing policy context from the 'tidal wave of inclusive intent' (O'Brien, 1998: 151) of the late nineties through to the recent concerns expressed by Warnock (2005), Ofsted (2004) and the House of Commons Education and Skills Committee (2006). These developments inevitably affect the emphasis of any national guidance to schools and the expectation of teachers in relation to the teaching and learning of pupils with special educational needs.

Much of the guidance issued since *Excellence for All Children* (DfEE, 1997a) has emphasised a move away from a focus on individual categories of need associated with a medical model of disability towards improving the quality of teaching, in order to improve the learning of *all* pupils, including those with SEN and other vulnerable groups. The inclusion statement within the National Curriculum (DfEE/QCA, 1999) sent a clear message that differentiation for a wide variety of needs and the planning of lessons to ensure access and participation were part of normal teaching for *all* teachers. It set out three principles considered essential for developing a more inclusive curriculum:

1   Setting suitable learning challenges
2   Responding to pupils' diverse learning needs
3   Overcoming barriers to learning and assessment for individuals and groups of pupils.

(DfEE/QCA, 1999: 30)

The depiction of these three principles in a Venn diagram in subsequent DfES materials (e.g. DfES, 2002, 2004b) is significant, as it conveys the message that inclusive practice relies on all three being present. For you as a teacher the challenge in developing your practice is to address the three elements as outlined in Figure 6.1.1. The National Curriculum inclusion statement (DfEE/QCA, 1999) sets out examples of approaches that might be undertaken within the three areas and reading these will provide a useful starting point.

SETTING SUITABLE LEARNING CHALLENGES

In setting suitable learning challenges you will need to place emphasis on giving every pupil in your class the opportunity to experience success in learning and to achieve as high a standard as possible (DfEE/QCA, 1999). Setting suitable learning challenges involves identifying appropriate learning objectives.

Learning objectives within the framework of the National Curriculum can be thought of in terms of what the teacher intends the pupil to learn (DfES, 2004b). For some pupils it will be inappropriate to work on the same tasks as other pupils in the class or the same learning objectives. In setting suitable learning objectives you may need to identify outcomes for particular individuals or groups, which are different from those set for the class as a whole. In taking this decision you need to be clear that, with appropriate access and teaching strategies, the pupil could not work on the same tasks and learning objectives as his or her peers. For example, some pupils with social, emotional or behavioural difficulties may lack skills in relation to their capacity to work as part of a group, but may have the cognitive ability to meet fully the same learning objective as their peers. For these pupils, giving them work of an easier level just because they cannot cope with the method of delivery (i.e. group work) may lead to boredom and lack of challenge that could result in increased behavioural difficulties.

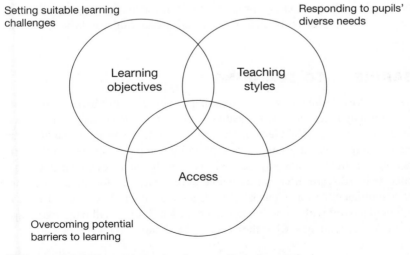

■ **Figure 6.1.1** Three elements of a more inclusive curriculum

Setting suitable learning challenges requires that you accurately assess the pupil's current level of attainment and make a judgement about the next step in learning. This may involve *tracking back*. 'Tracking back' is a phrase used within some DfES documentation (e.g. DfES, 2002) to describe the process of looking at earlier attainment targets in order to identify appropriate learning objectives. For those pupils, aged 5–16, with SEN who are working below Level 1 of the National Curriculum, the P level attainment targets (or 'P scales') (QCA, 2007) provide the means of identifying the next steps in learning.

Teachers of Foundation Stage pupils are able to draw on the descriptors from the Areas of Learning and Development within *Practice Guidance for the Early Years Foundation Stage* (DfES, 2007) when target setting. The descriptors from the Foundation Stage are also likely to be more appropriate than the P scales for target setting for pupils in Year 1 who are working below Level 1. In a typical Year 1 class there will be some pupils who have already started working on Level 1 at the start of school year and others who begin to do so as the year progresses. In most cases this is not indicative of SEN but simply reflects different rates of development. Usually the P scales would only be applicable to pupils in Year 1 who present with quite significant levels of SEN.

While, by practical necessity, you will need notionally to group pupils in order to make lesson planning and delivery manageable, you will of course need to be aware of each pupil as an individual learner, and be able to evaluate whether your inclusive teaching has enabled them, as individuals, to make the progress you have planned for them through the setting of appropriate learning objectives.

RESPONDING TO PUPILS' DIVERSE NEEDS

The National Curriculum inclusion statement requires teachers to take specific action to respond to pupils' diverse needs. This requires the teacher to use a variety of teaching methods to match the unique identified needs of individuals or groups and to secure motivation and concentration. Some pupils may require tasks that are of a more structured nature, or activities that are broken down into sequences of shorter tasks to match their current concentration span. Some pupils may need to overcome difficulties with personal organisation, so that they gradually become more equipped to tackle open-ended tasks or tasks requiring a problem-solving approach.

In responding to diverse needs other practical factors to consider include the clarity of verbal instructions, the length of the session, the proportion of time spent listening and the proportion of time spent doing, the mixture of individual, partner and group work, and the mix of closed and open-ended tasks.

OVERCOMING BARRIERS TO LEARNING

Providing access involves finding ways of 'bypassing' or overcoming barriers to learning. For a pupil with dyslexia it may mean finding alternative ways to provide access to the written word by the use of tape-recorded stories, visual planners, etc.; for a pupil with a receptive language impairment it may involve a teaching assistant giving extra support by going over the teacher's instructions to check understanding. Central to inclusive practice is the idea that many of the approaches developed to support pupils with SEN are effective as whole-class strategies for all pupils. For example, providing written reminders and/or pictorial representations of the key points from your lesson introduction will help a pupil with receptive language difficulties but will benefit *all* pupils as they will be able to check independently what they need to be doing.

National Strategy documents (e.g. DfES 2002, 2005) have increasingly used the phrase 'quality first inclusive teaching' to reinforce the principle from the National Curriculum inclusion statement that the class teacher should be seeking to make their *standard* class teaching as inclusive as possible by, for example, creating the 'dyslexia-friendly classroom' (DfES, 2002). The inclusive teaching checklist (Figure 6.1.2) can be used as a tool to evaluate your own teaching.

Quality first inclusive teaching fits within the waves model of provision (see Figure 6.1.3) presented in a number of government guidance documents. The waves model recognises that *in addition* to quality first inclusive teaching, some groups of pupils will require additional interventions and some individuals will need highly personalised interventions. The waves model originated from the National Literacy and Numeracy Strategies (DfES, 2002) and was primarily concerned with the management and use of 'catch-up' interventions at Wave 2. It has subsequently evolved into a model for the strategic management of a variety of forms of provision across the school, referred to as 'provision mapping' (DfES, 2005; Gross, 2008). The waves model does not readily relate to the *SEN Code of Practice*'s (DfES, 2001b) levels of intervention, though Wave 3 can be thought of as encompassing the types of additional or different interventions that characterise SEN provision.

DO PUPILS WITH SEN REQUIRE SPECIALIST TEACHING?

There has been considerable debate about the extent to which pupils who are categorised as SEN require special or different approaches. The DfES commissioned research in the form of *Teaching Strategies and Approaches for Pupils with Special Educational Needs* (Davis and Florian, 2004), which considered whether there is or should be a specific SEN pedagogy. The report was clear in its statement that:

> The teaching approaches and strategies identified during this review were not sufficiently differentiated from those which are used to teach all children to justify a distinctive SEN pedagogy. This does not diminish the importance of special education knowledge but highlights it as an essential component of pedagogy.
>
> (Davis and Florian, 2004: 6)

The report concluded that:

> questions about whether there is a separate special education pedagogy are unhelpful given the current policy context, and that the more important agenda is about how to develop a pedagogy that is inclusive of all learners.
>
> (p. 6)

1	Has the teacher identified appropriate and differentiated learning objectives for all learners?	
2	Is there use of multi-sensory teaching approaches, e.g. visual, verbal or kinaesthetic?	
3	Is there use of interactive strategies, e.g. pupils having cards to hold up or their own whiteboards or coming to the front to take a role?	
4	Is there use of visual and tangible aids, e.g. real objects, signs or symbols, photographs or computer animations?	
5	Does the teacher find ways of making abstract concepts concrete, e.g. word problems in mathematics turned into pictures or acted out or modelled with resources?	
6	Does the teacher use simplified and extended tasks, e.g. short, concrete text used by one group and long, abstract text by another, numbers to 100 by one group or to 20 by another?	
7	Are tasks made more open or more closed according to pupils' needs?	
8	Over time, does the teacher employ a variety of pupil groupings so that pupils are able to draw on each other's strengths and skills?	
9	Can all pupils see and hear the teacher and any resources in use, e.g. is background noise avoided where possible, is the light source in front of the teacher not behind, is pupils' seating carefully planned?	
10	Is new or difficult vocabulary clarified, written up, displayed and returned to?	
11	Does the teacher check for understanding of instructions, e.g. by asking a pupil to explain them in their own words?	
12	Are questions pitched so as to challenge pupils at all levels?	
13	Is the contribution of all learners valued – is this a secure and supportive learning environment where there is safety to have a go and make mistakes?	
14	Does the teacher give time and support before responses are required, e.g. personal thinking time, partner talk or persisting with progressively more scaffolding until a pupil can answer correctly?	
15	Where extra adult support is available for underachieving pupils, is it used in ways that promote independence, protect self-esteem and increase pupils' inclusion within their peer group?	
16	Are the adults providing the support clear about what the individual or group is to learn?	
17	Does the teacher work directly with underachieving groups as well as with more able groups?	
18	Are tasks clearly explained or modelled; are there checks for understanding, task cards or boards as reminders; is there time available and are the expected outcomes made clear?	
19	Are pupils provided with, and regularly reminded of, resources to help them be independent, e.g. relevant material from whole-class session kept on display, word lists or mats, dictionaries of terms, glossaries, number lines or tables squares?	
20	Is scaffolding used to support learners, e.g. problem-solving grids, talk and writing frames or clue cards?	
21	Has the teacher made arrangements (buddying, adult support, taping) where necessary to ensure that all children can access written text or instructions?	
22	Has the teacher planned alternatives to paper and pencil tasks, where appropriate?	
23	Does the teacher make effective use of ICT as an access strategy, e.g. speech-supported or sign-supported software, on-screen word banks or predictive word processing?	
24	Is appropriate behaviour noticed and praised or rewarded?	
25	Are all learners involved in setting their own targets and monitoring their own progress?	

■ **Figure 6.1.2** Inclusive teaching checklist

Source: DfES (2006)

An editable version of Figure 6.1.2 is available on the companion website:
www.routledge.com/textbooks/ltps2e

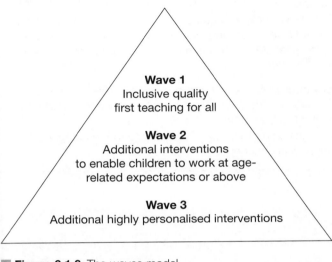

Wave 1
Inclusive quality
first teaching for all

Wave 2
Additional interventions
to enable children to work at age-
related expectations or above

Wave 3
Additional highly personalised interventions

■ **Figure 6.1.3** The waves model
Source: DfES (2005)

These perspectives support a focus on quality first inclusive teaching and, as the preceding section has demonstrated, this is where the emphasis has been placed within government guidance to schools (e.g. DfES, 2002, 2004b, 2005). While not departing from an emphasis on improving provision for all through quality first inclusive teaching, it is noticeable that the government has responded to concerns from teachers and others (e.g. Ofsted 2004; Warnock, 2005; House of Commons Education and Skills Committee, 2006) about SEN and the policy of inclusion by seeking to strengthen training in relation to individual types of SEN. The first tranche of Inclusion Development Programme (IDP) materials, launched in 2008, targeted dyslexia and speech, language and communication needs (SLCN) (DCSF, 2008), with materials related to autism spectrum disorders (ASD) and behavioural, emotional and social difficulties (BESD) scheduled to follow in 2009.

A focus by policy makers on 'improving provision for all' alongside 'strengthening SEN expertise' is a dual and interrelated challenge for schools and their teachers. For trainee and newly qualified teachers a core dilemma is whether the priority is to seek to strengthen quality first inclusive teaching or develop knowledge, skills and understanding in relation to particular areas of need. Ultimately, the conclusion might be that it is a question of balance and involves doing both. Developing strategies for quality first inclusive teaching will enable a whole range of learners to learn more effectively. However, an understanding, for example of how a pupil with an autism spectrum disorder may be viewing the world differently or a pupil with dyslexia may be processing information differently, is also likely to be beneficial in terms of the teacher's feelings of confidence and competence. The caveat to this is that, while pupils with a particular label or diagnosis are likely to share some characteristics with others with the same label or diagnosis in terms both of how they present and the strategies and approaches that they respond to best, they are all individuals.

Task 6.1.4 **USE OF TERMS**

The Scottish education system no longer uses the term 'special educational needs' and instead uses the broader term of 'additional support needs' (SEED, 2005), which encompasses a range of pupils who experience transitory and long-term barriers to learning and participation. Some writers (e.g. Corbett, 1996; Mittler, 2000; Booth and Ainscow, 2002) have questioned the compatibility of the continued use of the term 'special educational needs' within an educational system that claims to be inclusive.

■ Use a range of literature to critically explore the arguments regarding the continued use of the term 'special educational needs' and the associated processes of identification and assessment outlined in the *Code of Practice* (DfES, 2001b).
■ Where do you locate yourself as a professional with regard to the categorisation of some pupils as having special educational needs?

SUMMARY

Policy and guidance from the late 1990s has emphasised quality first inclusive teaching as part of a wider 'excellence' agenda (e.g. DfEE,1997b) that has moved away from the language of individual pupil needs and focused upon institutional improvement to secure better outcomes for individuals (Armstrong, 2005). It now seems that there is something of a swing back (e.g. DCSF 2008) towards individual categories of need and the assumption that pupils in each of these categories need specialist teaching.

In a frequently changing policy context, balance, feasibility, professionalism and rigour would seem to be the important guiding principles for practitioners (Ellis *et al.*, 2008). The emergence of the social model of disability that underpins inclusion has brought about important changes in attitudes towards, and treatment of, disabled people generally. It has also been a *necessary* trigger in the development of inclusive schooling, which has seen pupils who would once have been educated in special schools successfully included in their local mainstream school. However, there are biological and psychological variables in addition to social variables that contribute to individual differences. In embracing the social model of disability, it is important that these other variables are not overlooked. Although there is little evidence for a specialist pedagogy for pupils with SEN linked to a labelled category of need, knowledge of SEN and the involvement of a specialist teacher are reported to contribute to good progress for some pupils with SEN (e.g. Ofsted, 2006). This seems to support the view that the social model of disability, *if* interpreted as relating *only* to the removal of situational, generic barriers to learning, is not *sufficient* to address the needs of all pupils. You should, therefore, not be wary of recognising individual differences and addressing them through the design and delivery of provision when appropriate, drawing on expertise within your school and from outside agencies when necessary.

In terms of developing inclusive approaches, as the class teacher you will be implementing, monitoring and improving quality first inclusive teaching for *all* pupils. In *addition*, some small groups of pupils or individuals may require approaches that may be considered more 'specialised' in the sense of their required frequency, their intensity and the high level of individual monitoring by the adult of the pupil response. It will not always be feasible for you as the class teacher to directly deliver such interventions, although you should understand the purpose and intended outcomes in order that you can monitor the impact on the pupil's educational progress. As a class teacher you will need to work effectively with other adults such as the SEN coordinator, the teaching assistant and, in a few cases, other professionals such as speech and language therapists, occupational therapists and local authority advisers in the delivery and evaluation of provision. This way of working to support inclusive approaches and improve individual outcomes for pupils with SEN is intrinsic to *Every Child Matters* (DfES, 2004c) and the wider Workforce Remodelling agenda (e.g. TDA, 2007).

The final consideration is professionalism and rigour. How the ideology of inclusion is translated into effective practice is the responsibility of policy makers, schools and teachers. As a professional you have a unique opportunity to contribute to developing policy and practices for inclusion. Central to this development is the need for you to adopt a critical stance concerning emergent policy developments, to be clear about the 'purpose' of inclusion for the individuals you teach and rigorously to evaluate practice against that purpose. In so doing you will develop an evaluative stance to your practice that will enable you to contribute to the creation of a much-needed evidence base for the provision of effective strategies for the inclusion of pupils with diverse learning needs.

ANNOTATED FURTHER READING

Florian, L. (ed.) (2006) *The SAGE Handbook of Special Education*, London: Sage.

> This book is currently only available in hardback and as such it is more likely that you will wish to borrow it from a library. Featuring chapters by a number of well-known writers in the field, it is a source of authoritative information and ideas about current and future directions for special education. It examines the intricate relationship between theory, research and practice, and places a particular emphasis on what has been learned about providing for pupils who experience difficulties in learning, how these understandings can contribute to new conceptualisations of special education and the development of more inclusive schools.

Nind, M., Rix, J., Sheehy, K and Simmons, K (2005) *Curriculum and Pedagogy in Inclusive Education: Values into Practice*, Abingdon: RoutledgeFalmer.

> This book brings together a selection of previously published chapters and articles from a range of key writers in the field of SEN and inclusive education. It represents a useful starting point for the reader who wants to develop a critical understanding of the development of inclusive practice in a range of educational settings.

Wearmouth, J. (2009) *A Beginning Teacher's Guide to Special Educational Needs*, Maidenhead: Open University Press.

> This book recognises that for trainee and newly qualified teachers teaching pupils categorised as having special educational needs may seem a daunting prospect, particularly in the light of differing definitions of inclusion and variations between schools in how a pupil is defined as having SEN. Wearmouth succeeds in balancing supportive and practical guidance, focused on the immediate needs of the beginning teacher, with accessible, in-depth consideration of the many complex issues that exist within the area of special educational needs and inclusion.

Westwood, P. (2007) *Commonsense Methods for Children with Special Educational Needs*, 5th edn, London: Routledge.

> This book provides practical guidance on a range strategies and approaches for meeting children's SEN in mainstream classrooms. Importantly, the practical advice offered by the author is embedded within a clear theoretical context supported by research and classroom practice.

RELEVANT WEBSITES

Centre for Studies on Inclusive Education: www.csie.org.uk/
TeacherNet: www.teachernet.gov.uk/wholeschool/sen/
> This site provides guidance for teachers, carers and parents on removing barriers to achievement for children with SEN and disabilities.

Teacher Training Resource Bank Special Educational Needs: http://sen.ttrb.ac.uk
> This contains support for including and teaching learners with SEN or disabilities.

Visit the companion website www.routledge.com/textbooks/ltps2e for:

▪ an additional task for this unit;
▪ an editable figure from this unit;
▪ links to useful websites relevant to this unit.

REFERENCES

Armstrong, D. (2005) 'Reinventing inclusion: New Labour and the cultural politics of special education', *Oxford Review of Education*, 30(1): 135–52.

British Broadcasting Corporation (BBC) (2006) 'School inclusion can be abuse'. Available online at http://news.bbc.co.uk/1/hi/education/4774407.stm (accessed October 2008).

Blamires, M. (1999) 'Universal design for learning: re-establishing differentiation as part of the inclusion agenda?', *Support for Learning*, 14(4): 158–63.

Booth, T. and Ainscow, M. (2002) *The Index for Inclusion*, Bristol: CSIE.

Corbett, J. (1996) *Bad-Mouthing: The Language of Special Needs*, London: Falmer.

Croll, P. and Moses, D. (2000) 'Ideologies and utopias: educational professionals' view of inclusion', *European Journal of Special Needs Education*, 15(1): 1–12.

Davis, P. and Florian, L. (2004) *Teaching Strategies and Approaches for Pupils with SEN: A Scoping Study Briefing Paper*, RR516, Nottingham: DfES.

Department for Children, Schools and Families (DCSF) (2008) *Initial Teacher Training Inclusion Development Programme, Primary/Secondary: Dyslexia and Speech, Language and Communication Needs*. Available online at http://nationalstrategies.standards.dcsf.gov.uk/node/123019 (accessed October 2009).

Department for Education and Employment (DfEE) (1997a) *Excellence for All Children: Meeting Special Educational Needs*, London: HMSO.

Department for Education and Employment (DfEE) (1997b) *Excellence in Schools*, London: HMSO.

Department for Education and Employment/Qualifications and Curriculum Authority (DfEE/QCA) (1999) *National Curriculum: Handbook for Primary Teachers in England*, London: DfEE/QCA.

Department for Education and Skills (DfES) (2001a) *Inclusive Schooling: Children with Special Educational Needs: Guidance on Pupil Support and Access*, Nottingham: DfES.

Department for Education and Skills (DfES) (2001b) *Special Educational Needs Code of Practice*, London: DfES.

Department for Education and Skills (DfES) (2002) *Including All Children in the Literacy Hour and Daily Mathematics Lesson*, Nottingham: DfES.

Department for Education and Skills (DfES) (2004a) *Removing Barriers to Achievement*, Nottingham: DfES.

Department for Education and Skills (DfES) (2004b) *Learning and Teaching for Children with Special Educational Needs in the Primary Years*, Nottingham: DfES.

Department for Education and Skills (DfES) (2004c) *Every Child Matters: Change for Children*, Nottingham: DfES.

Department for Education and Skills (DfES) (2005) *Leading on Inclusion*, Nottingham: DfES.

Department for Education and Skills (DfES) (2006) *Inclusive Teaching Observation Checklist*. Available online at http://nationalstrategies.standards.dcsf.gov.uk/node/46320 (accessed October 2008).

Department for Education and Skills (DfES) (2007) *Practice Guidance for the Early Years Foundation Stage*, Nottingham: DfES.

Ellis, S., Tod, J. and Graham-Matheson, L. (2008) *Special Educational Needs and Inclusion: Reflection and Renewal*, Birmingham: NASUWT. Available online at www.teachersunion.org.uk (accessed October 2009).

Gross, J. (2008) *Beating Bureaucracy in Special Educational Needs*, London: David Fulton.

House of Commons Education and Skills Committee (2006) *Special Educational Needs: Third Report of Session 2005–06 Volume I*, London: The Stationery Office.

MacBeath, J., Galton, M., Steward, S., MacBeath, A. and Page, C. (2006) *The Costs of Inclusion*, Cambridge: University of Cambridge.

Mittler, P. (2000) *Working Towards Inclusive Education*, London: David Fulton.

Norwich, B. (2002a) 'Education, inclusion and individual differences: recognising and resolving dilemmas', *British Journal of Educational Studies*, 50(4): 482–502.

Norwich, B. (2002b) *LEA Inclusion Trends in England 1997–2001: Statistics on Special School Placements and Pupils with Statements in Special Schools*, Bristol: CSIE.

O'Brien, T. (1998) 'The Millennium Curriculum: confronting issues and proposing solutions', *Support for Learning*, 13(4): 147–52.

Office for Standards in Education (Ofsted) (2004) *Special Educational Needs and Disability: Towards Inclusive Schools*, London: Ofsted.

Office for Standards in Education (Ofsted) (2006) *Inclusion: Does It Matter Where Pupils Are Taught?*, London: Ofsted.

Pirrie, A., Head, G. and Brna, P. (2005) *Mainstreaming Pupils with Special Educational Needs: An Evaluation*, Edinburgh: SEED.

Qualifications and Curriculum Authority (QCA) (2007) *Performance: P-level Attainment Targets for Pupils with Special Education Needs Who Are Working Below Level 1 of the National Curriculum*, London: QCA. Available online at www.qca.org.uk/libraryAssets/media/qca-07-3315_P-scales.pdf (accessed April 2009).

Scottish Executive Education Department (SEED) (2005) *Supporting Children's Learning: Code of Practice*, Edinburgh: SEED.

Training and Development Agency for Schools (TDA) (2007) *Workforce Remodelling*, London: TDA.

UNESCO (1994) *The Salamanca Statement and Framework for Action on Special Needs Education*, New York: UNESCO.

Union of the Physically Impaired Against Segregation (UPIAS) (1976) *Fundamental Principles of Disability*, London: UPIAS.

Warnock, M. (1978) *Special Educational Needs: Report of the Committee of Inquiry into the Education of Handicapped Children and Young People* (Warnock Report), London: HMSO.

Warnock, M. (2005) *Special Educational Needs: A New Look*, London: Philosophy of Education Society of Great Britain.

Wedell, K. (2008) 'Confusion about inclusion: patching up or system change?', *British Journal of Special Education*, 35(3): 127–35.

Wearmouth, J., Glynn, T. and Berryman, M. (2005) *Perspectives on Student Behaviour in Schools: Exploring Theory and Developing Practice*, London: RoutledgeFalmer.

PROVIDING FOR DIFFERENTIATION

Eve Bearne

INTRODUCTION

Differentiation is one of those 'iceberg' terms in teaching – what you see on the surface covers something much bigger. But not only does it have underlying complexities, it is also one of those concepts that teachers assume 'everyone knows' the meaning of. However, there is no clear consensus about what the term means and implies. It is linked in many teachers' minds with 'mixed ability teaching', but there is still considerable debate about what it might look like in the classroom and just what 'ability' is. Some place greater emphasis on curriculum provision, while others see differentiation as more linked with individual progress. Most recently, differentiation has been linked with personalised learning (DfES, 2006). As with many classroom issues, the answer often lies in the combination of providing a suitable curriculum to ensure progression for all learners while catering for individual needs.

OBJECTIVES

By the end of this unit you should be able to:

■ see the links between differentiation, diversity and difference;
■ understand the importance of providing a differentiated approach to the curriculum for a diverse range of learners;
■ understand the main approaches to differentiation;
■ develop some practical strategies to provide differentiated approaches to learning.

So what does differentiation look like? Figures 6.2.1–3 show examples of how some teachers see differentiation.

Figure 6.2.1 shows how learning objectives relate to individuals. The teacher describes this as 'making one thing accessible to all, through an acknowledgement of different learning styles and experiences and a knowledge of individuals' "baseline" knowledge and skills'.

Figure 6.2.2 shows three different ways of reaching a learning destination. The teacher came across this in an in-service session and felt it aptly summarised her views. Route A is by bus where the passenger depends on the driver; Route B shows how a traveller might choose between a range of different vehicles; in Route C the traveller gets to the destination in his or her own way. The teacher writes: 'The transport enables all students to access the curriculum through means which suit their individual needs.'

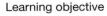
Learning objective

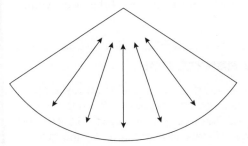

Individuals

■ **Figure 6.2.1** Description of differentiation – Teacher 1

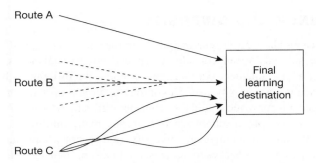

■ **Figure 6.2.2** Description of differentiation – Teacher 2

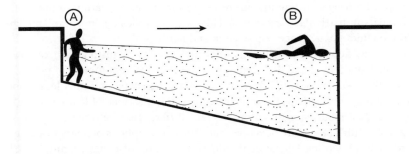

■ **Figure 6.2.3** Description of differentiation – Teacher 3

Figure 6.2.3 shows a swimming pool. The teacher writes: 'Differentiation is ensuring that every child can find their depth in every lesson but also challenging them to swim. If we don't support/encourage child A to take chances, [he or] she will never leave the shallows.'

The first teacher emphasises providing for the different qualities, knowledge and experiences of every learner while aiming for common learning objectives for all; the second recognises the importance of developing pupils' independence; the third sees it as important to create an environment that allows learners to feel secure enough to push themselves further. These descriptions indicate the variations that experienced teachers may have in mind as they consider differentiation. They also share a concern to provide for individual differences within a common curriculum.

Task 6.2.1 **DESCRIBING DIFFERENTIATION**

What does differentiation mean to you? How would you depict it? Draw a sketch or diagram and write a few words of explanation to describe differentiation. You might then compare your ideas with others in your group and with the examples in Figures 6.2.1–3 and discuss with your tutor the range of descriptions of differentiation gathered by the group. A group list would be a good starting point for a definition.

DIFFERENTIATION, DIFFERENCE AND DIVERSITY

In general terms, differentiation is about how far the curriculum is appropriate for groups of learners with particular needs. This does not only mean considering special educational needs (SEN), including the group defined as gifted and talented, but takes into account the differences between what a young learner at the Foundation Stage may need in contrast to an appropriate curriculum for pupils at Key Stage 2. Such a general approach would also consider differences between schools, settings and their communities. For example, a school where there are many multilingual pupils will adjust its curriculum to make the most of its linguistic diversity; or a school where pupils have to travel long distances may adopt specific approaches to home–school liaison. In this general sense, differentiation means providing an appropriate curriculum, within national guidelines, for the particular school.

In its more specific usage, differentiation refers to provision of learning opportunities and activities for individuals in particular classrooms. This often includes a concept of 'matching' the task or activity to the child's experience, knowledge and skills.

In policy documentation, differentiation is often linked with inclusion; for example, Ofsted emphasises educational attainment and the need to provide for 'different groups of pupils' to reach national standards (2000: 4). *Every Child Matters* broadens the scope and puts less emphasis on attainment, while retaining, and perhaps even sharpening, categorisations of learners (DfES, 2003). It is worth being cautious about categorisations of the 'differences' between learners. Ainscow *et al.* (2007: 9) argue that 'differences are never neutral', since descriptions of learners are necessarily constructed according to prevailing educational values. There are, of course, many links between differentiation and inclusion, but while inclusion is largely concerned with equity in terms of individual rights and curriculum entitlement, differentiation focuses on the management of teaching and learning, including:

- identifying pupils' knowledge, experience, skills and learning preferences;
- planning for a variety of ways into learning;
- classroom organisation for learning;
- using resources (material and human);
- response to the outcomes of activities or units of work and assessment of achievement in order to plan for future learning.

The Education Reform Act 1988 legislated for every pupil's entitlement to a curriculum that is broad, balanced, relevant and 'subtly' differentiated. In 1992 the National Curriculum Council referred to providing a curriculum suitable for 'differences in the abilities, aptitudes and needs of individual pupils' (NCC, 1992: 67). Over ten years later, the official definition of inclusion is to provide 'effective learning opportunities for all pupils' (QCA, 2005). Its key principles stress teaching in a way that takes account of the diversity of pupils' learning needs and preferences. In other words, differentiation needs to be thought of in terms of how the curriculum might cater for and build on differences in the needs of specific groups of pupils as well as the diversity of the learners in the classroom; and how teaching can accommodate the range. The recent DfES (2006) report on personalised learning puts it like this:

> Personalising learning means, in practical terms, focusing in a more structured way on each child's learning in order to enhance progress, achievement and participation. All children and young people have the right to receive support and challenge, tailored to their needs, interests and abilities.

> (DfES, 2006: 3)

Taking account of difference and diversity is complex. In addition to acknowledging that learners may use a range of approaches according to the task/ context and/or time of day, differentiation that genuinely allows for diversity needs to consider:

■ differences in learning approaches, strategies or preferences;
■ particular strengths and difficulties in some areas of the curriculum;
■ physical and medical differences;
■ variations in fluency of English, which may not be the first language;
■ gender differences;
■ the range of previous experiences brought to the classroom.

Providing for the needs of different learners means having some sense of where they are in their learning at any specific time. This in turn implies having some sense of where you want them to be. It means that, before planning for any unit of work or series of activities, the teacher will need to have a clear idea of learning objectives. This will need to be accompanied by useful pupil records of progress so that the learning can be matched to individuals or groups. Grouping pupils is common classroom practice, but the reasons for grouping have to be clear. Some activities require grouping pupils according to their common achievements, for example in guided reading, where grouping is determined by a perceived common level of reading competence. At other times, teachers will opt for 'mixed-ability' groups.

Grouping pupils can be trickier than it may at first appear, since, even if learners can be grouped according to common qualities, they may not form genuinely homogeneous groups. It is by no means a simple matter to group according to ability, because it begs the question 'ability in what?' There is a danger in making generalised judgements. It is all too easy to assume that someone who has difficulty with spelling, reading, writing or numeracy is 'less able'. Such convenient definitions are best avoided; they are inaccurate and misleading and, in the end, give no help to either teacher or pupil. It is better to be precise and to describe the skills rather than the pupil, for example 'less fluent in reading; accurate in mental mathematics'.

Not only does each person's 'ability' vary according to the task or curriculum area, it also varies according to what the teacher makes it possible for the pupil to achieve. Observing pupils at work – in physical education (PE), art, design and technology or as they work together on the computer – and listening to their talk in science or maths, for example, can reveal a great deal about the learning strengths and needs of particular pupils. Such observations help to provide descriptions of what learners can do that avoid unhelpful labels and over-generalisations.

Task 6.2.2 REFLECTING ON YOUR OWN ABILITIES

Think about your own 'abilities'. Are you good at everything? Some people are very good at reading the spaces in team sports, while others read music fluently. Some find mental calculations easy; some are good at constructing 3D objects; some express ideas elegantly through dance; others are successful at solving abstract problems.

■ What are your strengths? What areas of your learning need, or have needed, support? Make a few notes, then compare your reflections with others in your group.
■ How diverse are you as a group of learners? Discuss with your tutor the implications this diversity has for planning teaching and learning.

IDENTIFYING THE RANGE OF LEARNERS

Learning styles have been analysed and categorised by cognitive psychologists for some time, but they are now receiving even more attention, probably led by industrial and workplace studies and often following the thinking of Howard Gardner's 'multiple intelligences' (1993, 1999). Attention to learning styles over the last 20 years or so has taken on a momentum that is at one and the same time seductive (how neat to be able to categorise the learning styles of our pupils and so teach accordingly) and misleading, as many of the most popular instruments and models vary: in intended application (many were developed for industry); in theoretical underpinning; and in the extent to which they can be considered reliable (Coffield *et al.*, 2004). As with any categorisation there are dangers. Labelling pupils may not be helpful as this can take attention away from teaching approaches and the importance of learning contexts. Added to that, categorisations can ignore the fact that many learners use a variety of approaches to learning according to circumstances, prior learning and experience and what is on offer in terms of teaching. Rather than seeing these qualities as fixed, like the colour of one's eyes, it is better to take account of diversity in planning for teaching, but also to aim to extend the range of learning approaches through specific teaching. In addition, rates of learning differ as the *Independent Review of the Primary Curriculum* (Rose Review) notes: 'international evidence emphasises the importance of structuring a curriculum that is relevant and meaningful to learners, and monitoring progress to make sure that levels of challenge are appropriate to their different rates of learning' (Rose, 2008: 94).

Task 6.2.3 LEARNING STYLES

Read Coffield *et al.* (2004) *Should We Be Using Learning Styles?* (www.scribd.com/doc/20311529/Should-We-Be-Using-Learning-Styles). Although some of the survey is aimed at post-16 education, the analysis of the different instruments and models is appropriate for all phases. What are the implications for your own classroom practice? How might you cater for children's different approaches to learning without being too narrowly categorical about 'styles'?

Differences in learning approaches, strategies or preferences

Having offered those reservations, it is important to see learners as individuals with particular strengths and preferences. Some may approach learning by taking in whole concepts and then attending to detail, while others build from detail to broad concepts. The versatile learner is the one who has been able to develop both kinds of learning to fit specific purposes. Some learners show more of a tendency to take intellectual risks in learning, while others are much more cautious, at least at first. While learners may show a predisposition towards more innovative or more speculative approaches, education should help them to decide when it is best to be adventurous and when it is better to be more carefully decisive. It is important to remember that no approach is necessarily 'better' than another.

Task 6.2.4 **IDENTIFYING LEARNING PREFERENCES**

Have a look at these comments on their own learning made by a range of nine and ten year olds. What do they tell you about their learning preferences?

■ I worked it out by thinking about what we'd done last time.
■ I can't be bothered to work out all those fiddly bits.
■ I like to find out all the facts from the internet.
■ Being under pressure helps me to learn.
■ It helps me if I know what to do.
■ We've been shown how to do different investigations so I use the best way of doing it.
■ I like maths when things are hard.
■ I have a big blackboard of words in my mind that I know how to spell.
■ I like to make models and inventions.
■ I like trying things out . . . I don't like being interrupted when I've got a good idea.
■ I want to learn how to be a good social person; a good group would be a boff, two friends and me.
■ If it's got writing on it, I'll read it.

You may find it tricky to tie some of these down. That is perfectly understandable and simply serves to demonstrate the problems of trying to make hard and fast categorisations of learners. However, they should help you discuss with your tutor the issues about 'learning styles'.

Pupils' particular strengths and difficulties

Specific strengths or difficulties with learning can often be associated with pupils who give cause for concern. This can be because the pupil's learning may not be thriving, or because the teacher feels that more could be done to support or extend particular learners. 'Cause for concern' may include pupils with statements of SEN, but it can be wider than that. One teacher described the range of pupils who caused her concern:

K   Who was having difficulty with written work and not providing evidence of learning via written tasks or presentation. This pupil speaks Hindi as well as English.

L   Who was having difficulty with 'owning' information and tended to rehash knowledge rather than remembering and using it in imaginative writing or similar creative activities.

M   Who was achieving an excellent standard of written work and could remember facts of historical events, but showed no real sense of empathy.

N   Who was achieving an excellent standard of written and spoken work and needed to be extended and stretched.

(Reynolds, 1996)

A 'special educational need' can mean that we have to provide for those who take readily to school-based learning and those who excel at some aspects of the curriculum as well as catering for those who find learning difficult or burdensome.

Identifying pupils who might be described as gifted and talented is an aspect of diversity that has come to prominence over the last few years. Unit 7.5 provides an overview, but to ensure these pupils are not forgotten when thinking about differentiation, they are also noted here. Very able children often show outstanding potential or ability in one area or in several or all areas of the curriculum. This might not be in traditional academic learning, but could be in physical, creative, spatial, mechanical or technical learning. Pupils' abilities could be so well developed that they operate significantly in advance of their peers or a pupil might show outstanding talent in just one area of learning, again outstripping others of their age. Whether their abilities are in a range of areas or just one, such pupils require extra learning experiences in order to support and extend the identified ability.

Generally, however, it is often the 'strugglers' who come to attention first in the classroom. You might have observed pupils who:

■ have low self esteem;
■ are capable, but frustrated because they don't have the means, vocabulary, strategies or techniques to write what they want to say;
■ do not yet speak English fluently;
■ only skate on the surface of text when reading aloud and don't understand what they're reading;
■ 'can't think what to write' because they are paralysed by fear of failure; have poor techniques; do not value their own experience; lack motivation;
■ are restless – wanderers, diverters;
■ can write with technical accuracy but do not seem to have their own voice;
■ are naturally slow at working;
■ have hearing loss/sight loss/difficulties with manual dexterity;
■ are too proud to ask for help;
■ have language or neurological disorders;
■ have so many ideas they find it hard to follow one through.

Task 6.2.5 **HOW DO TEACHERS PROVIDE SUPPORT FOR DIFFERENT LEARNERS?**

■ Select one or two of the descriptions above and consider how pupils displaying these characteristics might be supported and moved on in their learning. If possible, recall any strategies you have observed teachers using, or that you have used yourself.
■ Discuss with your tutor the practical implications of offering support for strugglers.
■ Add to this list as you consider bilingual/multilingual learners and gender issues. What strategies have you seen teachers use to cater for language diversity and for gender differences?

Bilingual/multilingual pupils

Again, it is important to avoid generalisations. Bilingualism is perhaps best seen as a continuum of proficiency in speaking more than one language that varies according to the social contexts of language use, for example with peers who speak the same language; with peers who don't; with older people or relatives; or at school, work or worship (See Unit 6.5). Everyone, including apparently monolingual people, uses a set of language variations, so it is worth trying to find out about:

■ the languages/dialects used in school, in lessons, at break time and with friends;
■ the languages used in the home;
■ any language classes attended out of school.

Gender

Issues of gender often focus on boys' underachievement, although concerns about boys' achievements in learning generally are not new. While any underachievement is a proper concern for everyone involved in education – parents, teachers and pupils – it is wise not to take on generalised observations about boys, girls and learning without asking a few questions or gathering first-hand information (Bearne, 2007). Contexts differ and pupils' attitudes, motivation and achievements will be influenced by a variety of home-, classroom- and school-based factors. Careful observation and monitoring are essential so that teaching approaches can be developed that will support boys' – and girls' – achievements (See Unit 6.4).

Task 6.2.6 **MANAGING CLASSROOMS FOR DIVERSITY**

The survey by Ainscow *et al.* (2007) (*Cambridge Primary Review: Research Survey 5/1*, www.primaryreview.org.uk) argues that 'currently dominant constructions [of diversity] conceal as much as they reveal, and mislead as much as they guide' (pp. 17–18). After reading the survey, consider the implications for managing classrooms for diversity.

■ What does the emphasis on the role of practitioners mean in terms of classroom practice aimed at catering for the kinds of diversity that you have observed in the classroom?

APPROACHES TO DIFFERENTIATION

Considering diversity involves looking not only at the qualities and potential of different learners, but also at the provision that is made to support and build on that potential. Different individuals learn best in certain settings or environments and through different means or approaches. As you have already considered, some learners find diagrams, maps and webs useful in shaping and representing ideas; some read pictures more accurately than written text; some think best in sequences, using lists to help organise ideas and actions; others have a more random or spontaneous way of dealing with things. For sustained work some people need background noise, while others need absolute silence. The next move after identifying the range of learners is to identify the range of contexts and opportunities for learning that are on offer and that seem successful and effective.

Creating a school environment for learning

It is at whole-school level that the aspects of differentiation that balance issues of equity and entitlement with access to the curriculum are most apparent. If differentiation means taking account of the diversity of pupils' experiences, knowledge and approaches to learning, the environment is critical in allowing or blocking access to learning. In reviewing provision at whole-school level, it is worth considering first of all how hospitable to diversity the physical setting is. Figure 6.2.4 offers a checklist. You might think that these aspects of differential provision seem peripheral, but they are, in fact, a reflection of the general approach to diversity that will operate in the provision of learning, too.

The classroom environment

A good starting point for reviewing differentiated provision is to start with the question: What messages does the classroom give about the status or value given to the diversity of the pupils? Figure 6.2.5 provides a checklist of the classroom setting, since the physical environment reflects the thoughts of the teacher about what provision for diversity means.

■ Are the notices accessible to those who read iconic or pictorial texts more readily than print?

■ Are the languages of the school community genuinely represented?

■ Is there access for those whose mobility is hampered?

■ How is pupils' work presented and displayed? Is there 'only the best' – or a wider representation?

■ How accessible is the library or resource centre – what provision has been made for diversity here? Does it have books of maps, photographs, technical magazines and manuals, etc.?

■ How does the school reflect an environment for different subjects? Is pupils' work in maths, science, design and technology displayed as much and as frequently as art work and written work?

■ **Figure 6.2.4** The school as hospitable to diversity – review 1

Task 6.2.7 **OBSERVING SCHOOL APPROACHES TO DIFFERENTIATION AND DIVERSITY**

This task and the following two ask you to make some observations in a school. If you are not likely to be making a school visit soon, you will need to complete the review by thinking back to a school that you are familiar with.

■ When you have completed the review in Figure 6.2.4 discuss your notes with one or two colleagues. What differences did you find between the schools? What similarities? How can you account for these?

■ A second means of finding out the school approach to differentiation is to look at school policy documents. Ask the school for a copy of their general policy about differentiation. Look at the policy for one specific area of the curriculum. What guidance does it give about differentiation?

■ You may have found some gaps as well as some useful guidance. With your tutor, outline some guidelines that might be included in a school or particular subject policy to support appropriate differentiation.

■ Are there special areas for activities – technical, practical, role-play, listening, working on the computer, problem solving?

■ What do the displays suggest about accessibility to different approaches to learning? Are there pictures, diagrams, written texts, maps, photographs, three-dimensional objects?

■ What about the pupils' input into displays and the visual environment? Is the work or display material all selected and mounted by the adults?

■ Is there variety in the curriculum areas on display?

■ How does the classroom operate as an environment for inclusion? What about the height of shelves and displays and the use of space?

■ What messages about gender and culture are signalled by the materials and books used?

■ **Figure 6.2.5** The classroom as hospitable to diversity – review 2

It is worth remembering, however, that the physical context for learning is only part of the environment. Even more significant in supporting the diverse needs of learners is the environment of opportunity, expectation and challenge offered by the teacher. This might include:

■ modelling and demonstrating processes and approaches;
■ offering pupils chances to experiment and try things out for themselves;
■ creating an environment where failing is seen as part of learning and is a stepping stone to trying again;
■ building on successes.

Task 6.2.8 **REVIEWING HOW THE CLASSROOM ENVIRONMENT PROVIDES FOR DIVERSITY**

■ Complete the review of the physical environment of the classroom in Figure 6.2.5 and observe how your teacher creates an environment of opportunity, expectation and challenge.

■ Discuss with your tutor the relationship between the tangible environment of the physical setting and the intangible environment of the teacher's attitudes and aspirations for the pupils.

To be able to provide adequately for diversity means thoughtful and continuing intervention in learning based on a positive view of what the range of learners in the classroom can achieve. It is often assumed that intervention for learning is about teachers 'doing things' in the classroom. In fact, the most effective intervention happens before a teacher ever reaches the classroom – in the process of planning and organising activities and approaches.

Managing groups

Flexible planning for differentiation raises issues about how groups are constituted and how they might be varied. Strategies to organise groups may depend on social factors as well as learning objectives, so that pupils might be grouped according to:

- friendship patterns;
- expertise or aptitude relative to the task or subject;
- a mix of abilities relative to the task or subject;
- gender;
- home language;
- pupils' own choices;
- the content of the activity.

Whenever teachers plan for the management of learning there is an implicit question about classroom control. This is fundamental to successful group work, so it is important to teach pupils how to work productively in groups. This might mean:

- negotiating ground rules for turn-taking and dealing with disagreements;
- giving written prompts to guide discussion;
- developing ways of time-keeping for fair chances to contribute;
- using role-play and simulations;
- reviewing and evaluating with the pupils the ways in which they managed (or did not manage!) to work together. (See Unit 3.5 for further support.)

Task 6.2.9 **OBSERVING GROUP WORK**

Either by observing during a day in your current school or by remembering a particular classroom, make notes about the ways in which work is organised:

- Is there a balance between whole-class teaching, group work, paired work and individual work?
- Are the children working *in* groups or *as* groups?
- Following one pupil, note the variations in groups that that child is involved in during the day.

Compare your observations with those of others in your group. From your discussions, make a list of the criteria used by the teachers to decide on how to group the pupils. Was it always by perceived ability? Discuss with your tutor the advantages and disadvantages of grouping according to any specific criterion.

All the observations you make in school will help you to think about how best to manage group work in your own teaching. (See also Unit 3.5.)

Provision – planning for input and activities

For certain activities, differentiation is unnecessary, although attention to diversity will be important. In drama work, for example, activities are likely to be 'open access'; in PE, differentiation will be decided by criteria that will be different from those for maths. In long- and medium-term planning for classes and groups, teachers make decisions about learning objectives: the facts, concepts, strategies they want the class to learn in the course of a term or a year, as well as in the extended teaching unit in each subject area; what experiences they want them to have; what attitudes they want them to develop (see Unit 3.1). In terms of input, decisions might be made about factual information, the concepts and the vocabulary that will be used to help learners grasp content and ideas. At this point it is important to start with what the learners already know in order to build on existing knowledge. At the same time, planning will identify what new information or concepts individuals and the group as a whole might now be introduced to. Assessment for learning (AFL) suggests that 'Planning should include strategies to ensure that learners understand the goals they are pursuing and the criteria that will be applied in assessing their work' (QCA, 2005).

In shorter-term planning for specific learning outcomes (see Unit 3.2), teachers may differentiate by providing different tasks within an activity to cater for different levels of ability. In its worst manifestation, this version of differentiation is represented by three different worksheets – one with mostly pictures and few words; one with more words more densely packed and one picture; and a third with lots of words and no pictures. This kind of 'worst-case' practice gives very powerful negative impressions to all the learners in the classroom. It is more like division than differentiation. While recognising that these things are done with the best of intentions in order to cater for the range of pupils, it is wrong to assume that ability is linked only with reading print text. Also, if differentiated tasks assume that certain individuals or groups will only be able to cope with a limited amount of new information, this can run the risk of excluding pupils who might be able to cope with more ambitious learning objectives. The challenge to the teacher is to find ways of framing tasks that can not only genuinely stretch all the learners, but that might provide for the variety of approaches to learning.

These teachers describe their approaches to differentiated input and tasks:

When I plan for a unit of work I make sure that I include visual stimuli and IT, some activity-based and some print-based tasks and some group and individual work.

I try to vary the teaching approaches between and within lessons, scaffolding and extending where appropriate. When the children work in literacy groups I might ask them to do a storyboard on one day and some writing on another. That means that I can move around the groups and support and extend where necessary. In whole-class teaching I'll use a drama strategy for one activity and scaffold the learning, adjusting as I notice how individuals are doing. I might also read aloud to them for another so that they have a common experience.

I try to word questions differently on their activity sheets. I might use a general open question then provide additional bullet points and examples to support those who need more structure to help them think, but I'll also put some more challenging questions so that those who need extending can push themselves further.

Resources and support

While it is important to identify a range of material resources to cater for the preferences of all learners – for example, computers, tape recorders, videos, pictures, photographs, maps, diagrams and print – it is also important to acknowledge and use the range of human resources available in the classroom, for example teaching assistants (TAs). In some schools, TAs are given responsibility for planning parts of the teaching and the best practice is when practitioners and TAs plan jointly, particularly for group work. Although TAs are often used to support children who are experiencing difficulties, it can be just as effective, or even more effective, if the support is given to different groups, including those described as gifted and talented. The key lies in making sure that support time is carefully allocated according to the requirements of the subject area and the children involved. (See Unit 8.2 for a full discussion of working with other adults in the classroom.) However, support need not only be seen in terms of the adults in the classroom, or by peer support; it might also mean use of IT or other tools for learning. Perhaps the most critical element in considering this area of provision for diversity is to do with teacher time. There is never enough time to give the individual support that a teacher almost inevitably and continuingly wants to offer. Group and paired work, self-evaluation, support from adults or other pupils, collaborative revising and proofreading all help in offering differentiated support.

These teachers describe their approaches to differentiating by support:

> I find that I do differentiate by support, although with the older pupils I teach it has to be done subtly to avoid upsetting individuals. I tend to use paired work a lot, basing the pairs on different things – sometimes I suggest the pupils choose their own learning partners; at other times I select a more confident mathematician, for example, to work with someone who finds some of the concepts difficult. But I do think it's important to avoid making social divisions. In group work I'll sometimes select groups according to having someone who is more confident in literacy to take notes working with others who may not be quite so fluent and I also make the criteria for working in groups explicit so that everyone feels valued whatever role they take on.

> Of course, the TA is an important part of differentiated support but I don't really like the usual practice of putting her with the least able group – whatever that means. It's not good for her because it doesn't stretch her professionally and it means that I don't get to work with them and give them some focused support. We discuss things at the beginning of the week and sometimes she'll be working with the high fliers – she's particularly interested in science so I tend to ask her to work with the able scientists quite often. At other times I'll work with them and she'll work with other groups. She's also very good with IT so she might work with individuals at certain times either to bring their IT skills up to scratch or to push the really experienced pupils.

Outcome, response and assessment

Many teachers favour differentiation by outcome, but this can be seen as a less organised way to cater for the range. If differentiation by outcome is to be genuinely effective it has to be allied with response to help move learners on and that response has to be based on a clear view of the learning outcomes aimed for in a series of lessons or a unit of work. This teacher explains why she prefers to differentiate at this stage of the teaching process:

> I find differentiation by outcome the easiest because it leaves less room for error – any surprises about an individual's achievement won't have hindered learning; I mean mistakes can be made with provision if a child knows more or less than judged by the teacher, or the format of the activity has inhibited comprehension. Differentiation by outcome allows for more open-ended learning where pupils find their own level and their learning benefits from some more differentiated follow-up/reflection in order to further develop individual skills.

Outcomes can be both tangible and intangible. Tangible products (written or diagrammatic work, craft or art work, displays of physical activities or drama activities) provide obvious opportunities for assessment across a range of areas and kinds of ability. However, intangible outcomes are equally open to observation and assessment: increased confidence; the ability to carry out a particular operation or to present ideas orally; new-found enthusiasm or the articulation of concepts that have been understood; or the use of a language to talk about the subject or learning itself (metalanguage). Equally, response need not always be written. The end points of learning are often used to assess how well pupils have achieved, but if assessment is to inform future teaching and learning, there may be a need for a diversity of kinds of assessment and variation in times when those assessments are carried out. Response to the outcomes of learning, by teachers and pupils, makes the process of learning explicit and acknowledges different abilities. As AFL guidance indicates, response also encourages learners themselves to evaluate their work and leads towards future progress (www.qcda.gov.uk/4334.aspx).

Teachers are continually making assessments and judgements – minute by minute, hour by hour, day by day – as they work alongside pupils. Those assessments are based on implicit criteria of what counts as success and will necessarily be adjustable to take into account all the learners in the classroom. That is a teacher's professional expertise, but it is important to make criteria explicit. In doing so, a teacher can check that he or she is using a differentiated range of types of assessment that will accurately describe the achievements of a diverse set of learners (See Units 5.1 and 5.2).

A NOTE ABOUT TRANSFER AND TRANSITION

Every time children move to another class or phase of learning, they are likely to experience some upheaval. While the move to the secondary school is usually seen as offering the greatest disruption, often resulting in a dip in achievement (Galton *et al.*, 2003), some individuals thrive on the change. This may be to do with the opportunity to work in a wider sphere and on a more challenging curriculum, but it can also be related to the chance to work with different teachers. Within a school, even changing from one teacher to another or from one phase to another can have its effect. In catering for diversity, initial activities to discover children's 'funds of knowledge' (Gonzalez *et al.*, 2005) will allow for supportive differentiation and mean that individual and whole-class momentum in learning is more likely to be maintained.

SUMMARY

Differentiation involves providing a curriculum that allows for the progress of all learners, but that will specifically cater for the needs of different groups of pupils and the diverse strengths, needs and abilities of individual learners. It involves planning for teaching approaches that will build on the knowledge, concepts, skills and prior experiences of the pupils in the class. It also means balancing knowledge of the range of learners with the content of learning and managing and evaluating teaching and learning to try to move all learners on successfully. Judgements about lesson content, pace of learning, levels of challenge, management of groups in the classroom, use of support and response to individuals and groups for successful differentiation are part of the developed expertise of teachers. You are just starting on that professional journey; thoughtful observation and planning will help you to begin effective, supportive and stimulating differentiation.

ANNOTATED FURTHER READING

Ainscow, M., Booth, T. and Dyson, A. (2003) *Understanding and Developing Inclusive Practices in Schools*, Swindon: ESRC.
This study, carried out by a research network that was part of the Economic and Social Research Council's Teaching and Learning Research Programme, highlights the relationship between externally imposed requirements to raise standards and a school-based commitment to inclusion and equity.

Bearne, E. (ed.) (1996) *Differentiation and Diversity in the Primary School*, London: Routledge.

There are few books dealing with differentiation in the primary school. This edited collection has sections on definitions; differentiation and literacy; mixed ability learners; assessment; and school policies for differentiation. Although written some time ago, the content is still highly relevant and there are good practical suggestions and more reflective chapters.

Hart, S., Dixon, A., Drummond, M.J. and McIntyre, D. (eds) (2004) *Learning without Limits* Maidenhead: Open University Press.

This book isn't specifically about differentiation, but questions easy judgements about 'ability' and ability grouping. It is based on classroom research with Years 1–11 and in a series of case studies describes how teachers have developed alternative approaches to some of the limiting classroom practices based on ability judgements.

The magazine *Special Children*, published monthly by Questions Publishing, is a source of relevant articles, and the journal *Support for Learning: British Journal of Learning Support*, published on behalf of NASEN, is also valuable.

RELEVANT WEBSITES

Assessment for learning guidance: www.qcda.gov.uk/4334.aspx
This site also contains links to the ten principles of AFL.

Differentiation – guidance for inclusive teaching: www.ttrb.ac.uk
Type 'differentiation' into the search box and then follow the links to the relevant document.

Primary Special Needs: Differentiation: www.teachers.tv/video/5413
This is a 15-minute programme on a Newcastle primary school from Teachers TV.

Special Needs: Differentiation in Action: www.teachers.tv/video/21992
Again from Teachers TV, this 15-minute video features a primary school in London.

Visit the companion website www.routledge.com/textbooks/ltps2e for:

■ an additional task for this unit;
■ links to useful websites relevant to this unit.

REFERENCES

Ainscow, M., Conteh, J., Dyson, A. and Gallanaugh, F. (2007) *Children in Primary Education: Demography, Culture, Diversity and Inclusion (Cambridge Primary Review: Research Survey 5/1)*, Cambridge: University of Cambridge Faculty of Education. Available online at www. primaryreview.org.uk (accessed November 2009).

Bearne, E. (2007) 'Boys (girls) and literacy: towards an inclusive approach to teaching', in E. Bearne and J. Marsh (eds) *Literacy and Social Inclusion: Closing the Gap*, Stoke on Trent: Trentham Books.

Coffield, F., Moseley, D., Hall, E. and Ecclestone, K. (2004) *Should We Be Using Learning Styles? What Research Has To Say To Practice*, London: Learning and Skills Research Centre. Available online at www.scribd.com/doc/20311529/Should-We-Be-Using-Learning-Styles (accessed November 2009).

Department for Education and Skills (DfES) (2003) *Every Child Matters*, Cm5860, London: The Stationery Office.

Department for Education and Skills (DfES) (2006) *2020 Vision: Report of the Teaching and Learning 2020 Review Group*, London: The Stationery Office. Available online at www.publications. teachernet.gov.uk (accessed November 2009).

Galton, M., Gray, J. and Rudduck, J. *et al.* (2003) *Transfer and Transitions in the Middle Years of Schooling (7–14): Continuities and Discontinuities in Learning*, Research Report RR443, London: DfES. Available online at www.dcsf.gov.uk/research/data/uploadfiles/RR443.pdf (accessed November 2009).

Gardner, H. (1993) *Frames of Mind: The Theory of Multiple Intelligences*, 2nd edn, London: Fontana Press.

Gardner, H. (1999) *Intelligence Reframed: Multiple Intelligences for the 21st century*, New York: Basic Books.

Gonzalez, N., Moll, L.C., Tenery, M.F., Rivera, A., Rendon, P., Gonzales, R. and Amanti, C. (2005) 'Funds of knowledge for teaching in Latino households', *Journal of Teacher Education*, 56(4): 367–81.

National Curriculum Council (NCC) (1992) *Starting Out with the National Curriculum*, York: NCC.

Office for Standards in Education (Ofsted) (2000) *Evaluating Educational Inclusion*, London: Ofsted.

Qualifications and Curriculum Authority (QCA) (2005) *National Curriculum Statement on Inclusion*. Available online at www.curriculum.qcda.gov.uk (accessed November 2009).

Reynolds, J. (1996) 'An ear to the ground: learning through talking', in E. Bearne (ed.) *Differentiation and Diversity in the Primary School*, London: Routledge.

Rose, J. (2008) *Independent Review of the Primary Curriculum: Interim Report*, London: DCSF. Available online at www.dcsf.gov.uk/primarycurriculumreview (accessed October 2009).

Acknowledgement

My thanks to Shaun Holland, Ben Reave, Sara Tulk, Rowena Watts and children from primary schools in north Essex.

RESPONDING TO CULTURAL DIVERSITY

Pam Copeland and Des Bowden

INTRODUCTION

> Education for diversity is fundamental if the United Kingdom is to have a cohesive society in the 21st century.
>
> (Ajegbo, 2007)

This unit is for teachers who are hoping to develop an understanding of, and who are ready to implement a real commitment to, cultural diversity in their teaching. It explores the issues, challenges and opportunities that face schools, teachers and children in an ever diverse multicultural twenty-first-century classroom.

OBJECTIVES

By the end of this unit you will have understood:

- the issues surrounding diversity;
- entitlements to diversity;
- obstacles to entitlement to diversity;
- the value of diversity awareness;
- challenges in the classroom;
- teacher attitudes to diversity.

The population of the UK continues to be diverse in terms of ethnicity, religion, language and culture. This unit investigates this diversity and develops strategies for use in school for identifying, sharing and working with this wealth of difference. It develops an understanding of the issues concerned with identities that children inhabit. It tries to promote an understanding of the different people in the UK today, and how children contribute to this diverse society. Teachers have to help their children challenge and evaluate different standpoints from their own and educate them to develop an informed view of diversity and hopefully become part of a more cohesive society.

Children in the UK can inhabit a range of identities that are as confusing as they are defining, not only for themselves but for others. It is for teachers to gain an understanding of these dilemmas and to devise appropriate learning episodes that contribute to a curriculum tailored to the individual needs of the children in their unique setting. This should be their entitlement for education for diversity. Which national cricket team should a Bangladeshi boy living in Birmingham support? Where does his identity rest?

There is much encouragement from government educational policies to work towards the goal of more a cohesive and united society. The Ajegbo Report (2007), *Effective Leadership in Multi-Ethnic Schools* (NCSL, 2005) and the National Curriculum itself are strong in their encouragement of understanding diversity and working towards a cohesive curriculum that reflects, understands and celebrates the values of today's multicultural society.

CASE STUDIES IN MODERN DIVERSITY

The following case studies demonstrate the challenges and benefits of living a plural society on a range of scales. The example of Leicester shows the plurality of a modern British city. On a school level, the study of the Brook Primary School highlights the benefits and richness that a multicultural school can offer. The individual study of Neena Gill shows how people may have a range of identities determined by racial, cultural, social and economic circumstances.

Case study 1

URBAN DIVERSITY – LEICESTER

Based on the 2001 census data and supplementary evidence, Leicester is likely to become the UK's first plural city. If this trend continues, Leicester is likely to become one of the first cities in England to have a majority of people with an ethnic minority background. This is due to a range of factors, including higher birth rates among ethnic minority groups, increases in existing populations through family consolidations and increases in the numbers of new arrivals. If this trend continues, Leicester may reach this milestone some time after 2011. Among the ethnic minority people of Leicester, over 30 per cent have an Asian background. The Asian population is predominantly Indian, from either East Africa or from Gujarat in India. Other much smaller Asian populations include Bangladeshis and Pakistanis. The black population in Leicester comprises two groups – those of Caribbean origin and those of African origin. This range of ethnic groups has led to the fact that 45 per cent of the pupils in Leicester schools say that English is not their preferred language.

(www.oneleicester.com)

Case study 2

SCHOOL DIVERSITY – BROOK PRIMARY SCHOOL

Brook Primary School is a popular, oversubscribed, inner-city school that achieves excellent results, at or above the national average at Key Stage 1 (in 1997 – reading: 91 per cent; writing: 85 per cent; mathematics: 91 per cent) and well above the national average at Key Stage 2 (English: 80 per cent; mathematics: 80 per cent; science: 98 per cent).

Free school meals taken were higher than the local education authority (LEA) average (41 per cent) at 48 per cent in 1997, according to school data. Attendance was in line with the national average. Brook Primary is clearly a very good school, meeting the needs of its pupil intake.

This is particularly striking in the UK context given the profile of the school's intake. The children attending the school come from very diverse backgrounds. According to school data collected in 1997, 28 per cent were of black Caribbean origin; 6 per cent black African; and 12 per cent 'black other', mainly children of dual heritage. Children of South Asian origin make up less than 3 per cent of the intake (Indian: 1 per cent; Pakistani: 1 per cent). Only 37 per cent of children in the school were classified as from a UK white background. The remaining 17 per cent consisted of small numbers of children from a wide variety of other language backgrounds, including children with the following home languages: Arabic, Bengali, Chi, Danish, Dutch, Fante, Farsi, French, French Creole, German, Greek, Gujarati, Hindi, Italian, Luo, Norwegian, Punjabi, Polish, Portuguese (some from Angola), Spanish, Swedish, Tagalog, Yoruba, Urdu and others. One of the biggest groups was Portuguese speakers (nine children including those of Portuguese, Mozambican and Angolan parentage), followed by Arabic speakers (eight) and Yoruba speakers (seven).

At the time of the last Ofsted visit in 1995, 15 per cent of the children were assessed as needing English language support. By 1997 this had risen to 23 per cent, according to school records, but was still less than the LEA average of 30 per cent EAL (English as an additional language) learners.

However, this language survey data does not illustrate the true complexity of the school's intake. Many of the children were of mixed ethnic group parentage; for example, one child categorised as 'Indian' had a Goan father and lived with a white UK mother. This is not an exceptional case, for this is an inner-city area in which multi-ethnic cultural groupings and diverse new cultural forms are emerging, in which traditional or heritage cultures are only one element among other constructions of identity signalled in clothing, choice of music, choice of food and other affiliations.

This new urban and changing social background was also seen in the school records on the children's religious affiliations. While the majority (60 per cent) of parents claimed to be Christian, as many as 31 per cent claimed to have no religious affiliations at all. There were only 4 per cent Muslim, then 2 per cent Hindu, 1 per cent Buddhist and 1 per cent Jewish children.

(Adapted from the Standards Site, www.standards.dfes.gov.uk)

The challenge of diversity facing the teacher today varies across the country. Inner cities have a particular mix of ethnic groups and mixed-heritage children. With the expansion of the European Union (EU) and the right to work in any member state, there has been an increase in in-migration of new member states' workers and these are not always concentrated in large cities. The eastern European farm workers in East Anglia form significant minority groups amid traditional white British communities. Towns such as Slough and Reading have all received large numbers of Polish and other nationals.

Teachers are also faced with serious issues about the education of non-European nationals, both as refugees and as illegal immigrants.

Case study 3

PERSONAL IDENTITIES – NEENA GILL MEP

Neena Gill is a woman of Asian roots, with a home in the UK and representing the West Midlands as their MEP. She spends time in Brussels and Strasbourg. As president of the India delegation she represents the EU in southeast Asia. Additionally, she is an important member of her family. She is a person of multiple identities.

As the ethnic background of Europeans becomes more and more varied, there's never been a better time to recall the EU's founding motto: 'united in diversity'.

ENTITLEMENT TO DIVERSITY EDUCATION

Multi-cultural education that celebrates diversity is an important part of responding to the kaleidoscope of cultural attributes in the school and the community. Children will be living in a more globalised world where the old barriers of geography will no longer be relevant. Children in all parts of UK (rural, inner-city, suburban) need to understand and respect a range of different cultural heritages. Minority ethnic children, like all children, are entitled to appropriate diversity education through their experiences in school, both in the overt curriculum and within the ethos of the school (Claire, 2006).

Schools are under a legal obligation to promote good race relations and provide full equality of opportunity for all children (National Curriculum (2000) and Race Relations Amendment Act 2000). However, recent policy statements have improved on these baseline requirements. For example, the National Curriculum (2007) has a specific section on 'Identity and cultural diversity' which considers diversity in the curriculum, planning for identity and cultural diversity learning, and community cohesion. This comes from the cross-curriculum dimensions which:

> provide important unifying areas of learning that help young people make sense of the world and give education relevance and authenticity. They reflect the major ideas and challenges that face individuals and society . . . Dimensions can add a richness and relevance to the curriculum experience of young people. They can provide a focus for work within and between subjects and as a whole, including routines, events and ethos of the school.
>
> (QCA, 2009a)

Ajegbo (2007) recommends that schools recognise the 'pupil voice' and have systems in place so these voices can be heard (such as school councils and other mechanisms for discussion). Head teachers and their governors are required to meet statutory requirements for diversity and use *Community Cohesion Guidelines* (TeacherNet, 2008) as a check for their accountability. The National College for School Leadership ensures that training for diversity is an essential component of leadership. All schools are encouraged to audit their curriculum to establish their provision for diversity and multiple identities. The Qualifications and Curriculum Authority (QCA) report called *Respect for All* (2009b) provides an audit tool for this process that helps map the school's provision. Schools should build active links between and across communities with diversity understanding as the focus. Ajegbo further recommends the appointment of 'advanced skills teachers' with a responsibility for diversity training and suggests that points on the pay scale be awarded to teachers taking special responsibility for diversity.

The *Every Child Matters* (ECM) (2004) agenda put the emphasis on the needs and aspirations of each individual pupil so that they can make the best possible progress in developing as responsible citizens and making a positive contribution to society. The recent *Independent Review of the Primary Curriculum* (Rose Review) (Rose, 2009) confirms the learners at the heart of the curriculum, but all learners have a set of cultural diversity experiences that need to be understood and appreciated so that learning can be more effective. Teachers are encouraged to be more flexible and to develop localised curricula relevant to the needs and aspirations of their children, their schools and their communities. Learners are encouraged to be a focal part of their own learning journey.

The QCA's *Big Picture of the Curriculum* (2008), which is part of the government's *Children's Plan*, puts identity and cultural diversity as one of its overarching themes and this has a significance for individuals and society and provides relevant learning contexts.

The *Cambridge Primary Review* (Alexander, 2009) is a major independent survey and analysis of primary school education that has been continuing since 2004. Of their ten major themes,

Theme 5 is diversity and inclusion. They warn that recognising diversity in school may not be a straightforward exercise:

> differences between children are constructed rather than simply described, and ... the constructs embodied in official statistics and policy texts tend to dominate discourse in primary education currently. These constructions favour simplistic and evaluative categorisations which conceal as much as they reveal about diversity.

They go on to encourage individual schools to develop approaches to diversity that meet the needs of their children and the local community.

Task 6.3.1 **PROVISION FOR DIVERSITY**

Use these questions from the *Cambridge Primary Review*, Theme 5: 'Diversity and inclusion', to consider the provision for diversity in a school known to you.

■ Do our primary schools attend fairly and effectively to the different learning needs and cultural backgrounds of all their pupils?
■ Do all children have equal access to high-quality primary education?
■ If not, how can this access be improved?
■ How can a national system best respond to the wide diversity of cultures, faiths, languages and aspirations which is now a fact of British life?
■ Of what is identity constituted in a highly plural culture, and what should be the role of primary education in fostering it?
■ How can primary schools best meet the needs of children of widely varying abilities and interests?
■ How can schools secure the engagement of those children and families which are hardest to reach?

(www.primaryreview.org.uk/)

OBSTACLES TO ENTITLEMENT TO DIVERSITY

Ajegbo (2007) recognises that the quality of education across the nation is uneven, and suggests the following issues may prevent a coherent diversity curriculum being implemented:

■ insufficient clarity about flexibility and customising the curriculum;
■ lack of confidence by schools to engage in diversity issues;
■ lack of diversity training opportunities;
■ lack of proper consideration for the 'pupil voice';
■ tenuous or non-existent links to the community.

Other challenges facing teachers wishing to develop diversity awareness in their school include:

■ embedding it in a single subject, such as religious education, and not others;
■ lack of planning for integration of newcomers into the learning environment;
■ concentration on famous British people;
■ narrow selection of reading materials in the library;

■   stereotypes in school displays;
■   stereotypes in geography (all Africans are starving and live in mud huts);
■   lack of empathy in questioning children who are different from the teacher;
■   not recognising that some children do not have Christian names;
■   exoticising minority children;
■   tokenism;
■   language;
■   unwillingness to face controversial issues;
■   unacknowledged racism.

VALUE OF DIVERSITY AWARENESS: BEYOND TOKENISM

Ajegbo (2007) believes that 'education for diversity is crucial not just for the future well-being of our children and young people but for the survival of our society'.

If children are to develop as successful learners, confident individuals and responsible citizens (the *Big Picture* and ECM), it is essential for them to understand and have respect for cultures, religions and identities.

The most successful teaching and learning for diversity occur when there is a whole-school commitment. This includes governors and staff, children, support staff and the local community, working together on the whole-school ethos, which includes the taught and learned curriculum as well as the hidden curriculum. Too many schools celebrate cultural diversity without really understanding the nature of that diversity.

FLEXIBILITY AND THE CURRICULUM

Even since 2002, in the QCA's *Designing and Timetabling the Primary Curriculum*, schools have been encouraged to adopt more flexible approaches to the curriculum by customising the basic entitlement to learning to create their own distinctive and unique curricula. Some schools showed innovative ways to include this flexibility. Further encouragement to flexible and appropriate curricula came in 2003 with *Excellence and Enjoyment* (DfES, 2003). The *Independent Review of the Primary Curriculum* (Rose Review) (Rose, 2009) encourages schools to develop curricula promoting diversity.

In particular, the National Curriculum recommends the following:

1   Using appropriate resources such as artefacts and images to show diversity within and between cultures and groups;
   ▌ ensuring choice of examples provide balance.
2   Presenting a broad and balanced view of culture, identity and diversity;
   ▌ giving learners accurate and objective views;
   ▌ avoiding presenting minority groups as problematic;
   ▌ looking for commonalities between groups.
3   Questioning commonly held opinions and stereotypes (e.g. migration in the UK is a recent occurrence);
   ▌ challenging media portrayal of different countries and peoples.
4   Creating an open climate (using ground rules and distancing techniques when dealing with controversial issues);
   ▌ encouraging learners to take pride in their identity and culture;
   ▌ encouraging learners to draw on their own experience.

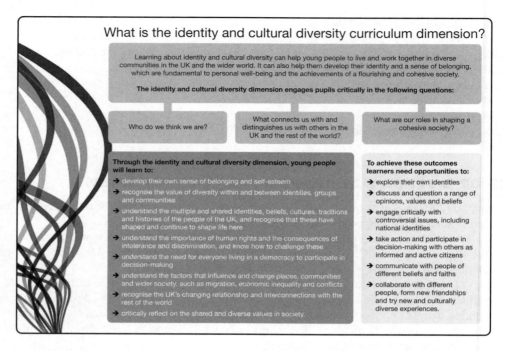

Figure 6.3.1 National Curriculum identity and cultural diversity overview
Source: http://curriculum.qcda.gov.uk

The National Curriculum diversity planning guidance (Figure 6.3.1) has been devised to help teachers develop strategies for introducing an identity and cultural diversity dimension in the school curriculum. Further, the National Curriculum offers guidance on the development of community cohesion (DCFS, 2007). TeacherNet produces a Community Cohesion Resource Pack and Ofsted (2009) produce a booklet for inspecting community cohesion. *Who Do We Think We Are?* (www.wdwtwa.org.uk/) is a readily available scheme of work designed to help teachers deliver diversity lessons at Key Stages 1 and 2.

Task 6.3.2 **RACISM**

Consider the influence of racism on people such as Mary Seacole, Nelson Mandela, Anne Frank and Stephen Lawrence and develop a scheme of work to include activities that will enhance the learners' empathy.

SCHOOL CONFIDENCE IN ADDRESSING DIVERSITY ISSUES

Many teachers feel that they do not have the experience or understanding to deal with diversity issues. At one level it is treating individuals with politeness and respect, but this can be compounded with language difficulties. In some cases, female teachers may not be shown the same sort of respect as male teachers by certain minority groups. Schools need to develop their staff to feel confident in their approach to dealing with controversial issues. This could be through taking a certain viewpoint, or playing devil's advocate, or adopting a neutral stance. At the beginning of any teaching episode every child needs to gain an understanding of which approach the teacher is adopting.

Lack of diversity training

Increased training opportunities are being made at school, regional and national levels. The Training and Development Agency for Schools (TDA) has spent more than £1.5 million between 2002 and 2006 in respect of diversity training. More opportunities are becoming available as the government pushes the diversity agenda. It is suggested that diversity training should be part of initial teacher training courses, giving newly qualified teachers the opportunity to spread their understanding to staff as they take up posts in school (Ajegbo, 2007).

The childrens' voice

This is concerned with giving a real say in what goes on in school. Most schools now have a school council. Some of these are strong and allow children to join in by making decisions on the nature of the school and its curriculum. Ajegbo (2007) reports that, in some schools, children are routinely asked for their feedback on all aspects of school life, being involved in staff selection processes and working with teachers on schemes of work. In these schools children are seen as part of the solution, not part of the problem.

Tenuous community links

These may be addressed by engaging children, their parents and the wider community in the daily life of the school. The extended school day, with breakfast clubs and after-school activities, offers opportunities for more people to come into school and for the school to play a more important role in the community.

CHALLENGES IN THE CLASSROOM

Teachers frequently encounter difficult classroom situations.

Various languages

Languages may be both barriers and bridges to learning. There are dangers for some to confuse not understanding a language with low ability. The child receiving language help and the other children need to be informed about the nature of the EAL support in the classroom.

Short-term children

Some schools receive more or less transient children, such as those from a travellers' community, army children or the children of short-term migrants. Their inclusion in the classroom needs to be carefully managed and their learning needs catered for. As they move on, a teacher should supply a report on their progress and achievement.

Task 6.3.3 **WATCHING CHILDREN**

Next time you are in school, take time to watch specific children who might be vulnerable, in the playground and on those occasions when children choose partners or group members. Isolation and marginalisation can be a signpost for more overt bullying away from teachers' eyes. Who is being left out? Who is hanging around on the sidelines?

■ Can you find out why some children are popular and others are not?
■ Does the school's equal opportunities policy have anything to say about bullying and name calling? How is this monitored and dealt with?

(Adapted from Claire, 2006)

BULLYING AND NAME-CALLING OF MINORITY ETHNIC GROUPS

Name-calling is probably one of the more frequently encountered expressions of racial hostility. Picking on individuals or small groups is also seen as bullying. Children need to be made aware that this type of behaviour is unacceptable – not only that, they need to understand why it is unacceptable. They may need to consider what their feelings might be if the situation was reversed. Moralising tends not to work in the face of opposing attitudes. Just to forbid such behaviour is controlling rather than educating. No Name-calling Week runs annually in January and is a week of educational activities aimed at ending name-calling in school and providing schools with the tools and inspiration to launch a continuing dialogue about ways of eliminating bullying (www.nonamecallingweek.org).

It is hard to counter entrenched attitudes of racism possibly learned from the family; nevertheless, racism is illegal and children need to be made aware of their right not to be bullied. Teachers need to be vigilant about bullying in their school and it may be a suitable topic for the school council to consider.

CONTROVERSIAL ISSUES

Teachers have to deal with controversial issues for many reasons and sometimes they are unavoidable. They may result in exciting classroom learning and, indeed, reflect partly what it means to be human, and they may help children make connections between areas of learning. They will help children develop value positions.

The QCA suggests that 'Education should not attempt to shelter our nation's children from even the harsher controversies of adult life, but should prepare them to deal with such issues knowledgeably, sensibly, tolerantly and morally' (QCA, 1998: 56).

A strategy for dealing with controversial issues is for the teacher to take a known stance and argue the issue with the children from there. The teacher may:

■ be an impartial chairperson (procedural neutrality);
■ speak from his or her viewpoint (stated commitment);
■ present a wide variety of views (balanced approach);
■ take an opposing position (devil's advocate).

Task 6.3.4 **TOKENISTIC GESTURES OR REAL UNDERSTANDING?**

Consider these issues:

■ Is learning a Caribbean song in music really improving diversity awareness?
■ Does circle time raise awareness of difference?
■ Are travellers' children ethnic minorities?
■ Do all children in your school celebrate Christmas?
■ Does making a curry make you more culturally aware?
■ Does dressing up in native clothes improve understanding of other people?

TEACHER ATTITUDES

Sometimes it is the teacher's attitude that is the concern in the classroom. Teachers need to acknowledge and decide how to deal with their own prejudices and viewpoints and to consider how to represent their personal opinions in the classroom. Low expectation of certain children and perceived typical behaviour problems are often associated with teachers' own stereotypical views. Children need children's diversity.

Task 6.3.5 **HUMAN RIGHTS**

Use the *European Convention on Human Rights* (www.hrcr.org/docs/index.html) and the United Nations' *Declaration of the Rights of the Child* (www.un.org/cyberschoolbus/humanrights/resources/child.asp) to critically evaluate the level of equality in society.

Task 6.3.6 **TEACHING DIVERSITY**

Critically evaluate the following paragraph and consider its implications for teaching diversity in the context of government policy and delivery in a specific primary school:

[T]eachers who are required to work within the framework of categorical constructions are nonetheless capable of moving beyond those constructions and of developing new responses in a 'spirit of transformability'. An example may serve to illustrate this point. Dyson and Gallannaugh (in press, 2007) report how a primary school participating in the Understanding and Developing Inclusive Practices project faced a situation in which many of its pupils appeared unable to make adequate progress in writing using the strategies that were favoured by the then National Literacy Strategy. Faced with this situation, and with considerable external pressure to raise attainment, the school could have opted simply to intensify its existing approaches. Instead, it sought to understand why its pupils were not responding, and came to the conclusion that they lacked the life and language experience they needed to profit from established approaches. Instead, therefore, of intensifying its teaching of reading, the school opted to embark on an experiential approach in which children participated in activities designed to extend their experience, in which they were then encouraged to talk about those experiences and in which only then, if at all, were they expected to write.

(Ainscow *et al.*, 2007: 16)

SUMMARY

This unit has started to address the dialogue currently surrounding diversity in the classroom. It has considered the challenges posed and suggests some solutions to help combat what is seen by many teachers, children and schools as one of the major issues in school today.

Encouraging multicultural education to be an integral part of the school ethos and embedding it in the curriculum is the first stage towards real inclusion and equal opportunity for all children. It should be part of the whole-school ethos embraced by all members of the school community. The unit highlights the need to be able to directly tackle racism and racial and other stereotyping, so that a relevant, meaningful and coherent curriculum can flourish. This curriculum needs to be designed to be appropriate for the whole school in the local community. It should be challenging, exciting and inclusive, meeting the unique needs of the children and helping all concerned to develop a cohesive society based on mutual understanding, tolerance and respect.

ANNOTATED FURTHER READING

Claire, H. and Holden, C. (eds) (2008) *The Challenge of Teaching Controversial Issues*, Stoke-on-Trent: Trentham.

This is an authoritative book that offers much practical support in teaching controversial issues, including diversity, in the primary school. It helps teachers to understand their own role and be equipped with effective approaches to sensitive and complex issues.

Elton-Chalcraft, S. (2009) *It's Not Just About Black and White, Miss: Children's Awareness of Race*, Stoke-on-Trent: Trentham.

This book provides research-based evidence on what children themselves think about cultural diversity and about efforts to counter racism in their schools. It is empirical, child-centred research that tells educators what they need to know. It was conducted with a sample of Year 5 pupils in two predominantly white and two diverse schools, all of whom were themselves involved in the research process. The book offers the children's voices and their surprising and challenging ideas.

Huddleston, T. (2007) *Identity, Diversity and Citizenship: A Critical Review of Educational Resources*, London: ACT. Available on line at www.citizenshipfoundation.org.uk/lib_res_pdf/0747.pdf (accessed November 2009).

This review aims to present a critical overview of what is currently available, with a view to helping teachers select appropriate resources for use with their learners. The usefulness of the resources in supporting teachers concerned with identity and diversity is appraised.

Maylor, U. and Read, B. (2007) *Diversity and Citizenship in the Curriculum*, London: London Metropolitan University/DfES.

This research report provides an up-to-date analysis of diversity in the curriculum. It includes relevant case studies and provides insight on the nature of Britishness.

RELEVANT WEBSITES

Cambridge Primary Review: www.primaryreview.org.uk/
EMMA: International Convention on the Elimination of All Forms of Racial Discrimination: www.emmainteractive.com/cultural-diversity-activities.html
European Convention on Human Rights: www.hrcr.org/docs/index.html
National Curriculum: http://curriculum.qcda.gov.uk
No Name-calling Week: www.nonamecallingweek.org

Standards Site from the DCSF: www.standards.dfes.gov.uk

TeacherNet Community Cohesion Resource Pack: www.teachernet.gov.uk/wholeschool/Community cohesion/Community_Cohesion_Guidance/

United Nations Declaration of the Rights of the Child: www.un.org/cyberschoolbus/humanrights/ resources/child.asp

Who Do We Think We Are?: www.wdwtwa.org.uk/

Visit the companion website www.routledge.com/textbooks/ltps2e for:

■ additional questions and task for this unit;
■ links to useful websites relevant to this unit.

REFERENCES

Ainscow, M., Conteh, J., Dyson, A. and Gallanaugh, F. (2007) *Children in Primary Education: Demography, Culture, Diversity and Inclusion (Cambridge Primary Review: Research Survey 5/1)*, Cambridge: University of Cambridge Faculty of Education.

Ajegbo, K. (2007) *Diversity and Citizenship in the Curriculum: Research Review*, London: DfES.

Alexander, R.J. (2009) *Towards a New Primary Curriculum: A Report from the Cambridge Primary Review*, Cambridge: University of Cambridge Faculty of Education. Available online at www.primaryreview.org.uk/Publications/CambridgePrimaryReviewrep.html (accessed October 2009).

Claire, H. (2006) 'Education for cultural diversity and social justice', in J. Arthur and T. Cremin (eds) *Learning to Teach in the Primary School*, London: Routledge, pp. 307–17.

Department for Children, Schools and Families (DCSF) (2007) *Guidance on the Duty to Promote Community Cohesion*, Nottingham: DCSF.

Department for Education and Skills (DfES) (2003) *Excellence and Enjoyment: A Strategy for Primary Schools*, London: DfES.

Department for Education and Skills (DfES) (2004) *Every Child Matters: Change for Children*, Nottingham: DfES. Available online at www.dcsf.gov.uk/everychildmatters (accessed November 2009).

National College for School Leadership (NCSL) (2005) *Effective Leadership in Multi-ethnic Schools*. Available online at http://publications.teachernet.gov.uk (accessed November 2009).

Office for Standards in Education (Ofsted) (2009) *Inspecting Maintained Schools' Duty to Promote Community Cohesion: Guidance for Inspectors*, London: Ofsted.

Qualifications and Curriculum Authority (QCA) (1998) *Education for Citizenship and the Teaching of Democracy in Schools*, London: QCA.

Qualifications and Curriculum Authority (QCA) (2002) *Designing and Timetabling the Primary Curriculum*, London: QCA.

Qualifications and Curriculum Authority (QCA) (2008) *A Big Picture of the Curriculum*. Available online at www.qcda.gov.uk/5856.aspx (accessed November 2009).

Qualifications and Curriculum Authority (QCA) (2009a) *National Curriculum: Cross-curriculum Dimensions*, London: QCA. Available online at http://curriculum.qcda.gov.uk/ (accessed November 2009).

Qualifications and Curriculum Authority (QCA) (2009b) *Respect for All*. Available online at www.qcda.gov.uk/6753.aspx (accessed November 2009).

Rose, J. (2008) *Independent Review of the Primary Curriculum: Interim Report*, London: DCSF. Available online at www.dcsf.gov.uk/primarycurriculumreview (accessed October 2009).

Rose, J. (2009) *Independent Review of the Primary Curriculum: Final Report*, London: DCSF. Available online at www.dcsf.gov.uk/primarycurriculumreview (accessed October 2009).

TeacherNet (2008) *Community Cohesion Resource Pack*. Available online at www.teachernet.gov.uk/ wholeschool/Communitycohesion/communitycohesionresourcepack (accessed November 2009).

RESPONDING TO GENDER DIFFERENCES

Elaine Millard

INTRODUCTION

This unit discusses the influence of gender on attitudes to schooling in general and the development of literacy in particular. While working your way through it, you will be asked to think carefully about the way in which society conveys its messages about what it means to be a boy or a girl and some strategies that you might adopt for ensuring that all pupils are encouraged to develop effective learning skills irrespective of their gender.

OBJECTIVES

By the end of this unit you should:

- be clear about what is meant by gender, differentiating its role from that of sex and considering its interaction with race and class;
- have an informed opinion of the role played by gendered cultural capital in determining school success and underachievement;
- be able to identify some common patterns of behaviour that militate against individual performance and know how to combat them;
- begin to connect children's experiences of home with their school learning;
- gain more insight into the part children's own (gendered) interests can play in motivating learning.

BACKGROUND TO THE ISSUE

It has not been possible to be in education in the Anglophone nations (Australia, Canada, USA, UK) at the beginning of the twenty-first century, either as a student or educator, without having encountered in some shape or form the strident public debate concerning the 'underperformance' of boys. Boys' underachievement in education in schools in general, and in literacy in particular, has become a global concern, evoking an anxious response from governments across the western world. In England, primary girls' literacy levels have remained stubbornly better than those of boys since the regime of national testing through standard assessment tests (SATs) and the reporting of performance in GCSE league tables began in the early 1990s and, although a whole raft of strategies have been in place to support boys' achievement for over a decade, boys have not yet 'caught up'.

In 2008 the National Literacy Trust prefaced its web pages on gender research with the following summary of statistical data for this period:

> Boys' attitudes to reading and writing have been the focus of much government and media attention. Girls started outperforming boys at GCSE when the exams were introduced in 1988. Then, in 2000, girls scored better at A-level than boys for the first time. In 2001 women achieved more first-class degrees than men. In 2007, government figures showed that 76 per cent of 11-year-old boys reached the expected level 4 in English, compared with 85 per cent of 11-year-old girls.

From the way the gender differences in examination results are reported in the media annually, you might be forgiven for thinking that not a single boy in your class will willingly sit down to read or write, nor will any boy be able to achieve his best. The anxiety over boys' achievements has been further fuelled by those, usually male, commentators who, speaking up for the importance of reforming boys' education, have suggested that schooling has become overly feminised through the predominance of female teachers (Bleach, 1998) and so does not cater effectively for the particular needs of boys (Biddulph, 1997; Hannan, 1999). Their recommendations include the abandonment of coursework (unfair because girls do it better!); boys-only classes; boys seated next to girls to discipline their learning; the recruitment of greater numbers of male primary teachers to create 'role models'; and a more 'boy-friendly' reading curriculum. The general burden of these accounts was that boys were being held back by the system and so it is the system that required modification. This was most vividly portrayed at the time by the late Ted Wragg's views on the subject, reported in the *Times Educational Supplement* (TES) and accompanied by an image entitled 'Chained males – How boys are held back'. It showed boys in short-trousered school uniforms, dragging a ball and chain behind them. Wragg's views can be taken either as providing a practical summary of issues raised earlier by research; or contributing to one of the periodic national moral panics about literacy-related issues (or basic skills). You can find Wragg's views and recommendations by searching the Archive section of the TES website (www.tes.co.uk) citing the date of its publication (16 May 1997). Interestingly, now more than ten years later, the American Michael Gurian, who describes himself as an author, business consultant and social philosopher, is promoting a similar message in *The Purpose of Boys* (Gurian, 2009).

Education policy makers in the UK have supported a number of research programmes to examine the differences in attainment revealed by the current system of assessment and, from them, produced a series of publications that address key aspects of boys' motivation and performance in relation to the literacy curriculum. These can be found most easily via the Teacher Training Resource Bank (www.ttrb.ac.uk) – look for 'Boys' motivation' as the search term. Research recommendations include suggestions about 'boy-friendly reading' and more appropriate writing genres and subject matter, using an interest in sports to motivate learning, greater use of new technologies and better male role models both in schools and in society in general.

However, it is also argued that this focus on boys can be divisive and cause schools to neglect the specific needs of girls, while ignoring their real gains in achievement. Critics of government policy insist that it is important to be clear about which boys and which girls are being discussed and that cultural and class differences need also to be considered. Nevertheless, despite such reservations, most commentators suggest that more boys would perform better if they were provided with different teaching and learning approaches from those currently dominating teachers' planning. The key to understanding the 'boys issue' is rooted firmly in the cultural differences inscribed in femininities and masculinities in society. Without this understanding, teachers may become trapped in a competing victims scenario, where either boys' or girls' needs are afforded primacy at any given time, and so one group is always regarded as underprivileged and the curriculum is merely tweaked to remedy the perceived problem without real thought being given to the underlying issues.

The irony of a 'moral panic' (Cohen, 1973) about boys' performance in school is that it draws its arguments from a theoretical basis for understanding differences in educational aspirations and achievements that is firmly grounded in the feminist perspective and a pro-woman lobby, which some of the commentators seek to challenge. As noted above, the 1970s' and 1980s' educational focus was on girls' underachievement, rather than any perceived problems experienced by boys, although looking back at examination results with hindsight, boys' weaker achievement in English literature and their poorer uptake of modern foreign languages were already marked.

As Carrie Paechter has suggested, in this period girls were regarded in many quarters as 'the other sex '(a process described as 'othering') or as 'boy(s) gone wonky' (1998: 7) and their achievements were often compared unfavourably with those of boys of the same age or simply left unacknowledged, for example in relation to their preferred sports, or their chosen areas of study. The emphasis was getting girls into science and technology and not boys into English literature or art history. Hilary Wilce, writing for the TES in 1995, summed up the conditions that prevailed for girls in school at that time:

> Boys dominated the playgrounds, the computers, the Bunsen burners, and teachers' time and attention; men dominated the headships and pay scales. A majority of all teachers, men and women, said science classes mattered less for girls than boys, while girls were less likely than boys to get the remedial help they needed.
>
> (Wilce, 1995)

Mercifully, most of these conditions have changed, particularly in relation to girls' achievements in maths and science and women teachers' achievement of higher status roles. However, it is still very important to think about issues such as the distribution of teacher attention, or the biasing of curriculum choices when planning a scheme of work or selecting a focus for learning.

As someone preparing to teach, you will need to be both well informed in your judgements and have a well-thought-out strategy for supporting all pupils' learning, rather than a dependence on the gender stereotypes that predominate in the popular press and in some current advice on managing boys' schooling. Therefore, before you consider what key researchers and curriculum advisers have had to say on the topic, I would like you to think through the influence of gender on education from your own standpoint.

Comment

I would hope that all of you now have found fewer differences in the access to education for all than were reported in earlier research studies and can report a sensitivity to the individual learning needs of boys and girls of whatever race, class or gender. You may, however, have noted that there are still differences in how boys and girls, men and women position themselves in relation to education and may have views on how this influences both their achievement in school and their future employment. This unit will look at the issues that lie behind these influences and offer ways of understanding the role that gender plays in shaping an individual's experience of school and engagement with her or his own education.

Task 6.4.1 **THINKING ABOUT THE INFLUENCE OF GENDER ON PEOPLE'S EXPERIENCE**

Your schooling

■ How far do you think boys and girls of your own generation were given equal opportunities to succeed in school?

■ Were there any times at school and in your later experiences of education that you thought you were treated differently from members of the opposite sex?

■ Did boys and girls of your generation share similar career aspirations?

■ Did boys and girls of your generation behave as well as each other, or as badly as each other in school?

■ Do male and female members of your family share the same interests, particularly in reading tastes?

■ Which family members were most proactive in helping you learn to read?

■ Have you observed any differences in the treatment of boys' and girls' achievements and behaviours in school today?

About teaching

■ Did equal numbers of men and women of your acquaintance 'always want to be a teacher'?

■ Now you have chosen to teach, what do your friends make of your choice? Do you think they would respond differently if you were of the opposite sex?

■ Do men and women choose similar subjects as their specialism in school – who, for example, is in charge of literacy, or in charge of ICT?

DEFINITIONS

The first point to clarify is the definition of gender as it is employed in the debate, distinguishing it from sex. Whereas the term 'sex' is used to signify the biological differences between male and female, 'gender' designates the patterns of behaviour and attitude attributed to members of each sex that are an effect of experiences of education, culture and socialisation. Whereas sex is conventionally categorised by binary oppositions of male and female, gender has a less determined division, embracing a spectrum of experiences and ways of self-presentation and identity markers, so that an individual may adopt a feminine gender without being biologically female and vice versa. This means that both sexes respond either in accordance with, or in opposition to, what they see to be the gender role ascribed to their biological sex. These roles tend to emphasise differences between the sexes rather than common patterns of similarity and correspondence. Glance at any children's television programme, toy catalogue or favoured internet website to see how aspects of masculine identity and femininity are clearly signalled to the participating reader/viewer.

Put simply, sex is a biological given but gender is socially and culturally constructed. All current evidence supports the idea that boys and men are more concerned to establish themselves as not female than vice versa, and that 'masculine' roles are therefore under greater scrutiny and more vulnerable to peer pressure. There have been several different explanations of how gender understanding influences choice and interest.

Gender regime

Gender regime refers to the accepted version(s) of masculinity or femininity as practised in a particular community or institution, such as the family, peer group, school or place of employment. It encompasses differences in patterns of behaviour, interests and relationships expected of boys and girls, men and women. In relation to schooling, Kessler *et al*. (1985) argued that young people were caught up in overlapping gender regimes, the most powerful influence of all being the peer group, which defines what is 'cool' for each sex both in and out of a school context.

Habitus

Related to this concept of a 'regime' is Pierre Bourdieu's theory of the habitus (Bourdieu, 1990). Bourdieu's term denotes taken-for-granted ways of thinking, which, although socially constructed, are so ingrained in an individual as a result of embodied action that they appear natural and 'durably incorporated in the body'. What this implies is that human behaviour is often heavily influenced by dispositions of action, thought and attitude, created from previous experiences of both success and failure in contexts influenced by class, family, education and social groupings. Such behaviours are therefore neither entirely voluntary nor completely determined.

Another way of thinking about the influence of habitus on gender-inflected behaviour is by using the concept of 'doing gender'. The following examples are given in the introduction to the Association of Teachers and Lecturers' 2005 publication, *Gender in Education 3–19: A Fresh Approach*:

> When a woman sits with her knees together and a man sprawls; when a woman stops talking because someone else has butted in, or jumps up to clear the table; when a man becomes the spokesperson for a mixed group, or takes over in managing a joint project – they are 'doing gender'. Girls and boys learn to do gender from the earliest age with positive and negative reinforcements at every turn, which, for most of us, are extremely difficult to ignore or unlearn.
>
> (Claire, 2005)

Cultural capital

This is another concept taken from the work of Bourdieu and his colleague Jean Passeron (1977 [1970]), which accounts for the cultural advantages bestowed on individuals from their own family and its position in society, rather than from mere economic power. It is used to understand and explain distinctions in cultural knowledge, taste and preference, which place individuals in positions of either social advantage or disadvantage in relation to dominant forms of education and experience. Cultural capital strongly influences educational opportunity and confers power and status on those whose capital is deemed to demonstrate their superiority. Further, Bourdieu argues that the value ascribed to specific aspects of cultural knowledge is dependent on the predilections, education and practices of the dominant elite already educated into particular tastes, as for example books rather than websites, classical rather than rock or pop music, theatre rather than television, world cinema rather than American movies. In terms of culture, men's activities often attract higher status than those practised by women.

You will find a fuller discussion of both habitus and cultural capital in relation to literacy in *Differently Literate* (Millard, 1997: 20–3).

Identity work

Sex and gender are key components of personal identity and, arguably, the first attributes that we register about someone we encounter, whether casually in the street or more permanently in relation to friends, colleagues and partners. Our upbringing and social interactions all provide us with strong messages about what it is to be a man or a woman and how we should present ourselves and interact socially. Carrie Paechter (1998) gives a very full account of the interrelationship of these two categories. Her chapter on 'Gender as a social construct' in *Educating the Other* will help you to understand these distinctions more fully. She argues that much of what is taken for granted as 'natural' in western society, as regards sex and gender, is not only socially constructed but also male-centred. Biological explanations have been used to support prevailing social inequalities by making gender roles seem to be a natural state (as in 'boys will be boys'). Further, she reminds us that, although in the majority of cases gender identity is related to biological sex, this is not a necessary relation and in some cases the two are unrelated.

Gender is therefore relational and, most importantly, the differences expressed in gender roles involve power relations in which, as argued above, 'masculine' activities are perceived to have higher status than feminine ones; for example, basketball is considered a more interesting sport than netball, carpentry more skilful than needlecraft or cookery. Because of the power relation inherent in constructed gender differences, boys are under greater pressure from their peer group to conform (Martino, 2007). However, masculine identity is more precarious, and therefore more constrained and defended than femininity; this leads to there being more restricted behavioural possibilities for males than for females with boys showing a tendency to be homophobic and misogynistic in classroom interactions and punitive of those who step 'out of line'. Becky Francis, who has shown how gender policing impacts on gendered power relations in both primary and secondary classrooms, reports:

> So, from pre-school ages onwards children engage in what Davies calls 'gender category maintenance work'. This involves behaving in stereotypical ways to demonstrate their gender allegiance, but also in policing other children to ensure that they do the same. It is this kind of behaviour that results in gendered trends in classroom behaviour and interaction.
>
> (Francis, 2005: 42)

It is clear that school plays a significant role in shaping children's sense of self and it is therefore important to take account of the role category maintenance may play in reinforcing, or maintaining, gender stereotypes in classroom interactions.

GENDER AND SCHOOL DISCIPLINE

In broad generalities, it has been found that many boys find accommodating to school expectations a far more difficult task than most girls. In particular, working-class boys and black boys are reported as finding school regimes oppressive and often seek to subvert the power of their teachers and other authorities (Phoenix, 2004). This has also been described by a number of sociologists, who identified key groups of boys who create their identities in opposition to schooling (Willis, 1977; Mac an Ghaill, 1994; Connell, 1995; Martino, 2007).

The findings of a wide range of studies related to behaviour are summed up below. Teachers find boys more disruptive in school and the attention they demand holds back girls:

Task 6.4.2 **ADULT–CHILD INTERACTIONS**

Take time to consider some of the ways tabulated below in which adults have been shown to interact with children and think about their consequences for learning, filling in the right-hand column with your views. Two have already been completed to provide examples; however, please think of your own examples and explanations for these items:

Adults through their earliest interactions treat boys and girls very differently.	*This reinforces gender roles and boys and girls begin to emphasise their differences from each other.*
Boys are encouraged to be more active than girls and participate more frequently in boisterous play.	*Boys find sitting down for an extended length of time tedious.*
Boys and girls are provided with different kinds of toys.	
Girls are provided with a wider range of writing and drawing materials.	
Girls often spend more time working with, and talking to, adults.	
The early reading of boys and girls, particularly in relation to popular culture, conveys different messages about what it is to succeed.	

- Boys use diversionary tactics to disrupt classroom management.
- Boys' peer culture endorses 'messing about' in class – it is 'uncool' for them to be seen to work and the dominant groups mock boys who wish to study.
- Boys are less diligent about completing homework (particularly 'learning' or 'reading' work).
- Boys seek to occupy the 'action zone' in the lessons they enjoy, gaining more opportunities for interaction with teachers (Randall, 1987; Shilling, 1991).
- Boys are reprimanded more often than girls – it is estimated that the ratio of praise to blame is as low as 1:3 for boys.
- Boys' disruptive behaviour annoys girls and prevents them from working as well as they intend.
- Boys' name-calling can deter less dominant boys and many girls from feeling confident in proffering ideas and comments in class.
- Girls are more quietly inattentive and so may slip out of a teacher's sight.

Think about which of these findings match your experience and decide what implications they may have for your practice. Discuss your ideas with your tutor and other teachers in training. Identify areas you might concentrate on addressing in specific lessons.

Comment

One of the most common issues raised by boys consulted by researchers is that they are 'picked on more than girls' and it is clear from classroom observational research that the teacher's gaze is frequently directed at the boys, focusing on their behaviour and using questioning as a closed disciplinary tactic (have you been listening?), rather than adopting a strategy that avoids confrontation (can you find your own solution to this problem?).

In managing classroom behaviour, you need to show fairness by dealing with both boys and girls in similar ways. Your 'ground rules' for the behaviour you expect should be applicable to all and when you deviate from them you need to be able to give a clear expectation of what has made you change your rules.

GENDER AND READING

It is in matters of literacy that most concern has been expressed about gender differences. Earliest attention to this difference focused on achievements in reading and every survey of children's reading interests conducted since the seminal work of Whitehead (1977) has shown that boys and girls have quite different reading tastes (Hall and Coles, 1999; Maynard *et al.*, 2008). In general, girls are also far more committed readers (Sainsbury and Schagen, 2004).

Further, it has been shown that girls' predominant tastes in reading choices, which favour narratives and life-like experiences, match the demands of the current English curriculum more closely, giving them a better start in school tasks (Millard, 1997; Barrs and Pidgeon, 1998). Both boys' and girls' interests need to be taken into account when selecting resources for both independent and whole-class reading, and these need to include a wide and varied range of texts, including non-fiction, magazines and screen-based texts. Further, it is important to ensure that all pupils are able to experience a rich diet of well-crafted narratives and hear them read well. The experience of reading aloud and 'performing' powerful texts embeds an understanding of the rhythms as well as the language of both poetry and prose and it is essential to create time for some texts to be tested on the tongue. Given an appropriate opportunity, the least able and the unwilling readers can enjoy reading to younger pupils if enabled to prepare properly. Parents and carers are usually very pleased to help with practice for performance.

When discussing issues related to reading and responding in writing, boys may be embarrassed if asked to reveal aspects of their personal lives and generally have less experience of sharing feelings with their peers than girls. Given appropriate contexts, however, boys can be interested in exploring their own concerns, but the choice of context for this needs handling sensitively. Drama, poetry and fiction allow many opportunities for discussing important personal issues through considering the interrelationship of characters, experiences and events. The importance of developing empathy, a cornerstone of social and emotional aspects of learning (SEAL), makes it important to share texts with both boys and girls that focus on character development and emotions, rather than always selecting for adventure, plot and action. It is also equally important to think about different cultures' responses to narrative and storytelling and weave other ethnic interests into your choices too.

A particularly useful way of categorising children's reading is provided by data from a sustained research project conducted by Moss and Attar (1999), in which the reading events in particular schools were analysed and related to children's understanding of what messages their attainment carries. They identified three distinct kinds of event, which they designated as: reading for proficiency; reading for choice; and procedural reading. Drawing out gender differences in the experiences they recorded, they suggested it is the proficiency frame for reading that creates most gender differentiation, with the less proficient boy readers masking their lack of competence by selecting non-fiction texts as their main reading choices. Moss (2008) later warns against a popular assumption that many weaker boys' interest in non-fiction, such as the very popular Usborne information texts, will support the development of their reading proficiency. She argues that their choice of text is picture-led and involves little more than scanning for impressive images to talk about with friends. To encourage a more thoughtful analytical response to non-fiction more appropriate to enquiry, you will need to set the reading of non-fiction within an appropriate context.

When catering for different reading tastes in individual reading, it is also important that a focus on gender does not simply reinforce the differences in range and breadth of the texts that all pupils encounter and that girls' preferences are not ignored when providing for boys' perceived interests. A recent example of negative reinforcement, created through providing stereotypical choices for boys, can be seen in the introductory rationale for a new reading scheme, Project X, by Oxford University Press. This reading scheme is specifically aimed at boys, so boys' interests in animé and computer games are dominant themes. Further, it is claimed that girls are happy with any kind of story, so three of the four main characters are male.

Task 6.4.3 **BOOK AUDIT**

Conduct an audit of all the books you are currently making available for sustained reading in your class.

▪ Ask yourself if you are providing your class with texts and their related activities that reflect a wide range of children's current interests.
▪ Take time to discuss the roles ascribed to men and women, boys and girls in these texts and help your children to think more critically about representation and stereotyping.
▪ Are there significant differences of representation from that in the books you read as a pupil in school?
▪ Are there particular issues related to access to learning that you need to address, such as access to computers, preparedness for writing and time to share ideas with others?

GENDER AND WRITING

Differences in reading choices have been shown to have consequences not only for children's reading in school, but also for developing confidence as writers (Millard, 1997; Barrs and Cork, 2001). More of girls' writing shows evidence of traditional narrative influences and structures, whereas boys frequently draw on film or oral narrative structures, producing action-packed stories (Marsh, 2003; Millard, 2005; Willett, 2005). This make boys appear less competent writers in relation to narratives produced in response to school criteria. Boys are often made aware of teachers' disapproval of their preferred content in story writing, which makes them less confident or motivated to write.

Again, it is important to ensure literacy activities from a wealth of different narratives, short stories, tales and children's novels are shared – not just a selection of excerpts to demonstrate specific language points. Digital and other multimodal texts, including the structure of computer games, can also afford interesting stimuli for writing (Millard, 2000). When discussing writing in literacy work, draw attention to successful uses of language in both boys' and girls' written work. For example, my research found that boys often employed a wider range of vocabulary and used action verbs more effectively, while girls spent more time developing the setting of a story or creating character. Help classes to analyse and comment on each other's work by sharing their most interesting pieces and highlighting achievements.

Here are some comments made by Year 5 girls on stories that had been written by boys:

My favourite part is where you find arrows firing across the room. I also liked the flame-pit room with a flaming fire. I think 'find a rope and swing for your life' is an original idea. I like the spiders and their sharp fangs. In fact I like everything.

I think your title is brilliant and so is your blurb. I like 'the mummy with gleaming eyes' and 'bubbly paper wrapped round it'. I like your pictures of the mummies. My favourite room is the dark chamber.

And a boy's comments on a girl's story:

I liked page two best. It has a brilliant description of the witch. I would have liked a picture of her though. The most interesting bit was where you discover the treasure. It was good how you could click your fingers to escape the magic.

Interestingly, only one boy in this particular group chose a girl's story to report on, whereas girls were equally interested in the stories written by both boys and girls (Castle of Fear Project; see Millard, 2005). It is important to get boys and girls sharing their work and understanding differences of language use in order to expand both groups' repertoires of image and vocabulary.

It is also frequently noted that most girls have greater concern for presentation in all forms of language work and often do more than is required of them, while many boys are happy with the bare minimum. To counter this you need to place greater emphasis on fewer finished pieces of work rather than completing numerous notes and exercises. Setting fewer set writing tasks will encourage both genders to see both the composition and presentation phases as more important. Encourage the use of word processing as well as handwriting to achieve well-set-out work and use the concept of design (Kress and Van Leeuwen, 2006) rather than handwriting alone as a way of judging good presentation. A range of media for creating meaning, such as PowerPoints, weblogs and simple poster designs, will help the overall development of both boys' and girls' use of appropriate language, design and presentation skills.

Make a class collection of stories and poems to promote both better presentation skills and an opportunity to learn from each other's work. Pupils can read this to children in other classes or share with parents and school visitors, as well as each other. Let the children make the selection themselves, giving specific reasons for the choices they make based on the language used. From the selection identify each pupil's writing strengths so that these can be drawn on for discussion in later writing sessions.

Comment

There is insufficient space here to consider in detail the particulars of differences in the affordances created by writing in a variety of modes, some of them electronic. However, these are important in understanding differences in pupils' responses to the written texts required in school. In research studies (Millard, 1997, 2000, 2003), I have concerned myself with differences in boys' and girls' approaches to writing, demonstrating that more boys than girls make use of visual forms to create meaning. It is important to understand each individual's writing preferences as thoughtfully as you do for their reading and encourage them in trying out varied ways of both planning and presenting texts. All pupils need to experience a wide range of ways of making meanings and to not be limited to what they already do as when, for example, boys are allowed to use graphics and girls to write reams. A focus on text types and ways of framing writing that inform much of the National Literacy Strategy, if not limited to a mechanical reproduction of form for practice, has proved very effective in supporting all children's written work, particularly, I would argue, that of boys. The challenge is to match the genre you are teaching to your pupils' interests and preferences in a process I have termed 'fusion' (Millard, 2000).

GENDER AND ORAL WORK

In oral work, it is girls who are more often placed at a disadvantage in both whole-class and mixed groupings. In whole-class settings, teachers have been found to direct more of their questions at boys, often for management of their behaviour, and in all kinds of group work boys manage to dominate talk even in small mixed groups, so that both girls and quiet boys may have problems in making themselves or their views heard. However, the same boys often leave the written recording of discussions to girls while taking charge of representations (Davies, 1998).

The first thing to do is to look closely at your own habits of questioning to promote more thoughtful responses from all pupils. In group work it is important not only to select members to work together and ensure that all your pupils have experience of working in both mixed and single-sex groups, but also to define their roles carefully. Talk is coming to be seen as an increasingly important aspect of pupils' school experience and has been emphasised as important by Sir Jim Rose in the final report of his *Independent Review of the Curriculum* (2009).

Boys have been characterised as particularly enjoying argument, competition and disputation (Davies, 1998). These aspects of language can be built into many classroom activities, particularly through the use of role-play and simulations. Girls will also benefit from safe challenges provided by working in role. You should be careful to 'protect' all children into role, especially the least confident ones. As Dorothy Heathcote argues: 'The soul of the artist protects the wood or stone, and the teachers' strategies must defend their class from feeling threatened, being stared at or exposed in negative ways'. For a fuller account of her thinking about drama in school, see Heathcote (2002).

Homophobic attitudes have been found to limit who speaks and what can be said in group work (Guasp, 2009). The ridiculing of alternative viewpoints should always be challenged and very clear strategies for cooperative work set out. It is more productive if you encourage your classes to draw up guidelines for good habits of working together, for themselves.

A ROLE FOR POPULAR CULTURE

Although English and language work in school concerns itself largely with what is judged by adults to be appropriate literature, out of school pleasurable narratives are available in a much wider range of forms, including comics, magazines, television, film, videos, computer games, and so on. Many of these texts are interconnected with each other so that a film, a comic, a computer game and a popular book may share a common narrative source and main characters. These narratives have wide currency with all groups of children and are important in the development of friendships and peer groups (Dyson, 1997; Marsh, 2003; Marsh and Millard, 2003, Willett, 2005). As Marsh argues:

> Popular culture, media and new technologies offer a myriad of opportunities for deconstructing these representations of gender and developing critical literacy skills, skills which are essential in order to challenge the stereotypes which perpetuate literacy myths, including those relating to underachievement.

(Marsh, 2003: 73)

Marsh and Millard (2003) have examined the role that popular media can play in creating motivation, particularly among pupils who find conventional school work unappealing (more frequently boys). You need to be aware of your own classes' popular interests and use them for these aspects of language work (see Dyson, 1997; Marsh, 2003; Millard, 2003; Willett, 2005). There are, however, disadvantages to popular texts as they are often more marked by gendered interests than resources more commonly made available in school. Commercial interests deliberately frame them to appeal specifically either to boys or girls by reinforcing ideas of typical interests; for example, football and Star Wars for boys, home-making and Barbie dolls for girls. However, because of their wide circulation and the personal interest invested in them, they provide a very rich source of ideas for writing and discussion and can provide good opportunities for challenging stereotypes that limit expectations.

GENDER AND CHOICE

In western cultures, girls are often freer to participate in activities that are seen as having a masculine bias, for example football or computing, than boys, who often feel unable to take up interests that are perceived by their peers as feminine, for example French or dance. Tomboys have more credibility than cissies! One example of such limitations occurs if reading in school appears to many boys to be associated with women and girls. This is because it is mothers and other female members of their families who, for the most part, help with early reading, and book choice in school sometimes seems skewed to the kind of psychological story in which nothing very exciting happens (Millard, 1997). If things are to change, such gender limitations need to be addressed in the same way in which earlier gender research addressed girls' disenchantment with science. The first step towards this is to consider how concepts of masculinity work to limit expectations in literacy.

Hegemonic masculinity

Hegemony is a term introduced by Antonio Gramsci to refer to prevalent ideas that have become naturalised, accepted without question and used to justify the status quo of an institution or cultural practice within a particular society. In the western world, there is a prevailing view that accepts gender as a binary division, biologically fixed, with masculinity occupying a dominant, assertive role. Hegemonic masculinity is present in the narratives of popular novels and films in characters such as James Bond or Batman.

Hegemonic masculinity in schools works similarly to validate a male peer-group culture based on music, technology and sport and which expects challenges to authority; it often rejects schooling as uncool and endorses messing about in class, expecting achievement through effortless ability (Mac an Ghaill, 1994; Connell, 1995; Martino and Meyenne, 2001; Phoenix, 2004). Mac an Ghaill caricatured this version of masculinity in older students as being dominated by the three 'f's (fighting, fucking and football (1994: 58, 108–9). Its binary opposite has been labelled 'emphasised femininity' (Connell, 1995). Connell suggests that the cultural ideal that is celebrated for women is about sociability, fragility, passivity and, above all, compliance with male desire. Emphasised femininity is constructed in a subordinated relationship to hegemonic masculinity in ways that reinforce masculine power.

It can be argued that one of the main reasons for girls' greater achievement in education and the workplace has been the result of changing conceptions of femininity in society as a whole, brought about by the educational work of the second wave of feminists, who focused on questioning women's role in society. In schools in the 1980s, the changing role of women and the possibilities opening up for girls in the professions were very much on the agenda. By contrast, there have been relatively few attempts in this or any other Anglophone country to challenge the traditional place of men in society or to understand the role that hegemonic (dominant) masculinity plays in determining and limiting boys' educational opportunities. This is an issue you may wish to begin to debate with your colleagues.

Warning: Because of the negative influence of peer-group pressure, which 'polices' the maintenance of this view of masculinity, attempts to address boys' relative poorer performance, particularly in literacy activities, using teaching strategies that focus on the interests associated with hegemonic masculinity will not change deep-seated attitudes and learning behaviour. It is important that, as a teacher, you make time to discuss with the boys how the world works for them and the difficulties they might encounter without greater flexibility in role and expectations.

I have concluded my discussion of gender by asking you to think about the current emphasis on boys' educational needs. It is equally important to keep in mind those of the girls in your classes. My own view is that most of the points I have raised about gender are as relevant to the sound development of girls' education as they are to that of boys'.

Both boys' and girls' interests should be catered for in resources and activities associated with literacy. It is equally important that girls are helped to make choices and judgements about their own work, preferred learning styles and competencies too. Avoid the easy adoption of supposedly 'boy-friendly 'resources that address a very limited set of expectations. Not all boys dislike reading or are interested in sport and conflict, for example. Boys' behaviour may present many teachers with greater difficulty, but the rules made for a good classroom ethos should treat both girls and boys fairly and equally.

GENDER, ETHNICITY AND CLASS

Gender identity and its relationship to boys' schooling and achievement has now been on the agenda for over a decade and many individual strategies adopted have proved effective in particular contexts, although always, it seems, limited by the constant need for 'raising achievement' that focuses on identifying key skills and providing explicit ways of teaching them. However, the focus on boys' needs has taken place at the expense of a more thoughtful consideration of educational disadvantage and an understanding of the intercalation of other markers of identity, such as ethnicity and gender. As Gillborn and Mirza stated in their 2000 report for Ofsted, *Educational Inequality*: 'social class and gender differences are . . . associated with differences in attainment, but neither can account for persistent underlying ethnic inequalities' (cited in Claire, 2004: 23).

The statistical evidence on which Gillborn and Mirza's judgements rest can be found in Hilary Claire's summary of the report (Claire, 2004). Nevertheless, Claire herself emphasises a point they make that 'in all the data, gender is a factor in unequal attainment and that their recommended strategies to reduce inequalities of 'race'/ethnicity are equally applicable to class and gender' (Claire, 2004).

The principles I have recommended in this unit emphasise the importance of understanding the cultural experience of each individual pupil in your classes and therefore questions of class and ethnicity that influence both interest in and orientation to learning should always inform both your understanding and planning.

Task 6.4.4 **TAKING IT FURTHER THROUGH RESEARCH WORK**

Those of you who are interested in conducting your own research in this area, whether as part of work towards an M level qualification or in order to address a specific need of your current context, may wish to consider working on a small project in your own place of work. Here are some ideas you might choose to follow up:

■ Investigate the current reading or writing interests of the boys and girls in your own classes and relate these to the findings of other research recommended in the unit. Use your findings to plan to increase the range and variety of literacy events you offer. How could you set about creating inclusive, sustainable reading communities?

■ Use Gemma Moss's (2008) categories of the literacy events focused on reading in school: personal reading, reading for proficiency and procedural reading to determine how reading is conducted in your class (or school). Observe boys' and girls' attitudes to the kind of reading expected of them. Is there strong evidence, as Moss suggests, that boys express no particular preference for non-fiction over fiction? What implications can you find from your data for your own planning and resourcing?

■ Devise a questionnaire to survey the literacy experiences and interests of your colleagues or fellow students. Analyse the responses in relation to teaching experience, age and gender. Do your findings hold any implications for planning the school's continuing professional development requirements?

SUMMARY

Western culture, despite the many changes that have improved the position of both girls and women in society, is still saturated with notions of gender difference, often with an accompanying assumption that there are 'natural' attributes of the sexes that are best acknowledged as fixed. Questions of masculine identity have not been analysed with the same amount of scrutiny, even when stereotypical responses result in poorer orientation to both schools and schooling. In helping you to think otherwise about the role of gender in education, I have stressed the importance of developing a pedagogy rooted firmly in the sociocultural lives of children, which is sensitive to their ethnicity, class, previous experiences and preferred ways of learning as well as their gendered identity.

ANNOTATED FURTHER READING

Millard, E. (1997) *Differently Literate: Boys, Girls and the Schooling of Literacy*, London: Falmer.
Many of the main concepts on which this unit are based are found in this book. It also contains the research methodology useful in guiding you in how to find out about your classes' interests in reading and writing. In particular, it recommends collecting 'stories of reading' from all the children you teach by asking them to write about their own journey into reading.

Moss, G. (2008) *Literacy and Gender: Researching Texts, Contexts and Readers*, London: Routledge.
Here, you will find an excellent analysis of further research methodologies, including accounts of important research findings of Moss's own. Her focus is on the structures of schooling and, in particular, the 'literacy events' that shape children's perceptions of what is expected of them in the literacy curriculum. Her analysis of types of readers and their response to classroom tasks is particularly useful in helping you understand how your organisation in the classroom contributes to the construction of readers and their self-identity.

Skelton, C. and Francis, B. (eds) *Boys and Girls in the Primary School*, Buckingham: Open University Press.

> In this book, you will find ways of developing your classroom practice in many of the areas discussed in this unit. It includes chapters on the following issues: working with children to deconstruct gender; the role of gender in the playground; aspects of transfer; issues of identity, status and gender; gender and special educational needs; and literacy, gender and popular culture.

RELEVANT WEBSITES

National Literacy Trust gender and literacy research pages: www.literacytrust.org.uk/Research/genderresearchindex.html

> A very comprehensive research index that you can use to follow up specific issues in relation to literacy and gender.

> The National Literacy Trust also hosts all the policy documents related to government research and initiatives to raise boys' achievements on:

www.literacytrust.org.uk/Database/boys/boysgovt.html#initiatives. See also same url suffixed with #research.

Teacher Training Resource Bank (TTRB): www.ttrb.ac.uk

> Look here for publications on key aspects of boys' motivation and performance in literacy; use 'Boys' motivation' as the search term.

Times Educational Supplement (TES): www.tes.co.uk

> **Visit the companion website www.routledge.com/textbooks/ltps2e for:**
>
> ■ additional questions for this unit;
> ■ links to useful websites relevant to this unit.

REFERENCES

Barrs, M. and Cork, V. (2001) *The Reader in the Writer*, London: CLPE.

Barrs, M. and Pidgeon, S. (1998) *Boys and Reading*, London: CLPE.

Biddulph, S. (1997) *Raising Boys*, London: Thames.

Bleach, K. (1998) *Raising Boys' Achievement in Schools*, Stoke-on-Trent: Trentham Books.

Bourdieu, P. and Passeron, J. (1977 [1970]) *Reproduction in Education, Society and Culture*, trans. Richard Nice, London: Sage.

Bourdieu, P. (1990) *The Logic of Practice*, Cambridge, Polity Press

Claire, H. (2004) 'Mapping "race", class and gender: a summary of the report by David Gillborn and Heidi Mirza', in H. Claire (ed.) *Gender in Education 3–19: A Fresh Approach*, London: Association of Teachers and Lecturers.

Clarricoates, K. (1978) 'Dinosaurs in the classroom: a re-examination of some aspects of the "hidden curriculum" in primary schools', *Women's Studies International Quarterly*, 1: 353–64.

Cohen, S. (1973) *Folk Devils and Moral Panics*, St Albans: Paladin.

Connell, R.W. (1995) *Masculinities*, St Leonards, NSW: Allen and Unwin.

Davies, J. (1998) 'Taking risks or playing safe: boys' and girls' talk', in E. Millard and A. Clark (eds) *Gender in the Secondary School Curriculum*, London: Routledge.

Dyson, A.H. (1997) *Writing Superheroes: Contemporary Childhood, Popular Culture, and Classroom Literacy*, New York: Teachers College Press.

Francis, B. (2005) 'Classroom interaction and access: whose space is it?', in H. Claire (ed.) *Gender in Education 3–19: A Fresh Approach*, London: Association of Teachers ad Lecturers.

Guasp, A. (2009) *Homophobic Bullying in Britain's Schools: The Teachers' Report*. Available online at www.stonewall.org.uk/teachersreport (accessed November 2009).

Gurian, M. (2009) *The Purpose of Boys: Helping Our Sons Find Meaning*, San Francisco, CA: Jossey-Bass.

Hall, C. and Coles, M. (1999) *Children's Reading Choices*, London: Routledge.

Hannan, G. (1999) *Improving Boys' Performance*, Oxford: Heinemann Educational Publishing.

Kress, G. and Van Leeuwen, T. (2006), *Reading Images. The Grammar of Visual Design*. London: Routledge.

Heathcote, D. (2002) 'Contexts for active learning: four models to forge links between schooling and society', Paper presented at the NATD conference, February.

Kessler, S., Ashden, D., Connell, R. and Dowsett, G. (1985) 'Gender relations in secondary schooling', *Sociology of Education*, 58(1): 34–48.

Mac an Ghaill, M. (1994) *The Making of Men*, Buckingham: Open University Press.

Marsh, J. (2003) 'Super hero stories: literacy, gender and popular culture', in C. Skelton and B. Francis (eds) *Boys and Girls in the Primary School*, Buckingham: Open University Press.

Marsh, J. and Millard, E. (2003) *Literacy and Popular Culture in the Classroom*, Reading: Reading and Language Centre Publications.

Martino, W. (2007) 'Policing masculinities: investigating the role of homophobia and heteronormativity in the lives of adolescent school boys', *Journal of Men's Studies*, 8(2): 213–16.

Martino, W. and Meyenne B. (eds) (2001) *What About the Boys? Issues of Masculinity in Schools*, Buckingham: Open University Press.

Maynard, S., Mackay, S. and Smyth, F. (2008) 'A survey of young people's reading in England: borrowing and choosing books', *Journal of Librarianship and Information Science*, 40: 239–53.

Millard, E. (1997) *Differently Literate: Boys, Girls and the Schooling of Literacy*, London: Falmer.

Millard, E. (2000) 'Aspects of gender: how boys' and girls' experiences of reading help to shape their writing', in J.Evans (ed.) *The Writing Classroom: Aspects of Writing and the Primary Child*, London: David Fulton.

Millard, E. (2003) 'Transformative pedagogy: towards a literacy of fusion', *Reading, Literacy and Language*, 37(1): 3–9.

Millard, E. (2005) 'Writing of heroes and villains: fusing children's knowledge about popular fantasy texts with school-based literacy requirements', in J. Evans (ed.) *Literacy Moves On*, Portsmouth, NH: Heinemann.

Moss, G. (2008) *Literacy and Gender: Researching Texts, Contexts and Readers*, London: Routledge.

Moss, G. and Attar, D. (1999) 'Boys and literacy: gendering the reading curriculum', in J. Prosser (ed.) *School Cultures*, London: Chapman.

Paechter, C. (1998) *Educating the Other: Gender Power and Schooling*, London: Falmer.

Phoenix, A. (2004) 'Learning styles and gender', in H. Claire (ed.) *Gender in Education 3–19: A Fresh Approach*, London: Association of Teachers and Lecturers.

Randall, G. (1987) 'Gender differences in pupil–teacher interactions in workshops and laboratories', in M. Arnot and G. Weiner (eds) *Gender under Scrutiny*, London: Hutchinson in association with the Open University.

Rose, J. (2009) *Independent Review of the Primary Curriculum: Final Report*, London: DCSF. Available online at www.dcsf.gov.uk/primarycurriculumreview (accessed May 2009).

Sainsbury, M. and Schagen, I. (2004) 'Attitudes to reading at ages nine and eleven', *Journal of Research in Reading*, 27(4): 373–86.

Shilling, C. (1991) 'Social space, gender inequalities and educational differentiation', *British Journal of Sociology of Education*, 12(1): 23–44.

Skelton, C. and Francis, B. (eds) *Boys and Girls in the Primary School*, Buckingham: Open University Press.

Times Educational Supplement (TES) (1997) 'Oh boy', editorial, 16 May. Available online at www.tes.co.uk/search (accessed November 2009).

Whitehead, F., Capey, A.C., Maddren, W. and Wellings, A. (1977) *Children and Their Books*, School's Council Research Studies, London: Macmillan.

Wilce, H. (1995) 'Different drums for gender beat', *Times Educational Supplement*, 15 September.

Willett, R. (2005) 'Baddies in the classroom: media education and narrative writing, *Literacy*, 39(3): 142–8.

Willis, P. (1977) *Learning to Labour: How Working Class Kids Get Working Class Jobs*, London: Saxon House.

RESPONDING TO LINGUISTIC DIVERSITY

Anny Northcote

INTRODUCTION

> Language is not only a tool for communication and knowledge but also a fundamental attribute of cultural identity and empowerment, both for the individual and the group. Respect for the languages of persons belonging to different linguistic communities therefore is essential to peaceful cohabitation.
>
> (UNESCO, 2003)

The languages that we hear and see around us in our communities and classrooms in Britain enrich society and contribute to developing all children's understanding of the wider world. Statistics show that 21 per cent of pupils in UK primary schools are of minority ethnic origin and 13.5 per cent of primary-age children, one in eight, speak languages other than English (DCSF, 2007); also, the number of languages spoken as a first language is this country is over 300. This multilingual society we live in should be as much recognised and supported within the education system as in all areas of government and society.

OBJECTIVES

By the end of this unit you should have:

- an understanding of the meaning of linguistic diversity;
- an understanding of bilingual children's range of linguistic skills;
- knowledge of key responses to linguistic diversity in education;
- an awareness and understanding of practical strategies to support bilingual learners in the classroom.

HISTORICAL RESPONSES TO LINGUISTIC DIVERSITY

In the UK, the response to children and their families speaking languages other than English has been predominantly regarded as a problem by successive governments. Even today, with advances made in our understanding of how children best acquire an additional language, there is still the demand that English should become the first language of families with other mother tongues.

The idea that bilingual families should speak in English at home stems from a notion, prevalent in the 1960s, that children and their families needed to be assimilated into the wider society through conforming to the language and culture of that society. To achieve this, bilingual learners new to English were withdrawn from the 'normal' classroom context and put into 'special' English classes (Levine, 1990) or 'language centres'. This took them away from their peers and a natural environment in which they could hear and engage in the new language. The focus was solely on learning new language skills, which ignored the actual linguistic competence of the learner (Levine, 1990). Children new to English were marginalised and without full access to the curriculum. There was at this time the danger of perceiving 'immigrant' children as deprived, disadvantaged and handicapped due to their own background and unfamiliarity of the wider society's language and culture (Gregory, 1996).

There was a shift in the 1970s that acknowledged a linguistic and cultural pluralism within the expanding move to comprehensive education. In 1975, *A Language for Life* (Bullock Report) (DES, 1975) presented a comprehensive study of language and English learning and teaching. This included a very powerful chapter on the importance of a child's home language, which stated that:

> no child should be expected to cast off the language and culture of the home as he crosses the school threshold, nor to live and act as though school and home represent two separate and different cultures which have to be kept firmly apart.

> (DES, 1975: 286, 20.5)

The next decade saw some advances in recognising bilingual learners in their acquisition of a new language within a more positive understanding of a multicultural society; one that recognised cultural and linguistic diversity. The support for bilingual learners became more sustained and specialist, although all teachers were considered to be responsible for the learning and language needs of the bilingual pupils. Mother-tongue teaching was introduced in some areas, particularly in the early years, but this was limited and seen predominantly as part of a transition from the home language to English. The Swann Report, *Education for All* (DES, 1985), reported that there were still major concerns around the lack of progress in the advance of a pluralist society that recognised diversity, achievement and minority ethnic communities in a positive way.

Since the Education Act 1988, Ofsted reports (Gillborn and Gipps, 1996; DfES, 1999b, 2003b) have continued to identify underachievement of some minority ethnic pupils. There has been some positive response to this issue over the last few years (DfES, 2006), which is beginning to redress the balance, although turning policies into reality is a complex process.

Legislative change has also come about as a result of the enquiry into the death of Stephen Lawrence (Macpherson of Cluny, 1999). This led to the Race Relations (Amendment) Act 2001, which gives a statutory general duty for public authorities to promote race equality. In schools this means that there should be an improvement in the educational experience of all children, in particular those belonging to minority ethnic groups. In practice, all schools must have in place a race equality policy that promotes and monitors the attainment of children from all racial groups. Even schools that may not have many or any Black or minority ethnic pupils in their school communities still need to be prepared. Any policy should also include an approach for *all* children to understand race equality as part of their education.

Since the 1960s there has been funding for supporting groups of children from countries outside the UK. Currently funding is available through the Ethnic Minority Achievement Grant (EMAG) (DfES, 1999) to employ local authority (LA) teams, teachers and assistants to work with minority ethnic groups, particularly those at risk of underachieving, such as speakers of English as an additional language (EAL) and refugee children. While responsibility lies with you as the class teacher to provide an appropriate curriculum for all children, the opportunity to work in collaboration with the EMAG-funded teams provides support for effective strategies to support bilingual learners at the early stages of acquiring English. In schools where there are only small numbers of bilingual learners, such additional support may not be available, therefore you need to be familiar with ways to plan for and support your bilingual learners, whatever the context.

With the revised National Curriculum (DfES/QCA, 1999) there has been a greater focus on inclusion as the way forward. The three principles of setting suitable learning challenges; responding to children's diverse needs; and overcoming potential barriers to learning and assessment for individuals and groups of children provide a framework intended to ensure that children from different backgrounds and with differing needs are considered by formulating an inclusive curriculum for an inclusive school.

WHAT IS LINGUISTIC DIVERSITY?

There has been much debate about the term 'linguistic diversity'. All children use a range of language when communicating with family members, friends and teachers, whatever the first language. The Standard English taught in school is one of these. Of course, linguistic diversity is diverse in itself and varies from school to school. In some areas there will be schools with a wide range of languages spoken by a large number of children. There will be schools where there is one main language other than English that is spoken by the majority and schools where there may only be a few speakers of a minority language other than English. The combinations are varied, but the key is that we live in a culturally and linguistically diverse country and, if you can acknowledge that your language is central to your identity, so is everybody else's.

It is a challenge for policy makers, concerned with ensuring that children are educated to meet the demands of society while at the same time protecting the right to be different in relation to the varied ethnic and linguistic population (UNESCO, 2003).

Task 6.5.1 **LANGUAGE SURVEY**

Find out about languages spoken by children in a school you know. What do you know about the languages? Choose one of them and explore the story of migration behind the speakers of the language now settled in your area.

■ Are there spoken dialects that differ from the written standard?
■ How and where do children study their home language?
■ How are children categorised in terms of their language?
■ Does the language relate to their religion and is this always the case?

Be careful not to make assumptions or apply the same conclusion to all speakers of a certain language.

BILINGUALISM AND BILINGUAL LEARNERS

This is an area within which definition and distinction are complex (see Baker, 2006). The focus for the purpose of this unit is to consider the individual bilingualism of a learner within the educational context. When we talk about a child being bilingual, this does not necessarily mean that the speaker is fully competent and fluent in at least two languages. While this 'balanced bilingualism' may be one end of the continuum, it is more likely that children in school may have varying levels of operating in two or more language domains. Children new to English do not have 'no language', as is sometimes said by teachers, but are likely to be highly proficient users of at least one language that is referred to as the first or home language in this unit. The term bilingual is intended to focus you on the potential of the learner and to avoid negative labels such as 'non-English speakers'. This more positive approach can also be seen in the shift from the term English as a second language (ESL) to English as an additional language (EAL), in which English is seen in addition to an already well-established knowledge and understanding of at least one other language. Also, you need to remember that bilingual learners are not a homogeneous group.

The rest of this unit explores the issue of linguistic diversity in our schools and classrooms and considers your knowledge and understanding of such diversity and, in particular, how to support bilingual learners, both in their acquisition of English and in ensuring that they have meaningful access to learning and the curriculum. The approach is one that starts from what bilingual children already know about language and the actual language that they bring to the classroom. Not only does this establish the foundation for the learner acquiring the new language, but also adds to the knowledge and understanding of language for all children. Questions frequently asked by student teachers are explored through what research tells us and what this might mean in action. There are ideas for the classroom as well as tasks for you to enhance your own research into the issues that affect and interest you in particular.

ACKNOWLEDGING CHILDREN'S FIRST LANGUAGE IN THE CLASSROOM

There is a considerable body of research that explores the relationship between acquisition of the first language and that of an additional language, particularly when that language is acquired subsequently rather than simultaneously. Cummins and Swain (1986) explore this relationship through a theory of interdependence, which suggests that second language acquisition is influenced by the extent to which the first language has developed. If the first language is strong, acquisition of the second may be relatively easily acquired.

Lambert (1974) considers that learning an additional language within the same set of cognitive and social factors as those of acquiring the first language, leads to 'additive bilingualism'. Positive values and high status given to the first language provide an enriched context in which the second language is an additional tool for thought and communication. The learner is able to build on what they implicitly know about language and how to use it and adapt or adopt this to the new language. Opposite to this is 'subtractive bilingualism', in which skills in the first language are not deemed as a basis for acquiring the second language and a new set of linguistic skills have to be learned. In this instance the value placed on the first language is low. Subtractive bilingualism can lead to a diminishing of the first language, while at the same time not allowing the additional language to be fully developed. This may result in difficulties in acquiring the additional language and prevent children being able to show their true cognitive level. Their capacity and potential for learning may be wrongly viewed in a negative light. Therefore, the concepts of additive and subtractive bilingualism are important when discussing the relationship between first and subsequent language acquisition. This also opens the debate on the positive cognitive aspects of being bilingual. The ability to speak two or more languages has been shown to contribute to cognitive understanding and to thinking, reasoning and problem-solving skills, as well as to being more confident in social intercultural contexts (Baker, 2006).

In fact, there is evidence that support for the first language of bilingual learners at academic levels is key to academic success in the additional language. Cummins (2000) shows how children's cognitive and academic language proficiency (CALP) in their first language can be transferred to an additional language due to the underlying linguistic proficiency being a key factor in learning.

Therefore, it is possible that older children who arrive in the classroom at the early stages of acquiring English, but with a strong command of their first language, are generally found to acquire an additional language more rapidly than those who are not as skilled. Once concepts are developed, making connections becomes easier – the new language gives new labels to the well-established concepts.

In reality, it can be hard to engage children in the classroom in their first language, particularly where there are small numbers of bilingual learners, or a range of languages spoken by individual children rather than groups. However, if you understand the role first language plays in the acquisition of an additional language, and the language skills are valued and recognised as key to learning, you need to make the experience of learning a positive one, building on the bilingual learners' linguistic backgrounds in their learning of English. The ethos of the classroom plays an important role here and recognising a child's bilingualism and, therefore, enhancing self-esteem can go some way to ensuring that the child's identity is seen as important and that diversity is beneficial for all children. As a teacher who encourages diversity and open discussion between adults and children and among peers, you will see that, when children use their first language with each other in the classroom, there is a positive effect on their learning. A school that values the languages and cultures of the community will find that the bilingual children are more likely to be successful in their acquisition of English and in their learning (DfES, 2003b). All this is not just for the benefit of the bilingual learners, but for all children and adults. It increases language and cultural awareness, supporting communication between groups and encouraging a positive response to a multicultural society. Where there are few bilingual learners in a school it may seem daunting to consider their needs, but the same principles can apply. An example of integrating a new bilingual child into the classroom where there are no other bilingual learners can be seen in the following case study.

Case study

YEAR 1 AND 2 CLASS (SPRING TERM)

Marco is a five-year-old Italian boy who started school in the UK in the previous autumn term. He was new to English when he arrived. At that time his mother spoke a little English and gave good support, which has continued.

Marco settled well socially in class and soon began visiting friends out of school time. The classroom context presented lots of opportunities for play and modelling of spoken English by peers and adults. Marco really enjoyed himself in this context and particularly enjoyed retelling stories, which he soon began to do in English.

The teacher included lots of resources in Italian in displays and other materials. The whole class became interested in Marco's language. They supported Marco well, sometimes using Italian words such as 'comprende?'

(Student teacher, Bath Spa University College, 2005)

There is now an additional opportunity to make languages central to the curriculum, particularly in Key Stage 2 with the introduction of primary languages. *Languages for All: Languages for Life* (DfES, 2002) established a commitment to language learning for every pupil throughout Key Stage 2. This is now becoming reality with such entitlement being in place by 2010. Not only does this strategy recognise that children starting to learn other languages early are more receptive to the new languages, but it also gives us the opportunity to promote the languages already spoken by numbers of children in school. The document states that 'learning another language opens up access to other value systems and ways of interpreting the world, encouraging intercultural understanding and helping reduce xenophobia' (DfES, 2002). The opportunity to introduce such languages as Urdu, Polish and even Mandarin alongside the more commonly accepted French and Spanish is evident in the new *Key Stage 2 Framework for Languages* (DfES, 2005). While learning a language is a central aspect, it also includes a strong commitment to knowledge about language and intercultural understanding. This provides a good platform for extending our awareness and understanding of the world and the people we share it with.

SUPPORTING HOME LANGUAGES IN THE CLASSROOM

To help develop a positive ethos, consider the following:

- Allow and encourage children to speak and work in their own language, recognising that the first language is valued.
- Learn some key vocabulary and phrases, such as numbers, days of the week, hello/goodbye, and encourage children to do this too.
- Explore stories, books and poetry through the first language, maybe with the help of a teaching assistant, and introduce the English version with props, puppets or through drama.
- Encourage talk partners to use home languages in whole-class and group work.
- Create a graphics/writing area with different scripts, giving all children opportunities to practise the range of symbols using different materials.

For more fluent bilingual learners, encourage them to continue to explore texts using the home language with peers or adults. Similarly, encourage pupils to use the first language as well as English when engaged with investigative and problem-solving tasks.

Task 6.5.2 **OBSERVING SPOKEN LANGUAGE**

Observe the use of language(s) of a bilingual learner in the classroom and playground. Record the different ways the child uses language to communicate with peers and adults.

- Does the context influence the child's confidence when speaking?
- What do your observations tell you about the child's understanding and use of home language and English?

TEACHING ENGLISH EFFECTIVELY IN A LINGUISTICALLY DIVERSE CLASSROOM

Acquiring an additional language has similarities to acquiring the first language. Learners of school age start by picking up words before putting them together in two- or three-word phrases as they tackle the syntactic structure of the new language. The similarities are important, but it is also important to recognise the differences. The most important of these is that bilingual learners already know implicitly how a language works and are generally proficient users. They will also have conceptual understanding similar to that of their peers, and will relate the language to the context. Bilingual learners are not less intelligent or linguistically disadvantaged (Baker, 2006). On the contrary – they have a skill in being able to speak and possibly read and write in more than one language as their understanding of English progresses. Not speaking English must not be viewed as a disability and should not be equated with special educational needs (SEN).

However, it is important to recognise that some bilingual learners may have SEN, not linked to their additional language acquisition. Children giving cause for concern need to be assessed carefully, preferably by involving professionals who know and understand the language and culture of the pupil (Hall, 2001).

Learning through play and experimentation is a successful approach for all young children and gives a strong context in which opportunities for the new language can be used for social and intellectual engagement. In the Foundation Stage this should be common practice, which can be enhanced through a range of resources that reflect the linguistic and cultural diversity of the community. Stories are also central to the primary curriculum and an excellent resource for supporting bilingual learners, particularly when supported by visuals, available on video, DVD or audio cassette, preferably in the home language as well as English.

Don't be surprised if some bilingual learners choose not to speak at these early stages. A silent period is quite common and, of course, during this time the child is engaging and, most importantly, listening. Bilingual learners acquire a new language most successfully if there is a meaningful context for learning to take place within which they can listen, experiment, hypothesise, adapt or adopt the language. In some cases in Key Stage 1, and particularly in Key Stage 2, you may need to reassess your planning and teaching approaches, providing more opportunities for investigative and problem-solving tasks, using visual and physical resources.

SUPPORTING BILINGUAL LEARNERS

Learners at different stages of learning English

This is a very common and likely scenario. As for all children, learning contexts should be carefully planned with the intention to build on the strengths of the learner and address their specific needs, which will vary from one bilingual primary to another.

One aspect to consider is how to group children, and frequently teachers may place the new pupil with speakers of the same language. While it may be appropriate to have a pupil new to English working alongside one with the same home language but more proficient in English, other factors need to be taken into consideration, such as experience, friendship, gender and interest. It is also important to consider the 'new' child's approach to learning. Research by Chen and Gregory (2004) shows how two Chinese girls, one aged nine and new to Britain, the other born here and now eight, work together. It sheds light on how children may perceive learning a new language and, when given the chance, control their learning. The newly arrived older girl's insistence on what she wants to know and how she wants to learn may come from her previous experience of schooling, as well as her wish and determination to take on a new language. The younger girl's need to act as translator and teacher stretches her language abilities, allowing her to become more aware of her own bilinguality. Chen and Gregory argue that the interaction can only be successful if there is an element of trust, respect and reciprocity between the two girls, which has to be in a setting that facilitates such interaction. They see the learning context not as one in which the 'able' English speaker scaffolds the other, but as one in which a synergy is created, in which the roles of the more experienced and the novice are more complex.

Placing bilingual children together in one group is rarely appropriate and is in fact a form of withdrawal in the classroom rather than inclusion. Labelling them as 'the EAL group', which may be common practice, is demeaning and misguided.

To understand this you need to consider further what has been stated previously – that children learn best when engaged in activities with speakers of English who can model the language appropriate to the task and to the cognitive level of the child. A collaborative approach to learning is one that is recognised as good practice for all children, and a stimulating learning environment that allows for children to take risks can give positive support for the bilingual learner. However, although some of their learning needs may be similar to those pupils whose first language is English, they also have different linguistic needs, particularly at the early stages, by the fact that they are learning through another language and come from cultural backgrounds and communities where there may be differing expectations of education. This means that, even if you only have one or two bilingual learners in your class, it is still important to find out about them and consider their needs.

Another important factor is how you assess children's development of English. The first thing to note is that no formal assessment should be done too early and, even then, any assessment of language has to start from the understanding of the child acquiring EAL. All LAs and schools should have descriptors that show the developmental steps against which to build a picture of each bilingual learner's achievements in the new language. However, at the heart of this must be an understanding that proficiency in understanding written texts takes longer than the spoken language and this will vary depending on each child's age, educational background and other factors.

Cummins (1984a and b) distinguishes between 'basic interpersonal communicative skills' (BICS) and the aforementioned 'cognitive and academic language proficiency' (CALP). BICS refers to the oral fluency of the bilingual learner, which may take up to two years to achieve. CALP is more concerned with the demands of the curriculum, particularly in terms of literacy skills, which take longer – between five and seven years. This is somewhat dependent on when a bilingual learner begins to acquire a new language and whether or not he or she is already literate in the first. The main point is that you will often hear teachers say that a bilingual pupil is good at speaking and listening but, in spite of this fluency, finds writing and reading tasks harder than monolingual peers.

In summary, you need to consider several areas when planning for bilingual learners (Gravelle, 2000). The social, cultural, linguistic and cognitive aspects need to be teased out alongside the learner's previous experience. The demands of the task need to then be considered for you to decide what support is needed.

Types of support

For children new to English:

- give them time to adjust to the new situation and to tune into the new language – don't pressurise them to speak, but include them in the established routines and activities of the class, making them feel welcome;
- allow them to be silent if they choose to and know that this is fine;
- ensure activities are considered for their linguistic content – but keep the conceptual element at an appropriate challenging level for their age; ensure that activities are considered in terms of their cultural content and relate to previous learning and social experiences;
- centre activities around spoken English until confident that the child is able to engage with written texts through their own reading and writing; this may be quite soon with children in Key Stage 2 who are already literate;
- ensure that activities include active participation of the learners – stories, songs, rhymes, turn-taking games, investigative and problem-solving tasks with good-quality support materials provide opportunities to engage the child and give a scaffold for the linguistic component;
- consider supportive grouping with children who will provide a language model and be encouraging in a collaborative learning context;
- always have high expectations – look at what children can do, are interested in and enjoy.

For children more advanced in spoken English, but who need further support with accessing written texts, particularly in Key Stage 2:

■　give plenty of opportunities to discuss language and linguistic devices in a way that builds on the children's own interest of a range of fiction and non-fiction texts, and their own reading and writing;

■　engage in language play, such as jokes, riddles, jingles and tongue-twisters, which give an understanding of the subtleties and nuances of language and develop a colloquial fluency;

■　set up discussion groups around literature that encourage children to focus on the text to support their comments and questions;

■　consider close work with subject-related texts.

Task 6.5.3 **PLANNING AND TEACHING TO SUPPORT BILINGUAL LEARNERS IN ENGLISH**

Plan a sequence of activities (Foundation Stage) or a unit of work (Key Stages 1 and 2). Consider the points above that are relevant to your context and plan two or three tasks to support the different bilingual learners in your class. Also consider the learning culture of the classroom as well as specific activities.

WHAT ABOUT PARENTS AND THEIR EXPECTATIONS?

Partnership between home and school is crucial to ensure bilingual learners and their families get the best help they can for academic success. All parents want their children to do well in school and, for families settling in a new country, where the majority language is not their home language, there is an added dimension to achieving that success. All schools will have an admissions policy, which should include gathering information about the child's linguistic and educational background and which should be available to you.

Learning to speak, read and write English is high on the list of priorities for bilingual families and one role of the school is to discuss with parents how that is done and the support they can give. Being aware of the issues around how their children acquire English and the value of being bilingual is often a relief to parents who think maintaining their home language may be disadvantageous to learning English. We need to show it is not, emphasising that communication in the child's first language is the best way to support children's learning in school.

However, some parents of bilingual learners may not feel comfortable coming into school and there needs to be some positive engagement to change such a situation. A tried and tested approach is one of sharing stories, culture and customs at bookmaking workshops, involving children and their parents writing stories in different languages. Projects that involve the community groups that bring together parents, siblings and teachers to discuss issues, as well as research into the children's range of literacy practices, have revealed a great deal about children's language and literacy experiences outside school, which are rich and varied (Gregory, 1996; Sneddon, 2003).

The relationship between siblings is another aspect to be considered when making links between home and school. It may often be the older sibling who, once settled in school, is able to support the parents and the younger children in making sense of educational practices. For example, understanding the literacy practices of the home has frequently been recognised as a way of mediating the familiarity of home with the new world of the school. Once again, the sociocultural aspects of learning a new language and recognition of different cultural norms are crucial in our understanding of diversity.

AN INCLUSIVE CURRICULUM

What this unit has aimed to do is give you some insight into the positive opportunities bilingual learners and a linguistically diverse classroom can offer.

The National Curriculum (DfES 1999) recognises some of the issues explored here and states that teachers should ensure access to the curriculum and assessment. The current emphasis in the Primary Strategy (DfES 2003a) is one that offers an inclusive curriculum. The three principles outlined in the National Curriculum (1999) give the opportunity for schools and teachers to consider effective opportunities for bilingual learners:

- setting suitable learning challenges – learning objectives and personalised learning;
- responding to pupils' diverse needs – teaching strategies;
- overcoming potential barriers to learning and assessment for individuals and groups of pupils – meaningful access to the curriculum.

Such an approach in relation to bilingual learners needs:

- a whole-school commitment to raising achievement through inclusion;
- recognition and understanding of the knowledge, culture, previous education and language that bilingual pupils bring to school and the learning context;
- support for pupils to access the curriculum, adapting where necessary;
- partnership in teaching and learning.

Task 6.5.4 **COMMUNICATION AND LANGUAGE**

Read the paragraph on page 325 above concerning Cummins' (1984a and b) distinction between BICS and CALP.

- What do you consider to be the key points of Cummins' research?
- How do other models of bilingualism referred to in this unit relate to this?
- How do these ideas relate to other theories of learning that you know?
- From this reflection and analysis, consider in your planning and through assessment how you can scaffold the learning for those pupils who may be causing some concern in their progress in reading and, in particular, writing in English.

SUMMARY

How we address and support the needs of bilingual learners is a politically charged arena. Underachievement of certain minority ethnic groups continues to be an issue and, in spite of all the research into heightening our understanding of how pupils acquire an additional language, there have been no major structural changes to support this. We do not live in a culturally neutral society or one that is free from prejudice and racism. Socio-economic status is also a strong determiner of success and this range of causal factors cannot be tackled solely within education.

This picture makes it more important that the curriculum and the types of interaction we can establish in schools and classrooms should be there to promote academic success for all children. An integration into the mainstream, while clearly positive, must be done systematically and with appropriate resources, including bilingual teachers and assistants, if we are serious about supporting bilingual learners to achieve their potential. Therefore, a greater understanding among all teachers of bilingual children, their linguistic and cultural backgrounds, their families and communities is essential if any sense of social equity can be turned into positive achievement.

Therefore, as new teachers soon to enter the profession, it is crucial that you are aware of the issues in order to support your own planning for bilingual learners. It is not as daunting a task as is sometimes perceived. As discussed in this unit, it is not about a separate curriculum for children with a learning disability, but about an enhanced curriculum for all children within which there are varied opportunities for children to extend their linguistic repertoires.

A greater understanding about how bilingual learners acquire an additional language and develop literacy skills gives insight into how all children learn to read and write, and how talk in educational contexts is part of an extended literacy curriculum. As was stated at the beginning of this unit, the range of languages spoken in this society and the cultures and communities in which they thrive can only enrich our schools and the lives of all children to become more tolerant and understanding of the backgrounds, linguistic and cultural, that present us with such diversity.

ANNOTATED FURTHER READING

Baker, C. (2006) *Foundations of Bilingual Education and Bilingualism*, 4th edn, Clevedon: Multilingual Matters.

A very readable and engaging text, which discusses comprehensively issues of bilingualism, learning and diversity as well as educational policies. The author draws on a range of established research into what it means to be bilingual and how to address this in schools and classrooms. He also discusses such issues as language minorities and whether we should consider linguistic assimilation or diversity. There are also study and practical activities suitable for student teachers.

Department for Education and Skills (DfES) (2006) *Primary National Strategy: Excellence and Enjoyment: Learning and Teaching for Bilingual Children in the Primary Years: Professional Development Materials*, London: DfES.

Although this is aimed at qualified teachers, there are many materials in this pack that are also useful to student teachers. It contains lots of ideas for the classroom based on sound research into the needs of bilingual learners, both in EAL and wider linguistic and cultural aspects relevant to all children.

RELEVANT WEBSITES

Multiverse: Exploring Diversity and Achievement: www.multiverse.ac.uk

An excellent initial teacher education resource, supported by the Training and Development Agency for Schools (TDA), this website covers a wealth of resource materials to enhance the educational achievement of pupils from diverse backgrounds. This includes research articles, debates and ideas for the classroom. Look here for the current statistics for languages spoken in your LA.

Visit the companion website www.routledge.com/textbooks/ltps2e for:

■ additional questions for this unit;
■ links to useful websites relevant to this unit.

REFERENCES

Baker, C. (2006) *Foundations of Bilingual Education and Bilingualism*, 4th edn, Clevedon: Multilingual Matters.

Chen, Y. and Gregory, E. (2004) '"How do I read these words": bilingual exchange teaching between Cantonese-speaking peers', in E. Gregory, S. Long and D. Volk (eds) *Many Pathways to Literacy*, London: RoutledgeFalmer.

Cummins, J. (1984a) *Bilingualism and Special Education: Issues in Assessment and Pedagogy*, Clevedon: Multilingual Matters.

Cummins, J. (1984b) 'Wanted: a theoretical framework for relating language proficiency to academic achievement among bilingual pupils', in C. Rivera (ed.) *Language Proficiency and Academic Achievement*, Clevedon: Multilingual Matters.

Cummins, J. (2000) *Language. Power and Pedagogy: Bilingual Children in the Crossfire*, Bilingual Education and Bilingualism series, Clevedon: Multilingual Matters.

Cummins, J. and Swain, M. (1986) *Bilingualism in Education*, London: Longman.

Department for Children Schools and Families (DCSF) (2007) *School and Pupils in England*, London: HMSO.

Department for Education and Skills (DfES) (1999) *Raising the Attainment of Minority Ethnic Pupils*, London: Ofsted.

Department for Education and Skills (DfES) (2002) *Languages for All: Languages for Life: A Strategy for England*, London: DfES.

Department for Education and Skills (DfES) (2003a) *Excellence and Enjoyment: A Strategy for Primary Schools*, London: DfES.

Department for Education and Skills (DfES) (2003b) *Aiming High: Raising the Achievement of Minority Ethnic Pupils*, London: Ofsted.

Department for Education and Skills (DfES) (2005) *The Key Stage 2 Framework for Languages*, London: DfES.

Department for Education and Skills (DfES) (2006) *Primary National Strategy Excellence and Enjoyment: Learning and Teaching for Bilingual Children in the Primary Years*, Professional Development Materials, London, DfES.

Department for Education and Skills (DfES) (2006) *Ethnicity and Education: The Evidence on Minority Ethnic Children Aged 5–19*, Research Topic Paper, London: DfES.

Department for Education and Skills/Qualifications and Curriculum Authority (DfES/QCA) (1999) *The National Curriculum Handbook for Primary Teachers in England Key Stages 1 and 2*, London: DfES.

Department of Education and Science (DES) (1975) The Bullock Report: *A Language for Life*, London: HMSO.

Department of Education and Science (DES) (1985) The Swann Report: *Education for All*, London: HMSO.

Gillborn, D. and Gipps, C. (1996) *Recent Research on the Achievements of Ethnic Minority Pupils*, London: Ofsted.

Gravelle, M. (ed.) (2000) *Planning for Bilingual Learners*, Stoke-on-Trent: Trentham Books.

Gregory, E. (1996) *Making Sense of a New World*, London: Paul Chapman Publishing.

Hall, D. (2001) *Assessing the Needs of Bilingual Learners Living in Two Languages*, 2nd edn, London: David Fulton.

Lambert, W.E. (1974) 'Culture and language as factors in learning and education', in F.E. Aboud and R.D. Meade *Cultural Factors in Learning and Education*, Bellingham, WA: Fifth Western Washington Symposium on Learning.

Levine, J. (ed) (1990) *Bilingual Learners and the Mainstream Curriculum*, London: Falmer.

Macpherson of Cluny, Sir William (1999) *The Stephen Lawrence Inquiry*, London: The Stationary Office, HMSO.

Sneddon, R. (2003) 'What Language do you speak at home?', in *The Best of Language Matters*, London: CLPE.

UNESCO (2003) *Education in a Multilingual World*, Education Position Paper, Paris: UNESCO.

7 RECENT DEVELOPMENTS

PERSONALISED LEARNING AND PUPIL VOICE

Carol Robinson

INTRODUCTION

In recent years there has been a growing move within the UK, as well as in other countries, to consider learners' perspectives and 'voices' on aspects of school-related issues, including learning and teaching. Learner voice work involves engaging with learners about issues that matter to them and that affect their experiences in school. This unit focuses on 'learner voice', what it 'looks like' in the school context and the significance of it for both teachers and learners. Stemming from work around learner voice and closely linked to this is the 'personalisation of learning', which involves learning being 'personalised' to suit the learning needs of individuals. Personalised learning is not about giving each child individual work, but more about allowing learners to have a say in how they would like to learn and in them taking on some responsibility for their own learning. Within this unit we start by outlining factors that have led to an increased importance now being placed on learners' voices. We then go on to identify ways in which teachers can listen to the voices of those they teach and consider how implementing such practices can enhance learner engagement and, as a result, improve the learning and experiences of young people in schools. We also consider the benefits of learner voice work from teachers' perspectives and give ideas on how teachers can work towards implementing personalising learning strategies within school.

OBJECTIVES

By the end of this unit you should:

- understand the terms 'learner voice' and 'personalised learning' and have an insight into the origins of this work;
- be familiar with school practices that promote, and those that inhibit, listening to learners' voices and the personalisation of learning;
- be aware of the benefits, for both teachers and learners, of incorporating learner voice and personalised learning work within school practices;
- have developed ideas about how you can listen to learners within your school, with a view to enhancing their engagement in, and enjoyment of, lessons.

WHAT DO WE MEAN BY 'LEARNER VOICE' WORK?

The term 'learner voice', also referred to as 'student voice' or 'pupil voice', refers to the move to consult learners and provide opportunities for learners to voice opinions about things that matter to them and that affect their learning and other school experiences. It is about teachers and other adults in schools wanting to know and learn from and about learners' experiences and is concerned with encouraging learners to participate in, and voice their opinions on, any issues that impact on their life in school. In extreme cases, in schools where learner voice work is fully embraced, this can result in schools being run in a democratic way, with learners' voices being equal to those of the adults in the school. In such cases, learners would have the opportunity to be involved in the decision-making processes of all aspects of schooling, including, for example, policy, financial and environmental decisions, as well as decisions about teaching and learning. For the purpose of our work in this unit, however, the terms 'learner voice' and 'pupil voice' will concentrate on learners' perceptions of issues around teaching and learning. They will be used to refer to cases where learners are given opportunities to voice their views and where the views of learners are specifically sought by teachers and other adults on matters relating to their learning and school experiences and where these views have the potential to influence teachers' pedagogies and practices.

LEGISLATION PROMPTING THE MOVE TOWARDS LISTENING TO LEARNERS

Agencies working with young people and government departments in a number of countries, including Australia, Canada, New Zealand, the UK and the USA, have placed an increasing importance on learners' voices in recent years. Much of this work has stemmed from the United Nations Convention on the Rights of the Child (UNCRC) (UN, 1989). In particular, Article 12 of the UNCRC states:

> Parties shall assure to the child who is capable of forming his or her own views the right to express those views freely on all matters affecting the child, the views of the child being given due weight in accordance with the age and maturity of the child.

Since this time there have been a number of acts and reforms within England that have recognised and promoted the importance of listening to young people in schools. These include the Education Act 2002 (DfES, 2002), which requires that schools consult with pupils; regulations for Ofsted inspections, which now expect inspectors to report on the degree to which schools seek and act upon the views of learners (Ofsted, 2005); and the expectations of the self-evaluation form (SEF), which all schools are now required to complete on an annual basis and which includes a section that asks: 'What are the views of learners, parents, carers and other stakeholders and how do you know?'

In addition, in 2003 the Department for Education and Skills (DfES) prepared a document entitled *Working Together: Giving Children and Young People a Say*. Within this, it drew up draft guidance notes on pupil participation. This guidance was designed to help schools and local authorities organise opportunities for pupils to develop their 'skills as active citizens' and to prepare them for involvement in decision-making processes (Rudduck and McIntyre, 2007: 8). Following this, in 2004 the government published *Every Child Matters: Change for Children* (DfES, 2004a), which brings together all the ways in which public services are working towards improved outcomes for children, young people and families into a national framework. Central to the *Every Child Matters* (ECM) legislation is that all children should have a say in decisions affecting their lives.

More recently, the voices and views of children and young people have informed the government's *Children's Plan* (DCSF, 2007). This plan reflects the general principles of the UNCRC and is aligned to the five ECM outcomes. Thus the importance of pupil participation is now reflected in the ECM agenda, making pupil voice work a recognised part of working with young people.

There has also been major investment in terms of research funding into issues around consulting pupils; in particular, the Economic and Social Research Council (ESRC)-funded project, *Consulting Pupils about Teaching and Learning* (www.consultingpupils.co.uk/) mapped the territory for the potential of consulting pupils and responded to teachers' needs for basic guidance in this area.

WHY IS IT SO IMPORTANT TO LISTEN TO LEARNERS?

Imagine a classroom in which teachers teach only what they think learners ought to know, where there is no space for learners to ask questions or voice opinions on areas of interest to them, where learners are not encouraged to learn through discovery, and where learners are simply passive recipients within a process. Alternatively, imagine a school in which learners feel listened to, respected and valued as individuals, where their views are important to the teachers they work with, where teachers want to know what interests and motivates the learners and where learners feel confident about taking responsibility for aspects of their learning – a school in which learners are encouraged to participate in assessing their work and setting future goals and where learners feel a sense of belonging to the classroom and the wider school.

Task 7.1.1 LEARNING ENVIRONMENTS

Of the two situations described above, in which of these would you expect learners to thrive? Why?

Task 7.1.2 TAKING PUPIL VOICE WORK FORWARD IN YOUR CLASSROOM

■ Define what you understand by the term 'pupil voice work'. Reflect on your experiences of pupil voice work in the classroom to date. Which learners participate? In what ways do they participate?

■ Identify one area of your work in the classroom in which you would like to move learner voice work forward (this could relate to either a curriculum area or an aspect of your practice, such as assessment). What do you hope to achieve by involving learners? What steps will you take to ensure the voices of all learners are heard?

HOW CAN LISTENING TO LEARNERS BENEFIT THEM?

Children and young people tend to enjoy school more when they are listened to and their views are taken seriously, when they are treated with respect and when they feel valued and included. Where schools enable learners to become active participants in the school and in their learning, and learners are provided with opportunities for them to have a say in their learning, this is more likely to result in them developing a sense of belonging to the school. Flutter and Rudduck (2004: 7–8), report on findings from Jelly *et al.* (2000), who consulted pupils in a special needs school. They found clear evidence that consulting young learners about their learning enhanced self-esteem and confidence, promoted stronger engagement and motivation to learn and encouraged pupils to become more active members of the school community. Similarly, Rudduck and McIntyre (2007: 152) found that pupil consultation tends to enhance pupils' commitment to and capacity for learning through strengthening self-esteem, enhancing attitudes to school and learning, developing a strong sense of membership and developing new skills for learning.

HOW CAN LISTENING TO LEARNERS BENEFIT TEACHERS?

Bragg and Fielding (2005) found that learners can give valuable feedback to teachers, which in turn can inform their future practice. Where learners' views are heard on teaching and learning issues, you and other supportive adults in school can gain an insight into learners' perspectives on what helps and what hinders their learning. Finding out about learners' perspectives on aspects of their school experiences, including learning, may take you outside your comfort zone in terms of the sort of dialogue you want to engage in with learners. The outcome of listening to learners, however, can be hugely beneficial, as you are able to receive helpful feedback that can increase your awareness of the learning needs of those you teach. An increased understanding and awareness of how pupils learn can be of great help when analysing and reflecting on your own performance and can serve to help inform and improve your own practice. Research has found that, where teachers listen to learners' opinions, this results in them being able to understand more easily how pupils learn most effectively and, as a result, leads teachers to reconsider and make changes to aspects of their own teaching practice (Flutter and Rudduck, 2004). Rudduck and McIntyre (2007) found that consultations with learners can lead to improved teacher awareness of pupils' capacities for learning; it can help teachers gain new perspectives and a renewed excitement about their teaching. A further benefit of consulting with learners is that, in most cases, a more collaborative relationship between the teacher and learners tends to develop, the outcome of which is likely to lead to improvements in the quality of pupil learning. Thus, the better you understand learners and their learning, the more effective your teaching and their learning will be.

Learner voice work is about teachers learning from learners about ways in which their teaching can become more effective and more meaningful to the learners. Creating listening classrooms can create a positive culture within the school and help teachers to identify factors that contribute towards helping pupils' learning and their enjoyment of learning, as well as identifying factors that create barriers to learning. Thus, learner consultations have the potential to transform teacher–learner relationships, to improve the conditions of learning and to lead to improvements in teachers' practices. They can also lead to learners having a new sense of themselves as members of a community of learners.

WHAT DOES PUPIL VOICE WORK LOOK LIKE IN SCHOOLS?

The processes involved in listening to learners within school should be more than features of inspection frameworks and merely ticking boxes on the SEF about learners' involvement and participation in school. Genuine learner voice work involves listening to learners about matters that are important to them, not just issues about which you and other adults in the school want to know.

In order to build 'listening schools', positive working relationships between teachers and learners are crucial. Learner voice work is based on the assumption that the adults and young people in the schools will engage with each other in positive and supportive ways. A great deal of literature has stressed the value of listening to young peoples' views and details the processes implemented by schools to develop a deeper understanding of how the voices of young people can be encouraged (Rudduck *et al.*, 1996; Fielding, 2001; MacBeath *et al.*, 2003; Rudduck and Flutter, 2004).

Some schools have a school council and many run circle times during which teachers listen to learners' perspectives on particular issues. In addition, some schools encourage 'pupils as researchers' projects, which involve learners conducting their own research within schools. The aim of these projects is to determine the opinions of others on issues important to the pupils, with a view to making changes in school as a result of the research findings. However, for pupil voice work to be embraced in a school, opportunities should be created for all learners to voice their opinions on all school issues of importance to them. There should be a real desire for teachers to hear learners' perceptions on any aspect of their school experience and to listen to the ideas they have on how to enhance these experiences. Learners can be involved in making decisions about the running of the school by, for example, taking on pupil governors' roles and by participating in management committees. Learners' views can also be listened to in 'formal' ways through, for example, questionnaires, surveys, focus groups, ballots and elections, sentence completion, drawing, paintings and photos, role-play, conversations, logs, video replay and posting views in boxes. However, in order to create a 'listening school', alongside these 'formal', specific means of listening to learners, teachers can encourage a culture of learner participation in the classroom by engaging with learners about pedagogy and practice in a way that empowers learners. For example, pupils can be invited to comment on their learning as well as on the teaching strategies and conditions for learning (Rudduck and McIntyre, 2007). You, as the teacher, can pose simple questions to learners during your day-to-day working with them in order to determine their perceptions of what motivates/demotivates them, what enhances/diminishes their enjoyment of lessons and what increases/reduces barriers to learners engaging in learning.

Task 7.1.3 **MOTIVATING LEARNERS**

Think about what interests you and motivates you to learn. Do you know what interests and motivates learners in your class? If not, spend some time finding out. You might ask learners, either individually, in small groups or as a class group:

■ What activities help you to learn best? Why?
■ Which activities do you enjoy the most? Why?
■ What stops you from learning? Why?
■ What would your ideal lesson be like? Why?

WITH WHOM AND HOW DOES LEARNER VOICE WORK HAPPEN?

When thinking about learner voice work it is important to remember that there is more than one voice; there are as many voices as there are learners and care must be taken to listen to the voices of all learners, not just the articulate, able, elite minority and those familiar with the language used by teachers. The views of all learners, including minority groups and less positive learners, are important.

Schools need to develop practices to encourage learners to voice opinions and to encourage the adults who work with them to listen to learners as part of their everyday practice. When talking to learners about their perspectives, learners should be allowed to speak freely and feel at ease to say what is on their mind, rather than feeling they ought to say what they think you or other adults want to hear. Learners need to know that, if they express their views, they will be taken seriously and this won't be held against them, no matter how controversial their views are.

Fielding (2008) suggests some questions for teachers to consider when embarking on learner voice work, for example: Who is allowed to speak? To whom? What are they allowed to speak about? What language is encouraged or allowed? Who decides the answers to these questions? How are those decisions made? How, when, where, to whom and how often are these decisions communicated? In relation to listening he suggests we ask: Who is listening? How and why?

When planning consultations with learners, in order to help think of ways to make learner consultations inclusive for all learners, it would be beneficial to ask yourself the above questions.

Task 7.1.4 **WHO GETS LISTENED TO? ABOUT WHAT?**

Consider the processes currently in place to listen to learners in your classroom about:

■ environmental issues, such as the school toilets or the playground;
■ learning and teaching issues;
■ policy/organisational issues.

Whose voice gets listened to? How often? How can less assertive and less confident learners be encouraged to participate and have more of a say in each of the above?

LEARNER PARTICIPATION

For learner voice work to be effective there needs to be a degree of learner participation; that is, adults and learners need to work together to ensure the voices and views of learners are heard and valued in relation to decisions that affect them. In 2008, the Department for Children, Schools and Families produced a booklet entitled *Working Together: Listening to the Voices of Children and Young People* (DCSF, 2008a). Within this, it suggested that different levels of learner participation take place in schools. Drawing on work by Shier (2000), it advocated that levels of learner participation could be viewed as shown in Figure 7.1.1.

Task 7.1.5 **LEVELS OF LEARNER PARTICIPATION**

■ At which level would you position the learners you teach?
■ Does this position vary in different circumstances? If so, why?
■ Think about the way you engage with learners on one specific aspect of work, e.g. the teaching of numeracy. At what level would you currently position the learners? Where would you like to position them in six months' time? What steps can you take to achieve this?

As we have seen, a key element of learner voice work is learner participation. Learner participation is also of great significance in the personalisation of learning, a specific aspect of learner voice work; learning cannot be personalised unless teachers and other adults in school engage

Children share power and responsibility for decision-making

Children are involved in the decision-making process

Children's views are taken into account

Increasing empowerment and responsibility

Children are supported in expressing their views

Children are listened to

■ **Figure 7.1.1** Levels of participation
Source: From DCFS (2008a: 5)

Task 7.1.6 **DEVELOPING LEARNER VOICE WORK IN THE WIDER SCHOOL CONTEXT**

■ What do you consider to be the main principles of learner voice work in relation to the wider school context (i.e. beyond the classroom setting)? In what ways do these correspond and/or conflict with your school's values and aims?

■ Using *Working Together: Listening to the Voices of Children and Young People* (DCFS, 2008a), under the section 'Principles into practice' (pp. 11–18), identify at least one way in which you could enhance pupils' involvement in your school. What steps could be taken to ensure that all pupils are given an equal chance of involvement? Can you foresee any barriers to their involvement? If so, how might these be overcome?

with learners. The personalisation of learning responds to learners' voices by building on pupils' prior learning and by considering the needs, aspirations and interests of learners.

WHAT DO WE MEAN BY PERSONALISED LEARNING?

The national policy on personalised learning in England was launched in 2004, when David Miliband described personalised learning as:

high expectations of every child, given practical form by high quality teaching based on a sound knowledge and understanding of each child's needs. It is not individualised learning where pupils sit alone. Nor is it pupils left to their own devices – which too often reinforces low aspirations. It means shaping teaching around the way different youngsters learn, it means taking care to nurture the unique talents of every pupil.

(Miliband, 2004: 3)

Underwood *et al.* (2007) sum up what is essentially implied in Miliband's and other definitions in a succinct way. Drawing on some of the working of the original Miliband speech, they defined personalised learning as:

The tailoring of pedagogy, curriculum, and learning support to meet the needs and aspirations of individual learners irrespective of ability, culture or social status in order to nurture the unique talents of every pupil.

(p. 13)

The personalisation of learning can involve learners having a say in the ways in which they learn by giving them the opportunity to, for example, decide what they would like to learn and choose how to present their work. The key challenge for the teacher with regard to the personalisation of learning is how to cater simultaneously for all the different needs of learners in one class.

WHAT DOES PERSONALISED LEARNING LOOK LIKE IN SCHOOLS?

For teachers to promote the personalisation of learning, they need information about the attainment and past progress of each of the learners they work with. Learning can then be personalised by learners, with the help of teachers if need be, identifying specific targets for them to work towards and deciding upon the best pedagogic approach to meet these targets. Within a 'personalised learning' classroom, learners have regular opportunities to discuss their progress with teachers, and teachers actively involve learners in the setting and reviewing of their progress towards these targets. Personalised learning approaches place demands on learners to be involved in their learning and in the decision-making processes about their learning. When using personalising learning techniques, there may be more diverse demands made of space within the classroom and the school generally, to respond to the needs and demands of learners.

For the personalisation of learning to be meaningful, learners need to be involved in the assessment of their work; that is, learners need to be equipped with the necessary skills to help them judge the quality of their work, and they need to be aware of what they are doing well, what they need to improve on and how they can work towards improving their work. Research by Black *et al.* (2002) demonstrated that learning is dramatically enhanced when learners know what it is they are aiming for and they do even better when they play some part in deciding how to set about achieving their aims.

According to the National College of School Leadership (NCSL) (now the National College for Leadership of Schools and Children's Services), personalising learning is a process in which learners are empowered with appropriate support and advice to decide what, where, when and how they learn. The NCSL considers the process of personalised learning to be made up of the following five key components:

1   *Learning how to learn* – 'Giving learners skills, strategies and procedures to enable them to become meta-cognitive and self-managing learners.'
2   *Assessment for learning* – 'Developing a wide range of assessment strategies, which place the emphasis on formative rather than summative approaches by engaging the learner in the

assessment process.' When employing assessment for learning strategies as a means of personalising learning, teachers and learners use data relating to the learners' attainment and progress to help define future targets for learners to work towards. They also make decisions about the most appropriate way for the learners to achieve these targets.

3   *Teaching and learning strategies* – 'Providing learners with a wide range of appropriate options to enable them to learn in the most effective way for them to experience the full portfolio of teaching and learning strategies.' Personalised learning aims to help learners to understand themselves as learners and to take some responsibility for, and control of, their learning.

4   *Curriculum choice* – 'This involves changing the curriculum experience from the 'set meal' to the 'à la carte' menu. Pupils are given increasing choice as to what they study and when they study it.' If learning is to be personalised, there needs to be some degree of flexibility in the curriculum to allow for learning to be tailored to the needs and interests of learners.

5   *Mentoring and support* – 'The one-to-one relationship is central to any model of personalising learning – it is the most powerful expression of a commitment to the learning of the individual. Mentoring may be used to monitor academic progress, support meta-cognition and provide focused support for aspects of the curriculum.'

(Quoted sections from NCSL, 2009)

Personalised learning takes into account prior learning and provides opportunities for learners to have some say in what, when and how they learn – a system that responds to individual pupils by creating an education path that takes account of their needs, interests and aspirations (DfES, 2004b: 7).

Task 7.1.7 **PERSONALISING LEARNING**

Think about a lesson you have recently conducted. Did the lesson give learners the opportunity:

(a) to have responsibility for deciding at what level to learn;
(b) to assess what they had learned?

If yes, what key factors needed to be in place for both (a) and (b) to happen? If no, how could you have planned the lesson differently to allow both (a) and (b) to happen?

BARRIERS TO LEARNER VOICE WORK AND THE PERSONALISATION OF LEARNING

For teachers, listening to the voices of learners means facing up to being open to criticism, which can generate personal and interpersonal insecurities. Teachers may be anxious about learners' criticism of aspects of their work and may be wary of the unpredictability of learners' comments and views.

As teachers, you may lack support from others in your school to work towards encouraging learner voice and personalising learning, and you may feel constrained due to the pressure of the curriculum you are expected to get through and feel you lack time to listen to learners as well. Some teachers may not agree with learners being given opportunities to express their opinions in relation to teaching and learning issues. They may believe that learners are not capable or mature enough to be consulted about teaching and may want full control of this aspect of their work and learning process. Some teachers may resent learners' voices being listened to if they feel they are listened to more than theirs. A further barrier to learner voice work and the personalisation of learning is the existence of power relations between staff and pupils in schools; this significantly affects the degree to which learners participate in school decision making, and the degree to which they feel valued as members of the school community. The greater the existence of the power relations, the less likely it is that learners will feel at ease to voice their opinions, especially in areas such as learning and teaching, which have traditionally been seen as a domain fully controlled by teachers.

Task 7.1.8 **DEVELOPING THE PERSONALISATION OF LEARNING**

■ Identify ways in which you could develop the personalisation of learning within one curriculum area throughout (a) next term and (b) next year.
■ Which learners or groups of learners do you think will be the most difficult to reach? What can you do to help reach these groups?
■ What resources/training would be of help to you in order to facilitate taking the personalisation of learning forward in your school?

Task 7.1.9 **ENHANCING THE DEGREE OF PERSONALISED LEARNING**

■ What are the main principles of personalised learning?
■ With reference to *Personalised Learning: A Practical Guide* (DCFS, 2008b), study the nine key features of personalised learning as outlined in the diagram on page 7.
■ Choose one feature that, if developed in your school, would greatly enhance the degree of personalised learning. Identify ways you could develop this feature (a) within your classroom setting and (b) within the wider school context.
■ Would you foresee any barriers to taking this work forward? If so, how might these be overcome?

SUMMARY

This unit has given you an introduction to how work around learner voice and the personalisation of learning can be incorporated into everyday classroom practices. If learner voice work is to be taken seriously and become embedded within your school, opportunities need to be provided for learners to be given a voice on all aspects of their school life. If schools are to listen to the whole body of learners, they need to acknowledge that there are multiple voices and that these voices are constantly changing. There should not be situations where schools favour only those with a language and culture similar to that of the school, or favour those with whom the school agrees.

The personalisation of learning promotes confidence and capacity building in individual learners. It gives learners some power over what and how they learn and encourages learners to take more responsibility for their learning, from the setting of targets to assessing their work. One of the demands of learner voice work and the personalisation of learning is to challenge the structures and processes of power that create barriers to the voices of learners being heard. It may be that, in some schools, teachers and learners will need to change their understanding of what it is to be a teacher and what it is to be a learner, in order to allow learners' voices and the personalisation of learning to play a more significant role.

ANNOTATED FURTHER READING

Arnot, M., McIntyre, D., Pedder, D. and Reay, D. (2004) *Consultation in the Classroom: Developing Dialogue about Teaching and Learning*, Cambridge: Pearson.
The book offers guidance on different aspects of pupil consultation and participation and reports on two projects, conducted within the UK, that were concerned with consulting pupils about their teaching and learning. It gives examples of learners' responses when questioned about issues relating to their learning. The book gives concrete examples of how the voices of learners can appropriately contribute to work in schools.

Department for Children, Schools and Families (DCSF) (2008) *Personalised Learning: A Practical Guide*, DCFS-00844-2008, London: DCFS.
This publication discusses the key features of personalised learning and how these can be promoted in schools. It covers, among other areas, target setting and tracking, assessment, pupil grouping, curriculum organisation and the extended curriculum. The publication was developed to support schools in implementing personalised learning and to help them move to a system based on progression, underpinned by assessment for learning, with relevant interventions such as one-to-one support.

Department for Children, Schools and Families (DCSF) (2008) *Working Together: Listening to the Voices of Children and Young People*, DCFS-00410-2008, London: DCFS.
This guidance discusses the principles and benefits of learner participation and outlines a range of opportunities that can be provided by schools to increase levels of learner participation.

Department for Education and Skills (DfES) (2004) *A National Conversation about Personalised Learning*, DfES/0919/2004, London: DfES.
This is a booklet intended to provide adults in schools with an understanding of, and ideas about, how personalising learning strategies can be developed. The booklet describes and outlines the key concepts of personalisation and personalised learning.

Fielding, M. and Bragg, S. (2003) *Students and Researchers: Making a Difference*, Cambridge: Pearson.
This comprises a book and DVD and includes guidance about how to provide training in research for students and how to run 'students as researchers' projects in schools. It contains actual examples of enquiries conducted by students and the impact of their work, including examples of enquiries into learning and the conditions for learning.

MacBeath, J., Demetriou, H., Rudduck, J. with Myers, K. (2003) *Consulting Pupils: A Toolkit for Teachers*, Cambridge: Pearson.
This book gives a range of examples of manageable consultation strategies for teachers to use with learners. The strategies include both written and talk-based approaches to consultations with young people in schools.

RELEVANT WEBSITES

Economic and Social Research Council (ESRC), *Consulting Pupils about Teaching and Learning* project: www.consultingpupils.co.uk/
National College for Leadership of Schools and Children's Services (formerly National College of School Leadership (NCSL)): personalised learning: www.nationalcollege.org.uk/index/leadershiplibrary/leadingschools/

Follow the links on this website to find ideas about how to make personalised learning real in schools. It includes videos, case studies and activities for schools to learn from and addresses such questions as: Why personalise learning? What is personalising learning?

Standards Site: Pupil Voice themes: www.standards.dfes.gov.uk/research/themes/pupil_voice/
Included here is a number of digests on pupil voice research, including one on 'Pupils as partners in learning'.

Teachers TV: www.teachers.tv/video/32624
This website includes videos of how special schools have enabled pupils to express their choices about their lives and learning. It also has links to various support materials.

Visit the companion website www.routledge.com/textbooks/ltps2e for:

■ additional questions for this unit;
■ links to useful websites relevant to this unit.

REFERENCES

Black, P., Harrison, C., Lee, C., Marshall, B. and Wiliam, D. (2002) *Working Inside the Black Box: Assessment for Learning in the Classroom*, London: Department of Education and Professional Studies, King's College, University of London.

Bragg, S. and Fielding, M. (2005) '"It's an equal thing . . . it's about achieving together": student voice and the possibility of radical collegiality', in H. Street and J. Temperley (eds) *Improving Schools Through Collaborative Enquiry*, London: Continuum. pp. 105–34.

Department for Children, Schools and Families (DCSF) (2008a) *Working Together: Listening to the Voices of Children and Young People*, DCSF-00410-2008, London: DCSF.

Department for Children, Schools and Families (DCSF) (2008b) *Personalised Learning: A Practical Guide*, DCSF-00844-2008, London: DCSF.

Department for Children, Schools and Families (DCSF) (2007) *The Children's Plan: Building Brighter Futures: Summary*, Norwich: The Stationery Office.

Department for Education and Skills (DfES) (2002) *The Education Act Statutory Instrument 2002*, London: DfES.

Department for Education and Skills (DfES) (2003) *Working Together: Giving Children and Young People a Say*, DfES/0492/2003, Nottingham: DfES.

Department for Education and Skills (DfES) (2004a) *Every Child Matters: Change for Children*, DfES/1081/2004, Nottingham: DfES.

Department for Education and Skills (DfES) (2004b) *A National Conversation about Personalised Learning*, DfES/0919/2004, London: DfES.

Fielding, M. (2001) 'Students as radical agents of change', *Journal of Educational Change*, 2: 123–41.

Fielding, M. (2008) 'Interrogating student voice: pre-occupations, purposes and possibilities', in H. Daniels, H. Lauder and J. Porter (eds) *The Routledge Companion to Education*, London: Routledge.

Flutter, J. and Rudduck, J. (2004) *Consulting Pupils: What's In It for Schools?*, London: Routledge Falmer.

MacBeath, J., Demetriou, H., Rudduck, J. And Myres, K. (2003) *Consulting Pupils: A Toolkit for Teachers*, Cambridge: Pearson.

Miliband, D. (2004) *Personalised Learning: Building a New Relationship with Schools*, Speech at the North of England Education Conference, Belfast, 8 January, London: DfES. Available online at http://publications.teachernet.gov.uk (accessed November 2009).

National College for Leadership of Schools and Children's Services (formerly NCSL) (2009) *Key Components of Personalised Learning*. Available online at www.nationalcollege.org.uk/index/leadershiplibrary/leadingschools (accessed November 2009).

Office for Standards in Education (Ofsted) (2005) *Conducting the Inspection: Guidance for Inspectors of Schools*, HMI 5202, London: Ofsted.

Rudduck, J. and Flutter, J. (2004) *How to Improve your School: Giving Pupils a Voice*, London: Continuum.

Rudduck, J. and McIntyre, D. (2007) *Improving Learning Through Consulting Pupils*, London: Routledge.

Rudduck, J., Chaplain, R. And Wallace, G. (1996) *School Improvement: What Can Pupils Tell Us?*, London: David Fulton.

Underwood, J., Baguley, T., Banyard, P., Coyne, E., Farrington-Flint, L. and Selwood, I. (2007) *Impact 2007: Personalising Learning with Technology*, Coventry: Becta.

United Nations (UN) (1989) *UN Convention on the Rights of the Child: General Assembly Resolution 44/25*, New York: United Nations.

LEARNING AND TEACHING LANGUAGES

Carrie Cable

INTRODUCTION

Many primary schools are now teaching languages and some have been doing so for many years. Language is very closely linked to identity and developing children's knowledge about language and their language skills will help learning across the curriculum. Languages are often seen as a means of enriching the curriculum and, increasingly, as a means of responding to diversity within our society and preparing children for participation in an increasingly globalised world. Languages can also make an important contribution to helping children achieve at least three of the core outcomes within the *Every Child Matters* agenda: enjoying and achieving, making a positive contribution and achieving economic well-being (DfES, 2003).

Teachers are often enthusiastic about teaching languages, either because they are linguists, because they have some facility in languages or because they feel they missed out on learning languages during their own school days. Learning languages and learning about languages in primary schools is not simply a preparation for more intensive study at secondary schools, but an opportunity to develop children's interest in, and enthusiasm for, languages and language learning in a context in which there are opportunities for more holistic and cross-curricular learning. While each school has the freedom to organise the teaching of languages in a way that best suits its situation, all primary teachers need to be able to teach languages to their classes either as discrete lessons or by reinforcing the teaching of specialist teachers and through developing language awareness and intercultural understanding.

OBJECTIVES

By the end of this unit you should have:

■ reflected on your own knowledge of languages and how you developed this knowledge;
■ developed your understanding of the importance of languages in society;
■ increased your understanding of the place and importance of languages in the primary curriculum;
■ increased your range of approaches to teaching languages.

HISTORY AND CONTEXT

Language teaching in primary schools is not new and some readers may remember learning languages when they were at primary school. However, the publication of the Burstall Report (Burstall, 1974), a longitudinal study of children's attitudes and performance, which suggested that children gained little from starting their study of languages prior to secondary school, had a major impact on primary provision across the country in the latter part of the twentieth century. It was not until the introduction of a National Curriculum at the turn of the century that guidelines and schemes of work for the teaching of languages were produced (DfEE/QCA, 1999; QCA, 2000), although these were non-statutory. The publication of *Languages for All: Languages for Life* (DfES, 2002) was a significant turning point, as the government accepted that there were strong social, economic and political arguments for learning languages:

> In the knowledge society of the 21st Century, language competence and intercultural understanding are not optional extras; they are an essential part of being a citizen. Language skills are also vital in improving understanding between people here and in the wider world, and in supporting global citizenship by breaking down barriers of ignorance, and suspicion between nations.

> (DfES, 2002:12)

As a result, the English government made a decision to introduce language teaching in Key Stage 2, for Years 3 to 6, although many schools have decided to also teach languages to children in reception classes and Key Stage 1:

> Every child should have the opportunity throughout Key Stage 2 to study a foreign language and develop their interest in the culture of other nations. They should have access to high quality teaching and learning opportunities, making use of native speakers and e-learning. By age 11 they should have the opportunity to reach a recognised level of competence on the Common European Framework and for that achievement to be recognised through a national scheme. The Key Stage 2 language learning programme must include at least one of the working languages of the European Union and be delivered at least in part in class time.

> (DfES, 2002: 15)

There has long been a debate about the optimum age at which to start learning another language, with some arguing for an early start because young children are more open to new experiences and others arguing that older learners can learn quickly because they have more finely developed language-learning strategies. Edelenbos *et al.* (2006), in a report for the European Commission, state:

> Empirical evidence has not yet definitively established an 'optimum age' for starting a foreign language. An early start offers a longer overall period of learning and has the potential to influence children's personal development when they are still at a highly developmental stage. However, an earlier start means an increase in the importance of continuity from one year to another. On its own, an early start is unlikely to make a substantial difference. These chances will improve if an early start is accompanied by quality teaching from teachers who have developed the required range of knowledge and skills.

> (p. 26)

Ironically, at the same time as proposals to introduce language learning into primary school were being considered, proposals to reduce the mandatory curriculum in secondary schools were also being considered and, in 2004, learning a language at Key Stage 4 ceased to be a mandatory part of the curriculum.

In Scotland and Northern Ireland, Gaelic and Irish have been introduced as subjects in the curriculum or the medium of instruction in some schools and English is taught as a second language. However, a study on the provision of community languages in Scotland (Buie, 2006) found 'a wide disparity in the well-developed resources and support available for Gaelic, compared to the minimal support for other indigenous languages such as Scots, including Doric, British Sign Language, and the language of travellers', and the picture is similar in other parts of the UK. In Wales in 2005–06, 20 per cent of primary-aged children were learning in Welsh-medium schools while the rest learned Welsh as a second language (Welsh Language Board: www.byig-wlb.org.uk). Children in the upper primary years in Scotland have the opportunity to learn another language and proposals are to be introduced for children to learn languages in primary schools in Wales. However, the study of community languages across the UK rarely takes place in mainstream schools. English is the main language taught in the majority of schools in Europe, largely because of the position of English as a global language. However, children in many European countries study a language for longer and for more hours in total than children in the UK (DfES, 2006; Edelenbos, 2006).

Task 7.2.1 REFLECTION ON LEARNING LANGUAGES

■ Think about your own experience of learning another language at home or in school. What made this a successful experience for you?

■ Think about your competence in another language. How does this make you feel?

Jot down your ideas and share them with colleagues.

METHODS AND APPROACHES

Approaches to learning and teaching languages have changed over time and have been influenced by different theories of learning and theories of learning language. You can explore these further in either of the annotated readings at the end of this unit. However, elements of many of the approaches briefly described below are evident in the teaching and learning of languages in primary schools today and in other language learning situations.

Grammar-translation method

This involves translating words and sentences from a text into English; instruction is in English and pupils aren't expected to learn to speak the language. Some teachers still use elements of this method when they draw attention to grammatical features in texts and ask children to translate words and phrases.

Direct method

This involves associating objects or visual representations with the word or phrase in the language being learned. The emphasis is on learning to speak the language and the use of English is discouraged.

Audiolingual method

This draws on behaviourist theories of learning and views language as a set of skills and procedures, which can be automated. It involves the repeated practice of words and phrases through drills and dialogues with the substitution of new vocabulary. There is a focus on correct sentence forms and correct pronunciation. The approach is often associated with language laboratories.

Total physical response

This emphasises listening comprehension and involves learners in listening to the spoken language a number of times before being required to speak. The teacher provides an association to go with different words and phrases, often an action, and learners are required to carry out the action or respond in some way when they hear the word or phrase to show they have understood. This method also draws on behaviourist theories of learning.

The big change in approaches to language teaching is relatively recent and relates to views of learners as active participants rather than passive recipients and the purpose of language learning to be some form of meaningful communication. Over time the importance of the social context in which the learning is taking place and the language is to be used has also become influential.

Communicative approach

This emphasises speaking and listening, but with the teacher providing authentic language and authentic situations or scenarios with the aim that learners will be able to use the language to talk to native speakers. Lessons often follow a set pattern, in which the teacher introduces the language associated with a particular scenario, sometimes with visual stimuli, such as a video sequence, and choral and individual repetition. Learners then practise the language through role-play, games and pair work and come together to present the learned language to the teacher and the rest of the class – a model described as presentation, practice and production. Greetings, verbal and non-verbal ways of addressing people and some knowledge of cultural conventions are also learned. Grammar is not taught explicitly, as many supporters of this approach believe that learners will acquire this understanding through practice. However, the extent to which learners can continue to use the language or are able to engage in real conversations with native speakers often means that the language learned remains formulaic and can be quickly forgotten.

Task-based approaches

These are ways of linking language learning to authentic situations by asking learners to carry out activities or solve problems. There is an emphasis on collaboration between learners and the use of ICT. Following an initial input from the teacher, learners may be involved in research on the internet, a physical construction activity, or the completion of a storyboard on the computer, and then be required to report back on their solution, procedures or findings to the whole class in the target language.

Content and language integrated learning

Content and language integrated learning (CLIL) is derived from immersion teaching – an approach used in certain parts of Canada for children to learn through French and English at the same time. It is interpreted differently across Europe, but initiatives in England have sought to teach an aspect of the curriculum or unit of subject material through the medium of another language. It is important that the children are learning new content and not just rehearsing knowledge they have already learned, as it is this new learning that supports language learning and motivates learners.

Task 7.2.2 **COMPARING TEACHING AND LEARNING IN LANGUAGES AND ENGLISH**

■ Consider these approaches to teaching languages/what you have observed in schools. Then consider what you have learned about teaching English/what you have observed in schools.
■ What are the similarities and differences between the two?
■ Individually or as a group you might wish to make a list under headings such as: role of teacher, role of learners, listening, speaking, reading, writing, whole-class activities, pair/group work activities, interactions, use of ICT, resources.

TEACHING LANGUAGES IN PRIMARY SCHOOLS

Across Europe different models for teaching languages can be found, but in England three models predominated in the primary schools studied by Driscoll *et al.* (2004) and Muijs *et al.* (2005): language sensitisation, language awareness and language competence. The language competence model, although widely used in secondary schools, was less frequently observed in primary schools at the time of these studies. The majority of schools were adopting approaches based on the language sensitisation model and, to a lesser extent, the language awareness model.

Language sensitisation

Variations of this model were the most commonly observed in the studies referred to above. The broad aim is to introduce children to other languages and cultures in a fun and enjoyable way. A different language may be taught each term or year and children are not expected to become competent in the language being taught, but to develop basic conversational skills and some knowledge about language, for example comparing and contrasting similarities and differences in languages and cultures, which they will then be able to apply to other language learning. Teachers do not need to be fluent speakers of the languages, other bilingual adults can become involved as well and the languages chosen for study may reflect the languages spoken in the local community. Cultural awareness is an important element in this model and includes developing knowledge and understanding of our own and other multilingual, multicultural societies and developing children's ability to reflect on their own assumptions, values and beliefs. Teaching is not necessarily timetabled, but takes place in short sessions and through incidental opportunities for learning linked to routines or projects.

Language awareness

The model owes much to the work of Eric Hawkins, who believes, as do others, that children need to develop sound foundations for learning languages before they focus on learning one specific language (Hawkins, 1999) and that this is best achieved in primary schools through a focus on exploring a variety of languages and making comparisons between English and other languages.

For example, children would be encouraged to examine the sounds, ways of expressing meaning, the scripts and writing systems, the roots of languages and how languages are used in different contexts and for different purposes in different societies and situations. There are overlaps between language awareness and language sensitisation, but both models emphasise the importance of developing knowledge about language.

Language competence

This model aims to develop skills in listening, speaking, reading and writing (often referred to as the four language skills). It is the model widely used in secondary schools, where the focus is usually on learning one or two European languages and where there are a number of timetabled lessons a week in which the language is taught as a discrete subject by a teacher with expertise in the language. There are staged objectives in terms of learning and usually some form of formative and summative assessment.

Task 7.2.3 LANGUAGE KNOWLEDGE AND AWARENESS

■ How much do you know about other languages spoken in the UK?
■ Ask someone you know to tell you about a language you don't speak, including a few common words or greetings.
■ Try to identify some similarities and differences between that language and English.
■ Prepare a short (two-minute) presentation and share your new knowledge with others in your group.

THE *KEY STAGE 2 FRAMEWORK FOR LANGUAGES*

The underpinning aim of language teaching as outlined in the *Key Stage 2 Framework for Languages* (DfES, 2005) is closest to language competence. The framework lays out the approach that the government expects primary schools to adopt with learning objectives, suggested learning opportunities and outcomes relating to three core strands: oracy, literacy and intercultural understanding. However, there are also two cross-cutting strands: knowledge about language and language learning strategies. The inclusion of 'objectives and outcomes' in the framework reflects an expectation that children will progress in their learning and achieve a certain standard in oracy and literacy in at least one language by the time they leave primary school. The Qualifications and Curriculum Authority (QCA) developed a new scheme of work to sit alongside this framework (QCA, 2007) and a number of commercial publishers have produced resources for teaching French and, to a growing extent, Spanish and German, which draw on the framework objectives and provide 'ready-made' schemes of work. The framework is non-statutory and achievement of the objectives relies on children receiving sustained teaching (the intention is for one hour a week). A degree of teacher language knowledge and confidence in teaching languages is also important and becomes increasingly so as children move through Key Stage 2.

Oracy

The *Key Stage 2 Framework for Languages* defines oracy as 'listening, speaking and spoken interaction' (DfES, 2005: 7) and suggests that this will be the focus in the initial stages of teaching and learning. There is an emphasis on exposure to the sound patterns of the new language. Initially, children are expected to listen, recognise, respond to and perform simple words and phrases, but by Year 6 they are expected to be able to understand spoken texts, read aloud or recite texts, initiate and sustain conversations and tell stories.

Literacy

Children are expected progressively to apply their developing knowledge of sounds to the letters (or characters) of the new language and gradually build up their reading and writing skills, so that by Year 6 they can read a range of short authentic texts and write sentences from a model and independently. They are expected to apply their developing knowledge to a range of text types, including 'simple stories, poems, information texts, advertisements, letters, messages – in paper and electronic form' (DfES, 2005: 8).

Intercultural understanding

The framework views intercultural understanding as an essential part of being a citizen and sees language competence as contributing to this understanding. The aims of this strand are to enable children to develop a better understanding of other people, their lives, traditions and cultures and, in so doing, identify similarities and differences and reflect on their own lives. Teaching of this strand is viewed as taking part in language lessons and more broadly as part of cross-curricular learning.

Knowledge about language

Children develop their knowledge about language through making comparisons between languages and reflecting on similarities and differences. This helps them to see patterns, rules and conventions in languages, can encourage reflection, questioning and experimentation and can contribute to children's understanding of how the new language, English and other languages they speak work.

Language learning strategies

A range of teaching and learning strategies are mentioned in the framework to support memorisation and recall, including using rhythm (chanting, clapping and beating out), rhymes and songs, gesture, actions and mime, physical response and mouthing words silently. Other strategies include making comparisons between languages, guessing based on context or prior knowledge and applying knowledge learned in one context to a new situation.

The government intends that languages will become a requirement within the revised curriculum to be introduced from 2010 (Rose, 2009). Languages will form part of one of the proposed six new areas of learning, 'Understanding English, communication and languages'. The current framework will be replaced by programmes of learning when the new curriculum is introduced, but it is likely that the strands will remain evident and that the objectives and outcomes will be reflected in any new guidance. Although the framework contains examples of the learning opportunities children should be provided with each year and suggestions for teaching activities, it *does not* prescribe which languages should be taught, who they should be taught by or how they should be taught.

WHAT THE FRAMEWORK DOESN'T PRESCRIBE

Although the *Languages for Life: Languages for All* strategy (DfES, 2002) recommended that children should learn at least one European language, other languages, including community languages, are not excluded. Also, because the learning objectives are skills-based, they can be applied to any language. In addition to the more common European languages, there are schools where children are learning Turkish, Greek and Somali, for example. The choice of language is often determined by the skills, knowledge and confidence of staff and the languages that children will be able to study at secondary school. Not surprisingly, the overwhelming majority of schools teach French.

Some schools employ secondary specialists to teach languages, especially where they have established good working relationships with secondary schools that are also specialist language colleges. The majority of schools prefer to employ teachers who are primary language specialists and familiar with primary pedagogy (Lines *et al.*, 2007). Some of these teachers are employed specifically to teach languages, while others are full-time members of staff who teach languages for part of their working week and their own class for the rest of the week. Another approach is for class teachers to teach their own classes, usually with the support of a subject leader who provides training, advice and suggestions for lessons to those who may initially lack knowledge, skills or confidence. Sometimes teachers are supported by foreign language assistants (FLAs) or bilingual parents. Alternatively, FLAs do the teaching supported by the teachers who then provide opportunities for reinforcement during the week. Different approaches suit different schools and a number of schools combine different staffing models.

The pedagogic approach varies according to the teacher's training and qualifications, both in terms of teaching generally and specifically in teaching languages in the primary school. However, the approach can broadly be described as communicative with an initial emphasis on speaking and listening. Key aims are to make language learning fun and enjoyable and motivate learners to develop language skills and understanding of other cultures. Teachers model language, provide lots of opportunities for repetition and revisiting vocabulary and phrases, and use rhyme, chants, songs, games and role-play to enable children to practise language in whole-class situations and in pairs. The interactive whiteboard is a key resource for teaching and learning in many classrooms, but teachers also use authentic artefacts, puppets, stories, flash cards, labels, dual-language books, poems, play scripts, matching and sequencing activities and individual computers to support literacy development and the development of intercultural understanding.

ASSESSMENT AND ACCREDITATION

Many teachers assess children's achievements and progress informally, but more and more teachers are looking for ways to keep some kind of more formal record. With the increasing importance given to personalisation, self-assessment and assessment for learning, a number of schools have found that My Languages Portfolio provides one way of doing this. This is a junior version of the European Language Portfolio developed by the Council of Europe and comprises:

- ■ *My Language Biography* – a personalised learning diary making children aware of their achievements as they learn.
- ■ *My Dossier* – where learners can file work and materials to illustrate the achievements recorded in the *Language Biography* or *Language Passport*.
- ■ *My Language Passport* – an overview of the learner's knowledge and experiences of different languages, based on a series of 'can do' statements, and of their cultural experiences.

(www.primarylanguages.org.uk/)

The Department for Children, Schools and Families (DCSF) has also been keen to develop a national recognition scheme for languages. The Languages Ladder is designed to endorse achievement in the four language skills at all levels of competence and for all ages in a wide range of languages. This recognition scheme is being developed for 25 languages. These include Arabic, Bengali, Chinese (Mandarin and Cantonese), Cornish, French, German, Greek, Gujarati, Hindi, Irish, Italian, Japanese, Panjabi, Polish, Portuguese, Russian, Spanish, Somali, Swedish, Tamil, Turkish, Urdu, Welsh and Yoruba. It is made up of six stages, with a series of 'can do' statements and different materials for primary pupils, secondary pupils and adults. A voluntary assessment scheme called Asset Languages has been developed to support the assessment of the 'can do' statements in the Languages Ladder. (For more information see www.dcsf.gov.uk and www.assetlanguages. org.uk, following the links to Languages Ladder.)

Task 7.2.4 **EXPLORING RESEARCH**

Go to the research and statistics section of the National Centre for Languages (CILT) Primary Languages website at www.primarylanguages.org.uk/policy_and_research/research_and_ statistics.aspx.

■ Choose a study, perhaps one of the longitudinal studies, and read the relevant report. Make a note of the key findings and be prepared to discuss these with your colleagues.

SUPPORT FOR TEACHING AND LEARNING

Resources

The resources teachers will use will depend on their role in teaching languages and the approach the school adopts to teaching and learning. Many teachers who are directly involved in teaching languages as a discrete subject make their own resources, but publishers have been quick to develop resources to support the teaching of the main European languages. There are also many web-based resources for teachers to download and use. The CILT Primary Languages website provides ideas for classroom practice, resources, professional development and networking for teachers (www.primarylanguages. org.uk/primary_languages/about_us.aspx). This site is a useful source of information for teachers who are teaching languages or reinforcing teaching throughout the curriculum.

Schools and local authorities (LAs) have also developed their own resources and many of these are available free or to purchase online. Some schools have adopted a language awareness approach, especially for younger children. For example, Coventry LA developed an approach called Language Investigation, which is now in use in many of its schools (www.language-investigator. co.uk/index.htm). This was described by Ofsted (2005) as:

> An innovative approach in one LEA to the Key Stage 2 curriculum supported teachers in teaching a multilingual programme, which built on pupils' work in literacy and developed their early understanding of language. Investigative activities enabled pupils to make links between languages and draw conclusions about how languages work. This provided a strong foundation for later, or simultaneous, learning of one or two specific languages, and pupils made rapid progress. The approach also provided an inclusive, non-hierarchical view of language and culture early on.

(Ofsted, 2005: 8–9)

Other websites provide resources for teachers to draw on in supporting language awareness and supporting children's awareness of the number of different languages spoken in our society today. These resources can be used by all teachers. For example, Newbury Park school has a Language of the Month website (www.newburypark.redbridge.sch.uk/langofmonth/).

Task 7.2.5 EXPLORING RESOURCES TO SUPPORT TEACHING

Access one of the websites mentioned above (if you are working in a group you might like to choose different sites or work in pairs). Along the way you may find other sites of interest. You should start to build up a list of websites that will be useful in the future and keep a summary of how they may be able to support your teaching. Share your findings with others in your group.

LANGUAGES IN THE COMMUNITY

Finding out about the languages children already speak is an important part of any teacher's role and it is also important to find out whether they are continuing to learn to read and write these languages at home or in community or supplementary schools. Language is an important part of everyone's identity and, in a world where we are trying to encourage children to learn new languages, we mustn't overlook the ones they already know and the ones they may already be developing literacy in (or are able to do so with appropriate support inside school as well as outside). Respect for children's languages and cultures is an important part of the *Every Child Matters* agenda (DfES, 2003). Over 14 per cent of children in primary schools already speak a language other than English and many will have considerable knowledge about language and language learning strategies – their knowledge and skills are a resource to be valued and drawn on. Consulting and involving parents, making contact with teachers in community and supplementary schools to share ideas and approaches, and investigating the languages spoken by all members of staff are important parts of developing your own language and cultural awareness.

> Learning other languages gives us insight into the people, culture and traditions of other countries, and helps us to understand our own language and culture. Drawing on the skills and expertise of those who speak community languages will promote citizenship and complement the government's broader work on the promotion of social cohesion.
>
> (DfES, 2002: 12)

ENTHUSIASM FOR LANGUAGES

Children in primary schools are overwhelmingly enthusiastic about learning languages, often because they see it as a fun and enjoyable experience and are motivated by the range of activities their teachers offer them (Cable *et al.*, 2008), including songs, games, stories and opportunities to engage in role-play, storytelling and activities on the interactive whiteboard. Children who are learning English as an additional language and those who have learning difficulties often excel, because most children are starting learning from the beginning together. Affective factors, such as developing a positive attitude to languages and cultures and to learning in general, are identified by teachers as key drivers for language learning in primary schools.

SUMMARY

All teachers will be involved in teaching languages in the future and need to prepare themselves by developing their own knowledge and skills. You may already be able to speak, read and write other languages, or you may need initially to learn alongside children and seek the advice of more knowledgeable others who may be advisers, other teachers, children or parents. This unit has introduced some of the developments and approaches to teaching languages in primary schools and provided ideas and suggestions for you to explore to develop your teaching.

ANNOTATED FURTHER READING

Kirsch, C. (2008) *Teaching Foreign Languages in the Primary School*, London: Continuum.
> This book combines coverage of theories of language learning and approaches to pedagogy with practical suggestions for teaching and case studies.

Martin, C. (2008) *Primary Languages: Effective Learning and Teaching*, Exeter: Learning Matters.
> This book expands the discussion of the optimum age to begin learning languages and supports teachers in exploring the requirements of the *Key Stage 2 Framework for Languages*.

RELEVANT WEBSITES

CILT sites

CILT: www.cilt.org.uk
> This is the website for the National Centre for Languages and National Centre for Information on Language Teaching and Research.

CILT Cymru: www.ciltcymru.org.uk/english/home.htm
> Following a number of pilot studies, the National Centre for Languages in Wales has recently published *'Getting Started': Guidance to Support the Introduction of a Modern Foreign Language in Key Stage 2*.

SCILT (Scottish Centre for Information on Language Teaching and Research): www.scilt.stir.ac.uk
> The revised Scottish curriculum – A Curriculum for Excellence – is currently being finalised, but languages provision generally starts later in P6 (Year 5 in England).

NICILT (Northern Ireland CILT): www.qub.ac.uk/edu/nicilt/
> The Department for Education (DENI) has recently commissioned a study to develop a languages strategy for Northern Ireland.

CILT Primary Languages: www.primarylanguages.org.uk/primary_languages/about_us.aspx
> This website provides information on training, continuing professional development, regional groups, networking, resources, ideas for best practice and links to many other sites and sources of practical information and support.

Other sites

Asset Languages: www.assetlanguages.org.uk/
Language Investigation: www.language-investigator.co.uk/index.htm
> This is an alternative approach to language teaching developed in Coventry LA that takes account of the needs of non-specialist teachers.

Language of the Month: www.newburypark.redbridge.sch.uk/langofmonth/
> This website offers free resources for promoting language awareness, including videos of children teaching their home languages, resources for putting up language displays and a booklet with 100+ ideas for celebrating community languages.

My Languages Portfolio: www.primarylanguages.org.uk
> This is a junior version of the European Language Portfolio developed by the Council of Europe.

'Our Languages' project: www.ourlanguages.org.uk/
> The 'Our Languages' project is a DCSF-funded initiative to develop greater synergy between language teaching in mainstream and complementary schools.

Welsh Language Board: www.byig-wlb.org.uk

Visit the companion website www.routledge.com/textbooks/ltps2e for:

■ additional questions and task for this unit;
■ links to useful websites relevant to this unit.

REFERENCES

Buie, E. (2006) 'Do mind the language gap', *Times Educational Supplement Scotland*, 15 September.

Burstall, C. (1974) *Primary French in the Balance*, Windsor: NFER.

Cable, C., Heins, B., Driscoll, P., Mitchell, R. and Hall, K. (2008) *Language Learning at Key Stage 2: A Longitudinal Study*, DCSF-RBX-08-08, London: DCSF. Available online at www.dcsf.gov.uk/research/ (accessed November 2009).

Department for Education and Employment/Qualifications and Curriculum Authority (QCA) (DfEE/QCA) (1999) *Handbook for Primary Teachers in England, Key Stages 1 and 2: Guidelines for MFL at Key Stage 2*, London: DfEE/QCA.

Department for Education and Skills (DfES) (2002) *Languages for Life, Languages for All: A Strategy for England*, Nottingham: DfES.

Department for Education and Skills (DfES) (2003) *Every Child Matters*, Nottingham, DfES.

Department for Education and Skills (DfES) (2005) *The Key Stage 2 Framework for Languages*. Nottingham: DfES.

Department for Education and Skills (DfES) (2006) *The Language Review*, Nottingham: DfES.

Driscoll, P., Jones, J. and Macrory, G. (2004) *The Provision of Foreign Language Learning for Pupils at Key Stage 2*, DfES Research Report RR572, London: DfES. Available online at www.dcsf.gov.uk/research/ (accessed March 2009).

Edelenbos, P., Johnstone, R. and Kubanek, A. (2006) *The Main Pedagogical Principles Underlying the Teaching of Languages to Very Young Learners, Final Report of the EAC 89/04, Lot 1 Study*, Brussels: European Commission. Available online at http://ec.europa.eu/education/policies/lang/doc/young_en.pdf (accessed November 2009).

Hawkins, E. (1999) 'Foreign language study and language awareness', *Language Awareness*, 8(3/4): 124–42.

Lines, A., Easton, C., Pullen, P. and Schagen, S. (2007) *Language Learning at Key Stage 2: Findings from the 2006 Survey*, DfES Research Brief RBX02-07, London: DfES. Available online at www.dcsf.gov.uk/research/ (accessed March 2009).

Muijs, D., Barnes, A., Hunt, M., Powell, B., Arweck, E., Lindsay, G. and Martin, C. (2005) *Evaluation of the KS2 Language Learning Pathfinders*, London: DfES.

Office for Standards in Education (Ofsted) (2005) *Implementing Languages Entitlement in Primary Schools: An Evaluation of Progress in Ten Pathfinder Schools*. Available online at www.ofsted.gov.uk/Ofsted-home/Publications-and-research (accessed March 2009).

Qualifications and Curriculum Authority (QCA) (2000) *Modern Foreign Languages: A Scheme of Work for Key Stage 2*, London: QCA.

Qualifications and Curriculum Authority (QCA) (2007) *Schemes of Work for French, Spanish and German at Key Stage 2*. Available from www.standards.dcsf.gov.uk/schemes3/subjects/primary_mff/ (accessed March 2009).

Rose, J. (2009) *Independent Review of the Primary Curriculum: Final Report*, London: DCSF. Available online at www.dcsf.gov.uk/primarycurriculumreview (accessed May 2009).

Welsh Language Board (2000/2004) *Welsh in Schools, SDB 3/2000 and SB 16/2004*, Cardiff: The National Assembly for Wales, Statistical Directorate. Available online at www.byig-wlb.org.uk (accessed March 2009).

CREATIVITY IN THE CURRICULUM

Teresa Cremin and Jonathan Barnes

INTRODUCTION

> Teachers and school leaders have to recognise that the development of creativity in pupils is an essential part of their job, and that an appropriate climate has to be established.
>
> (Ofsted, 2003: 11)

In a world dominated by technological innovations, creativity is a critical component; human skills and people's powers of creativity and imagination are key resources in a knowledge-driven economy (Robinson, 2001, 2009) and, as social structures continue to change, the ability to live with uncertainty and deal with complexity is essential. So organisations and governments all over the world are now more concerned than ever to promote creativity (Craft, 2005). It develops the kinds of skills that young people need in a rapidly changing world and can improve their self-esteem, motivation and achievement.

As primary professionals, we need to recognise that it is our responsibility to foster the creative development of the young. In recent years, creativity has been positioned more centrally in the curriculum; 'creative development' is named as an Early Learning Goal in the Early Years Foundation Stage (EYFS) (DCSF, 2008) and a high profile is afforded creativity in the primary phase where, within the personal development framework, children are expected to 'think creatively, make connections and generate ideas', as well as consider alternative solutions to problems (Rose, 2008: 77).

In addition, explorations of creative teaching and teaching for creativity are growing in number (see, for example, Jeffrey and Woods, 2003, 2009; Jeffrey and Craft, 2004; Grainger *et al.*, 2005; Dismore *et al.*, 2008; Cremin, 2009; Cremin *et al.*, 2009) and teachers themselves are seeking innovative ways to shape the curriculum in response to children's needs, new statutory requirements and the creativity agenda. A curriculum framed around your responses to global, national and local issues and resources, as well as the needs, priorities and interests of children, involves both risk and originality on the part of both teachers and younger learners. Teaching creatively does not mean short-changing the teaching of the essential knowledge, skills and understanding in the six areas of learning; rather, it involves teaching these in creative contexts that explicitly invite learners to engage imaginatively and that stretch their generative and evaluative capacities.

However, many teachers still feel constrained by working in a culture of accountability, and you too are no doubt already aware that the backwash of the assessment system markedly affects classroom practice. Such pressure can limit opportunities for creative endeavour and may tempt you to stay within the safe boundaries of the known. Recognising the tension between the incessant drive for measurable standards and the development of creative teaching is a good starting point, but finding the energy and enterprise to respond flexibly to this reality is a real challenge. In order to do so, you need to be convinced that creativity has an important role to play in education, and believe that you can contribute, both personally and professionally. You may also need to widen your understanding of creativity and creative practice in order to teach creatively and teach for creativity.

OBJECTIVES

By the end of this unit you should have:

- an increased understanding about the nature of creativity;
- an awareness of some of the features of creative primary teachers;
- a wider understanding of creative pedagogical practice;
- some understanding of how to plan for creativity.

CREATIVE PRACTICE

The class is full of focused learners, whose voices express urgency and interest as they collaborate in groups to create three-dimensional representations of two Egyptian gods. Earlier that morning, at this Northamptonshire primary school, the six and seven year olds had discussed the many options available to them, generated ideas and listened to others. They are now in the process of turning their ideas into action. They operate independently of their teacher, find resources in their classroom or in others, monitor their achievements in the time available (they knew they would have at least one more session to complete this challenge) and constantly evaluate and discuss their work. The groups create a wide variety of representations and new ideas that emerge during the creative process are added, celebrated and critically appraised. Later in this half term's unit on the Egyptians, the children write instructions for making these images and add them to their huge class book, which contains DVDs of the diverse cross-curricular activities undertaken; this also shows the total transformation of their classroom into an Egyptian museum. However, their ability to recall, explain and discuss the finer points of this creatively planned and executed project two terms later is an even richer testimony to the enjoyment and depth of the creative learning involved.

In this school, as in many others, the staff had adopted a more creative approach to the curriculum and placed creative teaching and learning at the heart of their practice, influenced by a developed understanding of the nature of creativity, by the significant achievements of creative schools (Ofsted, 2003, 2006; Eames *et al.*, 2006), by the report *Nurturing Creativity in Young People* (Roberts, 2006), by the House of Commons Education and Skills Committee (2007) considerations and by Rose's (2008) recommendations. As noted earlier, the EYFS states that 'children's creativity must be extended by the provision of support for their curiosity, exploration and play' (DCSF, 2008), the new primary curriculum profiles the development of learning and thinking skills and the secondary curriculum aims to develop 'creative thinkers' and 'independent enquirers' as part of the Personal Learning and Thinking Skills (PLTS) agenda.

However, the focus on creative learning (Craft *et al.*, 2007a and b; Sefton-Green, 2008) has arguably been renamed and relaunched as a new 'cultural offer' in the McMaster Report (McMaster, 2008). In essence, this seeks to involve children and young people as both spectators and participants in the creativity and cultural agenda. It also, somewhat erroneously, renames the significant Creative Partnerships programme, which demonstrated that collaborative projects inspire and foster creative skills, and raise children's confidence and aspiration (Ofsted, 2006), as a 'cultural learning programme'. Nonetheless, with a key role for creativity in the primary curriculum, teachers are currently seeking more innovative ways of teaching and are planning more explicitly to develop children's creativity.

SO WHAT IS CREATIVITY?

Creativity is not confined to special people or to particular arts-based activities, nor is it undisciplined play. It is, however, notoriously difficult to define. It has been described as 'a state of mind in which all our intelligences are working together' involving 'seeing, thinking and innovating' (Craft, 2000: 38) and as 'imaginative activity fashioned so as to produce outcomes that are both original and of value' (NACCCE, 1999: 29). Creativity is possible wherever human intelligence is actively engaged and is an essential part of an effective education: it includes all areas of understanding and all children, teachers and others working in primary education. Indeed, it can be demonstrated by anyone in any aspect of life, throughout life.

It is useful to distinguish between high creativity and ordinary creativity; between 'Big C Creativity' (exemplified in some of Gardner's (1993a and b) studies of highly creative individuals, such as Picasso, Einstein and Freud) and 'little c creativity', which Craft (2000, 2001) highlights. This latter form focuses on the individual agency and resourcefulness of ordinary people to innovate and take action. Csikszentmihalyi suggests that each of us is born with two contradictory sets of instructions – a conservative tendency and an expansive tendency, but warns us that, 'If too few opportunities for curiosity are available, if too many obstacles are put in the way of risk and exploration, the motivation to engage in creative behaviour is easily extinguished.' (1996: 11).

In the context of the classroom, developing opportunities for children to 'possibility think' their way forwards is therefore critical (Craft, 2001; Burnard, et al. 2006; Cremin et al., 2006a). This will involve you in immersing the class in an issue or subject and helping them ask questions, take risks, be imaginative and playfully explore options as well as innovate. At the core of such creative endeavour is the child's self-determination and agency as an active thinker to find and solve problems. From this perspective, creativity is not seen as an event or a product (although it may involve either or both), but a process or a state of mind involving the serious play of ideas and possibilities. This generative, problem-finding/problem-solving process may involve rational and non-rational thought and may be fed by the intuitive, by daydreaming and pondering, as well as by the application of knowledge and skills. In order to be creative, children may need considerable knowledge in a domain, but 'creativity and knowledge are two sides of the same psychological coin, not opposing forces' (Boden, 2001: 102) and imaginatively enrich each other.

Imaginative activity can take many forms; it draws on a more varied range of human functioning than linear, logical and rational patterns of behaviour (Claxton, 1997, 2006). It is essentially generative and may include physical, social, reflective, musical, aural or visual thinking, involving children in activities that produce new and unusual connections between ideas, domains, processes and materials. When children and their teachers step outside the boundaries of predictability and are physically engaged, learning through their minds and bodies, eyes and ears, this provides a balance to the sedentary and, too often, abstract nature of school education. In less conventional contexts, new insights and connections may be made through analogy and metaphor. Modes of creative thinking, such as the 'imaginative-generative' mode, which produces outcomes, and the 'critical-evaluative' mode, which involves consideration of originality and value (NACCCE, 1999: 30), operate in close interrelationship and need to be consciously developed in the classroom.

The process of creativity, Claxton and Lucas (2004) suggest, involves the ability to move freely between the different layers of our memories to find solutions to problems. They propose a metaphor of the mind based on the concept of three layers of memory that impact upon our thinking: an upper layer or *habit map*, which is a map of repeated patterns of behaviour; an *inner layer* comprised of individual conscious and unconscious memories; and an *archetypal layer* laid down by our genes. Others see the creative mind as one that looks for unexpected likenesses and connections between disparate domains (Koestler, 1964; Bronowski, 1978). Csikszentmihalyi (1996) wisely suggests, however, that creativity does not happen inside people's heads, but in the interaction between an individual's thoughts and the sociocultural context. When one considers examples of both big 'C' and little 'c' creativity, this explanation seems to make the most sense, since the social and cultural context of learning is highly influential.

Task 7.3.1 **CREATIVITY**

Read a chosen chapter of Vera John-Steiner's fascinating book, *Creative Collaboration* (2000). Consider the degree to which you see creativity as individualised or collective, subject-specific or generalised. Discuss with others the consequences of your views for classroom practice?

It is clear too that creativity is not bound to particular subjects At the cutting edge of every domain of learning, creativity is essential. It depends in part on interactions between feeling and thinking across boundaries and ideas. It also depends upon a climate of trust, respect and support, an environment in which individual agency and self-determination are fostered, and ideas and interests are valued, discussed and celebrated. Yet we have all experienced schools that fail to teach the pleasure and excitement to be found in science or mathematics, for example, or who let routines and timetables, subject boundaries and decontextualised knowledge dominate the daily diet of the young. In such sterile environments, when formulae for learning are relied upon and curriculum packages are delivered, children's ability to make connections and to imagine alternatives is markedly reduced. So too is their capacity for curiosity, for enquiry and for creativity itself.

Task 7.3.2 **OWNERSHIP OF LEARNING**

Relevance, ownership and control of learning, as well as innovation, have all been identified as key issues in creative learning in children (Jeffrey and Woods, 2003). Imaginative approaches involve individuals and groups in initiating questions and lines of enquiry so that they are more in charge of their work, and such collaboration and interaction helps to develop a greater sense of autonomy in the events that unfold.

■ To what extent have you observed children taking control of their learning, making choices and demonstrating ownership of their own learning? Think of some examples and share these in small groups.

■ To what extent was the work also relevant to the children? Were they emotionally or imaginatively engaged, building on areas of interest, maintaining their individuality and sharing ideas with one another?

■ If you have seen little evidence of these issues, consider how you could offer more opportunity for relevance, ownership and control of learning in the classroom.

CREATIVE TEACHING AND TEACHING FOR CREATIVITY

The distinction between creative teaching and teaching for creativity is a helpful one in that it is possible to imagine a creative teacher who engages personally and creatively in the classroom, yet fails to provide for children's creative learning. Responsible creative professionals are not necessarily flamboyant performers, but teachers who use a range of approaches to create the conditions in which the creativity of others can flourish. Creative teachers also recognise and make use of their own creativity, not just to interest and engage the learners, but also to promote new thinking and learning. Their confidence in their own creativity will enable them to offer the children stronger scaffolds and spaces for emotional and intellectual growth.

Research undertaken in a higher education context, with tutors teaching music, geography and English, suggests that creative teaching is a complex art form – a veritable 'cocktail party' (Grainger *et al.*, 2004). The host gathers the ingredients (the session content) and mixes them playfully and skilfully (the teaching style), in order to facilitate a creative party that is enjoyable and worthwhile (the learning experience). While no formula was, or could be, established for creative teaching, some of the ingredients for personally mixing a creative cocktail were identified, albeit tentatively, from this work. It is clear, however, that the elements are not in themselves necessarily creative, but that the action of creatively shaking and stirring the ingredients and the individual experience of those attending are critical if the 'cocktail party' is to be successful. The intention to promote creative learning appeared to be an important feature in this work.

The session content (the cocktail ingredients) included the themes of placing current trends in a wider context and extensive use of metaphor, analogy and personal anecdotes to make connections. The teaching style (the mixing of the cocktail) included the themes of multimodal pedagogic practices, pace, humour, the confidence of the tutors and their ability to inspire and value the pupils. In relation to the learning experience (the cocktail party), the themes included involving the pupils affectively and physically and challenging them to engage and reflect. Together these represent some of the critical features of creative teachers and creative teaching that combine to support new thinking.

Task 7.3.3 **TEACHING AS COCKTAIL PARTY**

■ Consider the metaphor of teaching as cocktail party for a moment. In what ways do you think it captures the vitality of teaching – the dynamic interplay between teachers, children and the resources available? Select one or two of the features, for example humour or the use of metaphor or personal anecdotes. Do you make extensive use of either of these features? Remember, as the research indicates, such features need to be employed with others in a flexible experiential encounter at the 'cocktail party'.

■ Consider your current tutors or previous teachers. Which are/were the most creative teachers? Do they/did they create successful cocktail parties in which you felt valued and were given the space to engage fully, to take risks, make connections and develop deep learning? How do/did they achieve this?

PERSONAL CHARACTERISTICS OF CREATIVE TEACHERS

It is difficult to identify with any certainty the personal characteristics of creative teachers. Research tends to offer lists of propensities that such teachers possess (e.g. Fryer, 1996; Beetlestone, 1998) or case study accounts of classroom practice (e.g. Jeffrey and Woods, 2003, 2009; Grainger *et al.*, 2004; Cremin *et al.*, 2006a; Cremin *et al.*, 2009). Common elements noted in these various studies include:

- enthusiasm, passion and commitment;
- risk taking;
- a deep curiosity or questioning stance;
- willingness to be intuitive and/or introspective;
- gregariousness and introspectiveness;
- a clear set of personal values;
- awareness of self as a creative being.

This list of characteristics encompasses many of the personal qualities you might expect in any good teacher, except perhaps the last. Sternberg (1999) suggests that creative teachers are creative role models themselves – professionals who continue to be self-motivated learners, who value the creative dimensions of their own lives and who make connections between their personal responses to experience and their teaching. In addition, a clear set of values, reflecting fair-mindedness, openness to evidence, a desire for clarity and respect for others are important and among the attitudinal qualities embedded in creative teaching. So too is a commitment to inclusion and a belief in human rights and equality. Such attitudes and values have a critical role in creative teaching and are perhaps best taught by example. Who do you know who models such values as a teacher?

FEATURES OF A CREATIVE PEDAGOGICAL STANCE

The intention to promote creativity is fundamental; you will need to place children in situations that help them make connections and then build on these, creating a climate of enquiry, of ideas and of sensible risk taking. You will also need to plan to develop their independence and ability to work in a community of learners. There are a number of features of a creative pedagogical stance that you may want to consider in relation to your teaching and observation of other creative professionals.

A learner-centred, agency-oriented ethos

Creative teachers tend to place the learners above the curriculum and combine a positive disposition towards creativity and person-centred teaching that actively promotes pupils who learn and think for themselves (Craft, 2000). Relaxed, trusting educator–learner relationships exist in creative classrooms and the role of the affect and children's feelings play a central role in learning in such contexts. Such relationships foster children's agency and autonomy as learners (Cremin *et al.*, 2006a). A learner-oriented ethos will also involve you showing patience and openness, reinforcing children's creative behaviour, celebrating difference, diversity and innovation, as well as learning to tolerate mild or polite rebellion (Gardner, 1999a). If you adopt such a person-centred orientation you will be shaping the children's self esteem and enhancing their intrinsic motivation and agency.

A questioning stance

Creativity involves asking and attempting to answer real questions and the creative teacher is seen by many writers as one who uses open questions and who promotes speculation in the classroom, encouraging deeper understanding and lateral thinking (Cremin *et al.*, 2006a; Cremin, 2009). In the context of creative teaching, both teachers and children need to be involved in this process of imaginative thinking, encompassing the generation of challenging and unusual questions and the creation of possible responses. The questioning stance of the teacher has been noted as central to children's possibility thinking, which, it is argued, is at the heart of creativity (Craft, 2000). Possibility thinking involves the shift from asking 'what is this and what does it do?' to 'what can I do with this?', particularly in relation to identifying, honing and solving problems (Jeffrey, 2005; Burnard et al., 2006). Work in this area demonstrates the importance of question-posing and question-responding in fostering creative learning (Chappell et al., 2008).

Creating space, time and freedom to make connections

Creativity requires space, time and a degree of freedom. Deep immersion in an area or activity allows options to remain open, and persistence and follow-through to develop. Conceptual space allows children to converse, challenge and negotiate meanings and possibilities together. For example, through employing both film and drama in extended units of work, teachers raised boys' standards and creativity in writing (Bearne et al., 2004) and in the early years when 'time was flexibly handled' and children's ideas and explorations were taken seriously, the youngsters' creative thinking and learning developed (Cremin et al., 2006a).

Employing multimodal teaching approaches

A variety of multimodal teaching approaches and frequent switching between modes in a play-like and spontaneous manner appear to support creative learning (Cremin et al., 2009). The diversity of pattern, rhythm and pace used by creative teachers is particularly marked (Woods, 1995), as is their use of informed intuition (Claxton and Lucas, 2004). As you teach, opportunities will arise for you to use your intuition and move from the security of the known. Give yourself permission to go beyond the 'script' you have planned and allow the children to take the initiative and lead you, for such spontaneity will encourage you to seize the moment and foster deeper learning (Cremin et al., 2006b; Jeffrey, 2006). Afterwards, consider the effect of this more responsive approach: did the children exert their autonomy, were they more fully engaged and intrinsically motivated?

Prompting full engagement, ownership and ongoing reflection

In studying an area in depth, children should experience both explicit instruction and space for exploration and discovery. Try to provide opportunities for choice and be prepared to spend some time developing their self-management skills so that they are able to operate independently. Their full engagement can be prompted through appealing to their own interests and passions, by involving them in imaginative experiences and by connecting learning to their lives (Cremin et al., 2009). You will find that, as the children realise that their questions make a difference, they will begin to ask more, ponder longer and reflect upon other ways to achieve a task or represent their learning. A semi-constant oscillation between engagement and reflection will become noticeable in the classroom as you work to refine, reshape and improve learning. The ability to give and receive criticism is also an essential part of creativity and you will need to encourage evaluation through supportive and honest feedback (Jeffrey, 2006).

Modelling risk taking and enabling the children to take risks too

The ability to tolerate ambiguity is an example of the 'confident uncertainty' to which Claxton (1997) refers when discussing creative teachers – those who combine subject and pedagogical knowledge, but also leave space for uncertainty and the unknown. You will gain in confidence through increased subject knowledge, experience and reflection, but your assurance will also grow through taking risks and having a go at expressing yourself. Risk taking is an integral element of creativity, and one that you will want to model and foster. The children too will need to feel supported as they take risks in safe non-judgemental contexts.

To be a creative practitioner you will need more than a working knowledge of the six areas of learning and the prescribed curriculum. You will need a clear idea of your values, a secure pedagogical understanding and a strong knowledge base, supported by a passionate belief in the potential of creative teaching to engage, inspire and educate. Such teaching depends in the end upon the human interaction between teachers and pupils and is also influenced by the teacher's state of mind. The creative teacher, it is proposed, is one who is aware of, and values, the human attribute of creativity in themselves and actively seeks to promote this in others. The creative teacher has a creative state of mind that is both exercised and developed through their creative practice and personal/professional curiosity, connection-making, originality and autonomy (Cremin, 2009; Cremin *et al.*, 2009). Such practice is, of course, influenced by the physical, social, emotional and spiritual environments in which teachers and children work.

Task 7.3.4 **CREATIVE ENGAGEMENT**

Read the first chapter of Ken Robinson's *The Element* (2009).

■ Consider with others when you feel in your 'element' and try to identify what are the features of your engagement in such contexts?
■ How do these relate to the aspects of creative practice described above – are there parallels and if not what might this reveal about the degree to which creative engagement can be prescribed or fostered?
■ Consider the similarities and differences between being in one's 'element' and in the 'flow', which is a term Mihalyi Csikszentmihalyi (1996) employs.

CREATING ENVIRONMENTS OF POSSIBILITY

You may have been to a school where creativity is explicitly planned for and fostered, and where there is a clear sense of shared values and often a real buzz of purposeful and exciting activity. Such schools have a distinctive character that impacts upon behaviour, relationships, the physical and ethical environment and the curriculum and are likely to tap into the potential of informal learning. An ethos that values creativity will, according to most definitions, promote originality and the use of the imagination, as well as encourage an adventurous attitude to life and learning. In such environments of possibility, packed with ideas and experiences, resources and choices, as well as time for relaxation and rumination, physical, conceptual and emotional space is offered.

The social and emotional environment

Taking creative risks and moving forward in learning is heavily dependent upon an atmosphere of genuine acceptance and security. As Halpin notes:

pupils [should be able to] feel confident enough to take risks and learn from failure instead of being branded by it . . . they should react positively to self help questions like: 'Am I safe here?' 'Do I belong?' 'Can I count on others to support me?'

(2003: 111)

The sense of well-being that offers a positive answer to these questions is promoted in creative schools by respecting individuals and involving both children and adults in activities that affirm both their individuality and their common humanity. Children's well-being now forms an important part of the curriculum; it is noted that 'as their confidence grows, they learn to respond positively to change, becoming more enterprising, finding new ways of doing things and developing a "can-do" attitude' (Rose, 2008). This kind of attitude is important to support their creativity, but can only be fostered by a secure ethos. However, creative schools may display apparently contradictory characteristics. The ethos may be simultaneously:

■ highly active and relaxed;
■ supportive and challenging;
■ confident and speculative;
■ playful and serious;
■ focused and fuzzy;
■ individualistic and communal;
■ understood personally and owned by all;
■ non-competitive and ambitious.

Since Plato, many have argued that there are links between involvement in creative acts and a general sense of well-being. More recent research in cognitive neuroscience (Damasio, 2003) and positive psychology (Fredrickson, 2003; Seligman, 2004; Huppert *et al.*, 2005) has suggested that the state of well-being promotes optimum conditions in both mind and body, and also ensures constructive and secure relationships. A perceived link between discovering one's own creativity and feeling a sense of well-being (Barnes *et al.*, 2008) has led some to make arguments for a re-evaluation of curricula, in favour of educational programmes that offer frequent, planned and progressive creative opportunities across every discipline (Barnes, 2005). The new curriculum (Rose, 2008) offers just such an opportunity to schools; much will depend upon the profession's response.

The physical environment

The physical environment in a school that promotes creativity is likely to celebrate achievement and individuality. Jeffrey and Woods (2003) have shown that it can affect every aspect of the environment, which is not only stimulating, but is also a valuable teaching resource. Children's views on this are important and deserve to be taken into account (Burke and Grosvenor, 2003). Projects have shown how creative thinking in the context of focused work on improving the school building, grounds or local areas can achieve major citizenship objectives and high-level arts and literacy targets in an atmosphere of genuine support and community concern (Barnes, 2005, 2007, 2009).

Active modes of learning and problem-solving approaches that include independent investigation require accessible resources of various kinds, so the richer and more multifaceted a range you can offer the better. This supports genuine choice, speculation and experimentation, happy accidents and flexibility. As well as good-quality equipment and resources for each discipline, you may want to 'collect' and involve the following:

- objects (e.g. crockery, etchings, machines and containers) chosen to suggest links between subjects;
- games and toys (commercial or home-made) to add amusement, challenge and variety;
- items (e.g. religious objects, fabrics, art and craft, foods, plants) representing the range of cultures in school and society;
- tools and artefacts (e.g. mystery objects from the local museum service) to encourage deeper thinking;
- tools (such as those used by geography, maths, ICT, science and design technology) that promote the use of hands and bodies;
- products that reflect current communication technologies to aid understanding and engagement;
- creative professionals from the community (e.g. hairdressers, architects, artists, town planners, website designers, advertisers, window dressers) who are willing to work with pupils.

An environment of possibility in which individual agency and self-determination are fostered and children's ideas and interests are valued, shared and celebrated depends upon the presence of a climate of trust, respect and support in your classroom. Creativity can be developed when you are confident and secure in both your subject knowledge and your knowledge of creative pedagogical practice; then you will seek to model the features of creativity *and* develop a culture of creative opportunities in school.

Task 7.3.5 **A CLASSROOM FOR CREATIVITY**

In groups of four, use the classroom plan in Figure 7.3.1, with 16 stickers to represent desks and 29 red 'blobs' to represent children, and design a classroom to promote creativity. You might want to consider the following issues:

- How are you going to make fullest use of the view?
- Where will resources be stored and who will have access?
- How are you going to group the desks for maximum flexibility?
- Will you need a teacher's desk?
- How can you make fullest use of the door to the playground?
- How might you create themed activity areas?
- How can the room design promote connection-making?
- How are the display spaces going to be used?
- How can you cater for the child who likes to be on his or her own sometimes?

PLANNING FOR CREATIVITY

The new National Curriculum, structured around the essentials for learning and life, personal development and literacy, numeracy and ICT, is supported by the six areas of learning. Together these could be seen to encourage more creative practice through cross-curricular planning across the EYFS and Key Stages 1 and 2. The intended holistic approach is perhaps best summarised in relation to the expectation to plan what the Qualifications and Curriculum Authority (QCA) describes as 'compelling learning experiences' (QCA, 2008). These, it is argued, at Key Stage 3 should:

- offer opportunities for autonomy, cooperation and collaboration;
- be real and relevant, connecting learning at school to the world beyond the classroom;

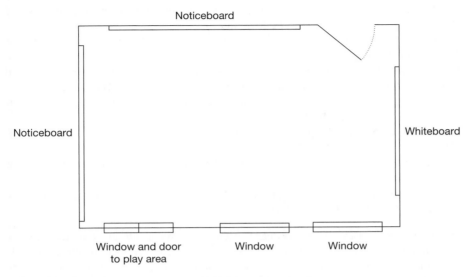

Noticeboard

Noticeboard

Whiteboard

Window and door
to play area

Window

Window

■ **Figure 7.3.1** Construct your own 'thinking classroom'

An editable version of Figure 7.3.1 is available on the companion website:
www.routledge.com/textbooks/ltps2e

- give learners a sense of autonomy, including the chance to think critically, make decisions, take responsibility and manage risks;
- have a clear sense of audience and purpose;
- provide contexts that draw together several aspects of learning: connecting different subject disciplines, focusing on a specific subject, or linking learning through cross-curricular dimensions or the development of personal, learning and thinking skills;
- have clear learning outcomes relating to what learners need to know and understand, the skills they will acquire and areas of personal development.

(QCA, 2008)

Such learning experiences are likely to be found in the primary phase also through extended and creative units of work, encompassing more than one area of learning and regularly involving the expertise of partners from the creative and cultural sector working alongside you and the children. Research from Creative Partnerships suggests that the involvement of significant others can enrich learning and raise children's expectations and achievements (Ofsted, 2006). In planning such creative units of work, you will want to build on insights from research. The following ten research-informed suggestions are worth considering:

- Create a *positive, secure atmosphere* in which risks can be taken (Seltzer and Bentley, 1999; Grainger *et al.*, 2005).
- Profile a *questioning stance* and frame the work around the children's interests and questions (Grainger *et al.*, 2005; Cremin *et al.*, 2006a; Craft *et al.*, 2007a and b; Jeffrey and Woods, 2009).
- Ensure a range of *practical and analytical open-ended* activities (Sternberg, 1997; Jeffrey and Woods, 2003; Cremin *et al.*, 2006a; Austin, 2007).

■ Emphasise *learner agency* and individual and cooperative thinking and learning (Bruner, 1996; Cremin *et al.*, 2006a; Craft *et al.*, 2007a and b).

■ Agree *clear goals*, some of which are set and owned by the learners (Csikszentmihalyi, 2002; Jeffrey and Woods, 2009).

■ Build *emotionally relevant links* to the life of each child, offering opportunities to discover *engagement and enjoyment* (Damasio, 2003; Fredrickson, 2003; Barnes, 2007).

■ Use a manageable number of *relevant subjects/areas of learning* to throw light on the topic (Gardner, 1999b; Barnes, 2007).

■ Involve developmentally appropriate *progression* in skills, knowledge and understanding (Thompson and Hall, 2004).

■ Set the work in a wider framework that includes *concepts, content and attitudes* (Grainger *et al.*, 2004; Cremin, 2009).

■ Provide supportive *assessment* procedures that build security and include time and tools for reflection (Adey and Shayer, 2002).

In this post-Rose Review era, primary teachers are reconsidering the advantages of more creative curriculum approaches, and planning coherent learning experiences in which 'school subjects [are seen as] resources in the construction of the curriculum, rather than determinants of its overall structure and emphasis' (Halpin, 2003: 114). Many plan in teams and maximise the relevance of their curriculum to the local community and the children's lives, using the rich physical, human and cultural resources of their locality and preparing significant shared experiences for children to interpret individually. Teachers are also focusing on developing the children's learning and thinking skills as they plan, specifically seeking to ensure that children learn how to:

■ *Investigate*, asking relevant questions, identifying problems, analysing and judging the value of information and ideas, questioning assumptions. They plan systematically using time and resources effectively, anticipating, taking and managing risks.

■ *Create and develop*, using their imagination to explore possibilities and generate ideas; they try out innovative alternatives, looking for patterns, recognising differences and making generalisations, predicting outcomes and making reasoned decisions.

■ *Communicate*, interacting with different audiences in variety of ways, using a range of media.

■ *Evaluate*, developing criteria for judging work and suggesting refinements and improvements.

(Rose, 2008: 77)

CREATIVE CURRICULA IN ACTION

Two examples bring such a curriculum centred upon creative learning to life. A whole school community from Tower Hamlets made a winter visit to Canary Wharf, less than 500 metres from the school gates. Many pupils had never been there. The event was grasped as an opportunity to collect as much information as possible. None of the collected impressions could have been gathered from website, lecture or written sources, so this visit was a genuine investigation involving every age group – traffic surveys, rubbings, observations of people walking, collections of geometric shapes, still images framed by 'key' describing words, moving images, sensory descriptions of sights sounds and smells, intricate 360-degree drawings, mosaics or trees imprisoned in stainless steel, stone and scaffolded containers. Every moment, morning or afternoon, was fully used in information gathering. Children and adult supporters collected digital, drawn, listed, tallied, acted and heard data from a variety of contrasting sites around the Wharf.

The library of collected and remembered objects, images and sensations were brought back to school and formed the basis of the curriculum for the next few weeks. Creating responses from these disparate sources involved very different paths in each class from nursery to Year 6. One Year 2 class made a 'sound journey' using mapping and musical skills and knowledge. Groups of five or six composed music to capture different places on their journey and linked them with other compositions of 'walking music'. Separate teams then mapped their journeys using techniques learned in the previous term and the resultant maps were used as graphic musical scores. A mixed group created large and imaginative abstract constructions from bamboo, tissue and applied decoration from rubbings and drawings, expressing their experience of the towering buildings at the wharf.

Children, along with their co-learning teachers, presented their compositions, artworks, mathematical investigations, stories and dramas to the rest of the school in a series of assemblies. These were especially appreciated across the school because everyone had shared in the same initial experience. The whole project was evaluated through a continuous blog kept by children, teachers, artists and teaching assistants. Their challenge, like yours, is to take account of individual differences in learning, help each child become a self-regulated learner, and ensure appropriate coverage of the areas of learning and their attendant knowledge bases.

In another context, a class from a rural school decided through discussion to concentrate on the value of community in a two-day project for the website Engaging Places (www.engagingplaces.org.uk/home). They divided into teams of five or six and went on walks up and down the street in which the school stood. Each group decided upon a sub-theme: improving the community, describing the community, the community in the future, problems in the community, or litter and the community. After this first decision the children used the walk as a data-gathering opportunity. The description group used cameras and viewfinders to record the different ages and materials of houses in the street, but also used sound recorders to collect the vastly different sounds at either end of the street. In class on their return, the children and their adult helper combined the sound-based and visually based impressions on a street map, which they constructed with great enthusiasm. Great bursts of creativity occurred as pairs decided how to represent the street, and how to present the sounds and images they had collected. Eventually, the group decided on a 3D street map with press-button recordings of different sounds in four different parts of the street.

The litter group arrived at a double focus. They decided to design and make attractive dustbins and make an anti-littering video. Their video decision involved storyboarding their video, rehearsal, acting it out, filming and editing. The wild and whacky litter bins were planned in detail and made in model form for a presentation in the school hall and eventually at a national launch of Engaging Places in London.

Evaluation was crucial at every stage of these activities. Children were encouraged to give their own (positive at first) assessments during each part of each process. At the end of the two days, the children and adult helpers were asked to complete a sheet saying what they most enjoyed, what new knowledge they had gained and how they would change the project if repeated in the future. Careful planning for such creative learning experiences is important and perhaps best done in collaboration with others. Some will last a term, others just a few days, but all will seek to involve the children in real, purposeful and imaginatively engaging experiences. As Rose argues, 'there should be considerable scope for imaginative approaches to curriculum design' and opportunities for 'disciplined curriculum innovation' (2008: 46).

Task 7.3.6 **A FIELD TRIP**

In groups, plan a short field trip very near to a school you know. Generate four 'problems' that children might safely be faced with in this context. Suggest the skills that would be needed to approach these problems and activities designed to help solve them. Decide on the areas of learning and personal development that this activity would address.

SUMMARY

Creative teaching is a collaborative enterprise that capitalises on the unexpected and variously involves engagement, reflection and transformation, patterned at such a rate as to invite and encourage a questioning stance and motivate self-directed learning. Creative learning involves asking questions, exploring options and generating and appraising ideas as the learner take risks and imaginatively thinks their way forwards, making new or innovative connections in the process. New thinking happens at the meeting places of different ideas and approaches and it also takes place when new links occur between people. Many of the examples in this unit show both adults and children involved in thinking and learning together, which can be a key generator of creativity. We hope you will choose to teach creatively and promote creativity through your planning and will build in choice and autonomy, relevance and purpose in engaging environments of possibility – environments both inside and outside the classroom.

ANNOTATED FURTHER READING

Craft, A. (2005) *Creativity across the Primary Curriculum: Tensions and Dilemmas*, London: RoutledgeFalmer.
> This is an informative and engaging read that raises more questions than answers as Craft explores principles and practice, policy and research and identifies an agenda for development, both at the level of the classroom and on a wider scale.

Halpin, D. (2003) *Hope and Education: The Role of the Utopian Imagination*, London: RoutledgeFalmer.
> A very accessible, passionate but philosophically sound argument for putting the hope back into education. Halpin concentrates on the need to change educators' attitudes towards a more child-centred, creative and culturally sensitive curriculum. In his mind, establishing an ethos of security where no child feels 'a loser' is central to promoting creativity.

Jeffrey, B. and Woods, P. (2009) *Creative Learning in the Primary School* London: Routledge.
> This book explores features of creative teaching and learning in the context of contemporary policy reforms in England. It is accessibly written and very well informed, highlighting the inventiveness of teachers and the role of pupils as a powerful resource for creative learning, for each other and for their teachers.

Scoffham, S. (ed.) (2004) *Primary Geography Handbook,* Sheffield: The Geographical Association.
> This handbook for teachers has a wealth of practical examples of creativity applied to geography. Chapters on 'Young geographers', 'Geography, creativity and place', 'Geography and the emotions' and 'Making geography fun' show how creative teaching and teaching for creativity are central to teaching knowledge and understanding of this subject.

RELEVANT WEBSITES

Education Act 2005: www.opsi.gov.uk/acts/acts2005/ukpga_20050018_en_1

NACCCE report, *All Our Futures: Creativity, Culture and Education*: www.cypni.org.uk/downloads/alloutfutures.pdf

(Note that the spelling of 'alloutfutures' in the url is intentional.) The National Advisory Committee on Creative and Cultural Education published this report in 1999, making recommendations for a wider national strategy for creative and cultural education.

Ofsted's *Expecting the Unexpected*: www.ofsted.gov.uk/publications/

In 2003, the Office for Standards in Education conducted this survey to identify good practice in the promotion of creativity in schools.

Visit the companion website www.routledge.com/textbooks/ltps2e for:

■ additional questions for this unit;

■ an editable figure from this unit;

■ links to useful websites relevant to this unit.

REFERENCES

Adey, P. and Shayer, M. (2002) *Learning Intelligence: Cognitive Acceleration from 5 to 15 years*, London: Open University Press.

Austin, R. (2007) *Letting the Outside In*, Stoke on Trent: Trentham.

Barnes, J. (2005) '"You could see it on their faces . . .": the importance of provoking smiles in schools', *Health Education*, 105(5): 392–400.

Barnes, J. (2007) *Cross-Curricular Learning 3–14*, London: Sage.

Barnes, J. (2009) 'The integration of music with other subjects, particularly in art forms', in J. Evans and C. Philpott (eds) *A Practical Guide to Teaching Music in the Secondary School*, London: Routledge.

Barnes, J., Hope. G. and Scoffham. S. (2008) 'A conversation about creative teaching and learning', in A. Craft, T. Cremin and P. Burnard (eds) *Creative Learning 3–11 and How We Document It*, London: Trentham, pp. 125–34.

Bearne, E., Grainger, T. and Wolstencroft, H. (2004) *Raising Boys' Achievements in Writing*, Joint Research Project, United Kingdom Literacy Association and the Primary National Strategy, Baldock: United Kingdom Literacy Association.

Beetlestone, F. (1998) *Creative Children, Imaginative Teaching*, Buckingham: Open University Press.

Bronowski, J. (1978) *The Origins of Knowledge and Imagination*, New Haven, CT: Yale University Press.

Bruner, J. (1996) *The Culture of Education*, Cambridge, MA: Harvard University Press.

Burke, C. and Grosvenor, I. (2003) *The School I'd Like: Children and Young People's Reflections on an Education for the 21st Century*, London: Routledge.

Burnard, P., Craft, A. and Cremin, T. (2006) 'Documenting "possibility thinking": a journey of collaborative inquiry', *International Journal of Early Years Education*, 14(3): 243–62.

Chappell, K., Craft, A., Burnard, P. and Cremin, T. (2008) 'Question-posing and question-responding: at the heart of possibility thinking in the early years', *Early Years: An International Journal of Research and Development*, 28(3): 267–86.

Claxton, G. (1997) *Hare Brain, Tortoise Mind: Why Intelligence Increases When You Think Less*, London: Fourth Estate.

Claxton, G. (2006) 'Mindfulness, learning and the brain', *Journal of Rational Emotive and Cognitive Behaviour Therapy*, 23: 301–14.

Claxton, G. and Lucas, B. (2004) *Be Creative: Essential Steps to Revitalize Your Work and Life*, London: BBC.

Craft, A. (2000) *Creativity Across the Primary Curriculum: Framing and Developing Practice*, London: RoutledgeFalmer.

Craft, A. (2001) 'Little c: creativity in craft', in A. Craft, B. Jeffrey and M. Liebling (eds) *Creativity in Education*, London: Continuum.

Craft, A. (2005) *Creativity in Schools: Tensions and Dilemmas*, Oxford: RoutledgeFalmer.

Craft, A., Cremin, T., Burnard, P. and Chappell, K. (2007a) 'Teacher stance in creative learning: a study of progression', *Journal of Thinking Skills and Creativity*, 2(2): 136–47.

Craft, A., Cremin, T. and Burnard, P. (2007b) (eds) *Creative Learning 3–11 and How To Document It*, London: Trentham.

Cremin, T. (2009) 'Creative teaching and creative teachers', in A. Wilson (ed.) *Creativity in Primary Practice*, Exeter: Learning Matters.

Cremin, T., Craft, A. and Burnard, P. (2006a) 'Pedagogy and possibility thinking in the early years', *Journal of Thinking Skills and Creativity*, 1(2): 108–19.

Cremin, T., Goouch, K., Blakemore, L., Goff, E. and Macdonald, R. (2006b) 'Connecting drama and writing: seizing the moment to write', *Research in Drama in Education*, 11(3): 273–91.

Cremin, T., Barnes, J. and Scoffham, S. (2009) *Creative Teaching for Tomorrow*, Margate: Future Creative.

Csikszentmihalyi, M. (1996) *Creativity: Flow and the Psychology of Discovery and Invention*, New York: Harper.

Csikszentmihalyi, M. (2002) *Flow: The Classic Work on How to Achieve Happiness*, London: Rider.

Damasio, A. (2003) *Looking for Spinoza: Joy, Sorrow and the Feeling Brain*, Orlando, FL: Harcourt.

Department for Children, Schools and Families (DCSF) (2008) *Statutory Framework for the Early Years Foundation Stage: Setting the Standards for Learning, Development and Care for Children from Birth to Five*, London: DCSF.

Dismore, H., Barnes, J. and Scoffham, S. (2008) *A Space to Reflect: Creative Leadership and the Science of Learning*, London: Creative Partnerships London North.

Eames, A., Benton, T., Sharp, C. and Kendall, L. (2006) *The Impact of Creative Partnerships on the Attainment of Young People*, Slough: NFER.

Frederickson, B. (2003) 'The value of positive emotions', *American Scientist*, 91: 300–5.

Fryer, M. (1996) *Creative Teaching and Learning*, London: Paul Chapman.

Gardner, H. (1993a) *Frames of Mind: The Theory of Multiple Intelligences*, London: Fontana Press.

Gardner, H. (1993b) *The Creating Mind*, New York: Basic Books.

Gardner, H. (1999a) *The Disciplined Mind*, New York: Simon and Schuster.

Gardner, H. (1999b) *Intelligence Reframed*, New York: Basic Books.

Grainger, T., Barnes, J. and Scoffman, S. (2004) 'Creative teaching: a creative cocktail', *Journal of Education and Teaching*, 38(3): 243–53.

Grainger, T., Goouch, K. and Lambirth, A. (2005) *Creativity and Writing: Developing Voice and Verve in the Classroom*, London: Routledge.

Halpin, D. (2003) *Hope and Education: The Role of the Utopian Imagination*, London: Routledge.

House of Commons Education and Skills Committee (2007) *Creative Partnerships and the Curriculum: Eleventh Report of the Session 2006–2007*, London: The Stationery Office.

Huppert, F., Baylis, N. and Keverne, B. (2005) *The Science of Well-being*, Oxford: Oxford University Press.

Jeffrey, B. (2005) *Final Report of the Creative Learning and Student's Perspectives (CLASP) Research Project: A European Commission Funded Project Through the Socrates Programme*, Milton Keynes: Open University Press. Available online at http://clasp.open.ac.uk (accessed November 2009).

Jeffrey, B. (ed.) (2006) *Creative Learning Practices: European Experiences*, London: Tufnell Press.

Jeffrey, B. and Craft, A. (2004) 'Teaching creatively and teaching for creativity: distinctions and relationships', *Educational Studies*, 30(1): 77–97.

Jeffrey, B. and Woods, P. (2003) *The Creative School: A Framework for Success, Quality and Effectiveness*, London: RoutledgeFalmer.

Jeffrey, B. and Woods, P. (2009) *Creative Learning in the Primary School*, London: Routledge.

John-Steiner, V. (2000) *Creative Collaboration*, New York: Oxford University Press.

Koestler, A. (1964) *The Act of Creation*, London: Penguin.

McMaster, M. (2008) *Supporting Excellence in the Arts: From Measurement to Judgement*, London: DCSF.

National Advisory Committee on Creative and Cultural Education (NACCCE) (1999) *All Our Futures: The Report of the National Advisory Committee on Creative and Cultural Education*, London: DfEE/DCMS.

Office for Standards in Education (Ofsted) (2006) *Creative Partnerships: Initiative and Impact*, London: Ofsted. Available online at www.creative-partnerships.com (accessed November 2009).

Qualifications and Curriculum Authority (QCA) (2008) *Personal Learning and Thinking Skills: The New Secondary Curriculum*, London: QCA.

Roberts, P. (2006) *Nurturing Creativity in Young People: A Report to Government to Inform Future Policy*, London: DCMS.

Robinson, K. (2001) *Out of Our Minds*, London: Capstone.

Robinson, K. (2009) *The Element: How Finding Your Passion Changes Everything*, London: Allen Lane.

Rose, J. (2008) *The Independent Review of the Primary Curriculum: Interim Report*, London: DCSF. Available online at www.dcsf.gov.uk/primarycurriculumreview (accessed November 2009).

Sefton-Green, J. (ed.) (2008) *Creative Learning*, London: Creative Partnerships and The Arts Council.

Seltzer, K. and Bentley, T. (1999) *The Creative Age: Knowledge and Skills for the New Economy*, London: Demos.

Seligman, M. (2004) *Authentic Happiness*, New York: Free Press.

Sternberg, R. (1997) *Successful Intelligence*, New York: Plume.

Sternberg, R. (ed.) (1999) *The Handbook of Creativity*, Cambridge: Cambridge University Press.

Thompson, P. and Hall, C. (2004) 'How an understanding of Bakhtin's theory of the chronotype can assist progression in classroom writing', *English in Education*, 38: 5–20.

Woods, P. (1995) *Creative Teachers in Primary Schools*, Buckingham: Open University Press.

THINKING SKILLS

Robert Fisher

INTRODUCTION

> We need to think better if we are to become better people.
>
> (Paul, aged ten)

In recent years there has been growing interest across the world in ways of developing children's thinking and learning skills (Fisher, 2005). This interest has been fed by new knowledge about how the brain works and how people learn, and evidence that specific interventions can improve children's thinking and intelligence. The particular ways in which people apply their minds to solving problems are called *thinking skills*. Many researchers suggest that thinking skills are essential to effective learning, although not all agree on the definition of this term (Moseley *et al.*, 2005). If thinking is how children make sense of learning, developing their thinking skills will help them get more out of learning and life. This unit looks at the implications of research into ways to develop thinking children, thinking classrooms and thinking schools.

OBJECTIVES

By the end of this unit you should be able to:

■ inform your understanding of 'thinking skills' and their role in learning;
■ understand some key principles that emerge from research into teaching thinking;
■ identify the main approaches to developing children's thinking;
■ see how you might integrate a 'thinking skills' approach into classroom teaching and research.

WHAT ARE THINKING SKILLS?

Thinking skills are not mysterious entities existing somewhere in the mind. Nor are they like mental muscles that have a physical presence in the brain. What the term refers to is the human capacity to think in conscious ways to achieve certain purposes. Such processes include remembering, questioning, forming concepts, planning, reasoning, imagining, solving problems, making decisions and judgements, translating thoughts into words, and so on. Thinking skills are ways in which humans exercise the *sapiens* part of being *Homo sapiens*.

A skill is commonly defined as a practical ability in doing something or succeeding in a task. Usually we refer to skills in particular contexts, such as being 'good at cooking', but they can also refer to general areas of performance, such as having a logical mind or a good memory, being creative, and so on. A thinking skill is a practical ability to think in ways that are judged to be more or less effective or skilled. They are the habits of intelligent behaviour learned through practice; for example, children can become better at giving reasons or asking questions the more they practise doing so.

If thinking skills are the mental capacities we use to investigate the world, to solve problems and make judgements, to identify every such skill would be to enumerate all the capacities of the human mind and the list would be endless. Many researchers have attempted to identify the key skills in human thinking, and the most famous of these is Bloom's taxonomy.

Bloom's taxonomy of thinking skills (what he called 'the cognitive goals of education') has been widely used by teachers in planning their teaching. He identifies a number of basic or 'lower-order' cognitive skills – knowledge, comprehension and application, and a number of 'higher-order' skills – analysis, synthesis and evaluation. Figure 7.4.1 shows the various categories identified by Bloom and the processes involved in the various thinking levels.

You could plan or analyse many learning activities in terms of the above categories. For example, when telling a story, a teacher might ask the following kinds of questions:

1	*Knowledge*	What happened in the story?
2	*Comprehension*	Why did it happen that way?
3	*Application*	What would you have done?
4	*Analysis*	Which part did you like best?

Cognitive goal	Thinking cues
1 Knowledge (knowing and remembering)	Say what you know, or remember, describe, repeat, define, identify, tell who, when, which, where, what
2 Comprehension (interpreting and understanding)	Describe in your own words, tell how you feel about it, what it means, explain, compare, relate
3 Application (applying, making use of)	How can you use it, where does it lead, apply what you know, use it to solve problems, demonstrate
4 Analysis (taking apart, being critical)	What are the parts, the order, the reasons why, the causes/problems/solutions/consequences
5 Synthesis (connecting, being creative)	How might it be different, how else, what if, suppose, putting together, develop, improve, create in your own way
6 Evaluation (judging and assessing)	How would you judge it, does it succeed, will it work, what would you prefer, why you think so

■ **Figure 7.4.1** Bloom's taxonomy

Source: Bloom and Krathwohl (1956)

| 5 | *Synthesis* | Can you think of a different ending? |
| 6 | *Evaluation* | What did you think of the story? Why? |

Bloom's taxonomy built on earlier research by Piaget and Vygotsky that suggested that thinking skills and capacities are developed by *cognitive challenge*. Teachers need to challenge children to think more deeply and more widely and in more systematic and sustained ways. Or as Tom, aged ten, put it: 'A good teacher makes you think . . . even when you don't want to.' One way in which you, as a good teacher, can do this is by asking questions that challenge children's thinking.

Task 7.4.1 QUESTIONS FOR THINKING

Choose a story, poem, text or topic that you would like to use with children as a stimulus for their thinking. Using Bloom's taxonomy create a series of questions to think about and discuss after you have shared the stimulus with them. List your questions under Bloom's six categories: knowledge, comprehension and application, analysis, synthesis and evaluation.

WHY ARE THINKING SKILLS IMPORTANT?

Thinking skills are important because mastery of the 'basics' in education (literacy, maths, science, etc.), however well taught, are not sufficient to fulfil human potential, or to meet the demands of the labour market or of active citizenship. Countries across the world are recognising that a broad range of competencies is needed to prepare children for an unpredictable future. These higher-order thinking skills are required, in addition to basic skills, because individuals cannot 'store' sufficient knowledge in their memories for future use. Information is expanding at such a rate that individuals require transferable skills to enable them to address different problems in different contexts at different times throughout their lives. The complexity of modern jobs requires people who can comprehend, judge and participate in generating new knowledge and processes. Modern democratic societies require citizens to assimilate information from multiple sources, determine its truth and use it to make sound judgements.

The challenge is to develop educational programmes that enable all individuals, not just an elite, to become effective thinkers, because these competencies are now required of everyone. A 'thinking skills' approach suggests that learners must develop awareness of themselves as thinkers and learners, practise strategies for effective thinking and develop the habits of intelligent behaviour that are needed for lifelong learning. As Paul, aged ten, put it: 'We need to think better if we are going to become better people.'

WHAT DOES RESEARCH TELL US ABOUT THINKING?

Research in cognitive science and psychology is providing a clearer picture of the brain and the processes associated with thinking (Smith, 2004). This brain research has some important implications for teachers. For example, we now know that most of the growth in the human brain occurs in early childhood: by the age of six, the brain in most children is approximately 90 per cent of its adult size. This implies that intervention, while the brain is still growing, may be more effective than waiting until the brain is fully developed. Cognitive challenge is important at all stages, but especially in the early years of education.

Dialogue is the primary means for developing intelligence in the human species. The large human brain evolved to enable individuals to negotiate through dialogue the complexities of social living. The capacity for dialogue is central to human thinking. Human consciousness originates in a motivation to share emotions, experience and activities with others. This 'dialogic' capacity is more fundamental than writing or tool use. It is through dialogue that children develop consciousness, learn control over their internal mental processes and develop the conceptual tools for thinking (Fisher, 2009). No wonder recent research emphasises that teacher–pupil interaction is the key to improving standards of teaching and learning (Alexander, 2006; Hattie, 2008).

Psychologists and philosophers have helped to extend our understanding of the term 'thinking', by emphasising the importance of *dispositions*, such as attention and motivation, commonly associated with thinking (Claxton, 2002). This has prompted a move away from a simple model of 'thinking skills' as isolated cognitive capacities to a view of thinking as inextricably connected to emotions and dispositions, including 'emotional intelligence', which is our ability to understand our own emotions and the emotions of others (Goleman, 2006).

There is also a growing realisation that we need not only to teach cognitive skills and strategies, but also to develop the higher 'metacognitive' functions involved in metacognition. This involves making learners aware of themselves as thinkers and how they process/create knowledge by 'learning how to learn' (see sections on 'Self-awareness' in the Primary National Strategy (DfES, 2004)).

Metacognition involves thinking about one's own thinking. It includes knowledge of oneself, for example of what one knows, what one has learned, what one can and cannot do and ways to improve one's learning or achievement. Metacognition also involves skills of recognising problems, representing features of problems, planning what to do in trying to solve problems, monitoring progress and evaluating the outcomes of one's own thinking or problem-solving activity.

Metacognition is promoted by helping pupils to reflect on their thinking and decision-making processes. It is developed when pupils are helped to be strategic in organising their activities and are encouraged to reflect before, during and after problem-solving processes. The implication is that you need to plan time for debriefing and review in lessons to encourage children to think about their learning and how to improve it. This can be done through discussion in a plenary session, or by finding time for reflective writing in their own thinking or learning logs.

The human mind is made up of many faculties or capacities that enable learning to take place. Our general capacity for understanding or *intelligence* was once thought to be innate and unmodifiable. As a child once put it: 'Either you've got it or you haven't.' The notion of inborn intelligence that dominated educational practice until the mid-twentieth century was challenged by Vygotsky, Piaget and others, who developed a constructivist psychology based on a view of learners as active creators of their own knowledge. Some researchers argue that intelligence is not one generic capacity but is made up of multiple intelligences (Gardner, 1999). Howard Gardner's Multiple Intelligence theory has had a growing influence in recent years on educational theory and practice, although not all are convinced of its claims. Whether intelligence is viewed as one general capacity or many, what researchers are agreed upon is that it is modifiable and can be developed.

Key principles that emerge from this research include the need for teachers and carers to provide:

■ *cognitive challenge*, challenging children's thinking from the earliest years;
■ *collaborative learning*, extending thinking through working with others;
■ *metacognitive discussion*, reviewing what children think and how they learn.

This research and the pioneering work of Reuven Feuerstein, who created a programme called Instrumental Enrichment, Matthew Lipman, who founded Philosophy for Children, and other leading figures such as Edward de Bono, creator of 'lateral thinking', have inspired a wide range of curriculum and programme developments (Fisher, 2008). These include a range of teaching approaches that you could use, including 'cognitive acceleration', 'brain-based' approaches (such as 'accelerated learning') and 'philosophical' approaches that aim at developing the moral and emotional as well as intellectual aspects of thinking – caring and collaborative as well as critical and creative thinking. These are discussed on pages 380–2.

By the end of the twentieth century there was a widespread realisation that 'key' or 'core' skills of thinking, creativity and problem solving lay at the heart of successful learning and should be embedded in primary and secondary school curricula. When the Department for Education and Employment (DfEE) in England commissioned Carol McGuinness to review and evaluate research into thinking skills and related areas, key points that emerged from her study were that:

■ pupils benefitted from being coached in thinking;
■ not one model but many approaches proved effective;
■ success was due to pedagogy (teaching strategies) not specific materials;
■ strategies were needed to enable pupils to transfer thinking to other contexts;
■ teachers needed professional support and coaching to sustain success.

SHOULD THINKING BE TAUGHT IN SEPARATE LESSONS OR ACROSS THE CURRICULUM?

Research suggests that one-off 'thinking' lessons are less effective than teaching thinking and learning strategies that can be applied in subjects (such as CASE; see page 380) or as dialogic strategies across the curriculum. McGuinness (1999) points out that the most successful interventions are associated with a 'strong theoretical underpinning, well-designed and contextualised materials, explicit pedagogy and teacher support'.

In England, the revised National Curriculum (DfEE/QCA, 1999) included thinking skills in its rationale, stating that thinking skills are essential in 'learning how to learn'. The list of thinking skills identified in the English National Curriculum is similar to many such lists: information processing, reasoning, enquiry, creative thinking and evaluation. Any good lesson or learning conversation will show evidence of some or all of these elements. They focus on 'knowing how' as well as 'knowing what', not only on curriculum content, but on learning how to learn. See Figure 7.4.2 for ways in which they can be related to Bloom's taxonomy.

In recent curriculum developments, such as the Personal Learning and Thinking Skills framework (QCA, 2009) and the interim report of the *Independent Review of the Primary Curriculum* (Rose Review) (Rose, 2008), in England, as elsewhere, the curriculum is no longer seen simply as

Thinking skills	Bloom's taxonomy
Information processing	Knowledge, comprehension
Enquiry	Application
Reasoning	Analysis
Creative thinking	Synthesis
Evaluation	Evaluation

■ **Figure 7.4.2** Thinking skills linked to Bloom's taxonomy

subject knowledge, but as being underpinned by the skills of lifelong learning. Good teaching is not just about achieving particular curriculum objectives, but also about developing general thinking skills and learning behaviours. Since the McGuiness review (1999) and the explicit inclusion of thinking skills in the National Curriculum, interest in the teaching of thinking has burgeoned in the UK. Research has shown that interventions work if they have a strong theoretical base and if teachers are enthusiastic and well trained in the use of a programme or strategy. Teachers are developing 'teaching for thinking' approaches in new directions, integrating them into everyday teaching to create 'thinking classrooms', and developing whole-school policies to create 'thinking schools'.

Task 7.4.2 **IDENTIFYING THINKING SKILLS**

Identify in a lesson plan, or observation of a classroom lesson, the thinking skills that are being developed as general learning objectives. Look for evidence that the children are engaged in information processing, reasoning, enquiry, creative thinking and evaluation.

The following proforma could be used for recording the evidence.

Identifying thinking skills

What thinking skills are pupils developing and using in this lesson? Identify examples of:

Information processing
Finding relevant information
Organising information
Representing or communicating information

Reasoning
Giving reasons
Making inferences or deductions
Arguing or explaining a point of view

Enquiry
Asking questions
Planning research or study
Engaging in enquiry or process of finding out

Creative thinking
Generating ideas
Imagining or hypothesising
Designing innovative solutions

Evaluation
Developing evaluation criteria
Applying evaluation criteria
Judging the value of information and ideas

HOW DO WE TEACH THINKING IN THE CLASSROOM?

Researchers have identified a number of teaching strategies you can use to help stimulate children's thinking in the classroom. These approaches to teaching thinking can be summarised as:

■ cognitive acceleration;
■ brain-based techniques;
■ philosophy for children;
■ teaching strategies across the curriculum.

Cognitive acceleration

CASE

Philip Adey and Michael Shayer developed the original Cognitive Acceleration through Science Education (CASE) project in the 1980s and early 1990s, applying the theories of Piaget on 'cognitive conflict' to Key Stage 3 science. Their work now extends into other subjects and age groups and has perhaps the best research and most robust evidence of the impact of thinking skills in the UK (Shayer and Adey, 2002).

The following is a typical format of a CASE lesson for thinking that builds in time for cognitive and metacognitive discussion:

1 *Concrete preparation*   stimulus to thinking, introducing the terms of the problem.
2 *Cognitive conflict*   creates a challenge for the mind.
3 *Social construction*   dialogue with others, discussion that extends thinking.
4 *Metacognition*   reflection on how we tackled the problem.
5 *Bridging*   reviewing where else we can use this thinking and learning.

CASE lessons have also been developed for young children under the title 'Let's Think!', and aim to raise achievement by developing Year 1 pupils' general thinking patterns and teachers' understanding of children's thinking.

During 'Let's Think!' lessons young children work with a teacher in groups of six and each activity takes about 30 minutes. The session is completely oral, with discussion based on a range of objects. At the beginning of the session the teacher helps agree a common language to describe the objects being used. Having established the vocabulary and the concepts involved, the teacher sets the challenge of the activity. One popular activity in this schema is called the 'hoop game', in which children are required to put orange toy dinosaurs in one hoop and T-Rex dinosaurs in another hoop. The challenge is that one of the dinosaurs is an orange T-Rex. This is very perplexing for pre-operational children because they have to utilise two pieces of information about the dinosaur and find a solution to the problem. The children work together as a group to come to a solution or a number of possible solutions to solve the task. They discuss their ideas and make suggestions. The teacher guides them, without being obvious, towards the idea of overlapping the hoops and putting the wayward dinosaur in the intersection.

As in other discussion-based approaches, children are encouraged to state whether they agree or disagree with each other by giving a reason. For example, they are taught to say, 'I think . . . because' or 'I disagree with you because . . .'. The activities are designed as problems to be solved, thus creating a context for developing thinking. Children are given a challenge and are required to work collaboratively, in order to plan and evaluate their own and others' thinking strategies.

The teacher then gets the children to think about their thinking (metacognition) through asking such questions as 'What do you think we are going to have to think about?' and 'How did you get your answer?', rather than 'Is your answer correct?' Of course, you do not need the 'Let's Think!' materials to apply this teaching strategy to any area of the curriculum.

What the 'Let's Think!' approach aims to do is to accelerate cognitive development between two types of thinking. The first type of thought is what Piaget called 'pre-operational', when children still find it difficult to engage in what adults perceive as rational thought. The next stage, which Piaget described as 'concrete operational', involves manipulating at least two ideas in order to produce a third, new idea, which is what the sessions encourage the children to do. 'Let's Think!' aims to accelerate the transition between the two types of thought in order to help pupils make better sense of their learning and improve general achievement. It does this by ensuring that teaching includes cognitive challenge, collaborative activity and children thinking about how they think and learn.

'Thinking maths' lessons for primary children are part of a related project called CAME (Cognitive Acceleration in Mathematics Education). These lessons involve discussion-based tasks in maths that aim to develop children's conceptual thinking rather than the mechanics of doing the maths. They differ from open-ended investigations in that each lesson has a specific concept to develop. The activities are planned to generate group and whole-class discussion rather than written work, with an emphasis on 'how did you get your answer?' rather than 'what is the answer?'. As the CAME approach suggests, if your emphasis in teaching is: 'How did you get your answer?' rather than 'Is your answer correct?', it is a far more productive way of generating children's thinking and learning.

Brain-based techniques

ACCELERATED LEARNING

Many educationalists are influenced by recent research into how the human brain works and draw on some of the implications of this research for teachers and schools. Accelerated learning and multiple intelligence approaches all draw on these broad ideas, together with research into learning styles. The common feature is the reliance on brain research to inspire teaching techniques in the classroom.

There are many theories of learning styles. They are rooted in a classification of psychological types and the fact that individuals tend to process information differently. Different researchers propose different sets of learning style characteristics, but many remain unconvinced by their claims that children learn best through using one preferred style (Coffield *et al.*, 2004).

Accelerated learning approaches include applying VAK learning styles to teaching. VAK stands for:

■   *visual* – learning best through pictures, charts, diagrams, video, ICT, etc.;
■   *auditory* – learning best through listening;
■   *kinaesthetic* – learning best through being physically engaged in a task.

For example, in teaching a class to spell a word a teacher might show them how to chunk the word into three pieces, and emphasise this by using different colours for each section of the word and asking them to visualise it in their heads. The teacher might also ask them to write the word in the air with their fingers. Accelerated learning emphasises the importance of including a range of learning experiences – visual, verbal and physical – in your teaching, so that children are challenged to think in different ways. (For more on Alistair Smith's approach to accelerated learning see www.alite.co.uk.)

These and other 'brain-based' teaching strategies, such as 'Brain Gym' (which uses simple but challenging aerobic exercises to focus the mind and stimulate the brain), offer much scope for research in the classroom (see www.braingym.org.uk).

DE BONO

According to Edward de Bono, we tend to think in restricted and predictable ways. To become better thinkers we need to learn new habits. His teaching strategy, known as 'thinking hats', helps learners try different approaches to thinking. Each 'thinking hat' represents a different way to think about a problem or issue. Children are encouraged to try on the different 'hats' or approaches to a problem to go beyond their usual thinking habits (de Bono, 2000). The 'hats', together with questions you might ask, are as follows:

White hat	=	information	*What do we know?*
Red hat	=	feelings	*What do we feel?*
Purple hat	=	problems	*What are the drawbacks?*
Yellow hat	=	positives	*What are the benefits?*
Green hat	=	creativity	*What ideas have we got?*
Blue hat	=	control	*What are our aims?*

De Bono claims that the technique is widely used in management, but little research has been published on its use in education. Some teachers have found it a useful technique for encouraging children to look at a problem or topic from a variety of perspectives. It encourages us, and our children, to think creatively about any topic and to ask: 'Is there another way of thinking about this?'

Philosophy for Children

A pioneer of the 'critical thinking' movement in America is the philosopher Matthew Lipman. Originally a university philosophy professor, Lipman was unhappy at what he saw as poor thinking in his students. They seemed to have been encouraged to learn facts and to accept authoritative opinions, but not to think for themselves. He became convinced that something was wrong with the way they had been taught in school when they were younger. He therefore founded the Institute for the Advancement of Philosophy for Children (IAPC) and developed with colleagues a programme called Philosophy for Children, used in more than 40 countries around the world (see http://cehs.montclair.edu/academic/iapc/). Lipman believes that children are natural philosophers because they view the world with curiosity and wonder (Lipman, 2003). It is children's own questions stimulated by specially written philosophical stories that form the starting point for enquiry or discussion.

STORIES FOR THINKING

Many resources have been developed that adapt Matthew Lipman's approach to Philosophy for Children to the needs of children and teachers in the UK. 'Stories for Thinking' is one such approach (Fisher, 1996). The aim, through using stories and other kinds of stimulus for philosophical discussion, is to create a *community of enquiry* in the classroom (see www.sapere.net). Encouraging children to question and discuss what they do not understand is fundamental to this teaching method. Researchers have reported striking cognitive gains through this approach in the classroom, including enhancing verbal reasoning, self-esteem and dialogic skills (Topping and Trickey, 2007).

In a typical Stories for Thinking lesson the teacher shares a 'thinking story' with the class. They have 'thinking time', when they are asked to think about anything in the story that they thought was strange, interesting or puzzling. After some quiet thinking time the teacher asks for their comments or questions, and writes each child's questions on the board, adding their name after their question. The children then choose from the list of questions which one they would like to discuss. The teacher then invites the children to comment, and who agrees or disagrees with particular comments made. If children do not give reasons or evidence from the story for their opinions the teacher asks 'Why do you think that?' or 'Have you got a reason for that?'

When asked the value of a Stories for Thinking lesson, one child said: 'You have to ask questions and think hard about the answers.' Another said: 'Sometimes you change your mind and sometimes you don't.' A third reply was: 'It is better than just doing reading or writing because you have to say what you really think.'

Teachers note that in Stories for Thinking lessons, in which they may also uses poems, pictures, objects or other texts for thinking, the children have become more thoughtful, better at speaking and listening to each other, better at questioning and using the language of reasoning, more confident in posing creative ideas and in judging what they and others think and do and more confident about applying their thinking to fresh challenges in learning and in life (Fisher, 2008).

What stories or other forms of stimulus could you use to really engage your children in thinking? How could you create an enquiring classroom?

Task 7.4.3 **CREATING A THINKING CLASSROOM**

What would a thinking classroom look like?

■ Collect words to describe what a thinking classroom might look like. These might include some reference to the teacher's behaviour, children's behaviour, classroom environment or kinds of activity that help children to think and learn well.
■ Sort your ideas into small groups and give each group a heading that you think appropriate.
■ Choose one idea from each group and consider how you could develop this in your classroom.

TEACHING STRATEGIES ACROSS THE CURRICULUM

A growing number of programmes and strategies aim to help teachers develop children's thinking and learning across the curriculum, such as the TASC (Thinking Actively in a Social Context) and ACTS (Activating Children's Thinking Skills). It is difficult to evaluate the success of these and other interventions because of the many variables involved in the teaching situation. There is much scope here for your own research into teaching strategies in the classroom and for developing new strategies.

A number of specific teaching strategies have been identified to help stimulate children's thinking in different subject areas and many of these are included in the Primary National Strategies guidance for teachers (www.nationalstrategies.standards.dcsf.gov.uk/primary/). For example, 'Odd One Out' is a teaching technique to identify pupils' understanding of key concepts in different subjects. A teacher might in a numeracy lesson put three numbers on the board, such as 9, 5 and 10; or in science three materials; or in English three characters to compare and contrast – then ask the children to choose the 'odd one out' and to give a reason. Teachers who use this strategy claim it can reveal gaps in the knowledge taught and the knowledge and vocabulary that the children are then able to use. The children think of it as a game and are used to thinking up examples and ideas that show their thinking in different curriculum subjects. This approach encourages creative thinking and reasoning (Higgins *et al.*, 2001). Can you think of three things and give reasons why one, two or each of them might be the odd one out?

Task 7.4.4 **EVALUATING CONCEPTS**

Choose a concept related to thinking or learning skills, such as creative thinking (or creativity), critical thinking (or reasoning), information processing, enquiry (or questioning) or evaluating (or assessment) as a focus for a small-scale investigation.
Try collecting data in the following ways:

■ *Find out from others*: Find out what others think of this concept through reading or internet research, and by interviewing children and/or colleagues, asking what this concept means to them.
■ *Investigate for yourself*: Observe a lesson to collect evidence about what happens in the classroom in relation to teaching and learning related to the concept you have chosen.

After collecting some data, evaluate what you find. Review, critically analyse and evaluate your data and draw conclusions about what you have learned from this investigation. Think in what ways teaching policy or practice might be modified in light of your research.

Mind mapping

Many approaches include the use of thinking diagrams – 'mindmaps' or 'concept maps' – as aids to making thinking visual and explicit.

Concept mapping is an information-processing technique with a long history. Tony Buzan developed this technique into a version he calls 'mind mapping' (Buzan, 2006). Concept maps are tools that help make thinking visible – and involve writing down, or more commonly drawing, a central idea and thinking up new and related ideas that radiate out from the centre. By focusing on key ideas written down in children's own words, and then looking for branches out and connections between the ideas, they are mapping knowledge in a manner that can help them understand and remember new information. A simple concept map might be used to map out the connections between characters in a story. Children might also draw maps from memory to test what they remember or know. Teachers have found concept maps helpful in finding out or revising what children know and the technique is especially popular when used in pairs or groups. Children can learn the technique from an early age and many find it motivating. As one young child put it: 'Concept mapping gets you to think and try more.' Concept mapping is a useful teaching and revision technique for extending thinking and making it visually memorable.

When you are planning your next topic or activity with children, think of ways of making your own or your children's thinking visible, for example by creating a 'mind map' of a story, a process or collection of ideas.

Computers and thinking

Research shows that there are several ways in which ICT could particularly enhance information-processing skills. ICT enables multiple and complex representations of information, for example allowing learners to think with a richer knowledge base. As James, aged eight, said: 'I didn't know there was so much to know!'

Educational software can act like a teacher to prompt and direct enquiry through asking questions, giving clues and suggesting avenues of investigation. It can also act as a resource while learners discuss and explore ideas, for example prompting reflection around a simulation. Networks via the internet, including videoconferencing, can allow children to engage directly in collaborative learning and knowledge sharing with others who are not physically present.

The main criticism of the computer as a tutor model is that directed computer teaching does not allow children to be creative learners, able to think and make connections for themselves, and so is unlikely to support the development of higher-order thinking. This can be transformed, however, by collaboration around ICT activities, which has been shown to have the potential to enhance the learning of transferable thinking skills.

Effective collaborative learning still needs to be structured. Learners should be taught how to reason and learn together before they are asked to work collaboratively with ICT, because having to articulate and explain strategies to others is more likely to lead to transfer than just doing things without thinking or talking them through. In the lesson plenary, by reflecting on this process of collaborative problem solving, the teacher can help children to 'bridge' their thinking from their experience with, for example, Logo or another computer program to different areas of the curriculum (see http://schools.becta.org.uk/).

Computers can help develop children's thinking skills when used as part of a larger dialogue about thinking and learning (Wegerif, 2002). The challenge for you as a teacher is to find ways to use the computer to encourage thinking with, and discussion between, children.

Task 7.4.5 **PLANNING FOR TEACHING THINKING**

■ Choose a teaching strategy or approach from published materials that aims to develop children's thinking skills.
■ Think how you might use this strategy or approach in a chosen area of the curriculum.
■ Plan a lesson that incorporates this strategy, identifying a specific thinking or learning skill in your lesson objectives.
■ Share your plan or teaching ideas with others.
■ Teach and evaluate your lesson for thinking!

Recent test results show that standards in schools are rising – but slowly. Could the teaching of thinking provide a key to raising achievement? The experience of many teachers suggests that, when pupils are taught the habits of effective thinking, they grow in confidence, their learning is enriched and they are better prepared to face the challenges of the future. Children think so too – as Arran, aged nine, put it: 'When you get out in the real world you have to think for yourself; that's why we need to practise it in school.'

Research suggests that the most successful approaches to teaching thinking are dialogic teaching methods (such as Philosophy for Children), Piagetian approaches (such as CASE) and assessment for learning (AFL) (Hattie, 2008; see also Unit 5.1 of this volume). Other approaches not so well supported by research may be found useful by teachers and provide a good focus for their own research. Good teaching is about helping children to think for themselves, which is why it is both a challenge and an adventure.

SUMMARY

In recent years there has been much research into ways of developing children's thinking and learning skills. This has been informed by growing knowledge about how the brain works, how people learn and how teaching approaches can help improve children's ability to think and learn. The phrase 'thinking skills' refers to many of the capacities involved in thinking and learning, skills fundamental to lifelong learning, active citizenship and emotional intelligence. Research shows that the key to raising standards in education is through teaching that promotes cognitive challenge, interactive dialogue with and between children and metacognitive review. These and other teaching strategies can help raise standards of achievement and create thinking children, thinking classrooms and thinking schools.

ANNOTATED FURTHER READING

Fisher, R. (2005) *Teaching Children to Learn*, 2nd edn, Cheltenham: Stanley Thornes.
> This book is a practical guide to teaching strategies that develop thinking and learning skills and provide a framework for active learning in the primary classroom.

Fisher, R. (2005) *Teaching Children to Think*, 2nd edn, Cheltenham: Stanley Thornes.
> This book discusses the nature of thinking and thinking skills and explores the development of thinking skills programmes and how they can be implemented in the classroom.

Fisher, R. (2009) *Creative Dialogue: Talk for Thinking*, Abingdon: Routledge.
> This is a guide to dialogic learning, presenting practical research-based ways of teaching children to be more thoughtful and creative, and to learn more effectively through talk for thinking in the classroom. It includes advice on using dialogue to support AFL and ideas for developing listening skills and concentration.

Hattie, J. (2008) *Visible Learning: A Synthesis of over 800 Meta-analyses Relating to Achievement*, London; Routledge.
> This, the largest ever overview of education research, suggests that raising the quality of teacher–pupil interaction is the key to improving education. Encouraging pupils to question their teachers on what they do and do not understand is identified as the single most effective teaching method. Other effective approaches identified include Piagetian programmes (such as CASE) and AFL.

RELEVANT WEBSITES

Accelerated Learning in Training and Education (Alite): www.alite.co.uk
> This site contains information on Alistair Smith's approach to accelerated learning.

Becta: http://schools.becta.org.uk/
> This site offers advice and guidance on how technology can be built into teaching and learning.

Brain Gym: www.braingym.org.uk
> This site focuses on the physical skills involved in learning.

Institute for the Advancement of Philosophy for Children (IAPC): http://cehs.montclair.edu/academic/iapc
> This site provides curriculum materials for engaging young people in philosophical enquiry.

Primary National Strategies: www.nationalstrategies.standards.dcsf.gov.uk/primary/
Qualifications and Curriculum Development Agency (QCDA): www.qcda.gov.uk/1841.aspx
> Visit this site for QCDA advice on thinking skills.

Society for Advancing Philosophical Enquiry and Reflection in Education (SAPERE): www.sapere.org.uk/
Visit this site for more on Philosophy for Children.

Visit the companion website www.routledge.com/textbooks/ltps2e for:

■ additional questions and task for this unit;
■ links to useful websites relevant to this unit.

REFERENCES

Alexander, R. (2006) *Towards Dialogic Teaching: Rethinking Classroom Talk*, 3rd edn, Cambridge: Dialogos.

Bloom, B. and Krathwohl, D.R. (1956) *Taxonomy of Educational Objectives, Handbook 1: Cognitive Domain*, New York: David McKay.

Buzan, T. (2006) *The Mind Map Book*, London: BBC Active Publications. See also www.mind-map.com (accessed November 2009).

Claxton, G. (2002) *Building Learning Power: Helping Young People Become Better Learners*, Bristol: TLO.

Coffield, F., Moseley, D., Hall, E. and Ecclestone, K. (2004) *Should We Be Using Learning Styles: What Research Has To Say To Practice*, London: Learning Skills and Development Agency.

de Bono, E. (2000) *Six Thinking Hats*, 2nd edn, London: Penguin.

Department for Education and Employment/Qualifications and Curriculum Authority (DfEE/QCA) (1999) *The National Curriculum for England*, London: DfEE/QCA.

Department for Education and Skills (DfES) (2004) *Primary National Strategies*. Available online at www.nationalstrategies.standards.dcsf.gov.uk/primary/ (accessed November 2009).

Fisher, R. (various) *Stories for Thinking* (1996), *Games for Thinking* (1997), *Poems for Thinking* (1997), *First Stories for Thinking* (1999), *First Poems for Thinking* (2000) *Values for Thinking* (2001), Oxford: Nash Pollock.

Fisher, R. (2005) *Teaching Children to Think*, 2nd edn, Cheltenham: Stanley Thornes.

Fisher, R. (2008) *Teaching Thinking: Philosophical Enquiry in the Classroom*, 3rd edn, London: Continuum.

Fisher, R. (2009) *Creative Dialogue: Talk for Thinking*, Abingdon: Routledge.

Gardner, H. (1999) *Intelligence Reframed: Multiple Intelligences for the 21st Century*, New York: Basic Books.

Goleman, D. (2006) *Social Intelligence*, New York: Bantam.

Hattie, J. (2008) *Visible Learning: A Synthesis of Over 800 Meta-analyses Relating to Achievement*, London: Routledge.

Higgins, S., Baumfield, V. and Leat, D. (2001) *Thinking Through Primary Teaching*, Cambridge: Chris Kington.

Lipman, M. (2003) *Thinking in Education*, 2nd edn, Cambridge: Cambridge University Press.

McGuinness, C. (1999) *From Thinking Skills to Thinking Classrooms: A Review and Evaluation of Approaches for Developing Pupils' Thinking*, Research Report RR115, London: DfEE.

Moseley, D., Baumfield V., Elliott, J., Higgins, S., Miller, J. and Newton, D.P. (2005) *Frameworks for Thinking: A Handbook for Teaching and Learning*, Cambridge: Cambridge University Press.

Qualifications and Curriculum Authority (QCA) (2009) *Personal Learning and Thinking Skills*, London: QCA.

Rose, J. (2008) *The Independent Review of the Primary Curriculum: Interim Report*, London: DCSF. Available online at www.dcsf.gov.uk/primarycurriculumreview (accessed November 2009).

Shayer, M. and Adey, P. (2002) *Learning Intelligence*, Buckingham: Open University Press.

Smith, A. (2004) *The Brain's Behind it: New Knowledge About the Brain and Learning*, London: Continuum.

Topping, K.J. and Trickey, S. (2007) 'Impact of philosophical enquiry on school students' interactive behaviour', *International Journal of Thinking Skills and Creativity*, 2(2): 73–84.

Wegerif, R. (2002) *Literature Review in Thinking Skills, Technology and Learning*. Available online at www.futurelab.org.uk (accessed November 2009).

GIFTED AND TALENTED

Deborah Eyre

INTRODUCTION

> We need to take particular steps to serve the needs of gifted and talented children.
>
> (DfES, 2003a: 41)

The idea that gifted and talented children need particular consideration during their primary schooling is one that has only recently been formally recognised. Yet, it has long been recognised that one of the greatest challenges for any primary teacher is to manage the learning needs of the various children in their class, especially when those children have very differing abilities.

'Gifted and talented children' is the term applied to those children who are achieving, or have the potential to achieve, at a level substantially beyond the rest of their peer group. It does not mean just the infant Mozart or the child Einstein, but rather refers to the upper end of the ability range in most classes. Every primary teacher, therefore, needs to know how to teach the gifted and talented and to be familiar with the techniques for creating high levels of intellectual challenge in the classroom. On the whole, these children can be some of the most rewarding to teach and, provided that you create a classroom in which they can thrive, they will generally repay you handsomely. Conversely, if they are under-challenged they can become disruptive and difficult.

This unit is designed to help you to create a classroom that meets the needs of your gifted and talented children by creating an intellectually lively and challenging learning environment. By creating this kind of environment to meet the needs of your gifted children, you will also provide benefits for the whole class and raise overall expectations. In this unit, we will consider how to identify the gifted or talented children in your class, ways to create an overall learning environment that encourages high levels of achievement and techniques for planning challenging tasks.

OBJECTIVES

By the end of the unit you should be able to:

- understand how to recognise gifted and talented children;
- know how to create a suitable classroom learning environment;
- develop techniques for planning challenging tasks.

DEFINING GIFTED AND TALENTED

The Qualifications and Curriculum Authority (QCA; see www.qcda.gov.uk/2346.aspx), based on the work of Excellence in Cities, identifies:

■ 'gifted' pupils as those who have abilities in one or more subjects in the statutory school curriculum other than art and design, music and physical education (PE);
■ 'talented' pupils are those who have abilities in art and design, music, PE or performing arts such as dance and drama.

Therefore, the pupil who is an all-rounder will be both gifted and talented.

The QCA defines 'gifted and talented' as:

Gifted and talented pupils are those that well exceed the expectations for their age group, either in all subjects or just one. The gifted and talented are a diverse group and their range of attainment will be varied; some do well in statutory national curriculum tests or national qualifications. However, being gifted and talented covers much more than the ability to succeed in tests and examinations. Therefore, it is impossible to set one way of identifying gifted and talented pupils.

In 2001, the QCA produced guidance to help primary schools in England to identify pupils who are gifted academically or have talents in the arts or sport, by the way they speak, listen, read and write. The guidance follows the Excellence in Cities requirement that schools identify the top 5 to 10 per cent of their pupils and offer them special programmes.

More recently, government policy starts from the expectation that there are gifted and talented learners in every year group in every school. It is up to each school to decide on the proportion of their population who are gifted and talented. Since we believe that ability is evenly distributed throughout the population, a school's gifted and talented pupils should be broadly representative of its whole school population.

It is important to keep in mind that children defined as gifted or talented are simply normal children with all the usual personality characteristics of their age group. They are diverse in their personalities and interests and it is no more possible to attribute an extensive range of personality characteristics to gifted children than it would be to children with, say, dyslexia. Don't be surprised if you find you have a gifted child in your class who is naughty or immature; giftedness is simply about intellectual ability and that is only one aspect of any child. As far as intellectual characteristics are concerned, most gifted and talented children are of above average ability generally, but have specific areas of outstanding strength.

WHO ARE THE GIFTED AND TALENTED?

Identifying who is gifted or talented is not as important in the primary school as making provision for them. You need to concentrate on making the right provision and then it is easy to spot who is gifted. The reason for this is that giftedness is not something that we are born with and that will always be evident whatever the circumstances; it is rather more complicated than that. Current thinking suggests that we are born with certain predispositions and that they give us the capacity to excel in particular areas. But this does not mean we will automatically excel – we will do so only if we develop those predispositions. For 'predisposition' we might substitute the more commonly used educational term, 'potential'.

An easy way to think about giftedness is as an equation:

potential + opportunities/support + personal drive = high achievement (giftedness).

Therefore, for giftedness to emerge, children must meet the right opportunities and be given appropriate support throughout their entire childhood. It is not a question of 'pushing' or 'hot-housing', but instead of coaching and supporting – not holding children back by having preconceived ideas about what a six or ten year old can/should do, but equally not pushing them forward at a rate that makes them uncomfortable.

Therefore, the main focus in primary education should be in creating the right opportunities, offering appropriate support and helping the child to develop a desire to learn and to achieve; also, acting as a 'talent spotter' in recognising indicators of outstanding ability as and when they begin to emerge. As you will already know, most researchers think that ability is multidimensional, so you don't have to be good at 'everything', just outstanding at 'something' to be considered gifted.

IDENTIFYING THE GIFTED AND TALENTED

Outstanding ability in some areas, or in some children, can be detected very early. If, in Foundation Stage, you have a child who uses an extensive vocabulary and exhibits an easy facility with language, they will stand out from others in their class. Equally, a child who, when introduced to simple number patterns, then makes up much more complex ones of his or her own, e.g. using large or negative numbers, is obviously mathematically able. These types of children who stand out from their peers are known in the literature as 'precociously gifted' and can usually be identified early.

A second group of gifted or talented children will start to emerge when they start primary school; in school, some children with the potential to perform highly will start to forge ahead of others as soon as their school introduces them to high-quality learning opportunities in the formal curriculum. They will readily acquire the knowledge, skills and concepts associated with their domains of strength. For these individuals, identification becomes a relatively straightforward process because the gap between their performance and that of their peers grows rapidly. They will be the 'star performers' in your class. They may well be recognisable in Foundation Stage or Key Stage 1, but will almost certainly be on the gifted and talented register by Key Stage 2.

The 'precociously gifted' and 'star performers' usually identify themselves, but there are other indicators that can help you as a teacher to spot who else might be gifted. One of the best early indicators is not so much about outstanding performance relative to others, but rather about substantial interest – for example, the child who is fascinated by music, numbers or language and seeks to play games with it (linguistically able children often, for example, make up terrible jokes using word puns). As formal school progresses, each stage brings a chance for children to collide with new opportunities and to discover their areas of particular strength. Playfulness is not restricted to Foundation Stage – you may be playful at any stage; in fact, the more skilled you become in an area the more scope there is to play. Once you know that a story has to have a beginning, a middle and an end, you can start to create ones that don't! A key technique for teaching gifted and talented children is to encourage them to be intellectually playful. Teach them the rules and then help them to move beyond them.

Families play a large part in the intellectual development of young children. Most families will nurture any signs of ability or 'playfulness', especially if the area of interest coincides with the interests of other members of the family. If a pair of professional musicians find their child shows an interest in music, they will encourage and support its development in quite a structured way. Equally, a family of academics might encourage questioning or investigation, or an

Task 7.5.1 **TALENT SPOTTING**

■ Spend a few minutes thinking about the children in your class. Can you identify any who fit the categories we have looked at? Do you have any 'precociously gifted' children, who are your 'star performers'?

■ Over a day or two, observe your class and see if you can spot any intellectually 'playful' children.

entrepreneurial family will encourage entrepreneurship, etc. This means that it is hard for you as a teacher to distinguish between raw potential and nurtured achievement. Howe (1995) suggests that, in the right circumstances, anyone can be coached to become gifted. This may be an extreme view, but nevertheless help from home can assist those with potential to appear 'precocious' and, perhaps more worryingly, can lead to some children being seen as gifted in their early years of schooling when in fact they are really just well coached. These children will inevitably begin to find schooling more difficult as they move through school; the conceptual demands will increase and their performance will become less remarkable.

The reverse of parent support is, of course, the results of lack of parental support. Gifted children from homes where intellectual support and opportunity is lacking are more reliant on the school making those opportunities and support available to them. These children will not show up in the 'precociously gifted' category and will never be your 'star performers' unless you as a teacher take action. You need to spot their 'playfulness' or insightful comments and structure their learning to help them make rapid progress in the formal curriculum. It is your job to look below the surface, especially with children from disadvantaged backgrounds.

Five ways to spot gifted children

■ Assessment of achievement through a variety of assessment measures (precociousness).
■ Particularly at Foundation Stage and Key Stage 1, children who are interested in an area and actively seek to pursue it, enjoying it for its own sake (playfulness).
■ Pupils who appear to master the rules of a domain easily and can transfer their insights to new problems (precision).
■ Pupils who observe their own behaviour and hence utilise a greater variety of learning strategies than others (self-regulation).
■ Pupils who exhibit any of the characteristics above plus a tendency towards non-conformity in the given domain (originality).

A very real problem in identifying gifted and talented children in primary school is the confusion between the acquisition of skills and real intellectual ability. Giftedness is about cognitive ability – the ability to think. Skills are important, but not all gifted children acquire basic skills quickly and this can hold back intellectual development.

In thinking about this, you may find it helpful to think of a particular skill, e.g. learning to read, as being like learning to drive. The length of time it takes you to pass your driving test is not an indicator of how good a driver you will eventually be. You can't be an expert driver without acquiring the basic skills (passing the test), but it is how you apply those skills later that makes the difference. So, too, in school. Acquiring the skills is important, but it is how you 'use and apply' them that differentiates between acceptable and outstanding performance.

Case study

Jack, aged seven, is a linguistically gifted child with an exceptional vocabulary. He learned to talk at 12 months and never makes grammatical errors. He never needs to redraft his ideas because he has immense fluency with language. However, he finds some of the skills associated with learning to read (decoding text) or to write (forming letters) difficult, even though he is expert at plot and character. This discrepancy is because the aspects he finds difficult require visual or physical coordination, which are not areas of strength for him. He needs support in these. This mismatch between ability and skill can lead to a very frustrating period for some gifted children, as they are accustomed to learning easily. If they are not helped to master basic skills, underachievement is inevitable. However, once these 'tools' are acquired, progress is very rapid. This inability to master some of the basic skills quickly is one of the reasons why some gifted children are not recognised at primary school. Jack may well have been overlooked if his teacher had not been 'talent spotting'.

Task 7.5.2 **LOOKING AT GIFTED AND TALENTED**

While on placement or during your first year of teaching, consider the following questions. Write a short response, addressing each bullet point, to share with your placement tutor or mentor.

■ Do current conceptions of giftedness have embedded within them the basis for the under-representation of groups outside the mainstream culture?
■ Is the gifted and talented register a microcosm of the school community?
■ Who nominates which pupils are gifted and talented? – Some schools have begun peer and self-identification: are there any issues with such an approach?
■ Might the existence of provision for gifted and talented pupils in a multicultural society with vast discrepancies in socio-economic status simply serve to increase the gap? – White boys from families with low economic status are under-represented on gifted and talented registers.
■ How can gifted and talented registers ensure fluid movement from year group to year group, and between key stages or schools?
■ Inequalities on gifted and talented registers arise from low aspirations, peer pressure, material deprivation, lack of support and low parental expectation. So how can your school identify untapped potential talent?

We have talked very little about the role of standard assessment tests (SATs) or other tests in the identification process. They are, of course, crucial and an integral part of the school's methodology for identifying gifted children. If a child performs well on the test, that should be seen as a key indicator. However, it is also important to look beyond test data, especially in Foundation Stage and Key Stage 1. Tests should be seen as one indicator rather than the sole indicator. Evidence-based teacher assessment is crucial in this process, so use the tests, but also keep your antennae alert for undiscovered talent.

Task 7.5.3 **ACTION RESEARCH**

In 2003, Ofsted evaluated government initiatives in gifted and talented education, in particular Excellence in Cities and Education Action Zones. The main findings of the report (Ofsted, 2003) include:

■ Pupils placed on the gifted and talented register are already high achievers. There are insufficient strategies in place to identify pupils who have potential for high achievement and attainment.

■ Few talented pupils in primary schools are taught by specialist teachers.

■ Schools have difficulty identifying talented pupils.

■ Provision for gifted and talented pupils is fragmented and disconnected from the main work of the school, so pupils' potential is not systematically developed.

■ Strategies for the primary/secondary transfer of gifted and talented pupils are not well developed.

■ For gifted and talented provision to be effective, it is vital to have a strong understanding and support from school leaders and managers.

Choose one of the above bullet points to carry out an action research project in your school. At the end of your report include an action plan that addresses your chosen issue as highlighted by Ofsted. Share your report, action plan and recommendations with your mentor and other senior members of staff.

CREATING THE LEARNING ENVIRONMENT

Gifted and talented children are, first and foremost, children and much of what they need is exactly the same as for other children. They need to be treated like other children and expected to behave accordingly. If the following is the basis by which you set your classroom climate for all children, then gifted children will also thrive.

Gifted and talented children need to:

■ have a secure environment in which they feel happy to display ability;
■ experience intellectual challenge, sometimes having to struggle to achieve;
■ take risks and sometimes make mistakes;
■ relax and have fun;
■ comply with the class rules and code of conduct;
■ know that they can ask searching questions and get a considered response;
■ receive praise when they do well;
■ be recognised as individuals with strengths and weaknesses;
■ be able to discuss meaningfully with the teacher.

Creating a secure environment

Each of the items in the above list is particularly important for gifted and talented children. The secure environment is perhaps the most important of all. Gifted children who are achieving highly do stand out, and this can cause difficulties. Sensitive children will notice that they stand out and may not find it easy. It is not 'cool' to be bright. In some schools, and in some classrooms, gifted children will learn that drawing attention to what you know leads to being called 'clever clogs' or earns you the reputation as the class 'boffin'. If you are a sensitive child this can be very damaging and such children soon learn to hide their ability and, in some cases, deliberately underachieve in order to remain unnoticed. Less sensitive children may continue to draw attention to themselves and become socially ostracised. Gifted children do need to learn how to manage their ability so that they do not continually 'show off' and try to outperform everyone else, but equally they should not have to be ashamed of their ability. It is something to celebrate. If you are really committed to celebrating diversity in your classroom, it should be easy to accommodate the gifted and talented children. Circle time is, for example, a good way of addressing the needs of gifted individuals and also can be used to help them recognise the different strengths other children have.

If you are to trying to 'talent spot', it is essential that you create a classroom climate where children are happy to reveal their ability. The best way to do this is to focus all your children on learning and deliberately draw attention to the different strengths individuals in the class bring to collective classroom learning. More generally, make it clear that everyone is expected to do their best and it is evidence of achievement through hard work that is rewarded, not just achievement. A piece of research (Eyre, 2002: 10), looking at primary school teachers who were very good at teaching gifted and talented children, found that all the successful classrooms were positive, pacy and purposeful, with a focus on hard work, fun and recognition of individual effort and achievement. They were not classrooms characterised by serious and earnest endeavour, but rather a context where children and teachers enjoyed the challenge of learning and the satisfaction of progress and success.

A classroom with high expectations

Of course, in order for gifted children to both emerge and to excel you have to have high expectations regarding what you think can be achieved. The learning objectives must be ambitious and clear and you need to ensure that the children are aware of them. Gifted children make intellectual connections between what they are learning now, what they learned before and the long-term learning objective. They like you to take them into your confidence and for you to tell them not only what is going to happen, but also why you are doing it and where it is leading. By Years 5 and 6 many gifted children will want an overview of the term or at least the half term, because this information helps them to gain control of their learning and become more independent. If they know you are going to 'do the Greeks', they may begin to read about them. They may line up their relatives to make sure they give them relevant presents for Christmas, and they are likely to help you make the lessons more engaging. Of course, you do not need to have a special conversation with your gifted and talented about the overall scheme of work, just tell the whole class.

A key element in creating a good learning environment is learning to value each child as an individual and knowing their strengths and weaknesses. Even the most gifted children are better at some things than others and they often suffer from people expecting them to be able to do everything equally well. They may find it hard to ask for help and some will be real perfectionists who find even minor failures hard to take. You can help here by creating an approach where 'having a go' is highly valued, even more than 'getting it right'. Make comments such as 'That's a really good suggestion, I can see why you thought that but . . .', 'I used to think . . . but then I found out", etc. Encourage children to take intellectual risks and not worry if they are wrong. Einstein said that clever people are those who make their mistakes fastest. Help your class to see that making mistakes is good if we examine them carefully and learn from them. It helps us move forward. Try using some examples of famous people who made big mistakes on the way to discovering great things. (Science can provide particularly good examples, since science is about refuting or confirming existing theories.)

Teacher/pupil interaction

Gifted and talented pupils like to work with people who have greater levels of expertise than themselves. In school this is usually the adults, and especially the teacher. It can also, in many schools, be other children of similar ability. Gifted children value teachers who habitually discuss with their class and who are willing, on occasion, to discuss in depth with the individual. To make this happen it is important to focus on four areas:

■ teacher questions;
■ pupil questions;
■ teacher explanation;
■ pupil explanation.

Teacher questions can stimulate thinking and are a very useful way to differentiate for the most able. Try directing a series of particularly searching questions towards a confident child whom you know to be gifted and let everyone listen as the argument is developed.

Task 7.5.4 **THE POWER OF QUESTIONS**

■ Discuss with your tutor your questioning technique. How frequently do you ask open questions, which require children to think or offer an opinion? Most teachers ask too many closed questions, which are designed merely to confirm whether the child understands rather than open up new thinking.

■ Look at how to improve your questioning skills. (Brown and Wragg (1993) is a good starting point, as is the guidance from the Primary Literacy and Numeracy Strategies.)

Asking the right questions is a two-way process and, as children move through primary school, you need to help them to become questioners. They need to pose questions and query findings, not take information at face value. This can begin very early and 'book talk' is a good way to engage with this agenda. If you begin by asking 'what questions could we ask about this book?', and doing this quite regularly, your gifted children will start to pose similar questions when they read. Aidan Chambers' book, *Tell Me* (1993) has a great set of ideas for this. This technique works equally well with a historical picture or a map. Any stimulus can be used in this way to get children thinking. In GCSE history, original sources are used and students judge the reliability of the source. This kind of technique can easily be used at Key Stage 2 and even younger. All children can take part when this is a general classroom activity, but with your gifted children you should encourage, and later expect, them to take this analytical approach to all their work, not just when you have set up a particular task. For gifted pupils it should become a way of thinking, not just an activity.

In a similar way, you can use your teacher explanations to create thinking. Don't just describe and convey information; try to set it as a query or use it to make connections with previous learning. Encourage your gifted children to describe what they have learned/found out in such a way as to make it appealing to others – perhaps for a specific audience, for example a younger class or the school governors. Explanations that have a real purpose are much more engaging than feedback sessions.

Classroom management

The key to meeting the needs of all the children in your class, including the gifted, is time management. Well-established classroom routines create the space for one-to-one work with individuals. Make sure the classroom is laid out in such a way as to enable children to collect materials independently. Ensure that you prevent disruptive behaviour by having a clear code of behaviour and a consistent approach to dealing with misbehaviour. Make sure your instructions are clear and unambiguous. Create ways of working in the classroom that everyone adheres to, for example where to put books for marking. Most of all, always make sure you have planned carefully and have everything you need for the lesson.

WAYS TO CHALLENGE GIFTED CHILDREN IN THE PRIMARY CLASSROOM

Much of what constitutes good classroom provision generally is also good provision for the gifted. You need to ensure that these elements are in place generally in your classroom before looking at specific challenges for the gifted:

- careful planning;
- clear learning objectives;
- target setting;
- high expectations;
- variety of approach;
- assessment for learning;
- good evaluation.

Gifted children need to be challenged both by the way in which they are required to operate in class and by the tasks they are given to do. These two elements support each other. In designing tasks for gifted and talented children it is useful to consider what we know about their learning:

- Gifted pupils do not seem to use strategies that others never use.
- Gifted pupils differ from others in the creativity and extent to which they draw upon a repertoire of intellectual skills that are nonetheless available to others.
- They demonstrate expert performance by using metacognition, strategy flexibility, strategy planning, hypothesis, preference for complexity, and extensive webbing of knowledge about both facts and processes.
- They think like experts even though they may lack some of the skills of experts.

(Shore, 2000: 173)

So there is nothing that is unique to the gifted children in your class. The above does, however, give some good clues on designing tasks to challenge the gifted. If gifted children think like experts, consider what experts in the subject believe to be important and try to include it. If gifted children are original and creative in their solutions to problems, give them tasks that encourage this and don't be surprised if they fail to give you the textbook answer. If they see learning as a complex interwoven web, help them to make those connections and allow them to complexify the original task to make it more interesting and demanding. Try differentiation by self – they suggest ways in which the core task set for the whole class could be made more demanding. Don't forget they are the ones with the brains; don't do everything for them.

Tasks to help children engage in advanced thinking

It is helpful to consider what, in addition to the acquisition of the knowledge, skills and concepts that we hope all children will achieve, we should expect of gifted children. The following are behaviours you should seek to engender:

■ greater reflection;
■ exploration of a variety of viewpoints;
■ consideration of difficult questions;
■ formulation of individual opinions;
■ problem solving and enquiry;
■ connections between past and present learning;
■ regular use of higher-order thinking (analysis, synthesis and evaluation);
■ independent thinking and learning.

How might you do this? A good way is by designing enquiry-based tasks:

■ Think independently – What do you think was the reason?
■ Reflect – Why do you think that happened?
■ Recognise connections in learning – Can you think of another time when that happened? Compare these two accounts.
■ Explore ideas and choose a 'best' solution – Which of these would be the most appropriate for . . .?
■ Justify ideas – Which of the following would be best? Give reasons for your choice.
■ Explain ideas using appropriate technical language – Yes, that's right, that is called a . . .
■ Solve problems and recognise the strategy used – What made that successful?
■ Think about real problems – How could we stop mud getting on the classroom carpet?
■ Encourage use of a wide vocabulary – Can you find a better word for . . .?
■ Order and marshal ideas – Tell me/draw/write the different steps you took to do that experiment.
■ Explore conflicting ideas – Was Robin Hood a good man?

This enquiry-based approach helps gifted children to develop the higher-level thinking skills that will enable them to perform at an advanced level. There is a variety of hierarchies of thinking skills in the education literature, but all share a view that higher-order thinking involves concepts such as comparison, analysis, reworking of ideas (synthesis), invention and evaluation of worth/value. The unit in this book by Robert Fisher (7.4) looks in more detail at the general use of thinking skills. When creating challenge for the gifted simply focus on the top-level skills.

These kinds of enquiry-based tasks are a good way to create challenge for the gifted, but they do not always have to be given to a specific group of children. Sometimes the task may require advanced reading or mathematical skills and, therefore, can only be offered to a specific group. But often enquiry tasks can be designed with challenge for the gifted in mind and then made available to all. The gifted will simply offer better, more sophisticated and more original solutions. This brings us back to identification. If you offer these types of tasks to all children, the outcomes may surprise you. You may 'talent spot' potentially gifted children you had not recognised before.

Breadth, depth and pace

There are three ways in which you could plan for gifted children to experience learning outside of that made available to all. You can add breadth, depth or pace to the normal curriculum offer.

BREADTH

Sometimes called enrichment, breadth can be defined as adding additional material at broadly the same cognitive level, for example studying more about a particular period of history or reading more widely around the core subject. It does not require the acquisition of new skills, but may emphasise the opportunity to 'use and apply' existing ones. Breadth can also include learning a completely new subject in addition to those studied by others. An example here might be a Key Stage 2 after-school Latin Club. Breadth is useful because using and applying learned skills is a good way to consolidate them and also creates a context for devising original ideas. Introducing children to new areas can also help them to discover their abilities by widening their horizons and, since this is a key role for primary schools, adding breadth to the curriculum for all children (as well as those identified as gifted) should be seen as a key strategy in challenging the gifted and talented.

In adding breadth to the curriculum, the greatest risk is, inevitably, overload. If you want your gifted children to experience additional learning, also consider what you could excuse them from. Gifted children are no more industrious than others and don't like having extra work.

DEPTH

Sometimes called extension, depth refers to an increase in cognitive level achieved by taking the existing focus of work and going into greater depth. It usually involves learning new material, including new skills and concepts. Good classroom provision should include a mix of breadth, depth and pace, but perhaps depth is the most important. It is about learning how to think intellectually. There are many ways to achieve depth, but here is an example you might like to try. Take a solvable puzzle, for example a crossword or a word search, and first ask all the class to solve it and then ask the gifted children to create one of their own. In order to create a puzzle you need to consider how the puzzle works and this requires you to deconstruct it. Talk about how it functions and why it works. Can they make one? Can they make one that is even better than the one they solved? Why is it better? This takes you into much deeper territory.

Equally, you might add depth by selecting an area that experts value but that does not appear in the primary curriculum. Historiography is a good example here. If you have very able children in Key Stage 2 looking at the Victorians, you might take a Victorian (maybe from your local area) who was considered a hero in his or her time and is now less valued (or vice versa) and consider how the society in which we live shapes our view of history. Use some first-hand resources such as newspaper articles. These are very easy to access on the web.

A practical way to increase depth is by bringing experts into the classroom: people from the wider community, staff from museums or science centres, authors or academics, parents or local experts. These events are great for all children, but think carefully about whether a proportion of the expert's time could be spent with a smaller group, developing high-level skills or exploring more advanced concepts.

PACE

Pace is about moving through the existing curriculum faster than other children and is sometimes called acceleration. (Acceleration should not be confused with accelerated learning, which is something quite different.) In practice, whatever strategies you adopt will involve the gifted children moving ahead of their peers in the formal curriculum and this is entirely appropriate. In general planning you should always look at the more advanced levels in the National Curriculum as a key way of creating challenge for the gifted and talented. The National Curriculum is a spiral curriculum, so concepts recur and skills are revisited. When planning a lesson you should consider what would be the next learning objective in this area and whether it would be suitable to include it, for some children, in the lesson.

The best provision for gifted children is through a mix of depth, breadth and pace. When planning the scheme of work it is usually easy to see which might work best, but ensure that you do not rely too heavily on any single one.

Task 7.5.5 **TASK DESIGN**

Create three tasks for use in your classroom. Task 1 must add *breadth*, task 2 *depth* and task 3 *pace*. Implement them and then reflect on the following with your tutor:

■ why you chose them;
■ how you created them;
■ who in your class experienced them and why;
■ how they worked in practice;
■ what you have learned from the process.

There is no single way to create challenge for your gifted and talented children, but make sure you aim high and use resources that will help you to create well-informed, thinking children. The following ideas may get you started:

■ Investigate or problem solve using a 'plan/do/review' approach.
■ Work from difficult texts or intensively on one text.
■ Use a variety of texts/pictures/artefacts to compare and contrast.
■ Record in an unusual way. Use fewer words rather than more.
■ Role-play. Think from someone else's point of view.
■ Provide choice in how children handle the content.
■ Create tasks that require decision making.
■ Create tasks with no single correct answer.
■ Provide the answer; they set the questions.
■ Create an element of speed. Use journalistic deadlines.
■ Introduce technical language. Speak and think like an expert.

SUMMARY

Meeting the needs of gifted and talented children is part of meeting the needs of all. By focusing on high expectations and talent spotting you may well find more gifted children than you expect and, at the same time, create a learning environment that is challenging and fun for all. The aim for a primary school is to ensure that their gifted and talented children reach secondary school with a desire to learn and the skills to do so, so that they can go on to achieve highly.

ANNOTATED FURTHER READING

Balchin, T., Hymer, B. and Matthews, D.J. (2008) *The Routledge International Companion to Gifted Education*, London: Routledge.

This is an up-to-date and very good source of strategies to support giftedness in children, providing practical ideas in an easy-to-use format. It contains a comprehensive range of articles on gifted and talented issues.

Eyre, D. (1997) *Able Children in Ordinary Schools*, London: David Fulton.

This is a practical handbook for teachers and head teachers looking to improve provision in schools. It includes chapters on management and classroom practice.

Eyre, D. (2002) *Effective Teaching of Able Pupils in the Primary Classroom*, Birmingham: National Primary Trust.

This short book describes the practice of five teachers who are considered to be very good at challenging gifted children in their classrooms.

Eyre, D. and McClure, L. (eds) (2001) *Curriculum Provision for the Gifted and Talented in the Primary School*, London: David Fulton.

This is an edited book with chapters offering detailed help and ideas on teaching English, maths and science.

Friedman, R.C. and Shore, B.M. (eds) (2000) *Talents Unfolding: Cognition and Development*, Washington, DC: American Psychological Association.

This is a substantial edited volume covering some of the key international research in gifted and talented education.

RELEVANT WEBSITES

Department for Children, Schools and Families (DCSF): www.dcsf.gov.uk

By typing 'gifted and talented' into the search box on the DCSF home page, over 100 links to information on identifying and teaching the gifted and talented are available.

Excellence in Cities: www.standards.dfes.gov.uk/local/excellence/gift/GT_summary.html

This web page has details of the *Gifted and Talented Children Policy*.

Qualifications and Curriculum Development Agency (QCDA): www.qcda.gov.uk/2346.aspx

This is the web page specifically for guidance on teaching the gifted and talented, but there are nearly 400 other links on the QCDA website to explore on this topic.

Visit the companion website www.routledge.com/textbooks/ltps2e for:

■ links to useful websites relevant to this unit.

REFERENCES

Brown, G. and Wragg, E.C. (1993) *Questioning*, London: Routledge.

Chambers, A. (1993) *Tell Me*, Stroud: Thimble Press.

Department for Education and Skills (DfES) (2003) *Excellence and Enjoyment*, London: DfES.

Eyre, D. (2002) *Effective Teaching of Able Pupils in the Primary Classroom*, Birmingham: National Primary Trust.

Howe, M. (1995) 'What can we learn from the lives of geniuses?', in J. Freeman (ed.) *Actualizing Talent*, London: Cassell.

Office for Standards in Education (Ofsted) (2003) *Excellence in Cities and Education Action Zones: Management and Impact*, London: Ofsted.

Shore, B.M. (2000) 'Metacognition and flexibility: qualitative differences in how gifted children think', in R.C. Friedman and B.M. Shore (eds) *Talents Unfolding: Cognition and Development*, Washington, DC: American Psychological Association.

E-LEARNING

John Meadows

INTRODUCTION

Most British schools are now equipped with a great variety of information and communications technology (ICT) tools and software (Becta, 2008). Most classrooms have interactive whiteboards (IWBs) to supplement and in many cases replace traditional black- and whiteboards. Many teachers use electronic equipment to prepare long, medium and short-term plans and to devise resources for each lesson. Children with special physical and educational needs use ICT-based equipment to support their inclusion in the everyday life and learning in the normal classroom and the final report of the *Independent Review of the Primary Curriculum* (Rose Review) recommends that ICT should be 'embedded throughout the primary curriculum and given greater prominence within the core of essentials for learning and life' (Rose, 2009).

This unit provides an overview of e-learning across the curriculum, as a resource for both teaching and learning. It presents some case studies as examples of ways in which teachers use the internet, IWBs, computer suites and laptops in classrooms to support children's learning in many different subjects and projects. It suggests ways in which creative teaching can be enhanced through e-learning tools and techniques.

The examples and case studies used in this unit all have a specific rationale for why e-learning enhances the pupil experience and the role of the teacher. Some contexts for learning are described so that teachers can recognise the potential for e-learning in a variety of settings.

OBJECTIVES

By the end of this unit you should have begun to:

■ recognise the diverse digital and visual literacy skills that young children bring to school;
■ understand how e-learning in the classroom affects the role of the teacher;
■ identify some links between technology and pedagogy;
■ realise how to integrate e-learning with cross-curricular themes and topics.

WHY E-LEARNING?

E-learning can be defined in a variety of ways, but for the purposes of this unit it will be dealt with fairly broadly, so that both teaching and learning with ICT are included in the examples, information, discussion and case studies. We also need to remember that children gain a lot of ICT skills and knowledge outside the classroom, in their homes, with friends, in libraries and in other computer-rich environments. The TIMSS 2007 survey (http://timss.bc.edu/TIMSS2007) reported that 95 per cent of families in Britain had a computer at home and 86 per cent had internet connection. The internet is seen as a social space as well as a source of objective information and the value of communication through the internet is now widely recognised, as much as the value of its information and presentation potential. Rose (2009) emphasises that a reasonable grasp of ICT is needed in education and employment and that children need to acquire ICT skills to prepare for technologies of the future.

However, research evidence indicates that even very young children have considerable experience of media and digital technologies (Rideout *et al.*, 2003; Marsh, 2005; Bearne *et al.*, 2007). In their homes and communities, as well as in school, children are surrounded by multimodal texts: texts that merge pictures, words and sound. In this 'new media age' (Kress, 2003) they learn early on to read images and design as well as print (Kress and van Leeuwen, 1996) and are frequently capable of handling the challenges of technology. Indeed, many have argued that some children are more assured than their teachers in this regard (Dowdall, 2003; Lambirth, 2003).There is also evidence to suggest that, when teachers build upon children's digital skills and competencies, and position them as multimodal designers, the young make use of their skills in a highly creative manner that supports their literacy learning (Bearne *et al.*, 2005; Walsh, 2007).

It has been argued that a knowledge-based economy requires skills that are both flexible and transferable (Becta, 2007). The purpose of an e-strategy, therefore, is to transform teaching and learning and help to improve learning outcomes for children, young people and adults through shared ideas, more exciting lessons and online help for professionals. As well as emphasising the skills involved in e-learning, it can be seen as a set of methods and materials that help teachers to plan and manage complex and creative environments in which children carry out tasks and activities with ICT, in order to learn more effectively right across the curriculum. E-learning can be used to support personalised learning and help children to become independent learners, which can lead to teachers raising their expectations of children's abilities and achievements. An open, accessible system of e-learning can also provide parents and carers with more information and services online, can foster more collaboration between organisations and can improve personalised choice and support.

In the context of the increasing digitisation of information worldwide, Rose (2009) suggests that children need to be helped to develop as digitally literate young people in order to enable them to participate fully in society. He uses an example of a small rural school, which encourages children to make use of podcasts and blogs as part of their lessons, but which also has a computer club open to the whole community and seeks to highlight that children need to learn to use specific devices and applications as well as to understand fundamental concepts of safe and critical use. Thus, effective ICT use is linked to lifelong learning.

Task 7.6.1 **KEEPING A PROCESS DIARY**

■ Keep a process diary over a week detailing evidence of three children's involvement in e-learning and visual literacy, enhanced by uses of ICT resources, such as digital cameras, animation techniques, PowerPoint work and so forth.

■ You might also consider inviting the children to document all their e-engagement over a period of 24 hours, first through sharing your own everyday encounters with electronic texts over the same period.

■ List, categorise and discuss the wide use of e-texts in your own and their own lives. Consider the skills they make use of in these contexts.

E-LEARNING SKILLS EMBEDDED IN SUBJECT TEACHING

Gillespie (2006) identifies six ICT-linked skills that learners need to acquire:

■ Basic skills
■ Skills with text
■ Skills with images
■ Skills with data-handling
■ Gaming and problem-solving skills
■ Creative and thinking skills.

(Gillespie, 2006: 95–6)

These skills need to be taught and then assessed in a variety of ways. She recommends that teachers, especially in Key Stage 1, need to plan for children to acquire the basic skills of using a camera, operating a mouse, using a keyboard and understanding how to print, save and open documents. I would add the basic skill of using a touchpad to this list. Although some Key Stage 1 teachers may think that some of these skills are too difficult for children with limited motor coordination, it does appear that most will be able to learn skills if they are given brief but frequent opportunities to develop them.

However, it is with specific contexts that children need to learn other ICT skills. Skills with images, for example, can be taught when children wish to make presentations, say in geography, using digital photographs and images, with captions added, to communicate their findings effectively.

The *Independent Review of the Primary Curriculum* (Rose Review) (Rose, 2009) recommends that subject lines can be crossed when teaching interesting topics to children, in order to make the learning as meaningful as possible. The *Independent Review of Mathematics Teaching* (Williams, 2008) reported that schools often provide too few opportunities for pupils to use and apply mathematics and to use ICT within their mathematics work. So here we see a proposal for making mathematics mean something more than abstract ideas and theorems. Mathematics can be used and applied in many contexts – not just in scientific and technological studies, but also in history and geography. For example, ICT, maths and history could be combined in working on a survey of common jobs in the local area now and 100 years ago. Rose suggests that children should learn how to 'create, manipulate and process information, using technology to capture and organise data, in order to investigate patterns and trends' (2009: 75). There are possible connections here between ICT, maths and science, if the data being collected arises from a scientific context, such as measuring and comparing pulse rates during exercise. The e-learning skills being used and developed in each cross-curricular context need to be identified by the teacher and the progress of children developing such skills also needs to be assessed and recorded.

Consider the example on the next page (Task 7.6.2) of mixing ICT, science and religious education with a Year 3 class.

THE ARTS AND ICT

Besides the vast array of visual treasures held in open galleries online, there are many examples of teachers using the arts and ICT together in more creative ways – helping children put a soundtrack and some plasticene animations to an image-filled poem, such as 'Jabberwocky' by Edward Lear, or create their own visual slide to run as a PowerPoint loop as a backdrop to a collection of children's poems.

Task 7.6.2 **VIDEO FOR LEARNING – AN EXAMPLE USING BUDDHISM AND SCIENCE**

Pete teaches a Year 3 class of seven and eight year olds. This lesson is one of a series about religions, drawing on resources from Espresso education (go to www.lgfl.net and follow the links to 'Faiths' under RE). During the previous lesson, the children had watched the video about the Buddha and discussed some of the facts about his life, where he lived and what he looked like. They compared themselves and their lives with the life and times of the Buddha. They compared the kinds of foods they eat now with the kind of food available to Buddha in his time. Pete started this lesson with questions to the children on what they remembered, where the Buddha lived and how long ago (an alternative might be to use a timeline to show other historical information, such as the Romans and Greeks, which the class had looked at before). He then introduced the main objective of the lesson – 'To learn about the teaching of the Buddha' – on the IWB.

During the plenary, the teacher used a multiple-choice quiz, from the website, to remind children of the main issues and to assess how well their factual knowledge had progressed.

■ How could you edit these ideas and strategies into a series of lessons to fit a current topic in science/maths that your class is studying?
■ Would it be useful to link this series of lessons to notions of 'education for sustainable development' and 'global citizenship', examining the effects of global warming on the changes in water around the world, including sea level rises as well as the melting of icecaps?

In each part of the session, there could be a separate learning objective. What learning objectives would you define for each part of this main lesson above? For example, in the initial question and answer activity with the whole class, the learning objective might be just revision and the teacher could use this part of the session for assessing children's prior knowledge, in order to use this as a starting point for further development. In the second part, the outcome might be – 'to be able to relate Buddhist teaching to your own life experience', while in the third part, the quiz, the objective could be – 'to be able to review and compare your own ideas and answers with those presented and to self-assess your own progress'.

One teacher, Iris, used simple digital cameras in their 'still' option, to get groups of student teachers to prepare animated films on environmental and sustainable issues. They made figures from paper, card or plasticene, with moving or stationary backgrounds to show simple stories, such as possible effects of global warming on a specific environment or scenarios with potential conflict and debates. These films were then saved for use in presentations at conferences as well as in the class itself.

It is good motivation for children too, if they can look forward to seeing their own productions on the large screen of the class IWB. The link with films that they watch from internet public sources, with their own films being shown on the same platform, helps motivate children and make learning more meaningful and relevant.

A common use of the school's website is as a gallery space for children's art work in two and three dimensions, on paper and as sculpture, as well as their digital art. In some schools, every class would have its own space on either internal or external web pages, with current topics and evidence of activities so that parents and carers can access the work of their own children. The online site might carry photos and drawings done by the children when visiting out-of-school physical sites, linking the ICT perhaps with the history curriculum, as well as with art.

Task 7.6.3 USING PICTURES AND ANIMATIONS

Prepare a presentation with animations and pictures from published sources – add sound files and, if possible, some resources you have prepared digitally, such as through your mobile phone camera. Suggest learning objectives and then learning outcomes to use as assessment for learning (AFL) criteria.

MOTIVATION, CHOICE AND COLLABORATIVE TALK

Motivation is often quoted as one of the reasons for using ICT with children, but it can be a short-lived phenomenon when children get used to the technology and as they tend sometimes to use more advanced and more interesting technologies outside the classroom. Allowing more pupil choice to take place within the classroom is seen by many as a more motivating teaching and learning strategy than a more passive approach to learning, where the teacher makes all the decisions and provides the learners with structured and precise tasks and activities.

For example, Rose describes an exchange of emails between a school in Oldham and another in South Africa, which, it is argued, not only 'helps them learn about other countries and cultures, but also develops their social skills, a powerful tool for learning' (2009: 92). During such exchanges, the content of the pupil exchanges should be partly determined by the pupils' own interests, as well as by the respective contexts and learning intentions set by their teachers. Such opportunities to communicate with others in another part of the world can foster choice, generate interest and offer authentic engagement and use of ICT.

In another context, a teacher working on Greek history asked the children to work in small collaborative groups to research, through specified internet sites, a particular character from Greek mythology and present what they found in a PowerPoint presentation for the other children in the class. Another teacher running the lesson might have done this research and then presented the material to the children through a textbook or with factual worksheets with a question and answer session for the whole class as a plenary. It is interesting to consider these two possible options and the advantages and disadvantages in terms of the children's learning, their agency and ownership.

Another key element of e-learning is the enriched opportunities for exploratory talk that arise (Dawes *et al.*, 2000) when children are using ICT collaboratively. These researchers define a concept of 'network literacy', to describe a person who is 'fluent in the uses of electronic communication' (p. 41), and who can use computers to gain access to resources, create their own resources and communicate with others. They consider the educational purposes of grouping children at computers, suggesting that friendship groups are not the best way of generating talk and encouraging decision making, as friends tend to agree too quickly rather than challenge each other in order to justify their ideas. In their Spoken Language and New Technology (SLANT) research, Wegerif and Scrimshaw (1997) found that group work can be difficult for children who may tend to compete rather than collaborate. Teachers can support them in agreeing the ground rules for talking in the context of using ICT. For more detail on the role of talk in learning and the ground rules for talk see Unit 3.5.

Task 7.6.4 **PREPARE AN ONLINE TEACHING RESOURCE**

Create a teaching resource to use with your own class, or to share with other teachers in the school, or through an online community. The resource could be a set of smartboard pages or a collection of web pages to deal with teaching a specific learning objective in a subject, or you could devise the introductory demonstration in the examples below and suggest how you would deliver it to your own class.

Make explicit the theories of learning that underpin the resource – see Unit 2.2. for an exploration of these.

CONTRASTING TEACHING STYLES USING E-LEARNING

Visual technologies, though hailed as innovations in classrooms, may sometimes limit classroom discourse and focus activity on the teacher as the presenter of information. If knowledge is presented to the students as a fait-accompli and as a series of objectives to be accomplished, rather than as something constructed or worked out through a demonstrable and reproducible process of reasoning, examining evidence and the use of logic, then the learning experience may inevitably be less rich and less meaningful for students.

(Reedy, 2008: 161)

In order to personalise your own approaches to e-learning and classroom practice, I now turn to two imagined examples of two teachers, Mr Blue and Mrs Green. Imagine they both work in a well-equipped school, but use the resources in different ways to reflect their own values and beliefs about education. Their classrooms are well equipped, with IWBs and ceiling projectors, PCs and laptops and broadband internet access, and they have regular access to a computer suite, equipped with 20 computers, IWB, carpet area and display area.

The following example is how these two teachers might start a lesson about weather – compare the different approaches with your own ideas about teaching.

■ At the start of the lesson, Mr Blue uses the IWB to demonstrate satellite images of weather pressure fronts and isobars and asks the class questions to establish their level of understanding so that he knows how to proceed with the rest of the time.

■ Mrs Green, on the other hand, starts with asking children, 'What do you think the weather is like in London, Reykjavik, Johannesburg?' Then she scribes some of the children's ideas on the IWB and uses this to display internet weather sites to see how accurate their predictions are.

It is clear that the teachers are using ICT very differently, and there may be benefits and drawbacks to both their approaches in relation to the children's learning and views of knowledge. It is possible, however, that either of the teachers might make more use of ICT resources as the lesson develops. For example, in the main part of the lesson children could be using laptops to write email messages to partner schools in Iceland and South Africa, predicting weather and temperatures and describing the weather in their own environment in the past week. Earlier in the week they might also have created online diaries of their visual observations and data-logged measurements, which they could use to prepare a presentation about the weather. They might also be involved in examining online weather and climate resources, including Google Earth and BBC weather sites, and could even participate in a more formal online discussion forum. It is evident from this brief example that a wealth of e-learning opportunities exist. Your challenge as a teacher is to capitalise upon these to enhance both your teaching and the children's learning.

Task 7.6.5 ICT AND SPECIAL EDUCATIONAL NEEDS

In relation to special educational needs, Allen *et al*. (2007) note that such children may have ICT hardware and software needs that should be identified as part of their individual education plan. Some examples include: a dyslexic child who may need software to address his or her needs; a child with motor impairment who may need hardware to allow access to the computer keyboard or a touch screen device; visually impaired children for whom browser windows with larger font may be useful; a specific child with very particular needs who may need to be assigned a laptop.

- ▪ Identify children within your own class/school who may benefit from special ICT provision to meet their specific educational needs.
- ▪ What sorts of specialist ICT could be available from the catalogues or websites of educational manufacturers?

E-ASSESSMENT

E-assessment can take a number of forms, including automating administrative procedures; digitising paper-based systems; and online testing – which extends from multiple-choice tests to interactive assessments of problem-solving skills (Ridgeway and McCusker, 2004). AFL is important in order to help children reflect on their own learning of ICT skills and understanding, as well as subject learning intentions. Rose suggests that we need to ensure that 'high-quality, personalised information about their learning follows every child; receiving classes and schools can build quickly on a child's prior learning' (2009: 83).

Many web-based teaching resources include 'banal' multiple-choice tests, which are often enjoyed by pupils, but which provide rather limited assessment of children's achievements, assessing mainly recall of information received, rather than more subtle thinking and problem-solving skills. An assessment of children's own alternative ideas is exemplified in the case study below, as Leila scribed the children's ideas about temperature on the IWB for the whole class to consider. This is a kind of formative assessment, done at the beginning of the main part of the lesson, so that children can develop these ideas as they make progress with understanding the complexities of the concept of temperature. Leila also taught some basic skills about the use of Excel before asking children to apply these to the scientific task.

Case study

Leila decided to integrate the computer suite time with a science and maths lesson both before and after the classroom-based science activities. Children aged nine and ten used Excel to record the changes in volumes of water in three cylinders that they had left on a windowsill in the classroom for three days and from which some of the water had evaporated. They knew how to use Excel to enter data and turn it into simple graphs. Using the BBC schools site (www.bbc.co.uk/schools), Leila found a resource called Pod's Mission: Hotter or Colder. She also downloaded some pictures from the internet to the IWB of water in nature in solid, liquid and gas form – ice in Antarctica, steam from geysers and water in seas and rivers.

They then used an interactive online game to try to answer some factual questions. Leila used the IWB in the classroom and included a whole-class discussion on what the children already knew about temperature: what it is, how you measure it, did they know any particular temperatures for things, such as how hot your own body is, or what it means when the doctor tells you that you have a high temperature. These questions were already on the IWB ready for children to see, and Leila wrote up some of their tentative answers during this introduction.

For the main activity, they were split into pairs and then moved into the ICT suite. Each of the children in a pair had a chance to control the mouse during the online activity and each had about 20 minutes of practice with the simulation and games. Leila used the plenary time to help them to raise further questions they would like to find answers to in the next lesson using the internet in the ICT suite. She saved these questions using a page of the IWB that is saved into her class section of the school's intranet.

Task 7.6.6 **THE COMPUTER SUITE**

Is there anything specifically about the computer suite that makes it valuable as a resource for learning and teaching? What alternatives are there for using computer suites in science, besides interactive quizzes and teaching specific ICT skills, such as the use of Excel?

■ Adapt the above case study to your own situation and evaluate your own use of the computer suite.
■ How would you ask the teaching assistant to help you in assessing the progress of children in achieving e-learning objectives?

Assessing children's progress needs to be carried out in a variety of ICT settings; social constructivist paradigms, linked to the theories of Jerome Bruner and Lev Vygotsky, propose that teaching and learning happen best within social situations involving interactions between learners. This can be planned for by using talk partners in classrooms or ICT suites. Learning is an active process linking not only the teacher and the learner, but also learners with each other. Teaching and learning have cultural implications as well as knowledge ones. The internet can be a social space as well as a source of objective information. The value of communication through the internet should be recognised, as much as the value of the information and presentation potential of ICT. The IWB is a tool for children to help them express their ideas and adapt their thinking, as well as a tool for teachers to present information and ideas to children.

SUMMARY

In this unit you have read about reasons for incorporating e-learning in primary schools, justified by the rapidly changing nature of technology, children's expertise in this area and the most recent review of the primary curriculum in England, which regards ICT as a core area alongside literacy and numeracy. Case studies have shown how teachers use ICT in their lessons and how they encourage pupils to learn and apply ICT skills and knowledge to support their learning across the curriculum.

The unit's overall argument is for a view of personalised learning through ICT that allows the child some choice, within a teaching and learning framework that seeks to provide access to relevant materials, since it is argued that teachers can motivate children through e-learning, encouraging ownership and increasing the relevance of their learning (Becta, 2007).

ANNOTATED FURTHER READING

As this unit concerns e-learning, there is no further reading as such. Instead, it is recommended that, in addition to the references below, you should consult the following websites, which specialise in different forms of learning appropriate for the primary classroom.

RELEVANT WEBSITES

BBC Schools: www.bbc.co.uk/schools/scienceclips
This website contains quizzes, games and other activities for Key Stage 1 and 2 learners.

Becta: www.becta.org.uk
Becta's 'Schools' section offers advice and guidance on how technology can be built into teaching and learning.

espresso education: www.lgfl.net
The London Grid for Learning 'espresso education' web pages contain modules covering the major faiths. Follow the links under RE to 'Faiths'.

Trends in International Mathematics and Science Study (TIMSS): http://timss.bc.edu/TIMSS2007
This provides data, every four years, about international trends in mathematics and science achievement.

Visit the companion website www.routledge.com/textbooks/ltps2e for:

■ additional questions for this unit;
■ links to useful websites relevant to this unit.

REFERENCES

Allen, J., Potter, J., Sharp, J. and Turvey, K. (2007) *Primary ICT: Knowledge, Understanding and Practice*, 3rd edn, Exeter: Learning Matters.

Bearne, E., Grainger, T. and Wolstencroft, H. (2005) *Raising Boys' Achievements in Writing*, Joint Research Project, United Kingdom Literacy Association and the Primary National Strategy, Baldock: United Kingdom Literacy Association.

Bearne, E., Clarke, C., Johnson, A., Manford, P., Mottram, M. and Wolstencroft, H. (2007) *Reading on Screen*, Leicester: UKLA.

Becta (2007) *Personalised Learning with ICT*, Coventry: Becta.

Becta (2008) Figures on equipment in primary schools and classrooms – numbers of IWTs, laptops, PCs in class, PCs in computer suites, etc. Available online at www.becta.org.uk (accessed November 2009).

Dawes, L. Mercer, N. and Wegerif, R. (2000) 'Extending talking and reasoning skills using ICT', in M. Leask and J. Meadows (eds) *Teaching and Learning with ICT in the Primary School*, London: Routledge.

Dowdall, C. (2006) 'Dissonance between the digitally created words of school and home', *Literacy*, 40(3): 153–63.

Gillespie, H. (2006) *Unlocking Learning and Teaching with ICT*, London: David Fulton.

Kress, G. (2003) *Literacy in the New Media Age*, London: Routledge.

Kress, G. and van Leeuwen, T. (1996) *The Grammar of Visual Design*, Routledge: London.

Lambirth, A. (2003) '"They get enough of that at home": understanding aversion to popular culture in schools', *Reading, Literacy and Language*, 37(1): 9–13.

Marsh, J. (ed.) (2005) *Popular Culture, New Media and Digital Literacy in Early Childhood*, London: RoutledgeFalmer.

Reedy, G.B. (2008) 'PowerPoint, interactive whiteboards, and the visual culture of technology in schools, *Journal of Technology, Pedagogy and Education*, 17(2): 143–62.

Rideout, V.J., Vandewater, E.A. and Wartella, E.A. (2003) *Zero to Six: Electronic Media in the Lives of Infants, Toddlers and Preschoolers*, Washington, DC: Kaiser Foundation.

Ridgeway, J. and McCusker, S. (2004) *Literature Review of E-assessment*, Bristol: Nesta Futurelab.

Rose, J. (2009) *Independent Review of the Primary Curriculum: Final Report*, London: DCSF. Available online at www.dcsf.gov.uk/primarycurriculumreview (accessed November 2009).

Walsh, C. (2007) 'Creativity as capital in the literacy classroom: youth as multimodal designers', *Literacy*, 41(2): 79–85.

Wegerif, R. and Scrimshaw, P. (1997) *Computers and Reasoning Through Talk in the Classroom*, Clevedon: Multilingual Matters.

Williams, P. (2008) *Independent Review of Mathematics Teaching in Early Years Settings and Primary Schools*, London: DCSF.

8 PARTNERSHIP IN PRACTICE

THE CHANGING ROLE OF THE TEACHER

Tony Eaude

INTRODUCTION

This unit considers how the work of primary school teachers has been affected by recent changes to legislation and policy. It needs to be read in the light of Hayes' earlier unit (1.2), since such changes are based on, and create, new views of what professionalism involves. The first part of this unit considers this further, with particular reference to the Training and Development Agency's (TDA) *Professional Standards* and other views of professionalism, to highlight that teachers need to use, and develop, a repertoire of professional attributes, knowledge, understanding and skills, drawing on those aspects of policy and guidance most relevant to their own situation. The second part looks at how three major aspects of recent government policy – on the curriculum, *Every Child Matters* and Workforce Remodelling – affect teachers in primary schools. While working with other adults in the classroom and with parents/carers, and the teacher's pastoral role, are touched on, these are covered in more detail in subsequent units in this section. The tasks are designed to encourage you to relate general principles to your own experience, given the importance of professional judgement, reflection and continuing professional development (CPD).

OBJECTIVES

By the end of this unit, you should:

■ be aware of how the nature of teacher professionalism has evolved and how the TDA's *Professional Standards* reflect this;
■ understand the importance of relating professional attributes, knowledge and understanding and skills to your own role and context;
■ have a greater knowledge of how recent changes to the curriculum, *Every Child Matters* and Workforce Remodelling have affected primary school teachers;
■ have reflected further on the challenges and opportunities of teaching in a primary school.

THE TDA'S *PROFESSIONAL STANDARDS* AND WHAT MAKES A GOOD TEACHER

In Unit 1.2, Hayes discussed professionalism, especially the attributes of a good teacher highlighted in the TDA's *Professional Standards*, emphasising the relationships that teachers create and how they conduct themselves in a variety of contexts. Published in 2007, these can be seen on the TDA website (www.tda.gov.uk) and are intended to identify the features of a good teacher and to show clearly what is expected at each of the five stages of a teacher's career, from gaining qualified teacher status (QTS), to successful completion of induction, to crossing the 'threshold', and to becoming an excellent teacher and advanced skills teacher (AST).

Each set of standards covers three main aspects:

■ professional *attributes*, which include:

- relationships with children;
- awareness of frameworks and policies;
- communicating and collaborating;
- personal professional development.

■ professional *knowledge and understanding* about issues such as:

- teaching, learning and behaviour management strategies;
- assessment and monitoring;
- subject and curriculum knowledge;
- achievement and diversity;
- health and well-being.

■ professional *skills*, for example:

- planning;
- teaching;
- assessing and giving feedback;
- reviewing;
- establishing a purposeful and safe learning environment.

As a primary school teacher, you may find yourself taking on many roles in any one day: a storyteller, a subject specialist, a shoulder for a parent or a colleague to cry on, a manager of a team of other adults, a wiper-up, a guide . . . It is very hard to capture exactly what makes a good teacher, because the necessary knowledge and skills, especially, vary according to the context and who the teacher is working with at any one time. So teaching a class of ten year olds in a large urban school will require a different balance of attributes, knowledge of policies and ability to liaise with other professionals from working in a nursery unit in a small town; and meeting the needs of a child with a physical disability will differ from teaching a class of high-attaining Year 6 mathematicians.

In Unit 1.2, Hayes discussed the professional attributes in detail. The knowledge and understanding, and to some extent the skills, required will depend on the needs of particular children you teach. These will certainly change from school to school and in the light of government priorities and policies. So, the TDA standards provide a useful starting point, even if there is bound to be disagreement about which attributes or what knowledge are most important. The General Teaching

Council for England (GTCE, www.gtce.org.uk) has also tried to define the essential features of teacher professionalism. However, no list can cater, entirely, for three key elements:

■ the specific role and context in which teachers operate;
■ the external expectations placed on them;
■ individual teachers' beliefs and understanding about teaching and learning.

This emphasises the importance of teachers being adaptable and thinking how best to use, and develop, their knowledge, understanding and skills.

THE HISTORICAL AND CULTURAL BACKGROUND TO PRIMARY SCHOOL TEACHING

Traditionally, teachers in British primary schools have worked with one class most of the time. This was based on the elementary schools of Victorian times, with one (usually female and unqualified) teacher covering a fairly narrow curriculum, for a whole class, aided, if at all, only by one or more older children.

While the introduction of more specialist teaching, technological changes and the involvement of other adults in the classroom, either as support staff or replacing the class teacher, has altered this model to some extent, it has remained remarkably durable.

In British primary schools, teachers have usually been seen as generalists, working with a class, undertaking a wide range of tasks, both academic and pastoral, and able to teach all of most subjects. Teachers in other countries have been seen differently. Especially in France and central Europe, the focus of the teacher's work is largely academic, with pastoral work delegated to others. In Scandinavia, it is expected that most teachers will be educated to M level, with an emphasis on pedagogy – how children learn. Alexander (2000) provides fascinating insights into how teaching approaches are shaped by, and shape, different beliefs about education in five countries. So, the cultural assumptions built into a curriculum or a school structure – as well as the teacher's own – affect how any teacher actually works with children.

Task 8.1.1 WHAT FACTORS AFFECT THE TEACHER'S ROLE IN A CONTEXT KNOWN TO YOU?

Think about factors that affect your job or the one you hope to have. You may not know the answers, but these are all things to consider, or find out, in applying for jobs and when you start.

Ask yourself how the following will affect you as a teacher:

■ the type of class or group and the age of the children you teach;
■ the area the school serves, the school's size, and whether it is a faith school;
■ the level of responsibility you are expected to take on;
■ school policies on planning, schemes of work and timetables;
■ the relationships among staff and more subtle expectations, such as how you might relate to the community, or how you are expected to dress.

Task 8.1.2 **MANAGING AND COORDINATING**

In your second year of teaching, you have been asked to coordinate (or manage) the humanities in a school of about 200 pupils, as well as being a class teacher. You do not have specific expertise in any humanities subject to degree level.

■ What might be the main challenges and tasks in the first year? Some areas to think about are resources, professional development (for yourself or others) and schemes of work, but add your own.
■ Where, and to whom, would you look for advice and support?

THE TEACHER AS A PROFESSIONAL

The twentieth century saw long struggles to ensure first that primary school teachers had to be qualified, and then that primary school teaching became a graduate profession. Although the TDA standards are all prefaced with the word 'professional', teachers have never been seen as professionals in the same way as doctors, lawyers or architects. One reason is the widespread belief that teaching is really just applied common sense, a view that no one would ever take of dentistry! Despite this, children's learning, and how to enable this, is very complicated.

As Hayes suggests in Unit 1.2, there is now less emphasis on teaching as a profession, and more on what it means to act as a professional. However, it is worth reflecting on the typical characteristics of a profession. Among these are:

■ mastery of a knowledge base requiring a long period of training;
■ tasks that are inherently valuable to society;
■ a desire to prioritise the client's welfare;
■ a high level of autonomy;
■ a code of ethics to guide practice.

(Adapted from John, 2008: 12)

Most teachers would agree on the importance of all of these, although many complain about the extent of interference in what and how to teach. Autonomy has reduced with the growing expectation that teachers will be accountable for what they do, especially in terms of results. While this is true of all professions, it has affected teachers especially, although they retain a good deal of autonomy in *how* to teach. Many teachers, especially when just starting, expect to be told what to do. However, exercising judgement remains an integral part of being a professional, because school and government priorities change; and, even more, because how children respond is never entirely predictable. This is one reason why teaching young children is so challenging and rewarding.

Sound judgement is based on becoming more reflective. Pollard and Tann identify six main features of reflective teaching:

■ an active concern with aims and consequences;
■ a process in which teachers monitor, evaluate and revise their own practice continuously;
■ competence in methods of classroom enquiry;
■ attitudes of open-mindedness, responsibility and whole-heartedness;
■ teacher judgement, informed both by self-reflection and insights from educational disciplines; and
■ collaboration and dialogue with colleagues.

(1994: 9–10)

These may look difficult at first, especially the third, but many are similar to the TDA's professional attributes. Many attributes of a good teacher are personal and harder to learn than factual knowledge, with their successful application depending on practice. These are features to develop over your career as a teacher, if you are going to act as a professional, rather than just a technician.

Schon's (1987) distinction between reflection-on-action (thinking back on what has happened) and reflection-in-action (thinking about what is happening to inform immediate decisions) is one that many people find useful. The former involves thinking about, and planning, how to teach in the light of school policies, schemes of work and experience; while reflection-in-action involves taking decisions on the spur of the moment, in response to particular situations. This is something good teachers are constantly doing, based on their knowledge and understanding, especially of how children learn, and of their own skills and experience.

Changes in the specific knowledge and understanding required makes flexibility and continuing professional development (CPD) especially important. CPD does not just involve courses, but reflection, reading, planning, moderation, coaching/mentoring and discussion, sometimes on one's own, where possible with others. In particular, take whatever opportunities you can to see teachers at work, whether with children, with other staff, or with parents/carers.

Task 8.1.3 WHAT ARE THE KEY FEATURES OF A SUCCESSFUL TEACHER?

Watch, and think about, the features of one teacher you have worked with, or observed working with young children. Consider the ones suggested below and add your own.

■ Which particular attributes did he or she demonstrate – enthusiasm, strictness, empathy . . .?

■ What professional knowledge did he or she use – subject expertise, behaviour management, knowledge of individual children . . .?

■ Which professional skills did you see – in terms of planning, giving feedback, asking questions . . .?

Be specific. For example, how did she use subject knowledge? Or what was good about his feedback?

Now, preferably with another person, do the same for yourself, but make sure you focus mainly on the positives – you will find there are plenty, even when a lesson has not gone well. From this, decide on your strengths and what you need to work at developing. But remember, we are all different, so it is not just a case of trying to copy one teacher you admire.

Task 8.1.4 A BORN TEACHER?

■ Sometimes, people talk about 'a born teacher.' Does this idea make any sense? If so, what are the key attributes?

■ Which aspects of the TDA's list (see page 415) do you think are hardest and easiest to acquire and develop?

■ Discuss this with another student or teacher. To what extent do your ideas and priorities coincide?

THE CURRICULUM AND THE ROLE OF THE TEACHER

The curriculum is one important factor in how teachers work. Elementary school teaching involved *delivering* a fairly narrow curriculum. In the 1960s and 1970s, there was more emphasis on *facilitating* the child's learning, with a lot of personal autonomy for both teacher and child. However, recent trends have emphasised *managing* a team of adults to ensure that all children can access a range of curricular opportunities, adapted to each child's own needs.

The introduction of the National Curriculum after 1989, based on a structure of subjects, led to a greater emphasis on curriculum content and measurable outcomes, especially in the 'core' subjects of English, maths and science. The rationale for this was to ensure a consistent entitlement for all children. The introduction of the Office for Standards in Education (Ofsted) in the mid-1990s was designed to make schools, and teachers, more publicly accountable and the National Literacy and Numeracy Strategies of the late 1990s were explicit about how teachers should teach. *Excellence and Enjoyment* (DfES, 2003) emphasised that children should enjoy learning and using their creativity as well as attaining high standards. Recent years have seen the increasing introduction of specialist teaching, notably in Years 5 and 6, which has altered the class teacher's previous responsibility for teaching all (or almost all) subjects. Future curricular changes will continue to affect how teachers work. For instance, the decision to introduce modern foreign languages (MFL) in primary schools from 2010, however welcome, will have considerable implications both for who will teach MFL and for class teachers.

Growing concerns, especially about overload, led to two reviews of the curriculum: the independent *Cambridge Primary Review* (Alexander, 2009) and the government-sponsored *Independent Review of the Primary Curriculum* by Sir Jim Rose (2008), with the final report published in 2009. These are discussed by Hayes in Unit 1.2, and in more detail by Wyse in Unit 4.2, so are not considered here. While it is uncertain to what extent these will change what, and how, teachers are expected to teach, there will always be a tension between how much content should be prescribed and how much left to individual schools' and teachers' discretion; and to what extent, and when, young children should be taught by subject specialists and how much by generalists.

Another recent initiative has been the expectation for schools and teachers to move increasingly towards 'personalised learning'. This should not be taken to mean individualised programmes for all, which is neither feasible nor desirable. Learning is a social process, where children learn together and from each other. However, it does entail adapting and differentiating the curriculum according to children's needs – for those with English as an additional language (EAL), those who are gifted and talented, and those with special educational needs (SEN). This is essential if the National Curriculum being an entitlement for all is to be a reality.

This section highlights that the curriculum is not static, emphasising what is deemed most important at any one time. For example, the current concern with Key Stage 2 attainment scores in English and maths leads teachers, especially in Year 6, to focus on these; and a greater stress on ICT and citizenship is based on the perceived needs of the world of work in the twenty-first century and concerns about social and cultural fragmentation. However, enabling all children to learn successfully depends crucially on the skill and judgement of teachers in deciding how to take children's different abilities, backgrounds and cultures into account and build on their prior learning.

Task 8.1.5 **HOW DOES THE CURRENT CURRICULUM REFLECT YOUR OWN BELIEFS ABOUT WHAT, AND HOW, CHILDREN SHOULD LEARN?**

We have seen how much the National Curriculum has changed in the last 20 years.

■ What are the advantages and disadvantages of having a National Curriculum?
■ What are the assumptions behind the current National Curriculum:
  ▌ about the teacher's role;
  ▌ about how children learn;
  ▌ about the aims of education for primary age children?
■ In which respects do you share these assumptions?
■ And in which respects do you differ?

Task 8.1.6 **PERSONALISED LEARNING**

The psychologist Jerome Bruner wrote:

we have learned that there is no such thing as *the* curriculum, there is only *a* curriculum; it is very specific to a particular situation and a particular student, and it will vary. For, in effect, it's an animated three-way conversation between a learner, someone who is somewhat more expert in an area of study and a body of knowledge that is difficult to define but that exists in the culture.

(2006: 141)

■ What are the implications for personalised learning?
■ How does this affect primary school teachers? What do they need to be experts in?

EVERY CHILD MATTERS AND HOW PRIMARY SCHOOL TEACHERS CAN SUPPORT VULNERABLE CHILDREN

Every Child Matters (ECM) (see 'Relevant websites' at the end of this unit) has become a shorthand term for a very important trend in government policy, not just in education. Lord Laming's report (Health Committee, 2003), which followed serious concerns after the death of Victoria Climbié, highlighted the need for different agencies (including schools) to work more closely together and for local authorities to reorganise. The Children Act 2004 establishes a duty on local authorities to ensure cooperation between agencies, and on key partners, including education, to cooperate. All professionals are expected to work towards the five ECM outcomes to ensure that all children will:

■ be healthy;
■ stay safe;
■ enjoy and achieve;
■ make a positive contribution;
■ achieve economic well-being.

Examples of how these have affected schools are a greater emphasis on:

■ enhancing physical, and increasingly mental, health through programmes such as 'Healthy Schools';
■ keeping children safe from physical, sexual and emotional abuse;
■ providing a wider range of opportunities for learning outside the classroom;
■ listening more to what is often called 'children's voice', for instance through school councils;
■ encouraging more links with local businesses and chances for children to run their own enterprises.

While ECM is important for all children, a major emphasis has been on protecting vulnerable children. For example, the Common Assessment Framework (CAF) is a procedure adopted nationally to identify more accurately and efficiently the additional needs of children at risk of not meeting the ECM outcomes, especially that of being safe. Schools, and teachers, are expected to work more closely with other professionals outside the school. Among these are:

■ health professionals, such as school nurses and doctors, whether general practitioners (GPs) or specialists;
■ teachers with specific expertise in a particular disability, such as sensory impairment or autism;
■ educational psychologists, who offer assessment and advice to schools and parents/carers, usually for children at the higher stages of identification detailed in the *SEN Code of Practice*;
■ educational social workers, who provide support especially in relation to school attendance;
■ social workers, especially with looked-after children (those vulnerable children whom a court (usually) has determined that the local authority has a particular duty to 'look after');
■ private and voluntary childcare providers.

Many of these professionals have specific expertise, which can be used to support individual children directly and/or help teachers meet their needs. Some have designated responsibilities in supporting parents/carers, or monitoring children's welfare. While much of the liaison with them is likely to be undertaken by senior colleagues, especially the head teacher or the SEN coordinator, teachers have an important place, for instance by reporting concerns or being part of reviews. The class teacher, as the professional who sees children and parents/carers most frequently, is absolutely vital in noticing possible indicators of concern. For example, irregular attendance patterns may indicate problems at home; or a child who becomes withdrawn or aggressive may need psychological support. Most serious is teachers' responsibility in relation to child protection, signs of which may be immediate, such as a bruise or a burn, or more long-term and harder to identify, such as emotional abuse. All schools must have a child protection policy, with which all teachers should be familiar. This must be followed – with the first action usually being to share concerns with a senior colleague. As a rule of thumb, if in doubt discuss your concerns with a more experienced teacher.

Working with parents/carers and the benefits of doing so are dealt with in more detail in Ryan and Griffin's unit (8.3). Liaising with them is a normal part of what teachers do. In the early years, especially, contact may be frequent, discussing children's progress informally and naturally. Reporting to, and discussing with, parents/carers more formally is an important part of every teacher's job. But the ECM agenda emphasises the importance of teachers being prepared to inform other professionals of, or involve them in, concerns about children's safety, a task that can, sometimes, be difficult and place a strain on relationships with parents/carers.

The teacher's pastoral role, especially the legal framework, is discussed further in Whitney's unit (8.4). The ECM agenda reaffirms and extends the belief in British education that teachers are not just concerned with 'academic' learning, but need to liaise more closely with professionals from other agencies, who may have different procedures and ways of working, for instance on confidentiality. The five ECM outcomes are a central part of what Ofsted inspectors focus on, but that, in my view, is not the main reason why you should be aware of these throughout your professional life. Rather, it is because these are central to the moral and professional responsibilities of all teachers.

Task 8.1.7 **SUPPORTING A CHILD WITH SEN 1**

This task is best done with someone else or in a small group.

Imagine that you are the teacher of a class of whichever age you are most familiar with. In the class, a little girl, Paula, has a hearing impairment and speech and language difficulties.

■ What information would you hope to have before you start teaching Paula?

List the other adults within and outside the school whom you would expect to be involved. As a prompt, look back at the list of professionals on page 421, but think about other staff in school (remember support staff and midday supervisors) and parent(s)/carer(s).

■ What would you hope to gain from each?
■ What do you think you can offer to each of them and to the process of assessment?

Task 8.1.8 **SUPPORTING A CHILD WITH SEN 2**

Which aspects of your classroom environment or your teaching may need to be considered to ensure that Paula is fully integrated into the class, and that her additional needs can be met? Think, for example, of induction, equipment, grouping, use of support staff, timetable, activities outside the classroom . . .

EXTENDED SCHOOLS

Every Child Matters has also led to what are often called 'extended schools'. This is intended to both extend the range of opportunities open to children and parents/carers and provide these at the most appropriate time and place. All schools will be expected to enable access (but not necessarily make provision on site) to a wide range of activities. The extent to which any particular school makes its own arrangements or is part of a wider partnership will vary.

Among the sorts of provision that may be included are:

■ breakfast and after-school clubs;
■ study and homework clubs;
■ opportunities for outside specialists, such as poets or artists, to work with children in curriculum time;
■ additional sports and leisure activities;
■ opportunities for specific groups of children, such as those with additional needs or gifted and talented children, outside school hours;

- community education;
- provision for other agencies, such as health services.

Much of this provision, such as breakfast clubs or after-school clubs, may not affect most individual teachers directly, apart from liaison with the organisers. Other opportunities are more directly related to the curriculum. Thus, this may involve:

- being aware of, and letting children and parents/carers know about, opportunities outside school from which children may benefit, such as holiday schemes or community groups;
- liaising with other colleagues on how best to extend children's learning, for instance in making arrangements for visits from 'creative partners', such as musicians or storytellers;
- planning with, and working alongside, creative partners, who may need advice and support on how best to work with a particular group of children.

Most primary school teachers have, for many years, seen their role much more widely than just in the classroom. The extended schools agenda formalises this. It has the potential to broaden and deepen children's learning and make provision suitable for particular communities. However, it also makes more demands of schools and of teachers. So, be prepared both to contribute to the new opportunities offered and also to ensure that you keep a good work–life balance by not taking on too much.

WORKFORCE REMODELLING

In 2003, the government, employers and most of the teacher unions signed an agreement usually called Workforce Remodelling (see www.tda.gov.uk). Intended to raise standards and tackle unacceptable levels of workload for teachers, it introduced some innovations that have been widely welcomed, such as all teachers having a minimum of 10 per cent of their timetable for planning, preparation and assessment (PPA). However, some aspects remain controversial, especially how support staff are used.

One major implication is in what school support staff do. In the past, there were far fewer than now, usually working with individual children or tidying up. In early years settings, staff such as nursery nurses always had much more expected of them. Workforce Remodelling has led to many support staff taking on much more responsibility – as librarians or technicians, or delivering programmes to support groups of children and, in some cases, taking a whole class. Some have gained additional recognition, and pay, by becoming higher-level teaching assistants (HLTAs). This has resulted in many support staff thriving in new roles and making a greater direct contribution to children's learning.

While most teachers have welcomed the introduction of PPA time, it has affected the class teacher's responsibilities, most obviously because he or she is not with the class for a significant part of the week. Most teachers welcome this, although some regret not teaching a subject area that they enjoy and/or are good at. In some schools, PPA time enables children to have sessions with those with particular specialisms, such as in music, arts, a foreign language or sports. For some teachers, it offers an opportunity to teach such a specialism to other classes. Where those covering PPA time are less skilled, teachers may find that they are asked to provide material, although this is not a requirement. However, whatever the model, PPA time presents challenges in knowing what has happened and the progress that children have made, so that how to report to parents/carers has to be carefully thought through.

Workforce Remodelling emphasises the importance of teachers working collaboratively and managing other adults. How to do so in the classroom is explored in more detail in Wood's unit (8.2). Planning will often involve working with other teachers in the same year group or key stage, but there are many other adults to plan with, or for, and to liaise with. Some will be highly qualified, others less so. Some may only visit the school occasionally. Some will work in the class, others with small groups or individuals, while others, such as learning mentors or specialist teachers, may offer individual support. While you will probably welcome such support, it makes demands on planning, liaising and feeding back. It may also make it hard to gather the whole class for a sustained period.

Other aspects of Workforce Remodelling include ways of reducing bureaucracy to ensure that teachers can be relieved of menial tasks that can be done by support staff, electronically – or not at all, if they are unnecessary. Both ECM and Workforce Remodelling emphasise teacher professionalism as involving *managing* the provision of a range of learning opportunities for children, rather than focusing exclusively on direct teaching, although that remains the most important part of what teachers do.

Task 8.1.9 **WORKFORCE REMODELLING – A CASE STUDY**

Read this description of how one class in a two-form entry primary school is organised to enable the teachers to have PPA time.

> The two class teachers with Year 4 classes are released on a Thursday afternoon. An HLTA takes half a class for one hour, then the other half, with the rest of the class having an external sports coach. The other class has a similar arrangement doing religious education with a teacher who works part-time and a different sports coach. Those taking the two classes swap after a six-week block.

■ Who does the class teacher need to liaise with?
■ What possible challenges and opportunities does this model offer:
  ▮ to the children;
  ▮ to the class teacher?

Think especially about:

■ liaison with other teachers;
■ curriculum continuity;
■ planning;
■ assessment;
■ children's behaviour;
■ reporting to parents/carers?

Task 8.1.10 **WORKING WITH NON-TEACHERS**

What are the specific challenges that teachers encounter when liaising or working with other professionals, especially those who are not teachers, in terms of:

■ interpersonal skills;
■ workload;
■ different belief systems and ways of working?

(It may be worth considering Atkinson *et al.*'s 2005 article – see 'Annotated further reading'.)

SUMMARY

This unit has considered recent changes that affect teachers in primary schools, especially in working beyond any one classroom and with others outside school. Deciding how best to enable a group or an individual to learn best, in a particular situation, requires teachers to draw on a range of the attributes, knowledge, understanding and skills highlighted in the TDA standards – and others. Learning to be a teacher may require you, initially, to concentrate on the mechanics of teaching. However, there is more to being a good teacher than this, developing, and relating, theoretical expertise and practical experience.

Good teachers are constantly drawing on a repertoire of professional attributes, knowledge, understanding and skills, making judgements as circumstances change. Especially with younger children, this requires both reflection-in-practice and reflection-on-practice, as well as being aware of the demands of the curriculum and policies. However, the relationships you build, with children and adults, are at the heart of successful teaching and learning.

You may need to undertake some roles outlined in this unit early in your career; and most of them (and others!) at some time in the future. Teachers will always have to exercise judgements and make policies and initiatives work in the real world. Even though this may seem demanding, do not be put off. Other teachers are usually happy to offer guidance and schools benefit from the up-to-date knowledge and energy that new teachers bring. The variety of the primary school teacher's role is one reason why it is so rewarding, offering the chance to enrich many children's lives – and your own.

ANNOTATED FURTHER READING

Atkinson, K., Doherty, P. and Kinder, K. (2005) 'Multi-agency working: models, challenges and key factors for success', *Journal of Early Childhood Research*, 3(1): 7–17.
    This is a fairly brief review of some of the complexities of working with other professionals, especially relevant to the *Every Child Matters* and extended schools agenda.

Pollard, A. and Tann, S. (1994) *Reflective Teaching in the Primary School*, London: Cassell.
    This book contains interesting ideas on the link between teachers' identities and how children learn, with practical activities designed to help you explore this. Read, especially, Chapter 4 (pp. 57–84).

RELEVANT WEBSITES

Cambridge Primary Review: www.primaryreview.org.uk
Every Child Matters: www.everychild.matters.gov.uk

This site includes all the *Every Child Matters* documents and many useful sources of advice. They can be downloaded or ordered on dcsf@prolog.uk.com or 0845 6022260, although most will be available in schools. Especially important are:

■ *Every Child Matters: The Next Steps*

■ *Every Child Matters: Change for Children*

■ *Every Child Matters: Change for Children in Schools*

■ *Choice for Parents, the Best Start for Children: A Ten Year Strategy for Children*

■ *Children's Workforce Strategy*

■ *Common Assessment Framework*

General Teaching Council for England (GTCE): www.gtce.org.uk

The GTCE's *Code of Conduct and Practice for Registered Teachers* gives their view of what teacher professionalism involves. Type 'Code of conduct and practice' into the home page search box.

Training and Development Agency for Schools (TDA): www.tda.gov.uk

Look especially at the *Professional Standards* (type TDA0600 into the home page search box) and information on the Workforce Remodelling Agreement, under the section 'Remodelling'.

TeacherNet: www.teachernet.gov.uk/wholeschool/extendedschools/practicalknowhow

The title of this website speaks for itself!

Visit the companion website www.routledge.com/textbooks/ltps2e for:

■ additional questions and task for this unit;

■ links to useful websites relevant to this unit.

REFERENCES

Alexander, R. (2000) *Culture and Pedagogy: International Comparisons in Primary Education*, Oxford: Blackwell.

Alexander, R. (2010) *Children, the World, their Education: Final Report and Recommendations of the* Cambridge Primary Review, Abingdon: Routledge.

Bruner, J. (2006) *In Search of Pedagogy Volume 11: The Selected Works of Jerome S Bruner*, Abingdon: Routledge.

Department for Education and Skills (DfES) (2003) *Excellence and Enjoyment: A Strategy for Primary Schools*, DCSF 0377/2003, London: DfES. Available online at http://nationalstrategies.standards. dcsf.gov.uk/node/88755 (accessed November 2009).

Health Committee (2003) *The Victoria Climbié Inquiry: Report of an Inquiry by Lord Laming*, London: The Stationery Office.

John, P. (2008) 'The predicament of the teaching profession and the revival of professional authority: a Parsonian perspective', in D. Johnson and R. Maclean (eds) *Teaching: Professionalization, Development and Leadership*, London: Springer.

Pollard, A. and Tann, S. (1994) *Reflective Teaching in the Primary School*, London: Cassell.

Rose, J. (2008) *The Independent Review of the Primary Curriculum: Interim Report*, London: DCSF. Available online at www.dcsf.gov.uk/primarycurriculumreview (accessed November 2009).

Rose, J. (2009) *The Independent Review of the Primary Curriculum: Final Report*, London: DCSF. Available online at www.dcsf.gov.uk/primarycurriculumreview (accessed May 2009).

Schon, D. (1987) *Educating the Reflective Practitioner: Toward a New Design for Teaching and Learning the Professions*, San Francisco, CA: Jossey Bass.

WORKING WITH OTHER ADULTS IN THE CLASSROOM

Elizabeth Wood

INTRODUCTION

Teachers work collaboratively with a wide range of adults in the classroom, including teaching assistants (TAs), specialist teaching assistants (STAs) for children with special and additional educational needs, professionals from other agencies, students in training, parents and caregivers. Under your direction, TAs will take responsibility for aspects of curriculum planning and implementation, observation, assessment and feedback, thus ensuring that the curriculum is differentiated for children's diverse interests, dispositions and approaches to learning. This unit focuses on three key themes of communication, collaboration and co-construction, which provide a framework for supporting personalised learning. Being able to work productively with other adults will make high demands on your interpersonal and managerial skills, and your professional knowledge. Practical tasks and case studies provide guidance on constructive approaches to using the professional knowledge and skills that TAs bring to the classroom.

OBJECTIVES

By the end of this unit you should:

■ understand the policy context regarding the role of TAs and other professionals, in the Foundation Stage and Key Stages 1 and 2;
■ know about the findings of research studies, and understand their recommendations for professional practice;
■ understand some practical skills and strategies that will help you develop a partnership approach based on communication, collaboration and co-construction;
■ know how to deploy TAs effectively to support children's personalised learning.

THE POLICY PERSPECTIVE

National policy documents support a partnership approach with families, TAs and other professionals. *Every Child Matters* (DfES, 2004) requires schools to develop multi-agency approaches to providing services for children and their families across education, health and social care. This 'joined-up' approach is significant for early intervention and support programmes, and underpins high-quality provision. The Children's Workforce Strategy, in *Building Brighter Futures* (DCSF, 2008), reiterates four key objectives that will help to improve outcomes for young people:

■ recruiting more high-quality staff;
■ retaining staff through better development and career progression;
■ strengthening inter-agency working;
■ providing stronger leadership and management.

A government aspiration is to ensure that all TAs and pre-school practitioners have at least a Level 3 National Vocational Qualification, but many assistants have no formal training, and learn their skills 'on the job'. TAs have a wide range of training and experience. Those who have childcare qualifications will bring specialist knowledge of child development, learning theory, policy and curriculum frameworks, and skills in planning, observation and assessment. Career progression includes opportunities for people to gain a range of qualifications, such as Foundation and M level degrees, and higher-level awards for teaching assistants (HLTAs). You will be responsible for supporting ongoing training and professional development, by sharing knowledge, modelling skills and engaging in reflective discussions about provision and practice. These strategies will also help you make effective use of everyone's knowledge and expertise.

In the Early Years Foundation Stage (EYFS) (birth to six) (DfES, 2007), the term 'practitioner' is used for teachers and early years professionals (EYPs) who work with young children. In children's centres and Foundation Stage units in primary schools, teachers and EYPs may work collaboratively, combining their specialist expertise. For example, teachers may take responsibility for curriculum management, while EYPs may have overall responsibility for centre management. The key principles of effective practice in the EYFS state that practitioners should:

■ meet the needs of individual children;
■ deliver personalised learning, development and care;
■ work with parents and families to support children;
■ provide regular information to parents and caregivers about children's progress;
■ provide opportunities for indoor and outdoor play (planned and spontaneous);
■ provide a curriculum that includes adult- and child-initiated activities;
■ observe and reflect on children's learning.

(DfES, 2007)

You will also be expected to liaise with a wide variety of professionals from outside the school community (such as educational psychologists, behaviour support specialists, English-medium advisory services, speech therapists and mental health specialists) and to share information and teaching strategies with TAs. They can provide continuous support for children's learning, well-being and development, drawing on curriculum frameworks, and the social and emotional aspects of learning (SEAL). These principles apply across the Foundation Stage and Key Stages 1 and 2, because integrated team working supports effective teaching and learning.

John's case study shows how communication and collaboration across multi-agency teams worked successfully to support his inclusion and progression in a mainstream school.

Case study 1

John had cerebral palsy, and joined his Year 1 class at age six, following additional time in the Foundation Stage. He had a statement of his special educational needs (SEN), and an individual education plan (IEP). His STA made this transition with John, and advised the Year 1 teacher on the range of resources needed to support his learning and development. The teacher reorganised the classroom to enable him to move around more easily. They acquired Dycem mats, which create an adhesive surface for books, paper and other resources, and they transferred John's computer with its special programmes and controls. The STA provided continuity with John's parents by sharing information across home and school. The teacher worked closely with his speech therapist, physiotherapist and educational psychologist, and shared information and recommendations with the STA. All team members contributed to records of John's progress and development. They worked collaboratively on removing barriers to learning, supporting his progress and achievements, and ensuring consistency of approaches across home and school.

THE NATIONAL STRATEGIES

The Primary National Strategy (DfES, 2006) defines key pedagogical principles, curriculum content, and guidance on their implementation in literacy and mathematics. In order to support personalised learning, teachers are encouraged to interpret policy documents in ways that are flexible and responsive, and respect children's diverse cultures and backgrounds. Personalised learning requires that planning is responsive to children's abilities, takes account of the dimensions of diversity (gender, ethnicity, social class, ability/disability, sexualities), and includes children's perspectives on their learning and development. One of the key principles to emerge from the government-funded Teaching and Learning Research programme is that effective teaching and learning foster both individual and social processes and outcomes:

> Learners should be encouraged and helped to build relationships and communication with others for learning purposes, in order to assist the mutual construction of knowledge and enhance the achievements of individuals and groups. Consulting learners about their learning and giving them a voice is both an expectation and a right.
>
> (James and Pollard, 2008)

In order to achieve this aspiration, TAs should work in close partnership with teachers as they plan and teach across the curriculum. STAs may have responsibility for supporting children who have SEN, or English as an additional language (EAL). All TAs can be involved in planning; for example, in literacy they can select texts and other resources to ensure differentiation, and support children's literacy skills across the curriculum. They can also observe and make notes about the children's progress and achievements in relation to the objectives for a lesson or scheme of work, develop further plans with you, and feed back children's ideas, interests and perspectives. Teachers can use their professional judgement in altering the balance between whole-class, group and individual teaching. Therefore, developing your own 'designer' version of national policy frameworks is essential to creative planning, accurate differentiation, and ensuring that children are motivated, engaged and involved. For example, if you teach a mixed-age class in Key Stage 1 or 2, you might consider a range of strategies to plan for differentiation and personalised learning:

■ reducing whole-class teaching time;
■ planning more time for groups (age/ability differentiation);
■ deploying TAs to an individual child or group of children, for specific support;
■ using TAs to lead small-group, rather than whole-class, plenaries;
■ using TAs for small group activities such as storytelling, music and language development (including verbal and sign languages).

The *Independent Review of the Primary Curriculum* (Rose Review) (Rose, 2009) is likely to bring further changes to how the EYFS and primary curriculum are planned and implemented. The recommendations place greater emphasis on cross-curricular planning through integrated themes or topics, alongside supporting children's social and emotional development (in line with SEAL). Recommendation 4 states that teachers should give children 'ample opportunities to use and apply their developing knowledge, skills and understanding in cross-curricular studies'. TAs can play a key role in helping to develop the contexts in which children can see the relevance and practical application of their skills and abilities, as shown in the following case study.

Case study 2

Children in a Year 6 class were involved in an action research project to improve the quality of outdoor play for all children in their school. With the support of the TAs and bilingual support assistants, they carried out a survey of children in Key Stages 1 and 2, asking what the main problems were with outdoor play areas, and what changes they would like. The TAs helped with the survey, and then supported the children as they entered their data into a database to present the findings to the school management team. The children also researched a range of websites for games that could be taught to children, and ways of making playtimes more beneficial. Children from ethnic minority communities contributed games that their parents knew about, thus widening the cultural repertoire of activities. The Year 6 children were then responsible for playing with children in other year groups to teach them the games, and gave feedback to the teachers and TAs about the success of their activities, and further improvements.

PLAY AND PERSONALISED LEARNING

The EYFS highlights the importance of adult- and child-initiated activities (including play), to which all practitioners contribute. There is consistent evidence from research (Wood, 2009) that adults can help children to plan their own activities, enrich and support play, extend children's agendas and interests, and act as co-players (as long as children's intentions are respected). Children's self-initiated activities also provide valuable insights into the ways in which they personalise their own learning through their choices and decisions. The following case study shows how a TA inspired play in 'Pepito's Pizza Place', with a focus on using literacy in the role-play area.

Case study 3

The reception children left the pizza café in a mess. The TA took this opportunity to develop and enrich the play theme, and planned some adult-led activities with the teacher. She closed down the café, and put up a notice from the 'Health, Hygiene and Safety Inspector', which listed all the reasons for the closure, with some imaginative touches: mouse droppings in the cupboard and mould in the fridge. This intervention led to further adult- and child-initiated activities; the children wrote a job specification for the cleaning and put it out to tender (this involved the school's cleaning staff). In science, they looked at different types of cleaning materials and ways of storing food safely. They planned to clean the café, then write to the inspector detailing their work and arranging another inspection. The TA wrote back, demanding to know who was responsible for keeping the café clean and what jobs needed to be done. The children drew up a roster of activities, and also took on the role of the inspector. These activities provided many opportunities for curriculum-based learning, as well as stimulating creativity, imagination, playfulness and inclusion for all children. Because the TA was involved as a co-player, she observed the children's activities, made notes on their learning, collaborated with the class teacher on planning further activities, and contributed to the children's Foundation Stage assessment profiles.

By using policy frameworks as a guide rather than a straitjacket, you can use your professional knowledge to decide where and how best to deploy TAs. This will be influenced to some extent by their training and experience, and by the nature of the task. For example, TAs or parents may be able to take a group reading session, but may not have the expertise to conduct a specific analysis and diagnosis of a child's reading difficulties. In contrast, an SEN support teacher, or educational psychologist, will be able to carry out more specialised diagnostic assessments that can inform personalised learning. TAs can support personalised learning by working collaboratively on planning, monitoring, taking responsibility for activities and making suggestions for extension, revisiting, practice or consolidation.

Task 8.2.1 **SHARING PLANNING AND ASSESSMENT**

■ Plan three activities in literacy and numeracy that will be managed by the TA with a group of children.

■ Ask the TA to annotate samples of work from each activity, and each child. Make time to discuss the observations and feedback, and extend the discussion to include evidence of each child's achievement and progress.

■ Record your 'next steps', decide how these might be mapped into the planning cycle, and decide who will take responsibility for planning and implementing the activities.

You can repeat this activity in any curriculum area.

Task 8.2.2 **CHILD-INITIATED PLANNING**

Discuss with the TA what particular approaches to learning the children showed in these tasks. Consider the levels of engagement and involvement, the children's strategies for persevering with challenge or difficulty, and what interests and ideas they discussed or revealed through their recorded work. With the TA, consider how your detailed knowledge of children as learners can inform your planning.

■ Can the children take some responsibility for planning to follow their ideas and interests?

■ How can the TA support child-initiated activities?

Schools should have a policy and job description for the effective use of TAs, along with guidance for involving parents in the classroom. You should become familiar with these policies so that you understand what can reasonably be expected of team members. For example, their hours of work may be different, so you will need to organise time for planning, preparation of materials, discussion and feedback. This aspiration is essential for supporting personalised learning, which involves recognising the different ways in which children learn, their attitudes and dispositions, their friendship and peer group relationships, what kinds of choices they make in free choice and play time, and their interests in and out of school.

WHAT SUPPORT MIGHT BE AVAILABLE IN MY CLASS?

TAs may be temporary or permanent, full-time or part-time. They may be shared across classes or phases, or may be attached to a specific class or to a specific child, or to a specific area, such as support for children with EAL. For those with SEN, the STA is likely to stay with the child, and move to the next class in order to provide consistency and continuity. Specialist teachers and assistants may be peripatetic within the school or within the local authority so that they provide targeted support for a child or group. The Ethnic Minority Advisory Service (EMAS) can ensure that TAs with relevant community languages are deployed in schools. They can be invaluable not just in supporting children, but also in liaising with family members, finding out about home-based child-rearing practices, religious beliefs and dietary requirements.

Parents are also a valuable source of support for learning, but remember to ask about your school's policy on this, particularly regarding Criminal Records Bureau checks. You need to clarify which parents or caregivers are available, and how much time they are willing to give. A couple of hours per week on a regular basis may be more manageable than whole or half days. Try to establish a clear pattern of who is available and when, so that you can plan accordingly. Most schools have a predominantly female workforce, so it is valuable to think about involving men, because they can be positive role models for boys, as Peter found with his Year 2 class.

Case study 4

Peter was concerned about the progress and achievements of a group of boys. They were demotivated in literacy, had difficulties with handwriting, and were not interested in imaginative writing. He arranged for some men to come into the classroom over one term – all were parents and family members. They were involved in whole-class and small-group sessions, and talked about the different ways in which they use literacy and numeracy in their everyday lives, including the workplace. They read and played alongside the children. Most of the boys subsequently showed significantly improved interest and motivation in their writing: they saw real purposes for their writing, and became more imaginative in what they chose to write about. The challenge for Peter was to develop this 'one-off' initiative into a more sustained whole-school policy.

TAs and specialist teachers may be involved in specific support programmes, such as:

- additional literacy and numeracy support;
- the Portage Programme (an early intervention, home–school partnership for children under five);
- Reading Recovery and other government initiatives;
- behaviour and social skills support (possibly with the support of a behaviour management team);
- counselling;
- extension programmes for gifted and talented children;
- specific support for children with SEN and EAL;
- speech/language therapy;
- homework programmes;
- peer tutoring, peer mediation and buddy systems.

Many of these support programmes require a multidisciplinary and multi-agency approach, where professionals cross the borders between home, school and community, as shown in Case study 1. The support that is available includes children's behaviour, emotional and mental health and all aspects of their learning and development. Children often experience short-term problems (such as an illness, accident or injury, family break-up or bereavement) that can impact on their progress in school. It is important to take a holistic view of each child in your class; this will enable you to work creatively with support staff and parents to address problems as they arise, and to provide the consistency that children need in times of stress.

Task 8.2.3 **FOCUSING ON CHILDREN WITH SEN**

Identify the school's coordinator for SEN. Make time to talk to her or him, and to find out the range of support services that are available from other agencies, and the support that is available in school. Ask the coordinator to discuss strategies that she or he has found particularly effective in working collaboratively with TAs.

HOW CAN I DEPLOY SUPPORT MOST EFFECTIVELY?

It is your responsibility to make decisions about how best to deploy TAs, bearing in mind that providing high-quality support for children's learning and development is the main aspiration. There are two complementary approaches:

- The TA provides support for the teacher, for example by preparing materials, taking on some of the class administrative responsibilities, photocopying, and researching websites and other teaching resources.
- The TA provides support for individuals/groups, thus enabling the teacher to focus on other areas (for example, whole-class teaching sessions or specialist input with specific groups).

Support staff may work inside the classroom, or take groups or individuals to another space – perhaps somewhere quiet or with special resources, or for outdoor activities. For example, all TAs in a primary school went on a Forest School training course in order to support the development and effective use of their own Forest School in the school grounds. An assistant or other adult may be assigned to a child to support positive behaviour. In these instances, it is tempting to have the assistant shadow the child constantly, and to correct behaviour almost continuously. While this strategy may make your life easier, it will not be productive in the longer term. Adults who work alongside children with challenging behaviour should be prepared to model appropriate behaviour, give praise and reinforcement, and talk though any difficulties. The main goal is to help children to develop their inner locus of control by taking responsibility for changing their behaviour, and acting independently of adults. Therefore, a balance needs to be struck between constant surveillance, establishing realistic, and achievable, expectations and creating trust. It is your responsibility to ensure that all adults in the classroom have consistent approaches to managing behaviour and maintaining routines. This does not rule out developing personal styles, but it is not helpful if you are a quiet, calm teacher and find that you have an assistant who shouts at the children.

DEVELOPING A PARTNERSHIP APPROACH: COMMUNICATION, COLLABORATION AND CO-CONSTRUCTION

The 'three Cs' – communication, collaboration and co-construction – provide some guiding principles to underpin your practice. Your first task is to establish good relationships with assistants and parent helpers, and open up channels of communication. Find out about their experience, training, personal interests and skills, what generic skills they might contribute, and their specialist skills and knowledge. If your TA has specialist qualifications, make sure that you capitalise on her or his strengths and knowledge, for example by asking them to carry out observations, liaising with parents and caregivers, or planning a programme of work for a group or individual child (Roffey, 2001). Aim towards co-constructing your knowledge and understanding about how children learn. Co-constructing means building knowledge together, based on sharing values, expertise and ideas; clarifying roles and expectations; providing feedback; and engaging in reflective conversations about children's learning, the success (or failure) of planned activities and the effectiveness of the curriculum offered. Remember to include the child's perspective as part of the assessment and feedback cycle. Schools should be seen as 'communities of learners', where adults are prepared to learn from each other, and from the children.

Sharing values and beliefs about children as learners will provide consistent principles and practices. Contemporary theories view children as strong, powerful and competent; learning is a joint endeavour, which involves co-construction of knowledge, skills and understanding, rather than a one-way transmission of a defined body of knowledge (Anning *et al.*, 2008). How adults view children profoundly influences how they behave and interact with them, what expectations they have and how they assess children (Fisher, 2008). For example, if you set up your classroom to encourage independence, decision making and problem solving, and give children a sense of agency in their learning and behaviour, TAs should understand the underlying reasons for your decisions and support these strategies.

By using collaborative approaches you will involve TAs in the cycle of curriculum planning, carrying out activities and teaching tasks, assessing children's learning and providing feedback. Following the recommendations from research, as well as policy guidance, ensure that you share the aims and intentions of learning activities, what learning outcomes you expect and how the activity will be assessed. Remember that you are not just interested in whether a child has achieved the defined learning objectives. Encourage TAs to identify children's interests, agendas, learning strategies, dispositions, misconceptions and areas of struggle. Ensure that they are 'tuned in' to noticing how the child engaged with the activity, whether he or she persevered with difficulty, how challenge was responded to, and what skills and strategies were used. You will need to model some of these skills yourself, so that you can co-construct shared, reflective dialogues about children's progress and achievements.

If an STA has been working in a previous class alongside a child with EAL or SEN, be prepared to listen and learn. STAs build valuable knowledge about particular conditions or syndromes that can extend your own professional knowledge. Voluntary organisations (such as the National Autistic Society, Scope, the Down's Syndrome Association) provide information that can be researched and shared within the teaching team.

Task 8.2.4 **DEVELOPING INDIVIDUAL EDUCATION PLANS**

With the STA, discuss a child's IEP.

■ Plan a range of activities that will help the child to achieve the next goals, identify resources and clarify areas of responsibility.

■ Decide how you are going to record the child's progress, areas of difficulty and achievements.

■ Discuss how you will communicate with the child's parents/caregivers, and how you will involve the child in assessment.

Task 8.2.5 **DETAILED CHILD OBSERVATIONS**

Plan with the STA to carry out some detailed observations of a child, using recorded notes or digital images (still or recorded). Make time to review and discuss these observations, focusing on any contrasting perspectives. Consider the following:

- what kind of language you both use to describe the child, and how you both understand the child's approaches to learning;
- how the child communicates through multimodal forms of representation;
- responses to challenge or difficulty;
- behaviour in different contexts.

The aim here is to develop fine-grained analyses of children's personalities and dispositions, and to check each others' perspectives and interpretations. Then move on to consider how you can use this knowledge to improve planning and provision.

You should use this 'feedback' assessment information to 'feed forward' into the next cycle of planning, which will develop further collaboration in reflecting on the effectiveness of your provision. Involving children in self-assessment is a highly effective strategy for supporting learning, so make sure that the TA receives feedback from the children. This can be multimodal (different forms of communication and representation), including verbal, written and sign language, drawings, paintings, maps, music, drama, plans, models and constructions. TAs can lead plenary sessions, or circle time with small groups. Some children are reluctant to participate in whole-class sessions; small groups can be less threatening, and provide a more intimate context in which children can achieve success. Again, sharing skills and expectations will help to make plenary or circle time more effective, for example by ensuring a mix of open-ended and closed questions to stimulate thinking and ideas.

Sharing assessment information is also integral to developing an effective partnership approach with parents and caregivers. However, this should not just be a one-way flow, from the school to the home. There is consistent evidence that schools undervalue the learning that goes on in the home and community, especially in minority ethnic communities (Brooker, 2008). Research studies recommend that teachers should build on children's home cultures and knowledge, which means finding out about children's lives, their family beliefs and traditions, and their orientations to schooling. TAs can help to make these valuable links by taking time to talk with children and family members, finding out about home-based child-rearing practices, and developing consistent approaches, particularly during children's transition between different phases of pre-school and school.

The following bullet points provide an aide-mémoire of skills and strategies:

- Find time to plan collaboratively, discuss the TA's assessments and evaluate the activity.
- Clarify where the activity will be carried out.
- Clarify who is responsible for preparing materials and special resources, and make time for this before the lesson or activity.
- Where children have IEPs, ensure that these are shared with the TAs, and develop a programme of work that will achieve the targets set.
- Liaise with TAs to differentiate activities, based on feedback from their observations and interactions.
- Find time to evaluate existing resources, and identify new resources, particularly to support inclusion and cultural diversity (for example, books, games, toys, puzzles, computer games and programmes).

USING TEACHING ASSISTANTS TO SUPPORT TRANSITION

In a report on the introduction of the Foundation Stage, Ofsted noted that TAs can be used to support transitions across phases:

> Teaching assistants frequently play an important role in the successful transition of pupils from Reception to Year 1. They contribute to assessment, support pupils with special educational needs, provide insights into the needs of individuals and maintain established routines where they change classes with pupils.
>
> (Ofsted, 2004: 2)

These principles apply equally to other transitions, from Key Stage 1 to 2, and on to Key Stage 3. Transition can be a stressful time for children: they worry about getting used to a new teacher or a new class, keeping up with the work, managing their books and equipment, finding their way around, losing touch with friends and finding new friends. TAs can be involved in supporting children across transitions by:

- being a familiar face in a new context;
- taking small groups of children to visit their next class;
- getting to know children before they make the transition – visiting the class to work with groups, tell a story, or just be available to chat and answer questions;
- helping children to settle and feel a sense of belonging.

TAs can also support teachers across the transition by being involved in:

- discussions about individual children;
- moderating judgements about children's work;
- contributing to the Foundation Stage Profile and Records of Achievement;
- helping to run workshops for parents;
- sharing good practice and supporting continuity in teaching approaches.

Task 8.2.6 **REFLECTION AND DISCUSSION**

These questions will help you to reflect on what you have learned from this unit, and to consider the practical implications:

- What are the skills and strengths of the adults in my classroom?
- How can their skills be used to support children's learning?
- How can I make time to discuss planning with the TA?
- How can I involve TAs in assessing children's learning, and encouraging children to participate in self-assessment?
- What information needs to be recorded, and how can we ensure that this feeds into planning for personalised learning?
- For children with EAL, can a bilingual TA provide a more accurate indication of children's knowledge and understanding in their first language?
- How can I use a bilingual TA to communicate effectively with family and community members?

SUMMARY

The key themes of communication, collaboration and co-construction provide guiding principles for involving TAs and other adults in the classroom. Sharing values and beliefs, clarifying aims and intentions and sharing assessment information are all effective pedagogical strategies. Schools and classrooms should be places where everyone has a sense of agency, belonging and involvement, and where they can make a contribution to the community. Developing a partnership approach and working as part of a team will enable you to share your challenges, concerns, achievements and enjoyment of being a successful teacher.

ANNOTATED FURTHER READING

Campbell, A. and Fairbairn, G. (2005) *Working With Support in the Classroom*, Buckingham: Open University Press.

> This edited collection of chapters covers early years, primary and secondary education, and is a valuable resource for thinking critically and creatively about managing support for learning. The authors use stories to illustrate successful practice, and provide a range of ideas and strategies for supporting children's learning.

Wood, E. and Attfield, J. (2005) *Play, Learning and the Early Childhood Curriculum*, 2nd edn, London: Paul Chapman.

> This book is aimed at early years teachers, and focuses on creating unity between playing, learning and teaching. However, there is much valuable practical guidance on pedagogy, curriculum planning, assessment and working collaboratively with other adults, which is useful across the primary age range. There are many research-based practical examples of children learning through play, and detailed exploration of the role of adults.

RELEVANT WEBSITES

Cambridge Primary Review: www.primaryreview.org.uk
Early Years Foundation Stage framework: http://nationalstrategies.standards.dcsf.gov.uk/earlyyears
Independent Review of the Primary Curriculum (Rose Review): www.dcsf.gov.uk/primarycurriculum review/

> The following websites will support teaching students in keeping up to date with research and policy changes:

Early Education (British Association for Early Childhood Education): www.early-education.org.uk
National Children's Bureau: www.ncb.org.uk
Tactyc (Training, Advancement and Co-operation in Teaching Young Children): www.tactyc.org.uk

Visit the companion website www.routledge.com/textbooks/ltps2e for:

■ additional questions and task for this unit;
■ links to useful websites relevant to this unit.

REFERENCES

Anning, A., Cullen, J. and Fleer, M. (eds) (2008) *Early Childhood Education: Society and Culture*, 2nd edn, London, Sage.
Brooker, L. (2008) *Supporting Transitions in the Early Years*, Maidenhead: McGraw-Hill.

Department for Children, Schools and Families (DCSF) (2008) *Building Brighter Futures: Next Steps for the Children's Workforce*, London: DCSF. Available online at www.dcsf.gov.uk (accessed October 2009).

Department for Education and Skills (DfES) (2004) *Every Child Matters: Change for Children*, DfES/1081/2004, Nottingham: DfES.

Department for Education and Skills (DfES) (2006) *The Primary National Strategy*, London: DfES. Available online at http://nationalstrategies.standards.dcsf.gov.uk/primary/primaryframework (accessed October 2009).

Department for Education and Skills (DfES) (2007) *The Early Years Foundation Stage*, Nottingham: DfES.

Fisher, J. (2008) *Starting from the Child*, 3rd edn, Buckingham: Open University Press.

James, M. and Pollard, A. (2008) *Learning and Teaching in Primary Schools: Insights from TLRP (Cambridge Primary Review: Research Survey 2/4)*, Cambridge: University of Cambridge Faculty of Education. Available online at www.primaryreview.org.uk (accessed October 2009).

Office for Standards in Education (Ofsted) (2004) *Transition from the Reception Year to Year 1*, HMI 2221, London: Ofsted. Available online at www.ofsted.gov.uk (accessed October 2009).

Roffey, S. (2001) *Special Needs in the Early Years, Collaboration, Communication and Co-ordination*, London: David Fulton.

Rose, J. (2009) *Independent Review of the Primary Curriculum: Final Report*, London: DCSF. Available online at www.dcsf.gov.uk/primarycurriculumreview (accessed November 2009).

Wood, E. (2009) 'Conceptualising a pedagogy of play: international perspectives from theory, policy and practice', in D. Kuschner (ed.) *From Children to Red Hatters®: Diverse Images and Issues of Play*, Play and Culture Studies, Vol. 8, Lanham, MD: University Press of America, pp. 166–89.

PARTNERSHIPS WITH PARENTS

John Ryan and Stephen Griffin

INTRODUCTION

This unit focuses on building effective, purposeful and long-lasting relationships with parents/carers. For the purposes of this unit, the term 'parents' should be taken to include carers also: single parents, grandparents, foster carers or older siblings.

After the Education Acts 1988 and 1992, parents have been increasingly described as 'partners' in their children's education. Coupled with the move towards greater parental choice in terms of the schools parents can send their children to, and increased transparency of school performance data via Ofsted reports, league tables and the publication of exam results, parents are viewed as key stakeholders in the educational process. Indeed, *Excellence and Enjoyment* (DfES, 2003) directly stresses 'partnership beyond the classroom', where primary schools 'review their strategies for involving parents in their children's education'. The power of parental involvement should not be underestimated – The Organisation for Economic Cooperation and Development (OECD) has suggested that family social background and involvement accounts for 29 per cent of variation in pupil educational outcomes (2001 Program for International Student Assessment (PISA) study, in Goldstein, 2004). Therefore, it is evident that greater collaboration with parents needs to be a key aim in improving educational outcomes for children.

OBJECTIVES

By the end of this unit you should:

■ have an understanding of the need to ensure that you develop secure relationships with the parents of pupils in your class, during school placement, the first year of teaching and subsequent years of teaching;

■ recognise and understand the importance of purposeful and structured working relationships with parents;

■ know of effective ways of liaising and communicating with parents;

■ have an appreciation of the need for trust and understanding as the foundation for successful relationships between parents and school;

■ know the range of partners and external agencies with which a primary school has to work with in order to support children and parents;

■ begin to have some strategies as an trainee teacher or newly qualified teacher (NQT) and begin to establish sound home–school links.

PROFESSIONAL REQUIREMENTS

It is important to recognise that not only is parental involvement desirable in achieving positive educational outcomes, but it is also a professional requirement of all teachers as detailed in the *Professional Standards*.

The qualified teacher status (QTS) (Q) standards (TDA, 2007) are divided into three sections:

- professional attributes;
- professional knowledge and understanding;
- professional skills.

Running through all these standards is a theme of being respectful towards all learners and considerate and committed to raising their achievement. Specifically, standard Q4 emphasises the need for trainee teachers to ensure the importance of working alongside parents:

- Communicate effectively with children, young people, colleagues, parents and carers (TDA, 2007: Q4).

This is further extended when you are fully qualified and, after your induction, you will be required to continue to meet core (C) standards in order to demonstrate a deeper understanding of professional attributes and skills. Within the context of working with parents, this is extended to three important areas:

- Communicate effectively with parents and carers, conveying timely and relevant information about attainment, objectives, progress and well being (C4b).
- Recognise that communication is a two-way process and encourage parents and carers to participate in discussions about the progress, development and well-being of children and young people (C4c).
- Recognise and respect the contributions that colleagues, parents and carers can make to the development and well-being of children and young people, and to raising their levels of attainment (C5).

The recent *Independent Review of the Primary Curriculum* (Rose Review) (Rose, 2009) outlines that, since September 2008, primary schools in England have started working with assessing pupil progress (APP) material. This is a major priority of the National Strategies and a large element of this is that every parent and carer is informed about how well their child is doing and what parents need to do to improve learning and to support their child and teachers.

HISTORICAL OVERVIEW

Historically, in England the home and the school have been two distinct and separate realms of a child's life. The role that parents have as educators has, therefore, been contentious in the past. The Hadow Report (1931) highlighted the importance of a child-centred curriculum, but it was not until the Plowden Report (DES, 1967) that recognition was attributed to the vital role that parents can play in their child's education: 'One of the essentials for educational advance is a closer partnership between the two parties (i.e. schools and parents) to every child's education' (DES, 1967: 102).

As well as highlighting parental involvement, it also suggested strategies as to how this could be implemented, the most significant being Parent Teacher Associations (PTAs) – a common feature of our schools today. More recently, Desforges and Abouchaar discussed the obvious link between input from home and attainment in school:

> Parental involvement has a significant effect on children's achievement and adjustment even after all other factors (such as social class, maternal education and poverty) have been taken out of the equation.
>
> (2003: 9.2.2)

As teachers you need to ensure that this is constructively built on and you have a secure understanding of pupils' cultural capital (Bourdieu, 1986). This can be understood as the set of dispositions that enable certain groups of pupils to succeed more readily at school than others; that is, they receive linguistic ability from their parents and have access to certain forms of culture, such as the theatre and the 'arts', which are reflected heavily in the school curriculum. It is these predisposed skills that give them the advantage, while pupils from less privileged backgrounds may struggle to access the curriculum for this very reason.

More recently, the government has actively encouraged strong links between parents and schools. More emphasis is now put on supporting parents by such strategies as Early Intervention and Sure Start. The way in which schools work nowadays is changing and, as an NQT, you will be working with many outside agencies, including parents, in order to support children.

The government's *Excellence and Enjoyment* (DfES, 2003) outlines three proposals to ensure that parental involvement is maximised. These are:

■ providing parents with information;
■ giving parents a voice;
■ encouraging parental partnerships with schools.

A wide range of strategies have been adapted in primary schools to ensure that the above have been implemented and followed. These will be discussed throughout this unit.

Approximately one in five children will have some form of special educational needs (SEN) at various stages throughout their school life (Dearing, 1993). As an NQT you need to become familiar with the *SEN Code of Practice* (DfES, 2001) and the philosophy behind the policy for inclusion and removal of barriers to learning. You will also need to be fully aware of SEN procedures, be prepared to liaise with the SEN coordinator (SENCO), as well as teaching assistants (TAs), and to communicate effectively with parents. The *SEN Code of Practice* provides guidance on your statutory duties in identifying, assessing and making provisions for children's SEN and outlines that:

■ the special needs of children will normally be met in mainstream schools;
■ the views of children should be sought and taken into account;
■ parents have a vital role to play in supporting their child's education;
■ children with SEN should be offered full access to a broad, balanced and relevant education, Foundation Stage and National Curriculum.

As a trainee teacher or NQT, you will definitely be involved with the above, all of which will be supported by the SENCO in the school. When you meet with parents of children with SEN to review their children's progress, you will also be involved in writing and explaining how parents can support their children's progress by constructing individual education plans (IEPs) for such children. IEPs are used for recording what is additional to and different from the 'normal differentiated curriculum plan', which is in place as part of the normal provision.

With the introduction of the Children Act 2004, it could be argued that most primary schools are more proactive than ever at investigating strategies to ensure parents are actively involved in their child's education. In January 2003, a national Workforce Remodelling Agreement was signed by school workforce unions, local government employers and the government. The purpose was to support schools in raising standards and tackling workload issues for staff. It also enabled many schools to have more autonomy as to how to organise the structure of their staff. One of the results was that many schools now employ a principal parent officer (PPO) or parent support adviser (PSA). Often these roles are carried out by class teachers or TAs and complement the common core of skills and knowledge for children's workforce staff of the *Every Child Matters* (ECM; see below) agenda and are aligned to the Children's Workforce Development Council induction standards. Roles concerned with initial training for staff working with children, young people and their families are receiving increased attention in relation to ensuring children receive the best possible start in education. Currently, the Department for Children, Schools and Families (DCSF) is funding the expansion of school-based PSAs, as outlined in the Children Act 2004 (DfES, 2004). The roles of teachers and parents may be different, but the ambitions that they have for children are very similar, if not identical. Teachers are contributing and adding to the learning process that has already, hopefully, been begun by the parents.

In 2003, the government published the ECM green paper (see DfES, 2004). This coincided with the public inquiry into the death of Victoria Climbié, known as the Laming Report (Health Committee, 2003), which outlined huge failings in systems in place to protect children. According to Reid, the ECM agenda 'Proposes the most radical changes in services for children and their families since the Children Act 1989' (Reid, 2005: 12). This agenda and its philosophy constitute a radical change, which incorporates protection yet places more emphasis on prevention.

One of the government's visions by implementing ECM is to support the principle of personalisation, as well as supporting the work schools are already doing in order to raise educational standards. Five outcomes have been identified that are significant to the well-being of children. As NQTs, and indeed as any grade of teacher, you will need to ensure that all children meet the following five outcomes:

- be healthy;
- stay safe;
- enjoy and achieve;
- make a positive contribution;
- achieve economic well-being.

At the heart of the ECM agenda is the recognition that parents play a significant role in supporting their child's education and are key educators themselves. The publication, *Every Parent Matters* (DfES, 2007), goes so far as to suggest that 'Parents and the home environment they create are the single most important factor in shaping their children's well-being, achievements and prospects'.

Common Assessment Frameworks

If, for any reason, a child in your class is not progressing towards the five ECM outcomes, you need to discuss your concerns with the designated teacher and Common Assessment Framework (CAF) procedures will have to be employed for the child. The process that this may take will vary in each local authority (LA) and may include:

- pre-assessment checklist;
- discussion with designated teacher;
- consent from parents;
- checking with other professionals/CAF;
- undertaking CAF;
- allocating lead professional;
- coordinating services.

As an NQT it is very unlikely that you will lead the CAF and be known as the 'lead professional', but as a class teacher your evidence and contributions will be very significant, which is why it is essential to keep rigorous and up-to-date records of pupils' progress in relation to all areas of the curriculum and the five outcomes of ECM. Parent permission must be sought before a CAF is carried out on their child and only CAF-trained professionals may undertake one.

The purpose of carrying out a CAF is to stimulate early intervention in cooperation with families and encourage multi-agency working. It is anticipated by the government that such an approach will prevent overlap or repeating information gathering and thus provide better and more appropriate services for families. For example, after completing a CAF for a child in your class, all practitioners may well help the parents access other services, such as health, social care or housing.

There are instances when a CAF may not be deemed appropriate. The most important one could be, for example, that you as a class teacher are worried about significant harm being done to the child. In such cases you need to raise your concerns with the designated teacher in school and adhere to confidentiality. Another reason may be that you are aware of the needs of the child or family, but your service, that is school, can meet these needs. In such a case you would need to involve outside agencies and be guided by senior members of staff or the designated teacher.

ADVANTAGES OF SECURE RELATIONSHIPS WITH PARENTS

Research (Bastiani, 2003; Desforges and Abouchaar, 2003) has shown that involving parents in their children's education can help remove barriers to learning, raise attainment and improve attitudes and behaviour. It is widely believed that primary schools working in partnership with parents to support their children's learning and development can expect significant and lasting benefits. Among these are improved, as well as consistent, levels of attainment, coupled with a more positive attitude towards behaviour and attendance.

O'Hara highlights the importance of communicating with parents and suggests six practical ways to ensure that teachers and parents have effective dialogue:

- regular parent–teacher contact;
- joint teaching/work in the classroom;
- home visits;
- whole-school events;
- school handbooks/prospectuses;
- letters, notices and circulars.

(2008: 14)

In a recent survey by Lewis *et al.*, primary head teachers were asked what were the most effective ways of involving parents in their child's education. The findings indicated that over 90 per cent of primary schools used the following:

Task 8.3.1 **AN INTERVENTION CASE STUDY**

Read the following and consider the questions afterwards.

Case study

BEFORE EARLY INTERVENTION

Jamie had been receiving help at school in Year 2 from the Behaviour Support Service due to his aggressive behaviour. However, over the summer his behaviour worsened and his mother was concerned that the transition to Key Stage 2 in a Year 3 class may mean that he would not get the same level of support. She contacted the PPO, who agreed to liaise with other agencies. A check on the data held for Jamie revealed incomplete records and Jamie's health visitor confirmed concerns about his sleep routines and an outstanding referral for speech therapy, while the school revealed concerns about Jamie's and his mother's difficulties.

AFTER EARLY INTERVENTION

The school undertook a CAF process with Jamie's mother and from that planned how services could come together to form a 'team around the child', including an education welfare assistant, a health visitor and a teacher. As a result, the education welfare assistant worked with Jamie at home and at school; a re-referral for speech therapy was made; and the health visitor continued to offer support to his mother, suggesting strategies for dealing with his behaviour. You, as class teacher, acted as the first point of contact for the family and information was shared on request with the other specialists about Jamie's behavioural difficulties. Due to this integrated approach to identifying and addressing the causes of Jamie's behaviour, Jamie's family now feels they are receiving coordinated support that meets his needs. His re-referral for speech therapy was prioritised due to his needs being set within a broader context of his educational and social development, and the team continues to work with Jamie and his family to achieve more improvement.

■ How do you think Jamie's school might have been more proactive in easing transition to Key Stage 2 for him and his family?

■ As Jamie's class teacher you are acting as the first point of contact. This means that you would have to make time to talk his parents. How do you enable face-to-face communication with parents?

■ You would also have to liaise with other professionals in order to deliver accurate information and to share it appropriately. What skills might you need to develop in order to do this effectively?

■ school newsletters;
■ special events for parents (e.g. information/discussion evenings);
■ gathering parents' views as part of school self-evaluation;
■ encouraging parents to contact/or visit the school.

(2007: 2)

The survey also described that the majority of primary schools actively sought strategies to involve their PTAs. However, the survey highlighted that socio-economic factors influenced the amount of involvement from the PTA or even if the school had a PTA. Whether on placement or when you qualify as an NQT, you need to ensure that you know the strategies employed by the school to ensure that parents are involved in their child's education. Recently, online communication and virtual learning environments (VLEs) have been identified as strategies to involve parents in school life. This is going to have an impact on your daily routine and you may be requested to contribute to such forums, so you need a confident and capable approach to ICT. Lewis *et al.*'s survey also outlines other strategies that head teachers feel they use to actively involve parents in primary education:

- ■ parents' forums/focus groups;
- ■ online communication/virtual learning environments (VLEs);
- ■ family learning/parent–child workshops;
- ■ as parent governors.

(2007: 3)

FIRST IMPRESSIONS

Recent initiatives at both a national and local level have encouraged greater collaboration between the two (schools and parents). For example, many schools now offer parents the opportunity to observe lessons and to discuss the new teaching methods employed.

To this end it is essential that you seek out opportunities to forge meaningful and appropriate links with parents of the children in your class. Outside formal meetings such as parent's evenings, this can be done effectively by taking the opportunity to be 'seen' at key times. It is often the case that many home–school partnerships never reach their potential because the school is seen as being remote and distant from the home. When you also consider that there may be significant numbers of parents whose own experience of schooling was negative, it is not surprising why they are reticent to 'cross the threshold' and approach teachers comfortably. For these parents, school may still represent an unhappy and less than productive period of their lives. Also, the demands on parents who may work full-time or look after younger children may mean that they are less active than they would like to be regarding the teaching and learning of their children. Therefore, it is your duty as teachers to reach out and open up the possibilities of home–school partnerships.

A key time to achieve this aim is at the beginning and end of the school day. While you need to be mindful of ensuring a prompt start to lessons, if you are visible and welcoming in the morning it sends a clear message to parents and children alike. This is especially important at the beginning of a new school year. Both the parents and the children will be keen to meet the new teacher and your presence will ensure that you have a positive influence throughout the year. As formal parents' meetings may not take place until later in the school year, a quick personal introduction is an effective means of establishing a relationship sooner.

Task 8.3.2 **RELATIONSHIPS WITH PARENTS**

- ■ Action point: Introduce yourself to parents at either the beginning or end of the school day – make a point of remarking positively on an achievement each child has made.
- ■ Task: During your non-contact time (or NQT time) visit other schools (or compare approaches while on school placements) to research how they ensure that parents are involved with their children's education. Report your findings to your mentor, line manager or tutor.

HOME READING

A considerable amount has been written about how to involve parents in school-based reading programmes. Halsall and Green (1995), Leseman and De Jong (1998), Hammett *et al.* (2003) and Dombey *et al.* (2006) have all sought, through their interventions, to increase children's academic performance by manipulating and maximising the home literacy environment (HLE).

The HLE is one of the child's first influences in learning basic literacy skills. The importance of this environment has been long recognised. Educators are stating that children must be read to and must have opportunities to improve their own reading (Badian, 1988; Burgess *et al.*, 2002; Dombey *et al.*, 2006). It is important that parents should feel confident in supporting their children's learning on an everyday basis, as children learn from those closest to them and care about the reactions that they receive from those adults. It is even more important that parents who do not feel confident in their role of supporting their child in reading or learning receive support from the child's class teacher and the school. There should be clear methods employed by the school to support parents in helping their children:

> This recognition of the importance of understanding the process of learning to read is both hopeful and liberating; it shows how important is the role of the parent as well as the teacher, and accepts that there are many things that can be done to help, most of which are not very technical or complicated.
>
> (Cullingford, 2001: 15)

While in school, whether on placement or in your first year of teaching, you need to become familiar with the school's policy on home reading and how this is encouraged. It must be acknowledged that the parents' role in all learning is crucial. The environment that they provide at home can help to cultivate their children's vital literacy skills. Many parents are willing to continue to help their children in many ways and it is your role as class teacher to promote these and to ensure that children benefit from them: 'Parental involvement in children's academic development is of vital importance, partly because it contributes to a sense of purpose and achievement' (Aunola *et al.*, 2002: 313).

DEALING WITH DIFFICULT SITUATIONS

As discussed previously, as teachers we are aware of the benefits that supportive parents have on the achievement of their children. Research (Edwards and Warin, 1999; Aunola *et al.*, 2002; Desforges and Abouchaar, 2003; Hammett *et al.*, 2003) also highlights the enormous benefits that parents can bring to school when the values and ethos between home and school are shared. However, we need to be aware of the problematic nature of school when this is not the case. The work of Edwards and Warin (1999) raises many issues concerning the assumptions that schools make considering adequate and appropriate support from parents. They reached the conclusion that many schools were keen to utilise parents as 'long arms' for the schools' own purposes and not as equal partners. They concluded that the ways in which schools enhance parental involvement is rather one-sided. This can be further problematic if parents and the school have opposing views and values. As an NQT you may find that not all parents are as supportive as you would hope.

A shared language of the nature of school is vital and staff in primary schools have to be aware that this may not be the case for the majority of parents, so schools have to take steps to ameliorate the feeling of failure, the feeling that education is of little or no value and that school represents a legitimate target for verbal and physical abuse. It is vital that, if you are abused physically or verbally, your line manager or a senior teacher is informed immediately. It is against this background that your role as an NQT or trainee teacher may sit. When you are appointed you will need a local knowledge of the school and an understanding of the issues that families may bring: domestic violence, child protection, alcohol and substance abuse, teenage pregnancies, joblessness, and so on.

You will also need a working knowledge of agencies and training opportunities for parents. The role of any NQT in a whole-school context is that of supporting families and children as well as staff. This is crucial in building and developing a shared vision, where the outcomes ensure that every day matters for every child and where parents and staff are given the tools, knowledge and understanding to enable this.

Task 8.3.3 **MANAGING PARENT HELPERS**

How would you respond to the following?

■ A parent helper begins to discuss their child with you during a science lesson.

■ A parent helper has led a design technology task (e.g. making puppets) with a group of children, but it has come to your attention that the children merely observed the process rather than becoming actively involved with the activity.

■ At the end of the school day, an agitated parent approaches you stating that their child is being bullied and that you have failed to deal with it.

Discuss these with a fellow NQT or your school mentor and decide upon a clear, structured course of action.

One of the most challenging yet rewarding aspects of your NQT year, after teaching and learning, is the relationship between yourself and parents. Research (Bastiani, 2003; Desforges and Abouchaar, 2003) shows that, where the partnership between home and school is supportive with shared values and expectations, this contributes greatly to the outcomes for the child. In order for this to happen, there needs to be a good relationship between home and school that facilitates open and honest communication. This does not just mean 'talking' to parents when there are concerns about the pupil, but taking the time to celebrate the child's achievements on a day-to-day basis, so that when the difficult conversations have to take place they do so against a background of 'perceived fairness'. It is imperative, therefore, that all school policies are consistently adhered to by all staff. Such policies may include the following; you should find and read these:

■ behaviour policy;
■ SEN policy;
■ teaching and learning policy;
■ whole-school policy;
■ assessment policy;
■ emotional literacy policy;
■ homework policy.

All policies should be followed with transparency so that parents are kept informed about their children's behaviour and attainment at every stage.

All primary schools need to work hard to develop positive relationships with parents. This can be a challenge. It is therefore important that, as part of the induction process or while on placement, you as an NQT or trainee teacher have the opportunity to sit in at both formal and informal parent discussions. This will provide you with an opportunity to observe how such a meeting is structured, to observe the body language and the language used by the teacher and to see how any issues are resolved. It is suggested that, should an NQT need to have a 'difficult conversation' with a parent, they discuss it with their mentor or line manager first, in order to 'rehearse' the points, and that the mentor or line manager should also be at the meeting with the NQT, whether this is formal or informal. There should be some reflection following the meeting to critically analyse your responses and set common agreements after such meetings.

If appropriate, it would be extremely useful for NQTs to attend any parents' coffee mornings (or similar activities) from time to time. This allows parents to get to know the NQT in a different setting and also provides NQTs with the opportunity to observe the other staff's relationships with parents. If the school has PPOs or PSAs, such professionals will be able to provide NQTs with a different kind of support. They will know the parents very well and may well have information about the whole family that the NQT needs to be aware of on a need-to-know basis before seeing the parents. You should be careful of making generalisations or labelling parents unduly.

PARENTS' EVENINGS

Parents' evenings form part of a teacher's statutory duties (DfES, 2009) and are an important fixture of the school year. Many schools will operate a termly parents' evening where parents are invited in to discuss their child's progress. It is also worth mentioning that parents' evenings may vary in their nature. Pastoral parents' evenings are often held at the start of the academic year to allow discussion around specific issues of transition and settling into a new class. These meetings may well be held with the acknowledgement that it is too early to discuss academic progress and, as such, the discussion will centre on the happiness and disposition of the child and friendship groupings. It may also be an opportunity for the teacher to share information regarding the curriculum. As was mentioned previously, these early meetings are particularly useful as a means of building purposeful relationships.

As with other aspects of school life, parent's evenings require careful planning to ensure success. It goes without saying that parents will expect to see their children's work marked effectively with purposeful comments. Also it will help to make a few notes about each child prior to the meeting and be prepared to make notes during the meeting should the need arise. Often parents may use the meeting to air particular concerns about their child that you may not be able to respond to immediately without some investigation (e.g. a bullying issue). In this case it is important that you offer the parents a particular time to meet at a later stage, when you have more information at hand.

It is always worth opening the meeting by asking the parents whether they have any particular concerns that they wish to discuss. This will allow for an open and frank dialogue. You must be also mindful that parents themselves are useful sources of information as the interim report of the *Independent Review of the Primary Curriculum* (Rose Review) states:

> Parents play a crucial role in children's early learning and throughout their education. Their role is particularly important in the early years. They have invaluable information and insights about their children of which teaching staff need to be aware when planning learning.
>
> (Rose, 2008: 2.91)

This highlights the need for the partnership between teachers and parents to be a two-way process.

Task 8.3.4 **AUDIT OF PARENTAL INVOLVEMENT**

■ While on placement, or during your first year of teaching, you may want to research the school's overall success at encouraging effective parental involvement. For example, an audit could be carried out by you and a working party on strategies currently being utilised by your school.

■ Alternatively, you may want to carry out action research on a group of parents' understanding of the ECM agenda. The results and findings of the research could be shared with the school's senior management team and governors.

Any results of your research could form the basis of revisiting existing school policies on parental involvement.

Remember that the purpose of the meeting with parents is to report on the child's progress, but it is also an opportunity to enhance pupil learning by empowering the parents with knowledge that will help them support their child. Therefore, you will need to communicate pupil targets clearly and make suggestions as to how these can be supported at home. As these meetings operate (for the most part) on scheduled appointments, it is necessary to keep an eye on the time. It is inevitable that you will, on occasion, run over time, but in the interests of all parents it is important to keep an eye on the clock. If you find that a particular issue requires more time, you may have to arrange to meet at a later date.

Task 8.3.5 **PARENTS' EVENINGS**

■ Consider what type of notes might be useful when preparing for a meeting with parents.
■ How would you explain to parents how best to support their child at home in the following areas:
  ▌ literacy;
  ▌ numeracy?
■ Consider what course of action you would take in the following scenarios:
  ▌ A parent complains that their child is being bullied by an older child from the local secondary school on the way home.
  ▌ A parent wishes to withdraw their child from the sex education lessons that are due to take place the following week.
  ▌ A parent is concerned that their child is not being challenged enough at school.
  ▌ A parent asks your advice about getting a home tutor to support their child with numeracy.
Discuss these with your mentor or tutor.

PARENT GOVERNORS

All primary schools are run by a governing body, which works alongside the head teacher and senior management team to ensure that pupils receive a high standard of education. The governing body in primary schools is made up of:

- parent governors (elected by parents);
- staff representatives (elected by school staff);
- local authority governors (appointed by the local authority);
- community governors (members of the local community appointed by the governing body);
- for some schools, people appointed by the relevant religious body or foundation;
- up to two sponsor governors (appointed by the governing body).

As an NQT, it is very unlikely that you will be a school governor; nevertheless, this is entirely possible. As all teachers, when you become an NQT you do need to become familiar with the role of the governing body. Governors probably form the largest volunteer group in major cities in the country, with around 350,000 governor places in England, so they perform an important job on behalf of the community.

The main role of any governing body is to ensure the smooth running of the school and to promote pupil achievement. Parent governors need to ensure that the views of the parents are reported to their local authority. Alongside other governors, they should also be involved in the following duties: setting the strategic direction of the school; approving the school budget; reviewing progress against the school development plan; and appointing as well as supporting the head teacher. As with all governors, a parent governor may be viewed as a critical friend. It would be beneficial as a new member of staff to be pro-active and informally introduce yourself to any parent governors at your school.

Schools have always actively sought the opinions of parents and, from May 2007, have had a duty to take account of the views of parents. All schools are encouraged to review their current practice in relation to this and consider enhancing such arrangements by setting up a parent council. Ultimately, the governing body will decide whether to set up a parent council and may appoint a working group to take responsibility for its establishment and management. The purpose of such councils needs to be clear and shared with all the school. One of the advantages of such an approach is that it opens up the school and allows parents who are less involved in the school, due to full-time work commitments, to become more active in their children's education. This allows the school to present ample evidence of engaging all parents, and to provide positive responses to the section of the self-evaluation form (SEF) relating to parental involvement.

Task 8.3.6 **HOME–SCHOOL AGREEMENTS**

With permission from the head teacher, obtain examples of home–school agreements from your school, consider the provisions in them and then explore any issues raised. For example:

- Are all parents able to support their children?
- Are there any cultural differences between the curriculum and values at home?
- What are the significant issues that parents have concerns about?

Use these as a basis for a discussion with your school parent governor with a view to proposing an action plan for dissemination at a staff meeting.

0.03

PARENTAL EXPERTISE

Another strategy to encourage closer relationships between parents and schools is to maximise on the expertise of parents and other members of the community. Contributions to the development of the curriculum by support from outside agencies and parents has become increasingly common over recent years. The willingness of parents to share their experiences with a group of children can provide a renewed vigour and inspiration to an existing unit or scheme of work. Parents who are, for example, nurses, postal workers, police officers, community artists, technicians or workers for the fire service could be utilised effectively by schools to enhance learning. Parents with particular interests or hobbies, or who have visited places of interest, or who have lived in different countries could also be involved by being invited to the class (or a small group of children if the whole class is too daunting) as visiting speakers.

It is vital that, if you are going to use the suggestions above, you arrange a meeting before any planned activities in order to ensure that the work or talk that any visitor is going to lead is appropriate for the children in your class. It is also important that follow-up work is planned for and shared with such parents in order to celebrate the impact that their expertise may have had on a group of children. This work does not necessarily have to be in written form, thus encouraging all children to express their engagement with the visiting speakers.

Such an approach could ensure that you value as well as respect parents' contributions and the children in your class will notice that you have a two-way relationship with parents.

Task 8.3.7 **USING PARENTS' EXPERTISE**

Read the case study and discuss the questions with a peer or mentor.

Case study

Yasmin's father is a staff nurse at the local hospital and the newly appointed class teacher, working in Year 5, is keen to use his expertise. Yasmin's father is invited to come and speak to the Year 5 class and the class teacher tells him to prepare 'something about healthy eating'. On arriving in school, Yasmin's father shares with the class a PowerPoint presentation of 33 slides (with mostly words) that he has used on a recent INSET day. He also talks to the children for 30 minutes on nutrition and dietetics. Throughout the talk, advanced scientific vocabulary and terminology are used. At the end of the talk, the children and class teacher cannot think of any questions to ask and there is a long, rather embarrassing pause until the teacher asks the class to thank Yasmin's father by giving him a round of applause.

■ How could the class teacher have avoided this situation?
■ What should the class teacher have done prior to Yasmin's father visiting the class or school?
■ How could the class teacher have maximised on the parent's expertise?
■ What follow-up activities could have been planned if the presentation had been pitched at the appropriate level?
■ Why is it important to liaise clearly and in advance with any visitors?

SUMMARY

In this unit we have endeavoured to highlight the importance of purposeful, open and structured relationships with parents as a means of ensuring the best possible education for the children in school. At the heart of this is the acknowledgement that parents are partners in their children's education and, as such, are key educators themselves. We have suggested that there are many ways in which these partnerships can be developed and supported in school, and the tasks are a good starting point for this. It is our view that establishing strong home–school links is essential when it comes to ensuring that the individual potential of pupils is realised.

ANNOTATED FURTHER READING

Department for Education and Skills (DfES) (2007) *Every Parent Matters: Creating Opportunity, Releasing Potential, Achieving Excellence*, London DfES.
> If you wish to understand better the key role that parents can play in education and the emphasis that government is placing on partnership, this publication is a useful starting point. The report offers a literature review of the research in this area and highlights the various initiatives that are taking place at present. In particular, the bibliography is a good source of references that provide further evidence of the efficacy of teacher–parent partnerships in improving educational outcomes.

Lewis, K., Chamberlain, T., Riggall, A., Gagg, K. and Rudd, P. (2007) *How Are Schools Involving Parents in School Life? Annual Survey of Trends in Education: Schools' Concerns and their Implications for Local Authorities* (LGA Research Report 4/07), Slough: NFER.
> This gives a clear overview as to how secondary and primary schools try to engage parents. It is a relevant up-to-date publication that highlights some of the contentious issues around this topic.

RELEVANT WEBSITES

Department for Children, Schools and Families (DCSF): www.dcsf.gov.uk
> Type 'parent support advisers' into the search box and follow the links.

Every Child Matters: www.everychildmatters.gov.uk
> Type 'CAF' into the search box to find links for the Common Assessment Framework.

General Teaching Council for England (GTCE): www.gtce.org.uk
> Here you can read the GTCE's *Code of Conduct and Practice for Registered Teachers* (effective October 2009) – type 'Code of conduct and practice' into the search box.

TeacherNet: www.teachernet.gov.uk
> Type 'teachers' pay and conditions' into the search box.

Training and Development Agency for Schools (TDA): www.tda.gov.uk
> Follow the 'Professional standards for teachers' link under 'Teachers' to find the standards for the award of QTS.

Visit the companion website www.routledge.com/textbooks/ltps2e for:

■ links to useful websites relevant to this unit.

REFERENCES

Aunola, K., Nurmi, J.-E., Niemi, P., Lerkkanen, M.-K. and Rasku-Puttonen, H. (2002) 'Developing dynamics of achievement strategies, reading performance and parental beliefs', *Reading Research Quarterly*, 37(3): 310–27.

Bastiani, J. (2003) *Materials for Schools: Involving Parents, Raising Achievement*, London: DfES.

Badian, N. (1988) 'The prediction of good and poor reading before kindergarten entry: a nine-year follow-up', *Journal of Learning Disabilities*, 21: 98–103.

Burgess, S.R., Hecht, S.A. and Lonigan, C.J. (2002) 'Relations of the home literacy environment (HLE) to the development of reading abilities: a one year longitudinal study', *Reading Research Quarterly*, 37(4): 408–6.

Bourdieu, P. (1986) 'The forms of capital', in J.G. Richardson (ed.) *Handbook of Theory and Research for the Sociology of Education*, Santa Barbara, CA: Greenwood Press.

Cullingford, C. (2001) *How Children Learn to Read and How to Help Them*, London: Kogan Page.

Dearing, R. (1993) *The National Curriculum and its Assessment: Final Report*, London: SCAA.

Department for Education and Skills (DfES) (2001) *Special Educational Needs Code of Practice*, DfES/581/2001, London: DfES.

Department for Education and Skills (DfES) (2003) *Excellence and Enjoyment: A Strategy for Primary Schools*, London: DfES.

Department for Education and Skills (DfES) (2004) *Every Child Matters: Change for Children in Schools*, DfES/1110/2004, London: DfES.

Department for Education and Skills (DfES) (2007) *Every Parent Matters: Creating Opportunity, Releasing Potential, Achieving Excellence*, London: DfES.

Department for Education and Skills (DfES) (2009) *School Teachers' Pay and Conditions Document 2009*, London: DfES.

Department of Education and Science (DES) (1967) *Children and Their Primary Schools* (Plowden Report), London: HMSO.

Desforges, C. and Abouchaar, A. (2003) *The Impact of Parental Involvement, Parental Support and Family Education on Pupil Achievement and Adjustment: A Literature Review*, Research Report RR433, London: DfES.

Edwards, A. and Warin, J. (1999) Parental involvement in raising the achievement of primary school pupils: why bother?', *Oxford Review of Education*, 25(3): 325–41.

Goldstein, H. (2004) 'International comparisons of student attainment', *Assessment in Education: Principles, Policy and Practice*, 11(3): 319–30.

Dombey, H., Ellis, S., Pahl, K. and Sainsbury, M. (2006) 'Handbook of Early Childhood Literacy', *Literacy*, 40(1): 29–35.

Halsall, S. and Green, C. (1995) 'Reading aloud: a way to support their children's growth in literacy', *Early Childhood Educational Journal*, 23: 27–31.

Hammett, L., van Kleeck, A. and Huberty, C. (2003) 'Patterns of parents' extratextual interactions during book sharing with preschool children: a cluster analysis study', *Reading Research Quarterly*, 38(4): 442–68.

Health Committee (2003) *The Victoria Climbié Inquiry: Report of an Inquiry by Lord Laming*, London: The Stationery Office.

Leseman, P.P.M and De Jong, P.F. (1998) 'Home literacy: opportunity, instruction and social-emotional quality predicting early reading achievement', *Reading Research Quarterly*, 33: 294–391.

Lewis, K., Chamberlain, T., Riggall, A., Gagg, K. and Rudd, P. (2007) *How Are Schools Involving Parents in School Life? Annual Survey of Trends in Education 2007: Schools' Concerns and their Implications for Local Authorities*, LGA Research Report 4/07, Slough: NFER.

O'Hara, M. (2008) *Teaching 3–8 (Reaching the Standard)*, 3rd edn, London: Continuum.

Reid, K. (2005) 'The implications of Every Child Matters and the Children Act for Schools', *Pastoral Care in Education*, 23: 12–18.

Rose, J. (2008) *The Independent Review of the Primary Curriculum: Interim Report*, London: DCFS. Available online at www.dcsf.gov.uk/primarycurriculumreview (accessed November 2009).

Rose, J. (2009) *The Independent Review of the Primary Curriculum: Final Report*, London: DCFS. Available online at www.dcsf.gov.uk/primarycurriculumreview (accessed November 2009).

Training and Development Agency for Schools (TDA) (2007) *Professional Standards for Teachers: Qualified Teacher Status*, London: TDA.

UNDERSTANDING THE TEACHER'S PASTORAL ROLE

Ben Whitney

INTRODUCTION

One of the key characteristics of the British system of education is that it is based on a holistic understanding of children. Despite continuous testing and using examination outcomes as the preferred way of monitoring schools' effectiveness, there are clearly many factors that will influence a child's ability to learn at school, not only their intellectual capacity or the quality of their teaching. Pressures from the rest of a child's life will also impact on learning. Educational outcomes for socially disadvantaged children in particular are often poor. The best hope of reducing the impact of these wider issues is to try to address them while children are still young, if at all possible.

Government thinking over the last decade (in, for example, *Every Child Matters: Change for Children* (DfES, 2004)), and the new focus on 'well-being' in the Education and Inspections Act 2006, have moved education professionals to the centre of the arrangements for meeting children's overall needs as part of a local authority *Children's Plan*. (This unit uses 'local authority' (LA) as it is no longer appropriate to talk about a distinct 'local education authority' (LEA) in isolation from other children's services.) All of the five key outcomes of the Children Act 2004, especially 'being healthy', 'staying safe' and 'enjoying and achieving', impact directly on education. Together with the development of extended schools, this has already led to a radical repositioning of schools to the heart of multi-agency family support.

Key responsibilities are:

- promoting and monitoring pupils' school attendance and the reasons given for their absence;
- determining whether absences are authorised or unauthorised according to school policy and ensuring appropriate responses;
- sharing concerns about children at risk of 'significant harm';
- helping parents to access services and support for 'children in need';
- understanding the role of key professionals both inside and outside the school under agreed inter-agency child welfare procedures.

While many of these responsibilities will also be addressed by non-teaching colleagues, you cannot teach a child you never see or if they are constantly preoccupied with the effects of their negative experiences at home. Making sure that children actually attend school as the law requires, and that all education staff play an appropriate part in carrying out the duty placed on children's agencies to protect them from harm and abuse, is crucial. This unit explores the relevant legal frameworks involved in these tasks and gives practical guidance about both managing attendance and dealing with concerns related to child protection and safeguarding.

OBJECTIVES

By the end of this unit you should:

■ be familiar with the legal framework within which the wider pastoral responsibilities of schools are carried out;

■ appreciate the appropriate duties of a teacher for monitoring attendance and working with both parents and non-teaching colleagues to ensure that absences are followed up and school or individual targets are met;

■ become more aware of the in-school procedures that should be in place to safeguard children and protect them from the risk of 'significant harm';

■ understand the role of the teacher when working with colleagues from outside the school, such as education welfare officers and social workers.

SCHOOL ATTENDANCE

Legal framework

Since at least the Education Act 1870, there has been a sense that education is compulsory between certain ages. In the early days, this was a gradual process of prising children away from the other activities that might occupy them as an alternative and holding parents in some way legally accountable for ensuring they received at least an elementary level of instruction. It is an open question whether there has ever been a total acceptance that education should come first in the lives of all children. (The rules were, for example, set aside during both wars, when many older children returned to the workplace, and some children and young people still end up out of school for a variety of reasons.)

Provision is certainly more universal with younger children, but the ever-greater numbers of children in pre-school education may give a misleading impression. It is only a generation or two since large numbers went through the system and into unskilled, if generally available, work, with little or no formal qualification to show for the previous ten years. Judging by the extent of poor literacy and numeracy in the current adult population, many must have been simply going through motions. The importance to every child's future prospects of what you do at school, and from age three or four, is a relatively recent idea.

Despite all the current concerns about 'truancy', unauthorised absence (the correct term) has risen only very slightly since the current recording system was introduced in the early 1990s. Attendance has certainly risen more. Children are having less time off than they used to (DCSF, 2009). But somehow the absence seems to matter more now. Even if a commitment to regular attendance cannot be assumed, it has certainly become the majority view, with an ever-increasing period of time over which the child is required to participate, and with a growing expectation that either training or further education should be the norm even beyond that.

Critics might suggest that, if our education system was good enough, everyone would want their children to go anyway! But some element of legal encouragement has always been retained and, along with it, the existence of the 'School Board Man' (*sic*) and the contemporary equivalent in the Education Welfare Service, in order to encourage the reluctant. Parents and children have a daily choice. Even the most stimulating and well-organised school needs to be aware of what may need to be done to ensure their pupils attend as they should. Early intervention at Key Stages 1 and 2 may reduce the risk of greater problems later. The signals you send then can make a real difference.

Absence is not necessarily an indicator of major family problems or evidence of an anti-social attitude in either child or parent. Some children just skip school occasionally, perhaps showing an entirely natural avoidance of something difficult or less than exciting, without necessarily repeating the behaviour over and over again. Parents sometimes have other more urgent priorities to deal with and school just has to wait till tomorrow. Much use of attendance and absence procedures is just a routine response to everyday problems and many situations are capable of relatively easy resolution through prompt action by school staff.

However, some cases of non-attendance, perhaps an increasing number, are but the tip of an iceberg in which not being at school is only the presenting problem betraying something much greater underneath. There are many vulnerable groups of children who cannot be expected to attend school while all else crumbles in chaos around them. These include those whose families are in crisis; those experimenting with drugs, alcohol or other substances; those with major mental health needs; many children in the public care system; the victims of abuse and of discrimination; child carers; and those grappling with the implications of homelessness, acute poverty and domestic violence. These children in particular will need 'joined-up' solutions to their problems.

The law seeks to be realistic in recognising that 100 per cent attendance is not necessarily required, allowing for 'sickness and other unavoidable cause' (Education Act 1996: s. 444). There is considerable discretion, given primarily to head teachers, but also, to a limited extent, to parents, that enables situations that are less than perfect to be regarded as nonetheless satisfactory. It is often more appropriate to adopt a 'welfare' approach where children have complex needs or there is major disruption to their family life.

However, there has been some pressure on LAs from the Department for Children, Schools and Families (DCSF), and through the National Strategies Behaviour and Attendance programme, to use their statutory enforcement powers more extensively. There are particular issues in relation to 'persistent absentees', that is, those with attendance under 80 per cent or at risk of it. Every school must have its own attendance target. These tasks cannot be done without teachers, so it is important that you get to know what these responsibilities are and the context in which they operate.

Registration regulations

Registration should be a significant part of the school day. Attendance registers are legal documents, which is why they must be kept strictly in accordance with the regulations (Education Act 1996: s. 434(6)). Should a parent be prosecuted for failing to ensure their child attends, head teachers will be required to account to the court for any discrepancies or mistakes in the register. Any dispute between the parent and the LA about whether, for example, a given absence should have been authorised, will require the personal evidence of the head teacher in explaining the criteria used.

As almost every classroom teacher at Key Stages 1 and 2 will be involved in actually marking the register, whether manually or by computer, schools *must* have written and consistently applied attendance policies that enable parents to know what the rules are and that ensure good practice by all staff. The decision about whether or not to authorise an absence determines whether or not the parent is committing an offence. Many schools authorise too generously or may never have established clear policies and procedures that are consistently applied. It should be clear to you whose responsibility it is to make a decision and what procedures are in place for clarifying any uncertainties or challenging parents' explanations for absence.

Registers have always had to be marked at the beginning of each half-day session. This is still the requirement for the morning, but there can be some flexibility about when to mark afternoon registers. This was intended to catch those who go missing during the afternoon, but also raises a number of problems and few schools have seen the need for change, although some schools have systems for lesson-by-lesson monitoring in addition to the sessional mark.

There are five registration categories, one of which must be used for every half-day session for every child of compulsory school age:

■ present on site;
■ authorised absent;
■ unauthorised absent;
■ approved educational activity off-site (counts as present);
■ school 'closed' for that session for that pupil (not counted).

The category of 'approved educational activity' enables schools to count those who are away from the premises for a legitimate reason, such as an educational visit, as 'present' for statistical purposes (provided they actually turned up!). The previous regulations classed all those not on the premises as 'authorised absent', even if the child was where they were supposed to be. This was plainly unreasonable and this change has given schools a welcome flexibility.

Education Act 1996

This outlines the basic legal obligations on parents and replaced the relevant sections of the Education Act 1944 and the Education Act 1993 from 1 November 1996.

DUTY ON PARENTS

S. 7 of the Education Act 1996 says, 'The parent of every child of compulsory school age shall cause him to receive efficient full-time education suitable:

(a) to his age ability and aptitude, and
(b) to any special educational needs he may have,

either by regular attendance at school or otherwise.'

PROSECUTION OF PARENTS

Parents (not children) commit an offence if a registered pupil does not attend 'regularly' (s. 444(1)). This duty includes any adult looking after the child, even if they are not actually related (though not staff from public agencies). Technically, any absence is an offence, unless authorised by the school. Enforcement is the responsibility of the LA where the school is (not now the LA in which the child lives).

ANTI-SOCIAL BEHAVIOUR ACT 2003 AND EDUCATION (PENALTY NOTICES) (ENGLAND) REGULATIONS 2004

New powers came into force from 2004 (in England only) that have given LAs the option of formalising their responses to non-attendance, but without the need for a court appearance. A penalty notice, along similar lines to a speeding fine, enables a parent to discharge their liability for unauthorised absences by paying a penalty. Penalties are currently £50 if paid within 28 days or

£100 if paid within 42 days (per parent and per child). Payment must be made in full, not by instalments. A written warning must be issued first, so most LAs are not using them 'on the spot', but as part of a procedure where the parent is deemed primarily responsible for the absence. This might be particularly in relation to younger children, or the response might be targeted at a particular school with the support of the head teacher.

There is also the capacity for parents to be summonsed for the enhanced offence under s. 444(1A) of 'parentally condoned unauthorised absence'. Some LAs may now use these more serious proceedings rather than s. 444(1), where an actual court appearance is considered appropriate. Convictions at this level carry a maximum fine of £2,500 and up to three months in prison, although this is very rare. The effectiveness of prosecution has always been a matter of some debate. Research suggests that prosecution is effective in about two-fifths of cases, in that the children concerned subsequently improved their attendance (NFER, 2003). But many LA officers also report that the proceedings often make little difference, that fines may be unpaid or that the threat of court action is often more effective than actually going ahead with it.

Task 8.4.1 **ATTENDANCE 1**

Devise an incentive scheme to raise attendance in a class or year group.

■ What kinds of prizes might be appropriate and how would they be awarded?
■ Will they go to the children with the best attendance or those who show most improvement? How will it work?
■ Is it the children, or the parents, who need the encouragement? What difference might this make to the kinds of rewards available?
■ How might peer pressure best be used to encourage those who find regular attendance difficult?

If your scheme is used, make sure it is included in the school's attendance policy and all parents are made aware of it.

Task 8.4.2 **ATTENDANCE 2**

Analyse attendance and absence figures in your school, perhaps for the current and previous year. There should be plenty of data available from computerised records and census returns.

■ Does the data identify any patterns or trends?
■ Is attendance rising or falling?
■ Are some groups of pupils more likely to be absent? What might be the reasons for this?
■ How many children are under 80 per cent present and what is being done about them?
■ How much of the absence is authorised by the school, and for what reasons, e.g. family holidays?
■ What is the balance between authorised and unauthorised absences?

What does your analysis suggest about which children should be the focus for the school's attendance-raising strategy?

Every school needs to establish a good working relationship with their education welfare officer (EWO), especially about referral criteria and to clarify the relative responsibilities of school and LA staff. A Parenting Contract may often be suggested as the first formal step, where parents are proving less than cooperative. Legal enforcement will be at the end of a long process, but should always be considered if problems are not being resolved. It is essential for everyone to maintain a focus on raising attendance and challenging absence as part of the everyday life of the school. Attendance should never be assumed; it always has to be promoted, encouraged and rewarded, just like any other achievement.

CHILD PROTECTION AND SAFEGUARDING

Inter-agency procedures

Teachers are not required to be experts at recognising child abuse, especially when new to the profession. That is not their responsibility any more than a doctor can assess a child's special educational needs or reading performance. Child protection is an inter-agency process from start to finish, but all those working with children must be clear about their own role, not act some other person's role. Despite a sometimes negative public perception, considerable progress has been made in recent years in child protection, but services are subject to almost continuous change.

A very large percentage of child protection concerns arise at school (CSCI, 2008). This is not surprising. Children spend more time there than almost anywhere else; relationships with the adults there are important, especially to younger children. S. 175 of the Education Act 2002, in force from 1 June 2004, requires staff in every school, whatever its status (including the independent sector), to cooperate with the agreed local inter-agency procedures for safeguarding and protecting children. In ensuring that this legal duty is carried out, the governors or proprietors must have regard to the guidance issued in December 2006 by the (then) Department for Education and Skills (DfES, 2006). Other LA officers may also be involved, but all school staff should expect to take individual responsibility for child protection in their own right.

The task of teaching (and non-teaching) staff is:

■ to be sufficiently confident to recognise those situations that give most cause for concern;
■ to refer them appropriately within the school's own and inter-agency procedures and support the child's need for longer-term protection if required.

Categories of abuse

Concerns about possible child abuse must be identified under four standard categories as outlined in government guidance *Working Together to Safeguard Children* (HM Government, 2006):

■ *physical abuse* – non-accidental cuts, bruises, fractures, wounds, burns, bites, poisoning, etc.;
■ *emotional abuse* – extreme denial of love, care, attention and security;
■ *sexual abuse* – not only sexual activity but may involve video, photography or 'grooming' (preparation for abuse) and the internet;
■ *neglect* – failure to meet a child's basic need for food, warmth, protection, safety, etc.

If your concern suggests the child may be at risk of 'significant harm' under s. 47 of the Children Act 1989, as outlined in the categories above, parental consent is not required to make a referral in the child's best interests. Parents should be informed of the referral, unless this would put the child at increased risk of harm. But prevention of abuse is always preferable to waiting for a more serious incident. Other welfare concerns are more appropriately seen as 'children in need' under s. 17 of the Children Act 1989. With parental agreement, referral may be made to other agencies for support on a voluntary basis. This process involves use of the Common Assessment Framework (CAF), which enables all professionals involved with the family to work together more effectively in meeting the child's needs according to agreed thresholds of concern. Schools will be central to this process.

The curriculum

A child protection concern may arise indirectly rather than by direct disclosure or because a member of staff sees an injury, and often when you least expect it! Almost any subject area contains the potential for the child to choose that moment to share what is on their mind. Children generally trust their teachers and do not always see the significance of what they are saying. They may write about their experiences at home in a poem; or give an indication in a practical lesson that the nutrition standards are unacceptable. They may talk about how their parents punish them, or use language that is attempting to describe sexual activity, when faced with a conventional topic such as what they did in the holidays or the worst day of their life. Children choose to disclose when they are ready; so the teacher must always be ready too, even if 'child abuse' was nowhere near their expectations for that particular lesson.

Making referrals

Referrals to a social worker or the police would normally be made by the school's senior designated teacher on receipt of information from the child, a parent, a colleague or other source, although action may still be required even if they are not available. If you have concerns about a child, you should always discuss them with the designated teacher or other senior member of staff to clarify whether referral under child protection procedures is appropriate. Never deal with it alone. Always pass on disclosures of abuse under the four categories above and any related allegations, together with children with significant or suspicious injuries.

You do not have to establish first whether or not it is abuse; that is the job of the investigating agencies, not the school. Evidence of possible physical abuse makes a referral particularly urgent, partly as the child may need medical attention, but also because any injury needs to be seen and assessed by a qualified medical practitioner as quickly as possible. These cases should be raised as early as possible in the school day to give maximum time for a response while the child is safe at school.

Children should not be promised confidentiality or, if you do promise it, be prepared to break it if the child then makes a disclosure of alleged abuse or you have other information that requires you to use the school's child protection procedures. You cannot protect such a child by yourself. Written records should be kept carefully within the school. When the child changes school, records should be passed to the new designated teacher as far as is possible. The ideal place for the child's whole protection history is in their current school.

Investigation and assessment

Following referral from any source, the social worker (jointly with the police if potential criminal charges are involved), will carry out an assessment of risk to the child. This will usually involve them contacting other relevant agencies that know the family, including other schools, and may include a strategy discussion/meeting with key professionals. The social worker will decide when to contact the family. (It is always helpful if they advise the school accordingly, and the referrer should receive a notification of the outcome of this initial assessment, even if no further action is being taken.) If necessary, they will make home visits, involve the child's parent, arrange to have the child medically examined, and so on. Where the child is old enough, they may be interviewed on video about what has happened. This tape can then be used as evidence in any subsequent court proceedings.

Many cases are resolved quickly with practical advice and support to the parents, or programmes to deal, for example, with basic care, alcohol abuse or domestic violence. Other cases, where sex offences or severe family breakdown and neglect are involved, will require much longer involvement. Court proceedings may be taken or arrangements made for the child to be cared for by other members of the family or foster carers. Where children continue to live in situations of risk, a child protection conference may be called.

Initial child protection conferences and child protection plans

Conferences are often required at short notice. It is essential that a representative of the school attends the conference for any school-aged child, even if other education officers have also been invited. A written report may be required. The conference is an opportunity for all professionals involved with the family to consult about how they may best be protected and, in particular, to decide whether the child needs an ongoing child protection plan. If so, a keyworker (social worker) and a Core Group will be appointed – someone from the child's school should always be a member of the Core Group. An outline plan will be drawn up immediately and the Core Group will all be responsible for meeting regularly and for undertaking a more extensive assessment.

When a child has child protection plan, the senior designated teacher must decide who needs to be told. This should be on a need-to-know basis and should certainly include the person with day-to-day responsibility for marking their attendance record. Procedures should be agreed about what to do if the child is absent or if further concerns are identified at school. The child's status must be reviewed every six months (after the first three months).

Policy issues

There must be a written policy for child protection within the school, which should be made known to all staff and parents. This will set out general principles, the duty to make referrals, and so on, including wider issues such as staff and volunteer appointments, the prohibition of corporal punishment, the use of restraint, curriculum issues and complaints procedures. Staff, especially those newly appointed, should have access to clear procedures within the school covering required documentation and defined responsibilities.

Ensuring such policy and procedures are in place is the responsibility of the senior management team, the governing body and the designated senior teacher, who must all work together to ensure a coordinated approach. Training should be available to both teaching and non-teaching staff as part of the induction process. This will normally be part of the role of the designated teacher, but additional training from LA and other agency specialists may also be available.

Allegations against teachers or other staff

Some child abuse cases raise additional issues because the abuse is complex, involves a number of adults or children, or because the person who is the subject of the allegation is a professional or volunteer in a position of trust, rather than a parent. This is the context in which any concern about an adult within a school will be investigated. There is always the possibility that someone may seek to exploit their position as a consequence of relationships established at a school. Especially since the Soham case and Ian Huntley, it is essential that a school's child protection policy and procedures include an awareness of such a risk.

There is understandable concern among many teachers that careers may be irreparably damaged on the basis of flimsy or malicious allegations by children. It may reassure you to know that this is actually extremely rare. Most allegations have their roots in an incident of some kind, although some do end up only as 'unproven' one way or the other, which is generally unsatisfactory. It is always better for a school to anticipate possible risks and to seek to prevent all reasonable risk of misunderstandings and false allegations. Proper policy and procedures are also likely to deter any individual seeking to use the school as a basis for inappropriate relationships with pupils. Agreed procedures should be applied both to teaching staff and to any volunteers and non-teaching staff who have direct contact with children, especially if they will be unsupervised or involved in high-risk activities, such as supervising children dressing and undressing or being alone with children in cars, and so on.

It is important to draw a distinction between complaints and allegations that involve misconduct or unprofessionalism, and those that specifically raise child protection concerns. Any concern that involves the possibility of physical abuse, emotional abuse or sexual abuse should always be discussed by the head teacher with senior LA officers and advice taken from outside the school. If child protection procedures are needed, investigations are carried out by social workers and the police as with any other referral. Head teachers, governors and LA officers must not carry out investigations themselves in these circumstances. If inter-agency action is required, there will be a strategy meeting at an early stage to agree a corporate approach. The views of the head teacher on any incident will be listened to carefully at this stage.

Corporal punishment, restraint and staff conduct

Teachers may occasionally need reminding that they are prohibited by law from using any form of punishment intended to inflict pain, including 'hitting, slapping or shaking' a child. Neither may they 'intimidate or humiliate' a child or make them carry out any kind of 'degrading punishment' (Education Act 1996: ss. 548–50). This is a higher standard than that applied to parents. Teachers are permitted to use 'reasonable restraint' to protect a child or other children, in ways that must be defined by clear, written procedures within the school.

Parents must be informed of the legitimate use of restraint where the head teacher is satisfied that the member of staff has acted appropriately. If parents are not satisfied, they may still choose to initiate an investigation under child protection procedures. It may also help to agree a staff general code of conduct to avoid the risk of any misunderstanding about, for example, sharing private mobile phone numbers, contacting pupils by email or meeting up with pupils outside school.

Task 8.4.3 **CHILD PROTECTION 1**

You have been asked to assist in providing a report on a child for a child protection conference. Ask to see a report that has been produced by another member of the school staff and consider what it includes. What do you see as the most important information for a school report to contain? Talk to the teacher or other representative who submitted the report and attended the conference and ask them what it felt like. If possible, attend a conference yourself, if only as an observer. Remember the need for careful confidentiality in all these discussions.

Task 8.4.4 **CHILD PROTECTION 2**

Carry out an evaluation of child protection procedures in a school where you are working.

■ What information is made available as part of induction?
■ Is there a written policy and who knows about it?
■ Are there children with a child protection plan and, if so, what does this mean for their class teacher?
■ Does the school, in your judgement, meet all the requirements of the guidance?
■ What strengths and weaknesses have you identified?

Discuss your findings with the school's senior leadership team and recommend any necessary changes in policy or procedures.

SUMMARY

These may not be the issues that initially attracted you to the idea of being a teacher. Perhaps you thought that other people would be responsible for these sensitive areas. It is true that teachers are primarily employed to teach and that schools may now contain a variety of other professionals in a supportive role, but the wider pastoral care of pupils still cannot happen without you. It will only enhance your effectiveness in the classroom if you can show the child that you understand them as a person. It may just have to be you who is needed to respond to a serious concern for their welfare. That is an immense privilege, but one for which it pays to be well prepared.

ANNOTATED FURTHER READING

Department for Education and Skills (DfES) (2004) *Every Child Matters: Change for Children*, London: DfES.

Department for Education and Skills (DfES) (2004) *Every Child Matters: Change for Children in Schools*, London: DfES.

These documents form part of the government's detailed response to the Laming Report into the death of Victoria Climbié, alongside the Children Act 2004. The original report and subsequent additions are available at www.everychildmatters.gov.uk.

Department for Education and Skills (DfES) (2006) *Safeguarding Children and Safer Recruitment in Education*, London: DfES.

Produced in conjunction with s.175 Education 2002, this circular provides comprehensive guidance to schools on safeguarding children and should be the basis of all local policy and procedures. It is available online at www.teachernet.gov.uk.

Whitney, B. (2007) *Social Inclusion in Schools*, London: David Fulton/Routledge.

This is an overview of a range of social and pastoral issues that may prevent children from accessing education and what can be done about them.

Whitney, B. (2008) *A Guide to School Attendance*, London: David Fulton/Routledge.

This is a summary of the legislation and examples of best practice in improving school attendance and reducing 'persistent absence'.

RELEVANT WEBSITES

Department for Children, Schools and Families (DCSF): www.dcsf.gov.uk
> This website contains examples of good practice, latest guidance, etc. For 'school attendance' go to www.dcsf.gov.uk/schoolattendance, and for useful advice on national and local safeguarding arrangements, type 'safeguarding children' into the home page search box.

Safeguarding Children report: **www.safeguardingchildren.org.uk/Safeguarding-Children/2008-report**
> This report details the results of a review led by Ofsted on behalf of the eight inspectorates involved in regulating and inspecting services for children and young people.

Visit the companion website www.routledge.com/textbooks/ltps2e for:

■ additional questions and task for this unit;
■ links to useful websites relevant to this unit.

REFERENCES

Department for Children, Schools and Families (DCSF) (2009) *School Attendance*. Available online at www.dcsf.gov.uk/schoolattendance (accessed November 2009).

Department for Education and Skills (DfES) (2004) *Every Child Matters: Change for Children*, London: DfES.

Department for Education and Skills (DfES) (2006) *Safeguarding Children and Safer Recruitment in Education*, London: DfES, in conjunction with s.175 Education 2002. Available online at www.teachernet.gov.uk (accessed November 2009).

HM Government (2006) *Working Together to Safeguard Children*, London: The Stationery Office.

National Foundation for Educational Research (NFER) (2003) *School Attendance and the Prosecution of Parents: Effects and Effectiveness*, London: NFER.

Office for Standards in Education (Ofsted) (2008) *Safeguarding Children: The Third Joint Chief Inspectors' Report on Arrangements to Safeguard Children*, London: Ofsted.

YOUR PROFESSIONAL DEVELOPMENT

APPLYING FOR JOBS AND PREPARING FOR YOUR INDUCTION YEAR

Jane Medwell

INTRODUCTION

Your initial teacher training (ITT) is only the first step in your career. Completing it is rather like passing your driving test – you will be safe to teach a class but will still have plenty to learn about teaching and very limited experience to draw upon. The next step in your training comes during your year as a newly qualified teacher (NQT). Towards the end of your training you will devote considerable energy to finding the right job for you. This is a job that you feel happy in and one that offers you the professional development you need to become a better teacher. By preparing your goals for your induction year thoughtfully, you can ensure you get the support you need in your NQT year. This unit should help you.

OBJECTIVES

By the end of this unit you should:

- understand the role of the NQT year;
- know how to look for a teaching post;
- be able to begin to write job applications;
- be able to start work on objectives for your NQT year;
- have considered the priorities for your NQT year.

APPLYING FOR A TEACHING JOB

During your training you may start to apply for jobs. This will necessitate some personal decisions about what area you aim to work in, in what sort of school you would like to work, how far your domestic commitments allow you to commute each day and whether you want a full-time post. This is the time to be realistic because your first teaching post is so important. It is no use finding the perfect post if you have to leave for work at 6 a.m. every day to get there, or doing your NQT year in a school that does not suit you and your educational beliefs. Deciding where to apply and what sort of schools to apply to is the first step.

Jobs suited to NQTs (starting in September) are advertised at any time from the previous October to the June or July before you start. If you have a target area, you must not miss the job advertisement for that area or job. Teaching posts are usually advertised by individual schools or by NQT 'pools', whereby a group of schools recruit together. You must make sure you check the systems in place in your target areas – it is not uncommon for schools to advertise individually *and* be part of a local authority (LA) pool. Look first at the websites for the borough or LA you are interested in. This will tell you where they advertise teaching posts – usually the *Times Educational Supplement* (TES) (Friday), a local newspaper and online. You may be able to arrange to have regular bulletins sent to you directly from the LA.

When you respond to an advertisement, the school or LA will send you an information pack and details of how to apply for a job. Your ITT provider will give you further information about how to apply for a job and you should also look at all the information offered by your union.

Applying for jobs will take time and raises a number of issues for you. You will:

■ want to use your training experience positively in writing your application;
■ need time out from your course for preparation, visits and interviews;
■ want to ask for references and ensure your referees are clear about what is required.

USING YOUR EXPERIENCE POSITIVELY IN YOUR APPLICATION FOR A TEACHING POST

You will be given support in applying for a teaching post in your ITT programme, but it is important that your application includes insights from your ITT course and placements because this shows that you can learn from your experiences. When you write in response to an advertisement for a teaching post or for details of an NQT pool you will receive a person specification for the job. This may be general, simply listing a number of attributes sought in a successful applicant, such as appropriate teaching practice experience, ability to plan, deliver, monitor and evaluate children's learning, and so on. Alternatively, there may be very specific requirements associated with a school. As an NQT, you cannot become a curriculum coordinator in your NQT year, but the school may well be seeking staff with particular areas of expertise.

There are two main types of written application for primary and early years teaching posts: the LA or school application form, which usually includes a personal statement or letter of application; or your own curriculum vitae (CV) and letter of application. The information pack you receive from the school or LA will tell you what is required.

Complete application forms neatly and accurately and in a way that demonstrates enthusiasm. The usual rules for form filling apply: read the instructions carefully and follow them; write a draft first (and keep it for future reference); do not leave gaps but write N/A (not applicable); check all your dates and have all your information to hand; make sure your writing is neat and correctly spelled and make sure your personal statement (or letter) is effective. Plan plenty of time to fill in your application and make sure you have done a thorough review of your record of professional development or training plan.

You will be required to write either a supporting statement or a letter of application as part of an application form. The first thing you should do to prepare this is to examine thoroughly the person specification and/or job description to work out what the school or LA is looking for. Then read the instructions for completing the form or letter very carefully. Filling out this form is a chore, but it is your chance to market your skills. Do not be too modest or make impossible, exaggerated claims. The completed form will be slightly embarrassing, because it spells out your achievements and qualities, but it should not be untruthful. Mentors, personal tutors and teachers will help you

---

Task 9.1.1 **REVIEWING YOUR PROGRESS TOWARDS THE STANDARDS**

You review your progress throughout your training, but just as you apply for jobs is a key review point, so we suggest you conduct a thorough review just before you complete an application. Doing this helps you to:

■ remember and revisit all the training tasks you have done – assignments, school tasks and even visits, some of which may have taken place a while ago;
■ bring to mind all the training opportunities you took up on placement;
■ identify progress you have made towards demonstrating the standards for the award of qualified teacher status (QTS);
■ decide what constitutes evidence of your progress towards the standards for the award of QTS and to store this appropriately;
■ prepare a portfolio of work in preparation for a job interview (see page 473);
■ begin to formulate your areas of interest, strength and weakness in your NQT year (see page 475).

Go through your record of professional development (or training plan), reviewing your placement reports and academic work against the *Professional Standards.* Identify four areas where you have made progress and four areas in which you would like to improve.

---

to prepare your application and you should discuss a draft of your letter of application, supporting statement or CV (whichever is requested) with your tutor or mentor. Arrange a time in advance, as you cannot expect staff necessarily to be available at short notice.

There are many ways of writing your letter of application or supporting statement and there is no perfect template, but there are some key points you should bear in mind. Give a brief overview of your training (but do not repeat everything you have put in the application form) and mention your degree and any relevant projects, experiences or previous work. It is important to identify why you would suit the post, so say why you are applying for this post in particular. Include any local links, faith issues or visits to the school.

Your teaching placements during training are very important, so reference to your formal school placements should include when you did the placement, what years you have taught and the level of responsibility you took, but do not use up all your letter space by repeating what you have put on the form. Refer to special features of the placement, such as open-plan schools or team teaching. You could also refer to your placements to illustrate an aspect of your learning or an enthusiasm you have developed during your training. Such references could be to examples of how you plan, teach, monitor and evaluate learning outcomes, your behaviour management strategies, work with parents, and so on.

Write a little about your vision or beliefs for early years or primary education and the principles that underpin your practice. This might include beliefs about how children learn, classroom management or teaching styles, for instance. If you can illustrate with an example of how you have learned this on your course or school placement, this can be very effective. This sort of information gives the school a flavour of you as a teacher.

Another part of your letter will include details of your personal experiences: leisure activities, interests or involvement with children. Make these relevant to your work as a teacher and be explicit about what skills you have.

One of the easier ways to organise this information is to identify a number of subheadings taken from the person specification or job description, such as:

- teaching experiences (placements);
- commitment to teaching;
- knowledge, skills and aptitudes;
- planning and organisation;
- strengths and interests;
- personal qualities.

Organise your information under these headings. You can then remove your subheadings and have a well-organised letter to discuss with your mentor, tutor or careers adviser. Write in the first person, check your grammar and use interesting adverbs and adjectives to lift the text. If in doubt, ask a friend to proofread your letter before you talk to your mentor or tutor.

Task 9.1.2 USING A PERSON SPECIFICATION

Using the suggested bullet points for a person specification (see above), review your experience, qualifications and knowledge, skills and aptitudes. Go through each point asking yourself the following questions:

- What evidence do I have that I meet this criterion?
- What have I learned about this on my placements and in my course of study?
- What else do I need to be able to do to achieve this?
- What do I want to focus on in my continuing professional development (CPD) during the induction year?

Use the headings below to organise your information:

- teaching experiences (placements);
- commitment to teaching;
- knowledge, skills and aptitudes;
- planning and organisation;
- strengths and interests;
- personal qualities.

Write a letter of application, of not more than two sides of A4, setting out your experience, knowledge, skills and aptitudes and views about education. Discuss this general draft with your mentor, tutor or teacher and ask them to tell you about the impact and impression it makes. This letter can then form the basis of other letters that are tailored to suit a particular post.

The curriculum vitae

In applying for your first teaching post, you may find yourself writing a CV for the first time. Your CV sets out the important information about you on two sides of A4. Preparing for this is similar to preparing to fill in a form, but you will need to print it out on good-quality, white paper. As with the letter, prepare a general CV well in advance, but adapt it for each application so that it matches the person specification.

There are some things you can omit from a CV, such as your date of birth, age, marital status or ethnic origin. Photographs of yourself are not necessary for CVs for teaching posts and can trigger subconscious prejudice. Do not include failures on your CV – aim to keep it focused on what you have achieved. You should also leave out previous salary information or reasons for changing jobs, which are irrelevant.

The following should be included on your CV:

■ Contact details. Make sure that these are guaranteed routes to reach you, so if you have an email address that you rarely check, do not include it. Ideally, include your postal address, any telephone numbers you have (landline and mobile) and your email address if you will check it frequently.

■ Your gender, if it is not obvious from your name.

■ A short skills summary or supporting statement (see next paragraph).

■ Your education. This is best organised as follows: primary, secondary, further, higher.

■ Your qualifications, listed with the most recent first, including results.

■ Your work experience and placement experiences, with the most recent first (any positions you held more than about ten years ago can be left out).

■ Interests. Include only real and genuine ones, e.g. any sports in which you actively participate. If these hobbies and interests can convey a sense of your personality, all the better. Include any non-teaching qualifications that may have arisen from your hobbies or interests here too.

■ Membership of professional associations (not including unions).

■ Nationality, National Insurance number and referee details can be included at the end of your CV.

A skills summary need only be around 200 words, but you can still cover a lot of ground. It should be written in the first person. Every word must have a use and grammar should be immaculate. Do not just repeat what experience you have had – your achievements, accountability and competence are more important and this is where you can really bring these out. Aim to give a sense of your creativity, personal management and integrity – the reader will want to see that you have strong communication skills and are perhaps even leadership potential. When writing a skills summary, some people prefer to include a short bulleted list of around six key skills.

With only two sides of A4, the layout of a CV is important and you need to be economical with space. While the page should not look cluttered, excess space will look messy and ill-thought-through:

■ Present your contact details across the top of the first page (like a letterhead) to preserve space.

■ Use a clear, standard font, such as Times New Roman or Arial.

■ Avoid abbreviations unless they are universally understood.

If you really cannot fit everything on to two sides of A4, try reducing the font size slightly. This will mean the print is still large enough to read, but will give you a little more room to play with. There really is not too much difference between 12 and 11 point in terms of readability.

When you have designed your CV on screen, print off a draft version and try to view it through fresh eyes. Is it likely to grab the attention of a reader within a few seconds? Is it visually pleasing? Are there any errors? It is a good idea to ask someone else to cast an eye over it, as it is easy to miss typos on documents you have been working on yourself.

Writing a CV is not a one-off task. Once you have completed your CV (see the sample in Figure 9.1.1), you will need to keep it up to date.

Paula Grey
Eastleigh Cottage, 35 Thornton Hill, Cardiff CF21 9DE
Telephone: 0128 213 3567, mobile: 07337 632077, email: Paulie@yahoo.com

I am a newly qualified teacher trained to teach across the curriculum with the 5–11 age group. My previous work experience as an accountant has enabled me to develop an understanding of management in a large multinational corporation as well as demonstrable communication skills. Part of my role was the delivery of internal training for new staff. During my initial teacher training I taught in an inner-city Key Stage 1 class and in two Key Stage 2 classes in a school with a large multiracial population. In addition to my teaching, I ran a successful 'Get Into Reading' after-school workshop for parents, which crossed age and cultural boundaries and was recognised by the head and governors as a constructive addition to the wider school culture.

Education

Primary:	1984–1990 Abbey Primary School, Cardiff
Secondary:	1990–1995 Newport High School for Girls, Newport
Further:	1995–1997 Newport Sixth Form College, Newport
Higher:	1997–1999 University of Reading BA
	1999–2007 Membership of the Society of Chartered Accountants
	2008–2009 Institute of Education, University of London PGCE

Qualifications

PGCE:	Primary
Degree:	Archaeology and Statistics 2.1
A levels:	Mathematics A, Statistics A, Physics B, General studies B
GCSEs:	Mathematics A, English literature A, English language B, Physics B, History A, ICT A, Art B, Geography B, French A, Biology B

Professional development

During my initial teacher training I completed an LA-run 'Levelling Mathematics' course and attended a 'Developing Storysacks' training day.

Work experience

2004–2005:	ITT placements: High Five School, Camden and Nelson Mandela Primary School, Westminster
1999–2004:	British International Bank, London, Accountant
1997–1999:	Vacation positions with Marks and Spencer and Dillons, Cwmbran

Interests

I have run a local Brownies group for some years. I also run to keep fit and have completed the London marathon.

Additional qualifications

Full, clean driving licence
South Glamorgan County Junior Football Coaching

Nationality

British

National Insurance number

TY123456B

References

Referees available on request

■ **Figure 9.1.1** A sample CV

References

You will usually be asked to supply the names, positions and contact details of two referees. The first should be a senior member of staff in your ITT provider. Check carefully who this should be. It is common for universities to use the name of the head of department, even though your tutor will probably actually write the reference. It is essential to get this name right for two reasons. First, if you do not get a first reference from your ITT provider, the job advertiser will usually assume you have something to hide. Second, the reference system in a large ITT provider will be geared up for a swift response, but it will only work if you get the right name. The wrong name will slow down your reference and may put you at a disadvantage.

Your second referee should usually be from your placement school – your mentor, class teacher or head teacher. Ask if the mentor or head teacher is prepared to offer you a reference. In most cases, a reference is offered gladly. Professionals will not write a bad reference for anyone, but would decline to offer a reference if they could not truthfully recommend you. Mentors and head teachers will never decline to offer a reference simply because they do not want the effort.

Be quite clear who you intend to name as a referee. You might want to discuss this with your mentor or head so that you get the best reference. Will you name the mentor him- or herself or the head teacher? Check that you know the full name, title and professional position of your referee and make sure that the mentor or head has your contact details and that you have theirs. You should contact them to let them know when you use their name as a referee in any application. Be clear about anything you would like your referee to mention, such as participation in out-of-school events, or avoid mentioning, such as a disability or illness. Say when you expect to be applying for jobs and whether these will be exclusively teaching jobs or will include things such as vacation jobs or voluntary work. It is a good idea to give your referee a copy of your CV and a summary of your strengths as part of the process of asking for a reference. Schools that you have applied to may ring your second referee for an informal reference, particularly if you are applying for a job locally. You want your referee to be prepared for this and speak warmly about you, rather than be surprised and feel caught out.

VISITS AND INTERVIEWS DURING YOUR TRAINING

When you are considering applying for a job, you may be invited to look around the school or you may ask to look around a school. Some schools schedule specific times and take a large number of applicants around the school together. This sort of tour is a very good way to find out about a school and whether it will suit you. However, it can present problems because of the time it takes out of your placement or taught course, especially if you are applying for posts at some distance. You must consider the impact of absence from school or university on your training and the cumulative impact of multiple visits, particularly as this is often a time when you are on school placement. You have to complete a certain amount of placement time in school and take sustained responsibility for the class on final placement and a large number of visits could affect the outcome of your placement. It may be better to try to visit schools after the end of the school day, or to explain to schools that your placement commitments prevent you from visiting informally.

You will almost always be given a tour of the school prior to interview and you would have the opportunity to withdraw from the interview after this if you did not think the school would suit you. If you apply for a job through a teaching pool, you will usually go for an interview for the pool first and may then be invited to look around schools that have jobs available. This is a different sort of school visit from the informal pre-interview visit mentioned above, because you will be looking at a school to see whether you would take a job there. You should go on these visits, but be aware of the time consideration mentioned above.

When you have applied for a post and are invited to interview during course time, you should ask your tutor or mentor for permission to attend, thus missing the taught sessions or school placement that day. In practice, this is a courtesy and you will always be given permission to attend interviews. It is a good idea to ask your mentor, tutor or class teacher to help you to prepare for interview and such preparation might take a number of forms:

■   Discuss 'hot' topics in the educational press or recent initiatives in school. Identify and discuss issues in the TES or another publication with a colleague, tutor or teacher. This will help you to explore the issues from another perspective. Consider what the effects of new ideas are for teachers, schools and children.

■   Role-play a 'mock' interview with the tutor, mentor, teacher or another trainee. This can help you to conquer nerves and prepare your interview manner. Practise framing your replies at interview – a pause to think, for example, rather than rushing in and babbling. What sort of body language do you want to exhibit – or avoid? Consider how you will conclude the interview and what your final impression is to be.

■   Your interview may include a task such as teaching a class or group, planning a lesson plan from information given or making a presentation to the panel. If the letter (or telephone call) of invitation states (or hints at) this, do not be afraid to telephone the school and ask for more details, such as the year group you will teach, subject required, technology available or length of lesson. Some schools leave these details vague and expect you to enquire.

■   Ask a tutor or teacher to help you to plan any teaching you are asked to do as part of your interview, but make sure you go to them with plenty of ideas and suggestions. It is not uncommon to be asked to teach something to a class. You will not be able to prepare a perfect lesson because you do not know the children, but you can still use a lesson plan to show that you know the relevant curricula, have good ideas, know a range of teaching strategies, are aware of a range of resources and have a good manner with children. Your tutor or mentor may be able to spot obvious faux pas or overambitious plans if you ask to discuss them.

INTERVIEW PORTFOLIOS

As a trainee you will be maintaining a training plan or record of professional development that contains evidence to demonstrate your achievement of the standards. This will contain placement assessment reports, observation notes, written assignments, mentor meeting notes and other evidence.

You may be asked to take this training plan or record with you to interview or to bring a portfolio. Even if you are not asked to bring a portfolio, you may want to do so. You can offer this to your interviewers – they do not have to spend much time looking at it, but it does indicate that you are well prepared and professional.

An interview portfolio can be a substantial document but, more usually, is a slim document containing some of the following:

■   Title and content page, preferably with a photo of you in a teaching situation.
■   Concise CV.
■   Placement assessment reports (one or more).
■   A really good lesson plan or two, some examples of the work associated with the lesson and the lesson evaluation.
■   A mentor, tutor or class teacher observation of a lesson that picks out a strength.
■   A sample mentor meeting summary (to show that you are focused and organised).
■   An example of a written piece of work (and the marking sheet) if relevant.

■   A few photos of you teaching. Choose these carefully as you really want to present a particular image. Generally, you might choose one photo of you 'at the front' teaching a large group or class, one of you looking sensitive with a group and, ideally, one of you teaching elsewhere – perhaps on a school visit or outside! Remember, choose photos to suit that job. If the school is very ICT conscious, make sure there is a picture with you using ICT. If the school is keen to improve its physical education, a photo of your gym session would not go amiss! Make sure you follow your placement school policy on photo use and that the school, teachers and children are not identifiable.

■   One or two photos of displays, school visits you have been on, after-school clubs or assemblies you have led.

■   Any evidence of your special interests – coaching certificates, first aid, cookery, etc.

In practice, interview panels do not spend much time on interview portfolios and usually just flick through the content, so consider how you can create the best impression to someone who does this (the flick factor). For example, anything on the back of facing pages is unlikely to be seen, so either put less important pages here, or have a single-sided portfolio with all pages facing the reader. Make sure your photos are well displayed, as they have a disproportionate impact. Although your portfolio may not command much time or attention, by preparing it you are not only demonstrating professionalism, but also getting the chance to present a tailored image of your achievements to the panel, in addition to your written application.

INDUCTION FOR NEWLY QUALIFIED TEACHERS

Induction for NQTs is compulsory, follows ITT and is the foundation for CPD throughout your career. The induction period must be undertaken by NQTs who wish to work in maintained schools and non-maintained special schools. The induction period may also be done while working in independent schools, but not all of them offer this. You can usually complete induction part-time, but it will take longer than the usual year. Check when you apply for a job, as failure to do a recognised induction will mean that you do not gain QTS. You do not have to complete your induction period immediately after your ITT, but time limits apply and you should check these on the Training and Development Agency for Schools (TDA) website (www.tda.gov.uk/induction). In the same way, not all types of supply work count towards NQT induction, so you must check this.

During the induction period you have to demonstrate that you have continued to meet the standards of QTS, and met all the induction standards. You will have an individualised programme of support during the induction year from a designated induction tutor. This includes observations of your teaching by school staff and induction tutors, you observing more experienced teachers in different settings, and a professional review of progress at least every half term. You will also have the opportunity to attend school-centred in-service provision and, often, external courses. During your induction year you will not teach more than 90 per cent of a normal timetable during the period, to allow your induction to take place.

The head is responsible, with appropriate bodies (for maintained schools and non-maintained special schools this is the LA, and for independent schools, it is either any LA in England or a special body, the Independent Schools Council Teacher Induction Panel), and will make a final recommendation as to whether you have passed or failed your induction period. The appropriate body makes the final decision, and there is a right of appeal to the General Teaching Council for England (GTCE). The revised Department for Education and Skills (DfES) guidance on induction, *The Induction Support Programme for Newly Qualified Teachers* (Reference: DfES/0458/2003), is now available online at www.tda.gov.uk/induction. You should ensure that you check it.

PLANNING FOR YOUR INDUCTION YEAR

Your goals for induction are your key induction tool. Until 2009, these were recorded as a Career Entry and Development Profile, but this format was not well used and a more induction-friendly format is being developed. It is the document you use to guide the process of reflection and review as you complete your ITT and go through your induction year. You will notice that the headings of the standards for the award of QTS apply not only to your ITT but also to your induction year, which is guided by the induction standards. During your transition from trainee to fully qualified teacher, you should review your goals at key transition points:

■ the end of ITT (Transition Point 1);
■ the beginning of your NQT year (Transition Point 2);
■ the end of your NQT year (or longer for part-time teachers) (Transition Point 3).

The personal development profile or record of professional development you have maintained throughout your ITT will help you to summarise your achievements and identify areas for further work. These can be turned into goals for your NQT year at Transition Point 1 – the end of ITT.

The induction profile prepared annually by the TDA will be given to you by your ITT provider near to the end of your training. It is also available as a package of online materials that you can access in advance. The web pages at www.tda.gov.uk provide information on the NQT year, format of goals and induction in general. Here you can find descriptions of the processes that you will be undertaking at each of the three transition points. The online materials have interactive elements and sample formats for recording your responses, setting objectives and writing action plans.

As you come to the end of your ITT programme, you will want to think about how far you have come in your professional development. This process is likely to be a natural part of your ITT programme. Your ITT provider will also help you to understand your own role in your induction. The formulation of goals for the NQT year will help you to think about your experience from before, during and outside your formal training programme, including your placements, and to identify your key achievements and aspirations in relation to teaching.

You should aim to set targets that:

■ reflect and build on the strengths in your practice so far;
■ develop aspects of the teacher's role in which you are particularly interested;
■ provide more experience, or build up your expertise, in areas where you have developed to a more limited extent so far.

At the end of ITT (Transition Point 1), you are not expected to write lengthy answers to the prompt questions. It is the processes of reflection and professional discussion with your course tutors or mentor that are important and these will be reflected in the notes you make. The main questions you should consider at this stage are:

■ At the end of your initial training, which aspect(s) of teaching do you find most interesting and rewarding?
  What has led to your interest in these areas?
  How would you like to develop these interests?
■ As you approach the award of QTS, what do you consider to be your main strengths and achievements as a teacher?
  Why do you think this?
  What examples do you have of your achievements in these areas?

■　In which aspects of teaching would you value further experience in the future? For example:

　　▌ aspects of teaching about which you feel less confident, or where you have had limited opportunities to gain experience;

　　▌ areas of particular strength or interest on which you want to build further.

At the moment, which of these areas do you particularly hope to develop during your induction period?

■　As you look ahead to your career in teaching, you may be thinking about your longer-term professional aspirations and goals. Do you have any thoughts at this stage about how you would like to see your career develop?

You will record your responses to these questions in the format that suits you best and some examples are available on the TDA website (www.tda.gov.uk). Each format helps you to focus your thoughts about your experience so far and is a place for you to collate conclusions based on the evidence from your record of professional development or training plan. As a rough guide, three to five points for each of the main questions is about right, in terms of offering a good range of material at the start of your induction year. Although the presentation of your training goals for the NQT year is not the most important aspect of these goals, it is the document you will be taking to show your induction tutor, so you may want to word process your answers and include evidence. This shows your induction tutor not only your IT skills, but your professional approach.

Task 9.1.3 USING YOUR RECORD OF PROFESSIONAL DEVELOPMENT TO PREPARE YOUR GOALS

Note down your response to the questions above, where you might find evidence to support your thinking, and/or the reasoning that led you to this response. You will want to draw on evidence that is already available in your record of professional development or training plan, for example:

■ reports on your teaching during your placements;
■ observation reports written by your mentor, class teacher or course tutor;
■ examples of your planning for placement;
■ records of targets and objectives set during your ITT programme;
■ your own audits of your progress towards the QTS standards;
■ course assignments or subject audits.

The end of ITT is also the time for you to review your achievements, needs and direction with a tutor or senior professional. Your ITT tutor should sign to confirm that a discussion about your goals for the NQT year took place.

Induction goals are an important product of your whole ITT period. They enable the school that employs you to:

■　understand your strengths and experiences by the end of ITT;
■　support your professional development through your NQT year;
■　support constructive dialogue between NQTs and induction tutors;
■　make links between induction, CPD and performance management.

Task 9.1.4 **FRAMING YOUR ANSWERS PROFESSIONALLY**

Consider an excerpt from the answers to some of the questions noted by Sophie and Alex, below.

■ As you approach the award of QTS, what do you consider to be your main strengths and achievements as a teacher?

Sophie: I think I am a caring person and relate well to the children. I have really got on well with teachers, but I have not had a chance to work with a teaching assistant. I want to work with a TA.

Alex: My placement reports identify my relationships with the children and teachers as one of my strengths. My final report suggested that good relationships with the children were part of my success at managing the class and my second placement report noted that I had worked particularly closely with other teachers in planning and assessment. I now want to develop my experience of planning for a teaching assistant in the classroom, as I have not experienced this.

■ In which aspects of teaching would you value further experience in the future?

Sophie: I have not really had the chance to teach children with English as an additional language during my placement and I would like to do much more of this and really cater for the EAL children in my class.

Alex: Although I have had training sessions and done an assignment about teaching children with English as an additional language, my practical experience has been limited. In my induction year I would like to develop my experience of planning for and teaching children with EAL with the support of a more experienced teacher. I want to develop a reasonable repertoire of practical strategies.

Which answers:

■ use evidence well;
■ emphasise experience;
■ balance strengths and weaknesses;
■ offer the best indication of what action might be required?

At the meeting with your induction tutor you will identify your specific targets, experiences and actions for the beginning of your induction, based on what is already in your goals. This simply continues the target setting, action, review cycle that you will be used to. Using your end-of-ITT goals well will help you to make the most of your first job and your induction year.

SUMMARY

This unit gives you a broad overview of the whole topic of moving on in your professional development and training. You will need to allocate a substantial amount of time and attention to securing the right first teaching post, but when you have, you have real opportunities to develop as a professional. To do this you must take a clear-eyed and realistic review of your achievements and CPD needs and summarise these as the basis for your future goals:

■ When applying for jobs enlist the support of your mentor or tutor. They can look at applications and offer you mock interviews.
■ Start considering applications early and allow plenty of time.
■ Prepare each job application carefully, making sure you use the application format they want and that you set out your abilities and skills appropriately.
■ Ensure that you name the appropriate referees and that you have asked them if you may use them as referees.
■ Use evidence from your training plan (or record of professional development) to prepare an interview portfolio. Make sure it presents the image you want for each job!
■ The induction year has its own standards for induction and setting targets for these is a final placement task.
■ Ensure that you know about your progress and what you want to cite as goals for the NQT year before you meet your course tutor or mentor. You are responsible for preparing your goals. Use the website and your records to do this so that you go to the meeting with your ITT provider well organised and prepared.

ANNOTATED FURTHER READING

Association of Graduate Careers Advisory Services (AGCAS) (2005) *Getting a Teaching Job in Schools: A Guide to Finding Your First Appointment*, Sheffield: AGCAS.
This contains detailed information about applying for a teaching post.

RELEVANT WEBSITES

Career Entry and Development Profile and support materials: www.tda.gov.uk/teachers/induction/cedp
This material will deal with 2010 while an alternative format is developed.

Induction Support Programme for Newly Qualified Teachers, DfES/0458/2003: www.tda.gov.uk/induction
This site also provides detailed guidance about induction.

The Daily Telegraph (Independent Schools): www.telegraph.co.uk
The Guardian (Tuesdays): www.jobsunlimited.co.uk
The Independent (Thursdays): www.independent.co.uk
The Times Educational Supplement (Fridays): www.tesjobs.co.uk
Most school vacancies are advertised in the above publications. Some of them operate an electronic job alert system.

Independent Schools Council Information Service (ISCIS) Job Search: www.isc.co.uk/JobZone_Job Search.htm
Incorporated Association of Preparatory Schools (IAPS): www.iaps.org.uk
The above two websites contain general information about teaching in the private sector.

National Association of Schoolmasters and Union of Women Teachers (NASUWT): www.teachersunion.
   org.uk
National Union of Teachers (NUT): www.data.teachers.org.uk
Association of Teachers and Lecturers (ATL): www.atl.org.uk
   Your union is an excellent source of help, advice and support in applying for a teaching post.

eteach.com: www.eteach.com
TeacherNet: www.teachernet.gov.uk
Prospects: www.prospects.ac.uk
   The above are additional useful online resources for finding a teaching post.

Training and Development Agency for Schools (TDA): www.tda.gov.uk/induction

Visit the companion website www.routledge.com/textbooks/ltps2e for:

■ additional tasks for this unit;
■ links to useful websites relevant to this unit.

CONTINUING YOUR PROFESSIONAL DEVELOPMENT

Kit Field

INTRODUCTION

The world of continuing professional development (CPD) is fast changing. With the emphasis on CPD within the *Children's Plan* (2007), subsequent documentation and literature has incorporated many proposed changes. The interim report of the *Independent Review of the Primary Curriculum* (Rose Review) (Rose, 2008) stresses the need for CPD focused on core skills and modern foreign languages. The Training and Development Agency's (TDA) proposals and pilot of a Master's in Teaching and Learning (MTL) represent a shift towards the development of teaching as an M level profession. The 14–19 curriculum and the introduction of vocational diplomas at one end of the compulsory education sector and the development of Early Years standards at the other illustrate the systemic change at present. New national professional standards for all teachers, coupled with relatively new performance management procedures, tie CPD in with a sense of professional entitlement and obligation. For new teachers, engaging with CPD represents an essential component of being a professional. CPD is multidimensional, and is a means of re-professionalising the teaching workforce, providing a degree of self- and professional esteem as well as the means of improving school performance and implementing a wide range of national strategies. Research has shown (Gray, 2005, for example) that CPD has not been a major success in more recent years, with teachers expressing little respect for what has been on offer and head teachers being prepared to divert funding towards more pressing priorities. With such an emphasis in recent legislative documentation, it comes as no surprise that built into the processes of CPD is a need to demonstrate a link between engagement by teachers and a positive and visible impact.

OBJECTIVES

By the end of this unit, you should:

- understand the complexity of, and the need to redefine, CPD;
- recognise the roles of the many professional agencies associated with CPD;
- acknowledge the need to be pro-active in organising your own CPD from planning stages to identifying the impact;
- recognise the links between CPD and performance management;
- appreciate the need for ongoing professional learning and development;
- appreciate what constitutes effective CPD from the perspectives of the 'system', the 'individual', the 'school' and the 'profession'.

REDEFINING CPD?

There are, self-evidently, three aspects to CPD: *continuing, professional* and *development*:

Continuing

Society is ever changing. If one goal of education is to prepare young people today for the world of tomorrow, no teacher can rely on lessons learned yesterday. Teachers must engage in learning for practical reasons. The CPD strategy (DfEE, 2001) mentions the need for pupils to develop an enthusiasm for lifelong learning, as it is seen to be key to success in adult life. Such an enthusiasm is more likely to develop if young people see their teachers modelling such practices.

O'Brien and MacBeath (1999) comment:

Teacher life-long learning in the form of continuing professional development (CPD) is increasingly regarded as an important means of contributing to the creation of more effective schools, and as integral to learning organisations.

The starting point for this argument is initial teacher education (ITE). The years 2007–08 saw the introduction of two forms of university-led teacher training. A *Professional* Graduate Certificate of Education provides training at degree level, whereas a *Postgraduate* Certificate in Education provides the opportunity to accrue a number of M level credits during the training process. Most institutions enable participants to gain 40–60 M level credits, whereas some offer 90 or even 120 credits. This enables participants to pick up further credits once in post as a newly qualified teacher (NQT) or even later in the teaching career. This provides a basis for *continued* studies from the outset. The logical justification for this is that lifelong learning leads to the development of a learning organisation, which continuously and collectively re-evaluates its purposes and seeks ways to develop the most effective and efficient ways of reaching its goals. Improvement is continuous if learning is ongoing.

Continuous and continuing learning is not problematic. It involves individual learning and developing along with colleagues, but also individually. The core 'business' of a school is teaching and learning. All teachers therefore have access to teaching and learning situations all day, prompting one Secretary of State for Education to assert that teachers learn best from and with other teachers (Morris, 2001). This does suggest the need for contact, communication and regular access to other teachers. A professional recognition for CPD is provided by the General Teaching Council for England (GTCE) through its awards scheme, the Teacher Learning Academy (TLA). The new national professional standards for teachers emanating from the TDA also strive to enable progression, and building upon existing successes and strengths. A career development plan can be built out of official performance management procedures and linked CPD. Putnam and Borko (2000) condemn the traditional view that teachers should 'find their own style' (p. 19) in that it encourages a paradigm of privacy. For them, the development of a community of practice (Wenger, 1999) leads to the establishment of a common theory and language, and opportunities to challenge assumptions. 'Continuing' professional development relies on regular interaction with colleagues.

Professional

The word 'professional' is problematic. Certainly Morris (2001) uses the term to draw approval for the strategy from teachers: '[CPD] . . . is part of the re-professionalisation of what teachers should do, shout as loudly as we possibly can that, yes, we demand a lot of teachers.' Rose (2008)

Task 9.2.1 **PROFESSIONAL DEVELOPMENT ACTIVITIES**

Which types of professional development activities are best conducted individually, and which in collaboration with others? What tools can be used to maximise the benefits of:

■ joint planning;
■ observation;
■ team teaching;
■ assessment levelling.

---

similarly commends existing practices and the attempts of teachers to develop as professionals, notably in processes associated with assessing pupil progress (APP).

Professionalising teachers for others (for example, Whitty, 2000) means providing independence and self-governance. Within the current government's CPD strategy, some allowance is made, in that teachers are encouraged to take responsibility for professional development, as, it is claimed, it is increasingly a requirement in other professions. The model of linking union learning representatives (ULRs) to school-based CPD leaders in Scotland (Alexandrou, 2006) is gathering some momentum. This does not go as far as Whitty would want – to have, as a profession, a mandate to act on behalf of the state. Education is, and will continue to be, subject to and regulated by market forces and supervision by the government.

To a degree, some features of a profession are in place:

■ teacher skills are based on theoretical knowledge;
■ education in the skills is certified by examination;
■ there is a code of conduct (DfEE, 2001) oriented towards the public good;
■ a new professional organisation (the GTCE) enjoys some power and influence.

(After Whitty, 2000: 281)

Day's (1999) analysis, drawing on Hoyle's (1975) definitions of professionalism and professionality, is less positive. Characteristics of the 'restricted professional' are applicable. Action is intuitive, and learning is derived from the work base. Experience rather than theory is used to justify action. Teachers are not encouraged by the CPD strategy to become 'extended professionals', that is, to locate practice in a broader political and social context. The extent to which teaching is 'value led' is also questionable. The 'values' are imposed; present in the latest official set of standards for qualified teacher status (QTS). The values have not emerged from the profession itself.

The new performance management procedures are very much tied in with school performance priorities, and the role of a mentor/coach serves the function of supporting individuals within the context of the need to link to school development plans, which themselves are engaged in implementing government-led strategies and systems. The recommendation that phonics should be the 'prime approach' to teaching reading in the report, *Phonics and Early Reading* (Rose, 2006), serves as an example. Proposals for the pilot of the MTL (Day, 2008) also define four 'content areas' to inform planning and development:

1   teaching and learning AND assessment for learning;
2   subject knowledge for teaching AND curriculum development;

3   how children and young people develop, how they learn and management of their behaviour AND inclusion, including special educational needs (SEN) and English as an additional language (EAL);

4   leadership and management AND working collaboratively, in and beyond the classroom.

The CPD developments are a move towards the professionalisation of teachers. They are contributing towards the professionality of teacher behaviour and practice, but, as yet, stop short of providing the decision- and policy-making powers traditionally associated with professions.

Task 9.2.2 **RESPONSIBILITY**

In which ways are you responsible and accountable to:

■ yourself;
■ your school;
■ the profession;
■ the community;
■ the government.

Does this sense of responsibility oblige you to do anything?

Development

Development can mean several things in the context of CPD. First, it can relate to personal growth and understanding within a community of practice, and therefore relate the unique contribution an individual makes (Tsui *et al.*, 2008). Second, it can relate to career development and, third, it can relate to school development, and the extent to which the school achieves its own priorities through improved, or more focused, teacher practice. From a government perspective, development can mean the extent to which schools and, therefore, teachers have successfully implemented national strategies. Last, and perhaps the least well covered in the literature, is the development of the professional, in terms of its prestige and the esteem in which it is held.

There have, no doubt, been attempts to integrate these four dimensions. Work undertaken (Field, 2007), through consultancy, to use the new standards and performance management procedures and to ensure that teachers as professionals 'buy into' the processes does illustrate the point. The work builds on the premise that engagement in CPD, both as a learner and as a contributor, is embedded in the standards. An analysis of professional standards at all levels reveals two dimensions:

■   that teachers will need to focus on personal, individual performance (*individual*);
■   that teachers will work with colleagues in order to support school development (*collective*).

Extracts from the standards for teachers having completed induction standards, maintaining induction standards, working towards and then maintaining threshold standards, and subsequently working towards excellent teacher (ET) and advanced skills teacher (AST) status inform the process.

A second set of dimensions is also contained within the standards: practical and reflective. Practical standards relate to those that demand the development and practice of classroom practice. Reflective standards relate to innovative and evaluative processes.

Drawing on these tensions and dichotomies, a developmental model for CPD can represented in the form of a matrix, recognising that real teachers will not fall neatly into each category, but may well display standards at more than one level. Types of CPD have been identified for those in need of development:

- individual and practical;
- individual and reflective;
- collective and practical;
- collective and reflective.

Figures 9.2.1 and 9.2.2 will assist the planning of CPD according to the needs in relation to defined professional standards. The direction of 'travel' from induction to AST, or through the maze of leadership pathways, may vary. Forms of CPD will differ according to the selected direction, and of course according to individual preferences.

The model designed for (aspiring) school leaders (Figure 9.2.2) also provides guidance to support movement to the next career stage. The lists of course types and CPD opportunities are hierarchical in each box. The overlap with CPD types within the learning and teaching model means that decisions to follow a leadership route are not final and decisive. The ET, for example, may well change his or her mind and revert to the learning and teaching model after an initial foray into leadership and management.

The development routes for leadership and management are not based upon existing standards, given that the leadership standards are all under review. They are, however, based upon the descriptors for 'stages of leadership' and the lists of programmes published on the National College of School Leadership (NCSL) (now the National College for Leadership of Schools and Children's Services) website (www.nationalcollege.org.uk).

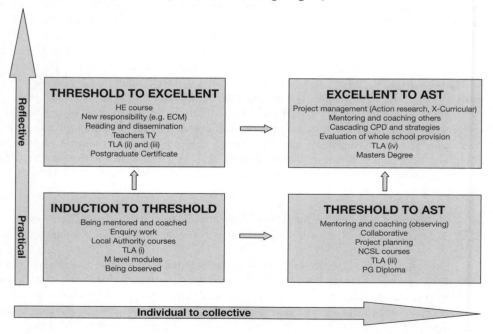

Figure 9.2.1 Learning and teaching route

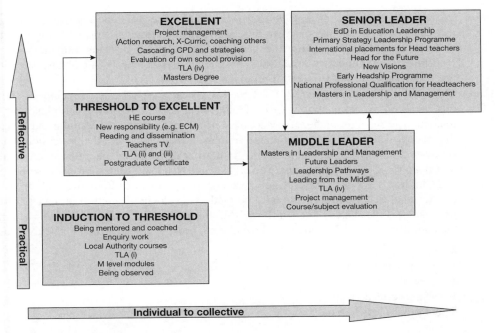

Figure 9.2.2 Leadership and management route

Task 9.2.3 **SETTING YOUR STANDARDS**

■ Using the models in Figures 9.2.1 and 9.2.2, select the set of standards to which you aspire.

■ Devise a self-audit tool in order to identify aspects in need of further development. This tool will need to be justified in terms of research methodology.

■ Can you identify the gap between where you are now and where you want to be in the future?

■ Identify the purposes and types of CPD most suited to yourself and your circumstances.

■ Indicate the types of evidence that will enable you to demonstrate the fulfilment of these standards.

■ What activities will generate the types of evidence you need, and how will you assure a reliable evidence-gathering process and validate the outcomes?

PROFESSIONAL AGENCIES ASSOCIATED WITH CPD

The Department for Children, Schools and Families (DCSF) clearly occupies a powerful position in CPD. However, CPD is a very cluttered playing field, and to assure maximum gain from the opportunities available teachers do need to understand the functions and roles of a range of institutions:

Department for Children, Schools and Families (DCSF): The DCSF is the government ministry that provides guidance and support for CPD. Its position in relation to CPD is contained within the *Children's Plan* (2007).

Training and Development Agency for Schools (TDA): The TDA is a government-sponsored independent body. Its purpose is to raise standards by attracting able and committed people to teaching and by improving the quality of training for teachers and the wider school workforce. Government representatives have requested that the TDA extends its remit to take responsibility centrally for CPD in England.

General Teaching Council for England (GTCE): The GTCE (2003) has also developed a framework that spells out what constitutes CPD. Teachers can use the framework to plan their CPD in relation to personal professional development needs, and evaluate the learning and development that occurs. The GTCE intends that the framework resonates with the professional standards framework as well as the qualifications framework offered by higher education institutions.

National College for School Leadership (NCSL): Now the National College for Leadership of Schools and Children's Services, the college's Leadership Development Framework (LDF) is centred on the belief that schools should be supported in developing leaders at all levels (distributed leadership). Five stages of school leadership form part of a non-linear model, within which the majority of NCSL's leadership development provision can be found. The five stages are:

■ emergent leadership;
■ established leadership;
■ entry to headship;
■ advanced leadership;
■ consultant leadership.

A portfolio approach to recording development and the impact of actions on educational leadership are essential components of development in this area.

HIGHER EDUCATION QUALIFICATIONS FRAMEWORK

Many teachers follow M level degree courses and programmes in education-related topics. Postgraduate professional development (PPD) consists of TDA-funded, 60-credit 'chunks' of study/development, and has to be planned, delivered and evaluated through partnership arrangements. The link between professional development and academic qualifications is becoming stronger, as professional bodies such as the NCSL and GTCE are seeking academic accreditation for teachers' engagement with their own 'frameworks'. In this way it is possible to use day-to-day professional experiences as a basis for study. The MTL is likely to replace and extend PPD in years to come.

■ *Local authorities (LAs)*: Local authorities, as the employers of teachers, have a responsibility for teachers' conditions of service and are also accountable for the levels of performance of the pupils in the local schools. The requirement to produce an education development plan demands that account is made of CPD and its impact in schools.

■ *Private companies*: Throughout the 1990s and early 2000s, private companies have entered the CPD market. Such companies are able to tender for national and regional projects as consultants and deliverers of CPD.

Task 9.2.4 **SCHOOL DEVELOPMENT PLANS**

Look at your school's development plan.

■ Work out the extent to which each priority is driven by external forces.
■ Now match up from which agency support for the achievement of each priority can be sought.
■ Are there fixed development programmes for each priority?

ORGANISING YOUR OWN CPD

CPD is complex and increasingly demanding of teachers' and schools' energies. It runs the risk of becoming a management tool, but can also be developed to support individuals. The autonomy and drive associated with being a professional suggests that teachers themselves should take control of the process. The process proposed below draws on the different dimensions, and also attempts to position CPD within the requirements of performance management and the statutory national professional standards. It is also based upon several premises, each demanding of a realistic and credible infrastructure (see Figure 9.2.3).

Consequently, the belief is that, by integrating national professional standards, CPD and performance management, the following purposes must be clear:

- there must be motivation and improvement in teachers' self- and peer esteem;
- development demands competence and understanding;
- part of professional development is to disseminate and share;

Premise	Infrastructure
Focus of performance management is positive, not to identify incapability	Clear protocols must include trade union agreement
Job descriptions can be related to national professional standards	Job descriptions may need revising
Evidence generated can be used to support school self-evaluation (SEF) and school improvement	An ethical code is needed to ensure confidentiality and anonymity when appropriate
The process includes an engagement with the appointed school improvement partner (SIP)	Clear and explicit role definitions in relation to performance management and CPD are needed
Localised criteria for effective learning and teaching are needed	Teachers should be involved in establishing these criteria, and they should not be imposed from above
All staff should have a sense of professional responsibility to improve and develop	Time, salaries and status must be reflected in the level of engagement
Schools must collate individual outcomes with an overall plan and report in mind	The member of staff with responsibility for performance management and CPD should have a strategic role. The recommendation is that these roles are conducted by the same person
Focus should begin with individuals, and expand to incorporate a team view and finally a school perspective	Clear channels of communication, with an appropriate ethical code, should be developed
Support and development opportunities must match teachers' needs and wants	Dedicated funding should be ring-fenced within a school budget
Confidentiality issues need to be agreed	Trade unions should be involved in formulating the ethical code

■ **Figure 9.2.3** Premises infrastructure underpinning and supporting effective CPD

■ improvement and development must be recognised and acknowledged;
■ organisational development is achieved through workforce development;

This process recognises key roles to be played by three stakeholder groups. Each 'stakeholder' must respond to and inform the others. Given the emphasis on the reviewee's performance and responsibility as a professional within the context of school development, the process is designed to support and facilitate. Reviewers may also have the responsibility for recommending pay awards, and therefore the process emphasises the need for responsibility, accountability and openness. All this must be within a positive and supportive environment, rather than within a negative, deficit model. This 'climate' must be established if the Rewards and Incentive Group (RIG) guidelines are to succeed.

A ten-stage process is recommended (see Figure 9.2.4). The 'critical path' explained below serves to analyse the process, and to enable the identification of training and development needs in relation to the agenda. It also offers a synthesis of the separate procedures and overall process.

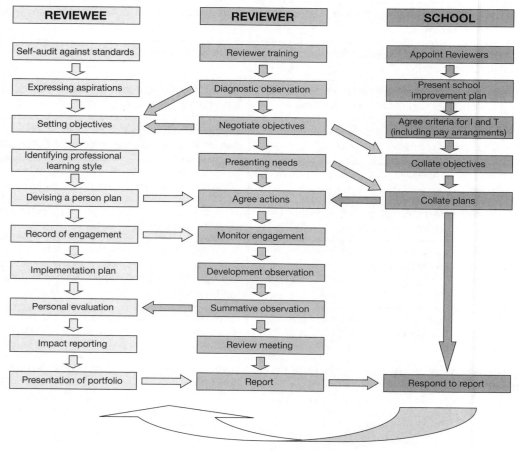

■ **Figure 9.2.4** The CPD and performance management process

The 'reviewee' refers to the teacher. A reviewer is what is traditionally referred to as an appraiser, but clearly incorporates the role of a coach and mentor. The 'school' is represented by the CPD leader. Each of the ten stages (reviewee) is explained below.

Stage 1 – Self-audit against standards
In order to support future career development, the teacher should rate his or her performance against the set of standards to which he or she aspires. One approach is to annotate each standard using an 'MIC' approach. 'M' means that a level of performance against a standard should be maintained. 'I' means that the teacher should strive to improve. 'C' means 'change', in that the school should attempt to provide opportunities for such a standard to be met.

Stage 2 – Express aspirations
Self-audits (see above) do lend themselves well to deficit approaches, through the identification of weaknesses. By stating aspirations, teachers may look to the future and build on existing strengths with defined purposes in mind.

Stage 3 – Set objectives
The negotiation of targets/objectives with a reviewer/coach/mentor is essential. With the need to demonstrate development, it is necessary to agree the criteria against which judgements relating to success are made.

Stage 4 – Identify professional learning style
Different people, in different circumstances, learn in different ways. It is important for professionals to have a role in determining how they will be supported in achieving the agreed targets. This means drawing from a wide range of CPD types as demonstrated in Figures 9.2.1 and 9.2.2 (pages 484–5).

Stage 5 –Devise a personal plan
A personal plan will consist of the identification of learning activities as well as the means and evidence by which the learning can be demonstrated. Timelines and feedback mechanisms should be agreed. This plan can be the basis of a personal log for future use.

Stage 6 – Record of engagement
It is recommended that a log of activity should be accompanied by reflective commentaries or a personal narrative to embed the learning, and to foresee advantageous future applications.

Stage 7 – Implementation plan
Too often, CPD loses its potential effectiveness once teachers return to their day-to-day activity. Reflection and implementation of new strategies and understandings in the classroom, through careful planning, should be formally recorded. This stage recommends judicial use of the coach/mentor to support development.

Stage 8 – Personal evaluation
This stage is related to the extent to which the individual has been stimulated through the CPD process, and the extent to which he or she has improved practice. This involves consideration of statistical and qualitative evidence. Often individuals benefit from an external viewpoint.

Stage 9 – Impact reporting
Impact reporting demands a consideration of how the CPD process has impacted upon others. These will include pupils, colleagues and other stakeholders. A claim of 'impact' will need to be evidence-

based and evaluative. It is recognised that direct causal links between CPD engagement and pupil learning outcomes cannot be firmly established, but correlations and narrative accounts can provide clear indicators of success in relation to the objectives agreed under stage 3.

Stage 10 – Presentation of portfolio

The presentation stage covers several factors. It enables acknowledgement and recognition – key factors in motivation and job satisfaction (Herzberg, 1987). It may be used for accreditation purposes, provides evidence for accountability purposes and should inform the next CPD/performance management cycle.

The pivotal point of the ten-stage process is the review/appraisal stages (3, 4 and 5). Working with a reviewer serves as a bridge between the individual and the organisation. The following case study illustrates how a teacher who meets induction standards, and who is working towards threshold, might interact with his reviewer.

Case study

Peter is a Key Stage 2 teacher, with an interest in improving boys' literacy. He works in a small primary school and is not a specialist in literacy teaching and learning. One objective is, therefore, to become more confident in the use of phonics, combined with a need to improve in the area of classroom management.

Reviewer: OK, Peter, we agree you need to work on your approach to teaching literacy, and that a continued focus on class management and learning styles could lead to an improvement in boys' levels of literacy.

Peter: Yes, but I haven't the time to devote to in-depth study. However, I do want to develop a way of working that suits me, and also that helps the school to meet its targets.

Reviewer: Do you feel that to *observe* an experienced teacher might help?

Peter: Yes and no. I really need someone to *observe me* and tell me how I could improve.

Reviewer: You may know already, but the local authority is focusing on boys' literacy and is rolling out *some short courses*. How about investigating these, and then follow up by being observed by the AST?

Peter: I think I need more than a couple of one-off events.

Reviewer: Fine. Maybe the school literacy coordinator could follow up with some *mentoring and coaching*. That way, you could evaluate the impact of any new approaches. Would you feel comfortable with that?

Peter: That would be great.

Reviewer: Great, now let's think about how you'll be able to demonstrate greater attainment by the boys. What sorts of level would you be aiming at? . . .You could even write this up as you go, and get some recognition from the GTCE *Teacher Learning Academy, level 1* . . .

DEMONSTRATING THE IMPACT OF YOUR CPD

Since the TDA has demanded an annual impact report from the providers of PPD, impact has become part of the discourse of education professionals. It is a relatively new concept, and its recent history can be tracked. Soulsby and Swain's (2003) *Report on the Award-bearing INSET Scheme* includes a section, 'The impact of training'. The subsequent Ofsted report, *Making a Difference: The Impact of Award-bearing In-service Training on School Improvement* (2004), also highlights the possible effects of award-bearing CPD, without really defining the concept. Philippa Cordingley *et al.*'s

(2004) EPPI report on the impact of collaborative CPD on classroom teaching and learning notes examples of perceived good practice through a systematic literature review. Armed with the belief that impact is possible, and that impact is good, the Teacher Training Agency (TTA) demanded that, to be funded, providers must plan, monitor and demonstrate impact. The Universities' Council for the Education of Teachers (UCET), on behalf of universities and in support of each other, have developed principles, models, frameworks and tools to aid the process.

It is worth tracking the emergence of the concept of 'impact', in order to fully understand it.

Soulsby and Swain

The basis of Soulsby and Swain's study (2003) was the (then) TTA and Ofsted principle that high-quality INSET (in-service training) 'should have a demonstrable and positive influence on classroom practice and/or whole school performance'. The findings were extremely positive and supportive of higher education instuition (HEI)-based CPD: 75 per cent of courses were deemed to be, in these terms, satisfactory or better, with 24 per cent being graded '1', 57 per cent '2' and 14 per cent '3'. Even when direct evidence was not available, Her Majesty's Inspectorate (HMI) noted that the potential for school improvement was likely to stem from the skills and attributes developed by the courses and that certain types of CPD lead to a positive impact.

Soulsby and Swain extend their study to suggest that impact is demonstrable through particular quality assurance activities, which include pupil satisfaction surveys, commissioned research, progress teaching, questionnaires after completion of courses, and the logging of examples of pupils' work that have had a perceived impact. Further evidence can be gleaned from the scrutiny of portfolios and assignments compiled by the participants.

Cumulative and long-term impact may be reflected by promotion, profile and the status of participants, but it would be wrong to make the assumption that these are direct consequences of participation in the programme. Indeed, short-term benefits may include a sense of reinvigoration and rejuvenation.

The 'hard evidence' of improved pupil performance, Soulsby and Swain explain; is even more difficult to prove. An impact evident in school performance data may not be apparent, in a stable environment, for a 'considerable time'. The value of Soulsby and Swain's study is that it provides indicators of impact, which relate to:

- *planning*: tailored, personal targets, negotiated outcomes;
- *provision*: school improvement-focused, portfolio-based, multiple members of staff;
- *quality assurance*: pupil satisfaction, post-course follow-up, commissioned research progress teaching, logging of pupils' work.

EPPI report

Cordingley *et al.*'s (2004) work breaks down the notion of 'improvements in student performance'. This includes the scrutiny of test results, greater ability in decoding and enhanced reading fluency. It also includes the need for qualitative study and judgements to make in respect of motivation, improved organised skills and more positive responses. The report provides examples of how research methods (lesson observation, teacher questionnaires, pupil analysis, big schools) can lead to increased self-confidence and greater satisfaction with work. The unanswered questions, which are not actually posed, relate to how teachers can incorporate this within their teaching. The assumption is that such activities become requirements of the CPD courses being followed. If so, it is teachers themselves who generate evidence of impact, rather than the providers of the CPD.

Cordingley *et al.* also focus attention on the impact on teachers rather than on their pupils. They note reports that outcomes of CPD include increased teacher confidence, self-belief in that teachers have the power to make a difference, an enthusiasm for working collaboratively and willingness to take risks and to experiment.

Cordingley *et al.*'s report does not reflect how CPD has an impact on teachers' attitudes alone. It also draws conclusions that collaborative CPD leads to improved teacher competence – developing a wider repertoire of teaching strategies, greater insights into pupils' thinking and improved planning skills. These positive effects are linked to specified activities – not individually, but collectively. In this way particular strategies for CPD that will have an impact are identified: observation and feedback, peer support and coaching, use of outside experts, teachers' ideology, the identification of technologies to facilitate professional dialogue, and achieving opportunities to experiment with, evaluate and enable new practices in the classroom.

Ofsted's *Making a Difference*

The Ofsted survey of HEI-based CPD, *Making a Difference* (2004), which followed up on Soulsby and Swain's report, reiterated that award-bearing INSET had a positive impact on standards of pupil work, thinking skills, pupil assessment and target setting; curriculum planning; and the implementation of national strategies and systems for review and self-evaluation. For teachers, engagement has resulted in increased subject knowledge, organisation, interpersonal and analytical skills, greater understanding of current initiatives and enhanced leadership and management skills.

With such a comprehensive list, one is moved to ask why all teachers should not be compelled to follow award-bearing INSET-type courses. After all, they can be seen to have a positive impact. The introduction of the MTL well may relate to this line of argument.

The Ofsted report also laments a lost opportunity to display impact. Evaluation reports are too often confined to the evaluation of course content and delivery, rather than assessment of their effect on participants. Despite the doubts expressed regarding the feasibility of linking improvements in pupil's attendance to course participation, there is an implicit view that the act of evaluating impact will and does lead to more positive effects than would otherwise be the case.

The Ofsted survey suggests that impact is visible and tangible. All teachers will need to contribute to impact studies. Evidence of a positive impact needs to be drawn from a range of sources (see Table 9.2.1).

A view of impact relates to the 'school effectiveness' paradigm. Many educationalists would not readily subscribe to this approach to performance management. Many engage more comfortably with the 'school improvement' movement, and most recently with 'school transformation'. Table 9.2.1 illustrates briefly the philosophical differences between each paradigm.

■ **Table 9.2.1** Sources of evidence of impact

	School effectiveness	School improvement	School transformation
Elements related to impact	• Performance • Attainment • Cohort-monitoring data • League tables • Statistics • Content	• Capacity • Motivation • Morale • Climate • Processes	• Empowerment • Distributed leadership • Autonomy • Agency • Professional learning • Networks and collaboration

'Impact' clearly provokes discussion and debate. The whole concept, as long as it remains undefined, will be understood in the context of the 'camp' with which education professionals align themselves.

An obvious solution is to suggest that none of the 'camps' is correct, and that none is wrong. Each could be seen to complement the other. Individual teachers will benefit from engaging with evidence of impact, and will also be able to inform and support school development through an active participation.

Task 9.2.5 **CONTINUING PROFESSIONAL DEVELOPMENT**

■ List forms of CPD you have undertaken. Give reasons for your choice of such activities.
■ In what ways has engagement changed your thoughts and behaviours as a teacher?
■ What do you think is the impact of each activity on others? How do you know?
■ What should your next CPD steps be, and why?

WHAT CONSTITUTES EFFECTIVE CPD?

> Our ambition is that all teachers should benefit from and contribute to professional development throughout their careers, and that professional development should be planned, appropriate to the individual concerned, and assessed for its impact on teaching and learning.
>
> (Kelly, 2005)

Engagement with CPD is to be linked to pay. Head teachers and teacher bodies have been asked to strengthen the obligation (which was previously only moral) to engage with CPD. There are likely to be good reasons, in terms of teachers' conditions of work and salary, to undertake CPD.

In a busy professional life, there are several factors that facilitate CPD and indeed motivate teachers to undertake continuing learning and development. The GTCE professional learning framework for teachers delineates the following aspects of teachers' entitlement to professional learning. Teachers, the framework suggests, are entitled to:

■ have time to engage in sustained reflection and structured learning;
■ create learning opportunities from everyday practice, such as planning and assessing for learning;
■ develop their ability to identify their own learning and development needs and those of others;
■ develop an individual learning plan;
■ have school-based learning, as well as course participation, recognised for accreditation;
■ develop self-evaluation, observation and peer-review skills;
■ develop mentoring and coaching skills and their ability to offer professional dialogue and feedback;
■ plan their longer-term career aspirations.

(Adapted from GTCE, 2003: 6)

The argument is that CPD is necessary, and under certain conditions can be stimulating and motivating.

One purpose underpinning teaching must surely be to help to prepare pupils for future adult life. Proponents of lifelong learning rightly recognise that reaching adulthood does not signal the end of learning. As Wenger (1999) succinctly puts it: 'Learners will inherit the earth. Knowers will find that they inhabit a world that no longer exists.'

CPD and professional learning surely should not only equip us to interpret and respond to the changing demands of practice and exercise our professional judgement in informed and creative ways. It should also be seen as a means for us to rejuvenate our practice to expand our professional repertoire, increase our self-esteem, self-confidence and enthusiasm for teaching or, for example, our level of criticality and, thereby, achieve enhanced job satisfaction.

Task 9.2.6 TEACHING: THE FUTURE

■ Why did you choose to come into teaching?
■ What do you think young people will need to know, understand and be able to do in the next 10, 20, 30 years?
■ In what ways will you need to act differently in the future without compromising the values that underpinned your decision to become a teacher?

In this respect, CPD is about capacity building. Moon (2001) also notes the benefits of CPD in terms of the enhancement of performance through improved self-esteem. A sense of professional control and personal well-being can be seen to be essential ingredients in job satisfaction.

On the other hand, leaving CPD entirely in the hands of the individual teacher is counter-productive. Pachler *et al.* (2003) point out that 'it is hopeless for those with responsibility for leading professional development simply to urge practitioners to reflect, reflect again, reflect more and reflect deeper'.

This 'caricature' serves to illustrate how empty a position can be that denies a body of learned knowledge that could inform and refine professional thinking (see also Lawes, 2003). Exposure to, and engagement with, relevant background literature can, therefore, be seen to be one very important CPD activity for us to engage in throughout our careers.

Working across different types of schools through networking and collaboration, to engage in research and enquiry into teaching and learning processes and to begin to develop leadership capacity are informative, enjoyable and become of greater interest if findings are relatable to existing bodies of knowledge and understanding. Learning and development through engagement demands, in simple terms, an integration of theoretical and practical perspectives.

SUMMARY

The very title of this unit emphasises the need for teachers to organise, plan and manage their own CPD. Much needs to go into the plans – account must be taken of purposes, approaches, requirements and the relationship with performance management and, therefore, national professional standards.

CPD is more than 'keeping up to date' – it contributes to job satisfaction, professional morale and status and school improvement.

Being a professional is, in part, concerned with professional autonomy matched by responsibility and accountability. Evaluating the impact of CPD undertaken can be seen to reinforce learning and development, and provide the opportunity to share and disseminate good practice. Impact studies do contribute towards a view of an evidence-based profession.

ANNOTATED FURTHER READING

Bolam, R. and Weindling, D. (2006) *Synthesis of Research and Evaluation Projects Concerned with Capacity-building through Teachers' Professional Development*, London: GTCE.

This synthesis of research and policy into CPD provides an excellent overview of what is seen to be successful in the field. It provides hard evidence to support successful approaches to CPD, enabling the identification of principles of best practice.

Bubb, S. and Earley, P. (2004) *Leading and Managing Continuing Professional Development: Developing People, Developing Schools*, London: Paul Chapman.

As the title suggests, Bubb and Earley provide an explanation of how effective, well-planned CPD can work hand in glove with school improvement. The book explains well how CPD can be informed by key players, including the TDA and GTCE. It offers very up-to-date guidance and advice, ensuring that any approach designed does meet statutory requirements. Bubb and Earley base their studies on the premise that CPD empowers teachers, thereby placing the emphasis on the 'professional' at the heart of CPD.

Gordon, S.P. (2004) *Professional Development for School Improvement: Empowering Learning Communities*, Boston, MA: Pearson.

Gordon provides an American perspective. He cleverly builds a view of CPD based upon an 'onion metaphor'. By unpeeling each layer, Gordon is able to examine the interrelationships between school leadership and CPD provision. The view that values and principles are at the core of CPD is reassuring and does help readers to build their own understanding based on their own stance as teachers. Strategies and approaches to suit the individual can be traced to the teacher's values, enabling a real tailoring from the practitioner perspective.

Guskey, T.R. (2002) 'Does it make a difference? Evaluating professional development', *Educational Leadership*, 59: 45–51.

For many, Guskey is *the* CPD guru. His views on evaluation have informed the debates concerning impact across the world. Guskey identifies five layers of evaluation:

■ participants' reaction;

■ participants' learning;

■ institutional support and change;

■ participants' use of new knowledge and skills;

■ student learning outcomes.

He explains the need for depth of evaluation studies and explains that to not address the five layers is to provide a superficial and insufficient evaluation report. For him evaluation is too often a brief one-off event. CPD must focus on the classroom, but the whole school culture, climate and structures need to be supportive. Consequently, Guskey explains that CPD can contribute in small steps towards a big change. When collective effort and collegiality are essential, CPD can bring teams together and affective factors (such as attitudes, enjoyment and motivation) usually follow recognition of success. In these ways, Guskey coincidentally provides the means to inform CPD planning.

RELEVANT WEBSITES

General Teaching Council for England (GTCE): www.gtce.org.uk

This site provides not only links to news and updates, but also to networks, enabling the sharing of ideas and problems with teachers at similar stages of their career development. Individual teachers, trade unions and many forms of comment and guidance make this an essential website for professional teachers.

International Professional Development Association: www.ipda.org.uk

This site contains updates on the world of CPD, an opportunity to join blogs related to CPD, and access to the association's refereed journal, the *Journal of Professional Development*. The site also provides information on the association's annual conference.

National College of School Leadership (NCSL) (now the National College for Leadership of Schools and Children's Services): www.nationalcollege.org.uk
Look here for descriptors and programmes for development routes for leadership and management.

TeacherNet: www.teachernet.gov.uk/
This site provides information and guidance on CPD for teachers. It includes access to statutory guidance, national standards and information for teachers seeking development opportunities at all stages of their careers. Of particular interest may be the page devoted to induction for newly qualified teachers.

Teacher Training Resource Bank (TTRB): www.ttrb.ac.uk
Although the TTRB has been designed to support initial teacher training, it has recently focused more on CPD. Articles, policies, research papers and commentaries, together with an excellent e-librarian service, provide ready access to very up-to-date developments.

Training and Development Agency (TDA): www.tda.gov.uk/teachers.aspx
This site has a section devoted to practising teachers. It contains information on CPD providers, performance management procedures, the new Master's of Teaching and Learning, induction procedures – and much more.

> **Visit the companion website www.routledge.com/textbooks/ltps2e for:**
>
> ■ additional questions and task for this unit;
> ■ links to useful websites relevant to this unit.

REFERENCES

Alexandrou, A. (2006) *EIS Learning Representatives: An Evaluation of the Educational Institute of Scotland's First Cohort of Learning Representatives*, Edinburgh: Educational Institute of Scotland.

Cordingley, P., Bell, M., Rundell, B., Evans, D. and Curtis, A. (2003) *How Does Collaborative Continuing Professional Development (CPD) for Teachers of the 5–16 Age Range Affect Teaching and Learning?*, London: CUREE/EPPI.

Day, C. (1999) *Developing Teachers: The Challenges of Lifelong Learning*, London: Falmer.

Day, M., (2008) *MTL Challenges, Opportunities and Progress*, Keynote speech delivered at the UCET Annual Conference, Birmingham, 8 November.

Department for Children, Schools and Families (DCSF) (2007) *The Children's Plan: Building Brighter Futures*, London: The Stationery Office.

Department for Education and Employment (DfEE) (2001) *Learning and Teaching: A Strategy for Professional Development*, London: DfEE. Available online at www.teachernet.gov.uk/_doc/1289/CPD_Strategy.pdf (accessed November 2009).

Field, K. (2007) 'Consultancy report for Swindon Local Authority', unpublished.

Gray, L.S. (2005) *An Enquiry into Continuing Professional Development for Teachers*, Cambridge: University of Cambridge Centre for Applied Research in Educational Technologies (CARET).

General Teaching Council for England (GTCE) (2003) *Commitment: The Teachers' Professional Learning Framework*, London: GTCE. Available online at www.gtce.org.uk/documents/publicationpdfs/tplf_commit_ptplf0603.pdf (accessed November 2009).

Herzberg, F.I. (1987) 'One more time: how do you motivate employees?', *Harvard Business Review*, 65(5): 109–20.

Hoyle, E. (1975) 'Professionality, professionalism and control in teaching', in V. Houghton, R. McHugh and C. Morgan (eds) *Management in Education: The Management of Organisations and Individuals*, London: Ward Lock Educational/Open University Press.

Kelly, R. (2005) Letter to the TTA expanding upon the TTA's extended remit for CPD, March 2005.

Lawes, S. (2003) 'What, when, how, and why? Theory and foreign language teaching', *Language Learning Journal*, 28: 22–8.

Moon, B. (2001) 'The changing agenda for professional development in education', in B. Moon, J. Butcher and E. Bird (eds) *Leading Professional Development in Education*, London: RoutledgeFalmer/Open University, pp. 3–10.

Morris, E. (2001) Keynote speech at the DfEE launch of *The National Strategy for CPD*, 1 March.

O'Brien, J. and MacBeath, J. (1999) 'Co-ordinating staff development: the training and development of staff development co-ordinators', *Journal of In-Service Education*, 25(1): 69–84.

Office for Standards in Education (Ofsted) (2004) *Making a Difference: The Impact of Award-bearing In-service Training on School Improvement*, HMI 1765, London: Ofsted.

Pachler, N., Daly, C. and Lambert, D. (2003) 'Teacher learning: reconceptualising the relationship between theory and practical teaching in Master's level course development', in J.J. Günther (ed.) *Quality Assurance in Distance-Learning and E-learning: International Quality Benchmarks in Postgraduate Education*, Krems, Austria: European Association of Telematic Applications.

Putnam, R.T. and Borko, H. (2000) 'What do new views of knowledge and thinking have to say about research on teacher learning', in B. Moon, J. Butcher and E. Bird (eds) *Leading Professional Development in Education*, London: RoutledgeFalmer/Open University, pp. 11–29.

Rose, J. (2006) *Phonics and Early Reading: An Overview for Head Teachers, Literacy Leaders and Teachers in Schools, and Managers and Practitioners in Early Years Settings*, London: DCSF.

Rose, J. (2008) *The Independent Review of the Primary Curriculum: Interim Report*, London: DCSF. Available online at www.dcsf.gov.uk/primarycurriculumreview (accessed November 2009).

Soulsby, D. and Swain, D. (2003) *Report on the Award–Bearing INSET Scheme*, London: TTA.

Tsui, A., Edwards, G., Lopez-real, F., Kwan, T., Law, D., Stimpson, P., Tang, R. and Wong, A. (2008) *Learning in School–University Partnership: Sociocultural Perspectives*, New York: Routledge.

Wenger, E. (1999) *Communities of Practice: Learning, Meaning and Identity*, Cambridge: Cambridge University Press.

Whitty, G. (2000) 'Teacher professionalism', *New Times Journal of In-Service Education*, 26(2): 281–96.

TEACHING, RESEARCH AND FURTHER QUALIFICATIONS

Cathie Pearce

> Live [teach] as if you were to die tomorrow.
> Learn [research] as if you were to live forever.
> (Mahatma Gandhi (1869–1948))

INTRODUCTION

What is the relationship between teaching and research? In what ways can you use your experience within research? How can teaching and research be thought about in overlapping, rather than distinct and separate, professional realms? And how can you, as an undergraduate, or as early career teacher, begin to make research matter, for your 'self', for your practice and in wider professional contexts?

This unit aims to interest you in the process of research within your own practice. It attempts to offer something more complicating than the usual research methods handbooks that set out examples of research acts: interviewing, observation, data analysis, etc., which help you speak the language of research, but which may bypass the important experiences that bring about some depth of understanding, for example imagining, anticipating, projecting, resonating and responding. Using a more holistic approach to experience, this unit aims to help you reflect on experience in ways that will enable research questions to emerge. It will also help you to understand in a research-informed way how aspects of your professional practice, the nature of teaching and variations of learning (including your own) can be meaningfully drawn into the research process.

OBJECTIVES

By the end of this unit you should be able to:

■ develop ways in which you might generate, explore, interpret and communicate professional-based knowledge in research contexts and practice;

■ develop an understanding of critical and creative engagements between teaching and research;

■ develop an understanding of the complexities that are involved in knowledge production (including claims to truth and meaning) and relate these understandings to educational inquiry;

■ offer some questions and problems that will enable you to develop your own rationale for inquiry within educational research.

'Learning to teach' asks that we also 'learn how to learn' and 'learning how to learn' is not a simple matter! We often do some important things without necessarily knowing why, not because we are rash, impertinent individuals but because it felt right to us in the situation, it mattered, and we had to act in a situation without the benefit of contemplative thought or hindsight. Teaching requires us to act in a million tiny ways, every session, every lesson, every day – and who knows what in those encounters will make a difference, what could be repeated with any certainty of outcome and what will be beneficial to someone's life and learning? We often act without knowing 'why' with any degree of certainty, and so perhaps 'not knowing' is a good place to start.

What is knowledge? What counts as knowledge? Who gets to decide what is knowledge? What ways of knowing get pushed out or put to one side? What can become knowledge? These are all questions that researchers have argued, debated and struggled with for some time. Various ways of framing and understanding knowledge (called research paradigms) come in and out of favour with research councils and funding streams, within different university departments and with changing government agendas. For example, currently much funded research in education is focused on 'What is practical?' or 'What works?', while questions such as 'What is going on?' or 'What is the situation/problem here?' have received less attention in many research forums. What we 'don't know' and therefore what we 'want to know' differs according to who is asking, what the agenda is and, importantly, how teaching is positioned in relation to research.

There is often a confusing and unhelpful set of terms that circulate around teaching and research. There is 'research-informed', 'research-led', 'experiential', 'practical-based', 'evidenced-based' research, and so on, each of which tries to 'capture' or privilege itself over the others. However, each in its own way tries to circumnavigate a relationship between lived experience and inquiry into that lived experience. Where they differ is in how that might be done, for what purposes and with what orientations in mind. Good research generates more questions than it answers and the aliveness of questions – the questions' vitality – is what sustains research.

So how to proceed? And where to start? Research that deals with being human – lived experiences, teachers, parents, classrooms, pupils and colleagues – cannot be neutral. There is no place where we can stand objectively and look in on such worlds as if we are not part of them, so perhaps our own experiences, subjective understandings, values and assumptions are places to start. Teaching is about movement and change if we are to aspire to make any difference at all, so it seems both appropriate and important for research methodology to be able to engage with such changes rather than try to stand outside the research in any neutral or so-called objective way. Using ourselves in the research helps to generate meanings, explore our understandings and engage ethically with others rather than data being 'poured into a given theoretical mould' (Smyth and Shacklock, in Etherington, 2004: 20).

THE 'QUESTION OF THE QUESTION'

Something matters to us, we get interrupted, we can't make sense, we don't know how to do something, we are curious about something or we simply fail and have to rethink. These are good places to be in research terms! Patti Lather (2007) refers to them as 'the stuckness of places' and perhaps this term works to emphasise that research often begins where our understandings fail, not where they are clear. The 'question of the question' opens up what kinds of understandings we are searching for and helps in focusing the kinds of approaches that would be conducive to responding to its task. The questions will inevitably change, but so too will the responses to them and it is in these 'movements and changes' that meanings are created and understandings are enriched.

The *emergent* nature of questions in research is an aspect that is often neglected in methods and approaches whereby linear models assume that a clear, researchable question must come first. Indeed, when it comes to researching practice, especially our own, it is both important and significant to think what comes before the research question by asking: What is it that significantly engages/grabs/interrupts me in my everyday practice as a teacher and that I would like to explore? What do I want to be able to do/understand/explain that I currently cannot? What aspects of myself (and my practice) within specific contexts would I like to understand better? (Pickard and Pearce, 1995; Pickard *et al.*, 2005).

REFLECTIVE AND REFLEXIVE RESEARCH

Becoming a teacher involves a degree of self-reflection in all that you do. You might write notes to yourself, complete journals and diaries as part of course requirements, self-evaluate lessons and sessions, read others' comments upon your 'performativity' or just think about your experiences. These are critical and crucial aspects in the learning process that, by and large, we do at a rational, conscious level by evaluating and judging how we are against what we know. When we do it well, we are able to perhaps open ourselves up to what we are less good at or what we need to learn; when we reflect in superficial ways we often confirm what we already know or what we would like to believe about ourselves! Understanding more about ourselves, our practices and our engagements within professional worlds requires a more careful and considered practice – one that we might call *reflexive* practice. The term 'reflexivity' will be more fully discussed later in this unit but, for now, I am taking the term to mean an interconnection between theory and practice that is more complex than just self-awareness or self-reflection. In order to understand reflexivity and how it might be used in research, it is necessary first to consider:

■ why using a 'self' at all in research might be more important than traditional, impersonal or purportedly objective accounts;
■ how a 'self' can be considered in ways that are constantly changing rather than in fixed, stable or reified ways;
■ how a disposition of 'not knowing' (rather than trying to fit or graft knowledge on to what we know already) can help us to think further about *how* we know and *how* knowledge is constructed.

In some research paradigms it is still the case that bringing your 'self' (subjectivity) into the research is considered to be contaminating and threatens to undermine claims to generalise or objectify. Such criticisms have been strongly argued against within the social sciences, particularly feminist, qualitative methodologies, which value openness, engagement, ethics, change, justice and fairness within research with other human beings.

However, at the same time, much research in qualitative studies in the last ten years has drawn attention to the problematics that are involved in having what may be called a 'romantic' notion of humanness; that is, any uncritical perspective that I am in charge of my own intentions and that I can say what I mean and mean what I say in an unproblematic way. Such thinking does not leave us much room for considering more complex aspects that contribute to us being human, such as imagination, affective dimensions, tacit knowledge (that is, what we feel, sense), our sense of values and, of course, our unthinking, habitual responses to events and situations. As we noted earlier, there is more to how we act than we know with any certainty, or can be conscious of at any one time, and this is important for both research and teaching.

TEACHING AS COMMUNICATION

One of the aspects that makes teaching an exciting, challenging and passionate activity is that we are dealing with other human beings. We are helping in the learning process and we try for that learning to make a difference to people's lives. If teaching was as simple as 'I speak – you hear and understand', we could exchange all manner of things in a very short space of time indeed. However, this is simply not the case and, as you reflect on any experience of teaching, just what goes on in that communicative exchange is a very complex and subtle activity. Language itself is very problematic. Words are very slippery things indeed and, for any given lesson, a teacher tries to reword, rephrase, give examples, illustrate via other means, ask questions and elicit responses all in attempts to circumnavigate our communication with each other. And, of course, the more the teacher does this, the more his or her own meanings and understandings of the phenomenon in question tend to move as well! So there is a sense in which there is an inevitable gap between what a teacher is meaning to say and what a pupil is hearing and understanding by it. These 'gaps' are not failures of clarity but *differences in themselves*. They raise interesting and provocative challenges for teachers who are interested in researching their own practices, the nature of learning and approaches to pedagogy. The research question shifts to ask: What is going on in such exchanges? How can I know what is being understood here? What perspectives are my pupils drawing upon? In what ways are they making sense?

MAKING SENSE

When we start from a position of 'not knowing', we often feel in a stuck place. How often do teachers hear a child saying 'I can't do it' or 'I don't know'? Research that looks for these stuck places is concerned not only with 'unblocking' these places, but also in understanding the ways in which we make sense and which can help us to explore how things could be otherwise. Consider what happens when you are confronted with an abstract image that you can't initially make sense of at all. You look at the image. The context may be making a huge impact. If you are in a classroom setting and expected to make a response, you may be busily trying out versions of sense that convey your confusion: 'It looks like chaos to me' 'It's a vast swirl of colours and lines' 'I haven't a clue what it's about". In the context of an exhibition, where others are wandering around with you, you might feel less pressured to make a response. You might find yourself trying to sense what is going on – 'Is the redness conveying emotion? In what ways am I being drawn in? What is happening to me when I look at this painting? How am I to respond?' Whether spontaneous or reflective, it is likely that you will first of all draw upon familiar worlds, of what you already know, in order to make sense of what you don't know . . . and this is no different when it comes to understanding practice. However, in noting how you are making sense, with what approaches and with which dimensions of knowledge, you are also able to note which aspects are missing, or which are absent or not being taken into account, and such thinking enables a whole variety of research questions to arise.

So questions arise, you think about less familiar aspects and sooner or later you begin to want to *make* sense. You have an inkling about what is going on, you want to tell a story about what you think you have found, you want to see how it resonates with other people and so you start to assemble what were previously disconnected bits into some coherence, into an account that you can present to others (in whatever form). Some may agree, some not, some will be puzzled or intrigued, but you have a new set of questions that make you think about your own ways of understanding again and about the account that you have constructed, or that might set you off in a new direction. Whatever others' responses are, they will have an effect/affect because research

501 ■

is inherently a social activity and, to that end, we are constantly exploring and experimenting with meanings, approaches and with what speaks to us as human beings, professionals, teachers and researchers, as well as within and from our understandings of race, class and gender.

THINKING ABOUT 'THINKING'

Evidence or data is never neutral or objective. It is always interested; that is, it has a context and a humanness that more traditional, scientific methods prefer to ignore! In any case, it would be of no use to research experiences if those very self-experiences were to be neutralised, sanitised or objectified, rather than informing or being meaningful to what we do. It helps to be suspicious about yourself – what values, assumptions and attitudes are you drawing upon, because in one sense all such things are social. There is unlikely to be a thought or stance that you have that is not already shared by others as well. This is a socially constructed view of reality through which we can explore just how we have come to know what we know, in what ways and with what alternatives at our disposal.

Task 9.3.1 **THINKING ABOUT 'THINKING'**

■ Try Google searches for any surrealist or abstract artists, such as René Magritte, Kay Sage, Jackson Pollock or Tim Head, and focus on an image that interests you in some way. Even the way in which it interests you is of interest! Does it make you think and feel? How? Why? In what ways does it connect? What sense can you make? Write down as many varied statements about it as you can.

■ Reflect upon the statements that you have made. What can they tell you about how you are making sense? What aspects do you mostly draw upon? Which are missing? In what ways are you making the 'unfamiliar' familiar?

There is often an *immediacy* to both acting and understanding within teaching. Such immediate concerns sometimes prevent us from getting interested in anything that might be longer term. The packed nature of the curriculum, the hectic pace of school life and the 'chore-like' nature of writing and text within the job itself mean that research that does not offer something immediately significant can be seen as 'another task', 'an additional burden' or a 'waste of time'. However, research that can parallel experience, speak *to* it rather than *of* it, means that there is a greater likelihood of being able to bring teaching and research into some kind of relationship – not as marriage (they are unlikely to lose their tensions!) or as friendship (neither should be a dumping ground for the other!) or as kinship (traditions within each need to be breached, traversed and brought into a creative production with each other!).

Thinking about what we do is already part of our professional experience and research that can help us think creatively, energetically, ethically, politically, responsibly, emotionally and playfully about what we do opens up conditions of possibilities for what is possible to be otherwise. However, what can be otherwise does not just arrive from nowhere. Research, if it is to be both serious and playful, both thought and action, both movement and change asks that we learn how to learn and as if we have never learned before. This way, we open ourselves up to what might be heard, understood or thought differently and that couldn't possibly have been before. The 'old' is brought into the 'new' – the familiar into the unfamiliar in ways that offer new junctions for both thought and action.

These are exciting times for educational research. Although the last decade has seen a period of almost manic policy reform and although this has brought with it a kind of Ikea-style mantra of 'out with the old and in with the new' with respect to new initiatives, methods, curricula and pedagogies – education is still an emotional business. Trying to make a difference, addressing inequalities, challenging individualisation, making teacher professionalism count, contesting the dominance of benchmarks and indices being used uncritically and questioning the relationship that education has with the economy and job markets are just some of the areas that educational researchers invest their energies in. They are not by any means the only ones or even the most important ones, but they may give you some idea about how your own research interests may touch upon various fields within educational research. The 'Annotated further reading' at the end of this unit gives examples of texts that try to connect experience, data and theory in research approaches that require nothing more than your own engagement, a willingness to think for yourself and a helpful scepticism towards any definitive attempts to make absolute sense – in other words, to be honest and reflexive about your ways of understanding and of how you come to know what you know.

Action research is a participatory, democratic form of educational research that is often carried out by practitioners within their own working contexts. Unsurprisingly, there are many versions of action research that are presented in the literature, some of which are included as annotated texts at the end of this unit. However, it seems less important to worry about what 'version' of action research you might best adopt and more useful to think of action research as a collaborative opportunity to do some research with colleagues and even with colleagues in different institutional settings. Action research places emphasis on the ongoing nature of an inquiry and helps to focus upon what possibilities there are for change. Theory and practice may be viewed as overlapping rather than separate, discrete aspects of research in ways that have been discussed in the sections above.

Action research is often described by practitioners as being a supportive form of inquiry that does not impose traditional research methods or prescriptions. It is *emergent* in nature; that is, the research arises from experience, over time, in collaboration with others, and so on. Questions emerge in the process and significances arise from engagements *within that process*. As we have been

---

Task 9.3.2 **QUESTIONS ABOUT KNOWLEDGE**

The following is a well-known quotation from Oscar Wilde (1854–1900):

Education is an admirable thing but it is well to remember from time to time that nothing that is worth knowing can be taught.

For both teaching and research, it is important to get a sense of the questions that are being asked as well as a sense of the problems that are being raised. Consider the quote:

■ What questions does it raise?
■ What areas, issues, problems does it touch upon?
■ What questions might make for an interesting research focus?
■ How, and in what ways, does this quote resonate with your personal and professional experiences?
■ What is knowledge?
■ Can knowledge be taught?

---

discussing throughout this unit, the emergent nature of research is crucial to *thinking otherwise*. In other words, it enables us to have new thoughts rather than folding or falling back into our habitual and reified ways of thinking and knowing. Keeping spaces open does not come as second nature in our hectic, professional lives.

THEORISING ABOUT THEORY

Generalised theories in education often have links with other disciplines. They may be theories about learning, behaviour, motivation, memory, social learning, rituals and meanings, humanistic development, perception, and so on, and may have first been applied in the fields of psychology, sociology or anthropology before being of interest in educational contexts. Such 'detached' theories are often derived from hypotheses or models that researchers then consider in terms of the data. However, trying to map or apply theory to data is a bit like trying to nail jelly to a tree! With critical thinking, studies that try neatly to apply theory to data are much more likely to invoke questions and metaphors of leakiness (what doesn't fit), messiness (the complexities that are being missed) and stickiness (what we can't disentangle from ourselves as researchers or the contexts we are in). Again, such stickiness is a good thing for researchers who are interested in lived experience, human experience or social and cultural contexts, for they help us to search for new perspectives. They also encourage us to go beyond our common-sense understandings or surmising from events.

Theory, like data, is never disinterested, neutral or objective (Stronach, 2005). Our theories are always pointing towards our desire to understand, to act, to change, to think differently and so it helps (as it does with data) to be reflexive about the ways in which we are making sense. Theory is nothing more than a way of making sense and it is important if we aspire to go beyond what we can immediately see, observe, measure, and so on. Within academic institutions theory can be portrayed in overly complex, dense and off-putting ways, but this need not be the case. Theorising from your own data is by far more empowering, more exciting, more challenging to do and more creative. This does not mean that more detached theories are not of relevance – it simply suggests that they can be brought into more productive conversations with your research. It therefore becomes possible to find connections and disjunctions, resonances and dissonances, rather than trying to 'prove', 'apply' or 'test' one theory against another. Putting theory to work means that theory always bases itself on the data and tries to illustrate where the central ideas/concepts have come from. Theory that emerges from data can help us to see situations, contexts and events in a different light. It is more than just a summary of common sense. Theory in action, meaning theory that emerges from your data, also enables different stories to be opened up and contradictory stories to be told (we can't just ignore what we come across). And perhaps, finally, 'emergent' rather than 'applied' theory helps us to relate things that don't easily or 'naturally' go together in our heads – in other words, it helps us break our habits of thought and think differently about things.

SUMMARY

This unit has attempted to convey the importance of the relationship between teaching and research, as well as the ways in which you might consider going about doing both!

Researching experience that is 'on the move' might be one way of thinking about it. Better perhaps to think of research as a space that enables things to get under your skin and to grow in your mind!

ANNOTATED FURTHER READING

I have included four very different readings, each of which conveys a different 'way in' to researching experience.

Altrichter, H., Fledman, A., Posch, P. and Somekh, B. (2006) *Teachers Investigate their Work: An Introduction to Action Research across the Professions*, London: Routledge.

This text is highly readable and practical and is a significant text that enables the reader to consider how action research can be used for both thought and change.

Clandinin, D.J. and Connelly, F.M. (2000) *Narrative Inquiry: Experience and Story in Qualititative Research*, San Francisco, CA: Jossey Bass.

As key authors in the field of narrative inquiry, this text is immensely helpful in understanding how narrative underpins many of our sense-making processes. It illustrates the textured nature of our 'stories' and offers some useful reflections of how to read both ourselves and others in more subtle and complicating ways.

Hammersley, M. (ed.) (1999*) Researching School Experience. Ethnographic Studies of Teaching and Learning*, London: Routledge.

Again by a key author in the field, this text illustrates the power of ethnography in trying to understand those aspects of school experience that can't be readily measured.

Stronach, I.M. (2010 forthcoming) 'Relocating early professional learning: the "invention of teachers"', in I.M. Stronach, *Globalising Education, Educating the Local: How Method Made Us Mad*, London: Routledge, Chapter 4.

This text is different from the above three in that it offers a way of thinking about your own learning from a more anthropological perspective. It explores resonances of experience and draws attention to aspects that are necessarily involved in trying to 'be and become' a teacher while also doing the job.

RELEVANT WEBSITE

Collaborative Action Research Network (CARN): www.esri.mmu.ac.uk/carnnew/

CARN is an international network for professional development that is committed to improving the quality of professional practice.

Visit the companion website www.routledge.com/textbooks/ltps2e for:

■ additional task for this unit;
■ links to useful websites relevant to this unit.

REFERENCES

Etherington, K. (2004) *Becoming a Reflexive Researcher: Using Our Selves in Research*, London: Jessica Kingsley.

Lather, P. (2007) *Getting Lost: Feminist Efforts Towards a Double(d) Science*, New York: State University of New York Press.

Pickard, A. and Pearce, J. (1995) MA in Teaching (by Research) unpublished definitive course document, Manchester Metropolitan University.

Pickard, A., Stronach, I., Shallcross, T. and Pearce, C. (2005) Educational Research Unit unpublished course documentation, Manchester Metropolitan University.

Stronach, I.M. (2010 forthcoming) 'Relocating early professional learning: the "invention of teachers"', in I.M. Stronach, *Globalising Education, Educating the Local: How Method Made Us Mad*, London: Routledge, Chapter 4.

INDEX

Relevant tables and figures are indicated by *italic* type; note also that text within task boxes is included in the index where appropriate.